D1001247

WAR ON THE RUN

Also by John F. Ross

The Polar Bear Strategy: Reflections on Risk in Modern Life

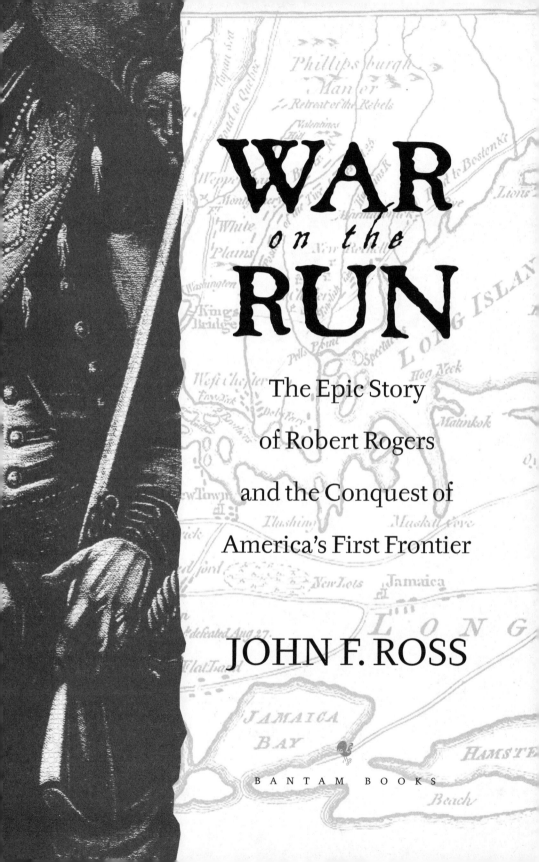

WAR
on the
RUN

The Epic Story
of Robert Rogers
and the Conquest of
America's First Frontier

JOHN F. ROSS

BANTAM BOOKS

Copyright © 2009 by John F. Ross

All rights reserved.

Published in the United States by Bantam Books,
an imprint of The Random House Publishing Group,
a division of Random House, Inc., New York.

BANTAM BOOKS and the rooster colophon are registered
trademarks of Random House, Inc.

ISBN 978-0-553-80496-6

Printed in the United States of America

Book design by Patrice Sheridan
Maps by Robert Bull

For Jane and Phil

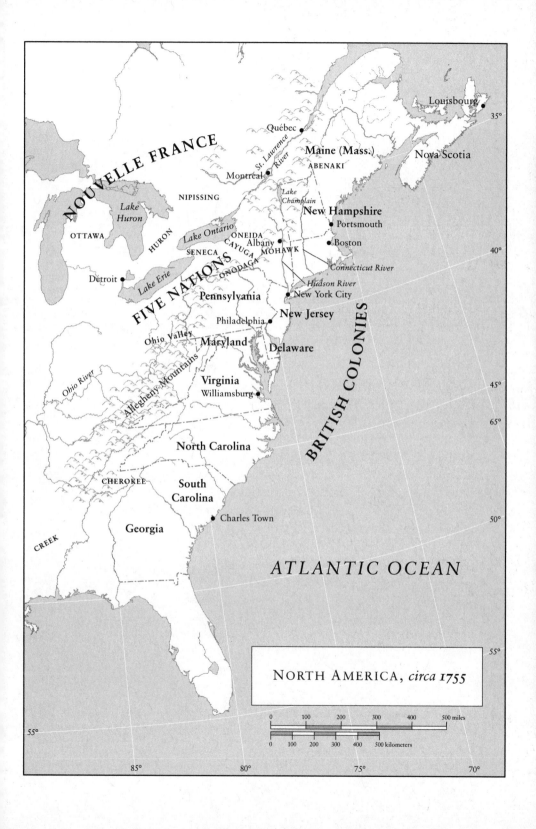

NOUVELLE FRANCE

Louisbourg

Québec

Maine (Mass.)

ABENAKI

Nova Scotia

St. Lawrence River

Montréal

NIPISSING

Lake Champlain

Lake Huron

New Hampshire

Portsmouth

OTTAWA

HURON

Lake Ontario

ONEIDA

CAYUGA

Albany

Boston

SENECA

MOHAWK

Detroit

Lake Erie

ONODAGA

Connecticut River

40°

FIVE NATIONS

Pennsylvania

Hudson River

New York City

Philadelphia

New Jersey

Ohio Valley

Maryland

Delaware

BRITISH COLONIES

45°

Alleghany Mountains

Ohio River

Virginia

Williamsburg

65°

North Carolina

CHEROKEE

South
Carolina

Georgia

Charles Town

50°

CREEK

ATLANTIC OCEAN

55°

NORTH AMERICA, *circa 1755*

0   100   200   300   400   500 miles

0   100   200   300   400   500 kilometers

55°

85°   80°   75°   70°

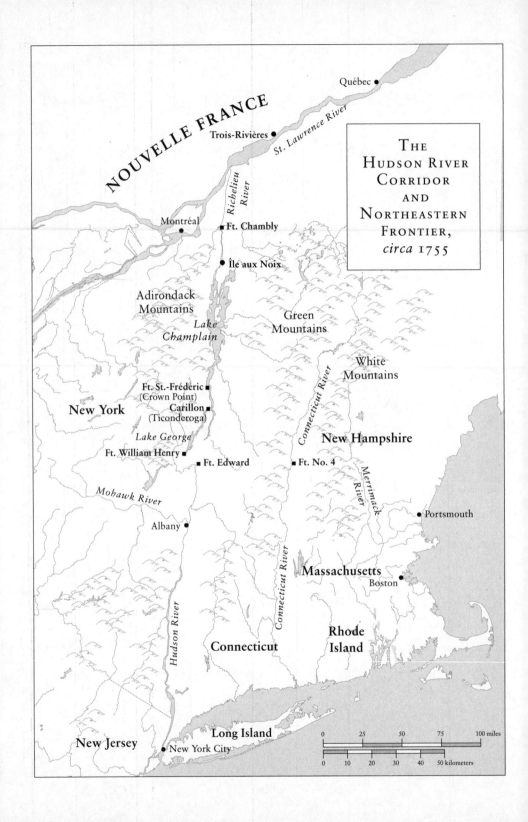

THE
HUDSON RIVER
CORRIDOR
AND
NORTHEASTERN
FRONTIER,
circa 1755

NOUVELLE FRANCE

Québec

Trois-Rivières

St. Lawrence River

Richelieu River

Montréal

Ft. Chambly

Île aux Noix

Adirondack
Mountains

Lake Champlain

Green
Mountains

White
Mountains

Ft. St.-Frédéric
(Crown Point)

Carillon
(Ticonderoga)

Connecticut River

New York

Lake George

Ft. William Henry

Ft. Edward

Ft. No. 4

New Hampshire

Merrimack River

Mohawk River

Portsmouth

Albany

Massachusetts

Boston

Hudson River

Connecticut River

Rhode
Island

Connecticut

New Jersey

Long Island

New York City

0   25   50   75   100 miles

0   10   20   30   40   50 kilometers

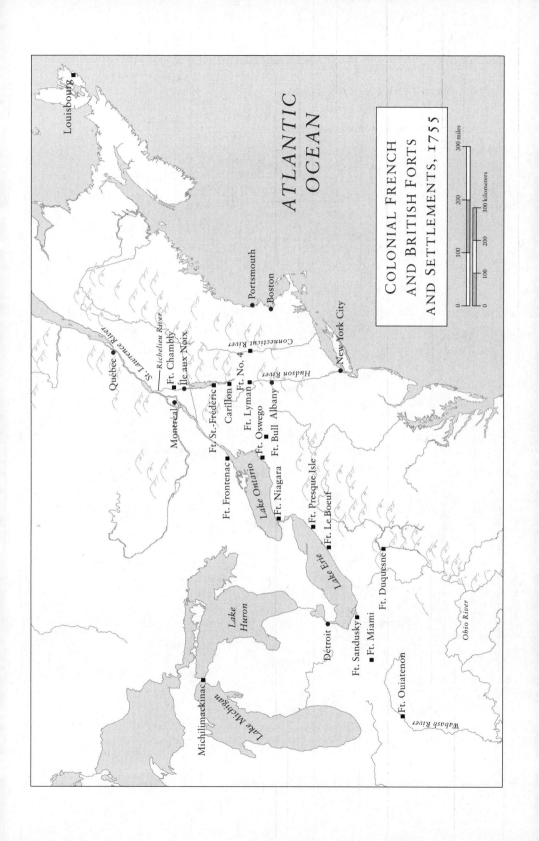

COLONIAL FRENCH
AND BRITISH FORTS
AND SETTLEMENTS, 1755

ATLANTIC
OCEAN

Louisbourg

Portsmouth
Boston

New York City

Québec
St. Laurence River
Richelieu River
Ft. Chambly
Île aux Noix
Connecticut River
Ft. No. 4
Hudson River

Montréal
Ft. St.-Frédéric
Carillon
Ft. Lyman
Ft. Oswego
Ft. Bull   Albany

Ft. Frontenac
Lake Ontario
Ft. Niagara
Ft. Presque Isle
Ft. Le Boeuf
Lake Erie

Lake Huron

Ft. Duquesne

Détroit
Ft. Sandusky
Ft. Miami

Lake Michigan

Michilimackinac

Ft. Ouiatenon
Wabash River
Ohio River

300 miles
300 kilometers
0   100   200
0   100   200

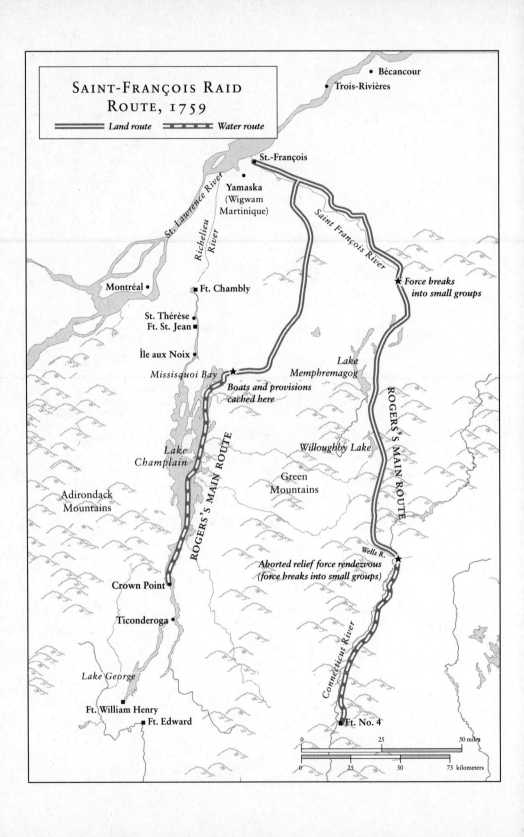

Land route   Water route

Bécancour
Trois-Rivières
St.-François
Yamaska
(Wigwam
Martinique)
St. Lawrence River
Richelieu River
Saint François River
★ Force breaks
into small groups
Montréal
Ft. Chambly
St. Thérèse
Ft. St. Jean
Île aux Noix
Missisquoi Bay ★
Boats and provisions
cached here
Lake
Memphremagog
ROGERS'S MAIN ROUTE
Lake
Champlain
Willoughby Lake
Green
Mountains
ROGERS'S MAIN ROUTE
Adirondack
Mountains
Wells R.
★ Aborted relief force rendezvous
(force breaks into small groups)
Crown Point
Ticonderoga
Connecticut River
Lake George
Ft. William Henry
Ft. Edward
Ft. No. 4

0   25   50 miles
0   25   50   75 kilometers

Contents

List of Maps

Dramatis Personae

Abercrombie, Capt. James. Nephew and aide-de-camp to Major General Abercromby (q.v.), he early discerned the value of Rogers's innovations.

Abercromby, James. Assumed command of British North American forces (1756–58) after Loudoun (q.v.). He suffered disastrous defeat at the hands of a far smaller French garrison at Carillon (later Fort Ticonderoga).

Amherst, Jeffery. Took over British North American command (1758–68) after Abercromby (q.v.). He approved Rogers's plan to attack the village of Saint-François, then later sent him to receive the surrender of western French garrisons at the end of the French and Indian War.

Atecouando, Jérôme. An Abenaki sachem and diplomat from Saint-François, who attempted to negotiate neutrality with the British before the French and Indian War.

Ayer, Ebenezer. Friend of Rogers's father, he mistook him for a bear and shot him dead.

Belestre, Capt. François-Marie Picoté de. Commandant of Fort Détroit, who surrendered to Rogers in 1760.

Blanchard, Col. Joseph. Commander of the New Hampshire provincials, he gave Rogers his first command.

Bougainville, Louis-Antoine de. Aide-de-camp to Montcalm (q.v.).

Bourlamaque, Brig. Gen. Francois Charles de. Commander of Carillon (later Fort Ticonderoga).

Braddock, Gen. Edward. After concentrating the first large British force in North America, he built a road toward the French stronghold at the Forks of the Ohio in 1755, where he was bitterly defeated and killed.

Bradstreet, Lt. Col. John. Commander of bateau men during the French and Indian War.

Brown, Thomas. A 16-year-old private when he fought alongside Rogers at the Battle on Snowshoes, he recorded his experience of being wounded and captured in a hair-raising journal.

Browne, Arthur. Portsmouth rector, Rogers's father-in-law, and fellow member of the Masonic Lodge.

Bulkeley, Capt. Charles. A ranger who pacified the mutiny on Rogers' Island and fought valiantly in the Battle on Snowshoes.

Burbank, Capt. Jonathan. A faithful ranger leader, whom the Indians mistook for Rogers and horribly mutilated.

Carver, Jonathan. Amateur mapmaker and surveyor, he served as Rogers's partner in his search for the Northwest Passage after the war. Later published his discoveries and did not credit Rogers.

Cheeksaunkun, Capt. Jacob. The son of Naunauphtaunk (q.v.), whom Rogers commissioned to form his own Indian ranger company.

Church, Benjamin. An innovative and early ranger during the King Philip's War (1675–76).

Dalyell, Capt. James. In command of the British force dispatched to relieve the besieged Fort Detroit during Pontiac's War; he died in the Battle of Bloody Run.

Dieskau, Maréchal-de-Camp Jean-Armand, Baron de. Swiss-born mercenary French commander, who was defeated and captured by William Johnson's forces at Lake George in 1755.

Dobbs, Arthur. Governor of colonial North Carolina (1754–65), he had spent decades supporting the quest for the Northwest Passage and aroused Rogers's interest in the venture.

Dumas, Maj. Gen. Jean Daniel. Led a mixed French Canadian and Abenaki force against Rogers's Saint-François expedition on their return.

Durantaye, Ensign Sieur de la. Of the Compagnies Franches de la Marine, he joined with Langy to deliver one of Rogers's most bitter defeats.

Gage, Thomas. Largely ineffective as a senior officer at two of the largest British military disasters—Braddock's defeat and Ambercromby's disastrous assault on Carillon—he raised a regiment of regulars to replace the rangers. A sworn enemy of Rogers, he pressed hard for Rogers's court martial. Became head of British North American forces (1768–75) after Amherst (q.v.).

George III. King of Great Britain (1760–1820).

Gill, Joseph-Louis, or "Magouaouidombaouit." A principal chief of Saint-François, who was away when Rogers' Rangers destroyed his village and took his wife and two sons prisoner.

Gladwin, Maj. Henry. Commander of Fort Detroit after the French and Indian War, he discovered Pontiac's plans to take the fort by surprise, then weathered a long siege.

Hale, Nathaniel. Young schoolteacher turned Revolutionary War spy, he was caught and brought to confess by Rogers.

Haviland, William. British colonel in the 27th Foot, he was a strong opponent of irregular forces. As commander of Fort Edward, his decisions to cut Rogers's unit helped lead to one of the rangers' worst defeats at the Battle on Snowshoes.

Henry, Alexander. Only the second British trader licensed to trade furs in the Great Lakes, narrowly escaped death during Pontiac's attack on Fort Michilimackinac, of which he survived to write a history.

Hopkins, Joseph. A turncoat colonial officer in the French service, he allegedly wrote a letter—almost certainly a piece of French intelligence troublemaking—that cast treasonous aspersions on Rogers's character and resulted in Rogers's court martial.

Howe, Brig. Gen. George Augustus, Viscount. British officer and early adopter of ranger practices, he became a close friend of Rogers's and was killed during the attack on Carillon in 1758. His brother William replaced Gage (q.v.) as commander in chief in North America in 1775.

Johnson, Sir William. Frontier agent among the Iroquois, he defeated and captured Dieskau (q.v.) at the Battle of Lake George (1755). Later, as superintendent of Indian Affairs, he became a rival of Rogers, conspiring with Gage (q.v.) to ruin Rogers in the "Hopkins" (q.v.) affair.

Langis, Jean-Baptiste Levrault de, or Langy. A formidable French partisan fighter who often matched wits with Rogers in fierce skirmishes in the woods.

Langlade, Charles-Michel Mouet de. A métis—half Indian and half French—he fought Rogers at the Battle on Snowshoes and other encounters.

Longueuil, Charles Le Moyne de. Governor of Montréal (1749–55), the French Canadian city that served as the center of the fur trade and gateway to the *pays d'en haut*.

Loudoun, John Campbell, 4th Earl of. In 1756, he assumed command of British North American forces after Shirley (q.v.). He asked Rogers to write down the principles of successful bush warfare, which produced Rogers's Rules of Ranging. (See Appendix 1.)

Lusignan, Paul-Louis Dazemard de. Commandant of Crown Point (1751–58) and afterward of Carillon, Île aux Noix, Saint-Jean, and Chambly.

Marin, Capt. Joseph de la Malgue. Officer in the Troupes de la Marine and a canny backwoods fighter, he turned the battle for the French against Braddock on the Monongahela River, and was perhaps Rogers's most dangerous adversary.

Millan, John. A London publisher, he put out Rogers's *Concise Account*, *The Journals of Robert Rogers*, and the play *Ponteach; or, The Savages of America*.

Montcalm, Louis-Joseph de, Marquis de. Commander of French forces in North America from 1756 to his death in 1759 at Québec. Successfully defended Carillon (later Fort Ticonderoga) against a much larger British army in 1758.

Naunauphtaunk, Capt. Jacob. One of the Stockbridge Indians for whom Rogers obtained a commission.

Ogden, Amos. Although wounded during the Saint-François Raid, he somehow recovered on the terrible march back.

Phillips, Billy. A backwoodsman of mixed Dutch and Indian blood, he served with Rogers with distinction as a sharpshooter at the Battle on Snowshoes. He was captured, thought dead, but escaped to rejoin the rangers for the Saint-François Raid.

Pitt, William, 1st Earl of Chatham. Imperially minded British secretary of state during the French and Indian War, he afterward became prime minister (1766–68).

Pontiac, or "Ponteach." An Ottawa chief in the Great Lakes basin, the keystone of a pan-Indian uprising against the British succession to the French trading posts after the French and Indian War. He so impressed Rogers that he made him the hero of the second oldest American play.

Pudney, Joseph, Sr. Family friend of Rogers's father, James.

Putnam, Israel. A captain of the Connecticut provincials during the French and Indian War, he joined Rogers on several scouts and was captured at the Battle of Fort Anne. Became a general in the Revolution, distinguishing himself at the Battle of Bunker Hill.

Roberts, Benjamin. Indian superintendent of Michilimackinac and implacable foe of Rogers; his false prosecution of Rogers as a British traitor led to Rogers's court martial.

Rogers, Elizabeth Browne. Daughter of a well-renowned Portsmouth minister, Arthur Browne (q.v.), who married Rogers on June 30, 1761. She gave birth to their son, Arthur, in 1769. Filed successfully for divorce in 1775, claiming long separations, drunkenness, and infidelity. Married sea captain John Roche.

Rogers, Richard. Rogers's younger brother, he served with him as a ranger commander until his death from smallpox in 1757.

Roubaud, Father Pierre-Joseph-Antoine. Curé of the settlement of Saint-François when Rogers attacked it.

Rowlandson, Mary. Carried off by Narragansett Indians in 1675, she wrote the first captivity narrative.

Sabbatis. Young Abenaki son of Gill (q.v.), the chief of Saint-François, who was carried away on Rogers's return from Saint-François and befriended by Rogers.

Shirley, William. The king's governor of Massachusetts (1741–59), he assumed command of all British North American forces (1755–56) and gave Rogers his first independent command.

Stark, John. Rogers's boyhood friend, who distinguished himself as a ranger, then served as a Revolutionary War general; the hero of the Battle of Bennington, 1777.

Stevens, Capt. Phineas. British colonial diplomat and commander of Fort No. 4, Britain's most northern post on the Connecticut River.

Stevens, Lt. Samuel. Ordered by Amherst (q.v.) to rendezvous with the remnants of Rogers' Rangers coming back from Saint-François, he abandoned the designated spot prematurely, only hours before the starvation-ridden group straggled in. He was court martialed and dismissed.

Sullivan, Owen. One of the most colorful and masterly counterfeiters in colonial North America, he enlisted Rogers in one of his schemes. Caught and finally hanged in 1757.

Theyanoguin, or "Hendrick." A Mahican sachem whose sage advice helped William Johnson (q.v.) shatter a formidable French column at the Battle of Lake George in 1755 at the cost of his life.

Tute, James. Served with distinction on the Saint-François Raid, later recruited by Rogers for an expedition to find the Northwest Passage.

Vaudreuil, François-Pierre de Rigaud, Marquis de. Governor-general of New France (1757–60).

Waite, Joseph. Fought alongside Rogers in the Battle on Snowshoes, then successfully commanded a group on the march home from Saint-François.

Walker, Reverend Timothy. First minister of Rumford (earlier Penacook, later Concord) from 1730 to 1782.

Washington, George. Commander of the American forces during the Revolution from 1775, and mysteriously set against Rogers at their first meeting.

Wentworth, Benning. Royal governor of the colony of New Hampshire and a fellow mason of Rogers's in Portsmouth.

Chronology

1728–31	Rogers's father, James, and his family leave Ireland and arrive in the New World
NOVEMBER 1731	Robert Rogers born
SPRING 1739	Family moves to Mountalona, on the New Hampshire frontier
MARCH 1744	France declares war on Britain, starting King George's War
APRIL 1748	Family farm is burned to the ground by Abenaki raiding party
JANUARY 1755	Rogers arrested on charges of counterfeiting
APRIL 1755	Rogers enlists 50 men into the New Hampshire militia and earns a captaincy
JULY 1755	General Braddock's forces routed by French at the Monongahela River
SEPTEMBER 1755	Battle of Lake George. British outpost resists attack by well-trained French regulars.
AUGUST 1757	Storming of Fort William Henry; major British fortress sacked
OCTOBER 1757	British commander Loudoun asks Rogers to write down his rules of rangering
DECEMBER 1757	Mutiny on Rogers' Island
MARCH 1758	Battle on Snowshoes, Rogers's epic midwinter fight against Jean-Baptiste Langy
JULY 1758	General Abercromby's large assault is fiercely repulsed by much smaller French army at Carillon
AUGUST 1758	Battle of Fort Anne
JULY 1759	Carillon falls to British, renamed Ticonderoga
SEPTEMBER–NOVEMBER 1759	Saint-François Raid and starvation-march home
SEPTEMBER 1759	Battle of the Plains of Abraham, Québec City falls

NOVEMBER 1760	Fort Détroit surrenders to Rogers
JUNE 1761	Rogers marries Elizabeth Browne, daughter of Portsmouth reverend Arthur Browne
AUGUST 1761– OCTOBER 1762	Rogers in South Carolina for the Cherokee Wars
1763–64	Chief Pontiac spurs pan-Indian attack on Great Lakes forts
FEBRUARY 1763	Treaty of Paris signed, official end of Seven Years' War (and its North American aspect, the French and Indian War)
JULY 1763	British forces sent to reinforce Fort Detroit are routed by Pontiac at Battle of Bloody Run; Rogers organizes retreat
1765	Publishes *A Concise Account, The Journals of Robert Rogers,* and America's second play, *Ponteach; or, The Savages of America*
AUGUST 1766	Rogers and Betsy arrive at Fort Michilimackinac
DECEMBER 1767	Rogers arrested at Michilimackinac on charges of treason
OCTOBER 1768	Exonerated of charges by court martial
FEBRUARY 1769	Betsy gives birth to their son, Arthur
JUNE 1776	George Washington orders Rogers arrested
JULY 1776	Rogers escapes from prison and joins Howe's army on Staten Island
SEPTEMBER 1776	Rogers unmasks the American spy Nathan Hale on Long Island
MAY 1795	Rogers dies in London

Those who have only experienced the severities and dangers of a campaign in Europe can scarcely form an idea of what is to be done and endured in an American war.

To act in a country cultivated and inhabited where roads are made, magazines are established, and hospitals provided; where there are good towns to retreat to in case of misfortune, or, at worst, a generous enemy to yield to, from whom no consolation but the honour of victory can be wanting—this may be considered as the exercise of a spirited and adventurous mind rather than a rigid contest where all is at stake and mutual destruction the object, and as a contention between rivals for glory rather than a real struggle between sanguinary enemies.

But in an American campaign everything is terrible—the face of the country, the climate, the enemy. There is no refreshment for the healthy, nor relief for the sick. A vast, unhospitable desert, unsafe and treacherous, surrounds them, where victories are not decisive, but defeats are ruinous, and simple death the least misfortune which can befall them.

This forms a service truly critical in which all the firmness of the body and the mind is put to the severest trial, and all the exertions of courage and address are called out. If the actions of these rude campaigns are of less dignity, the adventures in them are more interesting to the heart and more amusing to the imagination that the events of a regular war.

EDMUND BURKE,
ON THE FRENCH AND INDIAN WAR, 1763[1]

The French and Indian War was destined to have the most momentous consequences to the American people of any war in which they have been engaged down to our own day—consequences therefore even more momentous than those that flowed from the victorious Revolutionary War or from the Civil War. For it was to determine for centuries to come, if not for all time, what civilization—what governmental institutions, what societal and economic patterns—would be paramount in North America.

LAWRENCE HENRY GIPSON,
THE BRITISH EMPIRE BEFORE THE AMERICAN REVOLUTION

Introduction

The Bet

A waste and howling wilderness,
Where none inhabited
But hellish fiends, and brutish men,
That Devils worshiped.
This region was in darkness plac't,
Far off from heavens light,
Amidst the shadows of grim death
And of eternal night.

PURITAN POET MICHAEL WIGGLESWORTH,
GOD'S CONTROVERSY WITH NEW-ENGLAND (1662)

One raucous evening in 1765, two years after France had ceded its great North American holdings to the British, a dozen or so British officers comfortably scraped back their chairs in the plain back room of a London public house, quite interested to hear what the just-arrived war hero, Major Robert Rogers, had to offer these hard-bitten veterans of the line.

As in the countless other times when men like this gather, they consumed large quantities of alcohol, a process of lubrication here made the easier by servants circulating chamber pots around the table. These officers did not wear their uniforms on social occasions, a leftover reaction against Cromwell's strict Ironside rule, but dressed in the hose, breeches, and wigs of the landed class. The physical rigors of long campaigns during the Seven Years' War revealed themselves in the marks of the saber and musket ball, bodies tried to the limits by malaria's cruel fevers and chills, dysentery, gout, and teeth-shedding scurvy.

But even in that circle of hardy fighting men, Rogers stood out. His well-proportioned frame alone—pushing over six feet tall—was the equivalent today of a professional athlete's. He wore his hair back in a queue, or ponytail. Black gunpowder burns had seared parts of his face to sandpaper, and smallpox had left its distinctive mark, while a scar mapped the passage of a lead bullet across his forehead. A wound to the wrist had limited the use of several fingers.

Yet even more arresting was the catlike effortlessness of his movement, even if some of his permanently frost-deformed toes threw him off balance every now and then. Not a garrulous person, as some may have expected, he rather evinced the studied indifference of a presence that a contemporary described as "deliberate, of few words, generous to a fault, and desperate when roused."[1] Habit and disposition mandated that he sat facing the door. He quaffed the warm ale with relish, showing little effect except some softening around the eyes and an increasingly ruddier cast to his still-weather-chapped cheeks.

When his eyes met another's, the man so engaged often felt somehow silently challenged, as though the big quiet warrior were taking his measure. Like so many good combat leaders, Rogers left the impression that he knew more about others than they did of him. Rogers's coolness, even in the heat of the most desperate dangers, inspired many but deeply unsettled some, prompting one detractor to describe him as "subtil & deep as hell."

With those he liked, the bond closed instantaneously, as though old, long-parted friends had reunited. The men gathering around that scratched table, though brothers in arms and each holding the king's commission, shared little else with Rogers. Products of a proprietary military tradition descending from the feudal order, they had bought commissions from the colonel of the regiment to which they aspired. Only a very few might come up from the ranks. British officers viewed common soldiers as spineless, lazy oafs—"the scum of the earth, enlisted for drink," as the greatest British commander of the age would characterize them—to be flogged into minimal robotic performance by the most iron discipline. Only thus brutally molded could His Majesty's troops stand up to the hardships of the campaign and not break ranks when disease rotted their columns and cannon-balls tore holes in their lines. While they might be hammered into fortitude and ferocity, they would show little initiative or self-confidence when isolated and undirected.

Their officers gathered in formal institutions devoted to training them not just in tactics but in the carefully prescribed conduct appropriate to their rank, working their way carefully through Humphrey Bland's *A Treatise of Military Discipline*. Unlike them, Rogers had risen to seniority without benefit of a military academy or access to any corpus of the literature of war. Unfettered by such reflexive traditions or rote knowledge, Rogers practiced—and largely invented—a new form of deep woodland warfare, innovating and synthesizing techniques and tactics as he went, rising from command of a company to that of a battalion and then a regiment, then to divisional command, all within five years—on deadly merit alone—a breathtaking rise not possible in the Old World for a younger son.

His bold design and concert-pitch execution of long-distance expeditions, often under extraordinary duress, depended on his teaching a mixed force of provincial militiamen, raw woodsmen and farmers, British regular volunteers, and Indians, not to fight with dumb, lash-taught resolution but to think for more than themselves—a shattering break with past European practices. From the woods of New England emerged a new kind of war-maker, a path-breaker of new tactics, an innovator of new technologies, and perhaps most important, a motivator of warriors as individuals, who could draw them far beyond their perceived capabilities.

The war over, on the European continent as well as in North America, these survivors leaned forward to tell their whoppers at the fireside. As often happens among men of risk and action, the talk turned to wagers, and they quickly agreed to a round of storytelling: the others would pay the bill of the man who could tell the biggest lie or the most improbable story.

Rogers came last. His companions expected a war story, perhaps one about the already-legendary 1758 Battle on Snowshoes so assiduously reported by newspapers on both sides of the Atlantic. Rogers chose instead to evoke his boyhood in provincial New Hampshire, where he had followed rude blazes hacked into trees for more than ten miles to sell homemade brooms in Rumford, the town nearest to the family farm. Once, he explained to his now-rapt listeners, a hunter had tracked his mother for several miles, certain that her small footprints were those of a large wolf. Rogers paused for a moment, took a swallow from his tankard, and then with a lowered voice described how his father had met a worse fate when one dusk he approached the camp of his best friend, who mistook his hunched-over shape for a black bear. A single shot found its mark, and James Rogers died in his sobbing friend's arms. Rogers's tale had the effect of a ghost story told at night around a bonfire whose flames cast all too little light into the surrounding deep woods.

The audience met the story with hoots of disbelief; but, Caleb Stark, the grandson of Roger's good friend John Stark, reported, for that very reason they decided that the major "had told the greatest *lie*, when in fact he had told the *truth*." Rogers ate and drank free that night, revealing, as he had so many other times before, his uncanny ability to read a group of men.

No other man in that room could imagine growing up in a true wilderness: for the most part, the frontier had disappeared from Europe by about 1400, except for relatively small areas in northern Scotland, Scandinavia, and Russia, with a few pockets in Germany and Sicily. No human-eating animals roamed there, except occasional wolf packs in the central and southern continent, and by the eighteenth century, even those only rarely. Early accounts of North America's natural wonders often burst with a near-manic breathlessness: "Yea there are some serpents called Rattle Snakes, that have Rattles in their Tayles that will no flye from a Man as others will, but will flye upon him and sting him so mortally, that he will dye within a quarter of an houre after," wrote the Salem minister Francis Higginson in the early seventeenth century.

The North American wilderness recalled the stories of the ancient Skalds and Sagamen: Rogers evoked not only a world teeming with dangerous beasts, whose domain began a couple of strides outside the cabin door, but an environment in which men could be justly mistaken for these very creatures. This world blurred the line between savagery and civilization, perhaps the very difference between human beings and beasts—men skinned animals and scalped their enemies or were themselves eaten or scalped. This was no long-tamed forest of England, rich with folktales about fairies and Robin Hood's merry band, but a geography dark, unknown, and endless, capable of devouring those who ventured into it. Most notably, it fostered peoples even more exotic and alien than the Chinese, East Indians, and Turks, with which the British were already dealing. The Woodland Indians had never attained cities, nor sought to raise them: their minimalist patterns of land use and nonliterate traditions had created cultures inscrutable to the European mind.

What Rogers communicated that night would stay with these men, because he had opened up a fascinating vista into the world of the wilderness frontier, not merely unknown but absolutely unimagined. Few others had traveled as widely and knew as much about this increasingly crucial continent as Rogers. Not a single white European could challenge his claim that "no one man besides has traveled over or seen so much of this part of the country as I have done," and this hard-schooled author evidently needed no map to guide him through the northern woods of New England, which he had roamed on foot, snowshoe, and skate, first as an inquiring young man, then as an officer of rangers. He had pressed far westward across the greatest freshwater basin in the world to the Straits of Mackinac, which connect Lakes Huron and Michigan, and south into the still dangerously independent Cherokee lands that were rather nominally part of South Carolina. At the end of the French and Indian War, at one day's notice from General Jeffrey Amherst, he had marched, paddled, and rowed nearly 1,600 miles on a round-trip to Détroit from Montréal to notify the Great Lakes Indians and French garrison commanders of the British victory, losing only one man. No other expedition in pre-Revolutionary America would travel so quickly, safely, and far.

Rogers offered himself as the expounder of a realm never before made coherent by map or report, so vast and alien in its contours, fauna, botany, and human occupation that it resembled a new planet, "mostly a desart," he wrote (by which his age meant wilderness), "uninhabited, except by savages."

The same year he told his story, Rogers would bring out a battery of works about North America unique in their range and intensity: a play about the Ottawa chief Pontiac, portraying a man as formidable and extraordinary as the continent itself; his own journals elaborating in the first person his war experiences and unmatched journeys; and the first truly synoptic account of North America, a third-person disquisition on the continent's prodigious geography and an ethnographic description of its indigenous peoples. He would undertake to outline a credible plan to cross the continent, forty years before Lewis and Clark. In doing so, he became the first English-speaking continentalist, using multimedia approaches to help people wrap their minds around the Americas, visualize them, place them, make them somehow understandable. Certainly British colonists in Boston and Philadelphia could imagine vast stretches of forests, but understanding America was like understanding the solar system before spaceflight. People had a sense of the solar system as an immense place, punctuated by planets and stars, but not until ships blasted off into space and probes raced to its outer edges did humans look at the cosmos in new, revolutionary ways, most notably gaining the insight that the fragile orb of Earth is a finite place. And only when Europeans gained purchase on vast North America—through descriptions and explorations—could their perceptions change from dread to eager embrace of the immense possibilities.

All Americans think of themselves as birthright continentalists, so it is difficult today to imagine the dearth of simple information, let alone imaginative engagement, about the continent 250 years ago. Americans take for granted every Albert Bierstadt painting, Ansel Adams photograph, highway map, and roadside history sign, each of which affords another point of leverage to grasp the continent. Combining further input from the many images, ideas, maps, descriptions, and such creates a web of connections and interdependencies between history, geology, topography, biota, and weather data that simply did not exist then. The first novel featuring America as a background was not written until a few years shy of 1800.

In the early 1500s even the best maps of the world did not so much as display North or South America. No Europeans could entertain the sense that the discoveries of Columbus, Basque fishermen, and the Norse long before were anything more than small stretches of land, perhaps even islands.

As early as 1700 a British colonist could have traveled some 900 miles of tidewater lands from Portland, Maine, down to southern Virginia, stopping off in a village, town, or small settlement nearly every evening. Few contemplated undertaking journeys even a fraction of that length, such were the risks and difficulties associated with travel. Not until 1766 did a regular stagecoach run between Philadelphia and New York, and that took three days.[2]

A determined person traveling westward would have met no signs of civilization at its crudest more than 50 miles inland. Despite the 150-year European colonization of North America—most colonies were more than a century old by the 1760s—the settlers had barely reached beyond the sea-penetrated fringes of the vast continent. In contrast, the French had gone deep into the New World via the St. Lawrence, bringing the expertise of a culture used to plying rivers and building canals at home and deploying linguistically sophisticated missionaries. Yet even their presence remained largely limited to a chain of forts and trading garrisons near water sources.

Before the American Revolution the frontier stretched no farther west than the granite Appalachian chain, which shadows the east coast for some 1,600 miles, southwest from the Canadian Maritimes to the Gulf Coast plain of Alabama. Six hundred eighty million years of erosion had deeply creased and tangled a topography of ridgelines shooting off at oblique angles, smaller adjacent submountain ranges, odd glacial features, and twisted rivers and their steep valleys, which formed as formidable a barrier to British colonists attempting to move west as for centuries the Roman frontier zone held back the barbarians.

Oceangoing ships could carry English trade goods no farther inland than the fall line, the series of rapids formed as each river rages down the geological transition zone between the rocky piedmont plateau and the sandy coastal plain. Smaller-boat traffic upstream ran out of keel room when it encountered the eastern flanks of the Appalachians. No roads and but few tracks, except for buffalo traces in Kentucky and trails leading west from Albany, offered any practical assistance to westward movement, and even these accommodated only foot or horse travel. The Cumberland Gap—near where Tennessee, Virginia, and Kentucky now meet, a major artery for late-eighteenth-century westgoers—was not to be discovered by Europeans until 1750.

Despite its promise of wealth in furs and timber, grain and grazing, and perhaps in precious minerals, this vast wilderness remained too implacable, unmasterable, and dangerous for most colonists even to contemplate pushing deeply into it; its known dangers outweighed any potential gains. Many who ventured into it simply vanished. Most established colonists viewed the farther lands with deep apprehension; the frontier inched west, carried by outlawry, discontent, and the poorest elements of an excess population, not by visionary enterprise. Only generations later would it jump westward by leaps and bounds. The natural disposition of the established British coastal colonists during the mid-eighteenth century lay not westward into forbidding immensity but eastward, across the Atlantic to the British Isles, and, for those on the make, southward to the Caribbean sugar islands and farther east again to the slave coasts of Africa.

Not just physical boundaries kept most British colonists clinging to the coast: the New England colonies, largely formed as havens against religious persecution, sought to create highly regulated communities that would protect them and enforce their doctrines. Exploring or settling beyond the reach of their communities might result in less orthodoxy and moral decay. Even as the Puritan influence waned in the eighteenth century, the idea of what might be brooding beyond the far mountains terrified the established settlers on the coast.

The Puritans, for instance, imagined precontact North America as a land where Satan and his fallen angels lurked in the shadow of every tall pine. "A waste and howling wilderness, / Where none inhabited / But hellish fiends, and brutish men, / That Devils worshiped. / This region was in darkness plac't, / Far off from heavens light, / Amidst the shadows of grim death / And of eternal night," wrote the Puritan poet Michael Wigglesworth 40 years after the landfall of the Pilgrims but still a generation before the dark trials of Salem.[3] Wigglesworth's stark 224-stanza poem *The Day of Doom* became America's first best seller and a totem of early North American Puritanism, memorized by children along with the catechism.[4]

Meanwhile a new and peculiarly American form of expository work was emerging: the captivity narrative, detailing in the plainest prose the horrors undergone by settlers who had been torn from their homes by Indian raiders and marched into Canada and slavery, with cruel death the only alternative for those who could not keep up with their drivers. "Oh the roaring, and singing and dancing, and yelling of those black creatures in the night, which made the place a lively resemblance of hell," wrote Mary Rowlandson of Lancaster,

Massachusetts, taken by the Narragansetts in 1676. She—and the renowned Puritan minister Increase Mather, who wrote the preface to her book, *The Sovereignty and Goodness of God*—left no doubt in readers' minds that her eleven-week ordeal was biblical, she a latter-day Moses facing the trials of another wilderness.

Her story and those of other captives, including the bone-chilling accounts of the French Jesuits, provided nightmare glimpses into a capriciously cruel Dantesque world incomprehensible to European sensibilities. The Eastern Woodlands Indians spared some captives, even adopting them into their own families, but submitted others to tortures so hideous as to make death a joyful release. One can only imagine the response of English readers when they encountered early English explorer John Smith's matter-of-fact account of a Pamunkey healing process: "a man with a Rattle and extreame howling, showting [and] singing," circled the patient, then sucked the blood and phlegm from the infection. The artistically long-drawn-out torment of French missionaries, their fingernails chewed to bloody pulps by Indians with painted faces, their body parts hacked off and skins rent, recalled—indeed exceeded—the worst medieval terrors of the Inquisition and Reformation.

Even later, after the Revolution and the formation of the republic, the continent's vast interior remained outside the imaginations of most Americans. America's first two presidents seem never to have seriously considered sending exploratory parties west to the Pacific. When Thomas Jefferson initiated Lewis and Clark's mission in 1804, he told Lewis to watch out for giant sloths and iguanodons, for surely no species that had left remains in the coastal rocks could have died out in the unimaginably abundant interior. Few on the east coast would have been surprised had the expedition returned with word of a great Indian civilization rivaling that of the Aztec or Maya.

By proving that vast distances could be traversed, that the wilderness did not corrupt everything it touched with darkness and savagery but created such great leaders as Pontiac, Rogers was instrumental in changing his countrymen's sense of the wilderness from fear and darkness to possibility. Rogers acted as a "merchant of light," to use the English philosopher Francis Bacon's term for those who brought back understanding of the larger world. Rogers's writings revealed the wilderness as ultimately comprehensible and exploitable.

His ideas foreshadowed the Canadian explorer Vilhjalmur Stefansson's vision of "the friendly Arctic" by more than 150 years. Stefansson would argue that people of European stock could negotiate the extreme polar environment if they mastered the ways of the Inuit. Rogers unfolded extensive travels into clear-eyed discussion, revealing a world not dark and forbidding but fascinating, knowable, and deeply supportive to those who would learn its ways.

Rogers's depiction of his forest-clearing childhood marked one of the earliest renditions of the all-American "I grew up in a log cabin" theme that was to bewitch foreign audiences. By evening's end, drunk on rum and war talk, the soldiers fell out of the pub, most probably thrilled by Rogers's stories but also somewhat glad to separate from a man so fundamentally different from them, this unsettling and sometimes disturbing creature—and perhaps creator—of a new land.

Curiously, not one of those men, nor the thousands of others who met Rogers, ever wrote a physical description of the man (at least none that survives), although everybody remembered their encounter. Caleb Stark made a brief reference to his height, and years later during the Revolution a child referred to his "red eyes," conjuring up visions of a wolf. The portraits of him are all artists' fabrications created after his death. For a man whose extraordinary exploits had become frequent newspaper fare and whose fame and name recognition long rivaled that of Benjamin Franklin (the word *famous* was often appended to his surname), this silence is deafening—and telling.

No one seems to have set out to describe or explain him, because they could not get their imagination around the man, this master of nature and humans who could lead unimpressionable New Englanders to the edge of death over and over and could borrow money by hinting at dreams of larger things. People felt strangely subordinate to his forceful and strangely impersonal presence, focusing instead on his actions and stories, as though vaguely humiliated by the power he had exerted over them. Later, those who met him could not focus on the surface qualities of the man but rather concentrated on the way he made them feel, which left them often unsettled and occasionally angry, in recollection of this far stranger star around whom they had swung like planets.

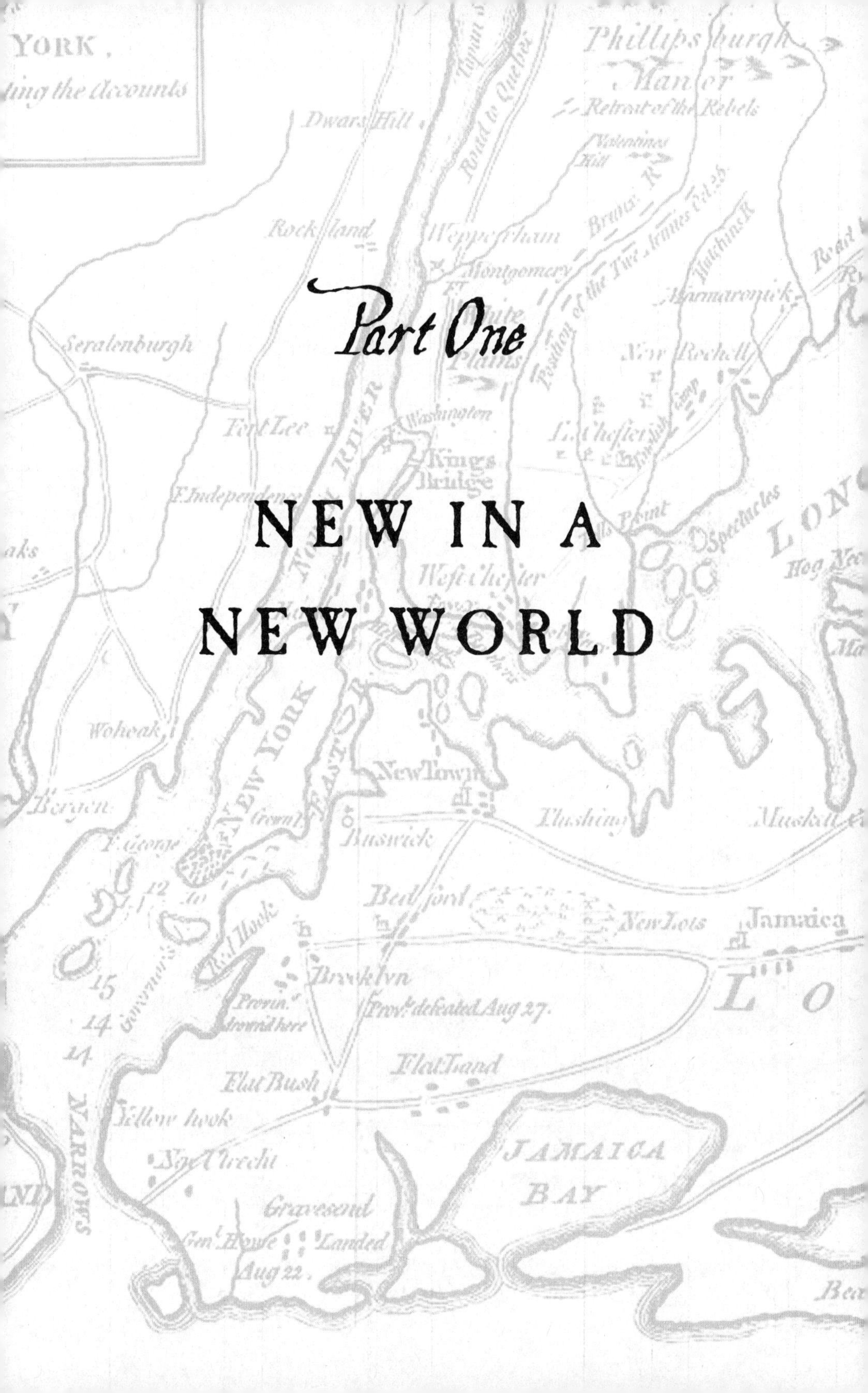

Part One

NEW IN A NEW WORLD

Chapter 1

Into the Wilderness

This is the forest primeval. The murmuring pines and the hemlocks,
Bearded with moss, and in garments green, indistinct in the twilight,
Stand like Druids of eld, with voices sad and prophetic,
Stand like harpers hoar, with beards that rest on their bosoms.
Loud from its rocky caverns, the deep-voiced neighboring ocean
Speaks, and in accents disconsolate answers the wail of the forest.

HENRY WADSWORTH LONGFELLOW, *EVANGELINE*

Early one spring morning in 1739 James Rogers cinched the knots securing his family's belongings to an oxcart. Several sacks of corn kernels, some to be used for food, others for seed, huddled among well-worn tools and implements: an ax, a hoe, an iron pot, and a skillet. On the wagon's sill he propped his heavy smoothbore, loaded and primed with powder and shot. The New Hampshire air still carried the lingering bite of winter. Nearby the Spicket River gurgled more quietly than usual, denied its usual springtime roar by two years of drought.

The fir-shaded clearing in front of the small log cabin bustled with even more activity than usual for this characteristically large frontier family. His wife, Mary, brought out the last belongings, while their 13-year-old daughter, Martha, looked after her mother's 2-year-old namesake. Their five sons—Daniel, 16, Samuel, 14, James, 11, Robert, 7, Richard, 5—dashed around. In November James the elder had bought a one-sixth interest in 2,190 acres of tallgrass meadow and evergreen forest 35 miles northwest of their present 44-acre homestead in Methuen.

During the long winter evenings James had read to the children from his small but choice library, which included the Geneva Bible that he had carried over from Ireland. He may have enthralled them with the resourcefulness of the shipwrecked hero of *Robinson Crusoe,* one of the few novels forever passing from hand to hand on the frontier. Buried in that grave but spirit-raising adventure lay a moral that resonated with those who ventured into any wilderness: things get done not by wishing but by willing. Perhaps for young Robert, as Friday passed out of the unknown into Robin's service, the story lent strength to the idea that friends could be found in the impassive wilderness.

James may have also read them *The Pilgrim's Progress,* Bunyan's allegorical epic, in which the highest qualities of worldly adventure sweep through the Slough of Despond and Valley of the Shadow of Death up Hill Difficulty and on to face "Apollyon straddling over the whole breadth of the way" and Giant Despair, fit enemies for journeyers to overcome. After the hardship of the passage on which many would fail, the traveler could expect to enter the truly Celestial City along its streets paved in gold. These tales unlocked doors in the mind that opened to reveal unending vistas of the strange and wonderful. By naming and depicting things dark and mysterious, at first glance unconquerable but that proved vulnerable to hope and light, these tales had the power to awaken energies capable of driving back the inescapable terrors of the unknown.

For years James had yearned to own something more than this little clearing. While the banks of the Spicket returned rich yields of corn, barley, and flax, so confined a tract provided barely enough for him to feed himself, his wife, and seven children and to meet town taxes and their share of the local minister's keep. He and Mary had left Ulster a decade earlier in search of something more than this.

Nonetheless, no one could call the Rogerses poor. They were lucky too. The diphtheria epidemic that ravaged the region between 1735 and 1737 had overleaped them. In those three years it had struck terribly close, choking the life from 256 children in the adjacent town of Haverhill, swelling throats and filling them with ash-colored specks. Death from "throat distemper" came quickly, sometimes in as little as twelve tortured hours, carrying off small children most readily of all. Some families lost five or six children in the space of one nightmarish week. Within one year 984 settlers, 800 of them children under ten, had been swept away, not quite five percent of the entire New Hampshire colony.[1]

James also looked forward to escaping the rarely hidden contempt shown by so many established colonists toward him and his fellow Scots-Irish. Ever since the Reverend Jamie MacGregor led the first wave of Ulster Presbyterians to northern New England 22 years before, the Puritans had made their lives difficult. In these proud, poor, and often violent newcomers, the older order found much to dislike: pride beyond their meanly assigned station and a spirited disregard for authority.[2] Antipathy ran so deep that the Puritans even regarded the potato, which MacGregor's flock introduced to the region, as a fruit of the devil, a pernicious root unfit for Christian stomachs, imputing to it—with an imagination that told more about the imaginers than it did about the humble esculent—aphrodisiac powers.

John Greenleaf Whittier would capture this hostility by quoting an anonymous balladeer's gloating depiction of how, in the spring of 1719, the townsfolk of Haverhill had watched with amusement as an immigrant canoe heading upriver to MacGregor's settlement of Londonderry capsized in the rapids:

They began to scream and bawl,
As out they tumbled one and all,
And, if the Devil had spread his net,
He could have made a glorious haul![3]

In 1729 a Boston mob prevented a shipload of Ulster immigrants from coming ashore, leaving the sea-weary people to work their way up the Maine coast before they could set foot on land.[4] Early-eighteenth-century New England was a homogeneous closed society, its coastal towns ruled by a religious elite who felt the hand of God's ordainments on their actions and policed obedience to the community with stifling social pressures. The newcomers struck at the heart of those iron conventions that had enabled the Puritan order to establish itself and survive in the New World. They spoke in a thick brogue, drank heavily, fought often, and spoke their minds when not asked. Their women often dressed provocatively.[5] They prayed standing, not on their knees, like warriors gaining a promised land.

Although they worshipped a Protestant deity, their association, if only by geographical proximity in Ulster, with the Catholic Irish awoke deep fears among the Puritans. These first New Englanders had contended for decades with the papists of New France, who periodically whipped up the more or less converted Eastern Woodland peoples into murderous raids on the English settlements.

Rogers's ancestors knew something about Old World bloodshed. For many centuries violence consumed the basin of the upper Irish Sea: northern Ireland, the southern lowlands of Scotland, and the hills and valleys of northern England. In the past 700 years only three English monarchs had not invaded Scotland or found themselves defending their bloody borderlands against their northern neighbors. These windswept and treeless lands harbored tough, poor people who operated as often as not outside the reach of the law. Clans frequently sent bands "reiving," or preying, on their neighbors. Cattle rustling and levying blackmail (then the term for protection money) was an enduring way of life, not an extreme remedy. Violence pervaded all aspects of these marginal men's lives to such a degree that weddings often featured simulated kidnappings of the bride, the groom and his friends joining together to "rescue" her. Such border violence hardened kinship relationships, often at the expense of allegiance to the distant Crown.[6]

In the early 1600s James Rogers's forebears and thousands of other land-hungry border Scots had crossed the Northern Channel to settle the nine counties forming the northernmost province of Ireland. By the early 1700s conditions for the Scots Presbyterians of Ulster had deteriorated. The "rackrenting" practices of their absentee English landlords opened up leased property, long deemed to be held by perpetual hereditary right, to the highest bidder. Often several Irish Catholic families combined to outbid one Scots-Irish family, generations of which had toiled to improve the holding. New religious restrictions under Queen Anne ratcheted up resentment, while drought and economic depression added to their settler woes.[7] In 1717 a first trickle of emigration to America began, swelling into a flood over the next 48 years as more than 150,000 people from Northern Ireland, mostly of Scots-Irish stock, set off.[8]

Sometime between 1728 and 1731 James Rogers, his young wife, Mary, and their four children, perhaps rackrented out of their home in Londonderry, joined the exodus, landing in Boston.[9] Luck blessed them with a safe passage, albeit of two long months, though many of their fellow voyagers fell prey not only to the seas but to the callous merchants who jammed their vessels far beyond capacity with human cargo. On average, nearly a third of the passengers died.[10] The parents of Robert Rogers's good friend John Stark lost all three of their young children to the foul holds.[11]

The northeastern town of Methuen, on the Merrimack River just west of Haverhill, did not exactly embrace the Rogers family, but practicality often overrode dogma in America's always labor-poor interior. The elders—some 65 taxpaying men[12]—sold them small parcels from the common pasture on the northern edge of town: these newcomers in their rough but defensible log cabins could serve as a first line of resistance to the fierce raiders from the north. Rogers's young sons would eventually enter the ranks of the all-too-often-mustered militia. On the Sabbathday, November 14, 1731, the town's young minister, Christopher Sargent, baptized one-week-old Robert, his family's first child born in North America, in the clapboard Congregationalist church on Meeting House Hill.[13]

James Rogers made friends with his neighbor Joseph Pudney, a former shopkeeper from Salem who also dreamed that the dangers of settling deeper into the wilderness would be more than offset by the scope and freedom there to be won. Pudney had much in common with Rogers, notably a houseful of children and a determination to better himself whatever the price in risk and labor. The two formed a plan to settle in the Great Meadows, a favorite hunting spot of theirs, 35 rough but promising miles northwest of Methuen: Rogers had purchased 365 acres for 11 pounds; Pudney received his title on an adjacent tract 12 days later.

The Rogerses' oxcart pulled out, followed by haltered livestock—a couple of cows and a horse—and the ragtag procession joined the Pudneys to trudge along the banks of the Merrimack to Haverhill, where they picked up what passed for a road leading northwest to Rumford (today's Concord, New Hampshire), which had been hacked through the forest 13 years earlier.[14] The travelers, perhaps the first oxcart party since the winter, encountered blowdowns—large toppled trees whose sprawling branches had to be axed away. The cart had no brakes, so James and his strongest sons had to

maneuver the heavy loads with care down every incline. The road
jogged around massive granite boulders, scattered across the landscape as if some Brobdingnagian child had been playing at marbles. A
traveler in the eighteenth century noted that moss grew so thick on
some trees that it fell in tufts like long hair.[15] In places the forest fir,
spruce, oak, yellow birch, elm, and sugar maple gave way to spruce
bogs thick with rotting tree trunks, their waters dark from the wood's
decay.

At the yet-smaller town of Chester, 15 miles from Haverhill, the
caravan turned west toward the Merrimack, along Cohas Brook, its
banks lined with magnificent specimens of arrow-straight white pine
(*cohas* in Algonquin), some towering 250 feet and stretching eight
feet across. The Crown had laid claim to these trees for the masts and
spars of its world-class Royal Navy. Every ship of the line required a
mainmast at least 40 inches in diameter and 40 yards in height, as
well as foremasts, mainyards, bowsprits, mizzenmasts nearly as formidable.[16] When a gust of wind passed through these cathedral
groves as yet untouched by ax, the canopies shook and sighed like the
murmur of a distant sea.[17]

Rogerses and Pudneys crossed the Merrimack on John Goffe Jr.'s
ferry, then took an even rougher track along the west bank to
Amoskeag Falls, the most powerful stretch of white water along all
the river's 110 miles. Half a mile north Black Brook, so named from
the inkiness of its water, fell into the Merrimack from the west,[18] and
as the weary party swung upstream, the reality of their commitment
now settled upon the youngest. Cutting back saplings and cajoling the
oxen, they embarked on the last eight-mile push, their pace by now a
crawl. They slept underneath the wagons, some kept awake by the
howls of a nearby wolf pack that smelled the uneasy livestock. Not
too many years before and not a dozen miles from where they lay,
Zerobbabel Snow had been treed by wolves at dusk while out hunting. Frantically he blazed away with his fowling piece, but the pack
stood its ground. His lead running out, he shot his coat buttons at the
gray shadows. Only the next morning's daylight finally chased them
away.[19] While wolves rarely if ever attack humans, black bears and
catamounts—mountain lions—do. Catamounts can measure up to
nine feet from nose to tail and weigh up to 200 pounds.[20] Around
that time a ten-square-mile section of deciduous hardwoods in east-

ern North America might have maintained 5 black bears, 2 or 3 catamounts, and 1 to 3 gray wolves, as well as 2 elk, 30 red foxes, 400
deer, 200 turkeys, and up to 20,000 squirrels.[21]

What relief must the incomers have felt when they finally parted
the last branches and beheld the Great Meadows, a beaver-cleared
opening of tallgrass in the interminable forest, reaching uphill and
enclosed by forest. A stream ran through it, filling a large beaver pond
at their feet. James and Mary Rogers named their homestead
Mountalona, in memory of the Mounterloney Mountains of the
Ireland they had left behind.

The two families threw up a crude log habitation known as a
"half-faced camp." Two forked posts dug into the ground about ten
feet apart supported a pole, up against which were stacked small horizontal logs, one side left open and roofed with bark. This makeshift
shelter would house the livestock once the cabin was built.[22]

The main cabin was wrought of tree trunks, split through the
middle or "squared on the rough," and placed on top of one another
to form a rectangle. Saddle notches cut into the ends of each log
afforded a basic fit.[23] The cabin required no nails to be hammered or
sockets to be made in the 80 some logs, 20 to 30 feet in length; split
logs were used for the roof.[24] The cabin the Rogerses built that spring
and summer consisted of a single large room, divided by quilts hanging from ropes stretched between hooks in the rafters.[25] At bed-
time the children climbed a ladder into a loft and fell asleep under
bearskins teeming with fleas and lice.[26] A plank door and shutters
closed out the elements. Bark shingles or pine clapboards covered the
roof.[27] Old World flourishes may have decorated the cabin, perhaps a
double cross on the door, witch hazel and lilac bushes in the yard, and
witch balls on the roof to keep away evil spirits.[28]

The settlers created a large fireplace by fitting a crib against a
crude hole cut in the side wall of the house, its insides lined with
stones bedded in mud.[29] A hearth of flagstones spread out from it,
ample room for the several fires that always burned there.[30] The fires
warmed the house, while raked embers boiled kettles of water and
heated a bake oven on the other side. From a hook driven into the
greenwood lugpole, which spanned the entire hearth, hung a large
iron pot, in which Mary Rogers always kept a simmering charge of
bean porridge—boiled beans or peas, enriched with beef or pork fat

and thickened with Indian cornmeal. Venison haunches, bear meat, skinned raccoon, rabbit, and other small game animals also thronged the lugpole. The youngest children took shifts turning the meat with sticks so it would cook evenly. As it savored, the drippings slid into wooden pans below.

When inside, James kept his musket, powderhorn, and shotbag dry on pegs over the fireplace.[31]

Men and boys harnessed the ox team to clear rocks from the open ground, fenced the hay meadows, and chopped firewood. Back in Methuen the minister expected the parish to supply him and his family with 30 cords of wood.[32] The Rogerses would need more than that, not counting timber to stock their plow, fix the wagon, make ox yokes and harnesses, and build the cabin's crude furniture. Mary and the girls sewed all the family's clothing. James and his family by necessity learned to be jacks of all trades, proficient if not skilled at the animal husbandry, masonry, blacksmithing, carpentry, and tool making that attended to this life of unremitting toil and isolation. The simple tasks of raising dwellings and barns, clearing the land, building fences, and making a rudimentary road could take a lifetime.

Time preyed heavily on the two families; they worked with speed, quickly expanding their cultivable land by using an Indian technique that did not require draft animals. Girdling trees—cutting deep enough into the bark at the base to interrupt the flow of sap— made the leaves and ultimately the branches fall off. They planted quickly maturing crops, such as corn in the meadows and among the already leafless and dying trunks. Corn returned a rich bounty without requiring much of a time investment. The kernels served as food, the stalks as rich winter fodder for livestock, the husks as mattress filling, and the cobs as tool handles. Once the cornstalks reached two or three feet, the farmers surrounded them with beans and pumpkins. In due course the stalks would serve as beanpoles and shade for the pumpkin vines.[33] The corn, in turn, brought deer to the fields, and the youngest Rogerses and Pudneys kept watch at dusk and dawn with muskets and butchering knives at the ready. With his own smoothbore Robert learned how to "bark" a squirrel, killing it not with a direct hit but with the concussive force of a close-in impact on the tree trunk to preserve the meat.

Already the boy had mastered basic lessons: he learned to "eye," or sweep his gaze to pick up unexpected patches of color, movement, or texture standing out against the forest tint; to sit quietly for hours on end to become invisible to forest creatures; and to identify the scat and prints of game animals.

Young Rogers became immersed in the rhythms and lore of the flora and fauna—the passage of migrating birds, the spawning of fish, the days when the sap ran richly from the sugar maples, and those when deer became more reckless and easier to hunt during the rutting season. He learned that an ideal time to kill a moose came when it stuck its head into a bog or pond to eat water-lily roots, and that its nose made particularly good eating.[34] Out of plain necessity Rogers came to understand how plants manage their energy, storing it according to the seasons in their roots, leaves, and seeds. The season-related behaviors of both plants and animals became waypoints around which to orient oneself in the woods and in life; in much the same way the Eastern Woodlands Indians might agree, at the end of the moon of the deer mating season, to leave on a scout.

The Rogerses' second winter in Great Meadows hit with a vengeance. On March 26, 1741, the Reverend James MacSparran climbed into his pulpit at Trinity Church in relatively prosperous coastal Newport, Rhode Island, looked down upon the drawn faces of his parishioners, and observed all too obviously that "the elements have been arm'd with such piercing cold and suffocating snows" that it were "as if God intended the Air that he gave us to live and breathe in, should become the instrument to execute his vengeance on us, for our ingratitude to his goodness, and our transgression of his law."[35]

Starting 150 to 200 years before the earliest British settlement at Jamestown, Virginia, and lasting until the mid-nineteenth century, North America and western Europe had felt the claws of the Little Ice Age, one of several climatic fluctuations since the end of the Pleistocene some 10,000 years before. In the winter of 1740–41 temperatures would drop to eight degrees below zero Fahrenheit on the coast and far lower yet on the exposed slopes of Mountalona. Twenty-seven storms lashed the coast, bringing snows that covered fenceposts and winds that whipped drifts above the second stories of houses, to suffocate chimneys. A sharp young merchant of 28, Francis Lewis, drove his horse-drawn sleigh over the frozen sea from

Barnstable, Massachusetts, in the crook of Cape Cod, all the way
along the coast to New York City, some 200 icebound miles. Thirty-
five years later this enterprising man would sign the Declaration of
Independence.[36]

To make matters worse, a December thaw and three weeks of
rain had liquefied the foot or more of crusted snow into a massive
runoff that overran every river valley in New England. The
Merrimack, which drains central and southern New Hampshire and
northeastern Massachusetts, rose 15 feet, bearing off many houses
and hundreds of tons of wood carefully stacked for the rest of the
winter. Everywhere the waters penetrated corncribs and barns, ruining livestock feed. "Our corn," wrote farmer Stephen Jacque of
Newbury, Massachusetts, "moulded as fast as six hogs could eat it."[37]
When the snow came back in earnest that February, the cattle
starved. Farmers told of finding sheep, lost for weeks, just alive beneath deep drifts, feeding on its sparse, frozen grasses. White-tailed
deer, exhausted by their struggles against the snowdrifts, made easy
prey for the equally desperate wolves and catamounts, severely de-
pleting a food resource that many inland settlers counted upon. At
Mountalona, even crowding near the fire did not guarantee warmth
against the damp and drafts.

Sleepless during those long nights, the wind howling bitterly outside, the family turned to storytelling and reading from the Bible.
Joseph Pudney added to the Old World tales with strange and unsettling stories of the New. His father, John, had testified in the trial of
Job Tookey during the Salem witch trials of 1692. Two young women
told of seeing five people—all murdered, they claimed, by Tookey—
arise from the dead and cry "vengeance, vengeance."[38] The magis-
trates ultimately spared Tookey's life, but 19 other convicted witches
went to the gallows, while others died after long spells in prison.

The elder Pudney had witnessed the brutal death of Giles Corey,
subjected to an old English ordeal to elicit a plea from the stubbornly
mute—*peine fort et dure*—by which the accused were pressed under
large rocks until they either pleaded or died. Young Robert Rogers
would never forget these stories, which drew the line between the
proud saltwater early-colonial families and the new breed of equally
proud settlers forging a livelihood on the frontier. Salem was an ex-
emplary reality tale about the dangers that boiled up when an Old

World society met the New and let loose fears and passions with which it could not come to terms.

To those icebound winter days, Robert and his brothers responded by fashioning snowshoes, bending inch-thick ash saplings into oval forms two feet long and one wide, then binding the ends to make a handle. Two pieces of wood were inserted at opposite points on the long axis, to which were woven strong elastic leather strings attached to the wearer's shoes.[39] They also sewed Indian-style moccasins, which they knew dried far faster in the fall and winter than boots. By rubbing deer brains into the skin, then drying it with wood smoke, they kept the leather soft and supple, even after repeated soakings. The brothers would brave the midwinter drifts and visit the lake at the foot of the Great Meadows, venturing offshore to cut holes in the ice near beaver lodges, through which they dropped iron traps. Or they would follow Indian practice and draw a beaver to the surface by disturbing its lodge. When a furry head appeared at an ice-hole, one of the brothers would beat it with a stick.[40] Snowshoeing slowly but steadily through the forests, they overtook deer and discovered black bears hibernating in their dens.

Spending more and more time alone, Rogers was learning self-sufficiency and how to improvise with limited materials.

Chapter 2

First Encounters on the Frontier

*Young man, there is America—which at this day serves for little more
than to amuse you with stories of savage men and uncouth manners; yet
it shall, before you taste of death, show itself equal to the whole of that
commerce which now attracts the envy of the world.*

EDMUND BURKE, "SECOND SPEECH ON CONCILIATION
WITH AMERICA," *THE THIRTEEN RESOLUTIONS*, 1775

In the winter evenings James Rogers and the older children carved
splint brooms from yellow birch, another craft learned from the
Indians. When the weather cleared, Robert strapped the brooms to
his back and followed a series of rude blazes on tree trunks over the
13 or so miles to the little Merrimack Valley trading town of
Rumford. Here he encountered Abenaki traders from the north,
come to barter beaver furs for English trade goods.

On the outskirts of town still dwelt the remnants of the
Penacook, the people "at the falling bank," a branch of the Abenakis,
who had once roamed over lands the size of European sovereignties
that were to become New Hampshire, Vermont, Maine, and the
Canadian Maritimes.[1] To the west the Penacook, Cowasuck, Sokoki,
Missisquoi, Winnepesauke, Ossipee, and Pigwacket hunted and harvested, while the Penobscot, Androscoggin, and Kennebec inhabited
the eastern realms of Maine and Nova Scotia. Squeezed between the
French colonial settlements pressing south from the St. Lawrence
and the British colonists hacking their way north and westward, the
Abenaki were ravaged by European diseases—smallpox, diphtheria,
typhus, influenza, measles. Within a few generations the never-

numerous Indians dwindled by as much as three-quarters, perhaps more. The Eastern Woodlands' already small and spread-out aboriginal populations would never fully come back. In 1748 the Swedish traveler Per Kalm wrote that a city dweller at any one of the seaside colonial towns might go without seeing an Indian for six months.

By the 1660s those Penacooks who had survived disease frequently died in Mohawk raids from the west. The remnants drifted southward to the upper reaches of the Connecticut or took refuge in the Jesuit towns of Saint-François and Bécancour along the St. Lawrence in New France. The townspeople of Rumford looked upon the handful remaining with paternalistic pity. The young son of the town's minister, Timothy Walker, would disappear for hours at a time, returning with his face painted many colors and his hair adorned with gaudy feathers.[2] Rogers, too, was drawn to the wigwams on the edge of town, haystacklike huts covered in birchbark to keep out the elements, with a hole in the top to let out smoke.[3] Their dirty inhabitants dressed in ragged European shirts, greasy from the bear and raccoon fat that kept away the cold in winter and mosquitoes in summer.[4]

But if young Walker was Tom Sawyer, Robert anticipated Huck Finn, a boy just on the edge of things, too independent for the town kids. Robert, his brooms sold and with no one feeling any need to watch him, may well have explored the ruins of the old Penacook fort atop a bluff overlooking the Merrimack not far from town, which in the 1660s had undergone a bloody siege by the Mohawks. Just to the north lay the tribe's burial ground, which frequently disgorged bones after heavy rain.[5]

An outsider himself, Rogers viewed the Penacooks with less contempt than his Puritan contemporaries. These curious, solemn, quiet men, when not overcome by rum, became the doorkeepers of a world beyond the small, orderly, yet crude compounds occupied by most of the Europeans on the frontier. Robert could not ask enough questions of them. He became a keen observer of Woodland Indian cultures, absorbing much lore about the forest and its remarkable abundance and even elements of Algonquin languages. "The Indians do not want for natural good sense and ingenuity, most of the Indians are possessed of a surprising patience and equanimity of mind, and a command of every passion, except revenge," by which he may have

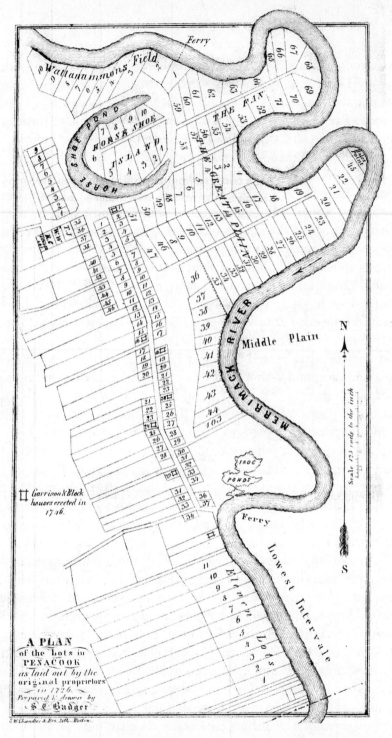

Penacook, New Hampshire (later Rumford and Concord)

meant rather more a sense of justice.[6] He studied their leaders and observed that success came to those who were "fortunate, brave, and disinterested,"[7] stressing that they would only follow one "in whom they firmly believe that these qualifications are united." He underscored the importance to them of "secrecy in all operations; in which art they greatly excel, their designs being seldom known to any but themselves, till they are upon the point of being executed." In years to come these principles would form the center of Rogers's own way of leadership.

With the help of his new friends, he began to understand that to those who could ask the right questions and knew where to look, the forest offered a feast of instruction. Without the light of sun or stars, Indians could find their bearings by any number of clues. Moss tended to grow more abundantly on the northern sides of trees; treetops generally inclined sunward, therefore to the south; branches grew thicker and larger on a tree's southern exposure, while the bark appeared darker, thicker, and more tender on the shadow side. Skunks coming in early for shelter under the barn, walnuts falling off the tree in bushels, and muskrat houses going up in great numbers signaled the approach of a hard winter. Cobwebs on the morning grass promised a clear, pleasant day.[8]

For Robert, the forest offered so much to learn. The cawing of crows gained in pitch before the coming of bad weather. Clouds that stuck atop the peak of a nearby mountain signified rain. When trammeled by snow and in need of shelter, he learned to look for hakmataks, natural mountainside refuges where the dense branches of hemlock and spruce interwove so thickly as to bear up under even the heaviest snowfall.[9] He became adept at setting up a culheag, or deadfall animal trap, in which a large rock is propped up by two logs and a baited stick.

As he later wrote to a friend, "by my own Slender Judgment and intimate Converse with the Indians I acquired a knowledge of Several Herbs plants and Shrubs that possess uncommon Virtues, and properties for General utility in the Medical Physical and Commercial States." Red, yellow, and black were the Indians' favorite colors, in which shades they had learned to create steadfast dyes from plants. A root with a small, smooth, deep green leaf of horse-hoof shape, which grows in swampy ground, formed the key

ingredient in a dye of the "most beautiful Red Colour" when boiled
along with red willow roots, hemlock bark, buds of the alder bush,
and an herb with a large hairy leaf and green stalk that when broken
bleeds "a Red Juice resembling the Colour of Claret." This dye re-
tained its color for years on "Beaver, blankets, Deer skins, Turkeys
Beards, Moose hair, and Porcupine Quils." Rogers learned the
Algonquin Indian technique of relieving frostnip by rubbing the affected area with the clear golden pitch of fir balsam.[10] He noted
"Prickley Ash" bark's effectiveness against fever and identified the
"Cohush Root," the white baneberry, by its "berry about the Size of a
Pea...the Taste is a pleasant bitter, and bears the sway from all other
Roots for its General healing and Salutary Qualities." His journals
and letters reveal time and again an amazingly alert eye for the details
of Indian culture. While advancing societies tend to demonize their
adversaries, particularly indigenous peoples, Rogers evinced no such
temptation, far too fascinated by the richness and strangeness of this
old New World.

In the woods he encountered Mohawk traders come eastward
with tales of the Great Lakes country, learning how long-repeated
Indian traditions reinforced the hunter's eye and observation: "Their
discourses run like a gentle flowing stream, without noise or tumult.
Their lips scarcely move through a whole speech."[11] He complained
about the Indians' tradition of rarely talking as they traveled, as much
out of awe at the land's overwhelming presence as from the fear of
alerting human enemies or animal prey—because this elected silence
prevented him from posing his incessant questions about everything
from whistling to attract prey to using animal skins as camouflage. "It
is very disagreeable travelling with them, on account of their being
enemies to conversation; for they not only never speak themselves
but when necessity obliges them, but are displeased with their company if they talk or converse upon a march by land, or a voyage by water."[12] If the Abenaki snacked on live rattlesnakes while jogging
through the woods, what other strengths might they draw on?[13] What
of men who scratched their skin with the sharp teeth of animals so
they could run through thickets full of briars and thorns with indifference?[14] What else might these eyes see in the forests?

His contemporaries certainly learned tricks of wilderness survival
out of necessity, but young Rogers's curiosity burgeoned into sus-

tained, systematic inquiry, energized to make sense of the endless body of instructed generalizations with which the Indians worked. These peoples, like the biblical patriarchs or the preliterate warriors in Homer, carried their stories orally across many generations, their bards and praise-singers capable of carrying thousands of lines of epic poetry or an equally rich storehouse of wisdom in their heads. "Their imaginations are so strong, and their memories so retentive, that when they have once been at a place, let it be ever so distant, or obscure, they will readily find it again."[15] By imagination Rogers meant not the ability to conjure up figments in the mind but the capacity first to see intensely, then to see into the implications of what is seen.[16]

He had learned from the Indians the habits of reviewing the vast knowledge-charged world for clues or (in later Western terminology) reading the landscape. The forest became not a dark and indistinguishable blur of green and brown but a vast, interactive virtual encyclopedia. Patches of similar tree species did not grow at random but suggested a certain soil composition, animal life, slope, and climate. A savvy observer could see that the green canopy of the Northeast, far from being coarsely uniform, was broken by the scars of fires both recent and ancient; large trees that blew down in winter storms created microclimates, and glacial remnants provided dependable landmarks. The sweep of the Milky Way, he learned, formed the "Road of Souls."[17]

Like all good hunters, he impressed upon his memory the contours of the land wherever he walked, not only its general characteristics but how and where game might browse, compete for mates, hunt, or sleep. On one single journey along a valley, for instance, his always-scanning eyes evaluated and stored thousands of pieces of information: How did the passing sun successively fall across the landscape? What sounds did the wind make when it was shifting directions? How did the game trails run?[18] All this would be stored away, to be drawn upon in the twinkling of an eye should a deer come into view. He could then make use of shifting shadows and wind patterns to stalk the prey unobserved. He had identified and remembered the places at which deer would never stop, as well as those where they might bed or feed, particularly the edges of blowdowns or among the tender shoots rising from burned-over ground. He learned how to calculate the time when the sun was hidden and worked out distances as he walked, and he picked up the Indian technique of breaking off tiny branches to help him retrace his steps.[19]

But the Indians and his own observations taught him not only good hunting practices but how to think about warfare. He scanned the terrain for the ideal spots where a hostile column of men could be ambushed, while simultaneously plotting escape routes and identifying places, such as patches of moraine boulders, where a staunch defense could be made. What was the fastest, most efficient, yet quietest way through this valley? What were the best spots for observing the surrounding terrain without exposing oneself too dangerously, as the tree cover thinned toward the crest? With experience, his woods vocabulary swelled, and his memory of places became a great library that he would often browse in the future. Hunting makes the Indian "strong, active and bold, raises his courage, and fits him for war, in which he uses the same strategies and cruelty as against the wild beasts," wrote William Smith, who had been an Indian captive in 1764.[20]

To the trained eye, human passage through the woods left a whole natural history that Rogers learned from his impassive teachers. The Jesuit father Joseph-François Lafitau noted that the Indians needed no more than a glance to "say without error of what nation, what sex and what stature are the people whose tracks they see, and almost for how long a time these traces have been there. If these persons are of their acquaintance, they will not be slow in saying, 'these are the tracks of such and such a man, or such and such a woman.' "[21] More than once in the future Rogers would save his life and others with such primitive profundities.

Once Robert grew old enough, his father took him and his brothers every mid-May to the oak-shaded banks of the Merrimack where it played through Amoskeag Falls. For perhaps 10,000 years the Algonquin and their precursors had gathered here to harvest the huge migrations of Atlantic salmon and shad that were fighting their way upriver to spawn in the cool waters. Eels, alewives, and sturgeon joined the race upstream, massing in such numbers below the falls that it was impossible to thrust one's arm into the water without touching a shad. And there were more alewives than shad, and more eels than both other species together.

The Merrimack drops 54 feet over a quarter mile of deep gray granite ledges, breaking into such roaring, furious white water that a century earlier Cotton Mather, the product of a culture with no word for *awesome* or *picturesque*, had simply dismissed this potent testimony to God's handiwork as "hideous." Below the falls the Merrimack spreads to thrice its former width and courses through a web of channels created by an ever-shifting riprap of jumbled boulders.

The Rogers men joined the hundred or so other New Englanders and Indians who hurried to the falls every spring to claim good spots on the rocks from which to harvest the natural bounty. The Rogers brothers scrambled up onto the large down-falls boulders, pocked by barrel-like shafts, some as deep as 16 feet. Today termed kettleholes, these features had developed when the rocks were underwater and the current spun stones in tight circles upon their surfaces, eventually wearing these deep pits. Those who stood atop Pulpit Rock—its religious overtones not lost on the boys—could command a view of the spring melt emptying out of a 5,000-square-mile drainage to their north as it crashed through this turbulent outlet.[22]

The best fishing occurred at night, when the men crowded the rocks alongshore brandishing lit torches of oil-soaked wood in a flickering otherworldly scene.[23] Some men were half-hidden in the gloom, while others were brightly lit, their torn and tattered clothes drenched with spray and slick with eel mucus. The uneven torchlight lent a strobelike quality, the frantic hunters dancing on the rocks in an unending slaughter of shad and salmon with swift spearthrusts, dragging out great seething masses of alewives with scoop nets and heaving armfuls of squirming eels out of pots. Some donned woollen mittens to pull the writhing lampreys directly from the water. Two decades later an observer asserted that one man swept out 2,500-odd shad with a single net-cast.[24]

The abundance, the triumphs of life in death, and the unceasing roar of the falls awoke a temporary insanity of hours-long shouting and striking and pulling. Fights often broke out, so-called Scotch arguments, because fists settled whatever issues had boiled up in that teeming place.[25] Sometimes the men fought for no reason at all, only perhaps to shed the boredom and loneliness left by many months of winter. Robert grew expert at chopping off eel heads (containing the only appreciable bone in the creatures' bodies) for his younger siblings to eat the remainder. The fish the family did not dry—which must have amounted to hundreds of pounds—they used as fertilizer to kick-start their summer crops. They may have copied the Indian practice of drying, smoking, and storing fish in underground birchbark containers for winter consumption.[26]

Eventually the frantic labor wore the men out, and they slumped around fires, soaked and exhausted, to gulp down rum and tell stories. The young Robert listened in the shadows to tall tales from the old country, told in rich Scottish burrs. The spring ritual became for the early frontier Scots-Irish, as it had for millennia of Indians, a time to exchange news and perhaps skills and to reawaken tribal bonding. These tough men and their steadily toughening sons, drawn together by such violent camaraderie, would form in later years the nucleus of the killer enterprise upon which Rogers would rely time and again in the worst extremities of frontier war.

Rogers and his friends had other opportunities to come together. Barn or meetinghouse raisings, where families gathered to help throw up a frame building, provided opportunities to escape the relentless demands of the farm, and the large barrel of rum that awaited the workers when the raising was done dissolved tensions. Fueled by the liquor, wrestling matches sprouted up to the cries of "a wrestle, a wrestle!" Within a small circle drawn in the dirt, the smallest boys began first. The winner was he who managed to stay within the circle or on his feet wrestling the next largest. Eventually the series culminated in a match between the biggest and strongest of the men.[27]

Games of strength, speed, and cunning played fiercely prominent parts in the semiannual Londonderry Fair, held on the common near the First Parish meetinghouse.[28] Small populations, dispersed over large areas, often spend their common time in trying to outdo one another, as one writer has said, "out-running, out-licking, and out-hollering one's neighbors"[29] or, as Benjamin Franklin put it, judging a man not by who he was but by what he could do. Whittier described it as a "wild, frolicking, drinking, fiddling, courting, horse-racing, riotous merrymaking."[30] The men lifted weights, pitched quoits, threw heavy pieces of iron, pulled sticks, and wrestled. By the time Robert entered his teens, he had grown into a powerful, athletic, and formidable competitor, a man "with bark on." The grandson of his good friend John Stark asserted that Rogers never lost a match, an exaggeration certainly but one that acknowledged an already legendary physical prowess.[31] In a thinly spread society scattered across vast and dangerous forest, superior physical strength and agility translated directly into better chances of living into the next week.

After ten years of backbreaking labor, the Rogers farm was finally paying off, its orchards yielding an abundance of cider apples. But such bounty would not be lasting. In March 1744 France declared war on Britain, prompting the Scottish Jacobites to rebel. New France and the British colonies braced for conflict.

Chapter 3

Savage Justice

They come like foxes through the woods, which afford them concealment and serve them as an impregnable fortress. They attack like lions, and, as their surprises are made when they are least expected, they meet with not resistance. They take flight like birds, disappearing before they have really appeared.

AN UNNAMED JESUIT MISSIONARY,
DESCRIBING THE IROQUOIS MODE OF WARFARE[1]

A dry, rainless, and hot midsummer raised dust along the rough road as Captain David Ladd led 30 militiamen into the town of Rumford. They were tired, filthy, and more than slightly frustrated. For the past five days of July 1746, they had been chasing shadows. Neither the shores of Isle-Hook Pond nor the woods near Suncook had yielded a trace of their deadly and elusive quarry: bands of eight to twelve Abenaki and Nipissing warriors sweeping down into New England from French-ruled Canada.

For the most part Ladd's men were farmers and shopkeepers from Exeter, a small town 35 miles to the southwest. Their ten-pound muzzle-loaders grew heavy; powderhorns chafed sweaty sides. Yet they could never let down their guard against such deadly and effective masters of ambush, who so skillfully blended into the blur of leaf clutter and tangles of branches that a man might not see a warrior only a pace away. Without any warning howls and musket shots would shatter the silence of the woods, inhumanly voicing triumph and destruction, evoking terror that sucked air from a man's lungs and paralyzed his limbs.

On the first days of patrol, every tree had seemed to hide an Indian, every animal trail across a brook to mark an ambush. But no quarry was to be found. "The Indians are all about our frontiers," wrote the exasperated Rumford militia leader John Goffe, who had come up just as empty-handed several months earlier. "It is enough to make one's blood cold in one's veins to see our fellow creatures killed and taken upon every quarter." Every one of Ladd's men was set on drawing blood, on dragging the enemy from the shadows. They had mentally rehearsed their response to every possible situation. But the brilliance of a campaign of terror is its uncertainty. Ambush could fall in the next five seconds—or perhaps just as likely, never at all.

Rumford reached at last, the party tramped south down Main Street from Horseshoe Pond to the ferry near Frog Ponds, glancing over their left shoulders at the sinuous curves of the Merrimack and taking in the startling changes that the town had undergone.[2] Among the dozens of clapboard houses lining the dusty street, most were empty, the furniture pulled out and valuables buried.[3] Only about 100 men—out of a normal population of 350 total inhabitants—still lived in the town.[4] The air smelled sweetly of recently split white pine; stout new walls of horizontally stacked hewn logs encircled seven of the town's largest houses. A chorus of dog howls greeted the militia. What was left of Rumford was an armed camp.

A hundred and fifty yards down Main Street, Ladd's little company halted before the grandest house of all, that of the town elder and Congregational preacher Timothy Walker, whose gambrel-roofed clapboard mansion soared above its new palisade, anchored by two solid chimneys crafted from big granite ledgestones from the river; Walker's was the first two-story house built between Haverhill in the Bay Colony and far distant Canada.[5] Its portly blue-eyed owner stepped out of the gate, musket in hand, to grip Ladd's hand and greet the second-in-command, 30-year-old Lieutenant James Bradley, by name. A renowned local brawler conceded of the parson that he "was the only man the Almighty ever made that he was afraid of."[6] Yet even this implacable cleric, who called himself a "moderate Calvinist," had been put to the test lately by news that French and Indian war parties had struck close by. Walker and his fellow town members had sent a hurried plea for help to Benning Wentworth, the governor of New Hampshire in Portsmouth, who had dispatched Ladd's force. Walker was damned glad to see them.

Barely had the militia arrived than word came of further menace. Knowing from much frustrating experience that such raiders often fled into marshes, Ladd and his men left hurriedly for a nearby wetland, where they indeed found moccasin tracks but no enemy.

To the distress of New England's frontier farmers and townspeople, two decades of peace had evaporated with the death of the Hapsburg Holy Roman Emperor Charles VI in 1740. The newly enthroned "King in Prussia," Frederick II, not yet "the Great," saw an opportunity to attack Charles's daughter and heiress, Maria Theresa, who now ruled over a vast tangle of feudal holdings in Austria, Bohemia, and Hungary. Within months he invaded Silesia, a central European Hapsburg property (now composing much of Poland). And so began the War of the Austrian Succession; France joined Prussia, as did Spain and Bavaria, while Protestant Britain and the Netherlands sided with Austria. The New England frontier people, living in barely formed and frighteningly exposed communities reaching into New Hampshire along the Merrimack and Connecticut Valleys, heard the news with growing alarm. Open conflict between France and Britain meant that war would spread across the St. Lawrence watershed. And although 200 miles of rugged forest and mountain lay between them and the French settlements, these small towns and isolated farms were the closest to, and had proved before to be within striking distance of, New France's habitants and Indian allies.

News of France's declaration of war on Britain in March 1744 took months to cross the Atlantic, and it reached Québec well before Boston. The French governor of Canada sent a fleet to launch a preemptive strike on Canso, a fishing village on the northeastern tip of Nova Scotia that housed a small British garrison. The North American arm of a European dynastic quarrel—King George's War—had begun.

Anticipating raiders, Governor William Shirley of Massachusetts raised ten 50-man companies of what were not yet called rangers— being still casually designated snowshoe men—to reinforce frontier defenses.[7] He placed a 100-pound bounty on each Indian scalp and called for volunteers to attack Louisbourg, France's pivotal gate fortress on the St. Lawrence estuary. Early in March 1745, 4,200 men sailed from Boston aboard 90 ships. Low on morale, with no hope of reinforcement, the French surrendered after 46 days of siege and bombardment. Humiliated at this disaster, the French Canadians beat the war drum, inflaming converted Northern Woodlands Indians in their missionary villages along the St. Lawrence with promises of their own bounties for white scalps. The Abenaki, Nipissing, Algonquin, Huron, Caughnawaga, and Mississauga needed little prompting to raid New England and upper New York, whose colonists had turned their ancient hunting grounds into towns and farmsteads.

That summer the French in Montréal welcomed more than 500 warriors from at least 14 tribes, including four far-journeyed buffalo hunters from the tallgrass prairies of western Minnesota, who had little trade contact with Europeans. Sixteen Menominees, whom the French called Wild Rice Indians, joined an extraordinary assemblage of Chippewa, Potawatomi, Winnebago, and Ottawa.[8] With some notable exceptions, such as certain Iroquois tribes and the Stockbridge Indians, the French colonists had engaged the native Americans more fruitfully than had the British over the past century and a half of European contact. Settled along the St. Lawrence, the Canadians enjoyed a direct water route to the Great Lakes, where fur traders known as *coureurs des bois* traded with the interior peoples, learning their languages and often marrying their women. Black-robed and fearless Jesuit missionaries penetrated deep into the wilderness, relying on the long traditions of their order's missionary work in Asia to find ways of speaking to the heathen, undergoing the most hideous tortures with superhuman courage and stoicism. It took the pope himself, for instance, to grant Father Isaac Jogues dispensation to administer Mass, so hideously mutilated were his hands. He then promptly returned to North America to die under the torments of those he had set out to save. Such conviction impressed the Northeastern Woodlands peoples with the power of the French god.

From the outset, the Puritans had little luck winning over the demonic pagans to a doctrine whose severely unpretentious religious ceremonies offered little compared to the rich and numinous rituals of the more ancient faith. Under French Catholicism the Indians could retain their customs and beliefs so long as they attended Mass, said a few prayers, swore allegiance to the king, and kissed the cross. In contrast, the Puritans thought this amounted to the merest lip service. Conversion, in the eyes of John Eliot, Jonathan Edwards, and their like, required the initiated not only to go through the motions but to understand what the words and rituals meant. But the French were fearful of alienating peoples who were able to sever the lucrative fur tradeways; hence the high officials sent out from metropolitan France to administer peasant Canada did not encourage deep-going agricultural settlement nor support claims to vast tracts of land. By contrast, such issues of displacement rent a large and violent divide between the Northeastern Indians and the land-hungry and unrestrained British colonists.

Supplied with new guns and plentiful ammunition, dozens of French Canadian and Indian bands left Montréal, most of them consisting of war-painted Abenakis and Nipissings, rarely numbering so much as 12 men to a party. They traveled light and, by the standards of the day, astonishingly fast, going almost naked in little more than a breechclout, leggings, and moccasins during the warmer months, their weaponry limited to light muskets, powderhorns, shot pouches, tomahawks, and scalping knives.

These Abenaki raiders Rogers would describe later as simultaneously romantic and terrible. Their heads were plucked bald, including the eyebrows, except for a "spot the size of two English crowns near the crown of their heads," the remnant lock adorned with wampum, beads, and feathers until it resembled "the modern Pompadour." Red paint blazoned their heads down to the eyes, "sprinkled over with white down." Their split ears were distended with wire or splinters, "so as to meet and tie together in the knap of their necks." Their noses were bored and hung with trinkets, their faces striped with many colors so as to give an "aweful appearance."[9] Another observer remarked that the warriors often slathered themselves with bear grease to make themselves "as slippery as the antient Gladiators."[10]

For two months tales—half rural legend, half understated fact— of grisly murders and wizardly attacks had seeped into Rumford. In Maine's Gorham Town twenty Indian raiders had shot a farmer named Briant tending his field in midmorning. *The Boston Evening-*

News reported that they then "went from the Field to Briant's House, and kill'd and scalp'd four of his Children; three of them were knock'd on the Head with an Ax, the other had its Brains beat out against the Hearth."[11]

On April 23, 1749, near present-day Keene in the southwestern corner of New Hampshire, a naked Indian had leaped from the bushes to drive a hunting knife into the back of Daniel McKenney's aged and corpulent wife as she walked home from milking her cow. Nevertheless she continued her deliberate passage up to the fortified settlement's gates, whereupon blood burst from her mouth and she pitched forward dead.[12] The raiding party fired six houses and a barn and killed twenty-three cattle, one more item in a growing tally of dozens upon dozens of homes and hard-won crop fields immolated along the frontier. The Indians tore out the fat-rich tongues of the livestock they slaughtered to devour on the trail. Dozens of colonists were scalped or borne off to uncertain fates in New France. In mid-May settlers were killed in sight of Albany. A diarist wrote, "So daring have the enemy become that they are daily seen about the settlements, and yet none of them are either killed or taken."[13]

The horrors were coming ever closer to Rumford. On June 11 Walker noted in his journal that Indians had scalped Benjamin Blanchard, on guard at a small fort just north of town. His entry the following day read, "Our Town was universally alarmed by ye hearing some guns discharged in ye woods."[14]

At the outset of the war Mountalona's isolation placed the Great Meadows out of the way of Indian raiding parties. But as attacks increased in the early summer of 1746, the Rogerses and Pudneys felt vulnerable. Between the two patriarchs and their 12 sons, they had improved nearly 98 acres of marshy meadow and another hundred of upland grazing and timber, and here James's wife had given birth to their final child. Still, James Rogers and Joseph Pudney decided to seek safety in Rumford. The saddened families buried what valuables they could not carry, hitched up their oxen, and set out two dozen strong on the rough path to town.

Governor Wentworth had appointed a Committee of Militia to assign families to garrisons in frontier settlements and plantations. Besides the seven fortified houses spread along the main road, Rumford contained a handful of others on the western edge of town, and another across the river. The Rogerses were assigned to a garrison at the house of the minister's cousin, Timothy Walker Jr. The Pudneys were dispersed among three strongpoints.

The Rogerses turned immediately to building quarters, along with the 22 families and individuals jammed into the Walker house and its adjoining lot. They threw up a small cabin against the palisades for its back wall, though Mary and her baby may well have merited a bunk in the house. At night Robert and his brothers took turns guarding the compound from two sentry boxes at the corners of the perimeter. Every morning except the Sabbath, armed men patrolled the farmlands. With no fields to tend of their own, the Rogerses acted as guard details scanning the woods, the monotony broken only when Robert or one of the other men returned to town to fetch bottles of rum for the farmers.

On Sundays families walked to church under heavy guard, the men stacking their muskets around a central post but keeping their powderhorns and bullet pouches around their necks as they sat across from the women on the long wooden benches. A dog tender policed the ubiquitous hounds. Parson Walker, suitably turned out in a large powdered wig, a three-cornered cocked hat, and shoes with large buckles, mounted the pulpit with a Bible and one of the finest guns in the colony to deliver his usual thirty-minute sermon, filled with scriptural instances of the duties required by a vigilant God.[15] The Scots-Irish immigrant slights that James had once felt so keenly in Methuen dissipated before the common struggle against a largely unseen but proven enemy. The congregation rose as the parson strode out, nodding to individual parishioners.

Used to hunting for the family, often on his own, Robert could not now roam the woods at will. Nearly 15, he had grown into a strong young man, keenly aware of the power of his limbs, the strength in his chest, and his easy ability to outpace competitors. Men have always differed in their capacity to stomach risk. Many shun it, preferring to live circumscribed lives. Others rise to the circumstances when community or country comes calling, shedding day-to-day identities as shopkeepers, scholars, or farmers to stare down the cannon's mouth. A very few seek out danger as a matter of course.

From boyhood Robert was to be found among these last. That

July, when Ladd's militia marched into town and the captain signed up men to scour the area, Robert looked on with a yearning and desperate excitement, for his father repeatedly turned down his insistent pleas to join.[16]

On Sunday, August 10, Ladd brought his men back to Rumford.[17] They might have picked up an additional 18 recruits, but otherwise the past month had proven fruitless. Provoked by rumor and fragmentary tracks, they had roamed the southern New Hampshire forests, enduring torrential rainstorms and steaming summer heat but spotting not a single enemy. They now joined the townspeople for worship, stacking their loaded muskets along with the others at the center post.

During the service a child named Abigail Carter fidgeted more than the rest, uncertain whether to tell her parents about what she had seen on the way to church. At meeting's end she blurted out that Indians lurked outside. Men grabbed muskets and pushed through the crowd. They quickly discovered that raiders had indeed hidden in a nearby alder thicket but had already left.[18]

Next day Ladd's second-in-command, Lieutenant Bradley, took six men on patrol to Eastman's Fort, about two and half miles distant. One Obadiah Peters, mustered in a Massachusetts militia company, joined the detail, intending to visit his father and family, who lived near the garrison. The eight moved out on horseback, most riding double, Lieutenant Bradley weakened from a bout of dysentery.[19] A mile and a half from town the road dipped toward Ash Brook. Daniel Gilman, riding foremost, spied a hawk fly down the road on the far bank and galloped across the makeshift bridge to take a shot at it, plunging past 30 or 40 Indians in a brookside thicket. Three hundred yards ahead of the main party, he heard shots and swung back, supposing his fellows had had the good fortune to bring down a deer: but on reaching the rise overlooking the brook, he recoiled in horror.

Six men reeled along the dirt road, their horses gutshot, Lieutenant Bradley crying, "Lord have mercy on me!" Thinking the enemy to be few from the limited first volley, the lieutenant had yelled, "Fight!" and discharged his musket into the bushes, as did the others. The Indians had waited for this move and rose howling upon the helplessly reloading Yankees. Gilman galloped off in a panic.

Peters, shot in the head by the Indians' second fusillade, lurched forward and collapsed. John Lufkin went down too. Another shot felled Lieutenant Bradley's younger brother Samuel, and yet another killed John Bean 75 feet from the road as he ran for cover. The Indians rushed the final three men and offered them quarter. Sergeant Alexander Roberts and William Stickney accepted, but Lieutenant Bradley refused.[20]

James Bradley had long ago decided that death would be better than captivity. He knew well what lay before him should he fall into the clutches of those who had killed his ancestors—five children, an infant, and three adults—half a century before. A generation later war parties had twice borne off his grandmother from Haverhill, near where the Rogerses first settled. The second time, on February 8, 1704, six Indians had burst into an unlocked stockade where she was boiling soap. One settler reached his musket and wounded the lead attacker. The then-pregnant Mrs. Bradley finished off the first Indian to reach her by flinging a ladle of scalding liquid on his head, but the others tomahawked the musketeer, then dragged Mrs. Bradley off through heavy snow to begin the death march to Canada. Toiling under a heavy burden and wretchedly clothed against the blizzards, the tough Yankee kept up, delivering her baby along the way. At one point, when it cried incessantly out of hunger, a warrior filled its mouth with burning embers. Later, she recalled, her captors asked if they could baptize the child, carving knifemarks surely unknown to the Roman missal into its forehead. Shortly thereafter she left it for a moment, then returned to discover it impaled on a pike. Despite these unimaginable horrors, she endured to Canada, whence her husband redeemed her in the spring.[21]

Leaving his brother dead on the road, Lieutenant Bradley now charged headlong among the tomahawks, wildly clubbing with his spent musket, whose heavy butt injured at least one Indian. But his opponents were too many, and Bradley was slammed to the ground by a blow to the back of his head. The Indians stripped off his clothes and scalped him.

Gilman got back to town and alerted the rest of the militia, who sprinted to the bridge. Before vanishing, the Indians had pulled intestines out of the sliced bellies, hacked off genitals and limbs, torn hearts from ribcages, and crushed heads so the brains spilled out on the roadside grass.

The dead men's comrades carried the barely recognizable corpses back to town in an oxcart, rolling down Main Street to the front of James Osgood's garrison; mothers and children peered at the mutilated bodies. Among the crowd were Samuel Bradley's year-old and three-year-old children. This was Robert Rogers's first view of bodies torn by war. Now that violence had struck so close, his father could not keep his headstrong teenager from enlisting. The next day the slain were buried in coffins quickly hammered together from white pine boards. Five days later Robert mustered into Captain Ladd's scouting and ranger company.[22]

He spent six weeks patrolling only as far as nearby Canterbury. Occasionally he tracked Indians, never quite running them down, but for the most part he guarded farmers and responded to alarms. He was being inducted into a long tradition of scouting and ranging that dated back to the early seventeenth century, when the first British settlers arrived in North America. Professional soldiers, such as Captain John Smith of Jamestown and Myles Standish of Plymouth, had organized the early colonies' defense. Smith made the first recorded reference to rangers shortly after Powhatan warriors ravaged 31 plantations and manors of the Virginia Colony, mostly along the James River. Forewarning reached the main settlement, but not those farther flung, where 347 people were killed, more than a third of the entire colony. Smith petitioned the Virginia Company to raise and maintain 100 outfitted soldiers and 30 sailors, writing that "these I would imploy onely in ranging the countries, and tormenting the Saluages [savages]."[23] He held forth elsewhere on the advantages that accrued to those who used the Indian technique of eschewing mass assault but keeping small groups perpetually on the move: "By their continuall ranging, and travel, they know all the advantages and places most frequented by Deere, Beasts, Fish, Foule, Roots, and Berries."[24] In 1648 the General Assembly of Maryland established a committee "to draw up certaine propos[ns] & conditions to be obserued by the raingers or scouts."[25]

The word *ranger* had emerged in the written record in thirteenth-century England, as applied to a far-traveling forester or borderer. By the late sixteenth century border rangers, units of irregular militia, patrolled the violent frontier between England and Scotland.[26] Northern immigrants to the New World brought these procedures along with them. By the late seventeenth century, as a series of Indian wars erupted, the colonists could not look for support to a regular army, and their ranger forces had to develop both offensive and defensive capabilities.

Captain Benjamin Church of Massachusetts figures in early colonial history as, in the general judgment, the first true practitioner of ranger recruitment, training, and operations, blending the woodcraft savvy of his adversaries with European combat practices. The son of a carpenter in settled North America, coming to the wilderness only in middle age, he had raised an independent mixed company of friendly Indians and irregulars in 1675 to combat a loose confederation of tribes led by Metacomet ("King Philip"), chief of the Wampanoags.

Church relied on his tribal allies—equal members of his company—to bring special skills to tracking and scouting. He admitted only the most sternly tested volunteers, demanding that they "be men of good reason and sense to know how to manage themselves in so difficult a piece of service as this Indian hunting is."[27]

Drawing on harsh past experience, he rightly concluded that men who were bunched together in the forest could be easily ambushed or encircled, and he therefore insisted that his rangers travel in a loose, spread-out formation—a tactic that required a transforming increase in the confidence and consciousness of European men toward the forest. A contemporary, Samuel Penhallow, observed that it was the custom of Church's men "to rest in the Day, and row in the Night; and never fire at an Indian if they could reach him with a Hatchet, for fear of alarming them."[28] Church also required his men to creep on their bellies until discovered, whereupon they must immediately leap roaring into the attack.[29]

Church finally cornered Metacomet in a Rhode Island swamp, paraded the fallen king's severed head through Boston, and lived on to fight in the succeeding Indian wars, including the raid that avenged the Deerfield massacre of 1704.

Mustering out in early October, Rogers joined his family at Mountalona. For the next two years the Rogerses and Pudneys worked their land in the winter and spring, returning for some part of the summer and fall to the Rumford garrisons. Robert served another month in the militia in August 1747, when the raiding parties again grew more frequent and deadly. Large armed details covered the harvesting farmers. That same month an Indian bullet broke Joseph Pudney's arm as he was returning from the fields.[30] The frontier was still ablaze. In 1748 the Marquis de La Galissonière, governor-general of New France, reported that his people had "experienced their usual success in enemy territory," bringing in 150 American scalps and 112 prisoners.[31]

In early April 1748, 17 Caughnawaga Iroquois from the small Jesuit town of Sault Saint-Louis, across the river from Montréal, prepared themselves for the warpath. Their chief—his torso, shoulders, and face blackened with charcoal—led his warriors in chants and a dance. They harangued A'reskoui, the god of war, as well as the Great Spirit. A pot boiled with the flesh of sacrificial dogs, which became identified in the braves' minds with that of their disdained enemies. Eating it stood for their joyfully anticipated devouring of their foe and the mystical incorporation of his strength.[32]

At Montréal the 17 warriors joined up with their French leader, Cadet Charly, who provided ammunition and food before they all set off in bark canoes downriver, then headed up the Saint-François past the village of the same name.[33] By paddling along small streams, cutting across lakes, and portaging frequently, they reached the Connecticut River, where they hid their canoes and moved west to the Merrimack Valley, thence dropping south toward Rumford. The small party gave the town wide berth and continued downriver.

On April 29 a patrolling ranger came across their tracks near Rumford and gave the alert. Such a party's return path could bring it dangerously close to Mountalona, so two men set out quickly to warn the Rogerses and Pudneys, who immediately left their hard-won farms. The two families stumbled yet again into the darkness toward Rumford, the men wondering whether their determination to hold the farms had cost them and their loved ones their lives; but they reached the town safely.[34]

The following morning the raiders came across two men and a boy in a field across from the junction of the Suncook with the Merrimack, only four miles east of Mountalona. They killed one and took the other two prisoner, then dispatched the oxen and cut out their tongues before sweeping on a wide loop westward to avoid retracing their tracks. Thus they came upon Mountalona.

Knee-high in the grass, the painted men surveyed the tidy farmsteads set in dense orchards of apple trees thick with white blossoms, land that had been theirs for generations to hunt and farm. Evidence that the inhabitants had barely escaped were spread everywhere. Two cattle, freed from the barn and shooed into the woods, returned to stare at the interlopers. Embers lay warm in the fireplaces, cream half formed into butter filled the churn, dinner preparations were abandoned. Time being short, Cadet Charly set immediately to work, pausing only briefly to drink deeply from the cider barrels in the cool stone cellars. They killed a steer and a heifer, torched the buildings, then carefully and systematically felled the orchards.

Well before the Rogerses and Pudneys returned under an escort of townsmen, they could see smoke rising against the clear spring sky. Discovering that the Indians had left but one fruit tree standing, Robert and his brothers wondered whether the Indians had missed it in the haste of their destruction or passed it up as an unsettling warning or even a taunt.

A decade's worth of toil was now ash and rot. In faraway London rich subjects could insure their ships against privateers, but ruin on the frontier of New England was just another impersonal, locally crippling casualty of war. It might not be paid for, but it could be avenged.

Chapter 4

Taken by Indians

The great and fundamental principles of their policy are, that every man is naturally free and independent; that no one . . . on earth has any right to deprive him of his freedom and independency, and that nothing can be a compensation for the loss of it.

ROBERT ROGERS WRITING ABOUT THE EASTERN
WOODLANDS INDIANS, ELEVEN YEARS BEFORE THE
SIGNING OF THE DECLARATION OF INDEPENDENCE[1]

On the afternoon of April 27, 1752, four young hunters and trappers gathered gloomily around a small stone fire ring uphill from where the Baker River cuts through the southwestern foothills of the White Mountains. A huge trophy of beaver pelts, deer hides, and black bearskins lay stacked like rugs not far from the pole-and-spruce-bough lean-tos that had served as their base for more than a month. But the day before, one of them had discovered moccasin tracks. Reluctantly they agreed to head home.

Six months after the wasting of Mountalona, France and Britain had made peace, exchanging far-conquered lands and signing a raft of documents. While the eastern Abenaki in Maine agreed to the treaty, their western brethren, embittered by decades of British encroachment, notably upon the beaver-rich hunting country of the Merrimack River basin, had implacably refused. The tributaries of the Merrimack teemed with beaver, and the forest edges provided exceptionally good deer hunting. For centuries the western Abenaki had hunted and farmed corn and squash along the riverbanks, which offered intervales (or *coos* as the Indians knew them), wide, sediment-rich meadowlands. Such a party as this, trespassing 60 miles deep into the very heart of the cherished hunting grounds, knew well what consequences discovery could bring.

Even so 23-year-old John Stark of Londonderry, his 28-year-old brother, William, of Derryfield, Amos Eastman of Rumford, and David Stinson of Londonderry tarried, understandably reluctant to abandon such ripe territory, which they reckoned had yielded 560 pounds sterling worth of pelts.[2] Across the middle belt of North America, beaver fur served as a universal currency, transcending mere political and ethnic lines and often superseding local tender. Around the Great Lakes in 1765 two medium-size beaver pelts could buy any one of the following: a pound of vermilion; a man's ruffled shirt; eight quarts of rum; a large trunk; or two fathoms of ribbon.[3] Hatters in Europe prized the fine underfur, which they stripped and processed into felt to surface stylish headgear. In 1750 the British colonies exported more than 60,000 beaver pelts to meet the fashion in hats.[4]

These young men, like Rogers, were typical of the adventurous colonial youths who set out to escape farm chores by roaming the creeks, rivers, and forests north of Rumford, trapping beaver and hunting deer, bear, moose, mink, and otter. Rogers and a very few ventured even farther afield. "Between the year's 1743 and 1755," he would recall, "my manner of life was such as led me to a general acquaintance both with the British and French settlements in North America, and especially with the uncultivated desart, the mountains, valleys, rivers, lakes, and several passages that lay between and contiguous to the said settlements."[5] He penetrated deep into the White Mountains, venturing so high up the flanks of one tall peak that he felt his lungs burn. He met French traders and learned how to speak with them. In the bright light of forest bonfires, he quaffed long draughts of brandy and drew maps in the ashes and on pieces of bark. He swapped furs, information, and stories with Indians both hostile and friendly. Traveling light, he learned to live with hunger cramping his stomach just as the Indians did. In the winter he watched as the northern sky lit up with the otherworldly colors of the aurora borealis, its glowing tendrils reflected off the snow like a rainbow come to earth. Listen closely, urged one attentive observer, and the spectacle exuded a soft noise not unlike that made by running a thumb and forefinger along the edge of a silk handkerchief.

He also lived in constant danger, often evading small Indian parties that were hunting more than game in the forest and were perfectly ready to kill him for his furs, musket, and scalp. Likely enough on many occasions, he simply ran from his pursuers, outdistancing them in the woods, while using woodcraft skills to erase his trail. Those not so wary often lived just long enough to learn how terrible the forest could be.

In time-honored male tradition the foursome delegated to its youngest the chore of collecting traps. Musket in hand, John Stark scrambled along the bank, occasionally stepping into the water in his moccasins, until he reached the trap farthest downstream, planning to pull it and work back against the direction of the current.

Back in the New Hampshire frontier settlements, Rogers knew John Stark well, a man three years his senior, of light blue eyes, bold features, and strong opinions, who compensated for his middling height with a pugnacious self-confidence that Rogers relished, never quitting easily, even when a stronger man—such as Rogers—wrestled him to the dirt.[6] Many decades later, long after Stark had made his name as a general officer at Bennington during the Revolution, he aptly coined a motto for New Hampshire, "Live Free or Die." Both Starks would serve as ranger captains under Robert Rogers in the coming war.

Stark and many of his fellow trappers favored a device of French Canadian design, consisting of a small iron plate, a spring, and a pair of iron jaws. Through a small ring it could be anchored to a stake driven into the creekbed, and baited not with beaver food—the bark and saplings they ate were far too abundant along the river's edge—but with castoreum, the musky hormones secreted by glands near the anus. Notoriously territorial, North America's largest rodent, which may reach 90 pounds or more, cannot help but investigate the perceived presence of a rival. Trappers painted the strong and bitter sexual attractant on a willow twig arched over the trap, its ends secured in the stream gravel. The beaver rose on its hind legs to sniff the twig, felt the crunch of the iron jaws, and fought in agony but eventually drowned.[7] The trappers, often short on calories, prized the high fat content of its tail meat, once the tough skin was scraped or seared off. In preparation for eventual sale, the trappers flayed the body, scraped the skin, then stretched it within a willow branch hoop.

Beaver plews, when dried and folded with the fur on the inside, weighed on average a pound and a half.

Amid the lengthening dusk Stark stood in the cold water of the Baker, sprang a trap with a stick, then pulled it up. The stream noises masked the approach of Francis Titigaw and nine other Abenakis from the Canadian mission village of Saint-François. Hearing a "sharp hissing sound" as of a snake, Stark whipped around to find himself staring into Titigaw's unblinking eyes, his naked forehead awash with splashes of bloodred paint, his earlobes dragged to his shoulders by silver baubles. Titigaw's presence shocked the breath from Stark's lungs and locked him woodenly into his crouch. Without a word the fearsome wraiths stripped Stark of musket and knife.[8]

Very slightly recovering his composure, Stark responded to Titigaw's gestures and walked downstream, leading his captors away from his brother and friends, a brave ploy that worked only briefly. The worried party fired their muskets, intending most probably to give him a bearing in the event he got lost.

At daybreak, Amos Eastman looked for the younger Stark along the riverbank, as his fellow trappers paddled downstream. Titigaw sprang his silent trap, and Eastman too was disarmed.

Ordered to call the canoe inshore, John instead yelled a warning. His friends frantically pulled away; the warriors raised their muskets. Stark knocked up several barrels, which sent most of the balls over his fleeing companions' heads. But two found their mark, killing Stinson outright and splintering William's paddle. John kept yelling for William to get away, until gun stocks beat him to the ground. The Indians reloaded quickly, but William had been given the time to bolt into the undergrowth.

Eastman and Stark watched the warriors strip and scalp Stinson and gather up the party's furs. Then they were dragged off to rendezvous with the canoe guards on the Connecticut. Long before William reached Rumford, the party had paddled upriver, crossed the Canadian watershed, and arrived on June 9 at Titigaw's home village. Saint-François stood on pine-shaded 60-foot bluffs overlooking its namesake river, about six miles before it falls into the St. Lawrence at Lake St. Peter. Stark and Eastman knew Saint-François as the jumping-off point of the war parties that had terrorized the New England border for decades, most recently destroying the Rogerses' and Pudneys' farms. Mostly Abenakis lived at Saint-François, in a loose alliance of displaced tribes chiefly from Maine and New Brunswick, the nucleus composed of Sokwakis and Penacooks.[9]

The small town's tidy appearance surprised them. No collection of mean huts, this was a settlement of more than 50 squared-timber houses arranged around a green. It also boasted a dozen or so frame houses, a few structures made of stone, and dominating the central area, a handsome white-painted Jesuit church, its slight steeple crowned by a plain cross. Nearby stood a fortified council house.

Stark and Eastman had little time to take in their surroundings. Within musket shot of the village, the returning raiders announced their advent with loud shrieks, which brought their joyful townsfolk pouring down to the water's edge, as the triumphal cry modulated into a terrifying chorus, which another captive described as "so sharp, shrill, loud and deep, that ... it makes a most dreadful and horrible Noise, that stupefies the very Senses."[10] There were live shouts, one for each prisoner, and a single dead shout for a scalp.[11]

The women, girls, boys, and older men gathered sticks, clubs, and rocks and formed two long parallel lines along the shore. The prisoners were to be compelled to run the gauntlet, the ritual induction of captives. The warriors stood aside and watched.

The canoes grounded on the sandy riverbank. If the raiders followed tradition, they had stopped earlier in the day, and now both captives, stark naked, bore stripes of vermilion and bear grease. The Indians pushed Eastman out of the boat; he had no choice but run under the drumming clubs up the embankment toward the village. Someone had thrust an eight-foot pole mounted with an animal skin into his hands. As he stumbled on, shielding his head with his arms, he loudly chanted an Algonquin phrase taught him by Titigaw, *Nen nuttattagkompish wameug nunkompeog*—"I'll beat all your young men"—which inflamed the already-excited villagers to hammer him even harder as he staggered by. He crested the bluff and collapsed.

Prisoners sometimes died under the ordeal, but most accounts suggest that the ceremony did not seek to maim or kill. Pierre-François-Xavier de Charlevoix, an eighteenth-century French Jesuit historian who traveled far into the wilderness, wrote that the

Iroquois, "when they seem to strike at random, and to be actuated only by fury, . . . take care never to touch any part where a blow might prove mortal."[12]

An Indian shoved a loonskin-adorned pole into Stark's hands and pushed him between the rows of fierce, excited faces. Unaware of its meaning, he sang, *Nutchipwuttoonapish wameug nonokkishquog,* or "I'll kiss all your young women." The first few blows brought his Scots-Irish blood to a boil, and he poled several Indians into the dirt—to howls of admiring laughter from his other captors; he completed the gauntlet untouched, then tended to the bruised and terrified Eastman.[13]

Captives of the Eastern Woodlands Indians, whether white or rival tribesmen, faced a range of fates, the most horrible being a slow and excruciating end under torture, a cathartic ritual savored by the entire village. Charlevoix described the Iroquois tradition of leading prisoners from one cabin to another: "Here they pluck off a nail, there they take off a finger, either with their teeth, or a bad knife which cuts like a saw; an old man tears off their flesh to the bones, a child pierces them with an awl wherever he can, a woman beats them unmercifully till her arms fall down with fatigue."[14] Another Jesuit, Joseph-François Lafitau, spared no detail in his graphic description of torture: "Several times in the same place, they pass and repass over him burning irons or glowing torches until they are extinguished in the blood or discharge running from his wounds. They cut off, bit by bit, the roasted flesh. Some of these infuriated people devour it while others paint their faces with his blood.

"Finally," he concluded, "after slowly burning all the parts of the body so that there is not a space which is not a wound, mutilating the face in such a way as to render it unrecognizable, cutting the skin from the head, tearing it from the skull, pouring on this uncovered skull a rain of ire, live coals or boiling water, they unchain the unfortunate being. They make him run again if he has the strength to do so and give him blows with sticks and stones or roll him in the braziers until he has given up the last breath of life remaining in him, unless someone, from pity, has torn out his heart, or pierced him with a knife-blow while he was tied to the stake."[15]

For a village that had lost men, ritual torture was a chance to exact retribution. Torture degraded not only its subject but his whole tribe. His death would also dishonor his entire ancestral tree as well as all of those akin to him yet unborn.

Yet this horrific ritual equally offered an opportunity for its victims to display unyielding manhood. "Even under those shocking tortures," Rogers wrote, "[men] will not only make themselves chearful, but provoke and irritate their tormentors with most cutting reproaches."[16] Eastern Woodlands Indian culture instilled a will to fortitude that reached so deep, he observed, that a newborn Indian would be stigmatized for life should his mother utter even a single groan or cry of pain during labor.[17] An early-seventeenth-century traveler reported a Powhatan song that ridiculed the "lamentations our people [the English] made when they killed them, saying how they would cry *whe whe* etc. which they mock't us for."[18]

On rare occasions, the village released a warrior who had borne up under its dreadful refinements. But in the end few could endure that roster of ingenuities that could involve placing hot sand or embers atop a scalped head, dropping a necklace of red-hot tomahawks around the neck, driving skewers into finger stumps, ripping out arm sinews, or touching off tar-soaked pine skewers deeply embedded in the victim's flesh. Following such a ritual torture, Rogers noted that the villagers ran from cabin to cabin, striking "with small twigs their furniture, the walls and roofs of their cabins, to prevent his spirit from remaining there to take vengeance for the evils committed on his body,"[19] thus finally conceding his common humanity.

But an altogether different fate awaited many captives: adoption. The sparsely populated subsistence cultures of the North American interior, already devastated by European diseases, felt the loss of even a single individual grievously—it placed severe hardships on the extended family and stressed the entire village. During Iroquois and Abenaki "mourning wars," raiding parties attacked other tribes with the express purpose of bringing back prisoners to replace their lost men. Generally, the women of the tribe made the choice between adoption or torture. In May 1755 some Mohawks bore off the 18-year-old Pennsylvanian James Smith and drove him through the gauntlet. Battered and shaken, he found himself encircled by a knot of warriors and knew that his time had come. One of them reached out, pulled a hank of hair from his head, and continued so pulling "as if plucking a turkey," occasionally dipping his fingers into ashes carried on a piece of bark to improve his grip. They left Smith with one lock of hair on the crown, which the whole band then adorned with beads and silver brooches, stripped him, wrapped him in a breechclout, pierced his nose and ears, and packed them with jewelry. After further long and painful ceremony, which included the women's washing him vigorously in a stream, the chief announced: "My son, you are now flesh of our flesh and bone of our bone. By the ceremony that was performed this day, every drop of white blood was washed out of your veins . . . Therefore you are to consider yourself as one of our people."[20] The involuntary adoptee had to assume the identity of a dead person, undertaking all that person's responsibilities. "I never knew them to make any distinctions between me and themselves in any respect whatever until I left them," wrote Smith.[21]

Caleb Stark later described his grandfather's continued intransigence. Sent to work in the cornfields, Stark, like Rogers a student of Indian culture, one day threw his hoe into the river with the declaration that "it was the business of squaws, and not warriors, to hoe corn." Far from taking offense, the braves applauded his boldness, released him from his menial duties, and took to calling him "young chief." The sachem adopted him.

For the rest of his life Stark remembered his captors' kindness. Before such romanticizations of the American Indian as Jean-Jacques Rousseau's depiction of the "noble savage," Chateaubriand's forest romance *Atala*, and James Fenimore Cooper's *Leatherstocking Tales*, colonists who came into intimate contact with their alien neighbors found a world impersonally terrifying, although the more imaginative found it sinisterly intriguing. To men of truly far-reaching curiosity, such as Rogers, who took one step further, the Indian cultures presented exotic wonders so rich as to draw them back again and again. Certainly unspeakable hardness lay at the heart of these cultures, but just as their peoples refined and elaborated pain, the richness of their religious customs, their extraordinary standards of courage, and their stern honesty invested them to some few early Europeans with a high degree of nobility. "No individual or family is allowed to suffer by poverty, sickness, or any misfortunes, while their neighbors can supply their wants; and all of this from the simple natural consideration," Rogers would record a decade later.[22]

Stark's chance to return to New England came later that summer when Captain Phineas Stevens, the now-legendary defender of Fort No. 4, reached Montréal as a representative of the governor of Massachusetts with authority to redeem captives. Stevens had set out from Albany, working his way for two weeks by canoe, bateau, and cart up through Lakes George and Champlain and by the way of the Richelieu River to Montréal, which stretched along the southern edge of a large island in the muddy St. Lawrence.

On July 5 he passed down the Rue Saint-Paul. The city extended three-quarters of a mile along the island shore but never reached more than a couple hundred feet inland. "The streets are regular, the houses well built, commodious and agreeable," Rogers would later write.[23] As Stevens strolled to meet the French governor and mayor of Montréal, he noticed that last year's heat and drought had withered the wheat growing outside the town's fortified walls: "The great probability of scarcity casts a sadness in all faces."[24] Most of the 400 or so residences, crowded along the two major streets paralleling the St. Lawrence, packed kitchen gardens into their yards, offering cleverly designed borders, paths, and the occasional compost barrel.[25] Spread up the slopes of Mont-Royal, to the northwest, the town gave the impression of a French provincial seat, with its convent, governor's chapel, and 18-foot revetted wall of stone.[26]

Occupying a strategic point on the great waterway into the interior, where the Ottawa River joins the mighty St. Lawrence from the northeast and not far from where the Richelieu discharges the north-flowing waters of Lake Champlain, Montréal served as a natural center for the French fur trade, the gateway to the upper wilderness country, or *pays d'en haut*, and as a point of departure for military expeditions into the continent and along other river systems that ultimately led down to Louisiana.

Stevens nodded affably to the pleasant French Canadian women rattling by in their tight-waisted, shortish skirts and in shoes so high-heeled and narrow that one observer was surprised "how they can walk on them." The most fashionable women carried dried turkey tails, with which they fanned themselves.[27] He counted 200 large birch canoes and bateaux heading upriver, each bearing five or six traders who would remain in country for three or four years, some traveling as much as 3,000 miles, drawing upon supplies sent annually to the wilderness garrisons at Michilimackinac, Détroit, and lesser posts often consisting of three or four log buildings surrounded by palisades. "All the inhabitants are addicted to the commerce of trade with the pays d'en haut," observed French engineer Louis Franquet, visiting Montréal that same year.[28]

Stevens called upon Charles Le Moyne de Longueuil, who at 64 had reached the pinnacle of public office in New France as governor of Montréal and acting administrator of French Canada. A servant conducted him to His Excellency, whose extreme corpulence and paper-colored skin gave a truly moribund impression: still, no one in Montréal mistook his physical frailty for a sign of weakness or lack of power. M. de Longueuil ruled over an elaborate patronage system rather more effectively than the Sun King's often frustrated successor ruled over the court at Versailles. A single nod could bestow a slice of the highly lucrative wilderness fur trade. Ever since the Treaty of Utrecht of 1713 had confirmed their hold on the great northeastern entryway, the French had cleverly managed the vast interior, penetrating as far west as the Rocky Mountains. Colonial regulars—Troupes de la Marine—manned the posts, which were overseen by commandants usually working under three-year contracts that afforded plenty of time to establish corporate partnerships with Montréal merchants. The latter coordinated the enterprises' logistics—hiring voyageurs, buying trade goods, and selling the furs.[29] In 1750, near the height of the French fur empire, maintaining a tenuous but clear claim to more than half of North America's vast expanse required only 261 officers and enlisted men in the far-flung garrisons.[30]

Longueuil's favor had fallen upon Paul Marin de La Malgue, a 59-year-old captain of the Troupes de la Marine, to whom he assigned the lucrative post of Baie-des-Puants, located near today's Green Bay, Wisconsin, Lake Michigan's inlet of that name. In 1751 Marin sent 400 stacks of beaver skins, 365 of prized female otter pelts, and thousands of other furs amounting to a total of 250,000 items back to Montréal.[31] Such experienced woodsmen would prove formidable adversaries in the coming war. Marin's son Joseph followed his father to Wisconsin and Michigan, learning fluent Sioux and several Algonquin languages. Over the next several years this woods-savvy man would become one of Robert Rogers's prime foes.

Longueuil plied his guest with excellent Bordeaux, of which Canada imported fully an eighth of the total vintage. They no doubt spoke of the drought, the price of beaver, and the state of European politics, trading hard news and gossip. Perhaps Stevens commented on how he had seen a brave murder a fellow Ottawa, and an Ottawa elder direct a boy to execute summary justice.[32]

Stevens found himself joining the governor in welcoming Jérôme Atecouando of Saint-François, and an Iroquois delegation from Sault Saint-Louis and the Lake of the Two Mountains.[33] Here, uncomfortably side by side in one room, stood representatives of three cultures that had grappled savagely with one another for more than a century, engaging in three declared wars, many formal battles, yet more skirmishes, and raids beyond counting, all of which had spilled the blood of tens of thousands. European greed—that of the French for furs, the English for land—and the Indians' understandable fears and bitter responses had set off much of the slaughter and cruelty. But the conflicts also originated in deep and tragic mutual misunderstandings, which left each party hardened if ill-informed realists and pragmatic opportunists.

Drawing himself up solemnly, Atecouando mustered all his formidable oratorical powers and addressed Stevens.

"We hear on all sides that this Governor and the Bostonians say that the Abenakis are bad people. 'Tis in vain that we are taxed with having a bad heart; it is you, brother, that always attack us; your mouth is of sugar but your heart of gall; in truth, the moment you begin we are on our guard."

Stevens listened as the words were rendered into broken English. His experience of the Abenakis had given him the gist without need for translation.

"We have not yet sold the lands we inhabit, we wish to keep the possession of them," Atecouando continued. "... You have the sea for your share from the place where you reside; you can trade there; but we expressly forbid you to kill a single Beaver, or to take a single stick of timber on the lands we inhabit; if you want timber we'll sell you some, but you shall not take it without our permission." He complained bitterly about the English surveying his people's traditional hunting grounds with predatory eyes.

But he presented Stevens with a belt of wampum, declaring that "it depended on yourselves to be at peace with the Abenakis." He added that the French father present had "nothing to do with what we say to you; we speak to you of our own accord," yet "we love that Monarch, and we are strongly attached to his interests." In fact, Phineas Stevens and many British colonists held the French largely responsible for British difficulties with the Indians. "Were it not for ye French," he wrote, "it would be Easy to Live at peace with ye Indians."[34] This gross simplification, which both absolved the British of being a threat to the tribes and drafted all local difficulties into the comfortable stereotypes of the struggle for world power, obscured reality: the Indians were less French mercenaries than uneasy allies drawn together against the advancing British.

Unlike the English, the French did not covet the Indian lands, establishing only small agricultural settlements at Kaskaskia, Détroit, and Cahokia. Longueuil and other administrators in New France knew that the best means to keep the advancing Britons at bay was to fuel the animosity that the Abenakis, Micmacs, Malacites, and other Northeastern Woodlands tribes already harbored against them. The terrorizing tactics of small-unit surprise worked well, tying up a large proportion of the frontier settlers especially during harvest season and keeping their towns in a constant state of alert and anxiety. With only a small investment in arms, ammunition, food, and bounties for English scalps, the French could indefinitely stimulate extensive raiding as a way of life.

Stevens met Atecouando's charges with what he probably considered a tough New England practicality: "Brothers Abenakis... Are you satisfied with the death of your people on account of your attacks on the English?" He added with some touch of conciliation, "I know that it is not permitted to go on your lands; those who have been there are young fools, without any character."

In reply Atecouando explicitly cited the Stark boys' trapping foray, although he wrongly assumed that Titigaw's party had dispatched William Stark. "The two Englishmen that we killed this year on the head waters of our river, and the two others that we have taken prisoner, must attribute their misfortunes to themselves, because they hunted Beaver on our lands, and on this point we repeat to you, with all the firmness we are capable of, that we will kill all the Englishmen we shall find on the lands in our possession.

"Our heart is good, and since we struck the blow our thirst for vengeance is extinguished."[35] Stark, Eastman, and the other prisoners would be ransomed. But as silence fell over the room, all present knew that such accommodations would buy only a little time. An apocalyptic fight to the finish loomed just over the horizon.

Days later Stevens ransomed Stark for a small pony and Eastman for objects of a lesser value. Shortly thereafter he led eight liberated captives back to the colonies.[36]

Chapter 5

The Counterfeiter

To Counterfeit is death.

INSCRIPTION ON MANY
COLONIAL PAPER MONEY BILLS

That fall Robert Rogers turned twenty-one, a coming of age that proved bittersweet. The razing of Mountalona had been a body blow: but now, as King George's War ran down, an even worse threat loomed over the Rogerses' livelihood. A long-simmering border dispute between the Massachusetts Bay Colony and New Hampshire threatened the Rogerses' and the Pudneys' very title to the land, which they had bought in 1739, when Massachusetts's claims sprawled west and north to the banks of the winding Merrimack.

In 1741 the Crown had ended the double governorship of Massachusetts and New Hampshire, granting the latter its own governor subordinate to London alone. The Massachusetts Assembly had then pulled back its boundary. Mountalona now fell under the authority of a colony that had chartered the land to Captain John Mason in recognition of his annihilation of the Pequots during the Pequot War of 1636–37. Mason's heirs had sold the grant for £1,500 to 12 of the richest merchants in Portsmouth, including the new governor's son. A tide of petitions for land deluged these ambitious proprietors, among them a proposal from John Stark's father, Archibald, and a group of Londonderry Scots-Irish interested in mapping and surveying a six-mile-square township within whose boundaries Mountalona would fall. In October 1748 the so-called Masonian proprietors authorized Stark's group to survey the area. Still rebuilding, the Rogerses and Pudneys confronted the survey with rage. Would the Masonian proprietors drive them off the land as mere squatters? Realizing that the other, better-connected claimants could take what the Indians had left, annihilating more than a decade of toil, the two families hired a Londonderry attorney and entered their own claim. By December the Masonian proprietors had granted James Rogers and Joseph Pudney each a share in the new town of Starkstown (later Dunbarton), along with one for each member of Stark's group, which included all his sons. The eldest Rogers and Pudney boys split another share.

None of their brothers received such title, which must have infuriated Robert and the other tough young men who had worked the land so hard, not only by breaking the ground and coaxing crops from it but by defending it against northern raiders. On the frontier, land was the only substantial wealth. For Robert especially, the verdict underlined the vagaries of law and justice as applied according to urban, book-learned, far-away principles, which merely enabled the rich, well-lawyered, and system-manipulating few to change the rules at will.

Rogers made his goodbyes and moved 20 miles south to a 60-acre plot that James had bought in his name when he was seven and had held in trust until he came of age. Close to the Merrimack and bounded on the west by Baboosic Lake, it bore thick stands of white oak. Robert set about taming the land and building a shelter. But before that winter ended, another catastrophe overtook the family.

One day as afternoon thickened into dusk, James visited the Walnut Hill hunting camp of his friend Ebenezer Ayer, not far from the newly rising Starkstown. James and Ayer, a veteran of Lovewell's Fight—a bloody encounter between New Hampshire militia and the Abenaki in 1725—often hunted together and met most every spring at the Amoskeag fish run. That day Ayer had finished hunting when James approached the camp, swathed in his usual black bearskin coat. Perhaps intending to surprise his friend, he refrained from calling out a greeting. Ayer misconstrued the silent, dark mass for an approaching beast and fired. James did not live through the night.[1]

Robert realized that his 60 acres would not secure him wealth. If the prospects of opening up the upper Merrimack country had sparked interest, the legendarily rich alluvial plains—*cowass* or *cohas* to the Indians—along the upper Connecticut River excited an outpouring of petitions to Governor Benning Wentworth of New Hampshire, who now could assign land patents. One such, to which Rogers probably subscribed, proposed that a group of 400 settlers should parcel out much of the best bottom country and settle it. In the vehemently expressed views of these petitioners, the Indians had long forfeited these lands by using them as a corridor to raid settlements. As Atecouando had made so eloquently clear, the Abenaki of Saint-François did not agree.

In November 1752 the New Hampshire Assembly authorized funding for two roads with bridges, one running from Canterbury northwest to the *cowass*, and another south from the *cowass* to Fort No. 4, the northernmost British colonial post on the Connecticut, in Charlestown. In March, Zacheus Lovewell, who 14 years earlier had sold the Mountalona tract to James Rogers, put together a group of surveyors and tough backwoodsmen, including John Stark as the "pilot" and Rogers as a guard. For 19 days the hardy band snowshoed up the Merrimack, blazing the proposed first road's course into tree trunks. Much as Stark had done the year before, the surveyors followed the Pemigewasset as far as the Baker, then overland to the Connecticut, where they could see the ice-choked river shining through a wide, flat valley. The true *cowass* began farther north, but there they stopped and returned safely.

Two months earlier six Abenakis had appeared at Fort No. 4 and asked for Captain Stevens. They had learned of the colonists' designs on the cowass in the face of Atecouando's explicit warnings in Montréal the previous summer. The "English had no need of that Land," they claimed, and "had a mind for War," which, they promised, would indeed be "Strong" if the white men further encroached upon the rich upriver lands. Nor would the Abenakis fight alone; the Mohawks and Ottawas would rally alongside them as members of that powerful confederation, the Seven Nations of Canada. Stevens voiced his grave concerns to the governor of Massachusetts, who in turn warned Governor Wentworth that any further activity within the *cowass* could mean blood indeed. The New Hampshire

Assembly voided its appropriations. Once more larger events intervened to dash Rogers's dreams of carving from the wilderness wealth and standing for himself.

Late in the summer of 1753 he signed a bond to his neighbor William Alld for 200 acres adjoining his present 60 and set about improving the land. He raised a house and barn, planted five acres of orchard, and let the house he had built on the original parcel to a tenant; but only six months later this house burned down and the tenant left.

No man to sit still, Rogers shook off the role of farmer as soon as the next friction with the Indians offered more full-blooded occupation. Rumors that the French were building a fort at the cowass prompted the New Hampshire Assembly to send another expedition north; it found no evidence of such activity but again inflamed the Abenakis, who retaliated with raids on Fort No. 4 and several settlements. Thereupon Wentworth ordered Colonel Joseph Blanchard to muster 60 men in defense of Rumford, Canterbury, and other vulnerable townships. Rogers enlisted as a private. A month of marches and patrols found no enemies but may have proved an effective deterrent.

Rogers got back to his farm late in September 1754, only to discover that William Alld had sued him for failure to pay the promised bond. A sheriff from Portsmouth had searched the property and, finding the only item worth taking to be a hat, left a summons for the defendant to appear before the court of common pleas in Portsmouth.

Great events have a way of entwining previously unrelated lives into contact at critical moments. Rogers's chance encounter with one Owen Sullivan, as he and his 20-year-old brother, Richard, returned from a hunting trip in late fall of 1754, nearly cost him his life but also goaded him into some of his greatest accomplishments. Unknown to the Rogers boys, Sullivan was perhaps the most notorious and colorful criminal in the colonies; his rich trappings and confident manner marked him immediately as an outsider to the frontier. He claimed that his watch alone cost £300. A gaudy ring of purple stone adorned his small finger, and a large pair of flowered silver buckles his shoes.[2] His elaborate hairstyle, wig, and hat obscured the letter R, for rogue, brand-seared on the upper edge of each cheek.

Punishment in the colonies matched the raw realities of life there—and branding, either on the cheek or the hand, served as a savage reminder of past indiscretions and yet was a crowning mercy compared to the gallows. Each county court in colonial Maryland disposed of a battery of irons: *SL* for seditious libeler; *M* for manslaughterer; *T* for thief; *R* for rogue or vagabond.[3]

The very same freedom that enabled immigrants from the Old World to remake themselves in the New also furnished ample opportunities for the criminally minded, who could bring off their scams according to the level of their cunning and audacity, then change their names and melt into the next undefined and ill-policed jurisdiction. In Britain men at the Stock Exchange and at Lloyd's of London could boast that their word was their bond; the fact that everybody with a stake in the country knew comparable people's family histories enabled them to seal large deals with a handshake. The colonies were much closer to being "a nation of strangers," if not several nations sometimes, under one vaguely respected charter.

Trouble had overtaken Sullivan and driven him, once more on the remake, to the New Hampshire frontier in search of fresh confederates for his counterfeiting schemes. The Rogers brothers played into the master manipulator's hands. Broke and down on his luck, Robert Rogers was fascinated not only by Sullivan's mind-stretching stories of the vast outside world but by the smooth and easy grace with which he enjoyed his wealth.

Even among his criminal peers, Sullivan knew few equals. In 1749, lying in Boston jail for counterfeiting, he audaciously cut a plate for manufacturing New Hampshire tenor, ran off a stack of 40-shilling notes, and smuggled them to an accomplice outside, who used them to buy his release.

In Providence in August 1752 one of his minions lost his nerve and turned king's evidence, instead of keeping his mouth shut: both men were convicted. The executioner was tasked with inflicting the sentence of public cheek-branding and ear-cropping—welcome entertainment for an eager rabble of townsfolk. But before he could begin, the fluent-tongued adventurer convinced those who had gathered to mock him that his punishment far overstepped the gravity of his crimes. A journalist recorded that his pleas softened not only the mob but the executioner, who inflicted a punishment far milder than he had been instructed, applying the irons above Sullivan's hairline and only nominally clipping the tops of his ears.

The artful Sullivan next convinced his jailers that it was a necessary deterrent for him to witness his partner's punishment. As
the executioner stood poised, glowing metal in hand, Sullivan shook
free from his guard, wrested a cutlass from a bystander, and strode
into the ring, railing against his partner's folly and perfidy and
brandishing the blade for emphasis. Turning to the executioner,
he exhorted him to char the man's cheeks and crop his ears with
a vengeance. Then he stood witness, and amid the screams and
smell of burning flesh, he cut his way through the crowd and disappeared.[4]

Now he flashed a fortune in paper bills before the eyes of the
Rogers brothers, playing expertly on the sucker's unending dream
of easy riches, or at least of easier living than clearing forest and
dodging Indian warriors. At an agreed-upon time Sullivan met the
Rogerses, John McCurdy, James McNeal, and four Martin brothers at
Nathaniel Martin's house in nearby Goff's Town.[5] After some mutu-
ally outrageous storytelling, Sullivan got down to business. There
would be some danger in the counterfeiting. At that point John
McCurdy brought up the illegality of pushing queer. Court records
catch Sullivan's response.

"Damn you for a pack of fools!" he yelled. "I never was concerned
with such a pack of damned fools before." Of course, he had been involved with many, but the accusation served to sort out the nervous
and untrustworthy.

McCurdy fled. The Rogers brothers remained under the spell,
mesmerized by the bluster. Pulling out a roll of bills, Sullivan shoved
a twenty-shilling note across to Robert in payment for pasturing a
horse at Mountalona, a plainly suspicious sum for so small a task. (In
the same year the average monthly wage of a seaman in Boston was
£1.39.)[6] As Rogers turned the bill over, Sullivan added, "It will go
through all the laws in any of the provinces." He wanted to buy three
yoke of oxen. Would Robert set this up for him?

While Rogers certainly knew that the implicit project was a hanging offense, his view of counterfeiters probably reflected that of
many people living in underserved rural societies, especially enterprising ones, particularly along the frontier. There never was enough
cash to move trade—and such currency as did circulate was a mix
of old tenor, or New Hampshire bills printed in 1709; new tenor,

printed in 1741; and British pounds sterling, Spanish dollars and pistareens, and Portuguese Johannas and moidores.[7] Britain kept the colonies on a short leash, restricting their foreign trade by limiting the circulation of internationally accepted currency. Specie earned in export soon made its way back to the mother country. The lack of circulating money particularly hamstrung ordinary people. Counterfeiters, especially in the backcountry, often emerged as folk heroes who sometimes enlisted whole communities in their illegal business.[8] Sullivan could count on many a loft and barn whenever he needed a place to hide.

Rogers agreed to pasture the horse, took Sullivan's note, and rode off to see John Stark, telling him that a man from Boston was interested in buying oxen. Stark sold him three yokes.

By the time Rogers goaded the oxen back to the Martin house, Sullivan had departed, perhaps not sanguine about his new accomplices' talents. Rogers could not keep the horse, because Martin had bought it from Sullivan. Stuck with the oxen for which he had paid legitimate money, Rogers probably had to sell them at a loss. But Sullivan had left behind some plates for making New Hampshire pound and shilling tenor, and his amateur sidekicks were soon at work. From Carty Gilman, an Exeter shoemaker, Rogers bought a wagon, a wig, and a pair of pumps.

On January 7, 1755, the New Hampshire House of Representatives, alarmed at the steady flow of bad paper, passed a resolution directing "all Justices of the Peace and other proper officers within this Province" to round up any persons suspected of forging or altering bills. By the twenty-fourth Justice Mesech Weare composed a list of nineteen suspects, including Robert, his brother Richard, Nathaniel Martin, and William Alld. On January 31 Sheriff Thomas Packer arrested the Rogers brothers at Mountalona. But before Packer arrived, Rogers dashed off a frantic note to his friend Carty Gilman:

> Mr. Gilman for gods sake do the work that you promised me that you would Do by No meanes fail or you Will Destroy me for Ever. Sir, my Life lays att your provdence now Ons more I adjure you by your Maker, to Do it for whie should such an onest Man be Killed Sir, I am a souned freiend
>
> Robert Rodgers

Despite this desperate plea, a virtual admission of guilt, Rogers interestingly still regarded himself as an "onest Man." There is always a cadre of operators—currency lubricators, bootleggers, chain-letter activists—who see themselves not just as remarkable risk-takers for profit but also as public benefactors.

Weare commissioned four justices of the peace, including Colonel Joseph Blanchard and Captain John Goffe—under both of whom Rogers had served on militia operations around Rumford—to examine the evidence. On February 7 Rogers pleaded not guilty to counterfeiting before the Rumford Inferior Court, but he did admit to having known Sullivan. John Stark took the stand—Rogers must have known that his upright friend would not lie—and testified that Rogers had bought oxen from him, "and some Time after he Saw Roger and askt him What he had Don With his oxon he said he Sold em but Not to the man he Purposed them for, and Said he Was Cheated for he Intended the oxon for Soolefin [Sullivan] & thot to have had a Large Quantity of Counterfeit money But said he wood not be Concerned any more In such things." Stark put the best possible face on it for his friend, but his testimony could not but confirm Rogers's complicity. Finding that Robert Rogers, William Alld, and eight others had knowingly made and passed counterfeit bills, the examiners nevertheless released Rogers and five others on bond, directing him to appear at ten A.M. on February 12 before the Superior Court in Portsmouth. Four principals remained in jail. The justices dropped charges against Richard.

Rogers realized that he was in dangerously deep and that ear-cropping or branding might be the best he could hope for. Many bills carried the unequivocal phrase "to counterfeit is death." Just a year later Sullivan would stand on the gallows, writing his script to the last, as he instructed the executioner not to pull the rope so tight, for it was hard for a man to die in "cool blood."[9]

For Rogers, Providence intervened in the form of war with France. On the day of his trial William Shirley, governor of Massachusetts, called for volunteers to seize the French holdings on the Bay of Fundy. The trial never took place. In short order Rogers rounded up 24 New Hampshiremen, paid them a small advance obtained from the Massachusetts recruiting officer, and started south. But by March the war drums were beating even louder, and an arc of new fronts was taking shape, including the possibilities of a campaign against the French stronghold on Lake Champlain. Come midmonth, New Hampshire called for 500 volunteers. Rogers might be a sorry conspirator when it came to crooked finance, but he was a magnetic young leader in the moment of war; as he marched up to Portsmouth, he drew into his ranks some 50 raw recruits. He might have left Shirley sputtering with anger about running off with "Massachusetts" men and the $30 commission fee, but the governor's angry letter to Benning Wentworth went unanswered. Rogers's men became the first company of the regiment commanded by none other than Joseph Blanchard, the New Hampshire justice who had presided over Rogers's hearing less than two months earlier.

For the moment the looming war trumped everything else—a very good thing for Rogers: luck finally seemed to have broken on his side. On April 24 Undersheriff John Light knocked on Carty Gilman's door in Exeter to serve a warrant; he found him stuffing a piece of paper into his mouth with one hand, while gripping two counterfeit six-shilling New Hampshire bills in the other. The sheriff wrestled him to the ground and pulled the cud out of his mouth— and found the half-consumed remains of Rogers's hasty but mightily incriminating injunction to his hapless accomplice.

But by then even such damning corroboration mattered little. Rogers had put together 50-odd men, a powerful argument for clemency, and had automatically earned himself a captaincy. He appointed John Stark his lieutenant, and the young men set about preparing for war.

Part Two

REINVENTING WAR

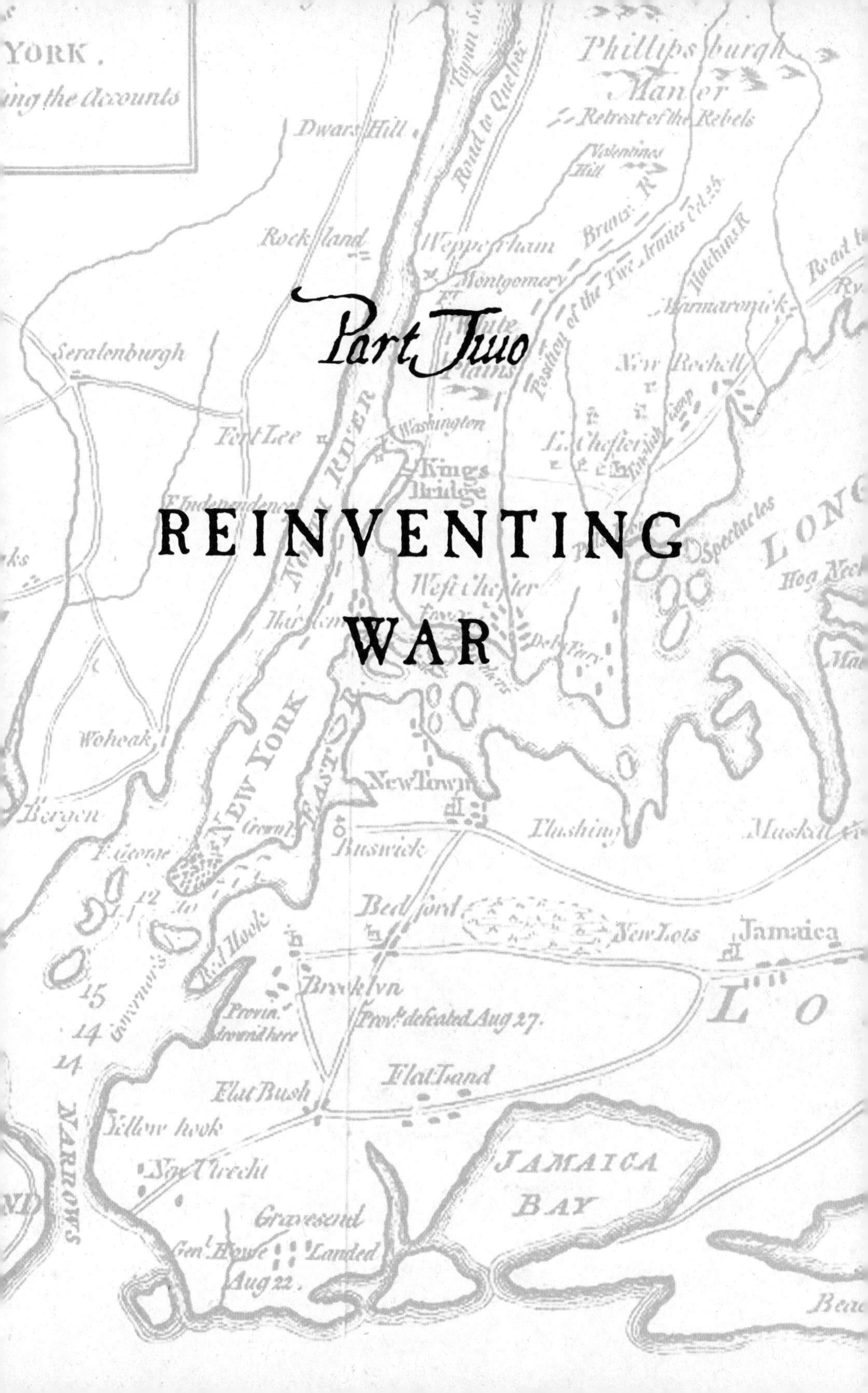

Chapter 6

The War Begins

In this country a thousand men could stop three thousand.

MONTREUIL TO VAUDREUIL,
JUNE 12, 1756[1]

On Tuesday morning, September 14, 1755, inside the palisaded British encampment where the Adirondacks cast their shadows over the southern end of Lake George, Rogers watched the carpenters' handsaws bite into lengths of freshly cut oak and white pine. Around them the high-curved ribs of Schenectady bateaux heaved out of the early morning fog like skeletons of great beached sea creatures. The geese had begun to fly south but only in small groups overhead; the wind blew gently from the southwest. The deciduous trees on the steep hillsides had just begun to turn purple. Provincial troops from the New England plantations stacked endless planking, while caulking pitch simmered in iron vessels atop large wood fires. Already more than a dozen of the straight-sided 30-footers of this aspirant inland navy were drawn up on the beach, ready for action; many had been deliberately submerged to swell the timbers and tighten leaky seams. Oars, paddles of different sizes, bailers, and iron-tipped poles for maneuvering through shallows lay in heaps.[2]

In their minds' ear, the boat workers could still hear echoes of the ferocious Battle of Lake George that had been fought on this spot only six days earlier in which the British had successfully withstood a concerted French attack; they cast occasional uneasy glances to the north, which, as the fog lifted, opened into a striking prospect of steep, pine-studded mountains embracing a dozen miles of clear lake water. Somewhere beyond lay the French army, with its formidable mission-Indian allies, perhaps at that moment planning another descent on the vulnerable British position. Major General William Johnson, who commanded the forces occupying this encampment and Fort Lyman (soon to be renamed Fort Edward), 16 miles by road to the south, was under orders to destroy the old French stone strongpoint of Fort Saint-Frédéric (present-day Crown Point) on Lake Champlain; his force was to be carried by a fleet of bateaux, including six that had been built more than 50 percent larger than the rest to carry 4,700-pound siege cannons capable of discharging eighteen-pound balls. No such fleet had ever cut these inland waters. But to Rogers's clear eye, this campaign of truly imperial ambition had little chance of being fulfilled. Far too few boats lay completed or had been brought up from Albany, and winter fast approached.

Rogers made no attempt to conceal his contempt for this design of boat, which his commanding officer, Colonel Blanchard, had called "clumsy, worthless things." Bateaux had no keels: their flat bottoms displayed only slight rocker toward their pointed bows and sterns, which might indeed ease their passage across shallows but made for sluggish steering and limited sailing to running before the wind. But at least their simple design had the merit of being easy to handle, even by unseaworthy soldiers.

Much to his disappointment, his and Blanchard's New Hampshiremen, stuck at Fort Lyman, the new fort guarding the portage between the Hudson and Lake George, had missed last week's battle. Blanchard's regiment had arrived at Lake George only just after sunset the evening before, rolling out their bark huts on the drier eastern side of the compound, not far from Johnson's white canvas marquee. They themselves abhorred tents, preferring the crude but dry, light, and portable bark lean-tos used for campaigning in the woods.[3] The newcomers quickly dispersed along the broad avenues of the ephemeral city of tents and shelters, to seek out friends and learn details of the fight.

They found last week's victors subdued—as Johnson would later write, "all fatigued both in Body and mind," despite a rich booty of tomahawks, caps, tumplines, belts, cutlasses, moccasins, and one sealskin pack. Promised freedom to plunder when they volunteered for service at Albany that spring, the New Englanders had taken up the task with vigor after driving the enemy back. "Our people and the Mohawks Went out to Plonder and Got a Great Deal," wrote Private James Hill of Massachusetts, "but the Mohawks got most of it."[4]

Details—some gruesome—came trickling out. The woods were scattered with the bodies of friends who, taken alive by the enemy, had been strangely bound together in threes and fours before being scalped and mutilated.[5] Burial parties told of finding dozens of the enemy dead on biers in a nearby swamp.[6]

Johnson's New Englanders formed one spike of a four-pronged strategy to crack the forward positions of New France in the summer of 1755. The overall British commander in North America, General Edward Braddock, had taken British regulars—the first major appearance of British soldiers upon the continent—against the strong strategic French presence at the Forks of the Ohio in July. While he pressed westward, Johnson's army, mustered and provisioned in Albany, was supposed to swing north against the lightly garrisoned Fort Saint-Frédéric at Crown Point, which commanded a crucial chokepoint on Lake Champlain.

France's North American empire hinged on control of the northeastern continent's major watercourses, which were critical not only as trade routes into the interior but also as strategic highways to counter and contain British land venturers. By the 1730s, while the British inhabitants were strung thinly along the eastern seaboard in patterns of local and relatively spontaneous settlement, the French, children of a state-centered culture, planted forts along strategic sea, lake, and river narrows, not to protect an ongoing frontier of settlement but to deny passage at will, based on centuries of abstract strategic mastery maintained on another continent. The massive fortress of Louisbourg protected the Atlantic estuary of the St. Lawrence; Fort Niagara closed off the Niagara River's entrance into Lake Ontario and with it access farther west to the Great Lakes; Fort Saint-Frédéric at Crown Point prevented the passage of hostile vessels from Albany, and ultimately from the continental gateway of New York City, northward into what was to become New France.

Of these three, Fort Saint-Frédéric and the stone forts along the valleys of Lakes Champlain and George would become the main southern battlefront of the French and Indian War, because the north-south orientation of these lakes, the river Richelieu, and the Hudson made a potentially manageable road of war between Montréal, the heart of New France, and New York City, center of the mid-Atlantic British colonies. A French army could paddle or sail down a virtually continuous 300-mile waterway from Montréal to Albany, slowed only by three portages: Montréal to the river Richelieu; Lake Champlain to Lake George at Carillon (later known as Ticonderoga); and Lake George to the Hudson. Controlling the latter two chokepoints became central to the war effort. For decades dozens of French raiding parties had jumped off from Fort Saint-Frédéric, including Paul Marin's raiders who sacked Saratoga in November 1745 and François-Pierre de Rigaud de Vaudreuil's command that besieged Fort Massachusetts in 1746.[7]

In early May 1755, aware of Britain's several intentions and indeed of Braddock's specific movements, the government in Paris dispatched Maréchal-de-Camp Jean-Armand, Baron de Dieskau and six of its 395 regular battalions, numbering some 3,000 Troupes de Terre, to the New World aboard 16 men-of-war. The Swiss-born mercenary commander Dieskau had served with some distinction as a cavalry officer under the famed Maréchal Maurice de Saxe during the War of the Austrian Succession. He planned not only to hold Fort Saint-Frédéric but to annihilate Johnson's dangerously extended force. At the head of battalions of the Queen's and Languedoc Regiments—the first French line formations dispatched to North America since 1665—along with some 1,600 Canadian militia and 700 mission Indians, Dieskau harbored little doubt that he could roll over his poorly trained provincial adversaries.[8] On reaching Fort Saint-Frédéric, he pared his 3,000-man force down to 1,400, leaving the rest in garrison. Meanwhile Johnson moved up the Hudson from Albany, reinforced Fort Lyman, then cut a road to the southern end of Lake George, at which he arrived on August 28 with at least four pieces of artillery. Twenty-two hundred men set about clearing the ground, raising rudimentary defenses, and building storehouses. Robert Rogers had arrived at Albany with his regiment only after Johnson had departed.

Both Fort Lyman and the advance camp on Lake George depended on resupply from Albany by Conestoga wagon trains driven by Dutch teamsters, fiercely independent hired hands with little inclination to manhandle their transport over the difficult road under the constant threat of Indian attack. Tasked with getting the desperately needed supplies north, Blanchard gave the 23-year-old Rogers his first taste of command responsibility by detailing him to escort a supply train from Albany to Fort Lyman with 100 men.

On September 7 Indian scouts reported the approach of Dieskau's army. Would it seek to cut off the Lake George encampment by attacking Fort Lyman or assault Johnson's camp directly? Johnson called a council of war, which resolved to send 500 men to destroy the beached flotilla from which the Frenchmen had come ashore, while another 500 moved to reinforce Fort Lyman. But the wise 75-year-old Mahican sachem Theyanoguin (also known under the Dutchified name of Hendrick), who had preeminence among the Iroquois, strenuously objected. A corpulent figure of great grim competence in two worlds, he wore English clothes, had visited London twice, and bore a savage knife scar across the length of his left cheek.[9]

The embodied wisdom of the Old and the New Worlds rose and, with some difficulty, leaned over and scooped up a handful of sticks on the ground at Johnson's feet. Conversation stopped as Theyanoguin bundled the sticks, then brought the faggot down smartly over his knee. He failed to break it but could snap any individual stick with ease. To disperse resources in the face of the enemy, he urged, was self-destructive imprudence. Concentrate forces and reinforce them; then they could meet the enemy with confidence. Johnson agreed to combine the two detachments but overruled Theyanoguin's pleas to send out a much larger force to meet the French. The advice would exact a great personal cost from the chief but would save Johnson from disaster.

At eight A.M. on September 8 the sachem led a thousand provincial soldiers and 200 Mohawks south; just two and a half hours later, only three miles from their encampment, they marched into an ambush. Colonel Ephraim Williams, in command of the provincials, died outright, shot through the head. (His estate would ultimately endow Williams College.) Another ball dropped Theyanoguin's horse, pinning him underneath it; the old chief lost both scalp and life.[10] Major Seth Pomeroy took command, later writing that "had not the Lord been on our side we must all ben swallowed up." Only a fierce rearguard action by Nathaniel Whiting's Connecticut regiment and some Rhode Island volunteers bought time for the other panicked columns to escape in wild disorder back to the Lake George entrenchments. Rogers, out scouting north of Fort Lyman, reputedly heard the firing.

The severity of the repulse threw Johnson's encampment into a frenzy. The log breastwork reached only knee-high along parts of the incomplete fort's perimeter. Johnson ordered his shaken men to bulk up the line with anything available. Bateaux, logs, trees, even wagons were heaved onto the rude barricades, rattling in the strong southern wind as the wild-eyed survivors raced behind them.[11]

The gunners checked and rechecked their four cannons—a 32-pounder and three of lesser caliber—that pointed down the road into a tangled pitch-pine forest and thicket.[12] They then watched in amazement as Dieskau's 220 regulars, bayonets shining in the sun, marched down the road in tight formation, six abreast and 300 feet deep with some seven feet between ranks.[13] Their close-order volleys riddled the boats and wagons, but Johnson's cannonballs, recorded a British provincial gunner, "made Lanes, Streets and Alleys thro' their army."[14] Dieskau's gamble that his best-disciplined line troops could break through the haphazard defenses failed; repeated heroic charges brought only a devastating casualty rate of one out of three men.

The engagement devolved into a prolonged sniping engagement, bullets flying "like hail-storms," wrote Thomas Williams, a camp doctor and brother of the slain Ephraim. He attended the wounded with little cover, protecting his face from pieces of wood sent flying when musket balls struck nearby tree trunks and the rude barricade. By about four that afternoon the French pulled back. Most of the provincials, too tired and frightened to pursue, huddled behind their barricades.

Two hundred and fifty New Hampshiremen, marching from Albany to reinforce Johnson, encountered the battered French and Indians licking their wounds and inflicted yet further losses—until the French fled into the woods, scattering their packs and belongings "like the Assyrians in their flight," observed Dr. Williams piously.[15]

The provincials found the Baron de Dieskau propped up against a tree with a hip wound and perforated bladder,[16] and they rounded up 21 of his wounded regulars.[17] In the infirmary, Williams fought for the lives of both sides' casualties over the next several days, infection now claiming many. He wrote bitterly about watching men slip away when their wounds were of themselves not life-threatening, and he proposed that French musket balls were poisoned with a solution of copper and yellow arsenic, evidence of which he claimed the provincials had discovered on shot left in bullet pouches on the field of battle. "I trust a righteous God will one day avenge their barbarous rage, cruelty & malice against us," he wrote his wife.[18] A more likely culprit was poor sanitary conditions and general malnutrition.

While Johnson's untested provincial forces had won a substantial victory over hard-disciplined metropolitan regulars, their success—indeed, survival—came at a heavy cost: the British had lost 306 men, the French 253.

Now, as Rogers watched the carpenters at work, Johnson held a council of war with the field commanders. His usually genial Irish spirit was still soured by a French musket ball in the hip that had driven him early from the battle line and that, almost a week later, the surgeon still had not found. But his hip remained the least of his problems; his pain and fever were constantly compounded by fear that the enemy was planning another attack, this time on artilleryless Fort Lyman, whose fall would leave the force highly vulnerable. Two of his dozen closest officers, the Connecticut colonels Ephraim Williams and Moses Titcomb, lay dead. But the loss of Theyanoguin posed a far greater problem.

Three days after the battle two Mohawk sachems had solemnly announced that "it is our constant custom after an Engagement in which we have any loss to return home for a little while and chear our People and then return with fresh vigour."[19] They had lost 33 men, a significant proportion of their whole force and no insignificant number of their whole people. Johnson's sustained entreaties did not change their minds, and he made matters worse by refusing to hand over the French general—the Indians believed, noted one observer, that they had the right to "kill, scalp, burn, and even eat" the wretched baron.[20] Even though Johnson moved Dieskau secretly from tent to tent, he only narrowly escaped death when a regular intercepted an Indian who had slipped in upon him and pulled a long knife.[21]

The Mohawks left next day, depriving Johnson of his prime

source of intelligence on enemy strength and movement. In desperation, he turned to Blanchard to provide woods-savvy New Hampshiremen of proven scouting ability. The colonel, pleased with Rogers's effective performance escorting the supply train, sent him to the general's marquee.

The 40-year-old Johnson stood just shy of six feet and bore himself with the air of an English gentleman; but his solid frame, culminating in a massive neck and broad shoulders, suggested something more of a yeoman farmer. The frontier-wise eyes that appraised Rogers were large and dark, cavernously intensified by the sleeplessness of strain and suffering. A female acquaintance described him as having a handsome countenance, "which, however, had rather an expression of dignified sedateness, approaching to melancholy."[22]

The British high command had chosen him for this assignment not for his military experience (which was limited to service as a paymaster for Indian warriors) but for his strong relations with the Mohawks as an unusually shrewd superintendent of Indian affairs. He wrote Braddock: "I am truly sensible of my own Inability to be at the head of this undertaking & I am afraid I shall have but few with me to assist & strengthen my Incapacity." A curious New World hybrid, Johnson ruled his estate on the Mohawk as half-squire, half-sachem, often garbed in the tribe's ceremonial robes. At any one time a visitor might find a dozen or more Indians wandering inside the manor house, an Old World touch on the far frontier. His many and much-frequented Indian concubines, observed one visitor, bore "as many children they had fixed upon you as the late Emperor of Merocco Muli Ishmale which I think was 700." To inaugurate the campaign at Albany, he presided over a gathering of some 1,100 Indian men, women, and children, who initiated a war dance, roasted a whole ox over a fire, and painted Johnson's face in the garish hues of war. As the dance ran down, Johnson hacked a piece of meat off the carcass with a cutlass, and the Indians followed suit with their axes.[23]

For all his exhaustion, Johnson managed to summon up some spark of Irish twinkle. The man in front of him, he noticed, exuded a quiet and powerful confidence unusual for someone so young. Would Rogers be willing to run the dangerous scout up to Fort Saint-Frédéric to assess enemy strength? That drew a grin from Rogers. Yes, sir!

Johnson immediately laid out a demanding agenda that would have daunted most other men. Would it be feasible to build an artillery-worthy road from the upper end of Lake George to Fort Saint-Frédéric? Were the French building new facilities? These crucial strategic data had to be gathered quickly, systematically, and accurately, not by sniffing around at long distance. Rogers should pick two men and leave at once in a bateau rowed by two Connecticut provincials.

As Rogers strode back to his camp under the steady rain, the mission's seriousness weighed on his shoulders. The British war effort was focused here now in the wake of an unthinkable catastrophe that had befallen it two months earlier: a far smaller French and Indian force had shattered Braddock's well-trained army in the western Pennsylvania woods just short of Braddock's objective, Fort Duquesne. A litter of wagons, provisions, clothing, personal effects, and corpses testified to the disaster; Braddock himself had been dragged away to die, and then his remains were shoveled into the roadbed, lest they be mutilated by the Indians.

How it came to pass was long debated. Ben Franklin, who had performed quartermaster work for the expedition, observed in his autobiography that while he considered Braddock a brave man who would probably have done well commanding in a European theater, he had "too high an opinion of the validity of regular troops; too mean a one of both Americans and Indians." Indeed, before the debacle, Johnson, the governors of Massachusetts and Virginia, and the bitterly experienced Colonel George Washington had urged Braddock to rely on Indian scouts. At first Braddock had responded, setting the Indian agents to ply several chiefs with presents. But by the time of the march west he retained only eight such recruits. While Braddock and his staff recognized that the North American environment demanded adjustments, they viewed aboriginal forest fighting techniques through a European spyglass, perceiving only crude improvisation and lack of offensive spirit, which led them to brush off suggestions that mass tactics be modified to suit the dangers and opportunities of the woodland world. Braddock did order his men to leave behind shoulder belts, waist belts, and swords and to reduce their spare kit, which considerably lightened the usual grenadier load of 65 pounds, and he supplied the troops with leather disks to place between their heads and their hat linings "to keep Them from the heat of the Sun."

On July 9, the British vanguard under Lt. Col. Thomas Gage crossed the Monongahela and approached Fort Duquesne. Gage inexplicably defied the basic manuals of war by neglecting to traverse highest ground—a small hillock lay uncovered on the line of march. Informed by only the most perfunctory scouting, he pressed forward, unaware that the French had sallied from the fort to meet their enemy. The two advance columns collided with great mutual surprise: indeed, the British gained an initial upper hand when the French commander was mortally wounded. But this turn of events curiously favored the French because their next most senior leader, the canny French Canadian partisan and woods fighter Paul Marin, was probably better prepared for the task at hand. He deployed the regulars as well as the Indians behind trees, directing them to flank their enemy.

The heat of battle did not melt British rigidity—bad as were the consequences, a shift to unprepared individual combat would have proven even worse. Tight formation doctrine assumed that the shock effect, order, and cohesion of the combat line would in the end break down conventional mass opposition or individual determination by sheer superiority of the institutionalized will to kill and die. But such brute exposure offered a woodland gallery of scarlet targets to the French and Indians. Gradually what was left of the advance guard collapsed back upon the main column, throwing themselves and the support troops into further confusion. Some troops never saw a single enemy during the three-hour-plus engagement. "The yell of the Indians is fresh on my ear, and the terrific sound will haunt me to the hour of my dissolution," wrote a badly shaken lieutenant of the 44th Foot.

The British public received the news of disaster with dismay and fury—the overall war was going badly around the world. What kind of army could profit by skulking behind trees and boulders? Only a decade earlier, at the Battle of Fontenoy in present-day Belgium, a Scots nobleman had drunk a toast to the French commanders as the armies closed upon each other, crying, "Gentlemen of the French Guards, fire first!" to the accompaniment of three cheers. The French reputedly replied, "Sir, we never fire first, please fire yourselves." That day more than 15,000 British and Hanoverian soldiers were killed or wounded. No wonder the subaltern of the 44th wrote, "We have lost gallant officers and generous friends, not in battle, for that we could bear, but by murder by savage butchery. The French dared not openly meet us; ours is the loss, theirs the disgrace."

Recent scholarship has questioned old assumptions. Had they stuck to the basic tenets of European warfare—using diligent scouting and systematically occupying high ground, for instance—the redcoats might have won the day. But British command deficiencies aside, the French, the Indians, and the Canadian militia proved quicker to adapt to the surprise encounter and used the terrain to their advantage.

Clearly the rules had changed in the North American woods. The British met peoples who had never been under the spell of the *Iliad* or of King's Regulations. Wholesale—and needless—slaughter was anathema to the subsistence-farming and hunter-gatherer tribes of the Eastern Woodlands. James Smith, captive of the Caughnawaga Mohawks of Ohio for four years, wrote that the Indians saw European military practice as dying "like dogs" and wholly unacceptable. Indeed, he continued, when fighting led to actual killing, the contending Indian parties would fall back, "but this proceeds from a compliance with their rules of war, rather than cowardice."[24]

European conceptions of war and manhood, if applied among relatively small peoples dispersed over a vast landscape, where the deaths of even a few hunters could bring on a winter of devastating famine, meant that one eddy of battle could cause the disappearance of an entire culture. The mark of success for an Iroquois war chief was the return of his entire party with "whole skins" to fight another day. Each side considered the other to be conscious and systematic violators of longstanding codes of individual behavior, group conduct, and ethics forged over centuries.

It would be Rogers's signature genius to see how a higher synthesis of Old and New World practices could create a new and formidable mode of warfare; the invisibility and sweeping range of the forest peoples would be cleverly united to the newcomers' technologies, strategic vision, and cultural appetite for innovation. By recasting both sides' rules of engagement—and consequently of clothing, travel, camping, and small-unit operations—Rogers would offer up his own systematized brand of North American warfare to match not only the continent's environment but also its magnitude.

Braddock's defeat at the Monongahela greatly strengthened the French relationship with dozens of tribes, whose raiders now poured south and east to ravage the new homesteads that had been tenatively erected west of the Alleghenies. They pushed the wilderness back east; hundreds of people of all ages perished, or if possible were carried northward for slavery, adoption, or ransom. Thousands of farmsteads were burned or rotted into ruin, and perhaps tens of thousands of homeless haunted the frontier towns.

For the British, the best hope of recovering the initiative lay with Johnson's army on Lake George. Rogers's upcoming scout would determine what they were up against and whether they could deal with it.

Chapter 7

First Sorties

The lakes and rivers are the only outlets, the only open roads in this country.

BOUGAINVILLE, JULY 1758[1]

Rogers's men loaded up nine days' worth of provisions, for the most part parched corn ground to powder, along with small hard biscuits, beef jerky, some sugar, rice, chocolate, and peas, all to be washed down with watered rum from their canteens and skins, into which it was customary to sprinkle powdered ginger in the belief that it was sovereign against the bloody flux, scurvy, and ague. Of these nascent rangers, rough-hewn men of the New Hampshire Regiment, a British officer would later write that they "have no particular uniform, only they wear their cloaths short." Each bore a musket, a tomahawk, and a long knife; a "bullock's horn full of powder hangs under their right arm by a belt from their shoulder." A leather or sealskin bag, buckled around the waist, carried some 60 lead rounds, weighing nearly five pounds, as well as smaller shot the size of "full green peas." Rogers may have carried a compass, which he would have affixed to the bottom of his powderhorn.

The men whetted their scalping knives, double-checked the contents of their small packs, and stitched reinforcing pieces of supple leather into their moccasins.

When night finally swallowed the soft glow of daylight a few minutes after seven P.M., men of the New Hampshire Regiment floated the five spies' bateau, whispering tension-relieving jokes about them coming back with scalps on. Rogers stood in the stern,

using a long oar to steer, as the other four dipped their oars into the
water, driving the boat north; at each stroke the tholepin rowlocks,
braided rope looped around brass stanchions, groaned softly into the
night.

Lake George gradually widens northward from its three-quarter-
mile-long beach terminus until after a dozen miles it appears to run
out against the green cliffs of the Tongue Mountain Range: but actually it only narrows, then doglegs to the northeast. Nine mountains
more than 2,000 feet tall crowd the lake's sinuous 32 miles, their
steep, pine-studded slopes often plummeting right into the water,
giving the impression of Old World fjords.[2] Nearly 200 rocky islands
interrupt the clear waters, often densely covered with pine, fir, sweet
gale, and juniper. The rugged topography bends storm winds into
strange patterns, which no doubt Rogers wished to avoid, especially
in a flat-bottomed bateau. The Swedish traveler Per Kalm observed
that within moments a squall could turn the quiet lake into "a boiling
kettle" of colliding breakers.[3]

Not concerned to muffle their oars while still within sight of their
own campfires, the small party swept briskly up to the narrows,
where a cluster of islets chokes the waterway and the mountains rise
even taller and more forbiddingly than before. The men no longer
spoke, and they may have muffled the oarlocks with small squares of
leather. Twelve hours later, as the first hints of sunrise spread across
the horizon, the bateau had covered another 15 miles. The tired oarsmen pulled onto a small promontory and hauled the boat into the
woods. The two Connecticut soldiers remained behind to guard the
boat and supplies while the three New Hampshiremen struck north
along the western edge of the lake with five days' worth of provisions,
glad to give their blistered fingers relief.

Sticking close to the shore, after two miles they encountered a
small bay and saw a smooth, exposed, mountainous granite dome
whose eastern cliff fell abruptly into the lake. Three years later this
rock would take Rogers's name as the setting for a feat that is disputed to this day.

From where they lay hidden behind the pine growth along the
bay's southern edge, the patrol could see several birchbark canoes
laden with Indians. Then they turned inland, following the contour
lines leading northward to Trout Brook Valley, then eastward to the

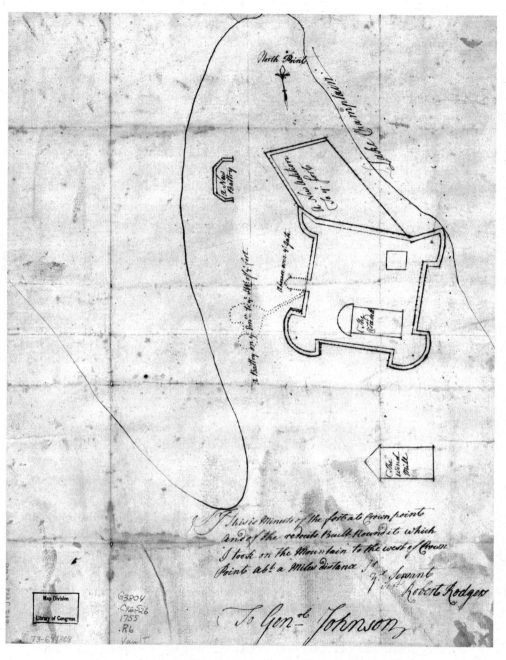

Rogers's sketch of the French Garrison at Crown Point, 1755

Ticonderoga peninsula, "the carrying place"; there they heard what could only be enemy activity and bore well to the west. On the rain-soaked second evening, after carefully negotiating a French-cut footpath between Carillon and Fort Saint-Frédéric, the trio emerged two miles south of the latter, which occupied the tip of a small peninsula jutting toward the opposite shore. They passed among wheatfields and four deserted houses until they were virtually beneath the fort's walls; they crawled into a newly dug trench that led some 500 feet from the fort's western wall to the crown of a small hill, atop of which the French had begun to raise a new redoubt. They spent an uneasy night, the wet mud sticking to their clothes in great clumps. With hearts racing, they pressed up against the mud to wriggle toward the major stronghold's solid limestone walls, which rose 18 feet into the dark night. From their vantage they could see an eight-sided, four-story tower pierced by many cannon ports and hear the sounds of the camp.[4]

At first light they scrambled a mile west to the flanks of Bulwagga Mountain or Coots Hill, from which they could view a panorama of the fort. A brigantine weighed anchor, raised sail, and tacked north. Between a large stone windmill 1,000 feet southward and the fort itself lay a field crowded with white tents, the acre within the walls by no means enough to accommodate the present complement. To the north was visible another enclosure, half as big as the fort's and just as full of tents; there must be between 500 and 600 troops and Indians all told. As the silent watch took in the French troops' muster and exercise, Rogers sketched a map of the complex, noting a new battery to the northwest. (See page 85.)

Work resumed on the redoubt that they had left just hours before, and pigeon-hunting parties came within 250 yards of their position. Rogers reported that the French roamed freely, apparently unconcerned about the possible presence of spies or raiders.

That evening the trio slipped off the mountain and worked their way south, pausing only briefly near the La Chute River, which starts from the foot of Lake George and descends five falls to empty into Lake Champlain. From a distance they observed much enemy activity, good grounds for suspecting that the French intended to fortify a fort at Carillon. They heard the surprising note of French—or at least hunting—horns, the Gallic soldiers filling the chilling void of the New World wilderness with the comforting warrior music of the Old.

The party hurried south to the rendezvous, out of time and provisions—scouting Carillon would have to wait—and arrived on the twentieth, only to find "to our great mortification" that the two Connecticut provincials had gone, taking with them the bateau and all the provisions.[5] Perhaps the immense quiet of the wilderness had pressed too hard upon them, a situation James Fenimore Cooper described in *The Last of the Mohicans:* "His awakened imagination, deluded by the deceptive light, converted each waving bush, or the fragment of some fallen tree, into human forms and twenty times he fancied he could distinguish the horrid visages of his lurking foes."[6]

Swallowing his anger, Rogers quickly took stock of their situation. Thirty miles of steeply contoured Adirondack forest lay between them and the southern end of Lake George. A front had moved in, delivering constant cold rain.[7] Their best option would be to follow a Mohawk war path skirting the lake's western edge. They shared what little food they had, understanding that they could do no hunting on the way home; one musket shot would surely give them away. They cinched belts around the clammy, wool blankets wrapped about their shoulders, heads, and chests and at a few words from Rogers pushed into the woods.

On the second day they stumbled upon a silent glen of quiet horror: the bloodied corpses of French and Indians, wounded on September 8 and left to die on the forest floor, lay stiffened in the cool air. The rain kept the stench from overpowering them, but wolves had already ripped much meat from the bodies. The trio ransacked the scattered packs for food, tainted or not.

Late on the evening of September 23 the three far-stretched men staggered into camp, "not a little fatigued and distressed from hunger and cold." Rogers made his report to Blanchard, then told his story to the eager men pushing around him. Likely Rogers paid his Connecticut ex-colleagues a visit and settled scores with a Scotch argument. Few sins equal leaving your comrades in danger of their lives.

Rogers's report disturbed Johnson. To build a road that could bear artillery from Carillon to Fort Saint-Frédéric at Crown Point across 20 miles of brutally rough and mountainous forest would be "impracticable." His army would have to portage all their bateaux, then approach Crown Point from the water. But the news of activity at Ticonderoga was even more alarming. A substantial force there would put an army laying siege to Fort Saint-Frédéric in severe difficulties.

Three days later Johnson sent Rogers out again, this time to check on activity at Carillon, that "verry dangerous and important place" to which the battered French regular regiments had retreated after the Battle of Lake George. (Fort Saint-Frédéric, old, small, and not defensible against siege guns, remained vulnerable, so it was at Carillon that Governor-General Vaudreuil, on September 20, ordered his nephew Michel Chartier de Lotbinière to build "entrenchments or other fortifications capable of assuring us control of this passage.")[8]

This time Rogers took a birchbark canoe and four New Hampshiremen, again slipping into the lake under cover of darkness. The canoe moved fast, quietly, and unnoticed past numerous campfires along the shore north of the narrows. Daybreak found them at or near the same point on which they had landed during the previous scout. Leaving the others behind, Rogers and a private pressed north, using the vantage afforded by the granite dome to enlarge their view. At the lake's far north end, where it narrows to a 500-foot strait, they discovered a thousand men encamped on both shores; the eastern complement were guarding the portage trail that met the La Chute below its falls, the quickest route into Lake Champlain.

The French had not cleared the dense oak and chestnut forest, so the two spies crawled between sentries on the western side to within 200 yards of the campfires, noting the absence of artillery. Working their way back, they traced a broad circle around the enemy and moved east, where they discovered the main French camp on a high rocky point above the little estuary where the La Chute falls into Lake Champlain. The small Ticonderoga peninsula overlooked only a narrow stretch of the lake but commanded the portage trail connecting the water route to Lake George. Again they infiltrated the sentries to within a thousand feet of the "Grand Encampment," finding a building and a "Number of Cannon Mounted." No question existed now of French intentions. Rogers estimated the camp's strength at about 3,000.

By nightfall the pair were tracking back along the west bank. As the sun rose, they spied a large canoe gliding south beyond the point where Rogers knew his men lay hidden. The canoe passed, and once reunited with the men, he recounted his adventures, then settled down to wait for darkness to cover their return. Soon enough a sentry was at his side with word that the canoe was back. Quickly sifting black powder from their horns into musket pans, the whole patrol sank into the shore undergrowth, each man propping both elbows on the ground, their musket barrels tracking the canoe.

Counting nine Indians and one French soldier, Rogers quickly ordered his men to pick individual targets. As the canoe drew within 100 yards' range, the rangers could clearly see the Indians' naked torsos flexing as they drove their paddles through the water. Then on Rogers's signal the rangers "gave them a salute," pouring in fusillade after fusillade, firing altogether "about Forty Guns," wrote Rogers. Then the New Hampshiremen launched their own canoe from its hiding place in the bushes, jumped in, and gave chase.

Six Indians lay dead or disabled in the bullet-riddled canoe, but the four remaining paddlers dug frantically into the water. Rogers's canoe gained on them, but the gunfire and cries had alerted the nearby encampment; three more canoes were suddenly racing to the site of the ambush. The rangers swung around and thrashed away on their own race for their lives; indifferent to their screaming arm muscles, they hammered along to Rogers's shouted cadence to outpace their pursuers. As they passed the narrows, the three canoes turned back.

When the rangers returned that evening, the camp lit up at the news of New England's first blow at the enemy since the battle of September 8. "A bold adventure It was," says Lieutenant Colonel Pomeroy's journal.[9]

Over the past several weeks, impatience at Johnson's reluctance to attack Fort Saint-Frédéric had been bubbling furiously behind the lines and at other British forts. William Shirley, who had succeeded to Braddock's command, pressed Johnson particularly hard. Johnson knew that, while his good fortune at Lake George had brought him close to the baronetcy he longed for, such excellent luck was unlikely to hold and further action could well jeopardize his standing. Besides, his many illnesses further bore on him; "I was seized with an

Inflamation in my head wch. gave me inexpressible Torment," he wrote to Shirley. "I have been bled, blistered & purged, wch. with want of Sleep & appetite confines me to the bed."[10] Shirley suggested that if Johnson's hip wound prevented him from taking the field, perhaps General Phineas Lyman could take over. Public opinion condemned Johnson even more heartily. A tagline from New Haven in *The New-York Mercury* of October 11 reported that "many of the good Women of this Colony are so enraged, that they declare if their Husbands come back without attacking the French in their Intrenchments, they shall not come near them; but that instead of receiving them with Joy, they will fling their P-s-pots at their Heads, as unworthy of the Name of New-England-Men."[11]

Meanwhile Johnson complained to Governor Stephen Hopkins of Rhode Island, "Our Men are quite homesick subdued & surfeited with the fatigues & hardships of a Military Life, no ways disposed to go forwards."[12] The weather grew yet colder, creating conditions nearly unbearable for a force that had little warm clothing. Rogers's report of a large French presence at Ticonderoga gave Johnson the out he needed. To attack a powerful entrenched enemy in the fall was not canny citizen warfare but was merely self-destructive.

Johnson dispatched his aide Peter Wraxall to Albany to quiet the recently knighted Sir Charles Hardy, governor of New York. A former naval officer, Hardy brooked no thought of retreat, dismissing Wraxall's summary of Rogers's intelligence on the grounds that such reports could "not be depended on" and insisted that Johnson send scouts out "again & again to be confirmed in the Truth of it."[13] The irritated Wraxall retorted that he "did not believe there was another Man in the Army woud go."

"Try if there is not," Hardy shot back contemptuously.

Wraxall's reliance on Rogers infuriated Hardy, who little understood the difficulties that constrained New England provincials in scouting the rugged no-man's-land. The vast majority of patrols not only failed to find the enemy but rarely even came near French positions; details led by Lieutenant Philip Lord, John Taplin, and Henry Babcock returned empty-handed after venturing no more than a dozen miles from camp. When Captain William Symmes's detachment, camped only three miles away, discovered a sentry shot and scalped with a hatchet left in his skull, he reported that he feared his men would "run off to night as they seem much frightened," and therefore he doubled the guards and urgently requested orders from Johnson. Fourteen men marched to Symmes's camp, whereupon Lieutenant Jelles Fonda, in command, ordered the shaken first party to proceed with its mission. The "distressed" men refused, whereupon Fonda ordered his men to confiscate their blankets and provisions. Still the demoralized outfit balked. "Cowards!" cried Fonda. "Come and I'll take your names down." To his surprise, Symmes's men surrounded him so thickly, preferring punishment to torture, that they had to return to the camp.

On October 1 a French deserter came into the provincial lines, having left Ticonderoga several days before Rogers's most recent reconnaissance. Confined by his various physical woes, Johnson left the task of interrogating him to a subordinate, then sent the man down to Albany on October 6 for additional questioning by Hardy. The deserter reported far fewer men and activity at Carillon than had Rogers. Where Rogers reported artillery at La Chute Falls, the deserter claimed there was none. By his account, Carillon presented far less a threat than Rogers had assessed.

This new information caused Goldsbrow Banyar, deputy clerk of the New York Supreme Court, to take a shot directly at Rogers, writing to Johnson, "I may be in Error but dont believe a single Syllable of Rogers's Information." It made more sense, he argued, to trust deserters, because "their Lives would have paid for any Misfortune the Consequence of their false Information."[14] And he may well have known about Rogers's counterfeiting troubles, which were no recommendation of the young captain's character or judgment.

By now Johnson was dancing fast. On October 6 the New Hampshiremen's period of enlistment had expired, and he had indeed let Colonel Blanchard and most of the contingent go; but he had retained Rogers, Captain Symmes, and some others, as he wrote to Governor Wentworth, because "they will be of a good deal of Service to us in the Scouting Way."

Wasting little time, he dispatched Rogers to Ticonderoga on October 7, this time at the head of a distinctly stronger party. Meanwhile he was working to protect his most valuable resource; "I have Understood some Insinuations have been made to his Disadvantage I believe him to be as brave & as honest a Man as any I have equal knowledge of," he wrote finally to Governor Hardy on October 13, "& both myself & all the Army are convinced that he has distinguished himself since he has been among us, superior to most, inferior to none of his Rank in these Troops."[15] To Spencer Phips, acting governor of Massachusetts, Johnson described Rogers as "a Gallant honest Man." In the meantime he lashed out against Shirley, whom he perceived as trying to undercut his authority, arguing in a long and rambling letter to the Lords of Trade that "from Govr. Shirley's late Behaviour and his Letters to me I am under no doubt that he is become my inveterate enemy and that the whole weight of his Power and abilities will be exerted to blast if he can my Character . . . Gross Falsehoods (such as he has already asserted in his letters to me,) artful misrepresentations, Deliberate malice, Resentment worked up by People in his confidence, whose Interest, nay whose very livelihood depends upon their inflaming him—these my Lords are circumstances which I own disturb me." (Years later Rogers would feel Johnson's considerable powers of antipathy.)

On the October 7 scout Rogers stayed behind with the boats and sent Israel Putnam and Samuel Hunt, both Connecticut provincial captains, to check on activity along the Carillon portage. Both confirmed Rogers's initial estimate of enemy strength.

Any knowledge that others questioned his accuracy and effectiveness seemed little to have concerned Rogers, whose continuing raids on several occasions flirted a little too closely with danger. On October 14 he and Putnam left three men hidden well behind in a thicket of dwarf willows while they adopted an Indian technique of night warfare, inching forward to within 300 yards of Fort Saint-Frédéric under uprooted bushes as camouflage, finally taking station behind a felled pine. The blue-eyed 37-year-old Putnam, who would rise to second-in-command of the Continental forces under Washington, followed Rogers's lead despite his 14 years' seniority.

First light revealed how far they had pushed their necks into a noose: large enemy parties were at work on all sides. Miraculously they avoided detection. At ten A.M. a big unarmed Frenchman strode right toward them. When he came within ten yards, Rogers vaulted over the log and pressed his fusee to the man's chest, offering him quarter if he came quietly. The man knocked Rogers's musket aside, pulled out a dirk, and lunged forward. Rogers grabbed his arm, and the two fell to the ground, the Frenchman bellowing for help. Putnam rushed out and knocked him on the head with his musket butt, then pulled frantically at Rogers's arm, for despite the general alarm that was bringing the enemy to them, Rogers had drawn his long knife; then, pausing to grab his enemy's greasy hair with one hand, he made a quick circular slash with the other. The scalp came off with a pop, leaving a bright flash of white skull. Carrying the bloody trophy in his hand, with a battle scream emerging on his lips, Rogers ran after Putnam toward the thicket, leaving the enemy camp now alive with self-confusing halloos and musket shots. The five men crashed desperately through the woods until Rogers slowed the party and moved it into single file; the last man covered their tracks, while the others strained to hear for sounds of pursuit.

The scalp created a sensation back at camp; indeed, word of this turnabout trophy rippled back to the settled lands, earning Rogers his first newspaper mention in *The Boston Gazette* of November 3: "Capt. Rogers . . . kill'd and scalp'd a Frenchman within 70 Rods [385 yards] of said Fort."[16] Up to that time the "hairdressers," as French Captain Duchat called them, had mostly been Indians. Breaking out of cover at the very lip of the enemy's stronghold in broad daylight and leaving so audacious a mark of disdain and deadliness dispelled their enemy's forest mystique. To coastal communities thirsty for any news of enemy blood being spilled, this tiny piece of savage craftsmanship was thrilling.

Later another French deserter, Captain Honoré Blanchard, reported under interrogation that Rogers's actions had changed French conduct. An advanced camp of 70 men had been moved down Lake George to an entrenchment on a sandy point, perhaps the beachfront of present-day Hague.[17] Canoes routinely patrolled the lake, paddling south to reconnoiter the British encampment.

Johnson ordered Rogers north with four bateaux to further assess enemy activity. To the gunwales and bow of each boat, the rangers had attached a wall-piece, an iron or brass swivel-mounted cannon capable of firing one- or two-pound balls or a charge of smaller shot at close range.

This venture would put the brash young ranger's leadership skills to a hard test and find them almost fully formed. He picked his team with care, tagging his brother Richard, Captain Putnam, Lieutenant

Noah Grant (great-grandfather of Ulysses S. Grant), and 15 others well known to him. As before, he intended to reach Friend's Point under cover of darkness and rest during the day. Winter had arrived— three inches of snow had covered the ground earlier that week. A cold northeast wind blew off the water, kicking up waves and shaking the trees. Rogers could take few chances with his tiny convoy. On a previous scout one bateau had become lost in the darkness and returned to camp. He assigned the men who were not rowing to the bow and stern, their sole job to keep eye contact with the boat in front and behind, all craft to keep close together. Should one capsize (and few frontiersmen could swim), the next in line could be there in seconds.

Before dawn they saw fires near Friend's Point and pulled ashore a mile and a half below their target; Rogers dispatched a high-caliber reconnaissance team of Captains Putnam, Fletcher, and Durkee to the north. That evening Fletcher returned, reporting that the enemy had only four small tents and "Sundry Small fires." Rogers sent him back to Johnson with six men to request reinforcements, also returning six "Invaleeds," perhaps fever cases or men who had been able to conceal injuries until the stresses of the expedition uncovered them.

"Un Easie" with Fletcher's report, Rogers rowed that evening with five men in a bateau to within 140 yards of the fires, finding a quarter-acre picketed fort enclosing several small log cabins, open to the water. The patrol rowed quietly back to camp, where they found that Putnam and Durkee still had not returned.

The next morning these two stumbled in exhausted; Durkee, wounded and limping, confirmed Rogers's observations. They had crawled on their hands and knees in upon the enemy campfires— which in British camps usually ringed the camp but which the French traditionally placed at its very center—suddenly discovering themselves in a hornet's nest. An aroused Canadian put a ball, still wrapped in the wadding, into Durkee's thigh at spread-arm's length.[18] Wadding usually comes free within 15 to 20 feet—the sheer point-blankness probably saved his life, though he was knocked backward. Adrenaline surging, the crackling night now ablaze with musket shots—Rogers's scalp had probably paid a heavy subscription—the pair dived into the forest, only to tumble into a wet clay pit that choked their muskets. Putnam raised his canteen to give Durkee a quick splash of rum but found that it had all dribbled out through shot holes.[19] Only darkness and plain harrowing endurance finally foiled their pursuers.

At dawn the pair began working their way back to Rogers and the boats, moving quickly now, aware that the French could easily rediscover their trail in deepening light. They arrived at ten A.M. on November 2. Shortly thereafter sentries spied two French soldiers watching them from a nearby hill; two large enemy canoes paddled past them, then hovered with unsettling oddness 200 yards apart in midlake.

Rogers smelled a trap. The behavior of the canoeists indicated that a land party was heading directly toward them, with an eye to squeezing the party in a vise. He quickly weighed his limited options: to abandon the boats, break his command into yet smaller groups, and melt into the forest would put them in the path of a column of unknown size; but to stay put and fight could only play directly into the enemy's hands, because the rangers could fold only after they had exhausted their ammunition. Crowding into the boats would only make them the target of every canoe afloat. Rejecting all the obvious options, Rogers instead ordered Putnam, the wounded Durkee, his brother Richard, and four others to stay with the camp and position themselves behind the pines crowding the shore. Then he, Ensign Johnson, and five men hopped into one bateau as he ordered Lieutenant Grant and the other five into the second.

They splashed out into Lake George, giving the pretense, according to Rogers's orders, of flailing in panic south down the lake. The French and Indians on the water rose to the bait, moving swiftly to cut their escape. But once they came within range, the rangers discharged a thunderous broadside from the wall-pieces, killing several men outright. The enemy canoes paddled furiously northward out of range before the rangers could reload. But in doing so, they drew close to Putnam's hidden detail, which according to a later newspaper description "gave them a smart Volly," killing yet more and riddling the canoes. Whooping with delight, the rangers rowed after the crippled craft, Rogers shouting for Putnam and the land party to get away in the third bateau. No sooner had they dragged the cumbersome boat to the water's edge and pulled away than the French ground force broke out of the woods and, reported Rogers, "made a brisk fire" on them. Later Putnam counted more than a dozen bullet holes in the blanket he wore around him.[20] Now all three boats chased the frantic enemy uplake, coming within 400 yards of the French outpost. A hundred or more troops massed on the shore, but carefully placed broadsides drove them headlong into the woods. Not daring to come closer inshore, Rogers let the battered canoes escape, then turned his bateau around and lay at rest in the middle of the lake. The much larger French force had wounded just one ranger. Halfway back the triumphant flotilla encountered their reinforcements.[21]

Not long after word of this daring victory made its way to Albany, Goldsbrow Banyar moderated his appraisal of Rogers, writing Johnson that "however exaggerated his acco[ts]. are thought here to be, every one says he is a bold useful man, and deserves well of the Publick."[22]

By November 22 the encroaching winter had extinguished all discussion of an attack on Fort Saint-Frédéric or Carillon. Poor morale, dwindling provisions, and a lack of bateaux served to abort the final effort—in the judgment of a general who had been reluctant to press on to the attack in the first place. Johnson discussed winter garrisoning with the officers of the New York, Connecticut, and Massachusetts contingents. Seven hundred and fifty men signed on for winter service at Forts William Henry and Edward, the ninety-five New Hampshiremen choosing Rogers as their leader. After the main force fell back, some thought better of a winter in the bleak garrison and deserted, leaving Rogers with a decimated force and only four Indians. If the enemy figured that the British would remain quiet, as tradition dictated during winter, they would soon learn otherwise.

Chapter 8

Honing Skills

These [the Indians' vaunted scalps] are their trophies, their obelisks, their arches of triumph; the monuments which attest to other tribes and consign to posterity the valor, the exploits of the warriors and the glory of the cabin.

BOUGAINVILLE'S JOURNAL, JULY 12, 1758[1]

Into the biting wind of a mid-January 1756 morning, a dark line of 17 hunched-over men swayed across the frozen surface of Lake Champlain. While a few articles of similar dress marked them as part of an outfit—some wore woolen hats, others fur, some surtouts of Bath Rug, others Indian blankets as capes—the overall impression suggested competent veterans steeled to subzero winter travel, each man having developed under necessity the combination of clothing that would keep his body warm yet give him full freedom of motion. Each man wore Indian-style moccasins that seemed oversize and swollen but were stuffed with scraps of heavy wool blanket liner, the soles and ankles reinforced with extra pieces of deerskin.

Strapped to their moccasins were rude iron skates, which had been fashioned by the garrison blacksmith out of quarter-inch-wide blades; they generally limited movement to skating head down and straight ahead. Grooved into a wooden, shoe-sized platform and pinned from the sides like a musket barrel, the blade reached only three-eighths of an inch deep, so the slightest pressure brought contact with the ice and stability.[2] The men took short steps, half-walking and half-running across the frozen lake. Some dragged a light hand sled or Indian toboggan, which they called "slays," loaded with packs, snowshoes, and food, each stout enough to transport firewood from the surrounding forest or carry a casualty. Three men shared the responsibility for one slay.[3] All had wrapped their muskets in greased deer- or moose-leather covers, some carrying them in their hands, others slinging them over their backs.

Rogers had taken advantage of certain rare periods of cold air— cold ice interface in upcolony New York when the ice of Lakes George and Champlain turns slick and smooth as a mirror. Just after first freezing—usually in mid-January—a quick thaw melts the surface, only to be refrozen by a north wind, which produces a singular uniformity. As in a slab of black Carrara marble, white veins weave across the deep black ice, which becomes particularly hospitable to skate blade and sleigh runner, remaining so until the next snowfall obscures the surface.

Rogers set a fast pace, leaving his men to scramble after his large form, adjusting their muskets and powderhorns, some using wooden staffs for balance, their breaths steaming into dry air. The speed of their start warmed them soon enough, loosening their strides, even though the cold seared their exposed cheeks and foreheads. Rogers often started a scout this way. Should a ranger be carrying a lingering cold or a touch of lameness or some other weakness disregarded or hidden in his eagerness to join the scout, a fast and early push would bring it to light. Time and again Rogers shed as many as half his contingent in the earliest days. The exhaustions ahead would make matters only worse, risking the less than totally fit men's lives and their comrades' too; by being too tough to be honest or sensible, a single man could jeopardize the mission and the security of the frontier.

The exertion of traveling under the bitter cold of an Adirondack winter made Rogers even more careful as to which men he chose. Winter proved so difficult in general that during the worst months the British and French observed an unspoken truce, hunkering down into stale and dirty but warm camp life inside their cramped but unthreatening garrisons, at least avoiding the frostbite and gangrene that could quickly claim fingers and toes when not life itself. The winter woods could exact dire trouble on ill-equipped men in short order. Later in the war, when Colonel William Haviland, then commanding Fort Ticonderoga, neglected to order a resupply unit of 100 men to change from regulation leather shoes into lined moccasins, a simple midwinter excursion of a mere dozen miles left the surgeon lopping off more than 100 frozen toes. Rogers's scouts would be woods-bound for many days, enduring many fireless nights for fear of alerting the enemy.

But Rogers's cantankerous Scots-Irish temperament relished the chance of getting around the rules. His own harsh knowledge of the cold and dark had made him anything but cavalier about risks. He inspected each soldier's equipment, suggesting such deceptively minor variants as donning an extra flannel waistcoat, the practice known today as layering, advice garnered not from a manual or book but from experience. He took special pains to inspect footwear, insisting that seams be double-sewed and that each man bring a sewing kit containing extra patches and the strings of leather known as whangs.

It took two nights to reach the northern end of Lake George. As darkness set in just shy of five P.M., Rogers had pulled his party off the ice two hours earlier so they could camp by daylight and set sentries. He led them up a nearby incline, searching for a site simultaneously high enough to escape the destructively cool and damp air that pools in ravines, yet low enough to escape most of the winds that beset higher, exposed elevations. Until they were nearing enemy country, they built and crowded around fires dug deep into the snow, sitting on bearskins thrown over piles of spruce boughs, pushing close to one another and dangling their feet over the flames, within a circuit of small lean-tos erected to break the wind.

Heating up pots of chocolate and water, they added sugar and forced down their barely appetizing rations. Severe cold and high exertion can often rob the body of its desire to eat, and Rogers had to prod his men to consume their salt pork and peas. Cold also insidiously wicks sweat from skin and sucks moisture from the mouth and nose—even the most experienced can become dehydrated without realizing it, which in turn leads precipitously to hypothermia, uncontrollable shivering, and often enough death.

Like all experienced small-group leaders, Rogers watched his men with an eagle eye: how much they ate and talked, their movements and body language. Most of all he watched their eyes for telltale signs of fear. Bitter cold—and in upstate New York of the mid-eighteenth century, temperatures then dropped to as low as 40 degrees below zero with wind chill—can chew around the edges of consciousness, hurting like an open wound without leaving a single mark on the body. Coping with really cold weather is often as much a mental as a physical task. The mind imagines terrible outcomes, becomes fixated on small things, obsesses about misplacing an article of clothing or equipment, and hears strangely dreadful things on the wind. Fear manifests itself physically first by constricting the blood vessels, then shuts down blood supply to the extremities in a bid to protect the body's core. Hands left out of gloves or mittens even for a few minutes take a long time to regain feeling. Fingertips, the nose, and even the tip of the penis grow numb and frostnipped.

Rogers probably insisted that his men use the Indian technique of rubbing bear grease onto their skin and required that they strip out of layers of clothes wet from sweat. He trained them to watch out for one another, particularly for disorientation or the loss of coordination and focus—symptoms of what was not yet known as hypothermia. That night their shivering shook the men awake again and again.

Close to the enemy on the third night, at the abandoned French and Indian camp at La Chute Falls, they slept on the snow without daring to light a fire, then rested for several hours before eagerly leaving their makeshift beds and warming up by snowshoeing well wide of Ticonderoga; they arrived about four P.M. on the banks of Lake Champlain, where they strapped on skates, then pushed up to a small point of land two miles south, and within eyeshot, of the French fort at Crown Point. Here they settled in to ambush traffic between the forts. They did not have to wait long.

At about dawn a farmer and a butcher setting out by horse-drawn sleigh from Fort Saint-Frédéric for Carillon met the nightmarish vision of gaunt, bearded men spilling out in front of them from the frigid woods. Grinding to a halt, the pair stammered their surrender, while rangers grabbed the reins and shoved them onto the ice.

As the captors exulted over the sleighload of fresh beef, they heard shots. The sentries on Crown Point's ramparts, helplessly watching the ambush unfold, became enraged by the arrogance of the strike and loudly awoke the garrison. Dark specks quickly appeared on the distant shore.[4]

For the French, long accustomed to mastery of the woods in contrast to the hapless English, the presence of a confident enemy so close to their walls must have come as a mightily unwelcome surprise. "The English colonies have ten times more people than ours," wrote a young French captain stationed at Carillon, "but these wretches have not the least knowledge of war."[5] That would soon change, and Rogers would be at the heart of it.

For now, his party had perhaps a thirty-minute lead. Grabbing one of the two stunned prisoners by the coat, he swung him around and under his compelling stare told him that he would die should he slow the group down. It is unclear whether the rangers attached extra skates to the prisoners' feet or roped them up and literally dragged them along, relying on raw terror. Whatever their technique, it worked.

Rogers sent most of his men and the prisoners south immediately, while he and several of his best skaters fell to their knees and, energized by the clamor from Carillon, hacked at the ice with their tomahawks, creating a storm of splinters. He may have slashed the horse's jugular, spilling the animal's hot life force onto the ice to weaken the frozen surface. In minutes they broke through the ice, and the sleigh slid noisily under the dark water, carrying with it a week's worth of winter well-being for Carillon.

Rogers and the rear guard stuck their tomahawks into their belts and took a deep breath. The enemy had gained considerable ground. They were now in a race for their lives against fresh skaters, still needing to get around Carillon before they could reach safety.

Exhilarated nevertheless by success, the rear guard closed the distance between them and their comrades, their thighs screaming in protest. Rogers knew where to jump into the woods, calculating that his pursuers would have neither the equipment nor the disposition to follow, once the rangers and their prisoners had melted into the snowy evergreens.[6]

At six-thirty in the next morning's predawn darkness, gunfire aroused the garrison at Fort William Henry. Men quickly lined the palisades, shaken into alertness, their muskets drawn and cocked. "Don't shoot!" cried familiar voices, and suddenly fear was lost in cheering as the exhausted raiding party trudged in with their captives.

Nine days later Rogers headed out again under orders from the acting commander, Lieutenant Colonel Beamsley Glazier of New York, to reconnoiter Fort Saint-Frédéric and upon meeting the enemy to "take them Prisoners or Kill them or distress them any other ways or Means your Prudence shall direct you." He was also instructed to "take Good Care of your men and not Expose them too much" and return immediately "if it should Snow." Rogers may well have found the last instruction rather amusing.

Since the last scout, the ice had thawed in places, forcing the party to track along the lake's western shore; but they still covered 18 miles the first day. Two men unable to keep up were sent back to the fort that evening. The rest arrived at Crown Point on February 2 and climbed either Bulwagga Mountain or Coots Hill, whence Rogers and others sketched a crude map of the defenses. That evening they sneaked down to take up ambush positions on the village road half a mile south of the fort, where at nine o'clock in the morning they jumped an unsuspecting soldier. Two men who had been following just behind the soldier took off flat out for the fort. Several rangers gave chase, but the Frenchmen flew over the wooden drawbridge spanning the 12-foot-deep dry moat and through the hastily opened portcullis. Their pursuers stopped within musket shot of the walls. Drums beat the call to arms, and the French peered through loopholes in the limestone out into the winter morning, uncertain whether the few rangers they could see defying them were just trying to lure them out.

Back in the village, deserted perhaps because of the earlier raid, the rangers rounded up fifty horses, cattle, and hogs, cut their throats, then set fire to houses and barns filled with "an abundance of wheat & other Graiens."[7] By the time they left at eleven A.M., flames engulfed most of the town. Farther away from resupply than the British colonists, the French would feel the want of the lost food all winter. A French Canadian deserter later reported that even during the summer, scurvy, a disease caused by lack of vitamin C and fresh food, took two or three lives every day at Carillon and Fort Saint-Frédéric, so the burden in midwinter must have been grievously worse.

On the next morning's return march, a man fell badly sick. Rather than slow the main force to the pace set by those carrying the invalid, Rogers sent the prisoner and all but a few men ahead;

the small contingent and the sick man made it back to Fort William Henry the afternoon following. Such an action sent the clear message that he would risk his life for any man in trouble and would not leave anyone behind when remotely possible. Correspondingly, he expected everyone in his outfit to go beyond what they believed themselves capable of. In this reciprocity, Rogers forged the ethics of the small-team commando, taking the hardest jobs himself and pledging that he would bring to bear all his powers, strength, and cunning to get the outfit back safely. Now, under the shadow of the wintry Adirondack woods, that pledge had been solemnly exemplified.

Going on scout might carry many risks, but life at camp offered its own. At William Henry "a bad cold & cough" affected everyone in mid-October, wrote Thomas Williams, an army surgeon, to his wife at Deerfield, Massachusetts. During that summer he had described how a shortage of kettles in which to boil meat had caused the men "to drop down one after another with Fevers & Fluxes, & Some Dysentaries." He himself suffered from fever and a constant "laxness of the bowels," probably caused by bacteria in the salted ox beef that served as the staple of their winter diet.[8] In the midwinter Drs. Bliss and Gott attended the sick, mostly by bleeding, applying poultices, and administering emetics—treatment often more likely to kill than cure. A contemporary medical treatise recommended bleeding for inflammatory fevers, topical inflammations, asthma, and coughs and after "falls, blows, bruises, of any violent hurt received either externally or internally"; in other words, for just about any condition.[9] Often it involved opening a vein with a scalpel, until the patient passed out. In early October a surgeon treated a painful inflammation of General Johnson's head by bleeding, blistering, and purging, which he later wrote "some what abated" his pain.

Journal writers record the tide of sickness, fever, and death with a matter-of-factness that is almost chilling to modern eyes. By the age of twenty everyone had witnessed dozens of deaths, very often of siblings, perhaps of one's mother in childbirth, and definitely of neighbors and friends to accidents and disease. Rogers suffered from recurring fevers, which suggests he had a serious affliction such as malaria. John Stark had rheumatoid arthritis. Smallpox, malaria, jaundice, and many other infections or systemic diseases that are

now considered unusual and grave were then considered "an unavoidable part of everyday troubles of life," as one mid-twentieth-century
medical writer has noted.[10] Far from being healthy and looking to
avoid getting sick, men carried with them simmering impairments,
perhaps malaria, or a lastingly septic wound, or the cold-induced
inflammations known as chilblains, which grew infected, or persistent intestinal distress. The discovery of germ theory pinpointing
the cause of many diseases to specific microbes still lay decades in
the future; troops stationed in remote frontier garrisons rarely used
soap and barely practiced even rudimentary prophylactic sanitary
measures.

For men under the stress of garrison life, Indian menace, cold
weather, and bad nutrition, the question became: would one of their
underlying conditions intensify? If one did, emerging perhaps as a
boiling fever, it would either blossom out of control and kill its host,
or subside after days of intense discomfort and perhaps leave the suf-
ferer impaired for life.

In January, when the sun disappeared before five P.M., camp life
offered no form of entertainment more complex than throwing dice,
very little reading material, no women, and long stretches of mind-
numbing monotony. Picking fleas and lice from bedding, hair, and
clothing became a matter of course; inside the barracks the men
would heat lice over candle flames until they cracked. The officers
and men, bunked apart from each other, whiled away hours before
fires in the weak light of tallow candles, sleeping and oversleeping,
plotting new raids, playing whist and loo, and dicing. Warmed by
rum, they would sometimes break into boisterous renditions of such
camp favorites as "Rule, Britannia" and "Over the Hills and Far
Away."[11] Perhaps they hammered out that marchers' staple "The
British Grenadiers," which robustly begins:

> Some talk of *Alexander*, and some of *Hercules*
> Of *Hector* and *Lysander*, and such great names as these:
> But of all the world's great heroes, there's none that can compare,
> With a tow, row, row, row, row, row, to the British Grenadiers.

And they would tell stories, each man pulling out a few chestnuts
to polish over and over again. In the dim light of the wooden block-

house Rogers probably leaned back on his crude stool and coaxed Israel Putnam to retell the story of the wolf. Old Put would agree with formal reluctance but would be unable to keep the gleam out of his eye. A renowned she-wolf had devastated farms in northeastern Connecticut for years, always avoiding retribution, although men killed many of her pups. They knew she still lived because of the irregular print that a trap had left on her. In the spring of 1743, when Putnam was 25, the same age as Rogers now, she killed 70 of his sheep and goats in one night at his farm in Pomfret. Put and his neighbors tracked her paw prints through the snow to a narrow cave into which their dogs plunged, only to emerge whimpering, scratched, and bleeding. Put stripped off coat, waistcoat, shoes, and stockings, tied a rope to one of his legs, lit a birchbark torch, and wriggled through the hole. Descending into the lair, he soon came eye to eye with its snarling occupant. His own howl of surprise spurred his comrades to pull him out with such force that he nearly lost his shirt and was badly lacerated. But down he went again, this time with a musket charged with buckshot. Those above heard a blast and a shriek and again drew him out. For the third time Put went down, this time pulling the dead beast out by the ears.[12]

Rogers launched into stories of his own, the recent raids furnishing topics for intense dissection and discussion. The heroes of these tales, standing up to great odds and surviving, served as rich tonic to the awed bystanders, building confidence against a world riven by seemingly random deadly power.

Accidents plagued the camp. Seth Pomeroy's journal records one particularly bad day, a Wednesday in early October, when a carelessly discharged musket mortally wounded a man in an adjacent tent. Later that day a sudden, violent thunderstorm set several soldiers adrift in their bateau, and only luck saved them from drowning. The storm also brought down two trees, one of which crushed a shelter with three men in it. All escaped with their lives, although they were injured; "wonderfull Interposions of Divine Providances are Dayly Pasing before my Eys in ye Deliverance of many from Sudden Death by accidents Surely we Carry our lives in our hands."[13]

On February 28, 1756, Rogers and his men, prepared for a fifteen-day scout, double-sewing their seams, smearing their bodies with bear grease, and perhaps most importantly sobering up. Captain

Jeduthan Baldwin, a recent arrival at Fort Edward who had served on the late February raid against Crown Point, kept a careful journal of his experiences. The 24-year-old Brookfield, Massachusetts, housewright, a man of some means, would maintain his record into the American Revolution, in which he served as a colonel of engineers. As the men worked their way northward again along the now-familiar western shore, Baldwin seemed enthralled by the north woods, jotting down animated observations of no newness to Rogers and his already-hardened veterans: a wolf chasing a deer into the water; how the party slept "not in a fither-bed but on hem lock boughs." They passed Captain Putnam's *enterueil*, a French term designating something that lies between land and air, which had come to mean an elevated blind used in hunting or to spy on enemy movement; most probably the term was new to the Bay Colony man, although it was not to Rogers, who had spent time trading with French hunters and trappers. The curious use of a French term—elevated blinds had surely served the earliest New England hunters—suggests the fluidity of vocabulary and technology among those who lived in the woods world.

The rangers skirted Fort Saint-Frédéric and slipped north of the fort at two A.M. on March 7, intending to cross the lake and press on in search of a reported village. While working his way down the bank to check on the thickness of the ice, Rogers slipped and fell 26 feet to smash through into the freezing water, from which, testified Baldwin, he extricated himself "with much Difficulty." Well aware that death often followed such immersion, Rogers scrambled to his clothes and warmed up as best he could without fire, which even under such circumstances was too dangerous to light so near the enemy.

The ice proved too thin to support any further northward probe, so the rangers slipped back to another village of the Crown Point complex, 12 miles to the south, and waited a day for any French soldiers who might show up. None did. At nine P.M. on March 8 they burned two houses and nine barns filled with wheat, oats, and peas. One of their company, an Indian, had fallen asleep in the second barn they torched and suffered burns so bad as to immobilize him. They carried him on a makeshift litter or by sled the next day, traveling 18 miles and at one point taking their delirious comrade across a river.

Again Rogers split the group, sending Baldwin and most of the men ahead.

As they closed with the French strongpoint at Carillon, Baldwin's force discovered ominous carvings on tree trunks, saying that any rangers taken alive would be burned. They had outraged the forest, and its most primal elements would consume them. But the sign continued more deeply and disturbingly: If the Englishmen captured any French or Indians, they should burn them too. Those who ventured into the forest must be able to endure its fates. The sign set a stern challenge: We are ready for the ways of the darkness. Were they?

Leaving his tiny band, Rogers crept beneath the walls of Carillon and eyed the sentries on their rounds. Thence he returned to his men and arrived in Fort William Henry two days after Baldwin's group; the Indian had succumbed to his injuries. Rogers's commitment to his dying comrade must have registered deeply with the troops. No provincial captain of the period, faced with a grievously injured native guide, would have been criticized for leaving him behind or for delivering a coup de grâce. But Rogers intuitively grasped that the more supreme the demands an organization exacts from its members, the more demandingly deep its obligations run toward them—and from each individual member to all others.

On March 15, 1756, the day after returning to Fort William Henry after his 120-mile midwinter scout, Rogers received a note from William Alexander, secretary to Governor William Shirley, the acting commander of British forces in North America, requiring him to visit headquarters in Boston. Thoroughly exhausted by a two-week scout of adrenaline-filled extremity across more than 100 miles of winter forest, he left for Boston on March 17.

As he negotiated New England's appalling roads, the drained captain pondered the meeting before him. A year ago he had taken two dozen fresh recruits, paid $30 apiece by the Bay Colony's coffers, to swell Lieutenant Colonel John Winslow's battalion north at New Hampshire's call. Shirley had been furious, calling for Rogers's arrest and complaining bitterly to Governor Wentworth. Rogers wondered if that incident would dominate Shirley's memory.

But he had reason to believe that the meeting would go well. Although he had led the merest handful of scouts, his daring and the successes it had brought his fledgling command had won much public attention. *The Boston Gazette* of March 1 reported, "We learn, that a Number of Officers at Albany, made a Collection and presented Capt. Rogers with a handsome Suit of Cloaths; and about 161 shillings New-York Currency to be laid out in Refreshments, for Him and His Men." On returning from his most recent scout he had discovered that the New York General Assembly had gifted him 125 pieces of eight "for my good Services done nigh and about Crown-Point against the French and Indians." Before he left for Boston, he dashed off a note of thanks, which was printed in *The Connecticut Gazette*. From then on journalists in all the colonial papers kept close track of his doings. He had become North America's first celebrity.

Chapter 9

An Independent Company
of Rangers

The brave Rogers is acquiring Glory to him-self in the Field, and in some Degree recovering the sunken Reputation of his Country.

THE BOSTON GAZETTE, FEBRUARY 14, 1757[1]

On Tuesday, March 23, 1756, Rogers strode over the cobblestones of Marlborough Street in Boston to his appointment. The following week *The Boston Evening-Post* would herald the arrival of the man "who has made himself famous in these Parts of America, by his Courage and Activity with his Scouting-Parties near Crown-Point."[2] He probably wore the fine suit given him by the New Yorkers. England's formal declaration of war upon France was still a month away, but the town bubbled with war talk. Early French victories in the so-far-undeclared war had badly frightened New Englanders, who were historically vulnerable to frontier assault. Braddock's disaster underlined how precarious was the British settlements' hold even on the continental edge. The emboldened Indian allies of the French were mounting increasingly audacious and brutal raids into Pennsylvania, Virginia, and Maryland, and the frontier was recoiling.

A real fear was growing that, as historian Laurence Gipson would later put it, the British colonies would become the Norway of America, an industrious country to be sure but limited to an existence clinging on the very margins of the western continent. Although the populations of the English colonies heavily outnumbered those of the French, victory on the field of battle was no certain thing. The depth of animosity and dread entertained by the British colonists toward their northern—and now western—rivals revealed itself on the same front page of the paper announcing Rogers's visit: "They ought to be considered Enemies to [the] Human Race, and to be extirpated from the Face of the Earth, or at least to be humbled as to be obliged to live peaceably with their neighbouring Powers." Urged an anonymous editorial writer, "Let us not, then, suffer a Ship to rest in our Harbour, nor a Gun to lie in our Arsenals, till the French are entirely driven out of North America."[3]

The town of some 20,000 inhabitants had built its quick and substantial prosperity on the shipping business, which inspired the Anglo-Irish statesman Edmund Burke to call New Englanders the Dutch of America, because they acted as carriers for all the British colonies on the continent as well as in the West Indies and indeed for some parts of Europe. If New England resembled the Netherlands, then Boston was Amsterdam, Rotterdam, and The Hague combined. Spread haphazardly over a mile and a half by two miles of hilly coastal peninsula, Boston was embodied by the Long Wharf, its north side choked with warehouses, which stretched nearly 2,000 feet into Boston Harbor to service thousands of vessels annually. Late in the decade before, 540 seagoing craft cleared the port in a single year, carrying the plain, bulky products of the stony hills and gray seas (fish, beef, pork, lumber, and fish oil) while 430 entered, those from the West Indies bearing more nearly tropical goods (rice, pitch, spices, logwood, rum, molasses, and sugar).[4] New Englanders refined the last two commodities into vast amounts of cheap rum, which did something to meet the insatiable Yankee appetite but above all lubricated the Indian trade and the slave commerce with Africa.

And every year an even larger fleet of coastal and fishing boats passed through the harbor; Rogers himself probably arrived by small boat from New York, then walked the busy wharf to State Street, perhaps stopping at the Bunch-of-Grapes Tavern, which served reputedly the finest punch in Boston.[5]

Besides the basics—70 warehouses, 1,800 houses, ten Congregationalist meetinghouses, three Anglican churches, and a single meetinghouse each for the Huguenots, Quakers, and Presbyterians stood on these three squares miles of city—the city boasted at least four schoolhouses, a workhouse, an almshouse, and a granary.[6] While later Boston would confuse visitors with its tangle of small streets, dead ends, and byways, the Boston of the early to mid-eighteenth century stood open and spacious.

An index of the city's rapidly mounting prosperity was Rogers's destination, the Province House, which stood on a lot 300 feet deep.[7] First among the many roomy, square mansions raised upon the riches won from the sea, it had been built in 1679, only fifty years after the city was first settled. A handsome, high-shouldered, three-story brick edifice laid in English bond, it commanded the corner of Washington and Milk Streets, its roof highlighted by dormered attic windows and an immense octagonal cupola. Atop it all swung a hammered copper weathervane bearing the symbol of the colony, an Indian with a glass eye fitting an arrow into his bow. Across the street towered the pointed steeple of Old South Church, and beyond that lay a series of open gardens. In 1719 the Province House had become the seat of the royal governors, who converted it into their own little piece of London.[8] Its present occupant, the 61-year-old William Shirley, had been governor of the Bay Colony since 1741; recently, on Braddock's death, he had been elevated to the temporary command of British forces in North America.

On Monday, March 29, Rogers passed between the tall oak trees that fronted this assertion of imperial power and climbed the nearly twenty massive red freestone steps leading to a portico supported by wooden pillars, well aware that he was about to meet the most powerful person in the colonies. He still probably felt the tingling numbness of frostnip in some of his toes.

He was shown, probably with a ceremony that grated upon his Scots-Irish spirit, into the grand sitting room to the right of the entrance, which was as foreign to him now as an Indian wigwam had once been. His appraising eye took in the ornate walnut carvings on the heavy furniture, the richly embroidered wall hangings, and the craftsmanlike wainscoting. Likely he had never seen a portrait before, nor trodden on rich carpets dense with design, nor seen the glow of dozens of candles massed in a candelabrum. A decade later John Adams would positively gush over the opulence of Nicholas Boylston's town house: "The Turkey carpets, the painted hangings, the marble tables, the rich beds with crimson damask curtains, and counterpanes, the beautiful chimney clock, the spacious garden, are the most magnificent of anything I have ever seen."[9] Rogers was not so much awed and deferential as fascinated, as he would have been in the longhouse of a sachem or the wigwam of a werowance.

Shirley's full face was divided by a prominent nose, jutting out between two kindly eyes. His warm handshake let Rogers know that he had moved beyond their brief past history. The two men took to each other immediately. Perhaps the young man standing before him, afire with possibility and ambition, reminded the weary governor of another promising young man: the French and Indians had killed William, Shirley's eldest son, who had had the misfortune of being General Braddock's secretary on the ill-fated march to the Monongahela. Perhaps they sipped brandy from German leaded glassware and climbed up to the cupola in the cold March air to take in its superb views of Boston Harbor, the scene of Shirley's glorious return to the Long Wharf eleven years before aboard the frigate *Massachusetts* after his improbable sacking of Louisbourg, France's premier North American fortress, in King George's War. The Troop of Horse, Troop of Guards, militia regiments, and local dignitaries had thronged to do the victor honor as the ships in the harbor thundered salutes and church bells clamored.

Rogers's brief description of their meeting says that he "met with a very friendly reception."[10] Much of the conversation centered upon conditions at Fort Saint-Frédéric and Carillon, on techniques of ambush and scouting, on interrogating prisoners, and how to initiate and motivate tough but uneasy greenhorns who had no love of fancy-dressed officers from overseas or often-savage forms of military discipline. Their conversation underlined to Shirley that Rogers was no mere brash bush-fighter but a leader capable of creating an elite to match the new demands of warfare—a ranger corps that had the capacity to gather critical intelligence and to stress the enemy by destroying his food supply and keeping him on constant fearful alert. Rogers's already-vast trove of woods knowledge and fighting skills was beginning to coalesce into a strategic vision of a mode of warmaking that well fit the peculiar geography of the Northeast and that countered the skills of the enemy, honed over centuries in the wild forests of North America.

Shirley, a pioneer New World imperial administrator who was forever angling for better ways of doing things, saw in Rogers the raw potential to put to work the as-yet-inchoate strengths of the New

England frontier and to forge a long-range force that could counter the acknowledged present superiority of the French and Indians in woodland combat. He "soon intimated his design of giving me the command of an independent company of rangers," Rogers recalled.

Such formation of an irregular military unit was not without precedent. A week earlier Shirley had authorized Lieutenant Colonel John Bradstreet to engage 2,000 bateau men and see to outfitting and provisioning the beleaguered British fort at Oswego, which had limped through a difficult winter. Bradstreet's command would serve Oswego well, even repulsing a sustained enemy ambush on the Oswego River, but would be disbanded once it had fulfilled its objective.[11]

The "independent company of rangers" was born into a curiously gray world. They were not provincial soldiers, because the Crown paid them and they served under the rules and regulations of the British army; but neither were they regulars. While ranger officers drew pay approximately equal to that of their regular counterparts, privates drew twice as much pay as provincial soldiers, who themselves earned more than regular privates. Most important, the company served at the pleasure of the commander-in-chief, who could dissolve it at will. Could Rogers create and define an organization that would step beyond the local and tactically immediate needs of a single campaign? Could this organization survive when the supreme command changed hands? It was a very real concern, because Shirley's successor, a short Scot named John Campbell, Earl of Loudoun, had been named in January and would arrive in the New World by summer. What might become of the rangers then would lie entirely in what Rogers had done with them.

Such questions remained far from his mind as he bounded down the Province House steps to set off in search of his brother Richard, who had arrived the week before with dispatches from Fort William Henry. The next day Rogers received his orders and the disposition of the new company, which was to consist of sixty privates, three sergeants, an ensign, and a lieutenant, each of whom was to receive ten Spanish dollars for outfitting themselves with arms, clothes, and blankets. Rogers was "to inlist none but such as were used to travelling and hunting, and in whose courage and fidelity I could confide," and he was to use this command "to distress the French and their allies, by sacking, burning, and destroying their houses, barns, barracks, canoes, battoes, & c. and by killing their cattle of every kind; and at all times to endeavour to way-lay, attack and destroy their convoys of provisions by land and water, in any part of the country."[12]

The brothers spent more than a week in Portsmouth, New Hampshire, which had rarely welcomed such a celebrated visitor. Many a cheer and glass of flip—a rum and butter concoction—was raised to the ranger captain at Stoodley's Tavern, the town's favorite watering hole. On April 9 St. John's Lodge No. 1 awarded him the degrees of Entered Apprentice and Fellow Craft. His fellow Masons included not only the governor, the king's attorneys Wyseman Clagett and Samuel Livermore, and eminent merchants and ship's captains, but also the Anglican rector Arthur Browne, later to become his father-in-law.

A few days later Rogers signed John Stark on, subordinate only to his brother Richard. Recruiting is surprisingly easy in places of blood and brawling, so Robert and Richard traveled to Amoskeag Falls to trawl the spring fish run. There the promise of three shillings a day for man-hunting under their leadership, plus the generous outfitting allowance, gathered 37 men. Sixty percent of the enlisted force that had been authorized was put onto the rolls at a single encounter.

But the enemy had not sat idle in the dour woods around Forts William Henry and Edward in Rogers's absence. A little after four o'clock in the morning of the very same day that Rogers signed John Stark, the sentries at William Henry heard a series of shots downlake, where a scouting party of four ranger sergeants and two privates had paddled the day before. Two loaded bateaux of soldiers dispatched at first light found grisly evidence on an island in the narrows: three men had been shot, scalped, and cut up, wrote Colonel Baldwin, "in the most awfull maner." *The Boston Gazette* spared no detail, reporting that the rescue party discovered one body "which the inhuman Savages cut his Breast quite a-cross, turn'd it under his Chin, and left his Inwards expos'd to wild Beasts."[13] Presumably the other three had been taken prisoner. That night the fort doubled its guards.

Rogers returned to Fort William Henry via Fort No. 4 on the Connecticut River and then Crown Point, where he and a small raiding force slaughtered twenty-eight of the enemy's cattle, then dispersed in the face of the enemy furiously pulling enemy bateaux. Throughout May and June large war parties, one consisting of 415 French Canadians, regulars, and Indians, moved toward Fort Williams and even menaced Albany.

By the time Rogers reached William Henry, news had spread that the king had replaced Shirley with Lord Loudoun. But even as a lame duck, Shirley continued to plan for the summer campaign on Lake Champlain and maintained a keen interest in the rangers: in late June, wrote Rogers, he "augmented my company to seventy men, and sent me six light whaleboats from Albany, with orders to proceed immediately to Lake Champlain, to cut off, if possible, the provisions and flying parties of the enemy."[14]

Under the worst of a pounding rainstorm on July 1, Rogers and his fifty rangers hunkered down on the eastern shore of Lake George beneath quickly-thrown-up spruce-bough shelters. Some crouched under the overturned hulls of Shirley's whaleboats—such a downpour would seriously complicate their task of wrestling these craft and their supplies over the all-too-close mountain country.

The men gave up trying to stay dry, instead turning all attention to keeping their muskets as functional as possible, wrapping them in leather sleeves. Most had stoppered the muzzles with tompions (another French term) to exclude dirt and water. Some muskets bore small metal dams to deflect raindrops from hitting the barrel and rolling down into the flashpan. But even so the men spent much of their time attempting to keep their muskets—and their powder—dry.

At least the rainstorm briefly washed the hosts of biting insects out of the air, and a few men fell asleep. Blackflies have a fondness for the soft skin around the eyes and left evidence of their work in grotesquely swollen faces. Wet mud soothed the bites, but the afflicted rangers appeared as though they had rolled in a swamp.

Rogers was forever moving around, rarely seeming to sleep, checking out the men's health, bucking up spirits, cracking raw jokes in an undertone appropriate to enemy territory, and preternaturally picking up when a man was ailing or doubting almost before the man himself. The harder the conditions, the more energetic he became.

Underneath the overturned cedar boats lay barrels of powder, some food, and a few curiously shaped balls trailing fuses, an
early form of hand grenade. At least one of the boats mounted swivel
guns.

His plan was either insane or brilliant. " 'Tis said," *The Boston
Weekly News-Letter* later reported, in an age in which months passed
between the order and the execution, that "Rogers designs to strike a
Blow in the Heart of Canada, or burn the French Brig on Lake-
Champlain."[15] Let him but sink the craft that he had watched off
Crown Point, and he could temporarily cripple resupply. But doing so
would involve somehow bringing his boats over to Lake Champlain—
no easy feat when Carillon controlled the Ticonderoga peninsula, the
chokepoint of the natural portage from Lake George.

Rogers knew an old Indian trace that climbed steeply from the
Lake George water's edge. A mile or so southeast of Sabbath Day
Point, it cut across the northern shoulder of Sugarloaf Mountain, paralleling a deep stream-cut ravine. The trace would need widening to
accommodate the whaleboats, so his men had spent the day before
clearing brush and rolling logs aside. The six-and-a-half-mile path to
Wood Creek flattened out for a mile or two, then dropped a steep
1,000 feet to the wet bottomlands, which afforded access to Lake
Champlain.[16] It was possible, yes, but certainly hard. The rainstorm
would make footing uncertain and dangerous.

Rogers at least had whaleboats, a good compromise between
birchbark canoes and clumsy bateaux. Whaleboats were superlight
but easily damaged and incapable of mounting serious firepower.
Their designs had been refined by generations of Nantucket carpenters to accentuate maneuverability, the better for whalers to hunt
down and kill their elusive prey. The symmetrically pointed bows and
sterns of these 30-foot-or-longer vessels enabled their oarsmen to re-
verse direction at a moment's notice, while the little more than five-
foot beam ensured that the hull cut the water like a shark.

It took the rangers four days to clear the boat path, first carrying
their packs and then returning for the largest task. Probably three
men shouldered a whaler on each side, plus two men to watch and
guide the bow and stern. Those left over acted as guards. Again
Rogers flew up and down the line, warning about upcoming logs and
lending a heave when necessary. It was punishing work to get up the

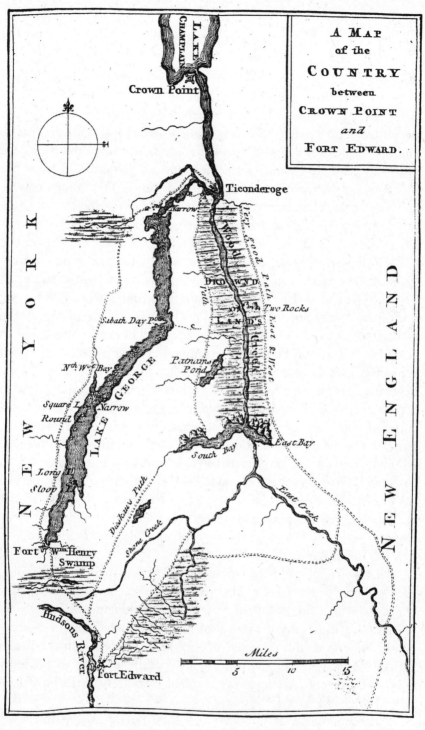

Fort Edward to Crown Point, 1759
("C" indicates route of Rogers's passage over the mountains)

800 feet from shore to crest. Moving downhill was somewhat easier, as they slid the boats carefully on their keels.

The channel of Wood Creek, north of South and East Bay, curved deep through drowned country, muddy swamp, and sodden grassland. At night Rogers and his men threaded their squadron through a 400-yard passage separating the new fort at Ticonderoga from the farther shore, virtually under the noses of some 2,000 French troops, as Rogers calculated from the number of campfires. The totally outnumbered rangers passed near enough to hear the sentry's watchword, then carried on for another five miles and took cover on the eastern shore to wait out daylight. There they watched several loaded bateaux pass south from Crown Point, perhaps hearing the strains of "Alouette" (The Lark), "M'en revenant de la jolie Rochelle" (Coming Back from Pretty Rochelle), and "C'est l'aviron" (It's the Paddle), the favorite shanties of the Canadian voyageurs. The rangers prepared to go uplake to Crown Point that evening, but Rogers called it off because the waxing gibbous moon over clear skies would have left the boats dangerously visible.[17] Next day the men, now beginning to wish for the bad weather that had plagued them over the mountains, counted more than a hundred boats—part of the supply train accompanying the new French commander, Louis-Joseph de Montcalm, who had arrived just the day before. At midday hands tightened on gunstocks as seven bateaux came abreast of their position, and the rowers entreated their officer to let them take a lunch break at that very spot. For whatever reason the officer had them pull in 150 yards along, where they ate under the rangers' eyes. Rogers gave no order to fire. He had bigger game in mind.

That evening, forty-five minutes after civil twilight had faded, they pulled out onto Lake Champlain. Rowing steadily north, they slipped through the 200-yard passage under the guns of Fort Saint-Frédérick, within easy musket shot of the sentries posted on either shore. Now two fully manned enemy forts lay between them and British-held William Henry, and the lake itself swarmed with enemy boats. Their only advantage lay in plain effrontery, with no rescue should things go wrong.

Ten miles north of Crown Point they pulled ashore and again waited out the daylight hours, camouflaging the whaleboats within the brush. A 30- to 40-ton schooner glided past, 30 boats streaming north after her. That night they pulled another 15 miles northward, to within a mile of another schooner lying at anchor. This treasure Rogers knew was worth breaking cover for, and the men removed packs and unnecessary equipment from the whaleboats. But just as they did so, two long flat-bottomed sailing galleys of the type known as lighters or shallops came up the lake and prepared to pull ashore right amid the rangers.

Having no other choice, Rogers hand-signaled an attack. A volley shattered the quiet, killing three Frenchmen outright. Rogers roared an offer of quarter to the survivors if they ceased resistance. The French signaled submission; then, unaware that the Yankees had watercraft, they quickly took to their oars and raced for the opposite shore. The enraged rangers floated their whaleboats and soon overtook the more cumbersome lighters. Swivel cannon at point-blank range elicited a more heartfelt capitulation. The whooping rangers jumped aboard, took the nine living men prisoner, and scalped the dead. The lighters bore some 800 bushels of flour and further stores of rice, pork, wine, brandy, oats, and wheat,[18] in addition to between 30 and 40 letters, which would provide useful intelligence. As his men ransacked the stores, Rogers lost no time interrogating the prisoners, who proved to be part of a 500-man contingent moving south on the lake; the remainder were right behind them. That information "induced us to hasten our return to our garrison," Rogers later wrote with the cool, remote understatement that typifies his journals. The men knocked the heads off the casks; pitched all the provisions overboard, except for some brandy, which they passed over to the whaleboats; and finished off a badly wounded prisoner who would have slowed them down. Perhaps Rogers himself knocked him on the head with his tomahawk, then quickly circled the man's crown with his long knife and stuffed the bloody prize into his coat pocket. Any thoughts of escape or obstruction passed quickly from the prisoners' minds.

The rangers scuttled the French boats, probably staving in the hulls, then rowed quickly south, already in grave alarm that the schooner or other vessels might be bearing down after them with the efficiency of sail and keel. Some six miles later Rogers motioned his company ashore to hide their boats, then began the long march to William Henry.

Three months later three Abenaki warriors returning to Montréal came upon four of the hidden craft, a discovery that deeply alarmed New France. Captain Louis-Antoine de Bougainville, Montcalm's aide-de-camp, dedicated a long passage of his journal to this ominous evidence. He ruled out any possible passage from Fort William Henry, perhaps because the portage was so brutal. Instead he entertained five rival possibilities, each more unlikely than the last, most involving secret lakes hidden in the mountains where British carpenters could work undetected. As the boats appeared to be old and well-used, Bougainville assumed that these invaders from nowhere must have been making free of French waters for some time. The French sent out two detachments in search of the secret waterway, one consisting of 80 Canadians and 20 regular volunteers.[19]

Rogers's raid rattled Montcalm also, who alerted the French secretary of war about "the necessity of using a little more precaution with our convoys," while thankfully acknowledging that it was "fortunate they did not take any more."[20]

With Montcalm in firm overall command in Québec, and Loudoun ready to engage, the next year would bring the first major encounters between the competing empires since the Battle of Lake George. Now Rogers would have a chance to match the rival woodsmasters in high levels of danger, testing the new instrument of war that he was painstakingly and painfully forging.

Chapter 10

Ambush in the Snow

*I receiv'd a Wound from the Enemy (the first Shot they made on us) thro'
the Body, upon which I retir'd into the Rear, to the Prisoner I had taken
on the Lake, knock'd him on the Head and killed him, lest he should
Escape and give Information to the Enemy.*

THOMAS BROWN, AGE 16, JANUARY 1757[1]

On January 21, 1757, just as the garrison at Carillon thought winter
had settled in for good, a front blew in from the south or east, bringing up a sudden thaw. Gusting snow deliquesced into sleet and then
rain, which collected in the footprints, hoofmarks, and road ruts concentrated in and around the fort. It rendered the thick Vergennes
clay—remnants of a fine glacial silt from the Pleistocene—into a yet
thicker and more gluey muck that clung wearingly to foot and hoof.
Nearly impenetrable fog made the morning air sodden and close.

That fog may have preserved a lone, terrified French Canadian
militiaman who pounded up the muddy trail that wound cliffward
from the southern shore of Lake Champlain to the rocky prominence
commanding it. The flogged draft horse was nearing its limit.

He gained the road that twisted through the oak-and-chestnut-
stump field up to the fort's gate; jolted past the huge 50-foot-long
wooden artillery shed outside the newly completed curtain walls; and
ducked his head under the stone tunnel roof into the courtyard,
horseshoes clattering on the limestone bedrock.[2] Startled French regulars and Canadians grabbed the reins as he slipped over his mount's
steaming flanks and stumbled to the engineers' quarters at the far end
of the courtyard to demand instant audition with the commandant.

The measured 65-year-old Paul-Louis Dazemard de Lusignan had stepped outside at the commotion. He gravely took in word of the ice ambush, which could be the work of no one but Rogers.

Only hours earlier he had sent a sergeant and 15 men by sleigh north to Crown Point for fresh supplies, particularly the brandy that quieted the pain of his rheumy knee.[3] Now he ordered an officers' call beaten on the tambour, or snare drum, and his regular subordinates came hurrying up: Captain de Basserode and Lieutenant d'Astrel, of the Régiment de Languedoc, their white uniforms trimmed with bloodred cuffs and collars and highlighted with blue waistcoats; and Captain de La Granville of the Régiment de La Reine, his white uniform bearing only blue trim. But their chief turned not to his brethren of the line but to a half-pay ensign of La Troupe de la Marine—the provincial militia—Charles-Michel Mouet de Langlade. Lusignan knew that the best chance of catching Rogers lay with this hard 28-year-old, who was just as tough as he looked. Langlade wore no grand cocked hat but a toque, a knit woolen cap pulled tightly over his head, a mark of the fur-trading *coureurs des bois* who for generations had threaded ever farther into the *pays d'en haut*, the wilderness upriver of Montréal.

A man with a foot in both cultures, Langlade was a half-breed, or métis—the fruit of the union of the rich fur trader Augustin Monet de Langlade with the Indian woman Domitilde. He was a consummate backwoodsman, a practioner of *la petite guerre*, as the French called small-engagement warfare.

Only five years earlier he had joined Chief Pontiac in leading up to 250 men of the Three Fires Confederacy—Ottawa, Potawatomi, and Chippewa—against the pro-Iroquois Miami village of Pickawillany (near present-day Piqua, Ohio), the crossroads of several trading routes. The Miami chief Memeskia had broken relations with the French and entertained British traders—a threat to French influence in the Ohio Valley. Langlade's party destroyed the village, ate the heart of one of the British traders, then killed Memeskia, boiled him, and devoured his body in front of his family. This act of strategic frightfulness cowed the Miami back to the French, helped secure the allegiance of other western tribes throughout the coming war, and defanged British trading in the Ohio Valley.[4]

Now the chance to run down the infamous ranger thrilled Langlade. Move fast enough, Langlade judged, and they might just catch Rogers pushing west of the fort. So Lusignan ordered de Basserode and some 110 regulars, Canadian militia, and Indians to join Langlade in pursuit. Ten soldiers would follow half an hour later with supplies.

Langlade strode out into the courtyard, the Ottawas and Potawatomies he half-commanded gathering around him. He and 90 Canadians and Ottawas had reached the fort late in December and been in the midst of planning a raid south when Rogers struck. The Ottawas' faces were neatly tattooed, dashed lines cutting across cheeks and bisecting the countenance from forehead down to tip of chin. They wore their hair short and upstanding in the front, long in the back; their ears and noses were pierced with stone, copper, and shell ornaments, the treasures of a trade network that reached over a quarter of a continent. Traditionally young Ottawa men had the fleshy edge of their ears cut through, leaving strips of skin that could be stretched to some four inches long with weights, then wrapped with such materials as brass wire.[5]

The joyous prospect of war and plunder had drawn these warriors more than a thousand miles from their longhouse villages in the rich hardwood forests of Michigan's Lower Peninsula, by canoe and on foot. Among the Ottawas, Langlade had an almost supernatural standing. It dated back to his childhood when his uncle, the influential chief Nissowaquet, had required him to accompany a war party down the Mississippi against the Ottawa's powerful enemy, the Chickasaw. The ten-year-old-boy, who had appeared in Nissowaquet's fasting dream before setting out, witnessed a triumph for the Ottawa, whom the Chickasaw had twice bloodily repulsed. Manitou, the Algonquin term for Great Spirit and the creator of all things, was deemed to have blessed the boy. In his old age Langlade would boast of having fought in ninety-nine battles.

He operated confidently between two worlds, that of the supremely polished Bourbon French and that of the matriarchal Great Lakes Ottawa, embodying even more than Rogers the cultural melding of the Old and New Worlds. The European demand for furs had turned Indian tribes against one another. After the Iroquois destroyed the Hurons in 1648 and 1649, the Ottawa took over the Hurons' lucrative trade routes, exchanging agricultural produce and trade goods for furs with the Assiniboine and Cree to the west and north along the lake-studded lands of Canada.[6] They remained loyal to the French but were less inclined to adopt Roman Catholicism than, for instance, the western Abenaki. Among the Eastern Woodlands Indians, they were known for their ferocity, which sometimes culminated in cannibalism.

Several of the Ottawas expressed concern that the French regulars' lack of *raquettes*—snowshoes—would slow them down and deny them the chance to overtake the raiders. Nevertheless, in minutes the regulars were filing out of the fort. The Indians, on their bear-paw-shaped snowshoes, followed.

Under the pelting rain, on the snowy and featureless Lake Champlain ice, Rogers stood cursing his luck, surveying his seven new prisoners and three haphazardly scattered French sleighs. Only minutes earlier the set of eight-horse sleighs traveling north had seemed like a gift. Now he faced a precarious situation. He had figured that Five Mile Point—so called because it was equidistant between Fort Saint-Frédéric and Carillon—would prove an ideal base from which to surprise any sleighing party and gain critical information about enemy troop strengths. So he had sent Stark and 20 men uplake at a dogtrot to head off any sleighs coming through. Captain Thomas Speakman and some rangers crept down to shore and set up an ambush, while Rogers's contingent hightailed it south to prevent the escape of any French sleighs.

But the curve of the lake and the heavy fog had obscured a further half dozen sleighs that had been following the first ones. Rogers promptly sent two of his fastest runners hurtling back along their tracks to warn Stark to "let the first Sledges pass," only to watch the first sleigh round the islet of Presquisle and spot Stark's men already streaming onto the ice. Major Rouilly, commander of the supply train, who was riding at the head of the second column of sleighs, roared orders to turn back headlong for Carillon.

The rangers bounded down the snowy bank and overwhelmed

the lead sleighs, capturing seven of the ten escorts and drivers. In the ensuing confusion, three cut the draft-horse traces, mounted, and galloped away; the other sleighs now careening home could not be overtaken on snowshoes through the rain-made mush, although one was abandoned.

Rogers split up the prisoners and pressed each one sternly for details about the numbers at Carillon, learning, his journal says, "that 200 Canadians and 45 Indians were just arrived at Ticonderoga, and were to be reinforced that evening, or next morning from Crown Point." These fresh troops were no doubt set on running down the man they all considered their most dangerous enemy.

Ranger officers gathered on the ice. Should they follow their tracks back to William Henry, or should they cross to the eastern shore, break a new path, and return via Wood Creek? Would the enemy see them outlined on the frozen white lake? They certainly couldn't wait for the cover of darkness; enemy troops would be on them long before that. Most important, however, were Rogers's very own oft-repeated words: never retrace one's previous route, because it was an invitation to ambush. The officers came to a quick consensus: they urged Rogers to cross the ice and take advantage of the deep woods opposite Carillon.

Rogers ran his eyes over the tired faces, the soaked clothes, and the beards bristling with freezing raindrops. Some were familiar— John Stark's, his lips pursed, and his own older brother James's—but many were new. To swell his ranks, he had accepted volunteers from Speakman's and Humphrey Hobbs's units, many of whom had not yet seen action or even winter service. There was one 16-year-old and a Spanish Catholic who spoke little English. He could count on Speakman, an experienced fighter. Lieutenant Sam Kennedy was a good scout but had never seen battle. His original rangers had had to help these new men make snowshoes.

He turned these considerations over in his mind. This marked their fifth day out. On that first evening on the trail Rogers had stood watching the column move past, pointing out one by one a dozen men who were not moving well, "injured on the ice," perhaps nursing twisted ankles or frostbitten toes. (Three days earlier, Bougainville had reported "frightfully cold weather" in Québec City of minus

29 degrees F. "Everyone who comes from even a short distance has his nose, ears, or chin frozen.")[7]

At first the recent rain and thaw had proved a bonanza for the rangers, but it had also soaked their clothes and wet their moccasins right through—ideal conditions to induce hypothermia, which would encumber awareness, initiative, and fine motor skills. Worse still, the black powder in their firelocks had thickened into a muddy dark paste; to use a modern term, such powder is hygroscopic, prone to absorb moisture. He doubted that more than a handful of the muskets could fire.

He had to give an uneasy and unsettling order: They must return to their campsite of the night before, about three miles southwest of the current position. But of course they'll never dare come after us, he added, with a dash of vintage Rogers confidence, the voice of a 24-year-old who had never tasted defeat.

For all his outward calmness, he had not deceived himself as to the difficulty of the situation. The French horsemen would reach Carillon in an hour or so, well before dark, and fresh, dry, and rested troops would soon be swarming after them.

In a little more than an hour—with "all possible expedition"—the seventy-four rangers, along with their seven prisoners, were back at the previous night's shelter. Rogers and Speakman saw to the division of labor: some men circled back along their inescapably marked passage to set up an ambush in case enemy scouts should pick up their trail; others marked a perimeter; and still others dragged in large branches. A handful coaxed the still-warm coals, lingering in the fire pits they had dug into the snow the day earlier with snowshoes.

Each man carried a "worm," two sharpened pieces of metal twisted together into a corkscrew, that fitted onto the end of their ramrods and were inserted into their muskets to scrape out any powder residue. Black powder rarely burned efficiently—sometimes up to 50 percent remained unconsumed in the barrel. Moisture (and there was more than enough) only made things worse. To dry out any remaining dampness, the men silently drew their weapons and placed them near the fire, while also carefully cleaning the frizzen pan, a small plate that held the few grains of powder necessary to ignite the charge when sparked by the cock's head of the firing mechanism.

Once their guns were back in working order, the men rammed down fresh charges, spilling powder from their powderhorns, followed by buck and ball, and several pieces of shot enveloped in paper or cloth to ensure a tight—and therefore maximum-velocity—fit to the barrel.

By one-thirty P.M. or thereabouts the rangers had packed up and crammed down some morsels of food, perhaps dried peas and ox jerky—not very supportive intake for stomachs probably sour with strain. Then they tucked their muskets underneath their coats and blankets against the pervasive rain and moved out, picking up the rhythmic, slightly rolling gait that characterizes snowshoe movement; the less experienced copied the veterans, whose exaggerated twisting of arms and torsos gave an impression of weighty purposefulness. By now, even the snowshoe novices knew that passing the raised shoe over the inside edge of the planted shoe cut down on the tendency to develop a dizzying bow-legged stagger.

When breaking new trail, Rogers sent four men abreast out in front to tamp down the snow. That exhausting chore once taken care of, he pressed everyone to keep close on the heels of the man in front, as they were now moving in prudent but time-consuming Indian file. On trampled snow an experienced snowshoer today can move at better than eight miles an hour—without a pack and with the benefit of the superlight carbon-fiber frames and titanium crampons that provide a traction wholly unavailable to the strictly organic fabrics of a preindustrial society. But heaving along on 30-inch Ojibwa-style shoes, which resembled stretched-out, old-fashioned tennis racquets put to emergency use, the rangers could not have maintained anything like such a pace. On a good track they might have been able to will themselves to maintain a strong walking speed of three miles an hour.[8]

The prisoners slumped along at the rear, their guards under Rogers's clear instructions to kill them should the enemy strike lest they pass along ruinous intelligence about rangers numbers and dispositions.

Rogers had placed his most trusted deputy, John Stark, at the rear. The brave and experienced but operationally lesser known Captain Speakman was in the center, while he himself was at the head with Lieutenant Kennedy. The rugged topography west of the

Ticonderoga peninsula offered them few opportunities to keep to a contour line and thus avoid the strain of going up and down. After a half mile over "broken ground," as the men's calves were burning from exertion, Rogers led them down a steep incline into a deep ravine only 250 feet wide and across a small frozen creek. Then he slowed slightly as they moved up the opposite side in a herringbone stance, feet slightly splayed, toes pointed outward, to gain better traction upon the frozen slope. Kicking their oversize shoes into the snow when the incline grew too steep, they created steps with a single hack. But barely had the lead men gained the crest, now comfortably warm, than a rattle of cocked muskets stopped them in their tracks, and the cold tranquillity of the winter afternoon disintegrated into gunfire and war whoops. Several rangers went down, shot virtually point-blank.

Langlade himself may have fired on Rogers, who took a ball across his temple; it ripped off his hat but left him standing.[9] As Langlade watched, the big man staggered like a great wounded elk, blood running down his face, bellowing orders to his men to rally on the far side of the creek. Lieutenant Kennedy lay wounded, as did Ensign Caleb Page, the son of a good friend of Rogers's. Young Private Thomas Brown took a ball in his side. Perhaps a dozen men lay dead, wounded, and dying on the slope.

Not waiting to reload, Langlade leaped out from behind an evergreen tree trunk and led his Ottawas against the disordered rangers with bayonets fixed. Wet snow dislodged by the uproar cascaded heavily upon the combatants.[10]

Rogers kicked one snowshoe into the air, rotated it, followed suit with the other foot, and then bounded with exaggerated steps down toward the creek, glissading, or sliding, down part of the slope. Some rangers who were not so adept looked agape at their attackers, discharged their muskets, then laboriously scattered downhill at all angles, some falling over and tumbling down to the water. The French regulars and Indians swarmed around the downed men and stuck them with their bayonets and tomahawks until the glen rang with shrieks of terror and pain. The men who were left on their feet tried to reload as they stumbled downslope.

It had taken Langlade's Ottawas and the French regulars nearly three hours to pick up Rogers's trail. But found it they had, in time to throw a horseshoe-shaped ambush around the ravine's western flank and take advantage of the smooth gray beech trunks and dark brown hemlocks. Still, the hours spent searching in the rain had cost them, rendering more than half of their muskets useless, especially those of the regulars less experienced in woodland warfare, dampening the impact of that first stunning volley.[11]

As the rangers recoiled, a deadly discharge had slammed over their heads into their pursuers. As soon as the ambush was sprung, Stark and Ensign Jonathan Brewer had quickly gathered the forty-man rear guard on the eastern ridge and moved to cover their beset comrades as they splashed and crunched across the broken ice of the creek and upslope. Captain Speakman went down but managed to keep crawling. Sixteen-year-old Private Brown, although wounded, stumbled with terrible purpose over to the prisoner he had helped capture earlier on the ice and shattered his skull.

But this act delayed his escape, and the Ottawas closed on him. He spied a large rock that might offer cover, but as he drew close, an Indian leaped out from behind it, so startling him that he fell backward, breaking his snowshoes. He managed to dodge a tomahawk while struggling back to his feet. Another Indian closed in on him, but kicking off his snowshoes and attached moccasins, Brown flew down the hill in his wool socks. Soon he picked out Rogers's commanding figure, taking refuge behind the thin trunk of a pine tree. He fired off six or seven shots before a musket ball broke his gunstock. Thirty minutes later the unlucky private took a bullet in the knee. And then as he crabbed to the rear, another slammed into his shoulder.

But overall the rangers, only minutes ago on the cusp of destruction, were making an astonishingly effective retreat. Stark's cool command and concerted rearguard action, along with the men's dry muskets, had knocked the élan out of the determined French assault.

Langlade directed a small band of his Ottawas to work around the rangers' flank, but Stark's woods-reading eye spotted them; he warned Rogers, who bellowed to Sergeant Phillips to enfilade the Indians uphill to the right with the outfit's best sharpshooters. Phillips, a backwoods hunter of mixed Dutch and Indian blood, did not let his comrades down, Rogers recorded in his journal, "giving them the first fire very briskly," which "stopped several from retreat-ing to the main body." The rangers had again held the integrity of their front.

The French regulars, their weight concentrated on boot soles rather than distributed over snowshoes, attempted a brave but leaden head-on charge through the deep snow. But their conspicuously uni-formed mass provided only plentiful targets to the enemy.

Seeing the folly of continuing the frontal assault, the French called out to Rogers, praising his force's courage but demanding immediate surrender; any further resistance would be met with massacre. Rogers declined with taunting relish, which drew laughs and cheers from his adrenaline-ridden men. The sniping resumed.

At dusk Rogers ordered his men to suspend firing and fall silent. Langlade's Ottawas crawled out to scalp the dead and the unrecov-ered wounded. Some crept toward the ranger line, perhaps thinking that the enemy had run out of ammunition or were mostly dead or disabled.

The rangers held their fire until the last possible moment, then blasted a deadly fusillade. In the ensuing counterfire a ball struck Rogers's wrist, smashing muscle, bone, and tendon before exiting his hand. A nearby ranger cut off Rogers's queue, or small ponytail, for a tourniquet, while Rogers sent a runner dodging through the trees with the news that he was fine, although he could no longer load his musket.

John Stark steadied the shaken and untested survivors by growl-ing that he would shoot any man who ran away. At that moment a bullet smashed his firelock. Spying a French soldier down nearby, Stark lumbered across, scooped up the man's weapon, and snow-shoed back unscathed.

By nightfall, the rangers' ammunition was running dangerously low. The wounded would not last the night, and Rogers knew that it would be folly to try to hold the position; Carillon was so near that reinforcements, ammunition, and perhaps even hot food for the en-emy had to be on the way. Indeed, 25 men carrying powder and bis-cuits were already moving toward Langlade's position, along with a surgeon and priest.[12] The overgunned and outmanned rangers had few options. "I thought it expedient to take advantage of the night to retreat, and gave orders accordingly," wrote Rogers, who detailed the strongest men to assist the six of the force whose upper-body wounds left them able to walk.

In the confusion and darkness, the rangers unwittingly left behind three of their worst hurt. One of them, the young Tom Brown, would later pen a wide-eyed narrative of what followed the main body's departure. In its deadly simplicity and honesty it ranks as one of the most chilling accounts ever written of frontier warfare and captivity.[13]

As the darkness swallowed the last light and as the woodland chill dropped below freezing, Brown, Captain Speakman, and Robert Baker, a volunteer from the 44th Regiment, huddled together, unaware that the others were gone. Unwisely, Brown kindled a small fire, and the men huddled around it. After about half an hour that preternatural instinct that registers danger when all is too still led Speakman to call out to Rogers. Only a far-off response in French broke the still air. Suddenly the trio understood that there would be no rescue. Of the three, only Brown could move at all and then only slowly; his sock-clad feet were already hard and painful. They decided to surrender—to the French, of course—well aware what could befall them should the Ottawas find them first.

Shortly thereafter Brown spied an Indian creeping up "towards us over a small Rivulet that parted us in the Engagement." A surge of adrenaline revitalized his stiffening body; digging into the snow with his hands, he half-pulled, half-crawled away from the dancing shadows of the fire, lunging free just as the Indian easily overpowered Speakman, cut off his clothes, and scalped him alive. Baker pulled out his hunting knife and brought it to his own throat, but before he could take his own life, the bloodied Ottawa had seized Baker's knife hand with a whoop, heaved Baker up, and dragged him across the snow and away.

Convulsing and naked on the ever-more-bloodstained snow, Speakman turned a destroyed face to Brown. "For God's sake!" he cried, then asked for a tomahawk, so that he could "put an End to his Life!" Horrified but no doubt also biblically well versed against the mortal sin of suicide, Brown refused, then "exhorted him as well as I could to pray for Mercy, as he could not live many Minutes in that deplorable Condition." Seeing Brown's frozen resolve, Speakman changed course, instructing the young man, should he live, to tell his wife about the "dreadful" way he had died. Brown's journal remains silent on what followed. Did he just limp away? Or did he indeed deliver a death blow once Speakman had finished his prayers? Certainly many badly wounded men on the frontier were set free from such dreadful extremity by a loyal friend, which was held as no crime.

Whatever happened, Brown rose unsteadily and hobbled away from that place of horror as quickly as his wounded knee would allow him. He came soon upon a fellow ranger dead in the snow. The shoes had already been stripped from the corpse, but the stockings remained, so Brown took them and put them on his numb feet.

That evening, still searching for a southward path, he staggered and crawled around a large fire that the exultant French had made, passing within 35 feet of a French regular. He found his bearings and set off, but the snow "put my Feet into such Pain, as I had no Shoes, that I could not go on." Sitting down by a brook, he bound them in his blanket, but the rest of his inactive body grew so piercingly cold that he got up and crawled, crippled knee and all, through the rest of the night.

At about eleven A.M. he heard cries and turned to see four Indians loping toward him; he threw off his blanket and struggled on, continuing even as he heard them cock their guns. The grisly image of Speakman in the firelight played through his mind, and he longed only that "they would fire and kill me on the Spot." The Indians got ahead of him and, seeing him so young and determined to escape, whooped with delight and "took me by the Neck and Kiss'd me." They found money in his pockets, and "in trying who could get most, they had like have Kill'd me." But then they kicked aside the snow at their feet, scratched up handfuls of leaves, and packed Brown's wounds.

His captors brought him into camp, where one of their fellows slashed him with a cutlass, cutting clothes but not skin. Others stepped back, the better to crash their heads into him. A French officer coming upon the scene grabbed Brown roughly away from his tormentors and brought him over to an interpreter, who had him identify a number of the dead. He saw Speakman's head on a pole. Not long afterward Brown found Baker, still alive but in "a distress'd Condition." Their initial joy at seeing each other evaporated when the Indians announced that they would march them to Carillon. One brave hustled Baker along, but he soon fell to the ground weeping in despair. Brown intervened just as the warrior pulled Baker's hair and raised his long knife. Drawing upon extraordinary reserves, Brown pulled Baker's arms over his shoulders, and thus doubly burdened, he resumed his struggle to the fort, which he eventually reached somehow, bringing Baker with him. Brown would return to his unit at Crown Point on November 25, 1759, after nearly three years in captivity.

Meanwhile on the evening of the battle, forty-eight exhausted rangers and their six badly wounded endured their own private hell, expecting at any moment to hear another chorus of war whoops presaging multiple tomahawk blows. Fear multiplied by fatigue eats away the spirit; Rogers called upon them as a group to reach beyond what they felt they could do individually. Himself woozy from loss of blood and from the gnawing of the cold on his open wound, he could nevertheless still summon his exhausted party to do what they could not have believed possible and turn disaster into opportunity. They stumbled after him in the darkness, somehow convinced that they could live up to his belief in them, that he would lead them out of it, if only they found within themselves the ability to do what they had once thought impossible. In that Dantesque struggle homeward, Rogers' Rangers were born.

Early the following morning, as the line of ice zombies reached northern Lake George, six miles south of Carillon, Rogers confided to John Stark, who had proved essential to keeping the column going, that the wounded could not survive the passage back. Stark volunteered to strike on ahead with two men and bring help, and soon the three were fast-diminishing specks on the ice. They reached the fort that evening.

The next morning, Lieutenant Charles Bulkeley of Hobbs's company appeared with 15 men and a sleigh to carry the wounded, including Rogers, upon whom the loss of so many good comrades weighed far more heavily than his exposed and throbbing hand. In his journals Rogers counted 14 killed, six wounded, and nine missing. Reports of French and Indian dead vary.

After the battle Captain James Abercrombie, aide-de-camp to his uncle Major General James Abercromby, Loudoun's second-in-command, wrote quickly from Albany: "I am heartily sorry for Spikeman and Kennedy, who I imagined would have turned out well, as likewise for the men you have lost; but it is impossible to play at bowls without meeting with rubs." In lawn bowling, rubs were the surface irregularities that put unpredictable twists on the course of a ball. "You cannot imagine how all ranks of people here are pleased with your conduct, and your mens behavior." Indeed, the popular acclamation went even wider and deeper than Captain Abercrombie guessed. "It is generally believed Rogers behaved extreamly well," noted a writer in *The New-York Mercury*.[14] Newspapers as far away as Williamsburg reported the story; *The Virginia Gazette* referred to him as "the brave Captain Rogers."

Chapter 11

Tragedy at Fort William Henry

It is impossible for an Army to Act in this Country, without Rangers; and there ought to be a considerable body of them, and breeding them up that, will be a great advantage to the Country, for they will be able to deal with Indians in their own way.

LOUDOUN TO CUMBERLAND, NOVEMBER 22, 1756[1]

So far, apart from Johnson's defeat of Dieskau at Lake George, the war had not brought much good news for the British. Braddock's disaster and the loss of Fort Oswego in 1756 formed a pattern of misfortune, along with the incessant Indian raids along the southern frontier, and Rogers's actions remained one of very few bright spots.

Upcoming months and more battles lost would bring a yet-more-dismal outlook to the English colonists. An American correspondent of *The Gentleman's Magazine* wrote that "the more we are strengthened from Great Britain, the more ground we lose against the French."[2]

Against what were widely and not unjustly perceived as the inhumanities and depredations of the French papists and their savage allies (the only problem being their close analogies to the British ways of war), Rogers acted as a figurehead for action. He also made good copy. The fledgling New World newspaper business drew naturally on the daring exploits, the desperate backwoods ordeals and triumphs, of men like Rogers to sell papers. For eighty-three years from the landfall at Jamestown, no British colony had had a newspaper: that was hardly surprising, however, since the most primitive journalism had emerged in England only in the late sixteenth century. War

coverage, usually at second- or thirdhand, provided the readership
needed to propel newspaper publishing into the New World. By 1750
about two-thirds of the forty newspapers established in seven of the
twelve colonies and Delaware had folded. But the war provided
the needed market, and the twelve papers operating in five colonies
in 1750 had doubled by 1765. Rogers's fame rose to near-mythic
heights, often out of proportion to his exploits. A New Bedford
whaler captain might not have much in common with a tidewater
Virginia gentleman, but they could agree that Rogers had sprung
ready-made from the heart of the New World and certainly earned
his pay. But his men followed him into grave danger not because
of his fame but because he knew his terrible but necessary business: he was the very best woodsman and small-unit fighter to which
more than a century of the British penetration of America had given
birth.

Rogers spent only a day—January 23, 1757—at Fort William Henry
before returning to Fort Edward, on the Hudson. Poultices and
bleedings had failed to heal his hand. The poor nutrition that plagued
most of those serving in winter garrison did not help: a body stressed
by a severe trauma needs extra vitamin C, which plays a key role in
collagen synthesis, the formation of strong bonds between protein
strands in muscle. A diet lacking in dark green and yellow vegetables
not only supplies little vitamin C but also reduces the levels of vitamin A, another important factor in such healing.[3] Grossly inadequate
sanitation is all too likely to have caused ongoing infection. Rogers,
fearing that gangrene could claim his hand, "was obliged to repair to
Albany for better assistance."

Rogers may have accompanied a wretched train of 70 wounded
who were loaded aboard sleighs and taken to the English forces' general hospital in Albany, where they arrived on February 1. Charlotte
Brown, the matron there, noted that of the 70 who had set out, "4
Died by the way with the cold." She welcomed the famous ranger
captain into her hospital, which she confessed to her journal was "no
better than a Shed" against the bitter cold.[4]

Not one to keep idle even while crippled, Rogers jumped at the
offer extended in Captain Abercrombie's cordially admiring letter:

"Please send me the names of the officers you would recommend for your own company and also to fill up the vacancies in the others; as I am certain you have the good of the service at heart, your recommendation will be paid great regard to." Beside Robert's and Richard's companies, William Shirley had raised three other ranger units, not under Rogers's supervision. Thomas Speakman had fallen in the ambush. Captain Humphrey Hobbs lay desperately ill with smallpox at Fort William Henry. Rogers saw an opportunity to seed these two companies with his own men.

As Rogers lay hospital-bound, his brother Richard visited Loudoun in Boston to ask that he enlarge the ranger units from 50 to 100 men. Loudoun spent much of that winter in Boston, planning a summer campaign in which he proposed to concentrate all available force against Louisbourg, supported by the royal fleet. Should he master that key stronghold, a British navy could press right up the river to assail Québec City and Montréal. His plan had a role for the rangers, because he knew that "whoever is Superior in irregulars has an infinite advantage over the other side and must greatly weaken, if not totally destroy them before they can get to the Point where they can make their Push."[5] Rogers was ordered to bring his companies up to one hundred men each, to be officered by a captain, two lieutenants, and an ensign. Loudoun also endorsed Rogers's recommendation that John Stark succeed Speakman. When word came of Captain Hobbs's death, Rogers recommended that Lieutenant Bulkeley, who had sledged out to relieve his hard-pressed comrades after the last engagement, assume command of that unit.

Rogers also took up with Loudoun a matter much on his mind: paying his men who had overwintered at Fort William Henry in 1755. Loudoun responded that "these services were antecedent to [my] command here" and thus it "was not in [my] power to reward them." Jeffery Amherst, who succeeded Loudoun, would take the same position, but the men of Rogers's company would hold him personally liable. (This New England relentlessness would unite with Rogers's unquestioning assumption of responsibility to push him steadily into a crippling cycle of debt.)

On the second or perhaps the third of March, Rogers spiked a high fever, which drained his energies further and confined him to bed, unable to keep food down. On March 5 Charlotte Brown or one of her nurses found red spots on his tongue and throat, telltale signs of smallpox, the deadliest disease in the New World.

The nurses moved Rogers out to an isolation ward or separate house with other victims of the scourge. A rash broke out on his face, spreading to his arms and legs, then his hands and feet. The fever broke, but over the course of several days the spots ripened horribly into fluid-filled raised bumps and thence into pustules, round and firm as though hundreds of pieces of buckshot were lodged underneath the skin. Fever returned, and Rogers sweated out the next several weeks as the pustules finally crusted over and scabbed. Once the scabs dried up and sloughed off, he was released as no longer contagious. He stepped outside for the first time on April 15 after forty-one days' confinement, his face now pocked with small round scars.

While Rogers lay sick, John Stark had stepped decisively into his new command at Fort William Henry. At two P.M. on March 19 his sharp-eyed sentries spied a light on the ice and heard the sound of scrapers. Some 1,500 French regulars, Canadians, and Indians were pushing uplake, most dragging sleds, or *traînes*, piled with winter equipment, including a bear and deerskin apiece, along with twelve days' rations. Officers' energies were maintained with three pints of brandy and two pounds of chocolate. Every soldier carried a five-foot-eight-inch scaling ladder, three of which could be fitted together to create an escalade device nearly 14 feet tall. The most substantial element lacking in this excellently equipped force was artillery.

Concerted fire from the rangers stopped any surprise in its tracks. Stark's biographer contends that his subject's decision to withhold rum from his rangers, while the largely Irish regulars lay hungover from St. Patrick's Day, saved the day; that assertion may be hard to assess, but certainly his rangers put up a stout and effective resistance. Snowfall and dwindling rations sent the enemy's much more numerous force back to Carillon, having lost barely one percent of its numbers—five killed, eight wounded, three captured. Their return to Canada, however, incurred "various sufferings," wrote Montcalm; many died from exposure, and a third returned to Canada snow-blind, having "to be led by their comrades."

The French operation had not lacked results. Bougainville wrote that "three hundred bateaux, four larger vessels, two storehouses" had been burned outside the stockade walls, hamstringing the British capacity to control Lake George next summer. The next time Montcalm came to Fort William Henry—sooner than the British thought possible—he would bring all the equipment necessary for a proper siege.

Not long after his recovery, Rogers received orders that Loudoun's Louisbourg expedition was going forward. By mid-May his, Stark's, and Bulkeley's units had traveled down the Hudson to New York City to join the expedition north. Stark, whose turn it was to contract smallpox, spent the trip belowdecks in delirious fever.

The rangers would not return to Albany until mid-September. Loudoun's expedition would prove fruitless: the fleet arrived much later than anticipated, and Louisbourg's well-manned and strong naval forces were thus given ample time to prepare. Hence Loudoun prudently if ingloriously called off the assault. The rangers carried out some small-scale scouts around Louisbourg and brought in some deserters but achieved little else.

In Robert's absence, the Rogers family suffered another disaster. On June 22, his brother Richard, close confidant and fellow leader of rangers, died of smallpox after only two weeks of fever. General Daniel Webb, commander of Fort William Henry, wrote to Loudoun that "his Death your Lordship must imagine, is no small Loss to us," robbing Fort William Henry of its most capable ranger officer.

Without Richard's guiding hand and with other ranger companies away, British intelligence floundered. On June 30, a successful scout by 55 men under Israel Putnam surprised 235 Frenchmen and Indians, killing a Canadian cadet and several braves, but otherwise the early summer probes after Richard's death proved ineffective. Six sorties in early July failed to bring in a single prisoner or even to get close to Carillon or Fort Saint-Frédéric. Charles Langlade and his Ottawas owned no-man's-land.

Frustrated at the lack of intelligence, Colonel George Munro, commander at Fort William Henry, ordered Colonel John Parker to take five companies of Jersey Blues—a New Jersey militia regiment noted for their blue coats—and a handful of New York militiamen, a total of some 350 provincial soldiers, north aboard 22 bateaux. On July 23 they rowed and sailed into disaster near Sabbath Day Point. Indians captured the three scouting bateaux before the rest of the British realized it and, probably under Langlade's direction, cleverly used them to lure their fellows into shore, where a large Indian and French regular force lay in wait. New Jersey had no Indian frontiers: its unseasoned militia must have found the murderous fire, delivering death invisibly from cover, nightmarish enough; but truly hellish were the swarm of canoes packed with screaming, painted Ottawa, Ojibwa, and Menominee braves bursting from the undergrowth to cut off any retreat. From the canoes Indians hurled themselves into the water and swam beneath the bateaux to capsize them, then speared the struggling provincial soldiers "like fish," wrote Bougainville. Most of the provincials surrendered without firing a shot. Only Parker's bateau and three others managed to escape.[6]

The Jesuit missionary Père Pierre Roubaud, camped among his faithful, counted 157 prisoners. Most had ropes around their necks and were "in a very wretched state, their eyes bathed in tears, their faces covered with perspiration and even with blood," as they were paraded by the victors, who had dipped deeply into captured rum. Père Roubaud walked up to a large fire and witnessed a horrifying scene. "But, oh, Heavens! what a feast!" he wrote later in his journal. "The remains of an English body, more than half stripped of the skin and flesh." As he watched, the Ottawas ate until their faces dripped with gore. Commanding the best seats in front of the fire were ten stone-faced bound provincials. When Roubaud attempted to intervene, a young Indian stopped him, saying in bad but perfectly comprehensible French, *"Thou have French taste; me Savage, this meat good for me."* Roubaud found what solace he could in the fact that his missionized Abenaki took no part.[7]

These goings-on paled in comparison with what happened only days later. While Lord Loudoun frittered away the summer with the cream of the British regular, provincial, and irregular forces in Nova Scotia, the canny Montcalm strengthened his army at Lake Champlain. His designs on Fort William Henry were no secret, but the fort was ill prepared to withstand a siege by an army deploying heavy artillery and was unaware of Montcalm's buildup. On the afternoon of August 3 hundreds of Montcalm's Indian allies paraded in clear sight of the fort. Their leader issued a letter under his seal clearly threatening that if the fort did not surrender immediately, it would be beyond his power to control "the Savages" once some of them had been killed. Chilling news about the fate of Parker's men left little doubt as to what Montcalm implied. His ultimatum would prove a horrible presage of things to come.

But Munro rejected Montcalm's offer, and the big guns began to roll into position. The British situation, however, deteriorated quickly. Promised reinforcements from Fort Edward never came; the overall commander, General Webb, feared on reflection that to dispatch relief columns would be to commit the cardinal error of dividing one's force in the face of the enemy and by so weakening Fort Edward might open the path to Albany and New York City. In the meantime news of the siege had mobilized thousands of provincial militiamen, who streamed toward Fort Edward.

After four days Fort William Henry was wrecked by cannon fire. Many of their own cannons had split open from the heat of too-frequent firings. The British commander surrendered on Montcalm's generous terms, which enabled the 2,000 soldiers and a considerable number of camp followers to go home on foot, carrying their colors and even pulling a single piece of artillery.

On paper this outcome reflected well on both sides. But trouble had brewed the night before when inebriated Indians had overrun the fort, killing and scalping the seventeen soldiers who had been too badly wounded to be evacuated. As the enemy marched out the next morning, laden with their private possessions, the Indian allies looked on with mounting agitation. Cheated of what they deemed their just rewards of victory, for which they had risked their lives and traveled many hundreds of hard forest miles, the Indians stripped the provincials of their belongings, arms, and even clothes. But they still felt entitled to more, particularly scalps, which a French officer would later write "are their trophies, their obelisks, their arches of triumph; the monuments which attest to other tribes and consign to posterity the valor, the exploits of the warriors and the glory of the cabin."

In short order, the looting burst out of hand, and those who resisted, and many who didn't, felt the sharp blow of the tomahawk and twisting cut of the scalping knife. Some two or three score died. The Indians stopped short of inflicting wholesale carnage, preferring instead to drag off prisoners that they might ransom in Canada. The French claimed to have been helpless before what many British colonists came to call a massacre. Father Rouboud saw a warrior who "carried in his hand a human head, from which trickled streams of blood, and which he displayed as the most splendid prize that he could have secured."[8]

The Indians even dug up the recently buried, including Richard Rogers, and took the corpses' scalps. Those trophies would prove costly indeed as they became vectors for the smallpox epidemic that would savage the Ottawas around the Great Lakes. The parish register at the Mission of Saint-Ignace de Michilimackinac, which adjoined the trading post of the French Far West—the meeting country of Langlade's two ancestries at the intersection of Lakes Superior, Michigan, and Huron—would list many dozens of deathbed baptisms, mostly of babies and the young.

Rogers heard of his brother's death and the fall of Fort William Henry on a troopship sailing south. The New Hampshire provincials, the last to file out of the fort on that bloody summer's day, had taken the brunt of the violence. Many of the dead had been Rogers's friends.

Chapter 12

Mutiny on Rogers' Island

The Americans are in general the dirtiest, most contemptible cowardly dogs that you can conceive. There is no depending upon 'em in action. They fall down dead in their own dirt and desert by battalions, officers and all. Such rascals as those are rather an incumbrance than any real strength to an army.

JAMES WOLFE TO HIS FATHER, MAY 20, 1758[1]

The evening of December 6, 1757, began normally as the four ranger companies assembled on the western shore parade ground of Rogers' Island, stamping on the packed earth to keep warm until inspection. The men could feel the cold presence of the Hudson that closed upon the 50-acre island, even as it lay beneath a mantle of ice. The Hudson was everywhere—its moist earthy smell in the nostrils, its fine clay discoloring moccasins, the shiftings and crackings of its ice in one's ears; it was somehow alive, like a wild animal trying to shake loose from its icy winter coat. Not only was the Hudson their lifeline to Albany and to resupply by boat and sleigh, but the big river and its many tributaries opened the way into the Adirondack interior. Its depths yielded rich harvests of trout as well as bony-plated six-foot sturgeons, often called Albany beef, whose lineage dated back to the dinosaurs. But the river took away almost as much as it gave, drowning more men every year than those who froze to death. When its surface rose in a winter thaw or in the warming breath of spring, the brown waters submerged the island's central and southern sections so quickly that it caught men inside their huts in a waist-deep grasp,

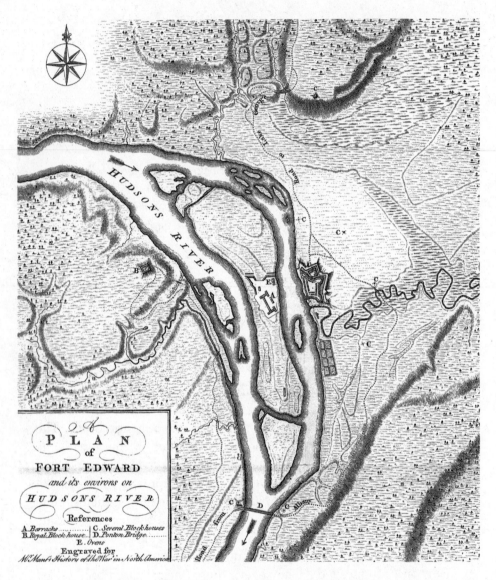

Plan of Fort Edward and Rogers' Island, 1759

drowning some with the briefest kick of its power before running off as quickly as it had come.[2]

Directly to the east, across the pontoon bridge of cabled bateaux, rose the dark outline of three-bastioned Fort Edward, now the northernmost British presence in the contested Hudson Valley. The island sat in a crook of the river's dogleg south, plunging over falls on its course through Albany 40 miles downstream. The river's wet breath, while often somewhat moderating the heavy falls of snow, lent the air a heaviness that cut through layers of clothing and chilled every bone.

By now, every one of the men assembled could recite their outfit's defining code of conduct, the 28 rules that Rogers had written at Loudoun's request three months earlier, a primer on backwoods fighting and soldierly conduct in camp and on the march.[3] The first rule required rangers to muster each evening, where an officer from each company would inspect each man "to see they are in order, so as to be ready on any emergency to march at a minute's warning," a pioneering example of the Revolution's Minute Men. A provincial diarist reported that they were expected at seven-thirty A.M. and seven P.M. musters, "our hats cocked up our guns Bright & our gloths cleen." There the men presented their tomahawks and regulation muskets, whose unwieldy barrels had often been sawed down from 46 inches to 38.[4] The officers poked into several of the men's cartouche bags, reiterating Rogers's standing orders that each man carry 60 rounds of powder and ball, then assigned that evening's guards.

That December night Martin Severance, a newly minted lieutenant from Deerfield, 40 years old, led a detail over to the guardhouse, where two rangers lay under punishment, recovering from a flogging administered the day before. Those selected for sentry duty probably dropped smaller-than-usual musket rounds into their muskets, a technique known as "running balls," which had the benefit of enabling men coming off sentry to unload without firing.

After parade those not on detail drifted in knots to their bunks, in the little log huts arranged in neat avenues by company, taking their muskets inside with them. Each 11-by-11-foot hut shared river-clay-chinked walls with the two adjacent ones. Once inside, the men rekindled the fires in the stone-mortared fireplaces, the flames illuminating the mice that raced around amid the detritus of camp life on the earthen floor, searching for scraps of food among the pieces of sprue, the wormlike lead tailings from musket-ball manufacture, fragments of clay pipe stem, and bone. Perhaps a chapbook lay on one of the bunks, the often sensational and always popular coarse-paper booklets clamoring about such timeless themes as murders, ghosts, the dangers of insobriety, and fairy tales, shipped over by the gross from London and passed from man to man until they fell apart.[5]

Intense eyes stared out of faces whose gauntness the scraggly beards did little to conceal. Several of the men further thickened the already-dense air by sucking on long-stemmed white tobacco pipes, stinging many eyes but at least masking the reek of men in long-unwashed close proximity. A visitor thrust among them unexpectedly might have thought himself visiting a trapper's isolated cabin.

That evening the men found solace in the passed bottle, perhaps the cherry rum that the Dutch sutler had recently come by. Winter garrison duty meant fewer scouts and less mobility; even marathon bouts of splitting oak and hickory for firewood failed to drive away the unshakable sense of being cooped up. Like other young men the world over, they broke their boredom with pranks and gambling. A private was caught urinating into a kettle of peas and was sentenced to a flogging. Another man ate three raw fish, guts and all, on a wager that won him four quarts of wine.[6]

There were the usual grumbles about the unsparing diet of salt pork, which came in 200-pound barrels of four-pound pieces, then was boiled furiously into some kind of soup, a process whose failure to tenderize the meat wrought havoc upon the men's sore gums and few teeth. When the cooks failed to knock off the salt clinging to the meat, the men woke up dry-mouthed, their hearts racing. Most could not stomach the "sass," or green vegetables, in the winter—for the most part a pathetic assortment of wilted turnip greens, a loathsome command diet that was vaguely specific against the scurvy but nearly as foul as the condition it was supposed to ward off.[7]

Yet among this long litany of complaints, none evoked more grousing and real cold anger than the proximity of the redcoats at the fort, whose contempt and caste disgust for North Americans knew few bounds.

Rangers had been camping on the island ever since the late summer of 1757, even before Montcalm leveled William Henry. Here, Lord Loudoun could keep them close at hand as the eyes and ears of his army, using them to scout northeastward up Wood Creek into South Bay and to Lake Champlain, or north to Lake George and thence up the Hudson's northwestern tributaries, and, of course, for maintaining efficient contact with Saratoga and Albany.

As the major staging point for operations against Carillon, Fort Edward would serve at various times during the war as a base for ten thousand or more regulars, besides thousands of provincials, rangers, and Indians. Given all the logistics entailed for such use, the banks of the Hudson often resembled a busy port more than an inland garrison. The regulars quickly filled the pair of long, two-story barracks within the walls and spilled out into tents pitched along fortified lines that spread northeast from Edward's wooden palisades. The complex would swell into British North America's third largest city, after only Boston and Philadelphia, boasting a large hospital complex and all the necessities of self-sufficiency: a blacksmith's forge, a powder magazine, a guardhouse, and provisions sheds. To the south spread extensive gardens for fresh vegetables; eight blockhouses guarded the perimeters on either side of the river. Dirt dug to create a moat formed embankments, from which sharpened posts rose another dozen feet.

In marked contrast with France's stone fortresses and bastions at Louisbourg, Crown Point, and Carillon, this temporary wooden-walled construction revealed the British conviction that the season's next campaign would drive the balance of power far northward—an assumption that deeply underestimated French capabilities. Edward sat near Hudson Falls. Boat traffic, working the 40 miles upriver from Albany to the falls, was forced to offload at what the Indians called Wahcoloosenchaleva, the Great Carrying Place, for the past quarter century the site of a Dutch fur-trading post.

The men in the hut and their comrades on the island were select rangers, recruited either from the provincial ranks or in the upcountry frontier villages. As Colonel Blanchard would write to Rogers three months later, "The enterprising Youths from our Frontiers, who have and are joining you for the Ranging Service, are not the Gleaning, but the first Fruits of North-America." Often the third and fourth sons of the usual large frontier New England families, they knew that their eldest brothers would inherit the ill-surveyed claims and brutally hard work of the farm. And so they signed up to bring terror and devastation upon the shifty French papists and the dangerous red men who had visited fear and misery upon the frontier for so many decades. But they were also mostly young men in their twenties, eager for adventure, for any tonic to fight the ongoing boredom and hardship of frontier life. If recruited in town by such men as Rogers, the chance to join a cause larger than one's own was intoxicating. It was these spirit-lifting possibilities, not a particular chivalrous loyalty to such a snobbish abstraction as the British Crown, that motivated these men to endure winter garrison duty and the extremities of wilderness combat.

Ask any of them (when officers were absent) about how well the redcoats were fighting their side of the war, and the question would have brought a sneer. For the first two years of the war the king's son, Cumberland, had played at North America like a novice in a game of dice, sending in a series of barely competent commanders. Braddock might have been the best of the lot, but it was provincial troops under the Virginian George Washington who had bailed out his shattered command after the debacle on the Monongahela. Who beat the French regulars under Dieskau at Lake George? Provincials, of course. And where was General Webb when Montcalm attacked William Henry? Panicked in Fort Edward, withholding all possible reinforcements to keep his precious scalp intact, not caring that this must doom the little fort to French occupation and its garrison to Indian massacre, all while Loudoun was taking the cream of the army on a fruitless expedition to Nova Scotia. The rangers learned with disgust how His Lordship had lived the high life in New York over the winter, replete with fancy balls, liveried servants, and carriages. In mid-February an editorial writer for *The Boston Gazette* seethed about the luxury enjoyed by Loudoun and his staff, "while the brave Rogers is acquiring Glory to himself in the Field, and in some Degree recovering the sunken Reputation of his Country." Asked the writer, "When we think of those Seas of Blood which have been inhumanly split in this and the Southern Governments, and the Numbers of our Countrymen ingloriously taken Captive:—One would think it a very impertinent Question to ask, *Is this a Time for Balls and Assemblies?*"[8]

The rangers might have added that Shirley, Loudoun—and now General Abercromby—were no doubt effective enough commanders in the European environment and mode, with its maps, accessible roads, and established channels of reprovisioning. But this was North America, for the most part trackless wilderness, and the British simply were not getting it, while, much to their fury, the French and their Indian allies inflicted one defeat after another. Meanwhile British officers and men continued to brush off the provincial regiments and rangers as little more than mobs in uniform.

With the integration of redcoat and provincial command earlier that year, the colonial and ranger soldiers had fallen under the rules and articles of war, which prescribed corporal punishment for a vast range of delinquencies, a roster of ingeniously brutal measures hammered out over centuries to keep the common soldier in his crudely rigid place. A few soldiers—probably more than enough to leave a lasting impression on the others—ran the gauntlet. For sleeping on guard, "Danniel Boake," as Private Luke Gridley described it, was forced to run between thirty whip-wielding men, a "sorrowful sight." Boake cried, "Lord god have mercy on me," as his blood flew at each stroke.[9] Other punishments, although practiced less than earlier in the century, remained in force, including riding the wooden horse, in which a transgressor was placed astride an elevated horizontal tree trunk with muskets tied to dangle from his legs. The insistent weight proved a source of excruciating pain and often dislocated joints.[10] One lieutenant from Boston had his sword broken over his head in punishment for "Disabligeing Langweg."[11]

Flogging proved the most common punishment, sometimes called "putting on a new shirt," and it was parceled out liberally for infractions ranging from sitting down on guard, wearing a dirty shirt on guard, drunkenness, cheating at cards, insubordination, and deserting to another colony's militia. One black man underwent ninety lashes for selling rum and telling fortunes to the regulars.[12]

On the parade ground stood the whipping post, a stout six-foot-tall pine log dug securely into the earth. Here prisoners were bound and flogged with a cat-o'-nine-tails, whose handle sprouted a medusa head of knotted leather thongs. The whipping post quickly became the most reviled symbol of the uneasy subordination of provincial soldiery to British regular authority.

British corporal punishment particularly galled the entirely volunteer provincials, who viewed themselves in essence as short-term
contract workers, hired to protect the immediate interests of their
community. In contrast, a high proportion of redcoats had often
chosen service to the king instead of going to prison for criminal mis-
behavior. Savage and often arbitrary punishment appeared to the
upper-class officer corps as the only way of keeping these hard cases
in dazed and wretched line.

Unlike their British counterparts, provincials earned their commissions on the basis not just of social standing but by their ability to
recruit, opening up opportunities for capable backwoods farm boys
such as Rogers. A Massachusetts or New Hampshire man might sign
up because he was solicited by a relative or someone of standing in
the community—and he remained in service, even when conditions
grew difficult, not out of fear of punishment but because of such initial obligations, reinforced by a steadily tightening attachment to the
outfit. Kinship and community ties softened military hierarchy,
deeply alarming British officers with their democratic implications.
Rogers capitalized on these conditions, building small-unit spirit
that catapulted his men to new levels of performance and commitment.

That evening the talk in ranger Joshua Atwood's hut turned to
the flogging of their company mates, Samuel Boyd and Henry
Dawson, on charges of illegally procuring rum. To men who routinely
risked their lives on extended patrols while the regulars often stayed
in camp, such an offense had to seem ludicrous. Every ranger in that
hut had come by rum outside the normal channels on occasion. Why
should rangers—and these two in particular—get beaten for such a
petty crime?

To make matters worse, floggings usually were delivered by
preadolescent drummer boys, but since the ranger companies had
no drummers over winter garrison, it fell upon the men themselves
to perform the double indignity of flogging their own comrades-in-
arms.

One of the hutmates may well have known one of the punished
men, or another could have burst into a spontaneous and elegant
summary of their collective humiliations. Perhaps the men had drunk

more than usual; whatever, something that evening turned easy talk and grumbling into violent action. Within moments the rangers' anger boiled out into the camp street. Other rangers picked up the note of mutiny and rallied to the spreading outcry.

Rogers's presence might have chilled the growing rage, but for the past several weeks he had lain bedridden in his hut, sucker-punched by scurvy, which incapacitates the legs with excruciating muscular pain, swells and bursts the gums, and can readily ripen into convulsions, fever, diarrhea, and death. That their leader, who seemed almost divinely impervious to bullet, tomahawk, and frostbite, could fall to an invisible agent had sent further unsettling ripples across the tight-knit ranger community.

The mutineers, by now armed with muskets and axes, coursed over to the whipping post. Grabbing another man's ax, Atwood swiftly hacked down the hated symbol of overbearing British discipline, to raucous cheering.

Looking for further objects upon which to vent their fury, the mob roiled to the guardhouse, where Lieutenant Severance, the acting officer of the guard, had the soldierly resolve to ask their business. Captain John Shepherd ran onto the parade ground, shouting, "Turn out, rangers! Turn out!"[13]

Surrounding the guardhouse, the mob demanded the release of the prisoners therein, probably the two comrades earlier flogged. One of the malcontents reached up and ripped a board off the roof, whereupon the rioters' momentum hit a crescendo, threatening to detonate into full-scale violence.

"Shoot the first man that touches the guard house!" roared Shepherd, who then turned to find Private Abraham Parrot covering him with a loaded musket. He angrily knocked the barrel aside while two men of Stark's company seized Parrot's arms. Shepherd pulled the musket out of Parrot's grip, then glared at the rest of the mutineers. At that point the riot tottered on edge of becoming a melee, as the angry soldiers swarmed around Severance's detachment and Shepherd's and Stark's men closed upon them. Shepherd commanded little respect from these New Englanders. Although he had been a captain in Colonel Nathaniel Meserve's New Hampshire Regiment in 1756 and had made a perilous midwinter escape from

Montréal after falling into Indian hands, he had served as a ranger captain for only nine months.

At that moment Captain Charles Bulkeley strode up to the thick knot of men and demanded explanations. Although Rogers had promoted the big Bay Stater to captain of Hobbs's company of rangers only in April, the men had respected him earlier, as a capable first lieutenant during the 1757 campaign in Nova Scotia. Now the mob's energy dissipated. Go back to your quarters, snapped Bulkeley, while Shepherd put Parrot, Atwood, and four others under arrest.

The roar and cheering carried over the water to the fort, whose commander, Lieutenant Colonel William Haviland of the 27th Foot, dispatched an officer across the pontoon bridge to investigate. After returning with news of the destruction of the whipping post, the officer went to Rogers's hut to demand that he send the six ringleaders over to the fort for interrogation. Rogers obeyed at once and detailed some rangers to escort the prisoners to the fort. Haviland's redcoats roughly corralled them into their guardhouse.

A portrait of Haviland shows pinched features, beady eyes, and a certain haughtiness of upper-class entitlement.[14] Temperament and position predisposed him toward dislike and contempt for the often-unruly rangers. Three weeks earlier news of another act of insubordination had reached his ears. While leading a reconnaissance of Carillon, John Stark ran afoul of Captain Abercrombie, who was accompanying the expedition along with two royal engineers set upon sketching the post. It was a scout that only the scurvy had prevented Rogers from leading himself. Where Rogers had experienced Abercrombie's high-handedness on such a venture the previous year and had jollied his imperial brother along, the taciturn and hardheaded Yankee Stark would do no such thing.

The 300-man scout had taken six days to reach Rattlesnake Mountain, but the view of Carillon from its summit was smothered by fog, frustrating any mapping. At about that time Abercrombie suffered a bad fall, and feared that he had broken his leg. Thereafter things unraveled. At camp near Carillon Abercrombie accused Stark of not posting sentries—hard to believe of someone with Stark's experience in forest warfare and his vivid recollections of walking into an ambush. Stark would have understood that frequent enemy patrols scouring the woods near Carillon made it virtual suicide not to take such precautions, and furthermore, along with most of his men, he could recite Rule Number XIV of Rogers's Rules of Ranging:

> When you encamp at night, fix your centries in such a manner as not to be relieved from the main body till morning, profound secrecy and silence being often of the last importance in these cases. Each centry therefore should consist of six men, two of whom must be constantly alert, and when relieved by their fellows, it should be done without noise; and in case those on duty see or hear any thing, which alarms them, they are not to speak, but one of them is silently to retreat, and acquaint the commanding officer thereof, that proper dispositions may be made; and all occasional centries should be fixed in like manner.

Far more likely the "centries" had exercised such "profound secrecy and silence" that Abercrombie and his tenderfoot subordinates simply did not see or hear them. Stark and his officers shot down Abercrombie's idea of creeping close to the walls in order to secure a prisoner, deciding instead to lay an ambush along the road leading to the fort. The next morning a team of woodcutters, escorted by 16 soldiers, came close but sensibly bolted at first sign of a hostile presence. Abercrombie described what followed with amazement. Stark, lying next to him, "set up the Indian hollow, upon that the whole party jumped up and yelled as if Hell had broke loose & all fell a firing at a few men running away." Leaping to his own feet, Abercrombie "did everything in my power to make them hold their tongues & behaves as they ought to doe," which included knocking several men over and damning their officers "as Scoundrels." Among the rangers, such activity must have come as a bit of a surprise, to say the least, because the rangers often employed such tactics not only to panic their foe into flight or surrender but to draw the main garrison into the open.

Abercrombie's contributions broke the edge of the rangers' charge, but they nonetheless taunted the garrison as cowards who had not rallied to their comrades in peril. When the French responded with cannon fire, Stark wisely chose to retreat, ranger style, which meant the command scattered in small groups through the forest to reassemble at some point fixed upon in advance—again a well-used tactic, clearly outlined by Rogers:

Rule Number X: If the enemy is so superior that you are in danger
of being surrounded by them, let the whole body disperse, and
every one take a different road to the place of rendezvous appointed for that evening, which must every morning be altered and
fixed for the evening ensuing.

Although his men were hardly surrounded, Stark probably calculated that the French would mount a large party in pursuit and that
breaking into smaller parties would confuse their ability to follow.
Abercrombie, at this point completely disgusted at what seemed a
wholly amateurish operation, put together a four-man rear guard and
marched upright and stiffly to the rendezvous. Again, he mistook
for disorder a careful technique of dispersed retreat designed to
disorient pursuers. Such spontaneity and reliance on the lower orders to do things effectively without supervision further reinforced
Abercrombie's already firmly bedded disdain for the rangers, a senti-
ment to which James Wolfe would soon give ample and more memorable voice: "The Pow-wow and pain, and howl operate too strongly
upon the Rangers." Even so, Abercrombie would claim some share of
credit for the raid.

For Stark and his men, this attitude smacked of the most stub-
born, patronizing, and dangerously rigid redcoat approaches to
warfare in an unfamiliar land. Exasperated at Abercrombie's fault-
finding, Stark led his force home, not resisting an attempt to tease his
enragingly obtuse colleague by appearing to confuse South Lake with
a beaver pond, not once but twice.

Stark may have expected that Rogers would respond to his account of Abercrombie's atrocious behavior with an indulgent
chuckle. Regardless, he could not have felt happy under Rogers's
long, hard stare. Such friction between his rangers and those who had
the ear of Loudoun and his second-in-command, Major General
Abercromby, could undercut all Rogers's efforts to raise the professional standing and the numbers of his units. Indeed, when Captain
Abercrombie reported on the scout to Colonel Haviland, he painted
such a dire picture of disobedience and disorder that the furious
commandant summarily discharged 12 rangers from Rogers's,
Stark's, Bulkeley's, and Shepherd's companies. Shepherd, his ears
still ringing from Rogers's dressing-down about the Carillon foul-up,

had come down hard on the two rangers caught stealing rum. The bedridden Rogers had asked Shepherd to oversee the case, but unable to disentangle conflicting stories, the unhappy captain had thrown up his hands and had the men flogged.

Over the next few days Haviland's contempt for and distrust of the rangers became yet clearer. On the eighth he appointed Rogers to head an inquiry but refused his request to bring the accused men before the proceedings, because he "would not trust them where there were so many Mutineers for fear of a rescue."[15] Accordingly Rogers found out little from the comrades of the accused; nor could Shepherd himself verify who had pointed the musket at him. After three days Rogers stopped the inquiry and sent Haviland his written report.

On the sixteenth Haviland summoned the haggard Rogers to the fort for orders to scout Carillon. Rogers brought up the recent incident, suggesting that Haviland go easy on the men still held. Haviland later recorded that Rogers "hoped I would soon put an end to the Affair for it had given him great uneasiness," but inflamed by reports of the Stark fiasco and the mutiny, he viewed Rogers as yet another embodiment of provincial impertinence, and retorted that it would be for General Abercromby to make any such decision.

This ominous response shook Rogers into saying that he "apprehends most of his men will desert," to which Haviland barked that "it would better they were all gone than have such a Riotous sort of people," adding for good measure that if Rogers "could catch me one that attempted it, I would endeavour to have him hanged as an example." Before dismissing Rogers, Haviland berated him for allowing his men to use up so much ammunition, to which Rogers replied that "his people could not do without practicing at marks."[16] Rogers retired across the pontoon bridge to pass on the orders for Carillon. The situation called for what he did best, making a deft and cunning strike into enemy territory. He would deal with the consequences of the mutiny and Stark's scout on his return.

Chapter 13

Taunting His Foe

In general, when pushed upon by the enemy, reserve your fire till
they approach very near, which will then put them into the greatest
surprize and consternation, and give you an opportunity of
rushing upon them with your hatchets and cutlasses to the better
advantage.

ROGERS'S RULES OF RANGING, NUMBER XIII[1]

As Rogers struck out on his raid with 150 men in early January
1758, he had to be deeply worried for his corps. Out of the original
rabble of contentious frontier misfits he had cobbled an elite long-
distance tool. Precisely the characteristic that the British loathed
about the provincials Rogers had wrought to singular advantage, building intense personal bonds among them and pulling them beyond
their own perceived capabilities as they came to belong to something
larger than themselves. In the making here was the special operations
commander and team, knit together initially by the leader's charisma
and strength but somehow transcending the sum of its constituent
parts.

But Rogers would make no headway with the British command
structure, most of his contact with it centering on having to explain
away disciplinary issues. Even though the British entertained a dismissive stereotype of the rangers as a malcontent corps, few had been
detected in really serious misconduct, and desertion rates were lower
than among provincial and regular formations alike.

Rogers knew that the British supreme commander in the New
World, Lord Loudoun, relied on his services. "It is impossible for an

Army to Act in this Country, without *Rangers*," Loudoun had written to the brutal but not stupid Duke of Cumberland, who had fought at Fontenoy in 1745, "and there ought to be a considerable body of them, and the breeding them up to that, will be a great advantage to the Country, for they will be able to deal with Indians in their own way"—an observation farseeing for its time.[2] Cumberland warned Loudoun about relying on Indians and rangers, instructing him to "teach your troops to go out upon Scouting Parties . . . and learn to beat the woods & act as *Irregulars*."[3] While Loudoun needed the rangers, he would have been foolish had he not set out at least to attempt to regularize ranger tactics, dress, and equipment and to bring these rough-hewn warriors into the fabric of the army proper. He decided to turn two companies in each regiment into ranger formations, implementing his plan by granting leave for 55 regulars who would volunteer to join Rogers' Rangers.

In September and October 1757 Rogers ran an informal school for these cadets, taking them on scouts and teaching them ranger techniques in training exercises. To distill intense rough experience into plain memorable instruction that could be "read and reread" (as Napoleon would later advise as the secret of decoding war), Rogers hammered out a 21-page document outlining 28 rules of conduct, which would become North America's first war manual, a clearly worded primer of minor tactics that resonates today. Manual writers and strategic analysts in Europe, such as Humphrey Bland and the Maréchal de Saxe, had articulated elements of *la petite guerre*, but none had so specifically, even scientifically, laid out the operational system of small offensive raiding parties. These European thinkers wrote strictly for highly literate, well-trained officers, whereas Rogers focused on the men themselves. The genius of the rules lies in their complete simplicity and clarity, statements and principles that any soldier might comfortably hold in his head, to be summoned up and naturally put to use when a man was tired and scared. And as befits a man who communicated much of his hard-won war experience through useful tales, the rules themselves are models of quiet storytelling, several of them clumped together about the same subject and enabling a soldier to follow their implicit reasoning almost visually; and these brief pointed precepts furthermore created a framework by which the rangers could analyze the successes and failures of past engagements.

This nearly self-contained tutorial ended with the admonition that most teachers will impart to their students once they've mastered the basics: that the greater part of what they learned would be subject to change according to "a thousand occurrences and circumstances which may happen" that will make it "necessary, in some measure, to depart from them, and to put other arts and stratagems in practice." Then "every man's reason and judgment must be his guide...and preserve a firmness and presence of mind on every occasion." This provision, which seems so plainly commonsensical today, contained the seeds of revolutionary thinking by giving "ordinary men" the tools, the rationale, and, above all, the firm confidence to think for themselves, an idea completely foreign to the British military system.

Just about everything about the raid against Carillon in late December illustrated Rogers's refinement of special force techniques—and revealed that his actions, however bold, were not rash, and however risky, were still well calculated. It is often so of men who push into the most dangerous corners of life—extreme mountain climbers, for instance, or those who plunge into the darkness and treacherous confines of deep caves; however much at first glance they appear to be reckless risk-lovers, the closer one examines them, the more careful and calculating they prove to be. The danger of death can never be exorcized: it will always take some of them. But that is the game on which they thrive, compelling them to match wits with the extremes, with the least predictable factors in an environment that can never be fully grasped in real time. Rogers responded strongly under the unrelentingly harsh rules of that sport, which was particularly unusual in a time when the business of merely surviving consumed so much nerve and energy. Compared to today, few safety nets existed then; needlessly drawing deeply on the slender physical resources available to most men was virtual suicide. The notion of throwing oneself yet further into harm's way on purpose—the idea of climbing a severe mountain, for instance, "because it's there," lay a century and a half in the future—would have struck most of Rogers's contemporaries as lunacy.

In late December 1757 eight days of hard marching in 15 inches of snow or more was arduous enough going for any venturer, and by the time the ranger party halted within 600 yards of the walls of Carillon, Rogers had sent back 27 men who were too tired to continue effectively, ensuring that none of the weakened members would compromise the unit's effort should they meet the enemy, nor slow down movement and bleed the high morale needed to push on deep and hard. The day before, Rogers had ordered the men to cache a day's worth of provisions lest they were repulsed—a clear-eyed anticipation of possible setbacks—which also lightened loads and provided a point of rendezvous. Most important, the cache afforded psychological reinforcement. Should the men find themselves stripped to their shirts and in flight for their lives, the food would give them a chance to rally and recharge before undertaking the long hard journey back to Fort Edward.

Nor did Rogers stop there. Early on the morning of their final advance he chose three rendezvous points "in case of being broke in an action," and he acquainted the officers and men with them, as outlined in his Rule Number X. Rogers used long-standing Indian techniques that acknowledged the savage randomness of warfare in a trackless geography. Thick woods and rugged terrain often prevented parties from registering one another's existence until it came virtually to unslinging tomahawk handles. Such was the general enmity of the "vast, unhospitable desert" toward its penetrators, wrote Edmund Burke, that "victories are not decisive, but defeats are ruinous."[4] Often necessarily small raiding parties encountered far stronger forces and had to melt instantly into the woods. Rather than disperse entirely, Rogers's men retreated in singles and small groups back to a first defensible rendezvous; then to a second, should the first prove untenable; and then, if necessary, "at the third," wrote Rogers in his journals, "to make a stand till the darkness of the night would give us an opportunity to get off." Such a plan could work only if each individual warrior could think for himself.

Late that morning Rogers set up an ambush along the road that led through the woods to the fort, selecting an advance party of 20 men and a rear guard of 15, which snared a lone French sergeant of marines, apparently in an act of desertion. Not long after Rogers finished interrogating the prisoner, a single hunter came into view. Rogers ordered the team to wait until he appeared in the clearing and then to dash in and take him, firing and calling out "in order to intice the enemy from their fort."[5] No one emerged. Captain d'Hebecourt doubled the watch and canceled Christmas Eve midnight Mass. For all these precautions, the rangers sneaked close to the walls and managed to pitch grenades onto five large piles of cordwood within the palisades. The fort ineffectively discharged its cannon while kindling and several outbuildings burned.

The next day the French ventured outside to find the rangers long gone and seventeen dead cattle, one bearing between its horns the following note:

> I am obliged to you, Sir, for the repose you have allowed me to
> take; I thank you for the fresh meat you have sent me; I shall take
> care of my prisoners; I request you to present my compliments to
> the Marquis de Montcalm.
>
> ROGER,
> Commandant of the Independent Companies[6]

The sheer espirit of Rogers's communication and its sparkling arrogance struck a nerve with the French, who were "much provoked at it," General Abercromby informed Loudoun. The recipients put an appropriately aristocratic and dismissive face on the message—"an ill-timed and very low piece of braggadocio," judged Paymaster General André Doreil; but d'Hebecourt did Rogers's obliquely defiant note the honor of passing it on to Governor Vaudreuil, and Montcalm himself wrote that Rogers's billet was "some of this partisan's customary gasconade. Perhaps we can dampen his spirit."[7]

It was the note's tone as much as its menacing physical closeness that made it so unsettling. In his hurried scrawl Rogers had managed to affect a French tone to the letter, as he duplicated the earlier French supremacy in surprise and shock along the frontier. What was more, he had inserted his ranger's long knife to gouge a crack through the French confidence in the supremacy of their partisan fighters. Here was a new kind of self-belief arisen among the New Englanders, whom the French and Canadians had long found to be ponderous and flat-footed in the woods. Rogers and his men had floated like fog closer under the walls of Carillon than any recently comparable French raid on a New England stronghold, striking demoralizing fear into its defenders, and all wrapped in musketeering panache.

The raiders lit up their camp with word of these latest accomplishments, replayed in detail in huts on Rogers' Island and the tents of Fort Edward. Rogers found a letter awaiting him from General Abercromby suggesting that Loudoun might consider expanding the ranger companies after all. Rogers mushed down to Albany through a late December thaw, which made going particularly difficult. The swelling waters of the Adirondack snowmelt drove up the Hudson's water levels, inundating Rogers' Island and flooding the Fort Edward moat.

General Abercromby received a "fatigued" Rogers, but nonetheless the pair enjoyed "a deal of Conversation together, and consequently a good Share of Nonsense," chuckling over Rogers's calling card. In the face of the damning instances of mutiny and the Stark-Abercrombie raid, Rogers explained his position: nine men had decamped recently under overly severe discipline, and "many more" would desert if such conditions persisted. At that point, Abercromby, however much he was carried along by Rogers's bonhomie, must have felt some doubts about conceding the rangers special standing. But Rogers then added that Colonel Haviland had ripened the already-heating animosities when he kept the mutineers locked in the Fort Edward guardhouse. Rangers charged with misdemeanors, Rogers argued, should be "tryed by their own officers, in the manner of the Regimental Court Martials," an approach with which General Abercromby could find little reason to disagree. He sent Rogers off to Loudoun with a sealed letter in which he reaffirmed the bearer's value as "so necessary and useful a Man" but still acknowledged sharing Loudoun's reservations.[8]

Rogers recorded in his journal that Loudoun received him "in a friendly manner," and in the next several days' meetings, while rebuking him over the mutiny business, Loudoun also examined him as to how many ranger companies he might be able to raise and who was fit to lead them. His Lordship was no fool. By the end of 1757 the colonial elites were alarmed at the tide of French success. Deeply concerned that the campaign of 1758 could bring disaster, even the colonies' submission to invaders, they were pushing London to make peace on any terms. Loudoun had recently dropped his idea of training two companies of rangers for each regiment when Thomas Gage of the 44th Foot had approached him with a plan to raise a new 500-man unit of Light Armed Foot, which would be known as the 80th Regiment, out of his own pocket. Many of the 55 graduates of Rogers's ranging school that fall would fill these ranks. No doubt Loudoun believed that light regulars of this kind, the first such corps in the British army, would eventually replace the colonial light formations; so he gave permission, which must have galled Rogers when he compared his record with Gage's to date. Still, the plans for a winter thrust against Carillon stood, of which the rangers remained an essential component.

Rogers returned with a proposal for eight new companies. Concerned about the expense of such independent units, Loudoun finally gave his approval for five, including one of Indians. The 100-man units would be captained by James Rogers, William Stark, John McCurdy, and Jonathan Brewer; Moses Brewer would put together 100 Connecticut Mohegans, all men to be "able bodied, well acquainted with the Woods, used to Hunting, and every way qualified for the Ranging Service."

Rogers also presented a bold plan of attack. He proposed to travel north with 400 men, skirting Carillon, and to surprise the first French sleigh convoy to show up. Changing clothes with the prisoners, Rogers and a selected sleigh-borne detail could then drive straight into the fort and secure it in a single blow. Once Fort Saint-Frédéric was in British hands, he argued, it could squeeze Carillon into submission. "I have heard him talk of this to M. G. Abercromby," Loudoun wrote in his journal, "who will tell him when tis proper to attempt it. I am forced to do this as he will break into my Plan of taking Ticonderoga if the Frost Permits."[9] Had Rogers's plan gone as intended, and assuming that he had an even chance of attaining his goal, the war might have been shortened by a year or more. As it was, Loudoun's winter attack never materialized, and with it went Rogers's opportunity.

When he returned to Fort Edward on January 25, 1758, the cold had reasserted itself. Snow obscured much of the flood damage, and the men had cleaned out the mud and silt from inside their huts and rebuilt the "necessary houses" carried away by high waters. The surge's only obvious remaining mark was the cracked and heaved in-shore ice along the riverbanks, but it had also swept away the wood supplies that the rangers had been seasoning to make hundreds of pairs of snowshoes for the proposed midwinter offensive.

While Rogers returned without a major's commission, he had reason to feel confident. Tailors in Albany were sewing handsome thick green woolen greatcoats, lined with green serge and adorned with white metal buttons, for his outfit. Officers' coats bore silver lacing and cord or braid. There were to be white silver-lace hats for parades and jackets, waistcoats, breeches, and leggings from thinner green wool. Rogers's new captains were out recruiting across New England. What was more, General Abercromby ordered Haviland to release the six mutineers to Rogers.

Haviland seethed. Not only had Rogers subjected him to an end run over the mutineers, he knew that Rogers's star shone at his expense. The tensions between the two continued to mount, soon becoming evident to everyone on the island. "Som of ye Rangers Went a Hunting & Fired Several Guns in Hearing of ye Garrison—About which Col. Haviland & Majr Rogers Had Som Diferance &c," confided Pvt. Jabez Fitch to his journal on February 19.[10]

Captain-Lieutenant Henry Pringle of the 27th Foot wrote admiringly that the rangers "shoot amazingly well, all Ball, & mostly with riffled Barrels. One of their officers the other day, at four shots with four balls, killed a brace of Deer, a Pheasant, and a pair of wild ducks—the latter he killed at one Shot." The rangers, he continued, went out in groups of six to scout, hunt, and sharpen their marksmanship. But Haviland, seeing only the cost of powder and ball, not the edge it imparted in the field, forbade shooting at marks on the island. Thereupon the rangers simply rowed across to the mainland and continued their practicing, pointedly within earshot.

In February unusually hard snows dashed Loudoun's winter plans. John Stark and forty-two rangers took Lieutenant Mathew Leslie of the Royal Engineers north and found four to five feet of snow burying the King's Highway on the eastern edge of the lake, whose own surface, reported Leslie, was covered with 17 inches of snow—hardly ideal offensive conditions. On the twenty-sixth Loudoun called off the expedition, ordering all "Stors that was Brought Up for that Porpos To Be Carryd Back &c.," wrote a disappointed Fitch. Over the next several weeks caravans of sleighs loaded with munitions, scaling ladders, and a mass of various equipment ground southward to Albany.

Rogers's plan of striking north with 400 men remained alive. Haviland publicly announced that Israel Putnam, captain in the Connecticut provincials, would lead a scout of 115 men, including some of Rogers's own people, north on the twenty-eighth. Rogers later noted with some bitterness that Haviland gave "out publickly at the same time, that, upon Putnam's return, I should be sent to the French forts with a strong party of 400 Rangers. This was known not only to all the officers, but soldiers also, at Fort Edward before Putnam's departure." Long had Rogers admired the Indian ways of secrecy, noting later that a chief must exercise "secrecy in all his operations; in which art they greatly excell, their designs being seldom known to any but themselves, till they are upon the point of being executed." He bristled at the public disclosure of plans and waited grimly for Putnam's return.

On March 6 his worst fears seemed confirmed, when a train of 30-odd sleighs that had left only an hour earlier returned in panic. In broad morning light, not far north of Saratoga, four Ottawa Indians had surprised one of the sleighs, killed and scalped two soldiers, and carried off the sutler's servant.

Well aware that this simple prisoner could spill the British plans, Rogers chose an extreme emergency detail, and in less than fifteen minutes they snowshoed off—"most of them stripped to their Shirts," wrote an Albany stringer for *The Boston Evening-Post*. Rogers drove them hard until at last they picked up the blood-bespattered trail. But the four-mile head start proved too much even for the much-motivated rangers, who came back at midnight with only "an Indian Cap, Tomahawk, and Snowshoes."[11]

Their return was greeted by yet more foreboding news: Putnam's raiders had returned not only without gaining useful intelligence but missing one John Robens, who had disappeared, noted Fitch enigmatically "in a Vary Strang Manner."[12] Robens had had a rocky past, marked by episodes of disobedience and drunkenness that had on occasion landed him in the guardhouse. A fellow ranger might have settled a score with him deep the woods, or the man may simply have gotten lost and died; the record does not show. But to the now-exhausted Rogers, Robens's disappearance, piling upon this desperate vain mission, could only increase the likelihood of disaster. It was hard not to entertain the fear that this chronic troublemaker had deserted, intending to spread word of the impending assault to sweeten his defection.

Haviland had one more surprise up his sleeve, enough to throw Rogers into the darkest mood. When Haviland handed him his orders for the attack on Carillon, Rogers discovered to his incredulity that his force had been cut to 180 men, only 65 more than Putnam's recent patrol. "As there was the greatest reason to suspect," he wrote later, "that the French were, by the prisoner and deserter above mentioned, fully informed of the design of sending me out upon Putnam's return: what could I think to see my party, instead of being strengthend and augmented, reduced to less than one half the number at first proposed. I must confess it appeared to me (ignorant and unskilled as I then was in politicks and the art of war) incomprehensible; but my commander doubtless had his reasons, and is able to vindicate his own conduct."[13] Haviland had emasculated the Carillon expedition, reducing it from a force capable of storming its objective to a mere reconnaissance unit even smaller than Stark's in the November sortie. Was Haviland purposefully sending them to their deaths? In light of what would soon come about in the winter woods, Rogers would not be unreasonable in entertaining such thoughts.

But it is hard to ascribe such forethoughtful malice to this all-too-average field officer, however deep his disdain for the rangers. He probably felt that they had little chance of success, especially after Putnam had fallen so far short of target in the bad weather. Yet he did know that Rogers was extremely capable, so he could imagine that the plan of taking Fort Saint-Frédéric might succeed. A bold coup by this man was something that he perhaps could not stomach, primarily because he had staked so much upon disparaging him to superiors. He could never forgive Rogers for circumventing punishment for the mutineers, for his ongoing insubordinate marksmanship practice, or for the rangers' behavior toward Captain Abercrombie.

Rogers gathered up his men and did what he knew best, preparing them for a tough, perhaps brutally compromised, scout. On the mid-morning of March 10 he marched northward with 183 men, filled "with no little concern and uneasiness of mind."[14]

Chapter 13

Battle on Snowshoes

On other occasions I fought for victory, but today
I fought for my life.

JULIUS CAESAR, ON HIS LAST BATTLE,
AT MUNDA, 45 B.C.

Not long before the hard late-winter noon of March 10, 1758, Rogers, 175 rangers, and eight British regular volunteers from the 27th Foot crested the embankment commanding the blackened ruins of Fort William Henry. The wide southern shore of Lake George stretched before them. A quick scope with a brass spyglass of the long ice down to the narrows disclosed no enemy patrols. As he rubbed his wrist, reducing at least for a moment the throbbing that cold awoke in the scarred flesh, Rogers posted sentries east and west of the main force.

Some of the men pulled off their snowshoes to tighten the ever-loosening leather-thong webbing; others dragged deeply on their two-quart canteens, the bite of ground ginger pinching their tongues. The remains of the fort's shattered walls broke through the heavy snow, a still rawly tangible memory to many rangers who had known men who were now skeletons along the lakeshore or starving prisoners in Canada.

Rogers's thoughts may have turned to his brother Richard that morning, dead here from smallpox and laid in the little cemetery, only to be disinterred and scalped by Montcalm's Indians. Perhaps he felt a momentary wish that his brother could stand beside him now and see how the men had shaped up, but such reflections would have proved fleeting: Rogers almost always displayed a close-to-disturbing power of moving on to the task at hand, dropping all but the most critical elements in light of the current plan. His synoptic focus enabled him to review all possible iterations, which he could bring before his mind's sleepless eye.

Upon Haviland's unsettling orders, he had quickly swept through the 400 ranger volunteers in their four companies, paring the expedition down to 180. Among those he included were veterans of ranger service such as Captain Charles Bulkeley, who had helped pacify the recent mutiny and could be counted on to keep cool under fire; and Lieutenant Billy Phillips, grimly proven in the snowshoe battle along Trout Brook, who had demonstrated again and again that when it came to marksmanship, he and his men had no peers among the British forces in North America.

Rogers also chose some promising tenderfeet, such as Edward Crofton, a newly minted second lieutenant in Stark's company, who had left Sir John Whiteford's regiment in England to come to North America, unattached to any corps, as a freelance volunteer. Crofton called out a superior officer to a duel, after which Lord Loudoun pushed the hot-tempered Englishman into the rangers' cadet cadre. Rogers liked this newcomer, as eager as he was explosive, who picked up ranging techniques quickly, exhibited no sense of British superiority over the provincials, and fit in well with the men.

For Lieutenant James Pottinger of the 44th, the rangers represented his last chance to keep a commission that he had forfeited by being "rendered intierly unfitt for Service by Drink," as Loudoun noted with hard Scots directness, which says something indeed in an army—and society—where hard drinking was the norm.[1] Pleading for a second chance, Pottinger wrote Loudoun that a camp woman had "led him into such a habit of drinking, that not only affected [my] understanding, but likewise [my] health, to such a degree, as to almost deprive [me] of the use of [my] limbs."[2] Loudoun determined that Pottinger could enroll in the rangers if he kept dry and if Rogers would have him. Rogers indeed welcomed him, not only for his combat record in the War of the Austrian Succession and with Braddock at the Monongahela, but less explicitly because Pottinger longed to fight and had no other outfit to do it in. That March his mistress had disappeared, leaving him with custody of their four-month-old baby.

Rogers also took along eight volunteers from the 27th, perhaps as a gesture to Haviland but also because he enjoyed the company of Captain Henry Pringle, with whom, unbeknownst to Pringle's stiff commanding officer, he had dined and drunk rum. Pringle's and Edward Roche's inexperience on snowshoes worried him a bit, but he figured that he could take care of them. So far he had not seen much injury among his men aside from some mild tendinitis, a consequence of hard going through winter country, but nothing to warrant sending any sufferers back, a crucial consideration given his drastically low-ered numbers.

Events of the past several days had forced him to table his bold plan to steal into Crown Point disguised as sleigh drivers on a provi-sion run. Haviland's reduction left him with a detachment neither small enough to move swiftly and invisibly, nor large enough to throw off a sustained attack. Rogers therefore made a more modest plan to harass the enemy, perhaps by ambushing a patrol rumored to leave Carillon every morning.

The rangers tied the snowshoes to their packs or onto their little sleds before attaching iron ice-creepers to their moccasins and begin-ning the familiar 12-mile scramble down Lake George, shadowing the eastern shore until they went into camp at the Narrows. After dark Rogers sent an advance party three miles north, who found no trace of the enemy. Nonetheless he "kept parties walking on the lake all night, besides centries at all necessary places on the land."[3] Rogers took no unnecessary chances, an essential quality of all effective field commanders, who worry about minute details that are within their control exactly because so many factors lie beyond it. In a day long before field manuals addressed themselves to mastering the minutiae of woods combat, Rogers dedicated himself not just to developing clever tactics but to ensuring that the men kept their musket pans clean, always secured the knots on their snowshoes, and sewed up tears in their moccasins at the earliest opportunity.

On March 12 he roused his command well before sunrise, in keeping with Rule Number XV, which specifies that since dawn was "the time when the savages chuse to fall upon their enemies, you should by all means be in readiness to receive them." Just before that moment temperatures fall to the coldest of the day, and all but the most comfortably sheltered—but especially troops on brutally demanding assignments—are peculiarly susceptible to sluggishness and dark thoughts. As the new sun awakened the landscape, the rangers packed up their frozen bearskins, massaged calf muscles still stiff from yesterday's exertions, and waited, steam issuing from their mouths at every exhalation, as a small patrol circled the perimeter for evidence of enemy activity. Each by then recognized the tightening and numbness of the face that marks the first stage of flesh freezing, followed by a pinging sensation, akin to a mild electric shock.[4] They set vigorously to rubbing their noses and cheeks with their rough woolen marksmen's mittens, the thumb and trigger finger separated,[5] to bring the blood racing back.

By first light the unit again struck north but stopped after three miles when Rogers spied a dog trotting across the lake, a common in-dicator of an enemy patrol. Careful examination of a forested island nearby revealed no evidence of activity, but the rangers made landfall anyway, strapping on snowshoes and melting into the woods to await nightfall before moving back onto the ice "to prevent any party from descrying us on the lake, from hills, or otherwise."[6]

In nearly impenetrable darkness the column advanced in close or-der to minimize the chances of accidental separation, while a flank party moved quietly between them and the western shore. Lieutenant Phillips and 15 men skated ahead. Eight miles shy of the southern outpost that the French had established on Lake George's western edge, near present-day Hague, word came from the advance guard of a fire on the eastern shore. Investigation turned up no evidence of the enemy, and the forward detachment acknowledged that their eyes might have been fooled by "some bleach patches of snow, or pieces of rotten wood ... (which in the night, at a distance resembles it)." The rangers would have known foxfire, the bioluminescence of certain fungi growing on decaying timber, but Rogers would later en-ter a footnote in his journal that "a small party of French, as we have since heard, had a fire here at this time; but, discovering my advance party, extinguished their fire, and carried the news of our approach to the French fort."

While the rangers camped fireless that March 12 on the western shore just south of Bald Mountain, Carillon bustled with the arrival of Ensign Sieur de La Durantaye of the Compagnies Franches de la Marine with reinforcements from Montréal. Thirty soldiers and 200

Iroquois and Nipissing Indians from Sault Saint-Louis and the Lake of the Two Mountains fell upon the garrison's hot food and brandy, vowing to go patrolling and raiding after a few days' rest.

That evening an Indian elder "went into a trance," recorded a French captain,[7] and came to with troubling visions. Such dreams, most often visiting the wise on a fast before battle, carried great weight among the Eastern Woodlands peoples, Rogers would observe in his *A Concise Account of North America*, serving as a "kind of religious ceremony" in which a "divine enthusiasm, and a kind of in-spiration" was often revealed. Shamans, not unlike some "Christians in Europe," he continued, "often persuade the people that they have revelations of future events, and that they are authorised to com-mand them to pursue such and such measures."[8] On this March night the shaman reported "seeing" an English party on the move toward Carillon. No evidence suggests that the captured sutler's servant or Putnam's possible deserter had alerted the French to Rogers's de-signs, but had information come into camp somehow? Whatever in-spired him, the possessed elder insisted that the garrison must not wait but must head out for urgent action on the morrow.

That next morning at seven A.M. Rogers and his men cached sleds and extra equipment near the shore. Then they snowshoed north-west and around the southern and western flanks of Bald Mountain into the wide contours of the Trout Brook Valley, keeping the steep-flanked, 1,200-foot Cooks Mountain between them and the French strongpoint over their right shoulders.

Bald Mountain lies right up against Lake George, extending be-yond by a saddle joining the northward-stretching pair of Cooks and Bear Mountains, along whose flanks there curves Trout Brook. It meets the La Chute River east-northeast around Bear Mountain where Lake George narrows, not far from the Ticonderoga peninsula and Carillon. French patrols often looped southwest from the fort, then south down Trout Brook Valley to cut across the saddle, then skirted the western lakeshore north back to base. In winter frozen streams often present the best surface for travel, because ice congeals level and snow accumulates there less than on the hard-frozen banks; so Rogers planned to set up an ambuscade along the streambank on the morrow.

At noon on that coldly well-lit day, after four hours of fighting four feet of snow that made for "very bad travelling," Rogers called a halt, calculating that by midafternoon the daily patrol from Carillon would have completed its circuit. At three P.M. he could move down the brook to take a strong ambush position to intercept the next day's patrol. The men ate a cold meal.

Unbeknownst to Rogers, earlier that day a 20-man Indian war party had come across broken snow caused by the passage of dozens of ice-creepers, disappearing into the woods just south of Bald Mountain; they raced back up the Lake George ice to Carillon and verified the shaman's vision, throwing the recently arrived warriors into a storm of preparation. Shortly thereafter Ensign de La Durantaye led a mostly Indian troop out of the fort, followed some minutes later by 200 soldiers and Indians under Ensign Jean-Baptiste Langy, a formidable French Canadian partisan fighter who Montcalm described as understanding *"petite guerre* the best of any man."[9]

The ranger column wound close to the foot of the mountain in single file that they "might better observe the rivulet, on the ice of which I imagined the enemy would travel if out," wrote Rogers. His advance party, about a dozen strong, was followed by Bulkeley's division, then his own; a rear guard of 11 men, commanded by the newly commissioned ensigns Joseph Waite and James White, came well to the rear.

After they had traveled nearly a mile and a half, a runner from the lead detail returned with news that an enemy patrol was moving up the brook. He was promptly sent "back again to See if they could ascertain the Number." The two divisions and the rear guard dropped their packs and blankets, undid the protective coverings on their muskets, pulled the tompions from the muzzles, and awaited orders. Word came that the enemy numbered 96, mostly Indians. The count was probably not as exact as indicated but was a fairly accurate eyeball by fast-moving scouts needing to gather intelligence quickly without being observed.

Rogers ordered his force to a depression immediately behind the brook's gently sloping 30-foot-tall bank, where men on the ice below would not see them. Hoarse whispers passed the word to stand and fire only after Rogers discharged his piece.

Arrayed along a front of several hundred yards, the rangers did not have to wait long for the blanket-draped, snowshoed Indians, faces painted bloodred and black, to glide by on the icy surface. First they passed Ensign Gregory McDonald's advance guard, then Bulkeley's unit. The lead Indians held their heads still and straight, but their eyes swept furiously back and forth, widening their range of vision as much as possible, alert for any anomaly in the pattern of the woods, perhaps a slight but uncharacteristic movement or a patch of unusual texture; but nothing jarred the winter stillness. The rangers' tightened breathing allowed them to hear all too clearly the soft slap of snowshoe on snow, the creak of leather thongs.

Rogers waited until "their front was nearly opposite to our left wing" before opening fire. Rising and scrambling over the lip of the bank with a roar, the rangers unloosed a volley into the mass some 60 yards in front of them. Some of the enemy pitched to the ice; the rest fled downstream, adrenaline driving them headlong over snow pressed by their own passage. Those rangers who had not fired in the first volley aimed their muzzles ahead of the fleeing men by several feet, then fired as though tracking a deer in flight.

Black-powder muskets discharge lead balls at somewhere between 1,000 to 2,000 feet per second, losing 500-feet-per-second momentum over 100 yards.[10] Add to that the "hang time," or lapse between squeezing the trigger and igniting the charge, which, although measured in fractions of a second, gave a running man up to half a dozen feet before the ball reached his distance. Knowing how much to lead came from instinct honed by experience. Unlike later automatic weapons, which can be adjusted quickly as the shooter registers whether the bullets are kicking up before or behind their target (and modern ammunition affords far more visible impact), musketeers or early riflemen had the one shot to bring down their prey, human or animal. Uncertain footing, nerves, and the need to aim downhill made targeting difficult. Tree trunks and branches deflected or intercepted many shots. Such difficulties explain why even now relatively few men are brought down in an ambush by the first and second discharges. Of the approximately 96 Indians, only perhaps a dozen took bullets.

"I now imagined the enemy totally defeated," Rogers later wrote.[11] He yelled for McDonald in fox-hunting idiom to "head 'em," but many escaped as the rangers stumbled down the steep bank to

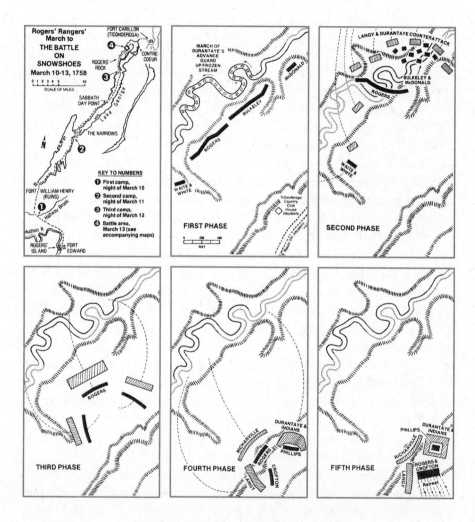

Battle on Snowshoes Schematic, 1758

the ice. "About one half of our people," reported Rogers, including much of Captain Bulkeley's unit, Lieutenants Increase Moore, Archibald Campbell, and James Pottinger, and Ensign James White, joined the pursuit, charging their muskets from their powderhorns as they plunged on. Perhaps winded, Lieutenant Crofton turned back after 50 yards to Rogers's company, which had set to killing the wounded and scalping the corpses. This act would save his life.

Then, as so often with the fortunes of battle, came a precipitate reversal. Bulkeley's and McDonald's men turned the brook's next snakelike bend—and came face to face with the roughly formed battle line of Langy's main body; up until then it had been masked by twists and steep banks, although it was closely following the advance Indian party. The moment of total shock dissolved into the flame and roar of a French volley delivered point-blank. More often than not it found its mark, tearing into skull and chest, shattering bone, and ripping large entrance and exit wounds that spilled blood copiously onto the ice. Lieutenant Pottinger went down, as did all the officers except two. Lieutenant Moore and Ensign McDonald managed to rally the survivors in retreat before falling dead from wounds that they had willed themselves to overcome until they had discharged their prime responsibilities.

Some 50 rangers perished, some from the volley, others crashing into one another and falling over in the panicked confusion, seconds before the French and Indians fell upon them with tomahawk and long knife. The fighters from Carillon slammed their snowshoes down on the fleeing rangers' footgear, stopping them abruptly, then dispatched them with tomahawk swings to the skull.

Black-powder muskets discharge clouds of dense whitish smoke that tend to hang when there is no wind to blow them away; so within moments a field of combat is obscured. Hundreds of flailing men were funneled into the brook's narrow course, the desperateness of their struggle unseen, only their screams and the bark of their muskets discernible. After twenty yards or so, low-velocity lead musket balls, fired with black powder, delivered devastating wounds without knocking their victims over. Time and again that afternoon men would see a bloody hole suddenly open in a comrade's face and the shock of realization sink in as the man stood his ground as he died.[12]

Winter warfare at close quarters with eighteenth-century weapons was terrifying in its intensity and demands on the human system, especially now for the rangers, who were a hard two days' march from reinforcement in the exhausting cold. Men exchanged deadly blows in a frenzy of noise and confusion. In a matter of seconds the quiet winter woods howled into a nightmare of sensory overload; the men's hearing was assaulted by screams of the wounded, by curses, grunts and groans, and musket shots; meanwhile the sickeningly rich, meaty reek of fresh-spilled blood, the stench of terror-discharged urine, the steam of intense body odor, the whiff of black powder, and most of all the reek of fear flooded their nostrils. In battle, respiration increases, men's faces grow ruddy, their voices rise in register, their hearts pound, and their mouths often flood with bitterness. In minutes Langy's men were caving in the right flank of Rogers's company.

Rogers' Rangers were on the verge of annihilation.

Chapter 15

Blood on the Snow

*If the enemy is so superior that you are in danger of being surrounded by
them, let the whole body disperse, and every one take a different road to
the place of rendezvous appointed for that evening, which must every
morning be altered and fixed for the evening ensuing, in order to bring
the whole party, or as many of them as possible, together, after any
separation that may happen in the day; but if you should happen to be
actually surrounded, form yourself into a square, or if in the woods, a
circle is best, and, if possible, make a stand till the darkness of the night
favours your escape.*

ROGERS'S RULES OF RANGING, NUMBER X[1]

Against this sudden horror Rogers stood, strangely undismayed.
His voice cutting the pandemonium, he roared his men back to their
packs beyond the stream-bank crest. If their command had been in-
coherently dispersed, the company would have been fast enveloped
and destroyed. (Dazed by the sudden and overwhelming violence of
the counterattack, Rogers later reckoned French strength at 600
men, although it was only a third of that.)

Cajoling and pushing, Rogers somehow managed to rally his men,
on the edge of dissolving into a doomed rabble, to retreat from the
carnage. As they scrambled upslope, he spread them out, to avoid outflanking and a general massacre. Thanks largely to his composure—
he had something of the command presence of Washington on
horseback—the fragmented rangers fell back "in pretty good order,"
claimed the higher ground, and checked the French pursuit with

brisk volleying. His men, Rogers reported, "fought with such intrepidity and bravery as obliged the enemy to retreat a second time."
Given the appalling casualties of the last fifteen minutes—more than
a quarter of the whole of his force down, and all but a handful of the
officers—there was no question of pressing the again-shaken enemy.
The counterattack had cut off the rear guard; only Ensign Waite and
two privates out of 13 men in all had broken through.

For a moment the gasping rangers, now protected by trees,
caught their breath, and shot nervous looks back toward the brook. In
the thirty seconds it took to reload, each man tried to work out
whether the enemy most obviously trying to kill him might be close
enough to cover the ground separating them. The survivors became
aware of the gravity of their situation, much as the dampness slipped
treacherously into the sweat-drenched wool and linen clinging sod-
denly to their skin. They heard the cries of rage as the Indians discovered the scalped corpses of the advance guard. A ranger's shriek for
mercy rose in high-pitched anguish, then stopped abruptly.

Adrenaline pulsing the beat of their hearts loudly in their ears was
no common sensation for most men in preindustrial societies. Such
rushes of quick decision, if they came at all, were perhaps experienced on a hunt or while negotiating a series of rapids in a canoe. But
they were certainly not nearly as common or as dangerous as the relentless guantlet of choices people experience today just by driving
down a highway or even playing a video game. The novelty would often send men bolting into the woods, propelled by the frantic need to
be anywhere else. Yet these men stayed still, coolly working their
muskets, partly because of the cohesion of their outfit but also out of
faith in their leader.

The wreck of Rogers's command faced a force now more than
double theirs, which quickly regained lost ground. Once more the enemy pressed on the rangers' center and wings, only again to be sent
reeling backward. No sooner had they pulled back for that third time
than Rogers saw a strong contingent of Indians purposefully kicking
their snowshoes into the ridge on his right. He could spare only
Lieutenant Phillips and 18 men, who hightailed it across the slope,
managing to retain their slight height advantage and to lay down an
accurate and withering fire that checked the Indians on their flank.

Rogers sent Lieutenant Crofton and 15 men, along with Pringle, Roche, and some of the volunteers from the 27th Foot, to secure the left against any other such move.

The fighting closed to 20 yards. The gunfire petered out to sporadic shots as both sides preserved ammunition and awaited clear targets, but sometimes the opponents heaved into one another, savaging each other with bayonet, tomahawk, and long knife in the deep snow. Rarely have men exchanged close-hand mortal blows under such exhausting intimacy for the more than ninety minutes it lasted.

Not just the attackers' plain superiority of numbers, but the capacity to extend and enfilade that such numbers provide, caused the ranger lines to dwindle. Rogers, now aware that eight officers and more than 100 privates were down in the bloody snow, ordered the crumbling center back uphill toward Phillips and Crofton, but the French pressed upon them "with numbers that we could not withstand." Durantaye and his Iroquois and Nipissings finally drove in between Phillips and Rogers to surround Phillips's remnant.

Realizing how close they were to being overwhelmed, Phillips parleyed frantically in French and soon could yell over to Rogers that they had been offered "good quarters" and that he thought it best to surrender, but if overruled he would "fight while he had one man left to fire a gun." Rogers probably shouted back his assent and wished Billy good luck. A leader's power to have his men fight to the death rests partly on his preparedness to let them yield in the face of pointless slaughter.

As soon as Phillips's helplessly isolated and disordered survivors, trapped along the right flank, had thrown down their arms, the Indians bound them to trees, probably with lengths of deerskin thong from tumplines. Their promised quarter would not long hold. Angered at their high losses, the braves set about hacking most of their captives to death "in a most barbarous and shocking manner,"[2] as Rogers would later learn. Only seven of those who surrendered, including Phillips, survived.[3]

Rogers surveyed his thinned ranks, as the men scraped their fouled guns. Their right cheeks were seared by powder, their eyebrows were burned, their shoulders were sore from dozens of smashing recoils, their clothing was pocked with scattered pinhole burns from sparked powder. Each passed a glazed glance back over the line, eyes sunk into the long stares brutally born of greater fear and stress than the system can handle.

At about six o'clock Rogers shifted his strategy simply to buy time, slugging it out until the approaching darkness thickened enough to cover some kind of escape. The sun had dipped below the far western ridge about an hour earlier. (True sunset had come at 5:58, but the powerful snow-diffused afterlight remained deadly present to the end of civil twilight at 6:26 P.M.)[4] But the line could hold no longer, and Rogers decided, in the characteristically understated voice of his journals, that it was "most prudent to retreat."[5]

Pringle urged that they make a last stand; his snowshoe webbing had loosened considerably, as had Roche's—which, compounded by their lack of snowshoeing experience, gave them no chance of moving fast. Rogers offered to detail a sergeant to accompany them.

At his word, such as were left of what at noon had been the finest Engligh-speaking special force in the world scattered upslope and along the ridge toward the saddle between Bald and Cooks Mountains, about a mile and a half directly south. Even exhausted and wounded men (if they were rangers) could snowshoe the mile-long passage across the saddle down to Lake George, overcoming the relatively gentle rise of 250 feet and descending that same amount. But the Indians knew that this was the only way out.

Pringle and Roche leaned against a large rock along the path and waited for certain capture or death. "Every instant we expected the Savages," wrote Pringle, but they did not come. "...What induced them to quit this path, in which we actually saw them, we are ignorant of, unless they changed it for a shorter, to intercept those who had just left us." The Indians may well have cut a lower and possibly faster way along the contour lines; besides, direct pursuit would have laid them open to ambush. Rogers noted that "the Indians closely pursuing us at the same time, took several prisoners." For the moment Pringle and Roche had escaped one horrible fate.

Rogers does not describe the following two hours, simply writing that "we came to Lake George in the evening, where we found several wounded men, whom we took with us to the place where we had left our sleds." But before reaching the ice at about eight o'clock, he had accomplished a remarkable feat. It was perhaps the most famous action of his life, and yet it must be pieced together by speculation.

Sheer animal power had enabled him to outdistance all but the toughest of his men; that the wounded beat him to the ice suggests that he had spent the two silent hours doing something else, perhaps fighting to win a last desperately needed margin for what was left of his command to lose themselves in the woods.

The waxing quarter moon shed all too much light over that clear evening, especially in the snow, for ranger and Indian alike.[6] The defeated force climbed up and back, trying to work as fast as possible along the southward contour lines toward the saddle. With death snapping at their heels, they drove themselves without respite, climbing over downed trees, pushing through low branches, praying that their snowshoe webbing would hold out.

It is not clear how the survivors gained the ice, whether by passing through the saddle around the south end of Bald Mountain, or by climbing up and over the mountain itself. Rogers knew it well, its naked granite cliff breaking off into a near-700-foot fall to the lakeshore, commanding a superb lookout up and down the watercourse.

Rogers boiled with fury that Haviland had sent him out so carelessly undermanned to unnecessary disaster and the butchery of so many good men who should have been by now celebrating under the guns of Carillon. Now, instead of planning to make the final leap at the enemy's throat, he had to put all his resources just into getting the survivors home.

A hike up Bald Mountain takes about twenty minutes; the scramble over boulders and around trees occasionally calls for the use of hands as well as feet. For a 26-year-old ranger captain with much to drive him, the climb would have presented few problems, though it might have taken slightly longer on snowshoes.

Should he have desired to distract the enemy warriors from their blood chase, one effective move, given his power and self-confidence, would have been to clamber upslope making a deliberate racket, then outlining his figure with artful carelessness among the shadows of the moon. Even under such duress, the hunter's pleasure in deadly play with those seeking his destruction energized Rogers's steps, and the climb gave the forest master ample time to shape a plan. He reached the moon-charged prospect of the frozen lake well ahead of his pursuers.

Some insist that he simply sailed off the cliff, but a jump like that, even allowing for a drift of snow heaped against the base of the precipice, would have been virtual suicide, barring wizardly good fortune—and Rogers's past shows no signs of reliance on blind chance. One student of his career has suggested that he raced to the lip of the cliff, then untied his snowshoes, turned them around, retied them, and backtracked to a spot where he could plunge into the snow undetected.

Such a stratagem would not have fooled the deadly woodsmen on his trail. More probably he moved quickly southwestward another 60 feet along the cliff face, where a crease cuts sharply into the rock; its harsh steepness still offers several small terraces and trees upon which a strong and agile man hurtling lakeward could gain braking purchase. Given the depth of the snow, and his familiarity with the mountain that may well have included descents in warmer weather, and his likely fate were he captured, it is certainly feasible that he improvised a sort of military triathlon, shoe-skiing, jumping, and climbing down this crude but masterable path—possibly masterable, that is, to someone like him. His pursuers may well have thought that he had flown off the mountain face, but certainly they would not have followed even if they had seen him descend the notch.

However he made it down—perhaps, for instance, he just continued along the ridge, which winds indirectly to meet the foot of the mountain—he may have decided not to mention it in his journals lest it appear too desperate. Yet again the feat may not have seemed noteworthy to a man whose record was maintained so publicly. It could have been a powerfully sound policy to omit such extraordinary feats of his own from journals and reports, meant to earn a reputation for conveying authority without strut.

After the battle, Bald Mountain became forever known as Rogers' Rock, and the face itself as Rogers' Slide. The legend of a superhuman escape spread across the trading routes of British North America, although just where the tale took shape remains for generations of historians to debate. Rogers himself neither took specific credit for the story nor denied it. Regardless of whether he actually negotiated that ancient, steep, and weathered dome, the capacity of people of his own time and of two centuries thereafter to think it possible is perhaps most telling, a tribute to Rogers's reputation for near-impossible escapes and superhuman endurance and athleticism. For his Indian pursuers who came to the cliff edge, the sight of Rogers on the ice far below must have indeed seemed supernatural and lent powerful new potency to Rogers's reputation.

On the ice, now safely out of the Indians' reach, Rogers took his measure of the perhaps 50 men remaining from the 280 and more who had turned out in that dawn's early light. He quickly dispatched two of them back to the fort for help. The rangers wrapped four of the most severely wounded in bearskins and laid each upon a sled; then they began the laborious trek southward over the ice.

Rogers's messengers reached the fort on March 14. "About Noon Som of Majr Rogerss Scout Came in & inform yt they Have Had a Hot Ingagment Such as Scarce Ever was Know in ye Country & Most of His Party are Distroyd," scrawled the Connecticut provincial Jabez Fitch.[7]

The rest of the ill-fated command had struggled through the night, the wounded suffering terribly. They continued their desperate journey until they encountered Captain Stark with three horse-drawn sleighs at Hoop Island, six miles from the southern terminus of Lake George, and attained the fort the following afternoon, as Private Fitch recorded: "About 5 oClock I Se ye Majr Com in Him Self Being in ye Rear of ye Whol—This was a Vast Cold & Tedious Day Especially for ye Wounded Men."[8] The sight of the grave, tall ranger captain grimly providing cover for his survivors' anything-but-happy return seared itself unforgettably into Fitch's memory.

Meanwhile Captain-Lieutenant Henry Pringle and Lieutenant Boyle Roche were still stumbling around in the woods, lost and slowly starving to death.[9] More than once they miraculously avoided capture, but they were still unable to move quickly on their broken snowshoes. All that night they searched for the lake under the quarter moon, and just before morning they ran into Rogers's servant, himself separated from the unit during the battle, who assured them that he knew the way back to Fort Edward because he had patrolled with Rogers "oftentimes all over the country." A ball had cut a superficial wound across Pringle's face, so he had thrown away his fur hat, convinced that it was serving as a target, and wrapped a silk handkerchief in its place. All three had also cast away their coats for greater mobility—or in the servant's case, because the green showed up deadly clear against the snow. They carried no blankets and had only a piece of bologna sausage and some ginger between them, all of which they quickly consumed. Given their exhaustion, shock, and hunger, it comes as no surprise that they made mistakes, any number of which could have done in the entire party.

They reached the ice, which the servant mistakenly believed was South Bay. Had it been so, Wood Creek would have been just before them, but in fact it was well to the southeast. Without checking up or down the lake, the trio plunged into the woods, Roche and the servant leaving their snowshoes behind, certain that they could travel faster that way. After many hours' struggle through the exhausting snowbanks, they built crude snowshoes by wrapping strips of leather around forked sticks: but, unsurprisingly, they kept breaking, leaving the men to sink waist-deep. For five days they labored on, every once in a while finding bark and handfuls of bitter juniper berries to chew on. Finally they staggered back onto the ice, only to realize that they had circled back to the spot whence they had set out. "Here I must own," Pringle later wrote, "my resolution almost failed me," to the point of deciding to find Carillon and throw themselves on the mercy of the French. Staggering up the ice for two miles, they then headed inland. Attempting to cross a creek above a waterfall, all three slipped on the wet rocks and pitched into the searingly cold water. Pringle, submerged entirely, lost his musket and only narrowly saved himself from going over the falls. Afterward, whenever they halted, even for a minute, "we became pillars of ice." Rogers's servant finally admitted that he was lost, but even more disturbingly he started imagining that Indians were stalking them—classic hallucinations of hypothermia.

Desperate for a fire, Roche used Pringle's pistol "to flash a little of the powder." But he held the cartridge too near and it exploded in their faces, nearly blinding Roche. With no means of making a fire and the night approaching, the wretched trio made a path around a tree and started circling it in a desperate bid to stay awake. At some point that night, despite their "repeated cautions," the servant stepped out of this frantic round dance, sat down, and died immediately, "tho' a strong man," a case, it seems, of the mind giving out and dragging the body with it.

The next morning, March 20, the seventh since the battle, Pringle and Roche spied the fort and came into the open with a white flag. A number of Frenchmen emerged and suddenly started running "violently towards" the Englishmen, whom they grabbed brusquely. Only then did the prisoners notice a band of Indians—perhaps who had been involved in the recent battle—dashing up from mere steps behind them. The French admitted that they would have been powerless to save them had the braves arrived first.

Eight days later Pringle wrote to Haviland detailing his experiences, which Rogers would eventually publish in his own journals. He dismissed any thought of Rogers's culpability for the costly defeat: "It was impossible for a party so weak as ours to hope for even a retreat."[10] The chaplain of the Royal Americans, John Ogilvie, wrote that "envy, that arch fiend, will not allow [Rogers] much merit" but that the facts offered "considerable proof of his bravery and conduct."[11] There is no record of Haviland's reflections about the battle. Perhaps he thought it better not to record them.

Rogers returned with perhaps 50 men; French casualty estimates vary but were significantly less than the rangers'. Nevertheless, D'Hebecourt wrote, "we had a wonderful result but it cost us dearly through the loss which we suffered."[12] The loss of these crack troops, many with records of service dating to the early days of the war, cast deep shadows over Rogers' Island, as the friends of the dead gathered up belongings and wrote to the families. The four most grievously wounded all died not long after reaching the fort.

Lieutenant Pottinger, wrote J. Macomb, "as he has left a young Child here of 4 months Oald which he had by the Girrill he formerly kept, I think what little Effects there is belonging to him cannot be better desposed off then toward the Mentenance of that helpless Infant, I will do anything I can to see it don Justice."[13]

For France, perhaps the most promising spoil of war was the discovery of Rogers's coat on the field of battle. It "gave me every reason to believe that he had been killed," wrote Governor Vaudreuil to M. de Massiac, the minister of marine.[14] What was more, he added, an Indian had personally assured him that he had himself killed Rogers. He, and with him all French Canada, were soon to be shown that Rogers was alive and well.

Part Three

ORDEALS OF EMPIRE

Chapter 16

Disaster at Carillon

All skill is in vain when an angel pees in the touch-hole of your musket.

GERMAN PROVERB

In the early morning of July 5, 1758, more than a thousand Albany-built bateaux, whaleboats, and three radeaux—cumbersome but formidable heptagonal barges not unjustly referred to by the men as "floating castles"[1]—crowded the calm waters of Lake George in orderly columns. Their frontage spread the mile and a half from shore to shore and extended, as *The Pennsylvania Journal* reported, "from front to Rear full Seven Miles."[2] They were laden in all with more than fifteen thousand soldiers, the largest army ever seen in North America. The dragonlike fleet had an enabling tail consisting of kegs of gunpowder and barrels of flour and salted pork, provisions enough for a month; its dragon's teeth consisted of forty-four pieces of ordnance of 2- to 24-pounders, the heaviest weighing more than 5,000 pounds and capable of casting a 5.5-inch ball 1,240 yards and penetrating a foot of earth at the target.[3]

To thousands of fresh young colonial recruits, many clutching the brand-new muskets issued to them only three days before, the spectacle was phantasmagorical. The sight of an acre or two of cleared land, or even of several dozen ships in the harbor of Boston or Portsmouth, had not prepared them for this spectacle. Maybe some had heard of the vast, massed formations that had beaten each other into bloody submission at Fontenoy, or of Hannibal crossing the Alps, leaving behind the skeletons of more men than lived in Connecticut. But nothing that they had experienced would have enabled them to imagine the sheer magnitude of this floating city that shadowed, even seemed to suffocate, the crystal lake waters.

Rogers rode at its head, standing grimly satisfied in the stern of a gently bobbing whaleboat, the forest of sails "a most agreeable sight." Time and again he had fought the enemy on uncertain terrain, rarely at times or places of his choosing. He had watched musket balls and hatchets wreak their destruction on so many friends—and on occasion he may even have dispatched a wounded comrade himself under the brutal codes of frontier warfare. He had lost not only friends but reputation at the Battle on Snowshoes four months earlier. But now, instead of skulking by night, his men proudly headed a truly imperial force, set on driving a weaker enemy back to Canada. Not that he had neglected training his men in irregular fighting. In a June journal entry surgeon Caleb Rea commented that "Major Rogers this Day exercised his men in Bush Fiteing which drew a great number out of ye camp, to view them." On another day "the Rangers exersize in Scout marches & Bush fighting which make a very pritty figure."[4]

Rogers felt comfortable with the intelligence estimates he had helped to form: the French boasted only 3,000 men, about one fifth the strength of the expeditionary force he now surveyed. Of course, nothing in so large an enterprise could run perfectly, and he had had some unpleasantness with General Abercromby over a scout gone awry—Rogers's 50-man probe up to Carillon to map the defenses and gather intelligence on enemy numbers. He had taken a small detail up Rattlesnake Mountain, overlooking the fort, drawn maps, and made estimates. While they came off the mountain, an enemy patrol had fallen upon their main party at lakeside, killing five rangers, taking three prisoners, and isolating Rogers, who himself barely escaped. Rumors of Rogers's death again stirred, until he limped into camp with even more hair-raising stories to tell.

The general expressed his deep dissatisfaction, concerned lest the captives reveal details of the upcoming campaign. He wrote to William Pitt, the newly empowered mainspring of the war effort in London, that Rogers, having surveyed Carillon from the mountain, was "not content with this Discovery, & out of Zeal for the Service." The ranger, "contrary to his Instructions, proceeded with his Whale Boats too far down the Lake, and fell in with a superior Force...an unlucky Affair, as they must learn a great deal from these Prisoners."[5]

Curiously, his orders had instructed him to proceed downlake several miles beyond Carillon if necessary, but he had stayed well south of the fort. Why Abercromby chose so to distort Rogers's actions, albeit with a touch of generosity, remains unclear; Richard Huck, chief doctor at the General Hospital in Albany, wrote, "It has been pretty much in Vogue lately to decry all Rangers and Rogers has come in for his Share of Discredit." Rogers himself seemed to have grown resigned to such criticism. He was operating with unorthodox techniques on geographical and institutional peripheries; the reports of his engagements were often thick with the contradictions inherent in first-person accounts of surprising and dangerous encounters in disorienting terrain. His very success in gaining intelligence galled the British troops. "Parties therefore of regular Troops," Huck continued, "commanded by such Officers as were judged the properest for that Service have been sent out to procure Intelligence, but returned without effecting any Thing, for which they blamed the Guides, and I believe are not a little sick of these Experiments."[6]

But now all was forgotten—at least for the moment. Conversation in the whaleboats among those men near Rogers was light and boisterous—a ranger occasionally shouted out to the major that they would show the French a thing or two. Rogers, rarely at a loss for a quip, boomed salty predictions of victory down the creaking column.

Three hundred of Rogers' Rangers—the truly select from Rogers's, Stark's, Burbank's, and Shepherd's regiments, joined by 100 Stockbridge Indians in two companies—rode in the van, each man gloriously arrayed in the new green regimental coats, most heads crowned with the rangers' signature Balmoral Scotch bonnet. Along with them came some 400 "leathercaps," members of the newly raised 80th Regiment—more exactly, Gage's Regiment of Light Armed Foot—and 1,600 of Lieutenant Colonel John Bradstreet's river-toughened Corps of Armed Battoemen.

Behind them paddled eight battalions of 5,825 regulars: the Highlanders of the 42nd Foot, their grenadiers wearing pointed bearskin caps, dirks fastened to belts over breeches,[7] buff facings on the red jackets; the 27th, 42nd, 44th, 55th, 80th, and Captain John Ord's Royal Artillery division; thereafter more than 9,000 provincials—six regiments from Massachusetts, five from Connecticut, and one each from New York, Rhode Island, New Hampshire, and New Jersey.

Anyone was a "desponding dastard," wrote Captain Charles Lee of the 44th, "who could entertain a doubt of our success."[8] Thick clouds broke the sun's glare that morning, promising relatively cool rowing conditions as the force pushed on. The uninspiring General Abercromby, lately Loudoun's deputy, now supreme commander of the forces in North America, had pulled off a minor miracle. Three months of hard work had funneled a mountain of supplies and a river full of boats to the southern end of Lake George, the portage of boats involving repeated, laborious round-trips of 173 teams of oxen and 35 "trucks," or four-wheel frames, over the high ground between Fort Edward and Lake George. Along that rough passage, the 22-year-old southern Connecticut private Abel Spicer noted "great numbers of whale boats and bateaux along by the road where the wagons break and drop them."[9]

This vast imperial fleet had other reasons for optimism. Back in London, the often-gout-ridden William Pitt, arguably the most brilliant global statesman of his age, now clearly held the reins of this multicontinental war, even if only as "Northern Secretary." In late December, as part of his efforts to transform British military priorities, Pitt had recalled Lord Loudoun, whose high-handed treatment as commander-in-chief of the colonial governments, the militia, and private citizens had caused much friction and even outright mutiny in North America. Private citizens in Albany, Philadelphia, and New York had bridled at the expense and invasion of privacy involved in quartering British troops, sometimes ridden with smallpox, in their homes. The colonial assemblies had pushed against Loudoun's assertions that only he and the royal governors could set the quotas for how many men each colony would supply the war effort.

Pitt recognized that the most profitable British path to victory lay not through the attrition of mass enemies on European battlefields but through hammering the French at sea and in their colonial holdings in North America, the Caribbean, Africa, and India. Conquering French North America became a high priority, and he backed it with thousands of redcoats. Even so, he realized, provincial soldiers must constitute the bulk of the fighting forces.

With Loudoun off the colonials' backs, Pitt set about healing the tense relations between the British military and the Americans, acknowledging the importance of their assemblies in the ongoing dialogue and, for instance, reversing earlier orders that often dangerously subordinated seasoned militia officers to junior commissioned regulars perhaps only a week or two in country. He convinced Parliament to subsidize colonial war expenditures. Soon 23,000 new recruits had enlisted in the militia, many of them now pulling oars on Lake George.[10]

In hindsight, Pitt's choice of James Abercromby as commander in North America seems less inspired. While Loudoun's sneering backhanded compliment that Abercromby made "a capable second" may have stemmed from bitterness at his recall, it did embody some truth. In an appreciation of the advancing offensive, "Strength and Composition of the English Army," Montcalm's aide-de-camp Louis-Antoine de Bougainville, described Abercromby—in the coolly but accurately diminishing vein of the French moral philosophers— as a man "more of courage than resolution, more of sense than of dash and of objective; age has lessened in him the fire necessary for the execution of great undertakings. He reflects sufficiently, operates slowly, and with too much precaution."[11] Provincial Rufus Putnam spoke more bluntly, calling him "an old man and frequently called granny."[12]

But, under Pitt's strategically watchful eye, Abercromby had been blessed with a deputy whose very personal characteristics compensated for his commander's defects. To Brigadier General George Augustus, Viscount Howe, the 34-year-old grandson of the king's father, a veteran of the War of the Austrian Succession and deeply popular among regulars and provincials alike, he had ceded much of the operational planning for the campaign. Howe's lean and dashing good looks provided an extreme contrast to the short, plump Scotsman. Howe was "a character of ancient times," wrote Pitt, "a complete model of military virtue,"[13] an anomaly among the British officer corps in his openness to, and even solicitous interest in, provincial expertise and leadership. A colonial carpenter called him the "Idol of the Army ... he frequently came among the Carpenters, and his maner was So easy and fermiller, that you loost all that constraint or diffidence we feele when addressed by our Superiours, whose manner are forbiding."[14]

Over Howe's year up to this moment in North America, he and Rogers had fallen into an easy relationship, spending hours discussing "the methods of distressing the enemy, and prosecuting the war with vigour."[15] While Shirley, Johnson, Loudoun, and Abercromby had expressed interest in Rogers's techniques, none so fully took them to heart as did Howe. Like most men of formidable intelligence, both listened well, and each learned from the other. "Any gentleman officer," Howe reputedly lectured his fellows, "will find his equal in every regiment of the Americans. I know them well. Beware how you underestimate their abilities and feelings, civil, social, and military."[16] It is difficult to believe that Howe did not have Rogers directly in mind, because his actions over the next several months leading up to the assault on Carillon came right out of the major's playbook.

He set out in short order to remake the regulars for North American warfare. "You would laugh to see the droll figure we all make," wrote an anonymous soldier in a letter published by *The Boston Evening-Post*.[17] Howe banished camp laundrywomen, himself going down to the brook to wash his own laundry. He cropped his "fine, and very abundant hair,"[18] ordering his men to do likewise, and forbade displays of gold and scarlet, himself setting an example by wearing an ammunition coat "cut short" as a "necessary precaution," wrote an observer, "because in the woods...the trees caught at the long and heavy skirts then worn by the soldiers."[19] In May Abercromby passed on orders that regiments proceeding to Carillon would not carry their colors; officers would not wear sashes, and furthermore they would limit their camp equipage to a tent, a small "portmantle," blankets, and bearskin, measures no doubt suggested by Howe.[20] "Many have taken up the Hatchet and wear Tomahawks," wrote Dr. Huck in Albany. Howe dictated that the best marksmen in each regiment receive new rifles and that each man carry powdered ginger to ward off malarial fever—or ague, as it was then known.[21] "The Art of War is much changed and improved here," wrote Huck in late May; "I suppose by the End of Summer it will have undergone a total revolution."[22]

By five P.M. the lead elements of the grand flotilla reached Sabbath Day Point, on Lake George's western shore, 25 miles from their point of embarkation, unrolled their canvas tents, lit great bonfires, and cooked a meal. Despite the confidence often afforded by overwhelming numbers, the landing proved somewhat sobering, for the camp lay amid the still considerable presence—"both in the water and on the shore," observed one officer—of white bleached bones and fragments of clothing, hair, and leather: bleak commemoration of Colonel Parker's ill-fated bateau expedition of a year earlier, which had left 300 provincials dead in an ambush. More frequently than they liked, the men shushed one another, straining their ears to hear the buzzing of the thick-bodied and highly poisonous timber rattlesnakes, "the greatest number of rattlesnakes I ever saw or heard of," wrote one provincial.

Rogers, Howe, and the commander of the bateau men, Colonel John Bradstreet, took no rest. While the presence of so massive a force might have eased the concerns of a different man, Rogers knew all too well that close-pressing woods and rugged topography could easily favor a smaller force with surprise and advantageous position on its side. Anyone familiar with this chokepoint between marauder-friendly forest and water indifferently ready to devour any panicked rabble would know that the enemy, perhaps in considerable force, would be occupying a commanding position atop the exposed granite of Bald Mountain, over which Rogers had made his own harrowing escape less than four months earlier—and that the options of a compact body of men using wilderness cover could be put to devastating use against a largely incoherent force who were still for the most part strangers to one another.

In a strategy that seems to display Rogers's trademarks, the invasion force packed up camp at about ten P.M., reembarked under strict silence, leaving its campfires burning to lull watchful eyes, and pressed downlake. Early the next morning it pulled ahead of a 350-man French scouting unit,[23] led by Captain de Trépezec of the Béarn Regiment and accompanied by Ensign Jean-Baptiste Levrault de Langis Montegron, or Langy, the tough partisan fighter who had done the rangers so much harm in the Battle on Snowshoes.

In the early morning light, with "gratest Dexterety,"[24] wrote a

EXPLANATION.

A. *Cheonderoga.*
B. *Intrenchment & front of the Attack in 1758.*
C. *Lake Champlain.*
D. *Wood Creek*
E. *A Mountain over looking the Fort.*
F. *Our Rafts with 3 Cannon & 1 Howhits.*
G. *Where the Army lay the 7th*
H. *Saw Mill & Fall.* The Carrying Place is from
I. *Ovens.*   {H. to I. & is about 2 Miles.
K. *Where the Army lay the 6th*
L. *Where the Army fell in with 150 of the*
   Enemy, and Lord Howe was Kill'd
M. *The Army marching in four Columns.*
N. *Landing Place.*
O. *Mutton Island.*
P. *Bare Mountain. Entrance of the Narrows.*
Q. *Saw Mill Creek.*

LAKE GEORGE

British Approach to Carillon, 1758

Massachusetts provincial, Rogers and his rangers stormed the French narrows, the northern tip of Lake George, where the La Chute's northward outfall on its way to the St. Lawrence marks the loading point for the portage road, which bypasses the rapids as it curls north and east on its way to Lake Champlain at Carillon. The attackers' nighttime passage caught the French by such surprise that they precipitously abandoned tents, letters, commissions, and even their swords. Provincials and light infantry of the 80th went in after the rangers, who pursued the French down the portage road to the sawmills and a few other redoubts along the river below the rapids.

Intending to bypass the sawmill complex, which he and Rogers figured would offer stiff resistance, Howe instead opted to swing west, then north, following the La Chute's left bank around to the fort, dispatching the rangers ahead to secure a passage over Bernetz (now Trout) Brook, which falls into the La Chute from the west. Here Howe and Abercromby made the first of a chain of ultimately crippling mistakes. By sending the rangers ahead, they deprived themselves of the men most familiar with this singularly resistant country, counting instead on the 80th, Gage's light infantry, as guides. But the "woods being thick, impassable with any Regularity to such a Body of Men," Abercromby later wrote, "and the Guides unskilled, the Troops were bewildered, and the Columns Broke, falling in on one another."[25]

That morning Trépezac's scouting patrol had also lost their way in the dense woods, recalled a French captain, by the "fault of his guide"—probably the canny Langy himself. That the veteran and woods-savvy ensign, who had matched wits so successfully with Rogers, should lose his bearing in the immediate vicinity of the fort gives some idea of what faced even the most experienced in the mapless, trackless, mountain-broken Adirondack deciduous forest.

The French finally found Bernetz Brook and decided to follow its south bank as far as the La Chute, their loss of time putting them into the path of the British advance guard.

Sure enough, a noontide conference between Rogers and provincial colonels Lyman and Fitch, whose regiments had just caught up with the rangers at the ford on the spring-swollen brook, was interrupted by a "sharp fire" to the rear of Lyman's command. Lyman and Fitch, forming a joint front, pressed a rapid counterattack, while the main body of rangers, leaving the crossing guarded, swung around to catch the attackers' left flank.

At first the French got the better of the equally startled rangers and provincials, clearly unaware that the bulk of the massive British army lay close by. At the head of his column Howe—his brigade major, Captain Alexander Moneypenny of the 55th Foot, at his side— raced to the scene "with great eagerness and intrepidity," Rogers later wrote.[26] Howe could not have helped but think about the lessons of Braddock's defeat three years earlier, where a failure of leadership at the initial encounter compounded problems for the British.

As Howe gained the crestline, Moneypenny later wrote, a ball "entered his breast on the left side, and (as the surgeons say) pierced his lungs, and heart, and shattered his backbone." Half a dozen paces away the captain watched Howe crash backward, his hand quivering only for an instant: "Never ball had more deadly direction."[27] Howe had taken Rogers's discussions to heart but not to mind; in his headlong plunge into the melee he had recklessly outlined himself against the sky as no veteran woodsman would have done. Some historians speculate that Howe took the musket ball from a green Connecticut provincial, wildly firing in the terror of first combat. Despite Howe's eagerness to learn the craft of woods warfare, he still could not shed the romantic notions of Homeric, sword-raised courage, dashing into the fray at the head of his men, doing a subaltern's work at the cost of his own life.

Rogers wrote that "his fall was not only most sincerely lamented, but seemed to produce an almost general consternation and langour through whole [army]." Even in the tangle of the forest environment, now further confused by gunfire and smoke, word passed from one man to another with uncanny speed. A contemporary British historian later wrote that "the soul of General Abercrombie's [sic] army seemed to expire."[28]

Even so, for the short term Rogers and his men—some the few survivors of the Battle on Snowshoes waged only four months before— must have taken deep pleasure in engaging the French with superior force; the battle in essence was decided in a bloody quarter hour, the woods and water thick with some 150 killed, wounded, or drowned, not counting the richest prize, "five officers, two volunteers, and one hundred and sixty men," reckoned Rogers, unwounded prisoners. Perhaps a little more than two score escaped by swimming the La Chute or disappearing into the woods, including Langy himself and Trépezac, who would die from his wounds the following day.[29]

At this moment the expedition, despite its costly but undoubted victory over Trépezac's patrol, began to unravel. Spread out across two square miles of forest, provincials and regulars alike found themselves in the now-darkening and disorienting woods. Parts of the 55th and 42nd fell back to the landing place, while other units in the forest reformed and marched toward Rogers's position. As the disordered columns stumbled through the woods toward some low ground near the brook, shots rang out, followed by what Major William Eyre of the 44th described as "a loud heidious Yell."[30] That inhuman cry sent hackles up the necks of the provincial soldiers, most of whom had only heard such sounds described in the soft light of a parlor fire. The Connecticut provincials shot blindly into the woods and received fire in return.

It all was a dreadful error. "At length," wrote Garrett Albertson of the Jersey Blues, the firing "was stopped by a universal cry through the army, 'All is well! All is well!'" "The fire that began this Confusion in the front was from Ourselves . . . not a Single Shot was fir'd against us by the Enemy," wrote Eyre. Albertson watched as the musket ball from a British regular sliced off the nose of the soldier next to him. "O, pray help me!" cried the injured man. So confounded was the 23-year-old that he replied, "I cannot, the army is now on the march," and ran off. The number of friendly deaths went unrecorded. By now darkness had descended; "we were seperated & had some difficulty to Join afterwards but in a very irregular Way, the regts intermix'd with each Other, a most wretched situation."[31]

The frightened, exhausted men "lay on their arms" that night, sleeping, if they could, on the dank ground. By morning, the scattered units had begun to straggle back to the landing place. The annihilation of Trépezac's scouting force had thrown the entire British army into disarray. For the French, the disruption of the advance "gave us twenty-four hours' delay," wrote Montcalm's aide-de-camp Bougainville. "This precious time was the saving of us and of the colony."[32] Drums beat the Carillon garrison to life at four-thirty A.M., rousing all 3,526 French, Canadians, and Indians, officers and men alike, who hefted shovel, pick, and ax and began digging entrenchments on the heights near the neck of the peninsula.[33] Their formidable defensive line of three-foot-thick logs laid horizontally and packed with earth, intersected with loopholes, would eventually stretch in a 230-yard horseshoe.

Howe's death advanced Brigadier General Thomas Gage to second-in-command, but at the moment when Abercromby could have best used the advice of a senior colleague, Gage disappeared. Not a single record of the upcoming battle—and many were written—mentions Gage, a silence not broken until August. Struggling in the woods, commanding the left flank of the Royal 80th and a passel of inexperienced Connecticut provincials, his commander dead, Gage must have choked on the haunting similarities to the situation with Braddock at the Monongahela. Perhaps this knowledge proved too much to bear; he probably broke down under the pressure, unable to summon a commander's resolution, that difficult-to-describe but critical quality of leadership in the field. Like Howe's death, Gage's absence on the field would ripple through the fabric of the English command with tragic consequences.

That day Bradstreet, who stepped into the role of Abercromby's tactical adviser, convinced the general to abandon the original plan of skirting the La Chute on the west side and instead to send him and his men along the far shorter portage road to storm the sawmills. After much reluctance Abercromby agreed; Bradstreet led a 5,000-man contingent, comprising his own men, Stark's rangers, the 44th Foot, two Massachusetts provincial regiments, and six companies of the 80th Foot, only to discover that the French had torched the mills and bridges. Perhaps fearing ambush, Abercromby ignored Bradstreet's pleas to press on. Instead Bradstreet's men rested as the bulk of the army marched up to the mills. That night, reported the 23-year-old Albertson, they "heard the French all night chopping and felling timber to fortify their breastwork."[34]

Late in the afternoon Lieutenant Mathew Clerk and Captain James Abercrombie, escorted by Stark and some rangers, climbed Rattlesnake Mountain, the steep eminence that overlooked the fort, from whence Rogers had spent much time spying on the French. It's difficult to understand why Rogers himself, who better than anyone else knew the terrain around the fort, indeed had stolen beneath its very walls on occasion, was not included in this critical mission. Most likely General Abercromby's inborn prejudice against provincials, and against Rogers in particular, removed the irascible major from consideration. Certainly Rogers did not have a friend in Colonel Haviland, who also accompanied the party.

The young engineer and Captain Abercrombie saw exactly what the French intended. Knowing full well that the British would peer down upon his defenses, Montcalm had taken pains to camouflage the breastworks with cut fir trees and bushes. From atop the 850-foot mountain, the two officers observed thousands of French soldiers digging and carrying logs, but only, it appeared, to reinforce rudimentary trenchwork. Evaluating vertical observation, most notably evident two centuries later in the age of aviation photography, has always proven difficult and required training to interpret the distortions of height and perspective. Properly reading the growing defenses, especially under camouflage, would have required experience and a detailed understanding of the preexistent topography. Had Stark seen fit to comment on their observations, it is hard to imagine that Captain Abercrombie, given the bad blood between them, would have paid him much mind.

On the morning of the eighth General Abercromby sent Bradstreet and "a foreign engineer" across the La Chute to peer at Montcalm's defenses for confirmation of the intelligence gathered on Rattlesnake Mountain, again an odd choice considering that neither had ever trodden that ground before. Why Abercromby did not send Stark, Captain Abercrombie, Clerk, or most obviously Rogers, all of whom had previously reconnoitered the peninsula, remains a mystery. It is difficult to believe that Howe, had he been alive, would have made a similar mistake, considering his avowed interest in intelligence-gathering.

A Highland officer reported that the pair found "that the enemy was encamped on rising ground about a half-mile from the Fort, but not fortified, only a few logs laid on another as a breast Work." This irregular fencelike obstruction was only a quickly-thrown-together temporary construct to protect the men building the serious complexes immediately to the rear. General Abercromby gathered his officers, notably absent any provincials. "Upon this Intelligence it was thought proper to attempt storming the enemy lines, without loss of time, and immediately the whole army marched." Wet conditions precluded lugging the heavy guns to the front lines; instead two sets of ten whaleboats would each tow a raft carrying two six-pounders down the La Chute and submit the fort's defenses to a murderous enfilade from the south.

Chapter 17

"Come Up, You French Dogs...
Like Men!"

*To hear the thar cris and se thar bodis in blood and the earth trembel
with the fier of the smol arms was a mornfullous as ever I saw.*

ARCHELAUS FULLER,
DESCRIBING THE BATTLE OF CARILLON, 1758[1]

Early on July 8 Rogers led an advance guard of nearly 2,500 men
forward with the design of skirmishing and providing protection for
the provincials, who, backed by regulars, marched up the road from
the sawmills to the enemy defenses on the heights of Carillon.
Captain John Stark's company led the force of rangers, Bradstreet's
bateau men, and Gage's light infantry. As the woods opened onto
the muddy Carillon heights, interspersed with stumps and tallgrass,
Rogers reported that within 300 yards of the breastwork they were
"ambushed and fired upon" by 200 Frenchmen, probably grenadiers
and *volontaires*, positioned to slow the advancing enemy. The musket
balls flew harmlessly over the rangers' heads through the trees, the
leaves fluttering gently down. In the face of this resistance, Rogers
drew up a line and marched forward, only to find the enemy hidden
behind formidable works—not the flimsy efforts reported by intelligence. What was more, the French had also built an abatis, a tangled
maze of large axed fir and oak trees that one participant described as
resembling the aftermath of a hurricane. From a nearby grove, or *bois
reservée*, kept for this eventuality, the French had felled hundreds of
trees, then sharpened the green and pliant limbs with fascine knives

into murderous points, forming an effective, organic barbed-wire entanglement, which, wrote Montcalm, gave them "the effects of the *chevaux-de-frise*," the deadly medieval barricades.[2] Behind that Rogers could see for the first time of all the British that the French awaited them behind strong entrenchments that were defended at key points by swivel guns. The British faced a murderous gauntlet.

His orders directed him to the left, but he kept the center around the road, driving in the remnants of the advance guard, perhaps finding it difficult to deploy leftward, most definitely concerned about the destructive power of the French position. The bateau men spread to the left, Gage's light infantry to the right. At around ten-thirty, Rogers notes, while still engaging in a scattering fire "between our flying parties and those of the enemy without the breast work," he heard a "smart fire" from the left flank: Colonel Oliver Delancy's New York provincials were shooting at the advance guard. Without General Abercromby, who was still well behind the lines, and with Gage simply not there, Haviland, commanding the right flank with the 27th, ordered Rogers forward to provide covering fire on the abatis, then to set down, so his men might march through them. Rogers knew that Haviland's decision to attack ran contrary to Abercromby's clear orders that the six divisions should not attack "till the whole Army was formed, & then a point of War would be beat for the attack," as one of his aides-de-camp later explicitly stated.[3] Somehow the New Yorkers' shouting and cheering on the left inflamed Haviland, causing him to send in his division long before all the divisions had gotten into position. In that moment Abercromby's and Howe's careful plan for a united frontal assault of six divisions perished.

The abatis stopped Haviland's front ranks head-on, leaving them easy targets; men "fell like pigeons," wrote one provincial soldier,[4] as they attempted to clamber over the frightening tangle of felled trees. The French, three deep behind their entrenchment, had placed their best marksmen at the loopholes; the men behind them loaded weapons and passed them forward, so that they could jump from a firing rate of two or three shots a minute to six or more. "A man could not stand erect, without being hit, any more than he could stand out in a shower, without having drops of rain fall on him, for the balls

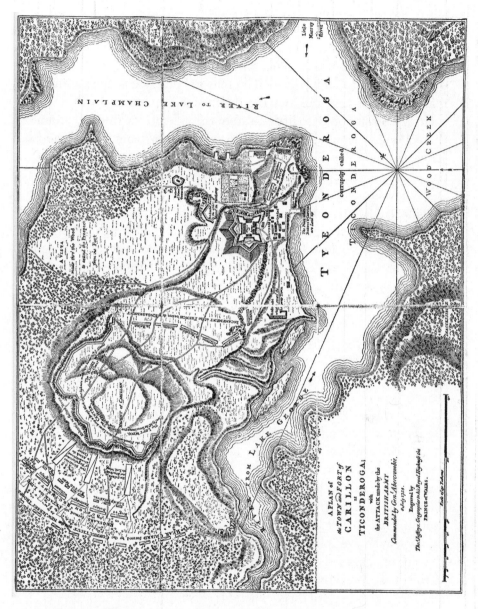

Jeffery's Map of Carillon and Attack by Abercromby's Forces, 1758

come like hands full," wrote a stunned 16-year-old Massachusetts soldier. "Whistling of balls and the roar of musketry terrified me not a little."[5] Rogers hunkered down behind the abatis to direct his troops' fire at the unsatisfying targets afforded by the occasional tip of a tricorne or ducking head. The rangers' practice with shooting at marks paid off and took out the determined defenders with deadly accuracy, but it could do little to stem the tide of slaughter all around them. Albertson recalled that "I felt a tremor or panic of fear, and I strove to conquer it but in vain; at length, I really thought my hat was rising off my head, I slapped my hand on my head to keep it down."[6]

When General Abercromby arrived at the battlefront by about one-fifteen P.M., the battle was fully, if raggedly, joined. No indication exists that he attempted to call off the now-haphazard attack; the record is all too clear that he retreated to a safe spot on the right flank. For the next four hours the regiments battered themselves headlong against the French position with appalling losses, each commander acting independently and by all accounts bravely. But, wrote Charles Lee, "we found that it was not in the power of Courage or even of chance to bestow success unless we alter'd our method: this was perceived very soon & had we profited of our early discovery, & beat the retreat in proper time, there was no loss sustain'd which was by any means irreparable." The command and control structure disintegrated, especially as great numbers of officers went down. "The Ded men and wounded lay on the grown, the wounded having some of them legs their arms and other Lims broken, others shot threw the bodey and very mortly wounded," wrote a 31-year-old Massachusetts man, Archelaus Fuller. "To hear the thar cris and se thar bodis in blood and the earth trembel with the fier of the smol arms was a mornfullous as ever I saw."[7]

Lee, who would later go on to serve under Washington in the Revolution, escaped death only by chance when a musket ball hit him in the chest, breaking two ribs and knocking him "senseless." He lay amid the carnage until dusk, when his servant dragged him to safety.[8] His criticism of the leadership on that fateful day was blistering: "no General was heard of, no Aid de Camps seen, no instructions receiv'd; but every officer left at the head of his division, Company, or squad, to fall a sacrifice to his own good behaviour and the stupidity of his Commander."[9]

The 42nd Scottish Highlanders, known as the Black Watch, threw themselves time and again at the French, several times breaking through to the trenches before they were slaughtered. "Even those that were mortally wounded, cried aloud to their companions not to lose a thought upon them, but to follow their officers and charge the enemy," recalled Lieutenant William Grant of the Highlanders.[10] "When advancing...they appeared like roaring lions breaking from their chains," wrote another observer.[11] The unit lost 647 men, fully 65 percent of its strength that afternoon, the highest casualty rate during the war.[12]

The promised artillery enfilade never came. Lieutenant Mathew Clerk, who now lay dying, had specified a landing place for the barges pulling the six-pounders, but the bateau men missed the spot that had been so clear to Clerk from his vantage on the mountainside, and they floundered right underneath Carillon's guns, which pounded the small flotilla and sank some of its craft.

By five P.M. Abercromby ordered a retreat—though even then word did not reach all the men until an hour later—detailing Rogers to cover with his rangers the battered divisions limping and staggering back to the boats. By seven-thirty the rangers had themselves to pull out, leaving hundreds of the terribly wounded, some still crying for help. "I suppose that soon as we left the ground, the enemy let loose his Indians upon them, for none of those that we left behind were ever heard of afterwards," wrote 16-year-old Private David Perry.[13] The outgunned and outmanned French chose not to pursue. Convinced that the superior force would return "the next day to take their revenge," wrote Bougainville, "...we worked all night to secure defilade against the neighboring heights by traverses, to perfect the abatis of the Canadians and to finish the batteries on the right and left [which were] commenced in the morning."[14]

The next morning eight grenadier companies marched out to reconnoiter, discovering "wounded, provisions, abandoned equipment, shoes left in miry places, remains of whaleboats and burned pontoons."[15] Wrote Captain Pierre Pouchot, "We found in the mud, on the road to the Falls, more than five hundred pairs of shoes with buckles, which strongly indicated the precipitancy of their flight."[16]

While nearly 2,000 of Abercromby's men died that bloody day, the expedition still constituted a formidable army, vastly outnumbering the French, but many of the fresh recruits were frightened and exhausted from two days without sleep. Even so, many were eager to revenge the losses of the previous day. The record remains unclear on why Abercromby pulled back. No French force threatened his position, nor could cut him off from the encampment on Lake George. The midsummer weather, although unusually wet, presented no serious problems. Abercromby did fear the reinforcements that he believed were coming from Montréal. Perhaps most important, he had lost so many of his officers that he felt the command and control system fatally compromised and no longer capable of mounting a sustained and coordinated attack.

The month's supplies, so patiently gathered, were destroyed and the great flotilla moved southward on the lake "with so much hurry, precipitation and confusion," wrote Charles Lee, "as to give it entirely the air of a flight."[17]

On the evening of the ninth, the battered army rowed ashore at the encampment on the lake's southern edge, "melancholy and still, as from a funeral," wrote Perry. The following day Abercromby delivered a message of thanks to the men, wrote Rogers, "for their good behavior," but their general's words did little to revive the camp's spirits. "Horrid cursing and swareing" boiled from the lips of everyone, "even among ye chief Commanders and those y^t were gasping for their last breath," noted the surgeon Caleb Rea.[18] Rumors flew about the camp, "almost as many sorts of news as there was men," wrote Abel Spicer.[19] Some provincial officers, disgusted with the regular leadership, vowed that they would indeed go back—but not if the redcoats came along. Jangled nerves took two lives from the careless flashing of guns.

By the eleventh "it was generally supposed that we should not go to Ticonderoga again, for it was said that the French had got to the place where we landed and entrenched and planted two cannon," wrote Spicer. Twenty men were placed under guard for threatening to go back and disparaging their officers' courage. Smallpox appeared in camp. "The men now grow sick very fast," observed Spicer.[20]

Rogers and his rangers had no time to melt into the general malaise. A deserter reported to the French that Rogers was out every day, "sometimes North, at other times, South." Montcalm, reinforced by 3,143 men who had arrived from Montréal three days after the battle, sent large teams out to harass the convoys supplying the entrenched camp at Lake George, intending to maintain the pressure after victory and drive the British back to Fort Edward and Albany.[21]

The large enemy presence around southern Lake George prevented French parties from taking that path south, so they instead traveled down to the southern end of Champlain, which winds south from Ticonderoga, shadowing Lake George's eastern shore for nearly two-thirds of its length. The southernmost extension, known as South Bay, sweeps southwest to a point less than five miles from Champlain's narrows. It was here that Rogers and his men had carried their whaleboats over the mountains, putting out from South Bay to row north. At the northern end of South Bay, Wood Creek cuts off and zigzags southeast, then southwest.

On the twentieth Rogers found evidence that a large party had passed near South Bay heading south. Too late: several hundred Canadians, Abenakis, Caughnawagas, and Ottawas had skirted the Lake George encampment and overwhelmed a detachment of provincials near the small stockade at Halfway Brook, an aptly named waypoint on the King's Highway between Fort Edward and Albany, killing three provincial captains and 20 men.

On July 28, two and a half miles shy of the Halfway Brook stockade, another raiding party fell upon a precious but woefully unprotected supply train of 138 ox wagons and carts. Colonel James Montressor, commander of Fort Edward, under intense pressure from General Abercromby to get through supplies to the Lake George encampment, had fatally chosen to dispatch the convoy before a newly arrived New Hampshiremen contingent was adequately rested. No records shed light on why Montressor, who certainly knew of the Indian attack along this same route only two weeks earlier, failed to detail an adequate escort. Only about three dozen soldiers accompanied the teamsters, sutlers, and traders delivering pork, flour, sugar, molasses, rum, and wine. The train included the lake camp's payroll, Abercromby's baggage and that of other officers, letters, regimental musical instruments, and hundreds of leggings. A dozen or more women and girls, designated to attend the great number of wounded at Lake George, also accompanied the convoy.

Six hundred Indians swooped down upon the convoy as they took a lunch break. "One little child, a girl, ran back in the path like a quail; a waggoner who cut his horse's ropes and cleared him from ye waggon rode back ye path, took her by ye hand, catched her up before him and saved her," wrote a captain in his journal.[22] A provincial chaplain reported that some of those that "got clear of the enemy being overheated with running dyed as soon as they got back to the Fort."[23] Some of the Indians got at the liquor supplies and turned on the captives, stripping the women and cutting them up with knives, slitting the throats of more than 150 oxen, taking the scalps of humans and animals alike.

Within an hour of hearing about the attack from a survivor, Rogers and Putnam had provisioned a team of 700 rangers and some regulars. They set out in bateaux to try to cut off the enemy's retreat by using Rogers's path west across the narrows to approach South Bay. Although they traveled all night and could hear the enemy's yelling and victory volleys, they stumbled into the empty camp. There they found taunting messages carved on tree trunks boasting that their scout of 1,800 strong had seven prisoners, two of them women. The pursuers had missed the raiders by probably no more than an hour.

Back on the lake on August 2, Rogers and Putnam received orders to sweep east to Wood Creek, then south back to Fort Edward, each of their 100 regulars, 150 light infantry, and 400 rangers receiving ten days' provisions. Aligned in three divisions led by Rogers, the rear brought up by Putnam, the force crossed through heavy rain in enforced silence. Aware that his less-experienced provincials and regulars could fall prey to the same panic that had turned General Abercromby's forces upon one another in the woods after Howe's death, Rogers assigned the identifying countersign "Boston" to prevent another tragic episode.

They lit no fires that night at the camp they had established halfway between the lake and South Bay. Scouts scouring the area found no enemy. The next day, stopping a half-mile shy of the bay, Putnam worked his way up to a prominence to check the water for bateaux. None being visible, the force camped at the head of the bay. The day following, scouts again detected no enemy, so Rogers took his men about five miles south to Wood Creek and camped at the site of Fort Anne, a small palisaded fort raised in 1709 during the Queen

Anne's War but burned to the ground two years later. A provincial imprudently walking down to fish in South Bay scared off a canoe full of Indians. That Sunday, the sixth, a regular spied another canoe on the creek and hallooed it, which sent the Indians racing off.

The morning of the eighth the parties rejoined at the ruins of Fort Anne, and Rogers responded to a challenge and shot at marks against an old tree. He probably believed that the enemy was gone. It was reckless, perhaps. But in that vast, sound-devouring forest, where forces could pass closely by one another undetected, a common ranger trick was to bait the enemy with gunfire. Rogers certainly knew that the French had been in the area, if only from their canoes and recent signs of habitation. Perhaps looking over a command soaked and moldy by an unusually wet summer, and anyway weary of chasing shadows in the forest, he wanted to provoke an encounter.

Rogers's column marched south that morning in single file down a path whose "each side [were] cloathed," wrote two provincial captains, "with thick low brush, interwoven with briers, brambles, and such like"—secondary growth closing over land that had been cleared at the fort decades before. Putnam led the vanguard, and Rogers brought up the rear of a line that soon spread to nearly a mile in length.

Unknown to the British, a raiding party of 50 regulars, 100 Canadians, and 150 Indians[24] under the experienced 39-year-old partisan leader Joseph Marin de La Malgue, had passed close to the ruined fort, wholly unaware of any other presence until they heard three shots. Marin swung his men into a half-moon ambush centering on a giant toppled tree, just outside the tangled thicket in the old-growth forest.

Not long after seven A.M. the advance guard walked right into the trap. Captain Putnam, a lieutenant, and three privates fell into enemy hands and were tied to nearby trees with leather tumplines. On hearing the musket fire, Rogers drew the rear guard into a line on the right side of the path and urged his men through the thicket; but the growth proved so dense that even while "Major Rogers was very expeditious in bringing up the rear," recalled two provincial officers, it took them half an hour to reach the forward position, where they found their comrades getting the worst of it. A Connecticut lieutenant named Worster took eight bullets in his body and fell stunned, face forward onto the ground. In moments he felt Indians grabbing his body; a tomahawk twice struck his head and then bounced off his elbow. He feigned death as the Indians stripped him and "made not the least resistance" while he was scalped, reported *The New-Hampshire Gazette.* Most remarkably of all, he lived to tell his story, with the top of his head missing to prove it.

Bullets from both sides tore holes through Putnam's clothing and the tree to which he was tied. A tomahawk hit the tree within inches of his head, but happily a French Canadian's musket misfired when shoved into Putnam's chest.

Rogers raced into the heart of the fray. Issuing orders, firing with deadly effect, he put heart into his justifiably shaken comrades and sent two runners headlong back to Fort Edward for reinforcements. The action's sheer ferocity had put 60 of the Canadians into headlong flight right before Rogers arrived, but the Indians kept up a stout front, anchored upon the large log. The British regulars fired a volley, but in superb defense a six-foot-four sachem jumped upon the log with a bloodcurdling yell and killed two men outright. In desperation, a regular officer swung his musket and hit the Indian in his head; to his amazement, the giant hardly wavered, for all the blood now spouting from his head, but raised his tomahawk to finish the officer off. Moments like these can turn the course of a battle, when a seemingly invincible man stands apart.

Without a second's pause, Rogers flung himself at the terrifying visage, who stood blood-bespattered and defiant atop the log. With his own inhuman cry Rogers shot the man dead at point-blank range.

"Come up, you French dogs...like men!" he roared, making the whole close battlefield ring with his challenge.[25]

Rogers turned his attention to the right, where the French had mounted four different attacks, and ordered 100 men to seize a small hill on that flank. That taken, he bellowed to the officer in charge about whether he wanted more men; if so, "he should have 500, which was to frighten the French," reported Abel Spicer.[26] The bluff worked, for the enemy "did not stand it but a little while longer but hallooed to get together and run off as fast as they could." Marin's forces retreated effectively in small groups, just as Rogers's had so many times before, frustrating attempts "to distress them by a pursuit," wrote Rogers.

But troops of this quality could still mount a counterattack, and so he ordered a breastwork of logs laid up on the right-flank knoll, then turned to burying nearly forty or more of the slain comrades, many of them horribly mangled by tomahawks. Some two dozen men were missing, including Putnam, whom the Indians had taken, but about twenty of these who had escaped the battlefield would straggle back into Fort Edward. More than fifty scalps bore bloody witness to the victory. A small ranger patrol visiting the site a week later reported seeing upward of a hundred bloated bodies in the forest; its commander wrote that "there might be many more, but the Stench was so great" that his men could not stand to make closer examination.

The survivors bundled up the badly wounded, carrying the mangled Worster on a quickly assembled stretcher, others on tumpline slings on their backs; and so the burdened column wound its way south, meeting the reinforcements, who helped shoulder their loads.

Rogers's actions in the field had won him another advocate among the regulars in Captain James Dalyell, whose favorable comments to Abercromby prompted the general to write William Pitt in London, "I must not omit, doing Rogers the Justice to say, that he merits much to be commended, he having, by Report of a very good Officer in the Light Infantry, who was on this Party, acted the whole time with great Calmness and Officer-like."

In a season of disaster for the British forces, Rogers had brought off the only victories in the Hudson River Valley campaign, and these over Langy and Marin, two of France's most talented partisan fighters. "The French Indians are not so forward in scouting as they us'd to be, before Major Rogers had the last skirmish with them," wrote Lieutenant Thomas Barnsley of the Royal American Regiment that fall.[27]

Perhaps a detail from the journals of the provincial preacher John Cleaveland gives the best insight into the unsettlingly powerful abilities of the ranger major. As smoke still hung over the bloody forest near the ruins of Fort Anne, Rogers interviewed two prisoners from the Régiment de la Marine. That's Marin, said one, pointing to a body—the leader of the French force, a name well known to Rogers.

Cleaveland reported that Rogers then scalped the corpse down the neck and, once the skin had dried on a stretcher, carved Marin's name into the grisly pale leather; these details were recounted without a single note of judgment. Yet the act was startling and noteworthy, not so much for its savagery—the war certainly had been full of worse—but because it so cleverly melded the New and Old Worlds: the lifting of the face representing the dark and largely alien arts of the Woodland Indian world, while the incised words spoke for the lettered Old World, of individual ownership and assertion. Here, withering flesh incarnate, was proof of Rogers's mastery over the ominous and forbidding forest world, his uncanny ability to turn woods magic back upon its inhabitants, to out-Indian the most terrible Indians.

It would turn out that Marin's death had been exaggerated. He had survived—skin intact—to fight another day.

Chapter 18

Allegro Guerriero

*If you determine to rally after a retreat, in order to make a fresh stand
against the enemy, by all means endeavour to do it on the most rising
ground you come at, which will give you greatly the advantage in point
of situation, and enable you to repulse superior numbers.*

ROGERS'S RULES OF RANGING, NUMBER XII[1]

On March 7, 1759, Rogers heaved himself up the last few icy feet of
Rattlesnake Mountain, the bitter wind plastering his blanket coat
against his body and searing his eyes. He could not remember such
cold—except perhaps that winter at Mountalona as a boy, when the
snowdrifts reached over the roof: weather "so severe that it is almost
impossible to describe,"[2] as he would later write. Four days in, he had
already sent 23 badly frostbitten regulars and rangers of his 358-man
command back to Fort Edward under direction of a "careful serjeant."[3]

In a few minutes another heavily clad figure joined Rogers atop
the smooth sedimentary outcropping—at a billion years old, it was
among the oldest exposed rock on Earth.[4] Lieutenant Diederick
Brehm, an engineer with the Royal Americans, was glad to have this
large, silent man next to him as they surveyed the snow-choked landscape spread before them. While Rattlesnake Mountain (today
Mount Defiance) rarely warrants listing among the array of high,
craggy peaks that crowd the Adirondacks, this modest height has
played a more strategic role in North American history than perhaps
any other. The killing field of the previous July, where more than
2,000 men died in the abatis and in front of the trenches on Carillon
Heights, lay nakedly exposed, as did the star-shaped outline of

Carillon in plain relief on the peninsula, whose outreach to the farther shore nearly closed the lake's north-south highway. Unseen, the
La Chute River ran right against the mountain's foot. On that ice-
clear winter day, Rogers and Brehm could see both Lakes George and
Champlain, a feat possible from no other location. That vantage
made the strategic denying power of Carillon inescapably clear: land,
lake, and river close upon one another, as geographically critical as
Fort Pitt's command of the meeting of three rivers was to the Ohio
Country. And affording the clearest overview of Carillon stood
Rattlesnake Mountain, the Achilles' heel of any eighteenth-century
nation that should occupy the fort, not only for the freedom it gave
spying eyes but also as an ideal perch for artillery.

Despite Rogers's many trips to the summit and his uniquely
vast experience with the tangled land running up to the fort,
Abercromby and his officers had all but cut Rogers out of the intelligence loop during July's disastrous offensive. But the situation had
now changed: in November William Pitt had reached out from
London and replaced Abercromby with Jeffery Amherst, the hero of
the brilliant capture of Louisbourg in July 1758. This cautious and
practical leader would not make Abercromby's mistakes.

Brehm noted that the enemy lines "appeared to me from the Top
of this mountain like a Fence of Rails about a Field and the Loggs
verry small," an acknowledgment of the tricks of perspective that had
so critically impaired Engineer Mathew Clerk's judgment.[5] Brehm
and Rogers discussed the lay of the land and the placement of artillery, which, Rogers pointed out, could deliver devastating enfilade
from Rattlesnake's lower flanks. Had Abercromby elicited such an
analysis from him the year before, Carillon might have fallen.

Rogers stationed five Indians and a ranger on the mountain so
they could observe any foot or sleigh traffic from the fort to the log-
ging glades on the eastern shore. On the way down he and Brehm discussed the importance of supplementing the engineer's detailed
observations with a reconnaissance of the fort's outer defenses.
Within hours the 20-year-old Lieutenant James Tute, a hardened veteran of the Battle on Snowshoes, and ten rangers infiltrated the fort's
unmanned external entrenchments under cover of darkness, returning safely by midnight. The regulars on Rogers's detail, under Captain
Samuel Williamos, a Swiss line officer in the Royal Americans, had

not fared well in the winter conditions. Finding them "extremely distressed with cold," Rogers directed Tute and 30 rangers to escort Williamos and all but one regular back to Sabbath Day Point and out of the orbit of the enemy's daily patrols, where they could build bonfires. At three A.M. Rogers, three lieutenants, 40 rangers, Captain John Lottridge, 46 Indians, and a single unnamed regular left to "attack the enemy's working parties on the east-side of the lake early in the morning."[6] But while Rogers's party battled the savage cold, a highly placed figure back in Albany was working purposefully to break up the ranger corps and take its leader out of the game.

As the creator of a new special formation, whose functions and possibilities each new superior had had to be taught, Rogers—who had watched three superiors come and go—reacted to Abercromby's departure with some resignation, writing that "I had now new commanders to obey, new companions to converse with, and, as it were, a new apprenticeship to serve."[7] In contrast, Brigadier General Thomas Gage saw the advent of a new commander as an opportunity. From his post in Albany he worked to establish himself as the filter through which Amherst, now based in New York City, would interact with Fort Edward and the Champlain front. Rogers's continued success and recognition throughout the colonies worked against Gage's plan to replace the rangers with a regular light infantry regiment—his very own 80th Foot, which he had created the year before. He primed the pump by writing Amherst that Rogers was "a good man in his way but his Schemes are very wild, & He has a new one every Day."[8] Rogers's way, Gage clearly implied, was not the king's way—or perhaps more important the army's. At first blush Gage's antipathy to Rogers and the rangers seems to reflect the dislike that most British regulars felt for the often-sloppy performance and discipline of the provincial soldiers. But it may have been the very sinister, unorthodox effectiveness of the forest warriors that pushed Gage beyond contemptuous impatience into deep and unsettled resentment. Indeed, Gage's clever and sustained operations even hinted at a more personal animosity; its bitterness would flower a decade hence with tragic consequences for Rogers.

Gage's 80th had failed to distinguish itself, particularly in the confusion that had resulted in Howe's death during the attack on Carillon the year before. Gage failed to understand that the rangers had morphed into a brand-new form of combat unit within a regular army under Rogers. Gage wrote to Amherst that the perfect antidote to marauding Indian parties was a "Light Infantry of the Regiment headed by a Brisk Officer." By all means mix in a few of the boldest rangers, he added, but only "to prevent their being lost in the Woods."[9] What Howe had certainly begun to see—even Loudoun and Shirley in their own ways—was that small-unit woods fighting required far more than developing way-finding skills and adapting woods-friendly uniforms and weapons; it involved a whole corpus of new skills in woodcraft and survival, micro-operational capacities, and an esprit de corps that enabled men to transcend their own perceived physical and emotional capacities.

Gage did have some legitimate gripes with ranger discipline. Rogers's command was gravely depleted: its 600-man nominal strength actually stood at effectively just one-third, brutally cut as it was by wounds, disease, desertion, and expired enlistments. "Rogers's Rangers are far from compleat and have so many Boys among them that they are not worth a Farthing," wrote physician Huck, who still fed Loudoun gossip from Albany.[10] Despite their sorely thinned standing, however, the ranger corps kept up a strategically high level of activity over the winter.

The past years of raids and battles had culled many of its finest leaders and men from the original high-hearted band, the brutal overhead exacted from a force required to go so often into harm's way. And as the natural talent pool of woodsmen sank lower and lower, Rogers and his officers drew more deeply upon men and boys with little or no experience and recruited volunteers from the militias. In contrast to the regulars, the rangers had no schools for officers, no standardized drills or training for other ranks, nor much in the way of indoctrination into life as a soldier. Increasingly, ranger duty resembled that of British airmen plugged into the Battle of Britain—woefully unprepared for life on the keenest of edges. So Rogers gathered new recruits as best he might, "the levies from the several provinces forwarded, the companies of Rangers compleated, and disciplined in the best manner I was capable of."[11]

Out of necessity as much as invention, Rogers shaped the changing landscape by instilling esprit de corps. A volunteer found himself joining an institution already full of shared stories, as well as resolute expectations and warrior ambitions. The rangers had bloomed beyond being simply Rogers's followers, however large his presence still loomed; they were now members of a team whose authority came from sharing the inexplicable and incommunicable experience of suffering, then overcoming and pushing beyond the humanly possible. Like marines or airborne today, the rangers were part of an exclusive group that had the express intention of redefining the possible, something that few outsiders could understand. Much later this quality would give the 75th Ranger Regiment its right to assert that "Rangers lead the way." Rogers had become the pack leader of a lone-wolf institution that could go out faster and compass actions beyond regular imagination or endurance.

Gage's most powerful resentments may have stemmed from a deeper issue. His command ability had come under great criticism during Braddock's disaster four years earlier, when he had led the advance force with striking lack of effect. Had he acted decisively in the first moments of the encounter and wheeled his men onto the hillside, he could likely have bought the main column time to rally and hold. Why had he not detailed men to occupy the height on their right flank? "It seems morally certain," wrote Shirley to Sir Thomas Robinson, secretary of state for the Southern Department and leader of the House of Commons, "that if the Eminence mark'd out in the Plans had been occupied in time by part of the General's troops, which it is agreed might have been done, he must have with ease defeated the Enemy."[12]

Nor did Gage's justification of his actions to Shirley answer the criticisms. The blame he cast upon his men rang hollow. In the end, he had thrown up his hands and concluded that the army had been undone by "the Novelty of an invisible enemy and the Nature of the Country, which was entirely a Forest."[13] (This remark reveals exactly the lack of imagination and active eye for terrain that rangers, and all special forces, possess and assume their enemies possess.) Then again, during Abercromby's debacle before Carillon, Gage seems to have disappeared, something noted by the soldiers who had been left behind to fight. The profession of arms across time has shown that personal courage is an indispensable element of leadership. Rogers, little educated and coming to terms with his calling as he practiced it, drew the complete loyalty of his men in a way that Gage never would.

Gage had been sowing discord well before Rogers's and Brehm's scout to Rattlesnake Mountain. Orders had come from Loudoun in mid-February to attack French positions that summer: Amherst was to strike north from Fort Edward to take Carillon and Fort Saint-Frédéric, while Wolfe pressed up the St. Lawrence with the fleet against Québec City. Needing intelligence on enemy strength, Amherst instructed Colonel Frederick Haldimand, commanding at Fort Edward, to dispatch Rogers and Brehm to make detailed drawings and descriptions of Carillon. Rogers would take 52 "Mohawks, Conojehery's, Schoharrys, Dilliways, Oneidas, and Seanekee's,"[14] under Lieutenant Lottridge. In addition, Captain Williamos would bring up 207 regulars from the 1st and 60th regiments.

Although the orders clearly dictated that Rogers would command the expedition, Williamos challenged his seniority, claiming that a regular captaincy overrode any ranger commission. A week and a half earlier Gage had written Haldimand exploiting a lack of clarity in the standing of the forces. Pitt had cleared up rank issues among regulars and provincials, so far as he could at 3,000 miles' distance, by determining that provincials were subordinate to regular officers of equal as well as superior grade. Technically, however, the rangers were not provincials. "The Rangers have, strictly speaking, no Rank at all, but as the Provincials had Rank, the Rangers assumed it, & were suffered to enjoy it last Campaign... You will avoid all dispute on this Subject as much as possible, for fear of disgusting the Rangers, but if You are forced to a decision, You must decide against the Officers of the Rangers as They have certainly no Rank in the Army."[15]

Even though Williamos brought more than twice as many regulars as the rangers, these men had little winter experience, and none of them had snowshoes: to Rogers's now-veteran eyes, that added up to the likelihood of disaster. He strongly contested Williamos's challenge, and the captain finally relented "to prevent all impediments towards their moving."

On March 8 Rogers moved out with his ninety-strong mixed unit, crossing Lake Champlain eight miles south of the fort by six A.M., then turning north until they approached the shore across from

Carillon. Creeping up close, two rangers and two Indians identified a party of woodcutters and guards. Rogers's men stripped off their blanket coats and packs and, at his signal, swept downhill, taking seven prisoners and "destroying most of the party."

At the sound of musketry a force of some 80 Canadian militia and Indians streamed out of the fort, followed minutes later by 150 regulars. Rogers moved south along the lake's eastern shore, keeping his force in an orderly but fast line abreast—no mean feat over rough terrain in the snow with a greatly superior and formidable enemy hot on their heels. After a mile the Canadians and Indians made contact, but their quarry swung to form a front along a hill; the pursuers advanced with resolution but were met with such steady fire, probably from a pair system in which one man fired while the other reloaded, as to be sent back reeling before the regulars came up. The march resumed in line abreast; within half a mile, when the first contingent gamely resumed the attack, the rangers doubled up to the crest of a long ridge parallel to the lake and resumed their stand. "The Canadians and Indians came very close" and displayed great bravery, wrote Rogers, but they "could not stand against our Marksmen."

Again the irregulars broke before the regulars could back them up; several Indians and rangers scrambled after the stragglers, as though running down deer worn out by wallowing through the deep snow. Traipsing abreast, the main group continued south unmolested. The enemy had had enough for that day. Rogers had lost two rangers and the sole regular; one Indian was badly wounded. He calculated that they had downed thirty of their pursuers. By deploying into line and making effective use of the topography, he had denied the enemy any chance to flank the retreat. And by moving fast, he had kept one step ahead of the slower regulars, who never got a chance to engage.

The withdrawal went on for the next twelve hours, as sensation agonizingly left first fingers and toes, then feet and hands. In time the marchers would forget how they moved their legs through the drifts, but they just kept doing it, keeping going because the major said they could. The rangers came through that cruel day in the teeth of adversity that, even with today's maps, clothing, and nutrition, would weed out most of those attempting it. Under such circumstances it is the spirit, not the body, that first succumbs: demons crawl out of the abyss of advancing cold and fatigue to implant dark thoughts that steal the will, then suck energy and life from the thighs and heart.

Two of the prisoners could not keep up and were killed without compunction, a detail Rogers did not mention in his scouting report but that he coolly lays out in his published journals. (No international agreement on the treatment of captives existed; only the possibility of reprisal and the disapproval of one's superiors regulated conduct.) At midnight, after twenty-one hours of slogging through subzero cold, several of them in fierce combat, and covering nearly 50 miles, the men stumbled into Williamos's camp at Sabbath Day Point, where "the Captain received us with good fires, than which scarce any thing could be more acceptable to my party." Rogers's journal refers only indirectly to the ordeal, commenting it was "excessive cold, and the snow four feet deep." But it had tried the toughest of his men. The next morning he sent the rested Lieutenant Tute back to Fort Edward with word of an Indian raiding party whose southward tracks they had encountered, and reported that "two-thirds of my detachment have froze their feet . . . some of which we are obliged to carry."[16] Haldimand sent 100 soldiers and 22 sleighs to bear off the disabled, one of them Rogers himself, along with a letter of congratulation.

Arriving at Fort Edward on the evening of March 10, Rogers and his officers were still "so fatigued" that they could not render Colonel Haldimand a lucid report.[17] A captain-lieutenant of the regulars recorded in his journal that "many . . . lost their limbs, and these chiefly rangers."[18] But what Amherst received shortly thereafter—Brehm's detailed engineering report on Carillon and its defenses; intelligence from the French prisoners about troop strength and their leaders' intentions; and an account of how the detachment had repulsed two and a half times its numbers—could not but please him. Even Gage grudgingly admitted the extreme nature of Rogers's undertaking.

Gage was still stinging from Amherst's approval of one of Rogers's "crazy schemes"—specifically, to enlist two companies of Stockbridge Indians and one of Connecticut Mohegans into the rangers. Rogers had urged both Gage and Amherst to reenlist the Stockbridges for the upcoming campaign, which only moved Gage to warn Amherst immediately that "these Indians were last Campaign so great a nuisance to the Army and did no Manner of service... neither orders nor Entreatys could prevail on them to do service, always lying drunk in their Hutts, or firing round the Camp"—allegations that more than stretched the truth.[19] One hundred Stockbridge Indians had joined Abercromby's army and fought in the attack on Carillon, as well as taking part in several scouts, which brought in prisoners and scalps. Amherst responded just as bitterly but modified his venom to meet a commander's needs: "I know what a vile crew they are, and I have as vile opinion of those lazy rum-drinking scoundrels as any one can have; I shall however take them into His Majesty's service for the next campaign... The French are afraid of them."[20] On Rogers's return he found a letter from Colonel Roger Townshend, Amherst's deputy adjutant general, approving the embodiment of the Indian units as ranger companies.

Of the recent scout, Rogers wrote that the Mohawks had "behaved with great bravery; some having been within pistol-shot of the French fort."[21] He thereby rated the Indians in the light of their performance in the field, a further application of dangerous New World evenhandedness that was distressing in principle to most British officers. Throughout the war Rogers would champion Indian membership in the rangers.

The captain of one of the Stockbridge companies, Jacob Naunauphtaunk, had indeed heard about Rogers's interest in signing up the Stockbridges and had come to Albany, refusing to negotiate terms with anyone else. And so Rogers, still able to walk only with difficulty from his frostbite, was dispatched by sleigh and horse. There, recorded Gage mockingly, "the two Chiefs [held] their conference"[22]—his disdain for Rogers could perhaps sink no deeper than to equate him with an Indian. Naunauphtaunk returned to Stockbridge with good terms and a letter from Rogers commissioning his son, Jacob Cheeksaunkun, to raise a company of his own. Rogers further wrote to King Uncas, head sachem of the Connecticut Mohegans, promising him a captain's commission, a company clerk, and the choice of an ensign and two sergeants from among the white ranger companies, should he put together a company of 50 men: "I heartily wish you success in raising your men, and shall be exceeding glad that you join me with all the expedition you possibly can." These high-flown sentiments came backed by a belt of wampum that gave his authority "credit or influence," as Rogers noted with true New England dryness.

Hearing about the early friction between Rogers and Williamos before the raid, Gage wrote pointedly to Amherst: "The Matter is loose & wants to be fixed."[23] His notion of fixing the issue was pretty conclusive; as Rogers recuperated in Albany and prepared for the summer campaign, Gage conspired to disband the rangers. Soon hundreds of new ranger recruits, some led by Rogers himself, would be arriving at Fort Edward, but Gage ordered Colonel Haldimand to have them report to a regular officer "& the six Companys leveled & distinguished from each other," which would break up Rogers's command.[24]

With indirection that would have been impressive in a better cause, Gage wrote Amherst on April 9 that Rogers "left this Place a few Days ago, with Orders to put his Comp'ys in some order, but as I know him to be a true Ranger & not much addicted to Regularity, I had before sent Directions on this head to Col'o Haldimand." And, he continued more explicitly, "I inclose you a Scheme for putting the Rangers in some better order, which I have got Major Moneypenny to write out; if you approve of it send your Directions, many Things more may be added."[25] Would Gage's gambit work with Amherst?

In public Rogers held his tongue, though privately he must have been furious at Gage's machinations, one of the most serious challenges to his command in the war. Perhaps he was somewhat reassured by Amherst's letter of April 1, which firmly declared that "I shall always cheerfully receive Your opinion in relation to the Service you are Engaged in."[26] Something had jelled in the relationship between the short, cautious English gentleman and the towering, roughhewn frontiersman where it had not with Gage—even though Amherst was no great supporter of provincials, let alone of Indians. It is also telling that Amherst, not hesitant to criticize those around him, never wrote disparagingly about Rogers. And his estimation of him soared after the American-loathing James Wolfe, at work on his plans for attacking Québec City, directly asked Amherst to have the ranger leader support him. Few British field commanders bore greater contempt in general for provincial soldiers than Wolfe, who had famously written that "they die falling down in their own filth."

"There are in America three or four excellent men in their way," wrote Wolfe. "Bradstreet for the Battoes and for the expeditions is an extraordinary man; Rogers is an excellent partisan for 2 or 300 men, and young Clarke under my Lord Howe . . . will make a good figure as an engineer for the field."[27] Amherst politely turned Wolfe down; he would need Rogers close at hand for the upcoming campaign. As for Gage's insistence on breaking up the rangers, Amherst seems to have simply ignored him.

Rogers's validation came in the second week of May, when he met Amherst in Albany and reported being "very kindly received." The general countermanded Gage by upholding Rogers's rank, affirming that he was "on all detachments to take rank as Major according to the date of his commission . . . as such, next after the Majors who have the King's Commission, or one from his Majesty's Commander-in-Chief." Rogers returned to Fort Edward having dodged a well-aimed bullet and in command of ten companies of rangers.

But he also heard the devastating news of the death of Captain Jonathan Burbank of New Hopkinton, New Hampshire, a comrade since mid-1756, and "a gentleman, I very highly esteemed, and one of the best officers among the Rangers."[28] An Abenaki party had jumped him as he led a scout of 30 men near the narrows, and left him and three other rangers scalped and "mangled in a shocking Manner," reported *The Boston Gazette*.[29] The ranger prisoners later reported that the savagery arose from the Abenakis mistaking Burbank for Rogers—a chilling reminder about what lay in store should the real Rogers fall into their hands. Rogers concedes in his journals his great uneasiness, "especially as I judged the scout he was sent out upon by the commanding officer at the fort was needless, and unadvisedly undertaken."[30] It was a situation with which Rogers was unfortunately all too familiar.

Chapter 19

To Carillon Once Again

Such Fury that the Logs Composing it Which Were More than 2½ feet and Some of them 3 Feet Diameter Were Flung Thirty Rods [165 yards] From the place Where the Magazine Stood and pitch'd Endways into the Ground 3 and 4 Feet and Cross'd in all manner of Directions Shivered as With lightning.

JESSE PARSONS, 3RD CONNECTICUT,
ON THE EXPLOSION AT CARILLON[1]

At six A.M. on July 21, 1759, an armada carrying more than 11,000 soldiers again spread across the waters of southern Lake George.[2] A number of the green-timber bateaux promptly took on water, forcing their complements to scurry and offload supplies; even so, a boat carrying 100 barrels of powder as well as a raft with two ten-inch mortars sank. Finally the *Invincible*, a heavy radeau, carrying four 12-pounders and four 24-pounders, hauled up a bloodred flag, signaling the fleet to row or to sail downlake. Amherst was irritated at the weeks of delay, but it had taken time to throw up a formidable series of five stockaded strongpoints between Fort Edward and Lake George to protect the army's vulnerable supply chain. Most especially, the construction of vessels capable of carrying heavy artillery had compounded the delay. Amherst would not repeat Abercromby's mistake of failing to arrive at Carillon with adequate firepower: the fleet bore 51 cannons, howitzers, and mortars.[3]

Nine days earlier Amherst had sent Rogers, Major John Campbell, and between 400 and 500 rangers, provincials, and Highlanders again downlake to the narrows in whaleboats and bateaux to clear the outlying islands. At the head of a curious fleet was a rowing galley mounting an 18-pounder. At eight A.M., as they approached their target, a small force of French and Indians opened fire, killing a ranger sergeant and wounding an Indian. The gunners on the galley discharged their piece prematurely, its shot falling harmlessly into the water, but the blast, along with the rangers now streaming onto one of the islands, sent the enemy fleeing. The force sank three enemy bateaux, killed a number of Indians, and burned the rudimentary breastworks and some stockades. Four days later they revisited their place of success to confirm that the enemy had not returned. Amherst's careful and deliberate use of the rangers, now and still more critically during the campaign, posthumously vindicated Howe's sense of the importance of intelligence.

In January Montcalm's aide-de-camp Colonel de Bougainville had got through to Paris bearing his general's desperate request for substantial reinforcements for the summer campaign. That winter the king's ministers, their attention fixed on the battlefields of Central Europe, deemed that France could ill afford to siphon off critical resources to the Canadian front, and they instructed Montcalm to cope with his present forces until the main French armies could gain major strategic victories on the Weser and in Brandenburg. Without reinforcements and with Québec City now under attack by James Wolfe's expeditionary force, Montcalm was in a bind.

On July 22 Rogers' Rangers landed in the van of the invasion force on the eastern shore of Lake George. Rogers' Rock loomed in plain view across the water, near the beginning of the portage road, which the French had blocked by felling tall oaks. Light infantry and grenadiers under Colonel Haviland followed Rogers, with orders to march "across the mountains in the isthmus; from thence, in a byway, athwart the woods to the bridge at the Saw-mills." The sight of the portly Colonel Haviland leading the advance guard stuck in the craw of many rangers, especially the few surviving veterans who remembered the fateful orders that had culminated in the Battle on Snowshoes.

Even though these citizen-volunteers had pushed time and again deep into danger and often suffered severely, they were once more sent out brusquely, often with inadequate numbers. That morning the ranger esprit kicked into high gear. Rogers's column struck uphill with relish, soon leaving Haviland's vaunted light infantry behind.

The capable commandant of the 2,300 men under arms at Carillon, Le Chevalier de Bourlamaque, knew of Amherst's approach. He had targeted the bridge across the La Chute River, where the sawmills clustered at the end of the portage road, as the best spot to make a stand; as he later wrote, "I wished to take advantage of that moment to make an attack on the troops in advance."[4] He himself led 300 Indians and about 100 other regulars and militia to the chokepoint at the bridge.

The speed with which the rangers stormed over the bridge and onto the opposite high bank caught the French quite off guard. In the face of sharp initial losses, Bourlamaque had difficulty motivating his Indians, losing vital moments that enabled Rogers's men to establish a formidable front. The French were left with no option but to fall back on Carillon under devastating fire.

When Haviland's grenadiers and light infantry finally arrived, they found the rangers in possession of the bridge and high ground—and waving several bloody scalps. While the French had planned to retreat anyway, Rogers's boldness while not losing a single man had defanged their power to make a damaging defense. Rogers's journals typically remain silent on the details of the attack, but the French most likely would have posted sentries at the bridge. Were these the four Frenchmen that several private journals say were killed, wiped out by a silent ranger detail dispatched by Rogers? His understated reporting leaves palpable silences and omissions. Perhaps the details of men crawling toward the enemy with scalping knives in their teeth to clamp a hand over the sentries' mouths, then slit their throats, might appear ungentlemanly and coarse, indeed boastful and murderous.

Yet Rogers's journals—what he chooses to tell and what he omits—reveal a man mysterious by design, who left the question of how he did things hanging in the air. Great stage magicians rarely reveal the tricks of their trade—how their assistant remains unscathed by the saw or how the elephant disappears—because the cold facts of technique shatter the illusion of supernatural mastery. Even Rogers's body of rules reveals precious little about the nuts and bolts of survival; they serve merely as guidelines along which to act. Time and again his journals have the reader wondering, How did he do that?

As the regulars marched up to the sawmills in perfect order, their contrast with the green-suited rangers could not have been more dramatic. Even the rawest recruit in the advance force could now share derisive smiles and knowing looks with his comrades. They stood apart.

Back where the portage road set in, provincials had cleared the abatis in only two hours, and soon the main army was marching up to the mills, dragging four pieces of heavy artillery. Amherst recorded his pleasure "with possessing a spot of ground so well fortified by nature, that the enemy with 2,000 regulars might have dispersed his whole army."

For the rest of the short campaign, wherever action took place, Rogers and his men were there, first attacking entrenchments, then furnishing the broad-gauged combat-exploration parties that circulated up to Crown Point that provided, as he wrote, "hourly intelligence from those posts." For three days after the attack on the bridgehead, the French pummeled the British with fierce cannonades while the British engineers built batteries for their own artillery placement. A cannonball clove Colonel Roger Townshend in two as he rode out to glass the enemy fortifications, costing Rogers another ally. Many of the Americans in Amherst's army would rise to prominence in the next war: Benedict Arnold, Ethan Allen, John Stark, Israel Putnam.

Under the cover of bombardment and nightfall, Bourlamaque evacuated the fort. His men rowed north, obeying orders to abandon so forward a position "as soon as the English army made its approach." Hébécourt and all but a skeleton force of 400 men remained behind "with orders to blow up the fort and to retire as soon as the enemy would have erected their first batteries."[5]

Indian parties provided further cover by mounting surprise attacks along the British line. During one encounter five regulars died and 11 were wounded, casualties exacted not only by Indian shots but by panicked "friendly fire" in defiance of Amherst's strict orders that "firing in the night must be avoided; the enemy must be received with fixed bayonets."[6]

Amherst seemed to lean on Rogers and his rangers throughout the next few days. On July 25 Rogers took 60 greencoats into the trenches by night to countersnipe enemy marksmen using a covered walkway dug into the glacis outside the fort. The hidden trench enabled the French to move at will and send out small raiding details. The rangers crept near that evening; their frequent and well-aimed shots exercised a most chilling effect.

On the twenty-sixth the British had pushed within 600 yards of Carillon's walls, but a log boom stretching from the Ticonderoga peninsula to the lake's eastern shore prevented their warships from cruising downlake to seal off the fort from the north. Again, Amherst turned to Rogers.

At nine P.M. Rogers used the cover of darkness to load some 60 rangers into three whaleboats and a flat-bottomed barge, armed with a swivel cannon. They pushed into the La Chute River near the mills, then wound silently and unobserved right beneath the fort, emerging into the lake. Just as they neared the lake's opposite shore, the stillness of the night was rent by an explosion, the sound and intensity of which North America had never seen. The French had slipped away, setting off fuses to the fort's magazine of hundreds of barrels of black powder, which had resulted in a conflagration that quickly spread to the barracks. The blasts continued for much of the evening, as the fort's cannon, each packed to the muzzle with powder and shot, exploded. The force of the initial explosion, wrote clerk Jesse Parsons of the 3rd Connecticut Regiment, went off with "Such Fury that the Logs Composing it Which Were More than 2½ feet and Some of them 3 Feet Diameter Were Flung Thirty Rods [165 yards] From the place Where the Magazine Stood and pitch'd Endways into the Ground 3 and 4 Feet and Cross'd in all manner of Directions Shivered as With lightning."[7]

Rogers and his men pressed north along the east bank of Lake Champlain and severed the log boom with large saws. Just before the explosion Amherst had been alerted to the garrison's intentions by a deserter and immediately sent out a messenger by boat instructing Rogers to attack any fleeing enemy. The party needed little prompting and rowed furiously north, soon espying a clump of bateaux. The rangers fired the swivel cannon and peppered the enemy with musket fire. Ten bateaux pulled ashore, their terrified occupants scattering into the woods: it was a relatively mild parting shot but one that had drawn blood. "A considerable quantity of baggage, and upwards of fifty barrels of powder, and large quantities of ball" had been abandoned with the boats, and the personal effects included a portmanteau belonging to Bourlamaque. The rangers brought in a cadet and 15 other prisoners.

The British had taken Carillon, so long a thorn in their side, without firing a single siege cannon. Inside they found, wrote Reverend Eli Forbush, "many monuments of Superstition which would Furnish a curious mind with aboundant Matter for Speculation."[8] Most prominently, on the entrenchments overlooking the scene of so much carnage a year earlier stood a taunting open grave. Above it towered a 30-foot-high red-painted cross with several Latin inscriptions carved into its side, including *Hoc Signum Vincit*, or "this sign conquers," recalling the vision of the Emperor Constantine before his triumph against the pagan Maxentius fourteen centuries before.

"The Whole is Such a place of Strength," wrote Parsons, "as Not hardly to be Equall'd in America and had I Known the Strength of it and I am Not alone in my opinion We Should Never have attacked it Without an Army of 30000 Men."[9]

Only Rogers' Rangers had engaged the enemy in any meaningful way and on each occasion with success. For this series of difficult and dangerous tasks, Amherst had turned not to Gage's light infantry or to Haviland's grenadiers but to the green-coated provincials, who all the while had continued to deliver critical intelligence. Had Amherst ever harbored any doubts about his chief scout's capabilities, he no longer did so.

Five days later a ranger forward patrol, led by Lieutenant John Fletcher of Brewer's Mohegan regiment, was approaching Crown Point when another detonation crumbled the four-story stone tower that dominated the small post. Inside the wall Fletcher's men found the grisly remains of horses, tethered so that they could not escape the explosion and fall into British hands. Fletcher surveyed the wreckage, and beyond it, fading far uplake, he saw a French fleet wearily making its way homeward. Finding the flagpole halyard cut, he claimed Fort Saint-Frédéric by carving his name into its mast. In the gardens his men found some cucumbers and apples that they brought back for General Amherst.

After maintaining a forward position for more than thirty years in the Lake Champlain area, the French had fallen back on their forts along the Richelieu River. Québec City remained under siege.

So far as Rogers was concerned, one target lay untouched, but still threatening, as it had for the entire eighteenth century: the Abenaki town of Saint-François.

Chapter 20

Mission Impossible

Only Men of Constitutions like Lions could ever have went through.

NEW-YORK GAZETTE, NOVEMBER 26, 1759,
ABOUT THE SAINT-FRANÇOIS RAID

A dozen miles north of Crown Point, on the eastern shore of Lake Champlain, amid the buttonbush, bulrush, and cattail wetlands that crowded Otter Creek's sodden delta, Rogers glassed downlake for the lateen sails of a French sloop or schooner. Pulled deep into hiding in the marsh lay 17 whaleboats, each carrying eight long oars and provisions for a month. The expedition soon to be launched would undergo perhaps the most grueling ordeal ever recorded in North American history, and in so enduring and surviving its members would write a new chapter in the roster of special operations. Amherst had finally approved Rogers's long-nurtured plan to make a bold and unprecedented strike against Saint-François, 150 miles north as the crow flies—but not as the woodsman labors—into Canada. By playing the enemy's own game of waging fast, surprising, and destructive small-unit warfare, Rogers was gambling that he could take the teeth out of the Indians' will to continue their alliance with the French. It was a bold gamble, indeed: no British ground expeditionary force during the war had even contemplated a long-range lunge of such operational scope or strategic intent.

As he and his nearly 200 handpicked men waited patiently, Rogers heard the shrill cry of a bald eagle. They watched as it swept from its broad nest amid silver maples and green ashes, beating its powerful wings in search of a fat chain pickerel or yellow perch. It was

Saturday, September 15, 1759. The fall weather, already unseasonably cold, had silenced the summer chatter of bullfrog and peeper
and brought early frosts that had at least blessedly killed off mosquitoes and biting flies.

Then Rogers's glass disclosed one sloop, then another, sails full,
tacking smartly within the lake's close confines. Soon they were
joined by a larger schooner. They were not particularly pretty ships;
the French had cobbled them together quickly, from sails, masts, and
fittings that they had stripped from merchant vessels at Québec; but
he could easily see the deadliness of their armaments. The 65-ton
sloops mounted swivel guns on their gunwales, and the iron noses of
six-pounders protruded from cannon doors. The 70-ton topsail
schooner *Vigilante* bore a brace of brass 12-pounders, as well as a
half-dozen iron six-pounders. Eighty-two seamen, especially brought
in from the Great Banks fishery, manned this tough little fleet of
three ships and one sloop. Sixty soldiers and 36 militia filled out
the complement.[1] A formidable sailor hardened in the privateer calling, Joannis-Galand d'Olabaratz, commanded the flotilla from the
Vigilante.

Had Rogers not pulled his craft inshore, these warships would
have made short work of them. In columns on the water the 17
whaleboats stretched upward of a tenth of a mile in slow parade—
easy pickings for an enemy that could top eight knots, when even
straining and frightened oarsmen found it hard to get whaleboats up
to three. A single two-pound ball that bounced over the water could
rip a large hole through the planking to wreak havoc among shoulder-
to-shoulder oarsmen. French swivel pieces, filled to the muzzle with
langrage—fragments of scrap iron forming a kind of giant shotgun
charge—would finish off any mutilated and unlucky survivors, all
well before the ship came within even ranger musket range.

The French might have abandoned Carillon and Fort Saint-
Frédéric, but they certainly had not ceded the lake itself to advancing
British power. Ranger scouts reported that three ships were ferrying
the evacuated garrison and its supplies north from explosion-wrecked
Crown Point. The squadron hovered around the chain of tiny islands
known as Isles aux Quatre Vents (The Four Winds Islands, or the
Four Brothers)[2], ready to pounce on any British raiding party or fleet,
as eager for plunder as they were to do their king's bidding.

The gauntlet that Rogers intended to run swung 75 miles from Crown Point north to Missisquoi Bay, at the lake's northeastern headwater. Over the first 20 miles Champlain keeps its thin figure, distending to more than three miles wide at only one point, and constricting to less than a mile at the Narrows, in the shadow of New York's Split Rock Mountain, and again between Split Rock Point and Thompson Point in today's Vermont, the most difficult passages in which to evade detection. North of Essex, New York, the lake abandons its mountain-valley character, swelling over the next ten miles to almost ten miles across. On the evening of the fourteenth, no clouds or fog masked the waning quarter moon,[3] so the impatient troops had to wait again. In wartime, inaction, especially in close proximity to the enemy, imposes a peculiar and difficult kind of stress. The enforced delay grated hard, especially on these men, who knew what lay ahead of them. Nerves jangled and tempers ran short.

The next day brought Rogers a raft of new headaches. He had already sent one sick Indian back to Crown Point; now he noticed that a couple dozen more men showed telltale signs of disease, perhaps the red eyes, the high fevers, and especially among people forced to pass up even rudimentary frontier washing, the maddening rashes of measles. Not two days into the expedition, he had a full-blown epidemic on his hands. Rendered impotent by the deadly corsairs and now menaced by mass ill-health, the men chewed on cold rations in the damp.

Disease had stalked Amherst's army all that spring and summer, in part moldering from uncommonly heavy rains, which, noted a camp reporter in *The Boston Evening-Post* with understatement, "has made the Troops (especially the Provincials) a little sickly."[4] Robert Webster of Colonel Fitch's 4th Connecticut Regiment at Crown Point frequently punctuated his brief daily journal entries with "I am in good health," as though he could not quite believe that he had again escaped the pestilences that were mercilessly robbing scores of men he knew of their lives. "Last night a man died in his tent and not one of his tent mates knew it. He belonged to Captain Stark's."[5] A devastating epidemic of measles struck, particularly at new recruits from isolated settlements, never before exposed to the virus. The Stockbridge Indians—like all native North American peoples—proved particularly susceptible to the originally European diseases that roiled through the crowded forts and encampments. Should measles get loose in this expedition, it might not kill many, but the high fevers and general malaise would mortgage its sufferers' energies and morale for weeks, to a degree that could not but compromise their commander's ambitious plan.

One further misfortune compounded his difficulties. Waiting had made officers and men edgy and careless. Captain Manley Williams of the Royal Americans, who commanded the raid's regular component, was "accidentally burnt with gunpowder," badly mangling his hand and severely searing his arm. Rogers does not elaborate, but a later newspaper account suggested that Williams and "a few more were wounded in stepping over some Logs by their Pieces going off"—neither a likely mass accident, nor specifically an easy way to burn one's arm, unless the weapon was being carried muzzle up, which even the rawest recruit must have known to avoid. Amherst's journal records that two badly wounded Highlanders made it back to Crown Point, where one succumbed.

Perhaps, on that day of hiding through the daylight hours at Otter Creek, the firearms discharged accidentally. Captain Williams's misfortune likely occurred because of those standard foul-ups, due to poor explosives discipline, that haunted seventeenth- and eighteenth-century warfare. Even though armorers took great care around the barrels of black powder in fortress magazines, wearing shoes without nails and using only wooden and leather tools, citadel after citadel vanished from a spark disaster; and field conditions proved anything but controllable, especially during letdowns in morale. Perhaps a bootstud struck a stone while Williams and others were rolling new cartridges.[6]

Rogers allowed accident and disease no further time to take their toll, however, posting forty-one men, mostly invalids, under a minimum escort of healthy rangers, back to Crown Point within forty-eight hours of setting out. Two score—stumbling, red-eyed, and some grotesquely powder-burned—filed back into camp, touching off rumors of a brutal surprise by an enemy lurking almost under the walls of the fort. A breathless correspondent in Albany told *The Boston Evening-News* that Rogers's scout had "soon fell in with 300 of the Enemy: He has taken and scalp'd 200 of them; but am afraid Major Rogers is either killed or wounded."[7] A week later the paper retracted. In the contested Champlain Valley thirsty rumor filled the void, pushed to a frantic pitch, but never more powerfully colorful and extreme than when it involved the ranger leader.

The return so soon of about a fifth of Rogers's force could hardly have lightened Amherst's frame of mind. Sketchy weeks-old communication indicated that Wolfe's siege of Québec was faring badly. Even worse news came from Gage, whom Amherst had directed to take over the garrison at Niagara, rebuild the fort at Oswego across Lake Ontario, then drop down the St. Lawrence to seize the post of La Gallette near the Oswegatchie River, which covered the Jesuits' particularly loyal Iroquois mission-village of La Présentation. That accomplished, Gage was to descend upon Montréal so that "the Enemy may be pressed and attacked in every Corner."[8] Amherst counted more on Gage's mobility because his own army lay bogged down at Ticonderoga and Crown Point, paralyzed by French naval control of the lakes and thus wholly unable to join hands with Wolfe in Québec. Any sensible commander in his position had to fear that his army could become dangerously stranded and overextended, should Wolfe have to abort his offensive along the St. Lawrence.

Much to Amherst's consternation, Gage directly contravened orders, insisting that to attack what he deemed a strong enemy at La Gallette so late in the season was foolishly hazardous, although intelligence correctly reported that the garrison was but lightly held. Rumors circulated that Gage and William Johnson were whiling away the campaign fishing and duck shooting.[9] "They have found difficulties where there are none," Amherst confided bitterly to his journal.[10] William Pitt and the king also wrote angrily that a fine opportunity had been missed.[11] When Amherst's army marched into Montréal the next year, Gage's command would bring up the rear, to his chief's lasting, profound, and public displeasure.

Communication between Wolfe and Amherst proved difficult that summer, the latter not even being certain whether the former knew of the fall of Carillon and Saint-Frédéric. His calls for volunteers to hazard an overland mission drew a tepid response. "Proposed to send one of Major Rogers People to try to get to Genl Wolfe but they would not undertake it," Amherst recorded on August 5.[12] He could hardly blame the unnamed ranger: Québec lay 200 miles to the north through unfamiliar and largely trackless wilderness, patrolled not by the French alone but by the Missisquoi and Saint-François Abenaki. Only when Amherst, desperate to contact the St. Lawrence fleet, offered 400 guineas for a volunteer did two Scots come forward—Captain Quinton Kennedy of the 80th Light Infantry and Lieutenant Archibald Hamilton of the 1st Foot. A Lowlander wounded on the Monongahela under Braddock, Kennedy had warmed to New World life, leading some bold raids and even taking an Indian wife. But these woods-savvy warriors realized that they could not make the run without a cover. Ultimately Amherst worked up a plan for them to travel disguised as Indians, accompanied by the real Captain Jacob Cheeksaunkun and six Stockbridge rangers. If caught by the Abenaki, they would wave a flag of truce and declare themselves ambassadors, ready to offer a handsome belt of wampum and negotiate peace. Once finished with their parley, the messengers would ostensibly carry the Abenaki response to Wolfe, while in fact delivering Amherst's secret correspondence. (Apparently abuse of the white flag was a crime only against white men.) The party left on August 9.

A month later Captain Disserat of the Régiment de La Reine appeared before Crown Point under a genuine flag of truce to inform Amherst that Abenakis had intercepted Kennedy's party near Saint-François.[13] While the men had quickly eaten Amherst's orders, they could not jettison two tin canisters of incriminating letters from British officers to friends in Wolfe's army. The French jailed the two disguised officers as spies. Word spread through the British ranks that an Abenaki had sliced off one of Kennedy's or Hamilton's ears. In fact, the French released the infiltrators quickly, having treated them far better than they were absolutely entitled to, while leaving the Stockbridge rangers in irons aboard a frigate. Montcalm's letter to Amherst gently mocked this distinctly marginal conduct. Embarrassed at being detected, and enraged at the rumors of his men's ill treatment, Amherst determined, says Rogers, "to chastize these savages with some severity."[14] His utterance was quite uncharacteristic of the officer of whom Sir Nathaniel Wraxall wrote, "I have scarcely ever known a man who possessed more stoical apathy."[15]

Sensing an opportunity, Rogers pressed Amherst with the plan to attack Saint-François, which he had harbored for several years. This initiative finally found its moment, and Amherst's orders dictated: "You will march and attack the enemy's settlements on the southside of the river St. Lawrence, in such a manner as you shall judge most effectual to disgrace the enemy, and for the success and honour of his Majesty's arms... Take your revenge, but don't forget that tho' those villains have dastardly and promiscuously murdered the women and children of all ages, it is my orders that no women or children are killed or hurt." Throughout the entire war no British raiding party had ever come close to penetrating Canadian territory by land.

Given Gage's inaction, and with the sawmill turning out the planks necessary for building gunboats only sporadically, it appeared that Rogers alone would be able to distract the French. Amherst would not learn for a month that the very same day on which the Saint-François party set out, Wolfe had launched a desperate storm of the Plains of Abraham and, through an unlikely chain of fortune, had reduced the great stronghold, albeit at the cost of his own life. Montcalm died from recklessly incurred wounds, and the French army retreated to regroup above the Jacques Cartier River, 32 miles west of Québec City, under the capable leadership of Brigadier General François-Gaston, Duc de Lévis.

Without a little luck or at least a dark night, Rogers would have gotten no farther than Otter Creek. But on the fifteenth, the French flotilla dropped past his position of concealment toward Crown Point, giving the rangers a small window of opportunity. The whaleboats hurriedly resumed their tortuous journey north, hugging the eastern shore; the oarsmen were ready to pitch their boats ashore and dive into the woods at the first sign of a sail. The French squadron's failure to detect Rogers's party must count as one of the largest intelligence bungles in the war.

Grand Isle and a chain of long, thin islands split the northern third of Lake Champlain nearly down the middle. The west branch leads north to the Richelieu River, and the French island fort of Île aux Noix, on its way to empty into the St. Lawrence. The eastern channel crosses a sandbar, passes just over the present Canadian border, and dead-ends in the shallows of Missisquoi Bay, which draws only two fathoms. On September 16 Bourlamaque, now commanding at Île aux Noix, led a scout to Missisquoi Bay and commented that "I would like to be in Mr. Amherst's place. I would launch an attack that way without difficulty."[16] Two additional scouts on the twentieth and twenty-first still showed no enemy activity there; but this was indeed where Rogers was headed.

The long train of boats, each kept close to the next according to Rogers's Rule Number XXV, not only prevented dangerous straggling but also made mutual assistance possible in the event that gummed seams burst or a westerly wave broadsided and capsized part of the column. Several days of bad weather had kicked up the lake water and made rowing yet more difficult, the boats forever shipping chill water and bringing the gunwales even closer to the hammering waves. "This lake is not like Lake-George, for the waves in it rise sometimes as high almost as in the main ocean," an unnamed correspondent from Crown Point would write a month later.[17]

The loss of so many men at the outset also meant that the rest had little break from rowing, which left legs and buttocks sore from bracing against the boats' pitch and roll; involuntary shudders gripped the men for hours on end, the only salve coming from pushing sore muscles just a little bit harder. Each man had made hundreds of false promises to himself that the destination was only another half-hour's effort away, only to find that the blades must still be pulled at least as hard as ever; then he made up a new set of fantasies while trying to keep in rhythm with the bent back in front. Each ranger, locked into his own cell of quiet personal misery, almost, but not quite, blocked out the burning fear that a deadly mass of French and Indians awaited in the wet brush that clothed each bend, muskets cocked and ready to steal his and his comrades' lives. So many scouts had ended badly; the Canadians and their allies had always played the deep-woods game better. And yet they trusted the unblustering major whose quiet authority kept them going.

In the morning hours of September 23 they pulled into the northern confines of Missisquoi Bay. A cold rain had pounded the open boats all night, soaking the wool blankets wrapped around heads and shoulders and leaving moccasins and leggings sodden and stiff with cold. Fingers that had grasped oar handles for so long, in the biting chill and damp, as to lose the capacity to extend took long minutes to uncurl and flex, as though a crippling arthritis had run through the whole detachment. Rogers indicated a landing spot among the marshy woodlands, under the shadow of a small ridge, beneath which now stands the town of Philipsburg, Quebec. One by one the boats ground ashore, the men just grateful to stagger on land. But they found little comfort in the dank woodlands, where considerations of concealment prevented their building fires. The officers signaled by hand as the boats were dragged ashore, the supplies were unloaded, and then the craft were overturned and covered with brush.

A hundred and fifty men in 17 boats could only be so quiet despite stern restrictions on talking. Rowlocks squeaked, and the gentlest splash of oars could not but carry far over water. A small party of keen-eared Abenaki hunters were hurrying for the warmth and brandy of Île aux Noix, some ten miles off; despite the insistent patter of rain, they heard some unmistakably human sound in the cool fall stillness and hurried yet faster. Before the war more than 20 Abenaki families had lived on the bay, five miles or so south of Rogers's position, and some of the party knew the area well.[18]

Unaware of this shadowy passage, the rangers parceled out at least a week's cache of provisions to tuck into the boats for the return journey. Rogers posted two Indian rangers to lie watch over the boats; should the enemy discover them, they were "with all possible speed to follow on my track, and give me intelligence."[19] The raiders' destination still lay 72 miles away; they would have to wind as much as a third more of that distance to follow any practical path.[20]

The small command moved directly east and away from Île aux Noix, out into the gently undulating hardwood forest of what is now southern Québec. While it still comprised a few more than 150 men, it had already lost much of the Indian ranger complement and two of its three regular officers. Amherst had required Rogers to pick his men from among the entire army, not just the rangers, a provision that may have galled him—but if so, he had wisely kept it to himself. A little more than half the original unit had been white and Indian rangers; Rogers filled out the cadre with some three dozen provincials from five regiments, all under the veteran Captain Ogden of the New Jersey Blues. Some twenty volunteers from the regular light infantry, led by Lieutenant William Dunbar of Gage's 80th, rounded out the party.[21] As was so often the case over the course of his military career, Rogers was struggling to build coherent working order among a disparate group while on the actual mission; the vast majority had never received formal military, let alone special irregular, training. Yet time and again he proved able to mold frontier individualists into coherent and effective battle formations by communicating effectively through his lieutenants and by imparting information and intent with clarity that all would understand, from the unlettered pioneer Scots-Irish and the praying Indian to the British regular and the flat-footed coastal provincial. Considering what they were now attempting, they would have to find much common ground merely to survive.

Of course, Rogers could count on some familiar faces. In some sort of miracle, Lieutenant William Phillips, whom Rogers had last seen tied to a tree by Indians at the Battle on Snowshoes, had turned up to lend a most unlikely hand. Most of Phillips's men had died in the March battle, many hacked to pieces, but he had survived and been carried to Canada, from which he had made a truly rangerly escape.[22] Finding his lieutenancy filled by another man, Phillips volunteered in Rogers's own regiment. Rogers could also count on Captain Joseph Waite, another hardened veteran of Snowshoes. These men and others, well versed in Rogers's code of conduct and in small-unit tactics, would do much to bring the promising but as-yet-untempered raw recruits into fighting trim.

Rogers's old friend John Stark had not joined the expedition, although he was present at Crown Point when it left. He would have been a logical choice, considering his intimate knowledge of Saint-François from his captivity there in 1752. But he may have declined because of his rheumatic knees, and also he may have felt somewhat loath to attack a village that had treated him well. Still, the hard-headed Yankee well understood that war demands a certain clear-eyed brutality. He certainly provided Rogers with critical information about the village's immediate geography and specific layout.

As the men marched ever deeper into the north country that first day, a French bateau patrol chanced upon a British oar floating in Missisquoi Bay. That discovery, complemented by the Abenakis' report, persuaded Bourlamaque to dispatch 40 men under his top partisans, the veteran ensigns La Durantaye and Langy, whose formidable force had nearly annihilated Rogers's at the Battle on Snowshoes. In short order they discovered the well-masked whale-boats, took tomahawks to most of the hulls, then burned the remains to ensure that no enemy could reconstruct that means of return. As La Durantaye and Langy watched their men at work, they must have wondered who had orchestrated so bold and effective a gambit under the very noses of a strong naval presence. As the French heaped the captured supplies into a few set-aside whaleboats, one name probably came to mind.

The destroyers left—some rowing away, others walking back to Île aux Noix—unaware that the two Stockbridge rangers had witnessed the operation. The discovery spurred Bourlamaque into a frenzy of activity. A sizable party heading north from Missisquoi Bay would have few logical targets—most likely Chambly, Yamaska, or Saint-François, Indian villages that acted as a sort of defensive perimeter for Canadian France. He immediately sent a courier to warn Vaudreuil in Montréal and alerted Paul-Joseph Le Moyne de Longueuil, the governor of Trois-Rivières, 22 miles northeast of Saint-François, that Yamaska and Saint-François should be reinforced. He also dispatched runners to warn Lévis that "all appearances indicate that they want to punish Saint-François for its loyalty."[23] Bourlamaque moved nearly 400 men to the whaleboat landing. The trap was sprung: the British expeditionary force would meet a warm reception in the north if the frontier garrison did not catch them first. Should they attempt to come back via Missisquoi Bay, they would be putting their heads yet deeper into a noose.

Oblivious to these mounting perils, Rogers and his men crossed the Riviére aux Brochets (near present-day Frelighsburg) and swung northeast. One day, perhaps two, later, the mud-bespattered and gasping lookouts overtook the column, crying out the password and then articulating Rogers's worst fears: 200 men lay in ambush at the whaleboat rendezvous, while another 200 had picked up the trail. All chance of returning via Lake Champlain was gone. Rogers looked over his men and called an officers' council of war, which mulled their suddenly bitter choices under the dark shadows of the spruce forest. "This unlucky circumstance...put us into some consternation," wrote Rogers, as usual in no way exaggerating his case.

Even should the rangers best their foes in direct encounter, no reinforcements could reach them—while the enemy could be "supported by any numbers they please." The destruction of the whaleboats had severed their best line of retreat, and the loss of provisions presented another "melancholy consideration."[24] Despite such concerns, the officers voted to carry on and "prosecute our design at all adventures." As Hernán Cortés knew at Vera Cruz, there's nothing like the destruction of their boats to focus men.

Rogers sketched out the only possible plan, which he acknowledged stood a good chance of failure. After ravaging Saint-François, the rangers would pass eastward by way of Lake Memphremagog and then south to the Connecticut River Valley and Fort No. 4, the northernmost outpost on the river. He calculated that starvation would nevertheless overtake them long before they reached the fort (that way to safety being a good hundred miles longer than the Champlain passage), and so he planned to summon a relief party from No. 4 to rendezvous 60 miles up the Connecticut at the west-bank infall of the Wells River.

Rogers charged First Lieutenant Andrew McMullen, an Irishman with two years' service, who already walked with some difficulty—a lameness that would only intensify over the coming weeks—to carry an outline of the Wells plan to Amherst, "that being the way I should return, if at all." He did not need to explain that the whole force's survival depended on effective coordination, but it is unclear whether he voiced the corollary: should the Indians capture McMullen and compel him to divulge his message, then every ranger would be doomed to the worst deaths imaginable. McMullen consented, and shortly thereafter he left at the head of six other rangers.

Chapter 21

Ordeal Through Spruce Bogs

No easy hopes or lies
Shall bring us to our goal,
But iron sacrifice
Of body, will, and soul.

RUDYARD KIPLING,
"FOR ALL WE HAVE AND ARE"

What brings some men together with great and lasting determination in the face of grave extremity, while others, on the face of things no less brave or enduring, falter or disintegrate as strident differences of opinion break them? An extraordinary chemistry may crackle into being among men in the field. It is too facile to explain the dynamics that spurred the rangers on that chill September day, hotly pursued deep in enemy territory, as the common determination of people who dreaded to appear weak or lose face in front of their fellows to whom they were bound by terrible but uniting fear and effort. In such circumstances a break east and south across the wilderness toward Fort No. 4 would have carried no stigma. So what explains the desire that pressed these already-desperate men onward, even deeper into the ever-sharpening teeth of danger, and that engendered that extreme belief in themselves that alone brings off ultimate achievement? The single-minded commitment of a leader does not itself guarantee that his companions will follow with steady nerves and consistent, effective morale. Somehow Rogers had focused the men's energy through a collective lens, preventing the natural human tendency under extreme circumstances to look out for oneself alone. And he did so, not by resorting to fear or punishment, but rather by turning adversity into a confident demonstration of preparation, skill, and character. Far from undoing the unit, the loss of the boats focused the raiders on their common goal. As with all the crack special-operations teams that would take shape 200 years later, extreme situations became an opportunity, a change of consciousness.

On they struggled north-northeast through the spruce bogs that laced southern Québec. As the land-changing glaciers of the Pleistocene had pulled north some 11,000 years ago, large blocks had broken off, the dying ice sheet dumping sand and gravel over them. Eventually they melted to form shallow, stagnant ponds or kettle lakes, which gradually became edged, then choked, with hardy sedges, cranberry, and Labrador tea and gave way to black spruce and tamaracks. Despite such development, the spruce bog still displayed more characteristics of subarctic desert than of boreal forest; the high acidic and anaerobic qualities of its water arrested organic decay, further limiting the availability of nutrients and maintaining an environment hostile to most animal life. Adult wolves often left their pups in spruce bogs during the summer months while they went hunting, reasonably confident that no predators would come that way.[1]

As the men stepped into cold, dark water the color of long-steeped tea, each step proved uncertain: one foot might gain good purchase, the next sink in above the ankle or knee. Submerged, unseen branches, roots, and logs ripped at moccasins and stubbed now-numb toes. Stiff, sharp black spruce needles raked weary, stumbling bodies. Human beings entering any desert habitat become conscious only slowly of the sheer magnitude of its life-sucking otherness. The glow of yellow tamarack needles in their fall splendor did little to temper the foreboding.

Rogers's Rule Number III instructed that troops marching over marshy or soft ground should go abreast so as "to prevent the enemy from tracking you (as they would do if you marched in a single file)."[2] Rogers had outfitted his force with two pairs of moccasins apiece; but under such punishment, footwear deteriorated quickly, so some probably stripped them off and walked barefoot. That way the cold blunted the poke and pinch of each step, "the water most of the way near a foot deep," wrote Rogers. Sleep proving difficult because "we had no way to secure ourselves from the water," they cut saplings and laid them down, overlaid by boughs and leaves "in Form of a raft"[3] or "a kind of hammocks"[4] on which they could grab a few hours of dreamless rest. As many as half the men lay down while the rest kept watch, some in six-man pickets on the perimeter. The weather continued wet and unseasonably cold.

For nine days they trudged, beginning before dark and camping well after dusk, gaining less than ten miles a day however great their effort. *The Boston News-Letter* later worked out that several died in the swamp, but of this Rogers's journal and other reports remain silent.[5] Fever and lameness may well have claimed good men's lives in that quiet purgatory. If any ranger delivered a heartrending mercy blow to a dying comrade, no one spoke of it afterward. Perhaps days into their grueling march, they could not even muster the will for that last noble duty but simply splashed away. All knew that the mission had gone beyond the point of no return. In the pervasive wet and cold, toenails dropped off, and despite the best efforts to keep feet dry, the initial signs of immersion foot became manifest, a condition marked by blue discoloration, swelling, and susceptibility to fungal infections. And meanwhile the tannin-rich water painfully knotted the gut.

They ate with abandon, visualizing the food awaiting them at Saint-François. The acid water they drank acted quietly and dangerously on their stomachs, preventing their systems from effectively absorbing iron and other nutrients. Seven days from Lake Champlain, noted Connecticut provincial Frederick Curtiss, most had run through their rations.

Yet Rogers's plan worked. Whatever rangers might do, La Durantaye's two hundred pursuers could not keep going against these bogs, in this frigid weather, with Rogers's head start. Quitting the drowned lands, they swung westward over dry ground, then drove north to catch the invaders as they emerged from the bog country.

Between this bog and the northward-running Richelieu River flows the Yamaska, a natural water highway and marker through the forest that leads directly to the Abenaki village of Saint-Michel-d'Yamaska, known to the English as Wigwam Martinique, some half-dozen miles south of where that river enters the St. Lawrence. None of the French or Indians could imagine that an alien raiding party could venture through this wilderness without keeping to its course—which made Wigwam Martinque the logical target.

Should such a force veer northeast toward Saint-François, it would have to cross the Saint-François River: and nine days after leaving the boats, the exhausted men indeed came upon that treacherous, rain-swollen watercourse, remarkably within a dozen miles of their target. Forceful and loud, several hundred yards across, it filled the remaining 142 rangers with dread.

The powerful waters of North America claimed more lives than did falling trees and accidental firearm discharges. All the rangers knew men who had drowned, even in benign pastoral lakes. Cleaveland reported the year before that a regular "was drowned as he was washing himself in the Lake."[6] This broad raging river could sweep a man off his feet and pitch him downstream, choking and banging him against rocks, until it finished him off in any of dozens of ways. Even if he could swim, his strokes—swimming being no science in those days—were rudimentary at best, no contest for this white water. The rivers of New England and southern Québec run rocky courses, malign with ledges, waterfalls, and log strainers. It was October 3 of a particularly cold fall, and not only was the water fast, but its icy grip would quickly suck the warmth and feeling from flailing limbs struggling for balance. Rogers judged the flood too wide at their present vantage, so the columns moved several miles upriver, where the channel narrowed. It was theoretically possible to build man-carrying rafts when tackling such a difficult crossing, but Rogers ruled that out here as too time-consuming and dangerous. They would wade across—although, he wrote, it would be "attended with no small difficulty, the water being five feet deep, and the current swift." Realizing that fires to dry wet clothes, a necessity in the cool fall weather, could prematurely announce their presence, Rogers told his lieutenants to have the men strip and bundle their clothes into their packs and carry them as high as possible on necks and shoulders. They may well have cobbled together some small rafts to transport their muskets and buckskin baggage.

Rogers motioned the corps's tallest man forward; he would step sideways into the river, facing upstream. Another large man behind him grabbed his waist, and behind him another, forming a human chain. Slowly they sidestepped across the torrent, losing purchase on the slippery and unsecured rocks, the entire endeavor depending on each man remaining a link in the chain. The shivering main force yelled hoarse encouragement above the clamor, their ribs standing out from pale and shrunken chests. At times the current broke a man's grip and threatened to send the hard-pressed line behind him spilling downriver. But somehow they held on and made it across, Rogers reported, losing only a number of muskets, some of which were recovered by diving.

Abenaki tradition declares that women scrubbing laundry at the riverbank that day noticed fresh-cut wood chips floating past, but that the ominous portent went unheeded.[7]

The next day's events, when put together from existing accounts, resemble a blurry action photograph, identities and particular tasks not quite assignable. Rogers's journals remain the most specific testimony. Other rangers' journals, some of them written years after the event, are subject to the so-frequent contradictions attending the memories of men pushed to extreme limits of fear and privation, then burnished in the retelling. Newspapers picked up first- and secondhand accounts but also passed along rumors and embroideries. Indian accounts offer other insights, although a wide gulf exists between how literate and nonliterate peoples make sense of their history, a difference, noted the Lakota author Luther Standing Bear, of the record "not stored in books, but in the living memory."[8] These stories, passed along and memorized by specially identified keepers of the tradition, have been handed down through the warp and woof of time; one observer commented that the Indians conceive of their past as "a collective dowry"[9] that future generations actively maintain, even as "a sort of cultural capital from which they can draw ideological, spiritual, and psychological interest." Historical facts sometimes are adjusted to fit the current sociopolitical climate, which makes oral tradition difficult to square with Western historiographical procedures. Yet these stories represent deep, newly accessible wells of historical understanding for the Western-trained historian, as well as largely unexamined perspectives not just on events but on the stakes, miseries, and indeed consciousness of the shadowy times before industrialization and pluralist humanitarian democracy.

The northern shoreland, soft but firm underfoot, proved a godsend to the shivering force, now aware that it was moving within range of its objective. After a several hours' march with the sun drawing close to the horizon, Rogers shinnied high up a tree and spotted smoke from cooking fires against the long light to the northwest, only five or six miles distant.[10] That evening they closed to within two and a half miles of the town, probably melting into a patch of second-growth forest where the original Saint-François had once stood, whence the war party had left to raid Deerfield on another fall day 55 years earlier.

At eight P.M. Rogers tapped Lieutenant George Turner of Moses Brewer's Mohegan company and Connecticut ensign Elias Avery, both of whom were reasonably fluent in Algonquin tongues. Stripping themselves of such telltale ranger dress as green jackets and bonnets, the trio walked toward the village, probably first swinging wide to pick out any signs of ambuscade. The night air proved cool and pleasant, and the town lay comfortably shaded by a canopy of tall pines atop its 60-foot bluff commanding the Saint-François, now a wide, deep, and scarcely ruffled watercourse on its way to the St. Lawrence.

From his hard experience of defending Rumford against the Abenakis, Rogers knew the difficulty of securing a town against a lightning strike by a highly mobile group. And he knew that the Indians' talents lay in the concerted, highly targeted offensive, not in sustained defense. He had to expect that warnings had reached the village soon after the whaleboats had been uncovered; messengers could travel by sloop from Île aux Noix up the Richelieu, and thence by way of the St. Lawrence, in a matter of days.

But as they crept closer, the patrol heard chanting and the clatter of turtleshell rattles from the stout council building in the center of town, indications, wrote Rogers, of "a high frolic or dance."[11] Such festivities, perhaps a ritual celebration of the fall harvest, did not suggest a community on the alert. That perhaps encouraged the three to walk into town, in brazen disregard of all standard procedures, where Rogers was "spoken to several Times by the Indians," reported one newspaper, "but was not discovered, as he was dress'd like one of them."[12] Were such stories crafted in the imagination or the rumor mill, which Rogers somehow always stirred? After all, striding directly into the heart of the settlement that he intended to attack the next day appears beyond foolhardy; yet such behavior was apparently not without precedent. Earlier that year Captain Joseph Marin had entered Fort Pitt, reported *The North Carolina Gazette*, "in Disguise, drest & painted as a friend Indian, treated well by the English, and shewn every part of the fort."[13] From past experience Rogers knew that French traders and Indians from other tribes often dropped in upon such frontier villages at the oddest times, so the appearance of three strangers might not have seemed unusual.

The newcomers quietly surveyed the three dozen wooden houses, the paths down the bluff to the canoes, the barns and granaries, and were back with the main body by two A.M.[14]

That evening, records Abenaki oral tradition as conveyed by Elvine Obomsawin Royce, a young woman lingered outside the council house, to take a break from the dancing within. As she turned to go back inside, an unknown voice came from the shadows, *Akwi sagezi*, or "Don't be afraid," continuing, "I am your friend and those enemies, those strange Iroquois, they are there in the little woods [planning] that when all [the Abenakis] leave for home they would kill them all, their husbands, and burn your village, and I come to warn you."[15] The girl rushed inside to pass on the warning, but "some did not believe her, because she was so young, because she was a child." Royce's tradition asserted that some adults hurried home from the celebration to gather their children and repair under the darkness to a nearby deep ravine in a place they called "the Pines."

It is highly improbable that Rogers's party would have warned the village, even had Rogers, quite conscious of Amherst's orders that the fewest possible number of noncombatants be killed, contemplated clearing the town. Such humanity could have destroyed the mission. Abenaki oral traditions say that the stranger was one of the Stockbridge rangers—but how had he got away from the camp unnoticed for a couple of hours?

Meanwhile Rogers passed out responsibilities; he himself was to command the right, Captain Ogden the left, and Lieutenant Dunbar the center. The three divisions parted and slipped across the last two and a half miles, their moccasins silent on the pine needles, until they came within 500 yards of the town; at that point they stripped off their packs, made a final check of their muskets, fixed bayonets, and adjusted the tomahawks and knives that hung around their belts. The officers paired the men up, each team to take one of the houses, while marksmen stationed themselves at key vantages to ensure that no one escaped.

Twenty minutes later, as the gray light began to kiss the tall riverbank pines half an hour before sunrise, shadows filed silently to their places at front doors and alongside the embankment paths leading to the water.[16] The struggling dawn revealed the grisly presence of some 600 or 700 scalps swaying in the light breeze atop house trophy poles; some even hung above the white-painted Jesuit church. The men held their breath.

Almost predictably, a musket discharged by accident. It precipitated the attack. Yet the men worked with grim efficiency, burst down doors, and "shot some as they lay in bed, while others attempting to flee by back Ways, were tomahawked or run thro' with Bayonets," reported *The Boston Gazette* with dispassionate relish.[17] The tribe's tradition says that some warriors defended the thick-walled council house to the death. "The major, who was never known to be idle in such an Affair, was in every Part of the Engagement encouraging his Men and giving Directions," declared *The New-York Gazette*.[18] Lieutenant Jacob Farrington and Sergeant Benjamin Bradley shouldered one door with so much force "that the hinges gave way, and Bradley fell in headlong among the Indians, who were asleep on the floor," adds another account.[19]

Handfuls of Indians fled down the embankment to their beached canoes, but "about forty of my people pursued them, who destroyed such as attempted to make their escape that way, and sunk both them and their boats."[20] Oral tradition reports that the early sun caught the hat ornament of Abenaki elder Obomsawin just short of the farther shore and a sharpshooter struck him dead.[21] The disorienting fusillade and clamoring burst upon the Indians as though their mythical winged beast Bmola had swept through the village on the wings of its ill wind.

Barely had the action opened than a musket ball ripped through Ogden's side and his powderhorn, but "it did not hinder him from doing his Duty, he took his Handkerchief and bound it round the Wound in his Body; two or three Men being near him, asked him if he was wounded, he answered only scratched, and encouraged them on."[22] Of Rogers's men, only one Stockbridge ranger died, although

Ogden's wound was severe and six others received slight injuries. In a quarter of an hour or so the action ended, the attack "done with so much alacrity by both the officers and men, that the enemy had not time to recover themselves, or take arms for their own defense, till they were chiefly destroyed."[23] A chief's two young sons had fallen to their knees crying "Quarter!" the only word they knew in English. The clamor subsided, and a handful of rangers stood with hot gun barrels and bloody bayonets and tomahawks, half incredulous at their success and braced for a counterattack. It never came. Several emerged from the French church, one brandishing a ten-pound silver statue of the Madonna over his head in triumph. Inside they had torn tapestries from the walls and trampled the host underfoot.

A little after sunrise Rogers ordered all but three corncribs torched. Some of those hiding in the cellars or lofts streamed out, the women and children joining a small huddle of terrified prisoners, but others chose to die in the flames. The rangers heard fierce death chants from within.

By seven A.M. Rogers considered the engagement over. Evidence suggests that the assault had met with considerably less resistance than expected. Having reason to believe that the village was at or near its full complement, Rogers claimed to have killed 200 Indians, a number which diverged significantly from the several French accounts, most of which settled on only 30 deaths overall. Father Roubaud, the village's Jesuit priest, who was away that day, reported that the rangers had killed ten men and 22 women and children.[24] Other French reports agreed.[25]

In fact, a town with 200 inhabitants present would most probably have given the rangers a harder time, certainly inflicting more than the few casualties actually sustained. Furthermore, in the wake of the massacre at William Henry and the way the two European powers were jockeying against each other to retain a moral edge, it is likely that the French would have taken the opportunity to question English morality should Rogers have slaughtered 200 people, mostly noncombatants, even given the general European disregard for the value of Native American life.

Field commanders throughout history notoriously overestimate the damage they have done; battle destroys perspective. For Rogers, even a small number of bodies, the awful odor of burned flesh in his nostrils, and the sense of others lost in the river and inside the charred houses could all have given the impression that many more died than actually did. He probably figured simply that the village had housed 200 and that he had destroyed it, so its inhabitants must all be dead.

Interrogation of the prisoners revealed that the village had been warned, even knowing the exact number of whaleboats that Rogers had left hidden as well as their location. Perhaps even Rogers's name had been invoked, the frontier bogeyman, and it is likely that many of the Indians knew his name and reputation, certainly if the claims of widespread glee at his death were any indication. If only 30 villagers died and twenty were prisoners, along with five released captives, then the town indeed carried only a fraction of its capacity. The others would have been in the woods somewhere, traveling to other villages, probably heeding word that came days before Rogers and his men gathered outside the village. Such a possibility suggests that the "frolic" Rogers heard before he struck was a harvest ceremony, a ritual celebration required to keep the cycles going, or perhaps some kind of anticipatory war dance.[26] The handful of those lingering in the village were those who chose not to leave, out of either stubbornness or disbelief.

The prisoners also claimed that a 300-man enemy party lay in wait for him only four miles distant. The visitors had made their impression. Now they must leave with all speed. Rogers ordered his men to stuff their packs with corn and warned against filling valuable space with loot, but many did not listen. They would pay for their greed.

The past three weeks had been awful. But now the true historic ordeal awaited them on the dark forest pathways, one that, far more than the razing of a single town, would carve their name in horrified memory.

Chapter 22

Starvation

The rest there fled into the wood
where they did dy for want of food
these men did grieve and mourn and cry
wee in these howling woods must dy.

"A BALLAD OF ROGERS' RETREAT, 1759"[1]

On the afternoon of October 5, the day after Saint-François went up in flames, 38-year-old Jean-Daniel Dumas and 60 Canadian militiamen from Trois-Rivières, 16 miles to the northeast, dogtrotted into the ruined town. Some of the dead lay prepared for burial, rolled full-length in bark tied up with cord. Although the ground was already hardened by autumn frosts, survivors and other Abenakis drawn by the smoke pouring into the sky had already dug the east-facing graves of their people. The dreaded Ghost Fire spirits of Abenaki belief attended the unburied dead, so the living did not dally. Tentlike structures topped a few graves. Boards would eventually name those whom they guarded. A woman walked silently among them, her hair cut to the scalp and her face rubbed black with ash, the signs of a mother bereft of a child.[2]

A wild-eyed figure in a heavy black wool cassock, pulling on the crucifix around his neck, ran up to the belated rescuers. The settlement's curé, Father Pierre-Joseph-Antoine Roubaud, could barely contain his fury at those who had destroyed his church and parsonage, set fire to the mission's valuable archives, and displayed violent contempt for the sacred host.[3] The nightcomers had looted silver-plated candlesticks and the silver Madonna, a gift from the Chapter of Chartres Cathedral more than half a century before, and they had defiled lovingly woven gold-cloth draperies, a silver shirt in a reliquary, and a banner depicting a life-sized Christ and the Virgin Mary in gold and silver wire.[4] The debased heretics had spilled and trampled the sacred host into the ground. Father Roubaud punctuated his lamentations with bitter reproaches at the failure of the king's soldiers to protect his people. How could this have come about?

Dumas walked over to the smoldering vestiges of the church and caught a glint of its brass bell amid the charred beams and fallen walls, tuning out the now hysterical rantings of the priest. Himself a man of strict principle, Dumas felt at best mixed sympathy for a pastor commonly known to take promiscuous advantage of his congregation. Yet the sacking of Saint-François appeared to push the man over the edge. In future months Roubaud would denounce the provincial authorities in a biting sermon, start spying for the English, and eventually surrender his cloth.

For all that, one detail of Roubaud's tirade stopped Dumas short. The major's stern stare caused the priest to repeat that the rangers had carried off Nanamaghemet, or Marie-Jeanne Gill, the wife of the white chief Jean-Louis Gill of Saint-François, and their two sons, Antoine and Sabbatis.

Clever of Rogers, thought Dumas. This complicated matters. While his own small force could catch up with Rogers's fairly easily, he had to move with unusual care lest he put the hostages at grave risk. He must begin a high-stakes game of cat and mouse, biding his time and moving carefully for fear of ambush.

Dumas was no stranger to battle or strategic raiding; his speed of mind had saved the French from certain defeat when Braddock's column had knocked into them outside Fort Duquesne and the initial volleys had cut down his commander, Daniel-Hyacinthe-Marie Liénard de Beaujeu, leaving the redcoats' advance guard poised to drive their equally startled leaderless enemy back in a rout. Had not Dumas quickly ordered 900 men on a flanking maneuver through the woods that enfiladed the exposed column with near impunity? A skilled orchestrator of Indian warfare, Dumas had long bedeviled British settlements.

Rogers would put as much distance between himself and Saint-

François as possible, but would he swing south and around back toward Missisquoi Bay and the cache that he might not know had been destroyed—or if he did know, would he make a southeast shunt toward the Connecticut River Valley? Two warpaths led from the Saint-François River, crossing over the watershed to the Connecticut.

The bitter Abenaki braves needed little encouragement to go with Dumas. The women were already at work grinding dried corn and forming the flour into bear-grease cakes. Unlike raw dried corn, which is difficult to digest, sagamite was a perfect food for traveling. Few but mercilessly driven, Dumas's party moved out of the savaged town, its bereft and angry priest urging them stridently to wreak a retribution for which they needed no encouragement.

Rogers's party, now swelled by six Abenaki women and boys and five newly unbound prisoners, had pushed southeast from the township, paralleling the river but this time a mile more distant, so as to avoid hunting parties returning home. The men, elated at the easy victory and exalted by the roar of violence, packed their cheeks with kernels of dried corn, letting their saliva soften the hard grain, the better to chew and digest it. At their infrequent halts they spat the mulch into their canteens for further soaking.

Wilderness warfare played out over an immense territory: the Saint-François raid, from its inception, had been a life-and-death contest. Rogers had had to make extraordinary calculations from constantly changing variables—the strength, position, commitment, and capabilities of his enemy; the climate and environment; the ever-pressed capacities of his own men; and the best ways to use the topography to advantage, especially for effective way-finding. His constant and intensive interrogation of these factors and the world around him yielded an ever-updated and fine-tuned economizing. He needed to anticipate misfortune at the greatest possible distance. Men such as Rogers and the Norwegian polar explorer Roald Amundsen are rare precisely because in them an insightful, interrogating mind is married to indomitable will, which enables them to go up against indeterminate extremity, grasp and wrestle its component dangers, and not only survive where others fail but become the instrument of survival for others. (See insert for a map Rogers commissioned on the route he took. It's the first time it's been published in the United States. See also Appendix 2.)

By the third or fourth day, after plodding some 30 miles, the column found the topography beginning to grow uneven and rugged as they entered the western flanks of the Appalachians. Rogers kept off game trails, so the going proved hard—dipping into ravines, negotiating the canopies of large blowdowns, pushing up steep inclines. Three weeks on the march with only a few hours' respite at Saint-François were starting to take their toll on the men's speed and fitness. Long drenching downpours did little to improve morale, and the euphoria of victory faded, just as it does among tired mountaineers on a difficult descent.

Had it been only a matter of lumbering back to the stash at Missisquoi Bay, they need not have supplemented their supplies. But the destruction of the cache and, worse, the boats entailed an inescapably longer and much harder journey home, forcing them to seek sustenance from the forest. Corn dwindled quickly. Despite Rogers's explicit warnings, some of his men had pretty much filled their small packs with loot at the expense of food. The frontier ethic of the irregulars guaranteed them the right to plunder, the age-old reward of high risks taken; and Rogers had no wish—not that he could have insisted—that they pass up the option, however self-destructive.

The British regular consumed on average 2,700 calories a day.[5] A cup of dried corn contains 955 calories, or about a third of the level necessary for daily sustenance, although the strenuous nature of the retreat would have demanded considerably more calories. Some percentage of the corn had to pass directly through the rangers' systems because they could not risk building fires to cook. Even if each man had been willing or able to squeeze 24 cups of dried kernels into his pack, after eight days—the point at which Rogers reported that "provisions grew scarce"[6]—they still could not have replenished anything like the energy that they were expending.

The long march took its toll in thousands of small ways. The soles of the feet grew sore from pounding the ground. Small cuts became infected by dirt and sweat. Pack straps dug into shoulder muscles and rubbed skin raw. Old long-silent injuries, such as a twisted ankle or strained back, reemerged. Upper-body weight drops first, and once-proud uniforms were now baggy and torn.

Rogers kept flanking parties and a strong rear guard at a constant alert, assuming that a well-fed and vengeful pursuit force could not be far behind. And something else bothered him as he urged the ragged rangers along: he had seen precious little game as they threaded through the woods. While their sheer numbers might have scared some animals off, good hunters whom he sent out after deer and bear came back empty-handed. The column found only an occasional partridge and red squirrel.

Over the past month the coastal papers had also been reporting many strange changes in animal habits. Dozens of black bears had invaded small frontier towns, eating corn and killing hogs, "more than was ever knowx," reported *The New-York Gazette*.[7] A bear mauled two children to death as they were picking beans outside Brentwood, New Hampshire, while Maine hunters killed seven bears near Kittery.[8] "It is said that some of these voracious Animals have ventured down even to some of the Seaport Towns at the Eastward," reported *The Boston Evening-Post*, one coming within two miles of Boston itself.[9] Some had white faces, probably a sign of age.[10] Over a ten-day period Rhode Island hunters shot 11,588 squirrels and filled 29 bushel baskets with their heads.[11] Perhaps some ecological disruption had rattled through the north woods, driving even sage older bruins to grub for food near dangerous human settlements. Perhaps a contagion had ripped through deer populations, or a blight had shaken the food pyramid and sent tremors through the whole web of mammalian sustenance. Whatever the cause, the absence of game haunted Rogers's weary column as it labored ever closer to the margin.

His men weakening by the hour, Rogers reviewed his options. Arguments and irritations flared between regular and provincial, in particular when a sergeant in Gage's 80th charged that Rogers "took away from Dunbar's party provisions and gave it away to others who had loaded themselves with Plunder after the Place was destroyed."[12] Incensed at the charge of favoritism, which was dangerously undermining to any commander, Rogers vowed to court-martial Sergeant Lewis when they reached home lines. But it was all too clear that it would be hard to keep his exhausted and famished command together for much longer.

Near present-day Sherbourne, Quebec, the river abruptly strikes northeast from its southernmost curve, and there Rogers convened a council of war. They had managed only eight or nine miles a day and were now falling short even of that.

His officers urged their commander to split up the party to make hunting easier. Even though Rogers had envisioned reaching Lake Memphremagog, just a dozen miles to the southwest, a point from which they could find an easier way to the Connecticut, he agreed. The food situation was dire.

Rogers had struck a devil's bargain. Divided, the rangers lost the advantage of numbers they would have had against almost any force likely on their trail, even while they gained the ability to move faster, more silently, and less obtrusively. Would he regret this decision? All now depended on whether McMullen had made it through to Crown Point and arranged for reprovisioning on the Wells River.

And so Rogers split his command into "Small Companies," each of less than 20 men, excepting his own. An experienced officer would direct each group, each carrying a compass. Rogers would take the least effective and sickliest, including 27-year-old Captain Ogden of the New Jersey Provincial Regiment, still struggling with his wounds. Rogers's group and most of the others would head toward the rendezvous on the Wells. Those led by Captain Joseph Waite, Ensign Elias Avery, and Lieutenants Abernathan Cargill and Jacob Farrington charted a roughly similar course to Rogers's south and southeast. Ranger George Turner and William Dunbar of the 80th Light Foot decided on the risky but faster Indian war trail leading southeast to the Connecticut. Billy Phillips and Lieutenant Jenkins of the Massachusetts militia would each lead a party back to Crown Point, southwest through the Green Mountains. Each detail bade the others a solemn farewell and faded into the forest—thus delivering to Dumas the break that he had so patiently been waiting for.

Soon enough he and his Canadians and Abenakis reached the point where Rogers's force had dispersed. His scouts quickly reviewed the signs and counted three diverging parties, not the ten at least that had set off. Quickly dividing his own column and surging with the energy of a predator, he began to hunt rangers in earnest.

Two days after Rogers broke up his command, Dumas's men overwhelmed Dunbar and Turner's group, killing both lieutenants and five men and taking three prisoner. Eight rangers fought their way out, as the Indians howled retribution, then scalped, stripped, and horribly mutilated the bodies, pitching the now-unrecognizable corpses into a nearby beaver pond. Eventually the shaken survivors fell in with Rogers.

At nearly the same time Dumas ran down Ensign Avery of Fitch's Connecticut Regiment and his detachment. Despite his men's eagerness to strike immediately, he bided his time. He could see that Avery's group had gone beyond the limit of their resources, the men stumbling along, eyes fixed on the ground right in front of their robotically moving feet. Corporal Frederick Curtiss would later recall how much they were "enfeebled by travail & destitute of provision save mushrooms & beach leaves for four or five days then past."[13]

The evening of the ninth day, listless and unfocused, Avery and two others went hunting, leaving eight men behind collapsed against logs and tree trunks on the forest floor, lost in their own private hells. Only then did Dumas give the order, and a handful of Indians plunged right into the midst of the worn men. One cried out when he locked eyes with an Abenaki warrior only two feet away. War whoops rent the air. Completely surprised, Curtiss and the others could not even struggle to their feet; Indian hands roughly pulled them up as long knives slashed off their blankets and leggings. The Indians and Frenchmen tied them naked to trees with tumplines, except Ranger Ballard, whose hands and feet they bound. Then the Indians plunged their knives into him, delighting in his screams, until suddenly they stopped.

Dumas's party scalped Ballard, loosened the living prisoners' legs, and set out. Sometime that evening two escaped, eventually falling in with Rogers's party. The next day the others came to a watercourse, probably the Saint-François, where the Indians and French built bark canoes. Curtiss climbed into the last one completed, along with four Indians and an "Indian Inglishman." On the evening of the fifth day he walked into the ruins of Saint-François and found five of his comrades lying butchered in the village center. An anonymous Frenchman wrote that "some of them fell a victim to the fury of the Indian women, notwithstanding the efforts the Canadians could make to save them."[14] Had Curtiss arrived earlier, he too would have felt the full wrath of the Saint-François survivors. "Upon seeing me the

Indians which were numerously gathered to the place demanded me to be Slain right out," Curtiss recalled. He prepared to meet his fate: "But my indian master being a Captain among them as he told me, who Could Talk inglish Well, he answered them no, Let it alone till morning. His Squaw also Interposed for me & Quieted them for ye present time."[15] The onlookers dispersed, satisfied that Curtiss would die on the morrow; but that night his owners helped him escape.

Meanwhile Rogers and his party had threaded their way southwest between Lakes Magog and Massawippi and shadowed the eastern shore of Lake Memphremagog. Rogers himself bore the slowly convalescent Captain Ogden across rivers on his back, his energy never seeming to flag anything like the others'. At every check he harangued stragglers with prospects of what awaited them at the rendezvous. Soon they broke into the rugged northeastern highlands of Vermont, a region so isolated that even today many mountains remain unnamed. Squeezed between the Green Mountains to the west and the Whites of New Hampshire to the east, the area is geographically speaking an extension of the latter, a tangled land underlain by light-colored granites pushed out originally as hot magma from the Earth's guts almost 200 million years ago.

Fortune had not entirely abandoned Rogers. In a marathon of their own and suffering from many ailments, McMullen's team had struggled the hundred or so miles back to Crown Point in nine days, arriving on October 3, the day before Saint-François fell.[16] Amherst detailed Samuel Stevens, one of Burbank's New Hampshire rangers who had risen through the ranks to a lieutenancy five months earlier, to march in all haste to Fort No. 4 with a dispatch ordering its commander, Major Benjamin Bellows, to provide him with whatever should be needed in the way of supplies, troops, and watercraft for the rescue mission. Stevens would paddle up the Connecticut to the rendezvous and "there Remain with Said party, so long as You shall think there is any probability of Major Rogers returning that way."

However improbably, such a possibility remained, as the wreck of Rogers's command passed through great groves of American beech, whose light-gray trunks resembled elephant legs. The pointed, veined leaves had turned golden. Patches of white birch filled in where fires or windstorms had devastated the old-growth forest. Among the changing patterns of tree cover—from 400-year-old red

spruce to maple saplings—the pressed and desperate men encountered their first starvation-induced hallucinations in the already-
strange shadows.

To counter the galling dryness of mouth that attends the early
phases of starvation, some of the men sucked on pebbles, their
tongues rasping their mouths like alien presences. Others cut holes in
spruce bark to gouge out gobs of primitive gum, which turned pink as
they chewed. All urinated frequently and copiously.[17]

They grew irritable, agonizingly sensitive to cold, depressed, and
simultaneously apathetic and easily offended. Angry outbursts only
gave way to prolonged ominous silences.[18] Game proved ever more
elusive. Every so often they killed a partridge, but such small game
could provide but little relief. An owl, for all its feathered bulk, offered only a morsel or two of meat. The men took longer and longer
breaks between marches. Many fell into listlessness, only mechani-
cally responding to Major Rogers's still astoundingly effective commands to get up and move along. By now he was pulling out all his
tricks, harvesting the oyster and chicken of the woods mushrooms.
They scraped the exterior bark off black birch trees and ate the
mildly sweet, wintergreen-tasting inside pulp.

Curiously, no survivors reported eating berries, which would normally have been in season, but then it was a strange, bad winter. As
hunger gnawed the guts with the intensity of a turning blade, they
doubled over on the march to find what little ease they could. Want
bit so deeply home that they resorted to roasting the Indian scalps
they had so recently taken and boiling their leather belts and straps,
chewing the tough material for any ghost of nourishment. Some ate
their moccasins and the nubs of candles they carried. They boiled
their powderhorns and drank the thin broth.

Once the metabolism has consumed its subcutaneous fat, it turns
upon the muscles and organs in the process of catabolysis, seeking to
keep the heart and nervous system going. Death can occur anytime
after 50 percent of the body mass is gone.[19] The rangers began to die:
some pulled into the fetal position during a rest break and just never
woke up. The weather granted them no kindness, continuing hard
and cold.

Knowing little of Rogers's woodcraft, Lieutenant George
Campbell's group could wrest virtually no nutrition from the forest.

The body needs a small amount of fat to maintain the functions of the brain, bone marrow, and cell membranes.[20] Some of Campbell's men lost their minds and "attempted to eat their own excrements," he later told a contemporary historian. After many foodless days the spectral column, crossing a small river, came upon the horribly mutilated bodies of Dunbar and Turner's hapless party, piled up floating among a tangle of logs in a stream running off a pond. "This was not a season for distinctions," wrote Campbell, and the men waded into the water, so ridden by hunger that they tore into the raw and rotting flesh as though it were the finest dinner they had ever eaten. Their cravings somewhat assuaged, "they carefully collected the fragments, and carried them off."[21]

How far Rogers's own struggling band broke the last taboo remains unclear. One rarely reliable source claimed that Rogers killed an Indian squaw and cut her into pieces,[22] although killing so useful a forager does not square with Rogers's practicality. Another ranger, named Woods, claimed that a black soldier died and was cut up; he himself ate the man's hand along with a trout he had caught, which "made a very good breakfast."[23] In his old age Ranger sergeant David Evans related a tale of horror, the hard-edged clarity of which makes it all too probable that the details never left his waking consciousness. One evening during the long nightmare, his hunger pains denying him sleep, he ruffled through someone's knapsack to make the horrific discovery of three half-eaten human heads. He quickly "cut a piece from one of them, broiled and eat it, while the men continued to sleep." That sustenance helped keep him alive where others died but instilled a deep guilt: "We hardly deserved the name of human beings."[24] These accounts, taken well after the fact, may suffer from embellishment or hallucination, yet starvation has historically imposed its own ethic, unimaginable until it is endured.

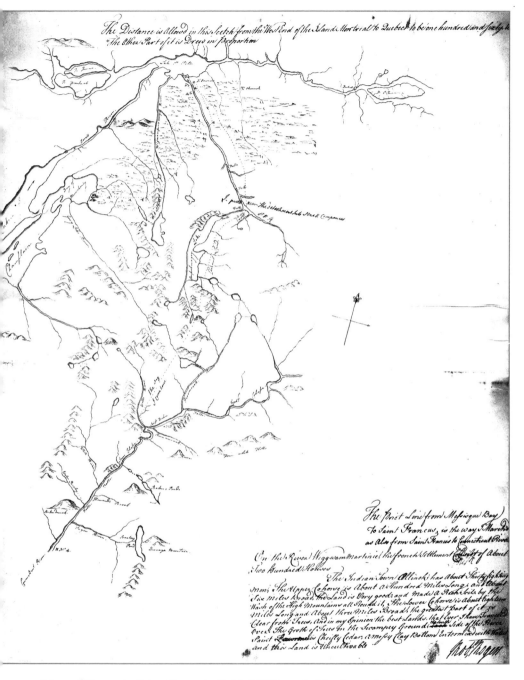

Map of Rogers's Saint-François Raid, 1759, probably drawn by Capt.
James Abercrombie. Contains notations in Rogers's hand.
See Appendix 2 for more information.
Courtesy of Bob Maguire

Brigadier General Augustus Viscount Howe by
an unknown artist.
Ft. Ticonderoga

Robert Rogers's wife, Elizabeth Browne
Rogers, by Joseph Blackburn, 1761.
*Reynolda House Museum of American Art,
Winston-Salem, North Carolina*

John Stark by Alonzo Chappel.
Ken Welsh, The Bridgeman Art Library

An eighteenth-century bateau based primarily on
archaeological examples from Lake George.
Mark L. Peckham

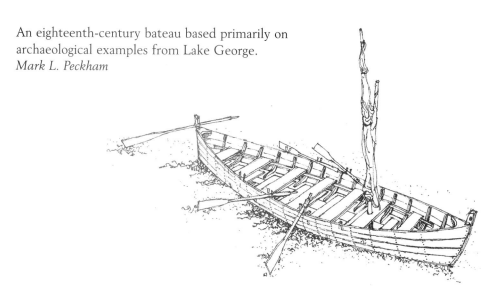

Contemporary woodcut of
Abercromby's 1758 attack
of Carillon.
Ft. Ticonderoga

*Embarkation of
Ambercromby* by
F. C. Yohn
*Chapman Historical
Museum*

An Iroquois warrior
scalping a prisoner.
*Peter Newark American
Pictures, The Bridgeman
Art Library*

War Party from Ticonderoga by Robert Griffing.
Paramount Press Inc.

Sir William Johnson by an
unknown artist.
From the frontispiece of the Sir
William Johnson Papers, *vol. 1.*

Sir Jeffery Amherst by
Henry Thomas Ryall.
The Bridgeman Art Library

General Thomas Gage by
John Singleton Copley.
*Yale Center for British Art,
Paul Mellon Collection, USA,
The Bridgeman Art Library*

Battle of Rogers' Rock by J.L.G. Ferris.
Chapman Historical Museum

Rogers' Rock, site of the legendary Rogers' Slide,
as seen from Lake George, New York.
Courtesy of the author

Rangers in winter dress.
Gary Zaboly

Robert Rogers by Thomas Hart, 1776. All existing visual
representations of Rogers, including this one, are imagined.
Ft. Ticonderoga

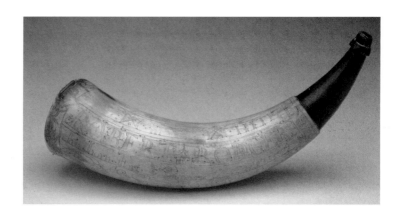

Robert Rogers's
powderhorn.
Ft. Ticonderoga

Chapter 23

Betrayal

The Misfortunes attending my Retreat from Saint Francois causes me great uneasiness, the Brave men lost I most heartily lament ... Lieut. Stephen's Misconduct in coming off with the Provisions hurt me greatly, and was the cause of so many perishing in the woods ...

ROGERS TO GENERAL AMHERST, DECEMBER 12, 1759[1]

For all these incommunicable privations, a map that Rogers drew indicates that he had kept a clear head. About 10 miles southeast of the southern end of Lake Memphremagog lies Willoughby Lake, a chili-pepper-shaped body of water that points to the Passumpsic River as it shoots through fairly good terrain directly to the Connecticut. There lay easier walking but also deeper danger, because the corridor had served Indian parties for centuries as a pathway to the rich intervales of the Connecticut, where they could grow crops and establish a baseline for raids against the advancing British settler frontier. Ambush patrols could make easy work of his weakened party on the Passumpsic path, so he kept the corridor well to the east, a "tedious march over steep rocky mountains, or through wet dirty swamps with the terrible attendants of fatigue and hunger."[2]

On October 20, some eight days after the groups divided, Rogers and his party encountered the steep-descending Wells River somewhere near present-day Groton. The distance from the dispersion point was some 80 miles as the crow flies, but they had traveled far more as the actual course had pulled them first southwest, then southeast. Five weeks had passed since they had left Crown Point. Tripping along the river course, the men heard gunshots and eagerly fired three or four rounds in response. Their growing joy pushed even the most morose of them to stumble the faster down the steep river-bank toward the Connecticut.

On a tongue of flat alluvial grassland, formed by the Wells's confluence with the main river and cleared by generations of Indian farmers, they came upon a deserted camp, its fire still burning. These survivors, who had given everything to get here, looked at one another with incredulous, sunken eyes. McMullen had clearly gotten back with Rogers's request for resupply, but the relief—and provisions—had left, at most only a couple of hours before. They fired their muskets in the air and hallooed with all the strength they could muster, but the wilderness quiet swallowed all noise, and they collapsed onto the forest floor.

By cruel fate, the relief party of Lieutenant Samuel Stevens and five other men had only just given up waiting after several days. Stevens had beached his large canoe three miles downriver from the Wells infall, lest the upstream rapids capsize it. Each day Stevens and some of his men had walked five miles overland to wait at the rendezvous.

What had prompted Stevens to abandon hope after so brief a vigil? The party did not lack for provisions. Perhaps they feared enemy patrols, or perhaps the still vastness awakened ancient terrors, as it had in so many men before them. Most distinctly, however, Stevens did not believe that even the great major could have pulled off so demanding a journey through that barren fall, a bleak judgment so absolute that he had decided not even to cache provisions.[3] His lack of belief would doom the weakest in Rogers's party. Just a few more hours, and the starving men would have been eating salted pork and slugging down great tots of rum—but the supplies lay unconsumed in the bottom of the big bark canoe now slipping quickly downriver to Fort No. 4. After Stevens reported in, Amherst noted in his journal that "he should have waited longer."[4]

Men under great duress and in danger of their lives can cling with almost maniacal tenacity to any shred of hope that promises deliverance from their suffering. It becomes the motivation that pushes each painful step, the focus that gives shape and reality to willpower, the crutch that holds back doubt and deep despair. Such is the power of the mind that salvation takes on an almost physical certainty.

When the dream is dashed, it is as if a kite string has snapped, letting all hope and endurance soar into the chilling sky.

"Our distress upon this occasion was truly inexpressible; our spirits, greatly depressed by the hunger and fatigues we had already suffered, now almost entirely sunk within us, seeing no resource left, nor any reasonable ground to hope that we should escaped a most miserable death by famine," wrote Rogers.[5] He kept such men as he could—and as were capable of responding—busy, even though the abandoned campsite must have been particularly crushing to him. A crude Jesuit church had once stood near the confluence; that and a stockade, now a pile of rotting logs, became the materials out of which they built a temporary shelter against the bitter sleeting rain.

Rogers pushed off to hunt with little effect, hampered by his own diminishing strength. The Connecticut, cold and fast, reminded the survivors hourly of the abundant food just 60 miles downriver.

After six days Rogers, rested but weakening further, decided to "push as fast possible toward No. 4, leaving the remains of my party, now unable to march further." Why did he wait so long? Had the disappointment sapped his own reserves? Six days of waiting made it clear that no rescue was coming. He was on his own. If any of his men, and the uncounted still struggling through the woods, were to come out alive, he would have to find a way down the rain-swollen river that chewed up even well-built bark canoes.

A day or two earlier he had gotten his men to fell uniformly sized pine trees with tomahawks, then cut them to length to form a raft that would support three men and a boy. Others of the unit dug up stringy but tough spruce roots, with which he bound the logs together near the water's edge. He selected Captain Ogden, who had healed fairly well but most importantly remained positive and clear-eyed, an unnamed ranger, and the Indian boy Sabbatis, taken from Saint-François.

He left a Lieutenant Grant in command of the withering remnant, reiterating the importance of keeping the remaining men occupied. He had already taught him where to look for groundnuts, a climbing perennial vine that carries starchy tubers, some as big as hen's eggs, sometimes stringing as many as forty along one root system, which boiled or roasted tasted like white potatoes.[6] Indians often planted them in wet areas near their settlements, and a good many of the Saint-François raiders probably owed their lives to the people they had set out to kill. They also dug up what the Indians called *sheepnoc*, the scaly white bulbs of the Canadian lily.[7] The men would have "to get such wretched subsistence the barren wilderness could afford," but the woodcraft gleaned by Rogers during his sojourns with the Indians of settled New England would keep the group busy and provide at least some rearguard sustenance to their wasting frames.

Some men could not even sit upright to wave their last hope off. The major, probably wondering how many he would see again, solemnly pledged to have food there within ten days. The foursome held makeshift paddles that "we had made out of small trees, or spires split and hewed."[8] The current bore them swiftly away; at first they spun in circles, learning quickly how to keep in the midline of the narrow river and avoid strainers—fallen trees athwart the water that look innocuous enough but can strip men from boats in a heartbeat.

On the second day they nearly shot right over the roaring White Falls (near today's Wilder, Vermont) but narrowly escaped by throwing themselves into the water and thrashing ashore. Their raft crashed over and broke into pieces, which the current dragged out of reach downriver. The sodden, exhausted crew worked their way around the boiling white water. Rogers sent Ogden and the other ranger off after red squirrels, while he and Sabbatis set about building a new raft—a challenging enough task even with adequate tools. The pair built fires around the bases of several pine trees and by sheer application brought them toppling down. Then they renewed the fire to divide the logs into roughly equal lengths. Perhaps Rogers had learned such a trick from his long journeys, or perhaps his quickly turning mind came up with the solution on the spot; either way, the weak man and the slight Indian boy with only their wits to rely on crafted the components of a workable raft with no tools except for a flint.

The hunters returned with a "partridge"—either a ruffed or spruce grouse—and that scrap of sustenance gave the four skeletal humans just the pathetically little strength to try again. The following day, the fourth since they had set out, the rangers bound the logs together, probably again with spruce roots, again risking the river's power.

The roar of Ottaquechee Falls, 50 yards of pounding cataracts, alerted the dazed foursome to this raft eater in time to make it ashore. Rogers and Ogden reviewed the situation, as the earthbound thunder nearly drowned out their enfeebled voices. Hunger ripped their midsections with cramps that bent them over and reduced their motions to a kind of pantomime. Sores and cuts would not heal, and their concentration was fleeting at best. Constant shivering sometimes seemed ready to knock their frail bodies to the ground. In his journals Rogers put it simply: they would not have been "able to make a third raft in case we had lost this [one]."[9] Their only chance—a steep gamble in itself—lay in getting it down the rapids. Rogers stumbled over to a bush, probably beaked hazel, pulled out his long knife, and harvested dozens of thin, wiry stems. By knotting the ends to one another, the men slowly braided a strong rope and hitched one end to the logs.

Ogden, the other ranger, and Sabbatis stared with the nearly total apathy of the starving as their leader, more a destitute refugee than a commander of a triumphant mission, crabbed down the embankment to the bottom of the falls. No longer could they hear one another, but Rogers waved his arm, and Ogden pushed the raft out into the current. He kept a drag on the current's power with the hazel rope while guiding it as best as he could through the tangle of rocks. At the bottom Rogers prepared "to swim in and board it when it came down, and if possible paddle it ashore."[10]

The raft bounced, bumped, and tumbled through the rapids, remarkably without coming apart. As it drew nearer, Rogers built up what head of steam he could and jumped into the icy water, kicking toward it as hard as he could.

"I had the good fortune to succeed," Rogers wrote with usual understatement. The raft's worn-out complement then worked their way toward Rogers's shivering figure who lay collapsed on the rocky shore beside the crude craft. The next morning they reboarded and once more shot downriver. Near Fort No. 4 they encountered woodcutters, who at first refused to believe that this haggard remnant could be the lead detail of a fine force that only a few weeks before had dared the wilderness. Providing arms and shoulders, the workmen helped the survivors back to Fort No. 4, where one anonymous observer noted that the major "was scarcely able to walk after his fatigues."[11]

At Rogers's steely insistence that a provision canoe must leave immediately, a detachment pushed off upstream within a half hour. It reached Grant's party four days later, on exactly the promised tenth day after the rafters had pushed off. Despite his own exhaustion Rogers coordinated other canoes to probe for survivors along the Ammonoosuc, dispatched couriers to Suncook and Penacook, on the Merrimack, with instructions to supply provisions to any rangers who straggled in, and wrote up his report to Amherst.

Two days later he himself canoed up the Connecticut in search of any other survivors. He indeed picked up the groups led by Cargill, Farrington, and Evans. Out of his own pocket, although eventually reimbursed, he bought them all shirts, stockings, shoes, and moccasins. All told, 63 struggled into Fort No. 4, and another 17 into Crown Point. Dumas's partisans and the bereft people of Saint-François had killed a dozen and a half rangers. Nearly a dozen known prisoners had disappeared, and starvation had claimed some two dozen, several during Rogers's desperate passage down the Connecticut. On November 26, 1759, *The New-York Gazette* announced: "We all here wait impatient for the safe Arrival of all those Officers and Men, that have behaved so gallantly in this Affair, and in particular that indefatigable Major, and a happy Recovery of Captain Ogden of his Wounds, such behaviour as only Men of Constitutions like Lions could ever have went through."[12]

The next few weeks weighed heavily on Rogers, as no further stragglers came in, while winter descended at its darkest and coldest. Rogers calculated he had lost three officers and 46 privates; the overall number may have been slightly higher, but clearly about a third of the 142-man command that had struck Saint-François had not returned—rather more than 50 percent of the number they had killed. It was a bitter reflection on the expedition's organizer: "The Misfortunes attending my Retreat from Saint Francois causes me great uneasiness, the Brave men lost I most heartily lament, and fear your Excellency's Censure as the going against that place was my own proposal, and that I shall be disappointed of that Footing in the Army which I have long endeavor'd to merit."

In April 1760 Rogers, still weak from the ordeal, traveled to Crown Point for the court martial of Lieutenant Stevens for "Neglect of Duty upon a Detachment to Wells's River in October last," before which he declared under oath that had Stevens "delayed but a day, or even some hours longer he would have saved the Lives of a Number of his party, who Perished in the Woods." Rogers's gaze set grimly on Stevens. By flouting his corps's prime directive of complete loyalty and never giving up on one's comrades, this weak-spined subaltern had doomed many good men to slow death. Under the harsh discipline of marathon wilderness travel and its concomitantly brutal warfare, Rogers instilled in his men—and relied upon—absolute faith that the mission could be brought off with ranger skill, endurance, and solidarity. That Stevens had departed because of a lack of faith in his comrades' power to overcome the French and the forest struck deeply and painfully at the spirit that he was attempting—with astounding effectiveness—to make ranger second nature.

Two rangers with Rogers claimed that no falls existed between the Wells and the point downstream where Stevens had beached the supply canoe, throwing unsettling questions on Stevens's claim that fall floods had kept him from paddling up to the rendezvous.

The depositions of three men accompanying Stevens from Fort No. 4 contradicted themselves about many of the dates, the days of waiting varying between three and five. Noah Porter's deposition swore that they had heard "three or four Shots fired from the North East Quarter," but that soon thereafter "a Batteau appeared with two Men in it, that were hunting, who told them they had been firing Guns." Not able to cross-examine the rescue detail from Fort No. 4, the court martial could not square the conflicting dates.

Stevens added little, claiming that he had expected that Rogers and his men would have returned in the time based on Lieutenant McMullen's calculations. The trial proceedings record that Stevens produced Amherst's orders "to go up to and remain at Wells River, as long as he should think there was any probability of Major Rogers's returning that way, and he says he Obeyed those Orders to the best of his Judgment."

The court found Stevens guilty and cashiered him from the service, "a poor reward, however," wrote Rogers, "for the distresses and anguish thereby occasioned to so many brave men, to some of which it proved fatal."[13]

The raid's success lay not in the crude number of lives taken but rather in psychology: it had shifted the balance of terror. None of the

Indian villages or French towns along the St. Lawrence could now feel safe from overland attacks. At the time Britain had prevailed in the French and Indian War west of the Atlantic, but the final outcome of the Seven Years' War on the European continent was still unclear. Events there could force the British to return their Canadian conquests, much as they had to Louisbourg in 1745.

The brilliance of Rogers's idea to undertake the raid lay not in any massive tactical effect but in its strategic ability to rob the enemy of his nerve. Outmatched in troop strength and resources, the French fought—as do all effective outnumbered armies—by employing speed and surprise to amplify what assets they possessed. Throughout the war the only British soldier thinking in the French frame of mind was Rogers, the consummate hunter and lifelong careful student of his prey, whose success lay in providing a mode of warfare that outmatched the other side in its strongest suit. Culminating its special-ops essence, the raid on Saint-François would deliver an attack as bold and terrifying as the Deerfield Raid of 1704 on the psyche of the St. Lawrence frontier settlements.

The raid sent a clear message to all Indians allied with the French: the French could not protect them—and the English could move where they wanted.

Rogers arrived in New York from Albany on January 12, 1760, with *The New-Hampshire Gazette* reporting under a New York byline that "Saturday last the brave Major Rogers arrived here from Albany."[14] *The Boston Weekly News-Letter* crowed, "What do we owe to such a beneficial Man; and a Man of such an enterprizing Genius?"[15]

Rogers brought the young Sabbatis to New York with him and put him into school to learn English.[16] The young Indian and Rogers had bonded, and he rarely left his patron's side.

Rogers's star had risen to new heights.

Chapter 29

Horror on the Ice

You will with 250 men land on the west-side, in such manner that you may get to St. John's (without the enemy at the Isle au Noix having any intelligence of it) where you will try to surprize the fort, and destroy the vessels, boats, provisions, or whatever else may be there for the use of the troops.

AMHERST'S ORDER TO ROGERS, MAY 25, 1760

On Tuesday afternoon, February 12, 1760, Rogers lingered for a few moments more at Fort Ticonderoga, which had been renamed after the British had taken it the previous summer. Then in the tight confines of the rectangular parade ground he mounted a horse-drawn sled. Piles of rubble from the magazine explosion still cluttered most corners of the small fort, even though reconstruction had proceeded briskly through the fall.[1] That day the major encountered men who knew those who had died on the way back from Saint-François, a memory still raw and tangibly weighing upon the shoulders of the hollow-eyed 29-year-old, which discouraged those around him from pressing too hard. Even so, he cast light upon the men he had left so unwillingly in the forest, finding it far easier to talk among the rough-hewn common soldiery than in Albany high society, which had lionized him.

Another good reason for dallying had been his dread of winter garrison duty at Crown Point under the insufferable Colonel Haviland: but not even he could anticipate the reception awaiting him only a few hours ahead. Needing Rogers's invaluable eyes and ears on the Champlain Valley frontier, Amherst had rejected his entreaties to take an expedition of 500 men into Canada. Rogers had brought 16 new recruits from Albany and had already begun, as so many times before, to indoctrinate them into the ranger life. They appeared willing enough, but few had experience with a musket, and some were little more than boys.

That afternoon Rogers dispatched the recruits under Sergeant Thomas Beaverly ahead with a caravan of 14 sutler sleighs, dashing the ten miles north to Crown Point. With the French well north at Île aux Noix, convoys stood little chance of being intercepted especially this deep into winter. Rogers promised to catch up.

Wrapped in a heavy blanket as the sleigh cut into the snowy landscape, he squinted through the stinging wind as Lieutenant John Fletcher's sleigh joined him to race out onto the Champlain ice. Relishing the bite of wind on his cheek and the clarity coming from escaping the confines of winter barracks, he fell easily into the tracks of the convoy well ahead. About five miles out, on that familiar stretch of ice where in January 1757 the rangers' ambush of a French supply train had precipitated the first Battle on Snowshoes, they pulled within sight of sleighs. As Rogers closed the distance, something did not feel right.

And then war whoops ripped the silent woodlands. Seventy Indians and Frenchmen in Indian costume, all under Rogers's great opponent Langy, charged out of the dark evergreens to bring the convoy to a skidding halt.[2] Sutlers fought to control their panicked horses, while the newly minted rangers, not yet issued their own muskets, watched helplessly. Within minutes five of them lay dead or dying on the ice.

Rogers smashed into the heart of the melee, unable to rally the shattered little command but still managing to point most of the sutlers southward toward Ticonderoga. He never recorded whether he recognized Langy through the turmoil, although he might have smelled the presence of so artful a woods warrior behind this consummate trap. Right now the disaster only grew worse; he could not save the moment, only avenge it, so he plunged flat out for Crown Point, which he reached in under half an hour.

Swinging his sleigh up across the beach, Rogers raced past the ruins of the old French post and up to the massive new British fort behind high earthen and rock walls 150 yards away. After taking

Carillon the previous July, Amherst had laid out ambitious plans to build "His Majesty's Fort of Crown Point," at least three times larger than Fort Saint-Frédéric had been, the king piece of a complex of blockhouses, fortified pathways, and three external redoubts.

A plan had crystallized already in Rogers's mind to cut off the raiders. It would not be difficult in the leafless woods that left unconcealed the print of their racing snowshoes. Less than a handful of possible routes north made sense, and Rogers knew them all, figuring that the enemy would be weary from the better part of a week's slogging, perhaps more, probably hungry, and slowed by prisoners. Soon he stood before Haviland.

Rogers's code of conduct and honor demanded that he undertake immediate retaliation for such an attack, or at the least make a spirited attempt to rescue the prisoners. But Haviland would give him no such satisfaction, refusing to risk his troops, the garrison having insufficient healthy men. Some indeed were suffering from scurvy and frostbite, due in part to his own poor management of winter provisions. Darkness began to settle over Champlain as Haviland remained impervious to Rogers's urgent arguments. He would later write to Gage that he thought the "idea had little possibility of success."[3]

Much of Haviland's skepticism stemmed from a natural and proper sense of responsibility for the welfare of this northernmost British strongpoint in the Champlain Valley; but the chance that the French, back on their heels after being dispossessed of Carillon, Crown Point, and above all Québec, would mount a winter counterattack on Crown Point was small. Some of Haviland's passive aggression lay in his blistering dislike of the all-too-active ranger major. Nothing would change his mind, and his considered reception gave Rogers a particularly bitter homecoming. The latter stomped off to his quarters, acutely aware that he had not done all he could for his men.

At sunrise, gathering enough volunteers to deter any likely enemy, Rogers set out uplake and found the scalped bodies of five recruits and the carcasses of four horses. In a wrecked sleigh the chest of arms had been broken open and some of the muskets therein looted. A little farther down the ice the men came upon a sight to haunt the strongest's dreams. From the outbreak of the war Indian prisoners taken by either side had never lived more than a few minutes from their capture: their very portable scalps possessed vastly greater value than their live bodies would have, either as intelligence sources or as laborers. No one would ransom or exchange them, in contrast to European soldiers or militiamen, and they were forever dangerous on the march. The Indian warriors knew this all too well, which added a particular ferocity to their deep-woods combat.

Here a squaw lay sprawled, scalped and frozen on the ice. Nearby, in plain view, the attackers had strung her husband from a tree, scalped but still alive. Before him hung a small mirror, placed (recorded *The Boston News-Letter*) so that he might "see himself die."[4] This artistically demonic detail supported the European view of Indians as savage animals whose nearest approach to human creativity lay in refining sadism. The looking glass certainly might have represented a cruel gesture and nothing more; but the European mind consistently misinterpreted many Indian acts, missing the complexities of carefully enacted ritual and other behaviors, either misunderstanding or choosing not to comprehend a worldview so remote from their own, a culture whose God sent his son to a torturous death. Perhaps the glass gave the dying man not so much the opportunity to examine his enemy's handiwork as the power to show himself that he could die with courage and bear his own witness.

The French had borne off the unit's leader, Sergeant Thomas Beaverly, and three other rangers, as well as a sleigh driver, but they had also taken the very sleigh, bearing 1,196 pounds in New York currency that he had brought from Albany for payroll, a third of it Rogers's own. Haviland responded typically to Rogers's claim: "This moment I heard Rogers' Money is Certainly taken by the French party, he says there was twelve Hundred pounds Currency, for my part I don't Credit it, as he is so very easy and indifferent about it."[5]

Despite appearances, Rogers was far from cavalier about the lost money. He could shrug off Haviland's aspersions but not those of Amherst's formidable secretary, John Appy, who kept the accounts of an army that was never efficiently paid. By this point the master of improvisational wilderness warfare had managed thousands of men, to many of whom he had advanced pay. Death had claimed more than a few, while others had deserted, reupped, or gone home at the expiration of their enlistments, implicitly trusting their leader to come through. Even in the best of circumstances, the paper trail and expense accounting, so well established in the regular army, proved extremely elusive in the remote garrisons of the New World, especially among such irregular outfits as the rangers, which employed Indians, frontier illiterates, and drifter toughs who responded to demands for receipts with a snort at best. A man's word and his handshake were what counted in a world where many were touchy about their literacy. As Crown and colonies repeatedly rejected Rogers's invoices, general rumor and angry rangers began to turn on him for breaking his word.

The situation was tricky. Rogers applied to the Crown for moneys advanced against pay to be earned under his command by men who had died in action. Appy countered that to make good on such claims, Rogers would have to track down the heirs, a task so difficult as to approach the impossible. Rogers again requested that his outstanding advances be met, at least for the 1755–56 campaign. The Massachusetts General Assembly turned him down, as did Amherst, who rightly pointed out that he had not at that point been in command. Rangers from that campaign had by now attached thirty-eight suits upon Rogers's property in Rumford.

Rogers later wrote to Amherst that he had "suffered greatly by means of his own Pay's being delay'd for so many years."[6] Time and again Appy had found fault with his accounting—which indeed was rough at best—mostly on the grounds that he furnished no documentation. Rogers won small concessions, but they fell far short of covering his costs. On one occasion he had explicitly told Amherst not to pay his Indian ranger companies before he got back, knowing full well that the only way to reclaim advances was to deduct them before disbursement. Amherst paid them anyway, which he conceded left unexacted debts hanging in the air, but that did nothing material to rectify Rogers's mounting money troubles. Consequently he had borrowed, and borrowed again, from merchants, friends, and family, to bridge his many gaps. However careless he was with money and receipts, he seems seriously to have assumed that the Crown would meet obligations incurred in its service. But the next year he would be writing angrily that "as I was kept in Constant Duty upon the Frontiers, it was out of my Powers to make a Seasonable Sollicitation for my Demands in that Way."[7] He naïvely believed that

things would work out in the end, but the intransigence of the
English paymaster and his borrowings to pay his men and outfit them
would prove an enemy over the long term far more dangerous and demoralizing than Langy or Langlade, dogging his every step and wearing away his hard-won standing, leaving in its place insinuation and ill
repute.[8]

All that winter Amherst worked on the upcoming seventh year's
campaign, which he calculated must be the war's last. One by one the
bastions of French power in the New World had come toppling down:
Louisbourg, Québec, Carillon, Saint-Frédéric, Niagara. The French
had abandoned all their Allegheny forts, while painfully maintaining
a post at Île aux Noix on the Richelieu and a few smaller garrisons
upriver. Montréal remained the last jewel in King Louis's Canadian
crown. A week and a half after the latest supply train disaster,
Amherst received word from London that he should take Montréal at
any cost. To that end he devised a three-pronged offensive that committed nearly every redcoat in the New World, along with thousands
of new recruits from New England, New York, and New Jersey.
Brigadier James Murray, commanding at Québec, would assemble
what regulars and militia he could, then move upriver with them and
with reinforcements from Louisbourg. Amherst would lead the main
body, some 12,000 strong, from Albany to Oswego, then down the
St. Lawrence to the objective. Meanwhile William Haviland, now acting brigadier general, would lead his 3,500 troops north by boat from
Crown Point to take Île aux Noix and the Richelieu garrisons, then
combine with the other forces before Montréal, which their united
power would squeeze into submission.

But of course the French commander, François Gaston, Duc de
Lévis, had different plans, calculating that he could buy time by re-
taking Québec. A treaty that settled the parallel war in Europe,
where England's main ally, Prussia, for a while had actually lost Berlin
to Russia, might nullify Britain's recent North American victories.
Certain factors indeed worked in his favor. Murray's garrison had suffered terribly during the winter; disease and cold had claimed 1,000
men and rendered another 2,000 unfit for service, which left less
than 4,000 men capable of bearing a musket. Although no support
had reached Lévis from France, he could count on many disaffected
farmers and colonists who had been dispossessed by Wolfe's destruc-

tion of the surrounding countryside during last year's siege. With angry warriors from Saint-François and the other St. Lawrence Indian communities, as well as two battalions of Troupes de la Marine and another of Montréal militia, Lévis cobbled together a force of more than 7,000 men. Lacking siege guns, he took a large gamble: in October he wrote to Paris for reinforcements, especially of artillery. Should a French task force beat the British into the St. Lawrence come April as the drive on Québec hit high gear, then the city would be isolated under overwhelming attack.

In early May Rogers, just back from a difficult scout of Île aux Noix, received an urgent summons to travel to Albany "as fast as possible." Amherst told him that Lévis had struck Québec hard on April 28, driving Murray's army, deployed outside the city's walls on the Plains of Abraham, back into the city in a defeat reminiscent of Montcalm's fatal mistake seven months before. The British lost 259 dead and 829 wounded, or some 28 percent of the overall force, whereas the French lost only 12 percent of theirs. In the haste of their retreat, the British had abandoned their field guns to the enemy, leaving the French engineers to set up siege lines in short order.

Amherst proposed to send Rogers into Canada "and by constantly marching from one place to another, try to draw off the enemy's troops, and prolong the siege till our vessels go up the river."[9] He was assigned 300 men, 275 of them rangers, to harass Île aux Noix and the garrisons along the Richelieu. Before he raced back to Crown Point, Amherst grilled him on the particulars of Île aux Noix, Oswego, and La Gallette, as well as details of the geography and the best places of passage critical to the upcoming campaign.

Back at Crown Point, Rogers met Haviland's by-now-expected resistance, receiving 14 light infantrymen—barely half the regular strength specified by Amherst. With a complement of Stockbridge Indians late in coming, Rogers found himself 30 shy of his approved outfit, but he decided not to wait. On June 1 he loaded the 270 available troops onto the brig *Duke of Cumberland* and three sloops, then tacked northward.

First they dropped off Lieutenant Robert Holmes and 50 men at Missisquoi Bay, charged with leveling the Indian village of Wigwam Martinique on the Yamaska. A sloop would pick them up on their return; meanwhile a five-man detail team set off with letters from

Amherst to Murray at Québec. Then the flotilla headed south and west.

On the northwesternmost arm of Lake Champlain, just north of Île La Motte, the lake rejoices in its last wide expanse before narrowing (near the present Canadian border) into the tight confines of the Richelieu. On the western shore, four miles from the Canadian border and 12 miles south of Île aux Noix, lies Point au Fer, a mile-long thumblike projection of southward-facing swampland, which forms shallow King Bay. The Chazy River runs into the lake opposite the point's extremity. Early on the morning of June 4 Rogers's command clambered aboard more than a dozen whaleboats offloaded from the sloops and rowed quietly into the bay. The *Duke of Cumberland* and one sloop held back around Île La Motte. Rogers sent the two shallower-draft sloops north and closer to the fort at Île aux Noix "to command the attention of the enemy till I could get into their country."[10]

Chapter 25

Pressing the French

*I . . . saw with pleasure, you was returned without the loss of a man of
your party, and that you had done every thing that was prudent for you
to attempt with the number of men you had under your command.*

AMHERST TO ROGERS, JUNE 26, 1760

The men pushed the provision-crammed whaleboats through the
cattails lining King Bay, startling some nesting black terns and a great
blue heron, and onto the sandy wet shore. Rogers selected a campsite
nestled up against the armpit of the point, the hardwood swamp on
his right providing secure coverage. Frequent rains had invigorated
the swamp's primeval-looking ground cover, a rich tangle of ferns,
swamp cabbage, sedges, and false hellebore beneath a canopy of red
maple, elm, and the occasional clump of northern white cedar.[1] A
slightly fetid smell of swamp maintained itself over the bustling
camp. Clouds of mosquitoes and gnats feasted on sweating bodies.

The rangers flipped the whaleboats and covered them with brush.
As they settled in, sentries established a perimeter in the thick alder
and holly undergrowth. Rogers sent a handful of the fittest men of
the party to monitor Île aux Noix, others along the sodden shore to
watch for French sails.

That evening and into the next day, sheets of rain spanked the
surface of King Bay until it kicked up in protest. Cold, dry air from
Canada had encountered sluggish, humid warmth from the south,
whipping up storms capable of releasing several inches of pounding downpour, which made "the bushes so wet," wrote Rogers, "that
both we and our provisions would have been greatly exposed by a

march."[2] He kept his men under their makeshift shelters, muskets protected by blankets.

That afternoon a lookout reported sighting warcraft. As darkness descended, Rogers glassed the enemy, hovering just out of cannon shot of the sloops that hung off Point au Fer. Rogers saw that his own sloops were drawing the enemy's attention, limiting the ability of his ground force to move; he and several men rowed out with muffled oars to the nearest sloop, quietly invoking the password, then instructing its captain to sail south toward Île La Motte.

For all the caution they took in rowing back into King Bay, vigilant French observers nonetheless saw the whaleboats pull ashore. Early the next morning runners from the advance scout crashed through the woods with word that more than 300 Frenchmen and Indians had landed just three miles downstream on the western riverbank. At midmorning patrols reported that the enemy had advanced in good order to within a mile of their position. By its nature, woodland warfare rarely gave opportunities for preparing a defense, but Rogers now took full advantage of the warning, supervising the construction of a makeshift bastion of overturned boats on the left flank. However well situated, he could not but feel pressed. Whereas the whaleboats might provide a means of escape if worse came to worst, the French gunships hanging like keen predators somewhere beyond the point could rip them apart in minutes should the sloops fail to beat up in a hurry; and he had no means of alerting them. A volley would betray their location with deadly certainty. Furthermore, the action would conclude in broad daylight, offering little chance of falling back under cover of night should things go wrong.

The attackers swung wide of the swamp as Rogers predicted, then pressed through the thick shrub to fall on the left flank, as one officer wrote, "with usual intrepidity and yelling," all of which the rangers greeted with brisk volleys. Over the next three hours combat grew so close as to leave the Indian front line crouched on one side of the whaleboats, the rangers on the other, blazing away almost point-blank. The cartridge-using rangers reloaded for the most part far faster than the Indians, who endured the painful awkwardness of crouching and pouring powder while trying to dodge bullets discharged barely a muzzle's length away. In their frustration the Indians started pitching stones as the rangers rose to fire. A participant noted that "our men halloo'd to them, that they would likewise fight with stones, and give them an equal chance, which routed them from behind the boats." This battle-line humor seems peculiarly characteristic of Rogers, to set his people laughing even at such dark and bloody quarters.

Rogers ordered the capable Lieutenant Jacob Farrington, a hero of the dreadful return from Saint-François, to take 70 men along the shoreline, then through the swamp, to fall on the enemy's rear—which they did with devastating effect, just as Rogers pressed hard from the center. The enemy line collapsed into disorderly retreat "with the same vivacity they attacked us."[3]

The rangers hounded the routed enemy for about a mile, but at that point the rival woods warriors pulled a tactic right out of Rogers's own rule book: they dove into a dense cedar swamp, perhaps at the egress of the Chazy River, and broke up into small groups. The thick bright-green sprays of cedar branches and the difficult footing smothered the momentum of attack, and by that time another downpour further obscured the enemy retreat. Rogers called off the pursuit. The frantic three-hour engagement had nearly exhausted their ammunition and killed 16 rangers, including Captain Noah Johnson and a light infantry ensign; nine rangers and two light infantrymen were wounded. The French and their allies lost at least double the number, including a prominent partisan fighter, Monsieur Longville, and the Canadian leader of the Indians, La Force. Over and above the three or four dozen discarded muskets and numerous packs, the rangers found Indian corpses, preemptively scalped by their own. The Indians "suffered greatly," reported The Boston News-Letter; "they all to a Man went Home, to bury their Dead," and "it was not in the Power of the French to detain them."[4] The stretched forces of Québec had suffered yet another blow.

The victors buried their own dead on Île La Motte and shipped the wounded back to Crown Point. Amherst's delighted dispatch to Haviland included an oblique but firm reminder that in the future he was not to shortchange Rogers: "I Imagine You have very likely Wrote me a Line or two and have forgot to Enclose it, in Sealing up Your Dispatches, and I don't doubt But You have Immediately Assisted M. Rogers with Everything he wanted to pursue his Orders."[5] Perhaps anticipating Amherst's criticism, Haviland sent 30 light infantrymen to join Rogers on the island, along with 25 lately arrived Stockbridge rangers under Lieutenant Caesar McCormick. The rangers unloaded ten days' worth of provisions from the *Duke of Cumberland*. Much of that day Rogers and the head of the small flotilla, Captain Alexander Grant, huddled together, discussing plans in lowered voices. On the night of June 11 the rangers gained the western shore and prepared to push north, Grant's squadron moving ahead to provide cover at the mouth of the Richelieu. That same day Amherst learned that a French relief fleet, attempting to reinforce the besieging lines around Québec, had been shattered by the blockading British forces and had withdrawn in disorder. Lévis's bold gamble had failed: no peace was on the horizon in Europe, no aid was coming from France. Amherst wrote to Haviland that Rogers was to continue his efforts to bedevil the enemy in Canada; but by the time the general's instruction crossed the wilderness, Rogers was already striking yet deeper into French territory.

Planning to bypass Île aux Noix 11 miles to the north, Rogers set out to Fort Saint-Jean, another 12 miles distant but across level ground. Saint-Jean marked the head of a dozen-mile series of rapids that culminated in a cataract, over which brooded the stone fort of Chambly. Both Saint-Jean and Chambly served as warehousing and loading points for the inescapable whitewater portage.

On the night of the fifteenth, Rogers struck the Saint-Jean–Montréal road and moved east on it "with an intent to surprise the fort,"[6] coming within 400 yards' range. The square wooden emplacement, enforced by sharpened 15-foot palisades made from largely rot-resistant stakes of white cedar, stood on the sandy low western bank of the deep, narrow river. Two riverward corner towers rose four stories high, pierced with cannon loopholes, while two lower towers provided defense against landward attack.[7] Without artillery Rogers had no chance of storming the fort, but he formed an alternative plan. If the light infantry reversed their jackets to display the white linings and marched in close order, then—just perhaps— the fort might mistake them for lily-white French regular reinforcements until it was too late. But as Rogers crept even closer, he found the fort on heightened alert; 17 "well fixed" sentries were patrolling a raised platform inside the palisades. Regulars from Lévis's aborted siege of Québec, fresh and no doubt eager for a toss-up, had recently

arrived and set up a tent city on the extensive glacis. Seeing something suspicious, a sentry or two pegged off a couple of shots in
Rogers's direction. Without a second thought Rogers pulled his party
back; by two A.M. they were marching hard to the north, even deeper
into harm's way. Now two strong enemy posts stood between them
and any chance of getting away by water.

His new target, Fort Sainte-Thérèse, a smaller version of the
square palisade of Saint-Jean, lay on the western bank of the
Richelieu, one-third of the nine-mile way to Chambly. The flat countryside now featured wide swaths of cultivated land in the classic
French Canadian layout, narrow strips stretching back from houses
on the river called ribbon farms. That morning Rogers observed ox-
drawn carts piled high with hay entering the fort and rolling back
empty, fodder for livestock in the upstream posts at Saint-Jean and
Île aux Noix. He also saw boats pulled up on shore, used to ferry provisions and materials between Chambly and Saint-Jean.

Crouched in a nearby copse, he quickly outlined a bold plan to
his most trusted lieutenants. Their dispatch of reinforcements to
Saint-Jean made it clear that the Sainte-Thérèse garrison did not feel
vulnerable, although the heavy gate swung shut after each haycart
pulled inside. Few sentries swept the open fields surrounding the
fort. Rogers eyed a creaking haycart moving ponderously down the
rutted road, a teamster flicking the rumps of his oxen with a long
whip; as it curved toward the river, the river-facing gate swung wide
open.

He hurriedly whispered orders. On his mark Lieutenant
McCormick and the fastest light regulars would swarm to one side of
the next wagon just as it rolled in, while Lieutenant Brewer and some
rangers sprinted to the other. The remaining rangers would overrun
the adjacent village of some fifteen houses, committing no unnecessary violence.

Finally the tensely awaited moment came, and Rogers gave the
sign: roaring green-clad figures broke from their position and sprinted
across the open ground just as the gate swung open. The teamster
watched in horror as the rangers poured onto the parade ground. The
remaining rangers swept through the stunned village.

Rogers knew well the power of surprise to rob its victims of
movement, resource, and resistance. As the grimly efficient lead

rangers fanned out to every corner of the fort, its 24 soldiers, fixated by their movements, gave up without firing a shot. Surprise worked equally well in the village, where the rangers pulled dozens of men, women, and children from their houses into a terrified huddle. Unknown to the conquerors, however, a handful of young men had taken off in headlong flight toward Chambly.

Rogers singled out some of the soldiers and interrogated them with the aid of McCormick, eliciting valuable information about the strength of Chambly, the losses incurred by Lévis during the attempt to retake Québec, and the bayonet and artillery strength of Montréal, Île aux Noix, and Saint-Jean. The prisoners all indicated independently that Chambly was a true strongpoint, so Rogers decided not to follow up on his initial success.

Looking over the frightened villagers, he conscripted three men and had their arms bound. The remaining 52 civilians received a sardonic "pass to Montréal" and were given a few minutes to gather up bedding.[8] The rangers set their homes ablaze, then torched the fort and the large hay magazine within it. They slaughtered all the livestock, stove in all but eight bateaux, and finished off "every other thing which we thought could ever be of service to the enemy."[9]

While smoke still smudged the sky and hay burned ferociously, the raiders ferried themselves and anything they found of use to the eastern bank in short order. Barely had the last ranger scrambled ashore than a strong column from Chambly sprinted into the ruined settlement. As the Frenchmen and Indians poked about the wrecked boats, realizing they could not get across after the rangers, Rogers's men set up a great mocking halloo.

Opposite Île aux Noix, far more serious interception awaited the rangers—about 800 ably disposed regulars in the forest. They fought off an advance party and continued southward fast and hard. Remarkably, the main force, a mile behind the advance guard, not only failed to close but actually recoiled, a cracking of nerve that indicated the ascendancy of Rogers's thunderbolt; but they recovered soon enough and gave chase down to Chimney Point, a hook of land a mile north of King Bay. Knowing that minutes counted, Rogers sent runners ahead to activate the signals worked out with Grant: quick smoky fires and three-shot sequences, spaced at one-minute intervals.

Unlike Stevens at Wells River, Grant was prompt to rendezvous, immediately sending boats to pick up his exhausted comrades. Their pursuers pounded up the shore just as their quarry scrambled aboard the warships. "I cannot but observe with pleasure," wrote Rogers, that "Mr. Grant, like an able officer, very diligently did all that could be expected of him for the good of the service."[10] On June 21 he sent his prisoners back to Amherst, along with a contingent of 50 soldiers and his intelligence report, while the rest of the rangers sailed up to Missisquoi Bay. That evening they collected Lieutenant Holmes, who had failed to find Wigwam Martinique.

Aside from Holmes's miscarriage, the expedition had made a truly telling mark. Rogers had not lost a single man; he had brought in prisoners filled with useful information; and he had demonstrated again his power to do harm so far into enemy territory. Amherst penned him a note whose praise rang markedly effusive for the cool supreme commander of the British forces: "I . . . saw with pleasure, you was returned without the loss of a man of your party, and that you had done every thing that was prudent for you to attempt with the number of men you had under your command."[11] Perhaps more consequentially, he wrote to Haviland that "Major Rogers has done very well."[12] Rogers had significantly rattled the French; *The Boston Weekly News-Letter* reported that the enemy had been "prodigiously alarmed, imagining it was an advanced Party of our Army."[13]

Unable to bear Rogers's mounting successes, even though it reflected well on him, Haviland, newly minted a brigadier general for the upcoming operations, attempted to bypass the major by reorganizing the light regulars, grenadiers, and rangers into a single battalion under a career officer. This scenario would essentially have sidelined Rogers, whose majority, by Haviland's calculations, had expired with the 1759 campaign. Reduced to junior, no longer field grade, Captain Rogers would find himself subordinate to all regular officers of comparable rank as a matter of King's Regulations. Understandably furious, Rogers sent in his commission with a cover letter promising to resign if demoted. Amherst promptly struck down this latest finesse with a furious dispatch, reaffirming to Haviland that "the order I gave last Year was not to any limitted time, & it of Course Sussists now . . . and You will be so good as to give in publick orders that Major Rogers is to Enjoy the Same Rank as was granted him last Year."[14]

The dust slowly settled. By August 16 Haviland's 3,500 men, with Rogers and 600 rangers in the van, had sailed up from Crown Point, bypassing Île La Motte, and landed a mile and a half downstream of Île aux Noix. Storms along the way swept some boats off from the flotilla, stove some as they crashed ashore, and split one canoe open, drowning seven or eight rangers, but did not deter the force from its northward path. Their possession of Île aux Noix, a narrow 210-acre island dividing the Richelieu, gave the French every reason to believe that they could check the offensive, even though Bougainville commanded only 1,000 Canadian militia and 600 regulars. Just five Indians rallied to their old allies—indirect tribute to Rogers's grim effectiveness over the last year; but strong log booms blocked passage beyond the fort. Sawyers attempting to sever the booms by night came under murderous cannonade. For days the hostile batteries exchanged ineffective fire.

Nine days into the blockade the booms remained intact, and Rogers received orders to take two companies of light infantry and four of rangers and manhandle two light howitzers and a six-pounder north through the east-bank woods. They pressed on with some difficulty until abreast the French warships. The improvised battery pounded the off-guard squadron at point-blank range; the six-pounder's first shell severed the mooring line of the powerful floating battery *Grand Diable*, and the west wind blew her ashore at the rangers' very feet. A French galley gallantly tried to come up, but the rangers poured murderous fire into her until she fled downriver with the sloop and schooner. The rangers swarmed over the radeau, taking it without firing a shot. Two miles away the retreating flotilla piled up on a muddy shoal.

Rogers and his men needed little prompting to leave the artillery and jog down the eastern bank—fording at least one feeder creek—until they drew opposite the stranded craft. At Rogers's word, his strongest swimmers stripped and dove in, tomahawk handles clenched in their teeth, to board one ship whose complement quickly surrendered; Colonel Darby brought up the captured radeau against her consorts, quickly overpowering both vessels. Infantry and artillery had all but destroyed Bourlemaque's navy. Two nights later the French withdrew, leaving only 50 soldiers to cover the evacuation, care for the sick, and obtain honorable terms.

That evening Haviland sent Rogers and his men to harass their retreat in the captured radeau. The next morning Rogers reached Saint-Jean; finding it already in flames, he landed 200 rangers there and pressed hotly on to make Bourlamaque "dance a little the merrier."[15] The rangers quickly overtook the rear guard, engaged them in sharp action, and captured 17 Frenchmen, including a major and a captain. Bourlamaque fell back across a tributary, destroyed the bridge behind him, and deployed along the opposite bank, matching Rogers's 400 muskets with more than 1,000 of his own. Rogers sensibly saw no point in pressing further without the advantage of surprise, and he let the enemy straggle the last dozen miles to Montréal. But he had made himself felt almost under the city's walls.

Haviland then dispatched him on a more strategic northward movement, in which he joined General Murray four miles south of Montréal. Shortly thereafter Vaudreuil surrendered to this overwhelming presence. "Thus at length, at the end of the fifth campaign, Montreal and the whole country of Canada was given up, and became subject to the King of Great Britain," wrote Rogers with satisfaction.[16]

Despite his exultation, uncertainties loomed. However glorious it had been for him, the war had exacted its toll. He had incurred wounds to his head and wrist, endured scurvy, smallpox, and severe frostbite, and still suffered from the memories of the hundreds of good men he had taken out but not brought back. He had repeatedly and without complaint served on the most hazardous missions of the entire war. Yet still he did not have a standing commission; nor had he been promised one. Victory entailed the disbandment of the rangers. He had earned no pension but had incurred overwhelming personal obligations and still struggled to recover shillings on the pound. While he might be the war's most famous North American hero, such fame might prove fleeting; indeed, the phenomenal success of this rough-hewn frontiersman, so far beyond his station, would bring him new problems, not just from haughty British officers under whom he served but also from elite coastal colonists who would not know what to do with a man who was so useful in war but was frightening and unsettling in the peacetime he helped win.

For Rogers, the fall of the last big cities had not ended the struggle. Amherst needed a man to push into the far western corners of the French empire, where it still spread a vast indeterminate presence around the Great Lakes basin, and to convince the garrisons there to capitulate. No British force had traveled west of Fort Pitt; a considerable strength of hostile Indians remained. The western French commanders might choose to take a stand and rally the tribes, particularly the British-hating Ottawa, against any assertion of the distant eastern conquerors. The journey must be undertaken as winter set in, over a landscape that was perilous even in kinder months.

Seven years of war had formed many men of promise out of capable provincials in Amherst's 17,000-man army, such as Israel Putnam and James Murray. But of them all, Amherst without hesitation reached for the out-of-nowhere young ranger who time and again had gotten the job done for him. This extraordinary journey— the longest and fastest expedition taken in British colonial North American history—would challenge even Rogers's considerable talents.

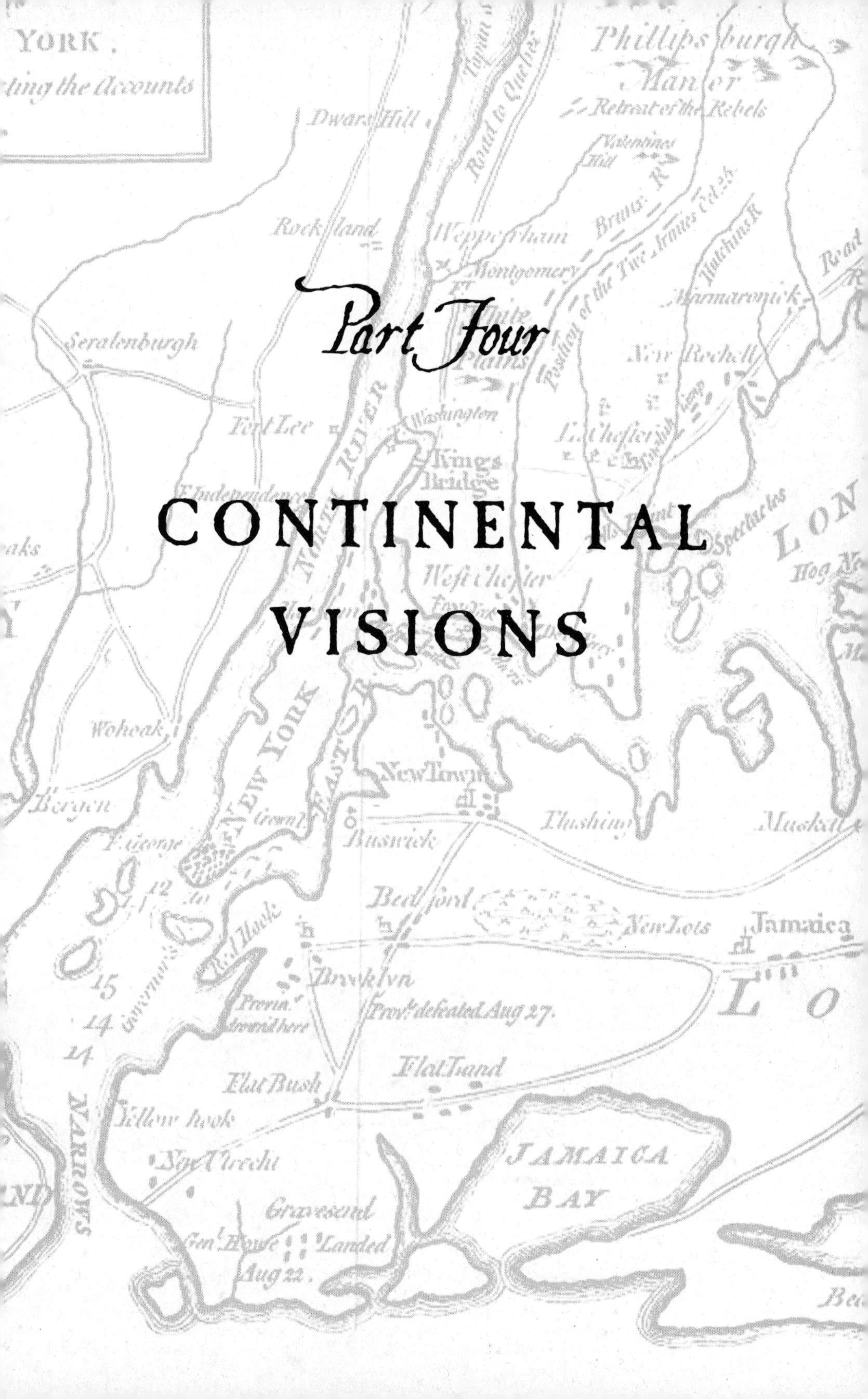

Part Four

CONTINENTAL VISIONS

Chapter 26

A Race West to Claim
the Continent for Britain

It is recommended to the soldiers as well as the officers, not to mind the waves of the lake; but when the surf is high to stick to their oars, and the men at helm to keep the boat quartering on the waves, and briskly follow, then no mischief will happen by any storm whatever.

ROGERS TO HIS MEN, NAVIGATING THE WINTER
WAVES OF LAKE ERIE GOING WEST
TOWARD DÉTROIT, 1760

A year to the day after he had left for Saint-François, Rogers and two companies of rangers, a detachment of Mohegans, a British engineer, a French guide, and an artillery officer with a talent for painting scenes—some 200 men in all—settled into 15 whaleboats and pushed off from Montréal's wharf against the dark, turbulent power of the St. Lawrence.

Behind them rose the tall, single-spired parish church and the lower, four-spired Jesuit church and seminary. A somewhat battered but truly garrison-sized Union Jack snapped over the city's small citadel, replacing the *drapeau blanc*, a field of golden lilies against white, for the first time in the 117 years since European stonework first marked this spot.[1] From this same location generations of *coureurs des bois* had paddled their large birchbark *canots du nord*, 25-foot-long vessels with gaudily painted bow decorations gunwale-deep, bearing a ton and a half of trade goods for the arduous journey into the heart of the continent.[2] Rogers had dreamed of this moment: now the lure of the vast unknown and the stories that had electrified him from childhood were at last drawing him magnetically westward.

Rogers left in the full noon light, less concerned than usual about prying eyes now that the French had been so largely defanged by the fall of Montréal and Québec, "a conquest perhaps of the greatest importance that is to be met with in the British annals," as he himself would write.[3] Yet in the single day's flat-out preparation for this epic journey, he had hewn to his usual policy of keeping his intentions quiet. Too many times information casually released had queered his plans—or even worse, soured them—with deadly result. While this time there was no canny French unit waiting in the woods they knew so well, a runner could possibly alert the undefeated wilderness garrisons of their coming and give them ample time to organize resistance.

A more cautious man might have balked at paddling and poling into the teeth of winter, a time of year when even the *coureurs des bois* overwintered in a king's outpost or an Indian village. Already the days had begun to draw in and the winds of winter to whip up the water and freeze the ground. *The New-Hampshire Gazette* reported that the "Major [has] gone to Lake Superior, a Journey the French say, never undertaken at this Season of the Year."[4] But Rogers had little time to worry: he had too many miles to cover, were this venture to be worthwhile. He was to see to "the relief of the garrisons of the French posts at Detroit, Michlimakana, or any others in that district, for gathering in the arms of the inhabitants thereof, and for administering to them the oath of allegiance" and to "bring away the French troops and arms," no small task. Amherst further directed that he return only after having "reconnoitered and explored the country as much as you can, without losing time unnecessarily."[5]

Five miles upstream they arrived at the Lachine Rapids and beached and emptied their craft. Heavily laden, they struggled over the well-used portage that skirted these formidable falls, named the previous century by French explorers who believed it the gateway to China. In 1535 Jacques Cartier, at the behest of His Most Christian Majesty Francis I, sailed up the St. Lawrence to these rapids and found them alien to anything in western Europe or on the North

American east coast. Great waves stood in place, roaring and froth-
ing, in season and out, as if hypnotized by a divine power. In the over-
wrought words of the nineteenth-century Kingston poet Charles
Sanger:

> Again the troubled deep heaps surge on surge,
> And howling billows sweep the waters dark,
> Stunning the ear with their stentorian dirge,
> That loudens as they strike the rocks' resisting verge.[6]

With its immense sweep and ledges of murderous white water,
the St. Lawrence embodied the uncontrollable wildness of a continent of unimaginable proportions.

Not even Cartier's imagination could stretch around the sober
Iroquois accounts of immense freshwater inland seas from which the
St. Lawrence, like some great umbilical cord reaching from the center of the continent to the Atlantic, fed the ocean. The St. Lawrence
is 800 miles long—shorter than Canada's Mackenzie and Yukon—but
when the five Great Lakes are included, it becomes a navigable 3,000-
mile waterway that stretches more than halfway to the Pacific.[7] For
the French, the river enabled fur traders, determined black-frocked
missionaries, and a handful of geopolitically minded officers to pene-
trate amazingly deep into the continent. The river never tired even in
drought, because Lake Ontario serves as its undepletable source. The
hardy men and women who built Montréal here at the rapids, beyond
which large boats could not proceed upriver, contended with the
dark river as friend and foe alike, especially in winter, when it backed
up against great ice floes and reached its icy fingers along the city's
streets.

The St. Lawrence begins benignly enough near the present-day
town of Kingston on Lake Ontario, spending its first four dozen miles
in a course that swells as much as 12 miles wide. But then it constricts
meanly, forcing this great volume of water through narrow chutes,
toppling over eroded ledges. Between Lake Saint-François and Lake
Saint-Louis, the Coteau Rapids drop on average more than ten feet
per mile for eight miles; by the time Rogers's party took their chances
on it, it and its brothers had already claimed untold lives. Only a week
and a half earlier, as Amherst's army bore down upon Montréal from

upriver, the rapids west of Lachine dashed 20 bateaux, 17 whaleboats, and a row galley to pieces and claimed 84 lives in the twinkling of an eye.[8]

The lakes-going party spent that night at the village of Lachine, shadowed by a small stockade containing a stone windmill, a chapel, a seigneur's house, and several small cottages. Some 30 such small garrisons formed a defensive belt around the city, built against Iroquois raids over the previous century.[9] Rogers writes that they "took a view" of two Iroquois settlements, which had sent so many hardened enemies against the rangers over the last seven years.

At the last stop on the western tip of Montréal Island, where the Ottawa River storms down into the St. Lawrence from the north, stood the small wooden chapel named for Sainte-Anne-de-Bellevue. Wrote fur trader Alexander Henry, she was "the patroness of the Canadians, in all their travels by water."[10] Near the door hung a small, well-worn box with a hole in the top in which *coureurs des bois* stuffed coins for the parish priest to say one more Low Mass for their safety.

Rogers's journals do not describe the difficulties they encountered as they worked upstream through the Coteau Rapids. They put ashore as much weight as possible and leaned on long poles with iron tips jammed into the riverbed. At the worst of it, rope parties were landed to haul the boats along the rough waters near shore, a miserable and dangerous business, the roar of the rapids all but drowning out the shouts of the weary men. Nevertheless, they had cleared the worst of the rapids by September 16.

Over the next two days of dark-and-daylight effort, the party pressed up and over numerous riffs interspersed over 50 miles. Over the years Canadian boatmen had improvised a device to help move craft upstream against the force of the river that was bad enough even at the lesser rapids; a ten-foot pole crossed at short intervals with small wooden bars, not unlike the rungs of a ladder. By gripping the bars successively from the bow end and putting their whole force into walking toward the stern, the boatmen could gain purchase and move their craft grudgingly forward.[11] Quick as they were to adapt effective technology, such as ranger James Tute's two-blanket sail system for whaleboats and bateaux, it is more than possible that Rogers's force put these devices to use.

On the nineteenth the bone-weary expedition reached Fort William Augustus (until recently Fort Lévis, near present-day Ogdensburg, New York), taken by Amherst's army in mid-August after a fierce weeklong siege and naval action. There the expedition rested for a day and repaired the battered and leaky whaleboats. Rogers sent ten sick and injured rangers to Fort Oswego, commanding that river's infall on the southeast shore of Lake Ontario.

A stiff wind from the south rocked the boats dangerously until they reached the riverine lake memorably studded by the Thousand Islands, patches of erosion-resistant rock threaded by scoured-away narrow chutes of softer stone through which the river raced. Not long after an evening encampment and meal, the wind died down, and Rogers ordered the whaleboats back into the water. The men silently paddled among the islands in darkness, so close to the sheer sides as to be able to touch them.

They continued with little break all the following day. Finally the water opened up into wide and wind-lashed Lake Ontario, and they pulled with relief into a safe harbor on the north shore, the site of the old Fort Frontenac, surrounded by 500 acres of cleared forest, now rocky pastures of clover interspersed with scattered pines. A vigorous wind blowing snow and ice horizontally pinned them to camp the next day, but the men complained little; a group of Indians camped by the old fort's ruins professed joy at hearing of the English victory and provided the rangers with a rich and welcome feast of venison and wildfowl.

So the journey continued, the whaleboats hugging the northern shore, the occupants barely able to register one another in thick fog, until the wind again forced them to lie over. Fifty Mississauga Indians materialized spectrally from the forest to present them with eight gutted deer, split in half, "which, with them, is a most elegant and polite present, and significant of the greatest respect."[12] That evening the Indians invited the rangers to watch as they filled large canoes with salmon in just a half hour, several men spearing the fish while another held a pine-pitch torch close to the water. Despite such apparent good relations, Rogers kept up his guard and maintained usual sentry rotations.

Whatever his coolness toward things human, a growing enthusiasm and curiosity seem to have awakened in Rogers the farther he paddled west. Finding the ruins of a French garrison on the Toronto River, he described the great oaks, hickories, maples, and poplars that abounded on clay soil, then mused that the site would make "a most convenient place for a factory [i.e., trading post], and that from thence we may very easily settle the north-side of Lake Erie."[13] For once his vision fell short: Canada's largest city, Toronto, would one day take root here. No wonder that he was amazed at the bounty of the western country, so different from the rugged, rock-clogged topography and thin soils of glaciated New England. All his life he had learned to interrogate the environment, questioning the land intensely for any clues it might yield as he moved through it. What he saw here, the abundant game even as winter closed in, springing from an ever-unfolding prospect of meadows and rich soil, overpowered him with a sense of possibility.

On October 1 they steered across the lake's western waters, coming upon the south shore at dark, some boats now "exceedingly leaky and dangerous." Before heading off the next morning, Rogers gave word that a red flag flying from his boat indicated strong winds and the need for the flotilla to close up for safety. The caution proved prescient that day: while under this tight formation, Lieutenant McCormick's boat sprang a bad leak. Despite the waves, wind, and inability of most aboard to swim, its whole company was rescued with the loss only of their packs.

The following day they arrived at Fort Niagara, a towering, many-chimneyed stone fortress set among outbuildings and bastions, just upstream from where its namesake river enters the lake. Its small garrison had surrendered to the British the previous July after a nineteen-day siege. The men rested, and the commandant provided them with "blankets, coats, shirts, shoes, magassins, &c."[14] Rogers traded two worn-out whaleboats for two bateaux, but complained that they leaked as well.

At the fort he met the English traders Edward Cole and Nicholas Stevens, who had arrived during the summer, eager to take advantage of the trade opportunities opening for the king's enterprising subjects in the moment of victory. As they sat outside one early October evening, the three men, joined by Lieutenant McCormick, fell into earnest discussion and soon agreed to form Rogers & Company. In Rogers the traders saw a nearly perfect partner. Their first client became the unit itself, the company selling them 256 gallons of rum, 170 blanket coats, some provisions, and other equipment.[15] Such an arrangement, although certainly not without precedent, walked close to the line ethically, even in this vastly looser world on the edge of empire.

Rogers, who had risked his life for the Crown and was owed much by it, probably felt little if any compunction in taking advantage of such dealings. No doubt in their fevered conversations the traders and soldiers speculated on the vast material possibilities embedded among the undiscovered lands.

As the rangers began moving supplies and boats down the portage trail skirting the falls, Lieutenant Brehm and Captain Thomas Davies surveyed the great cataract, as specified by Amherst: "No words can express the consternation of travellers at first view, seeing so great body of water falling... The vapour arising from the fall may sometimes be seen at a great distance, appearing like a cloud or pillar of smoak, and in it the appearance of a rainbow, whenever the sun and the position of the traveller favours."[16]

Amherst had ordered that they establish contact with Brigadier General Robert Monckton, now at Fort Pitt, well to the south, before continuing west to Détroit; and so Rogers decided, as the winter pressed in, to race ahead with a small command to Fort Presque Isle (now Erie, Pennsylvania) some 85 miles along Lake Erie's dangerous southern shore, and then head south, leaving Lieutenant Jonathan Brewer to lead the rest of the contingent west.

"As the winter-season was now advancing very fast in this country," the weather now became Rogers's chief opponent. Wind from the north and the severe chop caused by Erie's shallow waters combined to form a lee shore, against which the boats might at any moment be dashed to pieces by the surf. Speed became their chief weapon: they hammered down the southern shore, Rogers keeping a careful eye and ear on the mounting wind. Although the weather left them shorebound one morning and no doubt made for an entirely wet and miserable passage, they covered the 85 miles in two days. Arriving at noon, they gave word of the fall of New France to the Swiss mercenary Colonel Henry Bouquet of the 60th Regiment. Less than three hours later—barely enough time to dry their clothes— Rogers led his men out on the 120-mile journey south to Fort Pitt;

five rangers were sent back east to rendezvous with Brewer. The small group reached Fort Pitt by October 17, even though they had to negotiate a shallow stretch of the Allegheny River over endless shoals and fallen trees. Rogers found a detachment hard at work building a new palisaded fort in the shadows of Fort Duquesne, where the Allegheny meets the Monongahela; it had been burned by the retreating French eleven months earlier. He waited three days, uneasily no doubt in the face of winter's rapid advance, for Monckton to complete his elaborations on Amherst's orders, for several summonses to the orphaned western commandants, and for the text of an oath of allegiance to be administered to the inhabitants. Accompanying Rogers would be the nearsighted and overweight Captain Donald Campbell of the Royal Americans, a Scot who would administer the Détroit garrison over the winter, as well as George Croghan, the deputy northern superintendent of Indian affairs, to whom Rogers handed a letter from William Johnson. Croghan then dispatched Iroquois and Delaware couriers to Fort Détroit requesting that representative chiefs meet the incoming party at the Détroit River. Monckton rounded out his lengthy instructions with the direction that "you will keep up the Strictest discipline in the Troops under yr Comand, and not Suffer any of the Inhabitants to be disturbed or molested, as they are now become the Subjects of the King of great Brittain."[17] Rogers hardly needed reminding that he was walking into a volatile situation in which only his steady hand could prevent the eruption of violence.

Back at Fort Presque Isle ten days later, Rogers learned that Lake Erie had given his rangers some trouble, dashing several boats against the shore and ruining a good deal of provisions. Brewer and his whole party arrived "in a most shattered condition."[18] Furthermore a boat carrying supplies from Niagara to Presque Isle had never arrived and was feared lost. The rangers set to repairing their whaleboats. On November 3 Captain Brewer left with 40 oxen under an escort of 20 Iroquois, Shawnees, and Delawares to travel overland to Détroit, while Captain Waite returned to Niagara for more supplies. Rogers wrote his own extensive set of orders, carefully detailing troop dispositions, blue and red flag signals on the water, landing and embarkation procedures, and sentry rotations. He included a wry but serious note for the benefit of the new men, unaccustomed to travel on the wave-fraught lake: "It is recommended to the soldiers as well as the officers, not to mind the waves of the lake; but when the surf is high to stick to their oars, and the men at helm to keep the boat quartering on the waves, and briskly follow, then no mischief will happen by any storm whatever."[19] He quickly added that 10 of the best ranger steersmen would be at the helms of the boats that bore Captain Campbell's company.

Nineteen whaleboats and bateaux set out on November 4. "Itt is very Late in Ye Sason to Take Such a Journay Butt ye Bussness we are going on will Make itt agreeable anough," wrote Croghan,[20] who noted several days into the passage (which would take them by the present city of Cleveland) that a tranquil morning sail had curdled into a horrendous squall within an hour and a half, "the Waves run Mountains high." They raced into a protected harbor, with some of their flour provisions nevertheless drenched and the ammunition boat "allmost staved to Pieces."[21] Storm surges on Lake Erie can raise the water level by as much as seven feet, and 10-to-15-foot waves can lift the vessels traversing it a frighteningly unstable 22 feet.[22]

Before they reached Sandusky, during one of the enforced spells while waiting for the winds and rough waters to die down, a delegation of Indian chiefs walked into camp, escorted by ranger sentries. The Ottawas met Rogers just up from the shore, where large bonfires glowed under the swaying limbs of oak, hickory, and locust. Rogers surveyed the faces of these longtime allies of the French, a people "lusty, square, and strait limb'd"[23] who had so often battled his rangers to great effect, particularly under the half-breed kinsman and quasi-chieftain Langlade. Facial tattoos and the rags of stretched earlobes, long since pulled out, lent their countenance an ominous air. Their sometime penchant for cannibalism, as in the aftermath of the destruction of Colonel Parker's expeditionary force on Lake George in 1757, bestowed an unsettling reputation upon the Ottawas among the men.

It is likely that some of them, perhaps all, knew of Rogers. They advised him that Pontiac,[24] an important sachem, approached and desired that the detachment halt "till such time as he could see me with his own eyes."[25] Five years later Rogers would write of meeting a figure whose name by that time had become the human face of the largest and most enterprising Indian uprising north of the Spanish territories in American history. When they addressed each other on a blustery November day through an interpreter, Pontiac was as yet unknown to westerners but was an increasingly influential chief among the Ottawas; he would seize the stunned imagination of the new claimants to sovereignty just three years hence. Something about this man struck Rogers and those around him.

"He puts on an air of majesty and princely grandeur," Rogers later wrote,[26] and the handful of surviving accounts agree. Indian agent Croghan, never one to lavish praise upon Indians, described Pontiac as "a shrewd, sensible Indian of few words, and commands more respect amongst these nations than any Indian I ever saw."[27] Pontiac's straight black hair was probably cut short on the sides but was left heaped up on top in a sort of pompadour. He wore leggings and moccasins, with a French blanket coat wrapped around his midsection. The parts of his tattooed skin that showed glistened with rubbed-in bear fat. Colorful beads gleamed in his ears, and a stone pierced his septum. Rogers would be the first British officer to meet him.

Pontiac asked Rogers to state his business and to explain why he had not sought permission to pass through his land. Rogers replied that he had no quarrel with the Ottawas and intended only to "remove the French out of his country, who had been an obstacle in our way to mutual peace and commerce." Rogers handed Pontiac several belts of wampum; Pontiac reciprocated with a belt of his own, implying, wrote Rogers, that "I must not march further without his leave." As night fell and the Indians still posted themselves immovably across the westward trail, Pontiac inquired whether the rangers needed anything that his country afforded; Rogers replied that he would gladly buy any provisions offered. The rangers took up their posts nervously and spent a guarded and uneasy night.

The next day the Ottawas brought in several sacks of parched corn and other necessities, followed by Pontiac, bearing the white-feathered calumet of peace. Rogers sat down as Pontiac solemnly packed the red stone pipehead with either tobacco, bark, leaf, or herb. The journals may have been referring to Pontiac's pipe when they described a peace pipe as a brightly painted stem of "cane, elder, or some kind of light wood," from which hung the heads, tails, and feathers "of the most beautiful birds, &c." and which served "as an instrument by which they invoke the sun and moon to witness their sincerity, and to be, as it were, guarantees of the treaty between them."[28] The smoke, the Indians believed, carried prayers heavenward.

Pontiac assured Rogers that peace now subsisted between them and that he could pass through his country unharmed. Rogers had undergone an unarticulated test. Pontiac would detail an escort to accompany the oxen. "He would protect me and my party from any insults that might be offered or intended by the Indians." Rogers recorded several further conferences in which he registered Pontiac's "great strength of judgment, and a thirst for knowledge." Feeling out Pontiac's allegiance, Rogers found him "inclined to live peaceably with the English while they used him as he deserved" but that "he was far from considering himself as a conquered Prince."[29] The encounters would exert a profound effect on Rogers, leading him improbably to make this man the Aeschylean protagonist of perhaps America's first serious drama. As the vast lake country seemed so formidable and abundant, so did the power and richness of this Indian leader. In only two years Rogers would summon all his woods skill and command quality to fight against Pontiac's forces in terrible combat.

The party continued its slow passage over the wind-lashed, oceanic lake, arriving north of the iced-over Sandusky River on November 19, whence Lieutenant Brehm was dispatched to alert Fort Détroit of Rogers's approach. Nearly ten miles from Sandusky some Huron sachems and envoys sent by Croghan from Fort Pitt presented themselves and informed him that a body of 400 Huron warriors raised by the French commandant of Détroit awaited Rogers at the outlet of the Détroit River "in order to obstruct our passage." The embassy had come "to know my business, and whether the person I had sent forward had reported the truth that Canada was reduced."[30]

Rogers presented the chiefs with a large belt of wampum: "Brothers, With this belt I take you by the hand. You are to go directly to your brothers assembled at the mouth of the river, and tell them to got to their towns till I arrive at the fort... You live happily in your own country. Your brothers have long desired to bring this about. Tell your warriors to mind their fathers [the French] no more, for they are all prisoners to your brothers [the English]." But still he made it clear that the incoming master would look badly upon any Huron who abused the French.

The force made slow headway against the persistent wind, while the swamps that now lined the shore limited opportunities to gather firewood. Two days farther along the Huron sachems returned and announced that their warriors and some Ottawas had rallied to the French commandant, the 47-year-old Captain François-Marie Picoté de Belestre, whom they reported to be a strong man, set on resistance. Rogers knew that in the Lachine-born Belestre he had come up against a canny opponent; Belestre had fought alongside Montcalm at the fall of Fort William Henry and had led devastating raids in the Carolinas and against German settlers on the west bank of the Mohawk River in New York.[31] Still Rogers pushed on; two days later 60 Indians appeared, bearing the news that the French had confined Brehm's party and run up on a flagstaff the effigy of a man with a wooden head and a crow picking his brains. Belestre explained to them that he was the crow, Rogers the man. But the visitors, expressing confidence that it was Rogers who would pick Belestre's brains, agreed to accompany his men to Détroit.

On the twenty-fifth Rogers reached the mouth of the Détroit River and spent the next day "in conciliating their savage minds to peace and friendship."[32] The situation hung in volatile balance, the French commander and Rogers locked in a high-stakes game of poker. The Scottish fur trader John Porteous would write to his parents: "Capt. Belletre and the French commandant here bribed & sent all the Indian Nations about this place to cut off the English upon the lake, altho' they no sooner met Major Rogers who commanded the troops for said purpose, than they came & made an alliance with him & came along with him to Detroit & would have willingly sacrificed every French soul in the settlement if he had not strictly forbid them."[33]

The following morning Belestre requested that Rogers halt where he was and communicate Vaudreuil's letter and terms of capitulation. Shortly thereafter he further wrote, "Be not surprised, Sir, if along the coast you find the inhabitants upon their guard." Belestre himself had given permission to his Indian partners to arm themselves, in the light, he claimed, of rumors that Rogers had given the Indians accompanying him permission to plunder. "It is for your safety and preservation as well as ours; for should these Indians become insolent, you may not perhaps, in your present situation, be able to subdue them alone."

Rowing into a stiff, cold headwind, Rogers's party pushed five miles upriver, whence he sent Captain Campbell to the fort with the capitulation orders and a dispatch informing the commandant that he would await an answer until four o'clock the following afternoon. "Your inhabitants under arms will not surprise me," Rogers wrote, adding for emphasis that he had seen no hostile Indians, "only savages waiting for my orders." He made clear his displeasure at Belestre's failure to release Lieutenant Brehm's party but ended with the promise that no one in the garrison would be molested.

Chapter 27

Détroit

In Consideration of the Love and Good Will we have to him as also a
Desire we have To Convince the World that we will Grant him our
Bounty for Being the First English Officer that Ever Came into our
Country with Troops.

CHIPPEWA CHIEFS, ON ACCEPTING GIFTS FROM
ROGERS AND PLEDGING THEIR ALLEGIANCE
TO THE BRITISH, DECEMBER 1760

The next day Rogers drew up his rangers in their green wool and the regulars in their red coats on a grassy field. From there they had a clear view of the garrison's 12-foot-high oaken palisades, which sat on a high bluff overlooking the river, which ran deep and fast and 900 yards across. A slight disposition of three-pounders and small mortars guarded the 70 or 80 houses arrayed in orderly streets within, hardly the "Paris of the West" that Antoine Laumet de Lamothe Cadillac imagined when he found the outpost in 1701; yet the garrison of 200 or so, swelling to 400 in the summer, stood at a key location, overlooking the river that connected Lake Erie with Huron and Michigan and lying near the Maumee-Wabash river system, which gave access to the Indian cultures in present-day Ohio, Michigan, and Indiana. Croghan noted that the fort commanded "a very pleasant prospect for nine miles above, and nine miles below," a vista of cleared fields and whitewashed French Canadian houses standing on both sides of the river.[1] Across the river and behind some French houses lay a substantial Wyandot community, structures of long, wooden poles bound at the top and covered with bark and fur. An

Fort Detroit and Environs, 1763

Ottawa community existed a few miles upriver, a Potawatomi a mile below the fort.[2] Rogers could not help but taste the nature of the polyglot community here, far outside the tamed St. Lawrence River Valley. Here the regular ship-brought French presence, or certainly the British coastal colonial towns, the French regular soldiers, French habitants, half-breed métis, *coureurs des bois*, Algonquian-speaking Ottawas, Potawatomies, and Iroquoian-speaking Wyandots coexisted in a community forged over two thirds of a century. While the sharpened palisades of the fort might indicate the strength and power of a French occupation, it was the bonds forged by the polyglot population, not the walls and cannons, that kept these people together. The French had built Fort Pontchartrain du Détroit to dominate the river, not the cultures who lived there.[3] Rogers's careful approach to Détroit and his deft negotiations suggest he knew well the contours of these complex relationships.

Captain Campbell and a French officer approached the rangers from the fort, the French officer bearing Belestre's compliments and signifying that "he was under my command."

Rogers sent two lieutenants with 36 Royal Americans to take possession. The French laid down their arms. On November 29, in the fort's parade ground, the green-clad rangers lined up alongside the red-coated Royal Americans and across from a small and emaciated complement of white-coated French regulars. With drums beating, the white French flag dropped and the red Union Jack rose up the flagpole, "at which about 700 Indians gave a shout, merrily exulting in their prediction being verified, that the crow represented the English."[4] France's major western garrison had fallen without a shot being fired or drop of blood spilled.

By the next day the entire garrison had taken the oath of allegiance. Not one for lying idle, Rogers quickly drew up a plan: Lieutenant Holmes, accompanied by another officer, two sergeants, and 28 privates, would escort Belestre, two officers, and 35 men, along with 17 Englishmen who had been prisoners, to Philadelphia;[5] Lieutenant Butler and Ensign Waite would take 20 men and secure Fort Miami (present-day Fort Wayne, Indiana) and Fort Ouiatenon (now West Lafayette, Indiana); and Captain Campbell would overwinter at Detroit with a small contingent. Rogers sent the bulk of his men back to Niagara under Captain Brewer, retaining Lieutenant

McCormick and 37 men to go with him to Fort Michilimackinac. During these few days he also forged treaties with several of the surrounding tribes.

By early December winter had fully claimed the region, and many locals warned Rogers that his chances of reaching Michilimackinac (which held the Straits of Mackinac, where Mackinaw City, Michigan, stands today) were slim to nonexistent. Rogers left anyway on December 10, but snow and ice at Saginaw Bay forced him to turn back on the sixteenth, and then only his iron will and endurance got his frozen party into Détroit on December 21. Before the peripatetic major left for Fort Pitt two days later, he negotiated for parcels of land with the Chippewas, signing one deed for nearly 20,000 acres along the St. Mary's River northeast of Michilimackinac with traders Jean-Baptiste Cadotte and Alexander Henry and another for himself, 30,000 acres of what is now Michigan's Upper Peninsula. The Chippewa chiefs took away 250 blankets, 20 leggings, 60 pounds of vermilion, 300 barrels of rum, 30,000 beads of wampum, 400 pounds of gunpowder, and 500 pounds of ball and small shot. The Chippewa chiefs agreed to this "in Consideration of the Love and Good Will we have to him as also a Desire we have To Convince the World that we will Grant him our Bounty for Being the First English Officer that Ever Came into our Country with Troops."[6]

When Rogers performed the rough and perfunctory ceremony of accepting Belestre's surrender of Détroit, the symbolic centerpiece of the French west, he officiated over one of the most transformational moments in modern Western history. A nearly unimaginable swath of the continent had changed hands, the largest international transfer of land in history. When the peace was formalized in February 1763, the British Empire would swell larger than that of imperial Rome, most of its vast gains in the New World, where it now reached from the Atlantic west to the Mississippi River and from Hudson Bay south to the Gulf of Mexico. Large swaths of this land lay unmapped and largely unknown to the colonists and Europeans, the contours of the geography not defined in paintings, maps, or travel writings or even yet imagined in novels or plays.

The British had fought France in the New World on and off for fifty years. Only in the late 1750s did consciousness change and the British realize that they were not just parrying back and forth but

that Wolfe's effective navy could sail up the St. Lawrence and sack
the riverside towns constituting French Canada. So too, the idea of
long ranger combat units marching north into the St. Lawrence community was not even contemplated seriously in the 1730s or 1740s.
When Rogers marched his rangers into Canada and burned Saint-
François, the result was not strategically significant in the war effort
but was astoundingly new—the mastery of long distance, of the primal woods, and the ability to move there. Why the Saint-François
raid resonated with people was not merely the suffering of the attacked Abenaki villagers and the starving rangers but the vista of possibility that it opened up. Wolfe and Rogers had demonstrated that
new things were possible and that the French could be not only defeated but expelled, and the continent could be made their own.

For men of soaring imagination, the expulsion of the French kick-
started a series of events that would propel North America toward
revolution. It opened up the opportunity for an extraordinary generation of men to soar in many different directions; a small-town
counterfeiter could rise to a continental thinker. No one knew what
lay ahead. But Rogers, who came from the thin soils and battering
winters of New England, had had a taste of the deep soils, meadows,
and wide, gentle rivers of the Midwest, and he had a good idea of its
possibilities.

Rogers's description of his journey back to Fort Pitt seems almost
giddy. Certainly it must have seemed like a pleasant stroll after his
aborted struggle to Michilimackinac, but there's a sense of euphoria
in his words, as though he's seeing the landscape with new eyes. He
comments with exuberance on the large amount of game and on such
extraordinary sights as a spring that pulsed with a three-foot surge. "I
imagine it discharges ten hogsheads of water in a minute," reckoned
the practical New Englander. Along the western curve of Lake Erie
they walked amid rich savannahs that spread for miles without a single tree but were filled with "jointed grass near six feet high."[7] Even
in midwinter the Yankee was astounded by the open-air riches of the
Midwest, perking up corners of his imagination that soon would consume him. His father and brothers had labored at Mountalona for a
decade, fighting a living from a hardscrabble land plagued with devastating winters. Here Rogers could imagine enough for everyone, all
the latter-born sons of poor New England farmers, loosing their herds

of cattle on these immense pastures and watching them grow fat and rich with milk. To the son of Scots-Irish immigrants, the dream was all around him. "Had we, during the late war," Rogers noted in his journals, "either by conquest or treaty, added the fertile and extensive country of Louisiana, we should have been possessed of perhaps the most valuable territory upon the face of the globe, attended with more real advantages than the so-much-boasted mines of Mexico and Peru."[8] (By Louisiana, Rogers would mean the Mississippi basin and much more, the scope of land included in Jefferson's famous purchase.) This was a view very far ahead of the still-prevailing mercantilist emphasis upon precious minerals; not for a dozen years would Adam Smith disabuse his readers of the notion that a favorable bullion balance was the object of trade. Rogers's imagination was coming alive with a conception of the literally unimaginable possibilities of the North American continent.

By January 23 the patchwork watercraft pulled up to the Ohio River across from Fort Pitt, where they soon were welcomed by General Monckton, eager for details. Rogers had logged a remarkable 1,600 miles in four months during the fall and winter, several hundred more miles than Lewis and Clark covered during their whole first year's journey nearly a half century later. He had taken just one day to prepare and was missing only one man, a Royal American soldier lost overboard. All told, this expedition ranks as one of the most remarkable journeys involving a substantial command of men in colonial American history, not to mention the sensitive nature of the negotiations that ensued along the way and at Détroit. Yet it draws little notice, probably because Rogers made it look so matter of course.

Three hundred easy miles later Rogers and Lieutenant Brehm arrived in Philadelphia. "As soon as the Arrival of this Gentleman was known the People here, to testify their Sense of his distinguished Merit, immediately ordered the Bells to be rung, and Shewed him other Marks of Respect," reported *The New-Hampshire Gazette*.[9]

Rogers returned to find a grateful Amherst waiting for him with a commission as a regular in the British army. Amherst needed Rogers to settle the war's final business, the pacification of the Cherokees, so the commission designated him captain and commander of a South Carolina independent company. The independent companies enabled the Crown to raise individual companies without regimental organization for garrison duty both in Great Britain and in the colonies, formed of British soldiers raised on the continent as well as in the colonies. Rogers was jubilant with this long-sought prize, something many other colonists, George Washington included, had sought but had never been able to attain.

The Cherokee War of 1758–61 had severed a valuable alliance reaching across the first half of the eighteenth century. Concentrated in what is now eastern Tennessee, the Cherokee nation had traded the Europeans beeswax and river cane baskets and especially deerskins, which the Europeans turned into leather goods, such as gloves and knee breeches, for brass kettles, scissors, hatchets, knives, textiles, and guns and ammunition.[10] The British colonists pushing into the western Carolinas depended on the Cherokees as a buffer against French encroachment up the Mississippi and Ohio Valleys. The white men had brought the nation other gifts, including smallpox, which was reported to have wiped out half the Cherokee population in 1738 and that revisited in the 1750s and 1760. Disease and war had so devastated the nation that by 1763 a chief named Ostenaco said, "Our women are breeding Children night and Day to increase our People."[11]

The Cherokees had supplied several hundred warriors, many of whom fought with distinction against the French on the frontier; but in the moment of victory, Virginia frontiersmen killed some returning chiefs and warriors. Clansmen of the murdered settled the score brutally but entirely by the canons of Indian justice, which invoked an implacably collective responsibility, on the Carolina frontier settlements. Of course, the South Carolina government did not see it that way, proposing to exact a retaliation entirely consonant with the British vision of proper conduct. The highest Cherokee magnates hastened to Charleston to defuse tensions; but the governor of South Carolina put them in chains and offered to exchange them for the murderers. Events spiraled out of control after soldiers slaughtered 22 members of the peace delegation, culminating in Colonel Archibald Montgomery's leading 1,650 soldiers into Cherokee country, where they destroyed five towns. An Indian ambush in the mountains near Etchoee Town left 20 dead and 80 wounded, whereupon the army decamped precipitously to Charleston. A subsequent two-month defense of Fort Loudoun, a small post near the present-day town of Vonore, Tennessee, ended in early August 1760, when provisions ran out. The terms of surrender conceded safe passage for the fort's 100 men, 60 women, and uncounted children to the nearest British fort, some 140 miles away. Three days later Cherokee warriors rose from the forest and killed more than two dozen soldiers, reserving special retaliation for the leader, Paul Demere, captain of a South Carolina independent company, who was scalped alive, beaten with clubs, and forced to dance, then had his arms and legs chopped off. As incensed braves stuffed his mouth full of dirt, reported one eyewitness, they taunted: "You English want land, we will give it to you."[12]

Amherst had decided that Rogers would replace Demere and informed Lieutenant Colonel James Grant, commanding the 1761 punitive campaign, that Rogers would join him once he had settled his accounts, "which will not take him up long,"[13] although on that front Amherst and Rogers alike were sadly in error.

Rogers flew into an almost manic blur of activity. Concerned that he had not heard from his business partner Edward Cole for five months, Rogers designated former ranger sutler John Askin to exercise his power of attorney on March 19 to recover monies owed him. Rogers also created the partnership of Askin & Rogers, primed to take advantage of the western trade.

Soon on his way to Albany to collect receipts and vouchers, he met up with Caesar McCormick, lieutenant of rangers, already a member of the original Rogers & Company, and formed yet another partnership. The company borrowed 5,000 pounds on Rogers's name to buy bateaux and trade goods from John Askin, all of which McCormick was directed to take to Détroit and to return loaded with furs. Joining the crowd of postwar land petitioners, Rogers put in a bid for a tract on the western shore of Lake George. To a man accustomed to hand-to-hand combat in the forest, the tangle of growing debts at first appeared no more than a minor civil hindrance. But like a series of Lilliputian strings, these entanglements would begin to slow even the intrepid major in his tracks.

Rogers calculated that the Crown owed him 6,313 pounds, 14 shillings, and twopence for his outlay over the past half dozen years of war. Still unresolved remained the 615 pounds to the rangers who overwintered in 1755–56. Rogers listed 2,268 pounds for expenses he incurred remitting money for the room and board of 99 captured rangers, an advance of 400 New York dollars to Captain Solomon's Stockbridge company, 870 pounds for arms bought for his men, and miscellaneous charges for snowshoes, as well as the money lost to the French on the sleigh convoy the winter before.[14] On May 8 Rogers received news that must have outraged him. All during the war he had assumed that the Crown would be good for these expenses, monies borrowed (doubtless not at kindly public-spirited rates) from Albany moneylenders. Amherst tersely informed him that the Crown would reimburse only about one-third of his claims; a third of that would be held up until further receipts came in.

Three days later Rogers penned a ten-page letter, barely keeping his indignation at bay, which began, "Your Excellency's Written Objection of the 8th Instant to my Accompts Concerns and Distresses me Extremely." Then he laid out careful justifications for the expenses. He claimed that there were "Thirty Eight Attachments Against my Little Estate in New Hampshire" by angry rangers who were still unpaid from the 1755–56 overwintering detail. Untangling the intricacies of eighteenth-century British military accounting was difficult at best for a provincial untutored in that self-centered world of its own. (Senior officials in the Pay Office left accounts unsatisfied for years while drawing bankerlike interest on the appropriations.) There's no question that Rogers had been sloppy with his accounting and naïve in his expectations of reimbursement. Even so, when it came to the payment of rangers for early winter service, he had been neither particularly naïve nor overreaching. The system was lamentably unequipped to reconcile global warfare with glacially slow communications, kingdom with colony, urgent disbursements with a body of procedures that had an inbuilt disposition to save by stalling. He had fallen through the cracks of the imperial government and the provincial government, the action long gone and forgotten. Coming up with receipts for monies paid to rangers in captivity proved particularly difficult because the French rarely if ever issued receipts to prisoners. In addition Rogers needed to prove that their meals and clothing had not been paid for by their captors; that none of the prisoners had worked for compensation; and that the men had been captured and released on the exact days claimed. He needed evidence that the money paid to ranger captains in captivity had gone not to them personally but to their men; and furthermore, he had to provide receipts.[15]

It was a task likely beyond anyone, certainly beyond the harassed major. Amherst appointed three regular officers, including Rogers's friend Captain Pringle, to review the accounting, but in the end they would not disagree with Amherst's decision. Rogers had no recourse but to accept such money as was offered, which he used to pay off some of his creditors. On May 19 Amherst gave Rogers a 30-day furlough, and early the next month Rogers stepped onto the wharf at the foot of Queen or Court Street in Portsmouth, New Hampshire, for the first time since 1756.

That earlier year Portsmouth had received its first printing press; and if the encomiums heaped upon Rogers then had been superlative enough, this time his reputation had yet further crystallized. *The New-Hampshire Gazette* rarely mentioned his name without attaching the adjective "brave" to it.

The little seaport could not have been more different from the raw New Hampshire of Rogers's boyhood. A half-century of lucrative trade had turned this town, three serpentine miles upriver from the Atlantic, into a prosperous and bustling port. All manner of schooners lay waiting at anchor in the Piscataqua; sailors and laborers on the docks hoisted quintals of dried cod and long sections of lumber aboard craft moored at the wharves with forearm-sized lengths of tarred hemp; bewhigged merchants darted in and out of large warehouses packed with boards, house frames, oars, wagon spokes, barrel parts, and small boats destined for the West Indies, Spain, and Portugal. Rogers may have watched as a load of ramrod-straight white pine came downriver from the still-abundant interior forests, logs so immense that it had taken up to 72 oxen to drag a single one to the bank for launching. Specially designed ships would carry sometimes more than 500 trunks per year to the mast ponds of England and other colonies.[16]

While Portsmouth still boasted only 4,000 inhabitants, compared with Boston's 15,000 or so, trade had brought families such as the Wentworths, Chases, Jaffreys, Rindges, and Moffatts great wealth, manifest in the number of elegant mansions rising up along the dusty, American-chestnut-shaded streets. By happenstance, not design, this abundance stood casually amid early-settler plainness, the great houses next door to blacksmith shops, taverns, and flophouses. One hundred and thirty-one years ago a ship's captain had found the southern shore of the Piscataqua teeming with berries, probably encouraged by generations of Abenaki foragers, and named the first settlement here Strawbery Banke.[17]

Rogers would have been distressed to see that Stoodley's Tavern, a favorite ranger watering hole, had burned to the ground in January, when a nearby barbershop had caught fire. Rogers perhaps commiserated with the publican, watching as the mulatto housewright Hopestill March framed a new three-story, gambrel-roofed replacement, and he was surely buttonholed by many a passerby as the colony's most famous hero.

His brothers in Portsmouth's Masonic lodge held a party for him the day after he arrived at the Earl of Halifax Tavern, a public house to be immortalized in Longfellow's *Tales of a Wayside Inn*, from whose massive sign the scarlet-clad, periwigged nobleman haughtily reviewed all who entered. Fourteen of Portsmouth's foremost notables joined to toast Rogers's exploits. Among the many guests were Arthur Browne, the jowly Scots-Irish chaplain of the St. John's Masonic Lodge and incumbent of the Anglican Queen's Chapel, which occupied a pleasant height of land at river's edge; Rogers promised to attend the following Sunday's services.

On Friday he appeared before the New Hampshire legislature to request that it cover his obligations to the rangers of his 1755–56 winter corps; no doubt he received a clamorous welcome but a much less enthusiastic hearing on the substantive issue, which was met with a mumbling request for him to return in a month with better documentation.

On Sunday Rogers walked up the crest of Church Hill to the Queen's Chapel. From its steepled perch over a simple unpainted rectangular wooden building, the bell rang, a spoil of the capture of Louisbourg in 1746, presented by New Hampshiremen who had served on the victorious expedition.[18] There was more to the gathering than the austere readings from the Book of Common Prayer. Rogers could not take his eyes off Browne's comely eldest daughter, Betsy. Long brown hair cascaded down the 19-year-old's back, and her dark eyes flashed with liveliness and interest. A long aquiline nose mirrored her father's.

Browne no doubt noticed the electricity between the pair and did not discourage it. Such dashing suitors were few in Portsmouth, and besides he knew Betsy to be a strong-willed child. Life here was particularly difficult for young women, as he was all too aware. Not long after he had ascended the pulpit of Queen's Chapel in 1739, the discovery of an illegitimate infant's body in a well had stunned the community. Two young women near Betsy's current age were sentenced to die for "feloniously concealing the death of a...infant bastard child," although the identity of the baby's mother was never conclusively proven. Browne offered sanctuary and counseling to one of the young women in his church as the execution approached; he refused to conceal his feelings after the event, cautioning his parishioners, "may her Example and Sufferings answer the Intention of Law, and deter all viciously and wickedly disposed persons among you from incurring the like condemnation."[19] Browne had also counseled his flock through the terrible diphtheria epidemics that struck down so many New Hampshire children. And only the year before, an aged Governor Wentworth, stricken by widowerhood, had pressed the reluctant Browne into sanctifying a scandalous union with his poor housekeeper.

If Rogers's subsequent heartstruck letters are any indication, he fell passionately in love with Betsy at first sight. Once they were forced to separate, the normally reserved Yankee ranger commander laid bare his heart's deep longings in letter after letter: "Whenever I Set down to write to you Love and grief beyond degree together with pure gratitud and warm affection which I have for you my Dearest Betsy Invites from my Eyes a Shower. I often bid my passions all be gon and call fro thoughtless Rest but my fanceys Meet you a thousand times Every day."[20]

Over the next few weeks Rogers undertook a campaign to win Betsy's hand that was as worthy of any wartime expedition, spending much time at the Brownes' house on Court Street, often in discussion with the 62-year-old cleric. The blisteringly fast courtship ended when Betsy agreed to marry Rogers on June 30, her twentieth birthday, a date set with his impending departure for South Carolina in mind.

Four days before his wedding day Rogers again appeared before the New Hampshire Assembly, which determined that he still had not provided the requisite vouchers and that therefore it could not rule on his petition; then it hurried on to other business with an eye on that afternoon's summer recess. Rogers's frustration must have been turning into alarm as he perceived that no resolution would come anytime soon. Other financial troubles had popped up earlier in the month, when Rogers had taken a brief leave of wooing Betsy and showed up in Exeter to visit his family and property there and attempted to scare up vouchers from the men of the winter garrison. As Rogers walked onto his property for the first time in years, his tenant, William Alld, backed by an armed companion, forcibly ushered him off the land, claiming that he was delinquent on a past note for the property. As in earlier days, when challenged by such vicissitudes, Rogers went into overdrive, hiring a lawyer and pressing a countersuit.

But their wedding proved the high-society event of the summer, even meriting newspaper mention in an age without social columns. The backwoods youngster's star had burned white-hot, rising from the rugged frontier poverty of Mountalona to glaring zenith of the established coastal colony's highest social circles. No record exists of the event itself, but likely Portsmouth's elite all showed up at church in their liveried coaches, then retired to the Brownes' house for a traditional all-night party.

Rogers spent the next six days with Betsy before boarding a ship and sailing to South Carolina. Although he would terribly miss his wife, Rogers would meet a man there who would set his imagination on fire.

Chapter 28

To South Carolina

*When the sun breaks out, it is with the most intense heat; the most sharp
and heavy thunder and lightening frequently happen here, and very
sudden changes and alterations in the weather, which render the
summer-season very unhealthy for strangers, and subject the
inhabitants and natives themselves to fever, dysenteries, and various
distempers: add to all these the miriads of musquetoes, which are enough
to devour one during the summer-season.*

ROGERS'S DESCRIPTION OF SOUTH CAROLINA[1]

In the stultifying heat of a late August Friday in 1761, Rogers and
18 men marched up the Path, the sandy thoroughfare from the
South Carolina interior leading up the long narrow neck on which
sat Charles Town. Local laws forbade cutting trees along the road,
so at least the men moved beneath the shade of towering pine,
oak, tupelo, and sweet gum, which gave some respite from the un-
relenting blaze of the sun on South Carolina's coastal lowlands.
They peaked through woodbreaks at mansions with wide, encircling
porches, and grasslands and broken timberland threaded with thousands of grazing black, horned cattle. Horse-and-mule-drawn carts
probably brought up the column with its personal effects.

"A thick sultry air" rises in the forepart of a Carolina summer day,
wrote Rogers, "which those who are not used to it can scarcely
breathe in; when the sun breaks out, it is with the most intense
heat."[2] That time of year, the breeze blows from the south or southwest, driven by the heat of the seared sands of Florida and Georgia.
The roar of cicadas created a din.[3] These New Englanders had never

met heat and humidity joined in such miserable partnership. Their red wool uniforms with green facings, highlighted with the white-laced buttonholes and edgings that identified them as members of the South Carolina Independent Companies, grew heavy and itchy with sweat. More than a couple had felt the dizziness and nausea of heatstroke. The Stockbridge members of this small column refused to wear the red coats, partly from pride but yet more from practicality. Rogers stood out from the rest, not only in size but by the brighter shade of scarlet of his coat with light green trim, scarlet breeches, and white stockings. He wore a silver aiguillette on the right shoulder and black shoes with silver buckles. Silver lace adorned his black tricorne hat.[4]

A month ago the men had shipped out of New York Harbor aboard the sloop *Endeavor.* Its master, Captain Whitmarsh, had taken his time, hugging the coast with a close eye out for the French privateers that had recently plagued English commerce. He landed his small contingent at Cape Fear, the southernmost part of North Carolina, leaving it to work its way overland, the recruits staring uneasily at the scaly backs of the alligators. They saw the strangely flaglike pimento leaves burst out atop their cabbagelike stalks, and they experienced the theater of late-afternoon summer thundershowers.

The first sign of Charles Town rose above the trees, the newly finished and massively symmetrical, high-Georgian 186-foot steeple of St. Michael's Church, crowned by a seven-and-a-half-foot weather vane with a gilt globe itself topped by a dragon. For generations to come it would beckon sailors prowling the confusing coastline and lead them to the river mouth and to town.

Boots crunching on the sandy and gravel road, the men walked into Charles Town, the only large urban center south of Philadelphia. The soldiers marveled at the regularity of the streets, which "are wide and streight, intersecting each other at right angles,"[5] as Rogers would record. Of the large British colonial centers, only Charles Town and Philadelphia aligned to the right angles of a grid. The streets ran east-west, a mile between the Cowper River on the north and the Ashley on the south, which inhabitants with characteristic aplomb liked to say "united to form the Atlantic Ocean." Six-foot-wide brick sidewalks within posts flanked the sandy main thoroughfares. Looking out to the bay, the men could see all sorts of ships, rowboats, skiffs, and sloops, perhaps a canopied barge or British man-of-war.[6]

Some thousand or so wood and brick houses lined the streets in narrow lots, many with steeply pitched roofs and wide porches running around the first floor. "Near the center of town," wrote Rogers, "is a neat market-house; and near by it is the state-house, which is a stately commodious brick-building." The men marched to a nearby barracks, capable, Rogers noted, of housing 1,000 men.[7]

The entire town of some 8,000 residents, more than half African slaves, gave the impression of a city newly minted, even in the oppressive summer heat, perhaps because so many of the buildings were new. A decade earlier a devastating hurricane, the worst natural disaster in the British North American colonial experience, had nearly obliterated the town in two hours, driving many dozens of oceangoing ships into the streets, demolishing 500 buildings, ripping off roofs, destroying every wharf and warehouse, and taking some 95 lives.[8] Only three months before Rogers arrived, a "Typhone" ripped down the Ashley River with such force that it "lay the channel bare," noted one writer.[9]

The Virginia Colony thrived for a full sixty years before South Carolina saw significant development. By the middle of the eighteenth century, however, Charles Town and its environs witnessed the rise of a large white ruling class, lording over such several-thousand-acre plantations as Fenwick, Middleton Place, and Drayton Hall, all within 30 or 40 miles of the city, and creaming immense profits off an inhuman and brutal reliance on slave labor that turned swampland into rice paddies and the drier, loamy soil of the forests into sweeping fields of scraggly indigo plants, the source of a rich and valuable blue dye.[10] Slaves negotiated decked periaugers down the shallow inland waterways that threaded the coastal plain onto Charles Town's large wharves for the insatiable markets of Europe.

The presence of so many slaves on the wharves and streets or peering out windows would have taken the New Englanders aback. South Carolina held some 70,000 slaves, or about 60 percent of its people, dwarfing the 5,000 held in bondage in the far more populous and older Massachusetts Bay Colony. As ethnically mixed as colonial Europeans and native Americans, the black population ranged from lighter-colored Creoles to newly deposited Africans who bore ritual facial scarifications. Most of the new arrivals came in chains from the great western curve of Sierra Leone, Africa's Gold and Windward Coasts, the Bight of Biafra, and Angola, but some from as far away as Madagascar and Mozambique, imparting a welter of different languages and inflections to the town's streets and wharves. During Rogers's stay in South Carolina a planter would record that "a cargo of Angola's lately averaged £32 Sterling round & 50 prime Gold Coast Negroes bought in Antigua at £34 per head sold in one lot at £300 round."[11] A deep anxiety lay below the polished surface, however, as white plantation owners and gentry feared slave risings. When half of all white men in the Charles Town precinct between 16 and 60 went off to fight the Cherokees in 1759, the other half mustered to "guard against the Insurrections of their numerous Negro Slaves."[12]

A printer in Charles Town wrote, "The Planters here all get rich, which you need not wonder at when you see this small province export about 120,000 barrels of Rice worth 35/ Ster on average, and upwards of 500,000 wt. of Indigo worth 3/ sterling round."[13] The abundance of soaring wealth in this youthful city, unrivaled in the colonies, created a class of men with time and money on their hands. Rogers was "received and entertained in the genteelest manner by the Governor and the principal inhabitants," reported *The Boston Evening-Post*.[14] The handful of richest men, somewhat isolated in this far-distant colony, enveloped Rogers, and few moments were his own as he ate and spoke with the likes of Robert Smith, the sociable, Cambridge-educated rector of St. Philip's Church, and Peter Timothy, a fellow freemason and editor of *The South Carolina Gazette*. In the city's finest mansions Rogers could expect to eat beef, turtle, oysters, shrimp, and crab, washed down with Madeira and rum punch, then tuck into "peaches, Nectrins, and mellons of all sorts extreamly fine and in profusion," noted a Charles Town resident.[15] A rare contemporary ink drawing shows army officers of the South Carolina Independent Companies seated at a plain table after dinner, a slave boy asleep in a corner near a caged bird, a silver punch bowl brimming with liquid and decanters littered about the table, the men sipping from long-stemmed wineglasses.[16]

The town's most active time was between December and May, when the lion's share of rice and indigo was brought to town and shipped out, leaving not much for the quality to do during the summer.[17] Charles Town's men of weight created dozens of private societies, more than any other colonial city, including the Fort Jolly Volunteers, Smoking Club, Meddlers, and Laughing Club. The Fancy Society hosted its own poet laureate. One later visitor described a visit to the Sons of St. Patrick, where "at dinner six violins, two hautboys, and bassoon with a hand-tabor beat excellently well. After dinner six French horns in concert,—most surpassing musick!"[18]

Gambling was so prevalent that several South Carolina towns had to pass laws forbidding playing the Game of Fives in the courthouse, another banning gambling on "play at long bullet" in town confines.[19] One Charles Town resident, using a pseudonym, wrote a piercing assessment in *The South Carolina Gazette* of the social life: "There is not one night in the week, in which they are not engaged with some club or other at the *tavern*, where they *injure their fortunes* by GAMING in various ways, and *impair their healths* by the intemperate use of spirituous liquors and keeping late hours, or rather spending whole nights, sometimes in these disgraceful and ruinous practices, so that nothing more remains about them of the human species, but that they still retain the form of man."[20]

On Monday morning Rogers and his men set out to join Colonel Grant at Fort Prince George, more than 200 miles to the northwest, one of two interior forts used against the Cherokees during the recent troubles. Rogers carried a letter from Amherst to Grant, which read:

"Altho I conclude your operations will be over by the time Capt. Rogers can join you, yet if they should not, & you have any service for him, you will employ him as you shall see best; and if you find it necessary or proper to give him such a command as may regain the rank of Major, you will give it him in the same manner as I have done formerly for the campaign, or the time such service shall require."[21]

Amherst's consideration of Rogers's career bespoke an unusual relationship between a relatively low-ranked provincial soldier and the commander of all British forces in North America, probably stemming from fondness for the ranger captain as much as from practicality. Amherst knew from past experience that the officers over Rogers often had dismissed his considerable talents.

By the end of the month Rogers and his rangers arrived at Fort Prince George, on the bank of the Keowee River, a small garrison even by frontier standards at only 100 feet by 100 feet. Its palisade of yellow pine logs rose atop an earthen wall and was encircled by a five-foot-deep ditch, in which probably grew a honey locust hedge bearing two-inch sharp thorns.[22] Here in early 1760 the Cherokee conflict had escalated when Indians killed the fort's commander. In retaliation, the new commander ordered the execution of 22 Cherokee chiefs held hostage inside the fort.

The three-year conflict had ended after Grant's early June march with nearly 2,600 men, including an advance party of 13 New England rangers. Grant's 600-horse supply train, packed with a month's worth of food and ammunition, stretched a mile. "Heaven has blessed us with the great success on every occasion," noted a report of Grant's campaign in *The New-York Mercury*. They burned 1,400 acres of corn, destroyed 15 villages, "and near five thousand Cherokees, including men, women, and children, [were] driven to the mountains to starve; their only substance, for some time past, being horse flesh."[23] Under Amherst's explicit orders, Grant's men killed every prisoner, regardless of age or gender.

Grant's threat to continue on and destroy other villages brought in Attakullakulla (known to the whites as Little Carpenter), his brother the Mankiller, Half-breed Will, and the Raven, along with 17 others to sue for peace, and Rogers probably attended the negotiations that occurred in a "spacious bower prepar'd for their reception."[24] Rogers does not record his thoughts about the Cherokee peace process he witnessed and perhaps participated in, but he certainly was surprised and dismayed by the response of the rest of the regulars to his Stockbridge rangers.

Brought down south as a valued part of Rogers's team, the Stockbridges met only with sullen, hostile stares from the South Carolinian soldiers, who cared to make little distinction between them and the Cherokees they had fought for the past years. Even so, Rogers at first must have carried on, certain he could sway opinions, as he had many up north, including General Amherst, an increasingly dedicated Indian hater. But his meritocratic-based system held little traction here. Rogers reluctantly wrote Amherst with a request to discharge the soldiers, "as they will not be agreeable to the Soldiers of the Company."[25]

Rogers found other aspects of life in the southern colonies not to his liking. He endured what that locals called the "seasoning,"[26] several months or more during which newcomers contracted a variety of subtropical diseases and learned to cope with the heat. Rogers contracted malaria, running through its brutal episodes of fevers and chills, which weakened him at times to the point where he could barely walk.

"Myriads of musquetoes," Rogers wrote, caused the usually stoic ranger to complain that they "devour one during the summer-season" and "dinned and tormented" him.[27] Most white South Carolinians died before reaching the age of 40, in large part due to malaria and dysentery, which weakened the body and made it susceptible to other infectious diseases, leading to one of the highest mortality rates in the British North American colonies.[28] Wealthier South Carolinians slept in "Pavilions Made of Catgut Gause," but even a finger-size hole in the netting could result, observed botanist John Bartram, in "100 holes in our skin before morning."[29] The cycles of malaria caused one German visitor to observe famously that "Carolina is in the spring a paradise, in the summer a hell, and in the autumn a hospital."[30] Sailors also carried a variety of other diseases, sometimes including the dreaded smallpox, into the port town. A visitor to Charles Town not long after Rogers visited the area observed the pest house on Sullivan's Island, seven miles east of town, where smallpox sufferers were quarantined: "The most moving sight was a poor white man performing quarentine alone in a boat at anchor ten rods from shore with an awning and pretty poor accomodations."[31]

Rogers returned to Charles Town in October, the flush of his commission significantly faded, but recent news gave him an idea. Edmund Atkin, the superintendent of Indian affairs for the southern district, had died just before Rogers left Fort Prince George. Rogers dashed off a letter to Amherst suggesting that he might fill the position because "he would be able to act and conduct himself in such a manner as to give satisfaction to the publick and the savages themselves, not only by treating the latter in a proper manner, but by leading such of them as may be our friends, whenever your Excellency shall think proper, to war against other Nations that may be enemies or insolent to any of his Majesty's Governments." He cleverly suggested that Amherst could have a superintendent with dual skills—the ability to work with the Indians, but also the capacity to lead friendly Indians under arms against the hostiles, should that prove necessary.

That fall Rogers traveled to North Carolina ostensibly to recruit but in fact to gain the support of the colony's governor in obtaining the superintendency. The meeting would change Rogers's life.

Chapter 29

A Dream Is Born

So geographers, in Afric maps,
With savage pictures fill their gaps,
And o'er unhabitable downs
Place elephants for want of towns.

JONATHAN SWIFT,
POETRY, A RHAPSODY

Rogers may have met the 72-year-old Crown official on his arrival at Cape Fear in August 1761, the year before, his boat laboring up the wide sluggish Cape Fear River to Wilmington, thus passing the governor's mansion, Russellborough, on the western shore.

North Carolina had no fixed municipal governments and no capital; each town competed to attract assemblymen. The clever residents of the small, rough riverside trading town of Brunswick, up the Cape Fear River, offered Governor Arthur Dobbs a great deal in 1758 on the unfinished house of a recently deceased ship's captain. He paid five shillings and one peppercorn, the latter due in one year's time so as to guarantee that he would stay and ensure that this sleepy hamlet would host some degree of public doings.[1]

Dobbs finished building the two-story, 45-by-35-foot timber mansion, culminating in a handsome herringbone chimney. A number of outbuildings included stables and a carriage house. It's likely that Dobbs gave Rogers a tour of the gardens, of which he was justifiably proud, often producing such prizes as 17.5-pound muskmelons. Peach, plum, nectarine, and fig trees abounded in the yard beyond the kitchen garden. They talked about Dobbs's son, a major in the regulars back in 1756 in the Lake Champlain campaigns.[2]

Dobbs and Rogers may have sat outside on the 10-foot-wide piazza encircling the first floor, overlooking the low marsh to the wide river beyond. The contrast between the young man and the old would have been quite apparent. Nearly a decade in the malarial lowlands had sapped North Carolina's elder statesman. He still remained impulsive in speech; for all that his false teeth might clack, his mind was sharp, quick, and curious.[3] William Hoare's 1755 portrait shows a purse-lipped, bewigged gentleman extending a map of North Carolina with one hand and clasping navigational dividers in the other. At his right elbow sits a globe; over his left a ship under full sail sweeps on to the far horizon of open sea.[4] He radiates the stern self-confidence of a gentleman-adventurer of Elizabeth's day, God and the Crown on his side.

Arriving from the British Isles as the French and Indian War began, the new governor had deftly avoided antagonizing the colony's southern and northern factions, whose conflicts had hogtied his predecessor, by focusing them in union against France.

By 1760 goodwill had evaporated, and the contentious assembly had united in an effort to dislodge him. He managed to hold on, grumbling that the legislature "think themselves entitled to all Priviledges of a British House of Commons." A year after he met Rogers he would wed the 15-year-old daughter of a political ally.

Dobbs first came to the attention of Sir Robert Walpole, architect of the Whig supremacy, in 1730 when, as a new member of the Irish Parliament, he published the long and ambitious "Scheme to Enlarge the Colonies and Increase Commerce and Trade." It reflected his concerns that France and Spain could easily wrest control of the colonies from the quiescent, prosperity-minded Walpole administration. Among the instruments of his proposed muscular and aggressive colonial policy was treating the Indians fairly, an effective means, he felt, by which to expunge France's economic and religious influence.[5] Walpole's support helped advance him to the post of engineer and surveyor general of Ireland, but from then on he never seemed to lose sight of the New World. He engaged in 1745 with a partner to buy a tract of 400,000 acres in present-day Mecklenburg and Cabarrus Counties of North Carolina, nearly a decade before setting foot in

North America. As was the case with so many from this period, his vision of Britain's imperial expansion was inextricably tied up with his vision of advancing personal wealth and influence for himself.

Politically, the idea of supporting Rogers for Indian superintendent sat well with Dobbs. The South Carolina governor, with whom Dobbs had some friction over boundaries, had the previous superintendent in his pocket and presumed he could select the next one, even though Dobbs had also to contend with the Cherokees on his western borders. Rogers as superintendent would give Dobbs good political leverage in London and Charles Town. On December 9 Dobbs would write to Pitt that he and his assembly were "satisfied of Major Rogers' Zeal and Attachment to His Majesty's Service, his Knowledge and Experience in Indian Affairs, his Activity and Resolution, beg leave to recommend him to your favor, and request your soliciting His Majesty for his succeeding Mr. Atkins."[6]

Conversation between the two would soon have turned to other topics. However locked in the administrative details of a contentious colony, Dobbs still kept his strong curiosity about the world, a passion that had led him to publish five papers in the *Philosophical Transactions* of the Royal Society of London about such topics as the aurora borealis and the distances between Asia and the Americas, and to make prescient observations about bee pollination that anticipated Joseph Gottlieb Kölreuter's famous paper on the subject by 11 years.[7] His correspondence with eminent English botanist Peter Collinson on the "Catch fly sensitive" (today known as the Venus flytrap), only to be found on the coastal plain of the Carolinas, may be the first scientific notice of this remarkable carnivorous plant.[8] Rogers's comments about his travels, particularly to the Great Lakes, would have fascinated Dobbs. They recognized in each other the keen-eyed observer, the product of the aspiring scientific rationality of the advancing Enlightenment.

It would not have taken long for the two men to touch on a theme that had obsessed Dobbs for three decades: the Northwest Passage, the fabled waterway through the high latitudes of North America that could join the North Atlantic to the Pacific and its Oriental riches. He enlisted in an explorer-obsessing tradition dating back to the late fifteenth century in which marched such early luminaries as the Venetian John Cabot and the Florentine Giovanni da Verrazzano, the Frenchman Jacques Cartier, and the Englishmen Martin Frobisher, Henry Hudson, and William Baffin. The English merchants who sent out colonists to the New World envisioned their settlements in part as bases from which they could advance to the western sea and beyond.[9]

It is not hard to see why this addictive vision intoxicated generations of explorers: the route from the North Atlantic to the Pacific lay thousands of cruel miles southward and through the difficulties of Cape Horn, arguably one of the most dangerous of all voyages. A northern route would cut that journey to a fraction of its length, risk, and cost. Its discovery would bring untold wealth to those who found it, drastically restating the nature of intercontinental trade. Many expeditions in search of it disappeared altogether, and those who returned told of immense icebergs, shifting ice floes that squeezed ship hulls until they burst, and interminable horizons of broken ice and desolation.

For the past two decades Dobbs had been convinced that a water passage to the Pacific would open from the northwestern corner of Hudson Bay. His eyes sparkled at the thought of imperial Britain commanding such a seaway. Seizing upon any piece of information that would support his case, including the fanciful journals of long-discredited mariners, he imposed his will and imagination on the blank reaches of the northern latitudes with a visionary but ultimately factually bankrupt plan.

He did attempt to introduce scientific rigor into the mix—for instance, trying to integrate the behavior of the tides, presence of whales, the flow of currents, and the density of ice floes as indices of the passage's presence; but while his use of such data reveals an inquisitive mind, it also demonstrates an armchair explorer's impracticality. Unlike the man who sat opposite him, Dobbs lacked field experience that would have made him aware of the difficulties of taking accurate measurements aboard a pitching ship, the variations in winters and precipitation, and the accounting for the variability that hundreds of tangled miles of coastline brought.[10]

But a series of clever arguments, including that access to the Pacific would give England the opportunity to ravage its enemies the Spanish, resonated with George II, and he authorized funds to outfit two ships under Christopher Middleton, who left in 1741. Although

Middleton's and a second voyage under William Moor in 1746–47 failed to bring back any evidence of a Northwest Passage, Dobbs remained undaunted; he mounted a public campaign that ruined Middleton's career by claiming that the Hudson's Bay Company, not interested in finding a passage, had paid Middleton off not to reveal the presence of a passage. For all his bluster and hype, Dobbs supplied the emerging empire with the imagination to think big. Empire, one historian has written, "belongs to a geography of the mind as well as a geography of power. To construct an empire makes imaginative demands, and pays imaginative dividends, for the nation that undertakes it."[11] While the expeditions he set up helped map Hudson Bay in the great tradition of English explorers, they also gave voice to British imperialism in North America, which even at the time of Dobbs's and Rogers's meeting, when the French in Canada were all but vanquished, remained unfocused. In 1745, largely from Dobbs's doing, Parliament offered a £20,000 reward to any British subject who discovered a passage west from Hudson Bay.

Dobbs may have shown Rogers his 1744 book, which reviewed arctic voyages and outlined his ideas about the passage: *An Account of the Countries adjoining to Hudson's Bay, In The North-West Part of America: Containing A Description of their Lakes and Rivers, the Nature of the Soil and Climates, and their Methods of Commerce, &c. Shewing the Benefit to be made by settling Colonies, and opening a Trade in these Parts; whereby the French will be deprived in a great Measure of their Traffick in Furs, and the Communication between Canada and Mississippi be cut off.*[12]

Of great interest would have been the engraved map inside, detailing the inlets along the northwestern sweep of Hudson Bay that would seem to lead west to the Pacific. But Rogers's eyes were drawn to the rivers and lakes stretching southwest and connecting the bay to Lake Winnipeg and Lake of the Woods, beyond which, scraggly lines indicated, rivers ran westward. Out in Detroit, Rogers had already heard whispers from Indians about the lands beyond, and the presence of a large and long river leading to the Pacific.

Dobbs had drawn his map largely based on the word of a métis fur trader named Joseph La France, whom he had met in London around 1742. La France had earlier described a thousand-mile half-circle from the shores of western Lake Superior, along the present Minnesota-Ontario border, up to Lake Winnipeg, and around to York Factory on Hudson Bay via the Hayes River. He had overwintered with the western Cree beyond Lake Winnipeg, skilled birchbark canoeists quite knowledgeable about the vast drainage systems they paddled. Their trade with the Dakotan-speaking Assiniboine people of the upper branches of the Saskatchewan and southern Manitoba lakes threw a trading network over much of the north.[13] For Rogers, still flush with visions of the west, Dobbs's rhetoric, infused with imperial possibilities, struck a deep chord and brought him a long firm step from being a soldier with a sharp eye for possibilities toward an explorer of vision.

Rogers had finally discovered someone who shared his scope of vision and drank deeply of Dobbs's accounts of the possibilities of interior passage. In a pamphlet he published after his two failed expeditions, Dobbs had written that he would "hereafter retire, and leave the Prosecution of the Discovery of the *British* Trade to some more happy Adventurer."[14] Rogers must have appeared to the close-to-burnt-out senior as a dream, a man with not only drive and curiosity to reinvigorate his own passion but the practical tools and knowledge to make it happen and become the "happy Adventurer."

As Rogers returned to Charles Town, a plan was coalescing. In the town Rogers had made the acquaintance of the 36-year-old publisher of *The South Carolina Gazette*, Peter Timothy. Born in the Netherlands, his father a printing partner with Benjamin Franklin in Philadelphia, Timothy and 16 of his fellow citizens had established the Charles Town Library Society in 1748, a semiprivate organization modeled after Franklin's Philadelphia Library Company.[15]

In addition to publishing the paper and printing government documents, Timothy acted as a sort of literary and artistic marketplace in Charles Town. Among the advertisements in his paper appeared proposals to publish engravings of Charles Town, works of poetry, musical compositions, histories, and at least one play.[16] Timothy would take subscriptions, in essence preorders, that enabled him to pay printing costs, abandoning the project if insufficient orders came in. Printing was still extremely labor-intensive: each letter was set by hand within a composing stick, then the type was locked by page into a form and inked for each impression.

Emboldened by his dealings with Dobbs, Rogers engaged Timothy in conversation. Having brought his personal papers down with him to the Carolinas, he began to assemble his war memoirs from a mass of journal entries, letters, orders, and field reports. Timothy expressed interest in the material, perhaps making his own editorial suggestions as well. On February 27, 1762, Timothy ran a notice in his paper that advertised a four-volume set "octavo," a printer's term for forms folded into eight-page leaves, all sewn in blue paper, for one pound sterling (the equivalent of perhaps $240 today, in a world of very much less money and also very many fewer books).[17] The set would consist of his war memoirs; *A Description of the Soil, Produce, and Extent of several British Colonies in America;* and *An Account of different Nations of Indians that have an Commerce with the English.* The final volume: *Some Reflections on the great Advantages that would accrue by regulating a proper trade with them, and the great Value of the Interior Country on the Ohio, and betwixt that and the Country of the Illinois, and great Lakes northward to Hudson's Bay; and some Proposals for the Discovery of the North-West Passage by Land.* Notices for the book appeared in northern newspapers in April and May, catching the attention of Rogers's wife and father-in-law in *The New-Hampshire Gazette.*

The wording borrowed directly in tone and words from Dobbs's 1744 book. Finding the Northwest Passage by land would become Rogers's idée fixe, a plan grand enough to encompass his imperial, continental thinking, a means to wrap together his various senses and intuitions of the immense possibility of the continent.

The advertisement declared that the manuscript was finished. Even if it was nearly completed, Rogers must have been writing with furious intensity while he was wooing Betsy, while on shipboard, and in the dim candlelight of his room at Fort Prince George, while suffering the crippling fevers and chills of malaria.

That spring the prospect of enduring another summer clearly worried Rogers. In March he wrote to Amherst that he could not shake the malaria and openly wondered "whether I shall ever obtain relief from the same in this warm clime."[18] He would be glad, he added, to exchange commissions with someone elsewhere. But for the moment his plea fell on deaf ears. The War Office in London had ordered Amherst to assemble a quarter of the 16,000-man force necessary to attack the Spanish stronghold of Havana. In January Britain had declared war on its former ally Spain and intended to close a key Spanish shipping channel by attacking Cuba. Amherst needed Rogers's oft-demonstrated recruiting talents in the Carolinas.

In April and May Rogers traveled throughout North Carolina recruiting young men to the Independents, offering bounties, free drinks, and abundant war stories. He found it a tough sell, as he had anticipated to Amherst months earlier, because many of the potential recruits found easier and more lucrative employment as slave overseers on the plantations. But the same combination of persuasiveness, bounty money, and drink that worked well in New England had its effect on the young men of the Carolinas, and Rogers raised about one hundred. Even though Amherst's agent rejected a fifth as unfit for service, and another fifth thought better of it and deserted, his achievement far exceeded those of other recruiters in South Carolina and earned him a laudatory note from Amherst.

That spring several pieces of bad news arrived. Thomas Boone, governor of South Carolina, had succeeded in his bid to install trader John Stuart as superintendent; the Portsmouth Inferior Court had ruled in favor of the ex-rangers who were suing him for back pay; and his case for ejecting William Alld from his New Hampshire property had been rejected. Now he owed several hundred pounds more, plus court expenses.

Back in Charles Town as the heat intensified, he wrote Amherst more urgently about his desire to leave: "The fever and ague which I have been afflicted and have now upon me together with the heat of this climate have sunk my spirit and broke my constitution beyond anything I have ever suffered or cou'd conceive."[19] This assault on his phenomenal basal metabolism shook him to the core, and he realized that South Carolina held little else for him. He also desperately missed Betsy. If he was forced to stay, he wrote her, perhaps she could come down to be with him? In early May he put a happier face on Charles Town than he no doubt felt, writing: "I am sure that you will like Carolina much better than you expect as there is a very good set of people there and a very pretty orang garden in which I should be very glad to have some agreable walks with my Betsy, my Dearest Betsy will you come to me as soon as the scorching heat of summer is over."[20]

By late summer Amherst relented, showing concern about

Rogers's well-being and agreeing that he might come north "if you think it absolutely Necessary for the recovery of your health."[21] He could afford to be lenient: Havana had fallen, albeit at a horrific cost. Half or more of the British troops sent on the campaign would die of infected wounds, yellow fever, heat, overexertion, and the lack of good drinking water.[22]

In late October Rogers arrived in New York City, then detoured to Albany before continuing to Portsmouth. He was intent on visiting his partner John Askin and recouping the investment that they had made with Edward Cole. But trader Cole was still missing in the interior, though Askin had recently sent an envoy out to Détroit to track him down. Askin and Rogers borrowed £3,840 to pay back the Albany merchants to whom they were in debt. Rogers also learned in Albany that the Mohawks had denied his request to buy land along Lake George.

Back in Portsmouth he united with Betsy after an absence of nearly a year and a half. The pressure from his creditors mounted, including an aggressive bill collector hired by South Carolina merchants who wanted £23 sterling from Rogers. Cornered, Rogers spoke with his father-in-law, who agreed to buy nearly 300 acres of land near Concord, a house on its main street, and several slaves, including "one Indian Boy named Billy," who may well have been the young Sabbatis, whom Rogers had brought back from Saint-François. The £1,000 sterling from his father-in-law staved off the angriest claimants.

For the third time Rogers appeared before the New Hampshire Assembly, now armed with the muster roll and vouchers for the company's 1755–56 back pay. They awarded him £235—not much more than a third of what he owed the men, and much of which was eaten by his rapidly accruing legal fees. Somehow he managed to square the men, because they dropped their suits. But ugly rumors kept bubbling up. The "envious & the Malicious," reported Browne to Rogers, spread the word that Rogers's debts had been "incurred through prodigality & ye Gratification of unlawful pleasures and Passions."[23]

In mid-April came a blow from an unexpected quarter: his father-in-law, Arthur Browne, crumpled under the swirling accusations and sued his son-in-law for £2,590, writing him that "the vile aspersions that daily increased, and seemed indeed founded upon

Testimony not at all improbable." He arrived at the figure by reckoning that Rogers owed him £16 for room and board for himself and Betsy for thirteen weeks, as well as lodging and expenses for Betsy while Rogers was in South Carolina. Her father's exhortations that Betsy leave her husband until he settled his accounts did not dent her loyalty to her husband.

Later in the month, when Rogers's captaincy in the New York Independent Company came through, Browne wrote a conciliatory letter to the couple in Albany, perhaps realizing he had been quick to judgment. Neither Browne nor Rogers showed up for the hearing in June. In May more difficult news broke: all Rogers's work to gain a place in the New York Independents had come to naught. Peace brought reductions from London across the board, including the disbanding of the 80th Light Infantry, the 3rd and 4th Battalions of the 60th Royal Americans, and the slimming of other battalions and companies.[24] Rogers's new outfit was disbanded, further constricting his income to retirement half-pay of £280 annually.

Rogers did not blame Amherst. During all of his financial problems, Amherst never lost faith in the ranger, putting little stock in the stories of his purported excesses. Amherst would have entertained few qualms about breaking off communications with Rogers should he have believed the rumors. His silence on the matter, and his continued support, suggests a powerful faith in Rogers's character.

Late the year before Rogers asked Amherst to form a new ranger unit that could strengthen the Great Lakes garrisons and guard against the outbreak of an Indian war. Amherst wrote a note turning him down: "I must acquaint you, that Altho' I have a very good Opinion of You, & Shall Readily Employ You when the Service will permit me I have a very Despicable One of the Rangers in General."[25]

Rogers's request would later look prescient. A storm was brewing over the Great Lakes; at its destructive vortex was Chief Pontiac, who had impressed Rogers on his journey to Détroit. The war about to break out would cost thousands of lives and end Amherst's North American career.

When Pontiac descended on the weak western garrisons at the head of the Great Lakes war band, Amherst would again resort to Rogers, as he had so many times in the past. Yet again Rogers would drop everything and set off to serve his country.

Chapter 30

Great Lakes Tribes Declare War

We are well assured that very formidable Reinforcements are on their Way to the upper Country, which will be employed not only in securing the several Posts for the future, but in taking such Revenge *for the* Butcheries *committed by the* Barbarians *as shall be a* LASTING MONUMENT *of the Wrath of* INJURED BRITONS; *and be sufficient to deter the* BEASTS *from ever attempting the like hereafter.*

THE BOSTON GAZETTE, BYLINED "NEW-YORK,
AUGUST 4 [1763]," ON THE ATTACK BY PONTIAC
ON BRITISH WESTERN GARRISONS, AND ORDERS
TO SEND ROGERS IN RESPONSE[1]

On a mid-July Friday in 1763 at four P.M., after five days of rowing nearly 90 miles from Fort Niagara along the southern coast of Lake Erie, the 20-bateau expeditionary force of nearly 300 men pulled up at the mouth of Mill Creek in front of Fort Presque Isle (on the site of today's Erie, Pennsylvania). Bobbing in the waves with hands resting on their oars, the men turned their eyes in dread up the tall yellow-sand-and-gray-clay bluffs to the site of a fortress that was now silence and ashes.

Rogers stood in one of the flat-bottomed boats, surveying the scene of what must have been the fierce last stand of Ensign John Christie's 29-man garrison at the hands of a large force of Indians. He remembered the welcome that Colonel Bouquet's troops had given his cold and weary men nearly three years ago. They had pulled them from their whaleboats and warmed them inside the newly rebuilt fort. Even then Rogers had noticed the fort's vulnerability: only 350 feet from the lake, it was too close to the bluff, which offered places for would-be assailants to hide. But the large blockhouse had looked nearly impregnable, the linchpin of a strongpoint at a strategic cross-roads between Forts Pitt, Niagara, and Detroit. Let them try taking it, Colonel Bouquet had boasted.

Rogers remembered how the blockhouse conformed to traditional design, its second story overhanging the first. Holes carefully placed in the floor of the overhang enabled shooters to fire down on attackers from above. A sentry box stood at the apex of its shingled roof; defenders hidden there could pour water on flaming arrows. A small bastion built on one side gave the opportunity for enfilading fire.

From the small wharf at the foot of the bluffs, the men scrambled up the path into the cliff face 90 feet till they reached the fort and stood in its ashes.[2] Amherst's aide-de camp, the 33-year-old Captain James Dalyell of the 1st Foot, who was in charge of the expedition, had tried to reassure his men that the general had ordered the post burned, its complement evacuating to Fort Detroit. The morale-saving ruse did not fool a soul, as the grim evidence on the ground told a different story. On the lakeside and creekside bluffs stood a number of man-sized holes scrabbled out of the sand and protected by hastily heaped pine boughs, brush, and logs. A small trench, or sap, reached from the pits toward the palisade walls and the commanding officer's house that had once stood adjacent to the blockhouse.

Patches of unburned sod lay amid the blockhouse ashes, evidence that the besieged had placed green wet sod atop the blockhouse roof in a vain attempt to save it from the attackers' flaming arrows.[3] Later the rangers would learn that some 200 Chippewas, Ottawas, Hurons, and Mississaugas had participated in the methodical and deadly attack. One of Rogers's party would report that "we found going along several of their Camps, where they had trimmed and cut our Soldiers Hair,"[4] a grisly reference to the scalping soldiers received who survived the initial attack.

As Dalyell's force wandered among the wreckage, they could only guess at what had happened to Fort Detroit, farther west, where they were headed on a rescue mission. "Not the least Intelligence has as yet come to hand from Detroit," Rogers wrote Betsy.[5] The last shreds of information had come from Major Henry Gladwin, the fort's bullheaded commander, whose dispatch of May 14 told of how he had defeated a clever plot by Pontiac—the very same chief of the Ottawas whom Rogers had met three years earlier not far from Fort Presque Isle. No British officers then realized that Pontiac's bold move was the first salvo in a bloody uprising that would stretch from Michigan to the Ohio Valley and from the Susquehanna west to the Mississippi, a pan-Indian uprising to preserve their culture against the encroaching British.

In the three years since Rogers's men pulled up either the Union Jack or the red naval ensign atop the pole at Detroit and claimed the western posts for the king, British relations with the Great Lakes Indians had deteriorated badly. When they took over the French posts, separated by hundreds of miles of wilderness, the British also inherited a system that was expressly designed to facilitate the fur trade, pull in converts, and motivate the Great Lakes Indians against the British.[6] These French efforts had proved largely successful; the skids of peace and trade had been greased by a paternalistic relationship in which the French lavished their "children" with presents and ammunition. Over a half century the cultures had melded and morphed their ways by intermarrying and extensive trading. That changed overnight with the British victory. Squeezed by the extraordinary costs of the war, Whitehall had pulled the purse strings tight, and Amherst dutifully instituted a set of trade and settlement policies that were not nearly as generous as the French had been. The war years and the recent Cherokee action hardened Amherst into a resolute Indian hater, who now often referred to the tribes as "vermin" in correspondence.

For generations Indian cultures had regarded Europeans' gifts as the central mark of appreciation and respect from a grateful people to those who had generously opened their lands. The gifts themselves, rarely enough in quantity and value to be of significant economic impact, acted symbolically as a means of preserving a fragile hierachy of power. But now Amherst, no stranger to the power and importance of gift giving in native cultures, consciously changed the rules of engagement: "With regard to furnishing the latter with a little Clothing, some arms and ammunition to hunt with, That is all very well in cases of necessity; but as, when the Intended Trade is once Established they will be able to supply themselves with these, from the Traders, for their furrs, I do not see why the Crown should be put to that Expence . . . but as to purchasing good behavior either of Indians, or any Others, [that] is what I do not understand; when men of whatsoever race behave ill, they must be punished but not bribed."[7]

By reducing gifts of ammunition, Amherst intended to weaken the Indians and force them into a more productive trading relationship: that attitude was widespread among the British officer corps, who all resented the "ingratitude" with which the Indians had received their presents. These savages, whom the victors had spared and now deigned to support by trading with them, should display an altogether deeper practical appreciation.[8]

Amherst's subordinates operating in the far-removed garrisons may have equally despised the Indians, but they clearly saw the dangers associated with reduced gift giving and often protested to Amherst and Johnson. "I mention this as You are sencible how necessary it is to give the Indians a Little Support," complained the commander of Fort Niagara. "I have been at a great deal of trouble to Convince them of the good Intention that the English have towards them . . . You know they are a jealous people and Should we hold our hand intirely from them—they will Easily made believe We Intend them Some hurt."[9] Wrote another observer, about cutting off presents of ammunition, "They think it very strange that this custom should be so immediately broke off by the English, and the traders not allowed even to take so much ammunition with them as to enable those Indians to kill game sufficient for the support of their families."[10] Lieutenant Campbell, whom Rogers had delivered to Detroit, wrote to Amherst that "the Indians Sold all their skins at Niagara for Rum, and are now in a Starving Condition for want of Ammunition, Which I'm affraid may drive them to Dispair. They apply to me daily and cannot be convinced I have no Ammunition for that purpose, As they were accustomed to be Supplyed by the Commanding Officer, and Unlikely the Traders have brought very little with them."[11] Reports of Indians tricked out of their furs when drunk and of squatters setting up house on indisputably tribal lands added to the mounting tensions. The dangerous economizing of gifts confirmed the

Indians' worst fears that the British came not as friends and equals but as conquerors. When Pontiac and the western Indians united in war against the British, they would be fighting not to restore the old ways of exchange but rather for their very survival and way of life.

Henry Gladwin added to Pontiac's unease about British intentions. Sharing Amherst's deep contempt, a local eyewitness, probably a British trader, described how Gladwin had antagonized the Indians by calling them "hogs and other names" and telling them to leave because he "would not hear them."[12] Two weeks before hostilities broke out Gladwin ordered the public execution of a slave Indian woman who had been convicted as an accomplice in the murder of her new trader husband. Few neighboring Indians missed the clear statement of British authority. When Ottawa chiefs asked to see ceremonial pipes that had been given earlier to the commander at Detroit in recognition of their peaceful relationship, Gladwin sent them roughly away.[13]

Native dissatisfaction had found its voice in the nativist teachings of the Delaware prophet Neolin, who condemned alcohol and pressed for a return to precontact ways, a gospel that transcended Indian tribal differences and united a common, pan-Indian resistance. Talk became action on May 5, when Pontiac, until then only a powerful Ottawa war chief, convened a large council of Ottawas, Potawatomies, and Wyandots at a Potawatomi village just two miles south of Fort Detroit. There he gravely invoked Neolin's teachings, describing the many transgressions of the British against native peoples and announcing that war belts had been sent amongst tribes, compelling them to attack the forts in their areas. "It is important for us, my brothers, that we exterminate from our lands this nation which seeks only to destroy us," Pontiac said, according the journal of a French habitant. The chief expressed pointed contempt for Major Gladwin: "When I go to see the English commander and say to him that some of our comrades are dead, instead of bewailing their death, as our French brothers do, he laughs at me and at you. If I ask anything for our sick, he refuses with the reply that he has no use for us. From all this you can well see that they are seeking our ruin."[14]

Pontiac outlined a plan of attack that involved soliciting a meeting with Gladwin in two days' time. The warriors accompanying him would hide weapons under their blankets, as would the women and children. The Ottawas would enter the garrison, but the Wyandots and Potawatomies would quietly encircle the fort, while others would man a position downriver to repulse any reinforcements that happened to come that way. Pontiac expressly forbade the warriors to touch French traders and families.

If not for an informer—often identified with little proof as Gladwin's own Wyandot mistress and famously portrayed in a John Mix Stanley painting—the garrison might well have fallen on May 7, 1763.[15] Instead, Pontaic and his warriors were met by a fully turned-out garrison brandishing fixed bayonets. Gladwin and Pontiac engaged in a clipped conversation, and the chief left quickly. Even after this ominous development, Amherst remained unconvinced that the Indians presented any danger, writing Gladwin: "For my own Opinion, is, that they Never can Hurt Us."[16] Two days later Pontiac and his warriors attacked the fort.

News spread by courier across the *pays d'en haut*, precipitating attacks at the other garrisons. Wyandot warriors captured Fort Sandusky, at the west end of Lake Erie, on the sixteenth. A week and a half later Fort St. Joseph, about 170 miles west of Detroit, fell to Potawatomies. At the end of the month Fort Miami surrendered to Miami Indians, who then went on with the Kickapoo, Mascouten, and Wea to take Fort Ouiatenon on June 1. Few men in the thinly manned garrisons made it out alive.[17]

On June 2, a band of Chippewas playing a game of lacrosse near Fort Michilimackinac threw the ball over the palisades. When they entered the fort, supposedly to retrieve the ball, they pulled out knives and tomahawks and slaughtered most of the occupants in a bloody frenzy. Trader Alexander Henry, whom Rogers had met on his earlier trip to Detroit, sought refuge in the house of Rogers's old foe, Charles Langlade. Hiding under birchbark baskets in a small room, Henry looked out a crack in the wall into the fort's courtyard. "I beheld," he later wrote, "in shapes the foulest and most terrible, the ferocious triumphs of barbarian conquerors. The dead were scalped and mangled; the dying were writhing and shrieking, under the unsatiated knife and tomahawk; and, from the bodies of some ripped open, their butchers were drinking the blood, scooped up in the hollow of joined hands, and quaffed amid shouts of rage and victory." Moments later, all others dead, four Indians smeared with blood burst into his garret but did not discover him, although had one "put his hand, he must have touched me."[18]

Fort Pitt came under siege, and Fort Venango, Fort LeBoeuf, and Green Bay's Fort Edward August also fell. In less than two months every British stronghold in the west had fallen except for Detroit and Pitt.

The bad news pouring in showed Amherst just how badly he had underestimated the Indians. Now that the blood of several hundred soldiers and settlers was on his hands, his dispatches to colonial governors and his officers in the field grow increasingly shrill, racist, and extraordinary. He wrote to Gladwin that any captured Indians should "immediately [be] put to death, their extirpation being the only security for our future safety." To Bouquet, he suggested, "Could it not be contrived to send the small pox among the disaffected tribes of Indians? We must on this occasion use every stratagem in our power to reduce them." Bouquet wrote back enthusiastically that he could start an epidemic using infected blankets and that he would like to track Indians down with English hunting dogs. Amherst ordered him to "inoculate the Indians by means of blankets, as well as to try every other method that can serve to extirpate this execrable race." Hunting Indians with dogs sounded like a "good scheme," but unfortunately English packs were "at too great a distance to think of that at present."[19]

In large part due to Gladwin's brutal willpower, Fort Detroit held on. On May 28 Indians ambushed a 10-bateau, 97-man supply convoy on its way to Detroit from Fort Niagara, about 25 miles from the mouth of the Detroit River. Only the expedition's leader, Lieutenant Abraham Cuyler, and two boats filled with 40 men managed to escape. Back at an Indian village, the captured soldiers were "strip[ped] naked, and other Indians then discharged their arrows into all parts of their bodies...the poor victims had to keep standing till they fell dead in their tracks, and then those not engaged in killing fell upon the dead bodies and hacked them to pieces, cooked them, and feasted upon them."[20] The remains were thrown into the Detroit to float by the fort. "Was it not very agreeable, to hear every Day, of cutting, carving, boiling and eating our Companions! To see every Day dead Bodies floating down the River, mangled and disfigured, and Frenchmen daily coming into their Fort, with long wry Faces, telling

us of most shocking Designs to destroy us," an anonymous correspondent wrote in *The New-York Mercury.*[21]

Hearing about the Cuyler massacre, Amherst sent his aide-de-
camp Dalyell on a rescue mission to Detroit, along with Rogers.
Dalyell had served under Rogers in the August 1757 Battle of Fort
Anne, in which the last-minute appearance of the ranger leader had
turned defeat into victory. Rogers would later write that Amherst
had asked him to serve "under an inferior Officer, nominated to a
periodical Rank for the Occasion, it being Matter of Indifference to
whom the Credit of a dangerous Enterprize might be intended, so
that I stood signalized in a prompt Obedience to the Calls of my
Country."[22] Yet no evidence exists that Rogers strongly reacted to
working under Dalyell, most probably indicating that rank did not
cloud a master-pupil relationship. As so often in the past, Rogers's in-
volvement inspired the newspaper editors to print all sorts of rumors,
including a report that "Major Rogers, who was in Pursuit of the
Indians, having a Party of 500 Men with him, were cut off."[23]

Chapter 31

Encounter with Pontiac

So ho! Know you whose Country you are in?
Think you, because you have subdu'd the French,
That Indians too are now become your Slaves?
This Country's mine, and here I reign as King;
I value not your Threats, nor Forts, nor Guns;
I have got Warriors, Courage, Strength, and Skill.

PONTIAC TO COLONEL COCKUM, IN ROGERS'S
PONTEACH; OR, THE SAVAGES OF AMERICA[1]

Leaving the ruins of Fort Presque Isle, Dalyell and Rogers led their relief expedition west, covering the 150 miles to Fort Sandusky in nine days. The slow pace probably resulted from Dalyell's inexperience and extra precautions they took against ambush by Indians. Landing at daybreak, they found the small garrison burned to the ground. Dalyell, Rogers, and 173 men marched inland toward a Wyandot village, eager to surprise the enemy; the ranger commanded the advance guard of light infantry. They found the ten-hut village deserted but uncovered a small cache of beaver and raccoon pelts that Rogers valued at "about 40 Pounds York Currency," which they carried off, he noted, "for the Benefit of the Soldiers." They burned the huts and nearby cornfields, marched back to the boats, and rowed another five miles. The next day a strong wind from the south filled their makeshift sails and carried them smartly 60 miles north to the mouth of the Detroit River.[2]

In the darkness of a foggy dawn the 20 bateaux quietly rowed up the Detroit River, keeping squarely to the middle of the channel, 300 yards from either side, in an attempt to sneak past the Wyandot and Potawatomi villages. Not far into the river, scattered gunshots, followed by howls and screams on the shore, broke the still morning air. The men pulled even harder on the oars while bullets whizzed overhead. In the cramped confines of the boats, made smaller by the thrashing of the men at their oars and the provisions underfoot, the rangers shot at the dark shadows on the bank; the regulars fired orange-flamed blasts from four gunwale-mounted swivel pieces. They ran the gauntlet all the way to Fort Detroit. Surprised and confused by the haze of the early morning light, the fort's defenders fired a cannon. The relief expedition responded with a cannon blast themselves, at which time huzzahs arose from the fort, overjoyed to see unexpected reinforcements. The foggy conditions had helped minimize casualties: 11 men lay wounded by gunshots, some unaware of their injuries until they laid down their oars; another six bore burns, probably from a small powder explosion.

The reinforcements, who more than doubled the strength of the garrison, could not fit in the barracks, so they were lodged among the habitants inside the palisades. Through one of these Frenchmen Rogers sent a bottle of brandy to Pontiac with his compliments. The go-between reported that Pontiac's counselors had advised him not to drink it, implying, as Rogers wrote later in his *Concise Account*, that it was poisoned. "But Ponteak, with a nobleness of mind, laughed at their suspicions, saying it was not in my power to kill him, who had so lately saved my life."[3] In the same way fourteen years hence George Washington would return General William Howe's dog before the Revolutionary battle of Germantown. By sending his gift, Rogers acknowledged something that Amherst, Gladwin, and other English officers would not: that Pontiac was a man of great weight, a most worthy adversary. But also inherent in the gift lay the courtesy of the confidently strong. The dignity of the act added formidability. Rogers's small gesture showed a deft touch.

Perhaps Rogers had other things in mind as well. The war would not last forever. He may have imagined the development of a powerful and lucrative partnership. In the paragraph following his account of the gift of brandy, he noted that Pontiac had devised a rudimentary monetary system; he had designated a commissary to create bark money or bills of credit bearing his symbol, the otter. "Were proper measures taken, this Indian might be rendered very serviceable to the British trade and settlements in this country, more extensively so than any one that hath ever been in alliance with us on the continent."[4]

But Rogers's arrival was too late at that point to change the events, as would become painfully clear over the following two days. No sooner had Dalyell arrived than he began badgering Gladwin, his superior, to permit him to take out a force against Pontiac immediately. A heated argument ensued, Gladwin urging caution. Wounded with Braddock and then again with Abercromby at Carillon, burdened with recurring malaria, and having endured two and a half months of siege, Gladwin had no illusions about life and warfare in North America. He had narrowly escaped losing the entire garrison to Pontiac's treachery. Yet somehow he had met his match in Dalyell.

The only known painting of James Dalyell shows quick eyes, handsome good looks, and the unshakable confidence of one to the manor born. His eldest brother, the baronet of The Binns, a handsome estate outside Edinburgh, had gone to India to seek his fortune, while James had traveled to North America. As was customary then, Dalyell had used family connections to become Amherst's aide-de-camp. Although he was not as battle experienced as Gladwin, he did not underestimate the Indians but thirsted to engage them; the past several weeks they had come tantalizingly close to encounters but found only recently abandoned villages, burned outposts, and shadowy shapes firing from afar.

A quick, surprise attack on Pontiac made sense implicitly. What finally caused the tough-minded Gladwin to yield to Dalyell's request for an immediate sally is not recorded, but his subordinate's relationship with Amherst, the inborn authority of a great military family, and just plain weariness were surely factors.

Anticipating such a move, the Wyandots that Saturday, July 30, had cleverly made a show of loading up their camp, burning all the trash, and paddling around the bend of the river. Then they sneaked back to set an ambush for any pursuers.

At two in the morning on Sunday, July 31, 1763, Dalyell and 278 men filed out of the fort's water gate two abreast.[5] Prying eyes, watching from the high ground across the river, counted the soldiers in the light of a waning but quite bright gibbous moon.[6] Each man stripped to his waistcoat in the sultry weather and affixed bayonet to musket tip. Most of the men came from the 55th Regiment, supported by complements from the 60th, 80th, and Queen's Rangers. Rogers and a handful of his own rangers joined the latter. Two bateaux with bow-mounted swivel guns pulled out into the river.

The men marched east-northeast up the river road toward the Indian encampment at Cardinal Point, some three and a half miles from the fort.[7] Sometimes fenced-off fields of wheat and orchards rose on their left, a patchwork quilt of four or five fields stretching from the river before reaching the forest.[8] On their right a sandy beach sloped gently to the river's edge.[9] Two French guides showed the way, while Lieutenant Archibald Brown of the 55th led an advance team of 25 men 20 yards ahead of the main body. Captain James Grant of the 80th directed the rear guard. Dalyell placed Rogers, by far the most experienced Indian fighter, in the main body—one of several tactical mistakes that would prove his undoing. No scouts marched on their flanks. Dalyell clearly envisioned the final push against Pontiac as regular business; as had so often happened before, a British officer's arrogance about redcoat invincibility blinded his ability to soundly assess the enemy's fighting skills. Only 24 rangers joined the whole force.

About two miles from the fort the road crossed Parent's Creek over a narrow bridge. By this time the men had formed into platoons. They were instructed to fire in the way of street fighting, which meant the front rank would fire, then pass to the rear and reload, so as to deliver nearly continuous fire.[10]

Across the creek stood Baptiste Meloche's farm and a slight ridge. A picket fence faced the creek and protected the habitant's garden. Behind the fence hid several dozen warriors, their muskets trained on the bridge; others deployed behind trees on the ridge. Pontiac's intelligence system around Fort Detroit had kept him carefully informed of Dalyell's movements. He had time to set up at the bridge and to send an additional 250 men in a broad sweep behind the enemy force.

Once Lieutenant Brown and his advance guard reached halfway across the several-dozen-yard-long plank bridge, a whizzing fusillade of lead bullets knocked them down in heaps. Caught entirely by surprise, the main guard fell into confusion, firing blindly into the night, their ears now filled with horrible sounds of dying men and whoops of the Indians. With nothing to hide behind, some of the men fell to their knees to reload. Dalyell managed to rally the men, although a bullet had creased his thigh. The British fired several volleys across the creek and then charged across the bridge, stepping over comrades shrieking from their wounds. Dalyell gained the ridge and found the Indians gone, but the damage was done. Blood dripped so copiously through the planking and into Parent's Creek that it turned it red. For generations to come the watercourse would be known as Bloody Creek.

Then musket fire broke out behind Dalyell, who realized to his horror that the Indians had attacked his rear guard to cut off the whole column. A house 20 yards off Grant's left flank, which had appeared empty when the main body marched by, suddenly erupted with shots. Grant wheeled his company and that of Captain Joseph Hopkins around to return the fierce fire into the houses and the piles of cordwood behind a fence. A messenger from Dalyell ran up to Grant with orders for him to take the houses, which he was able to do. Inside one of the houses he discovered two French habitants pressed to the floor and quaking with terror. When questioned, the pair revealed that the Indians, more than 300 in number, had known the British designs and planned accordingly.

A runner reported Indian intentions to Dalyell. Lieutenant Jehu Hay wrote that Grant "begged of him either to push on immediately [or] make a retreat without loss of time."[11] Meanwhile the exposed main body came under increasingly hot fire from Indians hidden along the roadside. The news apparently undid Dalyell, who froze for more than forty-five minutes before ordering his men to "face to the Right about and march two abreast back to the fort."[12] Dalyell and the light infantry would bring up the rear.

The men retreated down the river road from whence they had come, marching as close as possible to the rail fence separating the road from the fields, their only cover. Shots flew at them from dark houses, from the hedges in front, and from cords of wood stacked for the winter. Splinters of wood flew in their faces. Each man had seen others mowed down and wondered if he would be next.

Half a mile down the road the Indians mounted a concerted attack, and the line broke up. Captain Gray took a company over the fence to rout the Indians, but several of his men and then he himself went down wounded. In the meantime Rogers and some men sprinted to a nearby house opposite the British center from which Indians had been blazing away; yelling and firing on the run, they finally drove the Indians out, but only after losing several men. Survivors of Gray's company dragged their wounded captain and several others into the house.

Meanwhile in the rear Dalyell and Captain Grant had led a charge against a fortified position. Dalyell, who by all accounts fought bravely, took a fatal bullet when he apparently rushed to aid an injured sergeant. The loss of this brave but not-woods-savvy officer would remind Rogers of how his friend Augustus Howe had needlessly taken a bullet years ago near Carillon.

The bateaux, one of them commanded by Rogers's friend Lieutenant Brehm, pulled up alongside the embattled position. The wounded lay along the benches and in the bottom of the boats, river water and blood sloshing together. Careful blasts of grape canister by the three-pound swivel guns mounted on the bows scattered the Indians, enabling Rogers to lead Captain Gray, Lieutenant Brown, and others aboard.

Meanwhile Captain Grant, now in charge, directed the retreat down the river road, as a new day slowly dawned. But the distance between front and rear had grown dangerously wide. Rogers hurriedly sent a runner telling Grant to stop so they could catch up. As Rogers and the rear of the column beat a fast retreat down the road, the Indians nipped closer and closer at their heels. The boats had returned to the fort with the wounded to pick up more ammunition, so the British now had little or no protection. The growing daylight offered fewer opportunities for the soldiers to hide against the steadily more numerous enemy. Rogers took a lieutenant, an ensign, and 30 men into another house with designs to make it a strongpoint. The ranger commander, now in full blood, scanned the interior. The large windows dismayed him. He detailed men to pull boards off the roof and to reinforce the walls. He was in luck: the habitants had collected thick bound packs of beaver pelts. He ordered the men to wrestle these into place in front of the windows.

In moments he sprinted down to Captain Grant, telling him that their only hope was to hold the houses, falling back from one to the other. He would hold off the onslaught as long as possible until the gunboats might offer relief.

Then he pounded back to his comrades, who were taking much fire from a nearby barn and some defiles. Inside, the men were jammed next to one another on the floor; they passed along loaded muskets to those putting up a steady fire at the windows. Black powder now clouded the interior. The full brunt of the Indian force, some 200 strong, fell upon the improvised blockhouse, Rogers recorded, finally surrounding it. But the men fired on for two hours, suffering only two deaths. Finally Lieutenant Brehm's boat reappeared and blasted rounds and grapeshot into the Indian left, which forced them to fall back. By eight-thirty the remnants of Dalyell's command were straggling back into the fort.

Dalyell's body was found headless the next day by habitant Jacques Campau. Reports came back that the Indians had cut out his heart and rubbed it on the faces of their prisoners and set the head itself atop a pike; rumor had it that Pontiac had celebrated his victory by serving the flesh of dead British soldiers. Rogers would report that "Pindiac, who is the Indian Chief, calls himself King from the Rising of the Sun to the Setting; is encamped 4 Miles above the Fort, where he well entrenched, and declares he never will leave that Ground till he has got Possession of the Fort."[13]

This last great uprising of Eastern Woodlands Indians would soon wane, as new forces came west and dissolved much of Pontiac's coalition. But on that day he delivered a devastating blow to the British. If not for Rogers's quick thinking and the bravery of many men, the outcome could have been much worse than the already-grim butcher's bill of 25 percent casualties.

Rogers would soon head back east; the Battle of Bloody Run would be his last Indian engagement. His head swirled with desperate images and strong opinions about the British policy in the Great Lakes region. They would take extraordinary shape and form, almost unbelievably for this backwoodsman, in a play he wrote and published in London. *Ponteach; or, The Savages of America* would set out to distill the vastness and extremity of his experiences into an unprecedented body of reflection. As Pontiac's War further demonstrated for the

British colonists the savagery of those who had inhabited the continent first, Rogers went out of his way to praise the nobility of his mighty opponent as symbolic of the wonder and possibility of the West. It would be a curious presentation by a man who had long been stereotyped as only a natural-born destroyer of savages.

Chapter 32

Imperial Capital

So much one man can do
That does both act and know.

ANDREW MARVELL, *AN HORATIAN ODE UPON*
CROMWELL'S RETURN FROM IRELAND

On a summer day in 1766 the 34-year-old Robert Rogers saw London for the first time, probably when his lurching post coach crested Highgate Hill from the north. The mighty ribbed dome of Christopher Wren's 365-foot-high St. Paul's Cathedral would have immediately commanded his eye, as would the two western towers of Westminster Abbey added just two decades earlier. The spires of St.-Mary-le-Strand, St. Clement Danes, and more than three hundred other churches sprang from a "forest of brick, bisected by a river and filled with a teeming horde of people who cherish a thousand different passions," wrote a later German visitor.[1] Innumerable rounded chimneys sprouted amid the steeples, feeding the coal haze that smudged the skyline. Masts crowded the Thames near London Bridge. Fifteen inns of court, more than a dozen hospitals, some forty banks, several colleges, royal palaces, artillery grounds, and two dozen prisons packed the city hugger-mugger. The same view, three years earlier, had so thrilled the 22-year-old James Boswell—on his way to meet Samuel Johnson and improbably thence to become his unsurpassed biographer—that he laughed and flew into a rapture about future sexual conquests.[2]

Nine years of war, however, had beaten any boyish exuberance out of the cool-eyed Rogers. Even so, the city's magnitude must have astonished him, as it did all thoughtful men from the still-empty New World.

No English-speaking city between the Rio Grande and the St. Lawrence—and Rogers knew them all—came close to London in size, frenetic energy, wealth of civil and religious architecture, and crushing poverty. A new and relatively modern metropolis had risen from the ashes of the Great Fire of 1666, which devastated 15 of London's 26 wards. In the mid-eighteenth century London eclipsed Amsterdam as the world's most important financial center and surged past Paris as Europe's largest human gathering place, its 700,000 souls more than a third of the entire number of British colonists and slaves living in the colonies. So concentrated was its population that it took no more than a twenty-minute walk to reach the country from any point in the city.[3] Bureaucrats, bankers, and entrepreneurs at the Bank of England, the East India Company, and the Stock Exchange dynamized and more or less policed a brisk international trade that kept London's quays crowded with ships bearing tobacco, tea, spices, silk, and sugar.

No single factor played a more critical role in Britain's rise to power and empire than its victory in the recent Seven Years' War, the longest and costliest since the fifteenth century. Hostilities had begun in the North American wilderness a decade earlier when British regulars, joined by North American colonial militias, challenged French Canadian control of the beaver-rich but otherwise barely tapped resources of the Ohio Valley. This remote conflict erupted into what Winston Churchill would later dub the first world war, as Great Britain and Hanover joined forces with Prussia to fight France, Austria, Sweden, Saxony, and sometimes Russia, in Europe, the West Indies, and Asia. Britain's eventual victory brought it possession not only of France's great holdings along the St. Lawrence but also of French forts and of claims reaching down into the Ohio Valley; it gained the power to conquer chaotic India without organized European competition, the West Indies, and, at least as a trading partner, the Spanish colony of the Philippines as well. Great Britain was blossoming from a powerful if disorderly multinational state into the second empire upon whose dominions "the sun never set." The geopolitical reshuffling set the stage for the American Revolution a little more than a decade later, and beyond that for the French Revolution beginning in 1789.[4]

The well-muscled six-footer, a full head taller than the average European, now approaching London cramped into a coach designed for a far smaller generation, had played a vital role in Britain's North American victory in the Seven Years' War. "Few of our Readers we apprehend, are unacquainted with the name, or ignorant of the exploits, of Major Rogers," crowed London's *Monthly Review* in January 1766.[5] The New Hampshire backwoodsman had won a commission in Britain's hidebound, class-conscious army. The heroic young British general James Wolfe, who sealed the conquest of Québec with his life in 1759, commanded more troops; and Jeffery Amherst, the supreme commander, played far more important strategic roles in the final victory. But no North American figure captured the imagination of George II's still-undivided subjects all around the North Atlantic world than Rogers. Newspapers and broadsheets acclaimed his exploits on snowshoes, in bloody ambuscade, and on grueling long-distance raids. His unmatched—perhaps unprecedented—mastery of the prodigious, untamed North American wilderness not only showed the British how to win but revealed that they could outmatch the woods-savvy French *coureurs des bois*, with their long-dreaded mystique, and native warriors of the Eastern Woodlands. In a 1759 issue of *The London Chronicle*, Benjamin Franklin boasted that "one ranging Captain of a few *Provincials*, *Rogers*, has harrassed the enemy *more* on the frontiers of *Canada*, and destroyed *more* of their men, than the *whole* army of *Regulars*."[6]

In the London of 1765, two years after France had been brought to a humiliating peace at Paris, Rogers's fame exceeded that of any other North American, Franklin and George Washington included. He was a soldier of great ability, yet something more as well: a new type of American, sprung from the wilderness that still brooded along the narrow frontiers of settlement.

Just a year earlier, the great hero had been languishing as a prisoner for debt in the "New-Gaol" on Murray Street in New York City. His predicament had come to the ears of soldiers in the 1st Battalion of the Royal Americans and the 77th Highland Regiment quartered nearby. At nine-thirty P.M. one January evening, fueled by

rum and refusing to believe that any paltry bill-server had the authority to jail their hero, a mob of more than a hundred strong grabbed
muskets, fixed bayonets, stuffed pistols and tomahawks into their
belts, and assailed the three-story prison. In the attack a musket ball
grazed Rogers's eyebrow, which would scar him for life. Once free,
he reputedly shouted to his liberators in a no-doubt-scripted moment, "I am afraid that they will ruin me," and galloped off into the
night—"Indian style," it was said—a £200 reward on his head, which
amounted to one pound of the king's silver for each pound of his
flesh.

He arrived in London as "broke as a bankrupt's bastard." In
his journal future president John Adams noted Rogers's straitened
circumstances with some amusement.[7] London's *Public Advertiser*
reported that "this Gentleman was the first Person in America who
raised a Body of Troops at his own Expence, and headed them against
the Indians who were in the Service of our Enemies.—His regard for
the Welfare of his Country, however, utterly exhausted his private
Fortune."[8] Part of the reason for Rogers's coming to London was to
seek such money as he believed the Crown owed him for outfitting
his own ranger corps. Other newspapers suggested that he harbored
grander ambitions. "A gallant office," reported *The Boston Evening-
Post*, "has a most important proposal to lay before a great board."[9]
Rogers indeed cherished a master plan, which he pursued with the
same relentlessness that he exhibited against European rivals and
aboriginal warriors in the New World.

Like many men of action, Rogers was best when left with only
his wits to draw on. In London he borrowed either from fellow
Freemasons or from officers who had served alongside him in the
war. He took rooms in the West End enclave of Spring Gardens at
Charing Cross, located at what would become the southwestern corner of Trafalgar Square.[10] Rogers's arrangement probably resembled
Boswell's, who wrote that he rented three rooms in a family house;
dinner with the family cost an extra shilling.

Charing Cross marked the center of the city, the point from
which all distances were measured. The Palace of Westminster,
which housed Parliament, Westminster Abbey, and the Admiralty lay
only a few minutes' walk away. Just outside Rogers's front door
coursed what Samuel Johnson called the "full tide of human exis-

tence." Hackney coaches raced, and sedan chairs lumbered, along Whitehall and Cockspur Streets and the roaring Strand, coming within inches of people "every where, rambling, riding, rolling, rushing, justling, mixing, bouncing, cracking, and crashing in one vile ferment of stupidity and corruption—All is tumult and hurry," as the novelist Tobias Smollett put it.[11] Pedestrians ignored at their peril the shouts of sedan-chair bearers—"Have care!" or "By your leave, sir!" Bellmen and news vendors bellowed the latest occurrences, while metal-shod carriage wheels clattered over the cobblestones, and those who had to cross the street picked their way around horse droppings or clacked noisily on pattens, large platform shoes. Men and women hawked hot spiced ginger, taffety tarts, brick dust, watercress, and doormats.[12]

Most Londoners in the Georgian metropolis lived in such slums as were immortalized in Hogarth's 1751 engraving "Gin Lane," which pictures gaunt, disease-ravaged men, women, and children amid the pestilence, poverty, and overcrowding of St. Giles. By the time of Rogers's visit, several new hospitals and charities had opened their doors, but a tide of death carried off so many, the parishes' Bills of Mortality revealed, that it required almost half the natural increase of England to keep the swelling metropolis' numbers even stable. All too frequently mothers abandoned babies on the street. All humanity, whether rich or poor, spilled out into the "two thousand streets" in a kaleidoscope of human suffering, resourcefulness, and villainy. Sooty-faced and cancer-ridden chimney sweeps and ragpickers shared, and often disputed, the right of way with foppish "Macaronis," young men of wealth wearing tight pants and absurdly large wigs crowned by minute hats.

As one whose fortunes would depend on the impression he made upon the influential, Rogers must have attended to his wardrobe immediately, replacing his worn clothes with a new frock coat. Rogers, like Boswell, knew he had to keep up gentlemanly appearances. Boswell complained repeatedly about the costs associated with maintaining a clean suit of linens and the morning shave at the barber's. Perfumed wigs, constructed from horse, yak, or human hair, anchored the well-dressed gentleman's wardrobe. Hot and uncomfortable to wear, each cost more than a coat, shirt, breeches, shoes, and hat combined and required constant professional toning. Rogers wore a silk shirt underneath a dark woolen coat with a small turned-down collar and narrow side pleats. Tight-fitting pants came down just below the knee, the calves turned out in white stockings, and shoes were emphasized with large buckles.[13]

A well-turned sleeve and a penny bought access to any one of the dozens of coffeehouses that served as information hubs across the city. At Lloyd's and the Baltic Exchange men tinkered with creating novel forms of insurance and financial instruments. That summer Rogers frequented the New England Coffee House on Threadneedle Street behind the Royal Exchange, where a tall pot steamed over the hearth; there men talked and wrote while sipping dish after dish of the brew, often drawing on long clay pipes until the smoke hung so thickly that the house smelled, wrote one wit, "like the cabin of a barge."[14] Before the systemization of the postal service and the emergence of serious journalism, coffeehouses served as places where men read broadsheets and newspapers. Bulletins announcing auctions, ships' sailing dates, and notes of auctions plastered the walls. Rogers penned letters to Betsy back in New Hampshire.

Coffeehouses also served as the most conspicuous public centers of the rising Enlightenment. Ever since the fire, London's high culture of writers, painters, philosophers, poets, and thinkers had no longer centered at court, relying on the sovereign's patronage, but spread into the city's rapidly multiplying coffeehouses, taverns, clubs, and playhouses. Anchored by new scientific insights, most powerfully by Newton's formulation of the laws of gravity and optics, and by the provocative writings of Locke and Voltaire, Enlightenment philosophy promised to carry Europe out of superstition and persecution into a life of reason and the command of nature. "I seem to have been only like a boy playing on the sea-shore," Newton reflected, "and diverting myself in now and then finding a smoother pebble or a prettier shell than ordinary, whilst the great ocean of truth lay all undiscovered before me." Across western Europe men with powerful insights, who had once lingered on the edge of things, were making their way to the center. The ideas of a watchmaker's son, Jean-Jacques Rousseau, once might not have gained traction but now did: his ideas about the "noble savage" would forever change conventions about human and material nature. Rogers felt the tidal pull of this environment.

In London the traffic in ideas and commerce, inseparably mixed with visions of empire, was awakening an insatiable appetite among patrician and middle-class Londoners for news, plays, novels, and general entertainment. In the evenings gentlemen flocked to the theaters. When the curtain rose at six P.M., Rogers could watch David Garrick perform *The Country Girl* or *Cymon* at Drury Lane Theater under circular chandeliers each ablaze with 300 tallow candles. Villains could barely make themselves heard for the catcalling. The audience pelted bad actors with apples sold between acts. Following a tragedy, the audience shouted for lighter entertainment; the company then often indulged them with frolics of music and dancing, or with farcical pantomimes based on Roman and Greek mythology but presented in anachronistic perukes and knee breeches.[15]

After the theater, the gambling halls, the bull-and-bear baitings, and the whores of St. James's Park beckoned. Noblemen gathered elbow to elbow around the circular stages of the Royal Cockpit, throwing down gold-sovereign bets as bloodied cocks ripped at each other with needlelike silver spurs for up to forty-five minutes. In streetside attractions men fought with sharp but light broadswords, their feet fastened to a scaffold so they could move only their bodies; the audience howled its pleasure when blood gushed from a superficial wound.

Early in his stay Rogers stepped out of his apartments with a sheaf of papers under his arm, his towering presence an immediate target for the flocks of prostitutes who prodded him with fans and plucked at his sleeves. The equestrian statue of Charles I rose above the fray, framed by the imposing Corinthian colonnade of St.-Martin-in-the-Fields. In the early seventeenth century Charles's heavy-handed high church policies had finally broken down in civil war, but only after driving thousands of religious dissenters to New England.

Old and new lay under Rogers's gaze. The square held pillories where criminals endured sometimes fatal torments from the public. Toward the Thames, just north of Westminster Bridge, rose the curious multistory spire of the York Building Water Works, shaped like an erect wizard's hat punched with large round holes. Inside, a clanging Newcomen steam engine sucked in river water for the use of residents of Piccadilly—an early marker of the Industrial

Revolution that would transform the city and nation over the next century.

He walked south down Whitehall toward the Houses of Parliament. After just a few more minutes the Admiralty rose on his right. The three-story brick pile with a U-shaped setback hardly counted as one of London's architectural landmarks, yet the bloodred flag with a gold anchor flying atop proclaimed the seat of the vaunted Royal Navy. In the next couple of years the Lord High Admiral, John Perceval, 2nd Earl of Egmont, would help launch the Pacific explorations of James Cook.

Across the street from the Admiralty, Rogers stepped inside the shop of John Millan, bookseller and printer. Oddly shaped animal skulls, snakes curled up in tall jars of alcohol, and swarms of brilliantly colored butterflies pinned to boards were scattered among stacks of books. The 64-year-old proprietor, like many affluent gentlemen across western Europe, was given to assembling natural history cabinets of curiosities, cases filled with objects of beauty or of terrifying wonderment from the plant, animal, and mineral kingdoms. Many of them would later form the nuclei of full-scale natural history museums. The antiquary Richard Gough described Millan's collection as "a future Herculaneum," a most complimentary comparison to the rich little city that had perished with Pompeii under the fires of Vesuvius and was now yielding extraordinary treasures to generations of antiquarians. Millan's collections no doubt also contained carnival-like oddities, perhaps the fetus of a two-headed calf in a bottle of spirits or the penis bone of a walrus won from the already-legendary whale fisheries. In Millan, Rogers found a kindred spirit.

Pulling the manuscript from beneath his arm, Rogers laid it on a clean surface: it was the draft, he explained, of a work recounting his travels in North America as well as his journals during the war just passed. Would Millan be interested in publishing them?

Millan may have recognized the same raw talent that he had seen earlier in his friend the Scottish poet and playwright James Thomson. After all, Millan had made his name at 25 by publishing Thomson's poem *Winter*, whose blank verse broke with the arch, artificial style of the poets of the day, anticipating the romantic school that would flourish two generations later in its evocation of the dour pleasures and grim lives of Rogers's own Scottish forebears:

Wish'd, wint'ry, Horrors, hail!—With frequent Foot, . . .
Pleas'd, have I wander'd thro' your rough Domains;
Trod the pure, virgin, Snows, my self as pure:
Heard the Winds roar, and the big Torrent burst:
Or seen the deep, fermenting, Tempest brew'd,
In the red, evening, Sky.

Thomson's later poems had included "Rule Britannia," which Thomas Arne set to music in 1740. Millan also published the work of military men, such as *A System of Camp Discipline* and *Lists of the Forces above 40 Sovereigns, &etc. Ranks, Uniforms, Number of Officers, Private Men, &c. Neatly coloured*, fit companions for an age of alliance-shifting world wars.

Millan was intrigued, finding Rogers's prose clean and direct, a style honed over years of filing reports to busy superiors describing scouts and fights undertaken on terms well outside authority's experience. His books, Rogers gladly admitted, represented the work not of a writer or scholar but of a soldier; they were written not in "silence and leisure, but in desarts and rocks and mountains, amidst the hurries, disorders, and noise of war, and under the depression of spirits, which is the natural consequence of exhausting fatigue."[16] With a knack for writing succinctly under stress, Rogers had formed a vibrant, immediate first-person narrative style highly unusual for his day. Not until far into the next century would travel writers, foreign correspondents, and such military leaders as Ulysses Grant develop comparable powers of plain exposition.

His second manuscript laid out the human, animal, and physical geography of North America in an entirely different voice: objective, third-person authority. Rogers promised to take the most interesting and important facts and "reduce them to an easy and familiar method, and contract them within such narrow limits that the whole may be seen, as it were, at once." Take a look at North America, Rogers urged the reader, and it can be imagined whole, not just as a collection of random facts and rumors.

Thomas Jefferson, who would recommend that it be included in the new republic's nascent Library of Congress, modeled the layout of his *Notes on Virginia* on Rogers's monograph. It would be part of the first generation of natural history texts in the New World, which later writers would build upon in their search to describe this new land. For Europeans and Americans alike, *Concise Account* began to fill in the blanks of the North America map, giving shape, context, and meaning to a continent barely imaginable to his readers.

Hardly an Indian hater, Rogers wrote that North America's natives "do not want for natural good sense and ingenuity, many of them discovering a great capacity for any art or science, liberal or mechanical." He promised to dispense with false information and mention only "such as I thought most distinguishing and absolutely necessary to give a just idea of the genius and policy of that people, and of the method in which they are to be treated, in order to our having any safe and advantageous commerce with them."[17] He described not merely clothing and hunting techniques but deeper distinctions between the inhabitants of the New and Old Worlds. For the northern Indians, he wrote, "avarice, and a desire to accumulate . . . are unknown to them; they are neither prompted by ambition, nor actuated by the love of gold; and the distinctions of rich and poor, high and low, noble and ignoble, do not so far take place among them as to create the least uneasiness to, or excite the resentment of any individual; the brave and deserving, let their families or circumstances be what they will, are sure to be esteemed and rewarded."[18] Yet here too was a cautionary tale: "It is observable, that, in proportion as they lay by their savage customs, and conform to our methods of living, they dwindle away, either because these methods are disagreeable and noxious to their constitutions, or else (which I am inclined to believe is the case) when settled among the English, they have greater opportunities of procuring spirituous liquors."[19]

In his geographical descriptions Rogers threw in ideas not before discussed on paper, more definitively nailing down a vision of the continent. Most notably, he wrote, the continent contained mountains that were "situated in the center, and are the highest lands in North America." Rivers flowed from these heights, and "by those rivers the continent is divided into many departments, as it were from a center." Here were nascent ideas of watersheds and the continental divide.

Millan agreed to publish the manuscripts. As the economics of book publishing then dictated, Rogers paid a small cash advance for work to begin.

Chapter 33

A Concise Account of
North America

The work is concise and yet full: and the knowledge it contains is acquired with pleasure, and retained with ease, by the regularity of the method, and the perspicuity of the stile.

THE GENTLEMAN'S MAGAZINE, ON THE RELEASE OF
ROGERS'S CONCISE ACCOUNT, DECEMBER 1765

In short order Rogers received many invitations from Londoners curious to see the hero of backwoods America. Many Americans visited London, such as the planters who, flush from the triangular traffic in slaves, molasses, and rum, packed their sons over for a suitably quality British education, but Rogers proved an exception to the usual fare of coastal townsfolk and squirearchy. Benjamin Franklin, dressed in his signature simple frock coat, had cut a very different but at least equally wide swath ever since he arrived in London eight years before as a spokesman for the colonial war effort. The British patronized Franklin—a clever fellow indeed, but in the long run altogether too much like a member of their own middle class. Rogers, with blood on his hands, bore an authority that Franklin and others could not match. With rare exceptions, such as most recently a delegation of Cherokees in 1763, viscerally impressive in their finery of raw alien power, most Londoners had not encountered North Americans from the frontier. To those who could look beyond his sometimes-coarse manners, Rogers represented something tantalizingly new: a self-made

American man of indomitable self-confidence, independence, and large appetites. He exuded an abundance of what the ancient Greeks called *thymos*, or "spiritedness," which formed, as Plato famously argued, the third element of the soul along with reason and passion; it was the source of the craving for recognition, of pride, indignation, and shame, the driving power of all great natures.

Rogers sought patronage, engaging the interest of Charles Townshend, lately a lord of the Admiralty and secretary at war. Rogers had served alongside his brother in the last war; Charles had told a correspondent that "Major Rogers marches thro' the prints [newspapers] in a thousand various Shapes." And he cultivated John Campbell, agent for the colony of Georgia and author of such well-regarded books as *Lives of the British Admirals.*[1] One observer informed Sir William Johnson, sensitive to the currents of power in the British world, that Rogers was "looked upon at London As...very intelligent." Rogers's entry into London society was highly unusual for an American provincial, even if he did hold a commission in His Majesty's forces.

Yet more than curiosity drove influential men to cultivate Rogers. To such men as Townshend, Campbell, and Benjamin Franklin, Rogers candidly unveiled his dream of mounting an expedition overland to find the Northwest Passage, the fabled waterway that could link Europe with Asia and for which men had died and squandered fortunes for two and a half centuries and would do so for another century. With a passage Britain could challenge Spain's trading relationships with East Asia but also with Russia, which recently had set to exploring the western North American coast.

Rogers claimed to have gleaned special knowledge from the Great Lakes Indians, themselves passing on word of mouth, that a great river, the Ourigan, might reach across a great section of the continent. Rogers proposed that a three-year expedition of 228 rangers could find the passage to the western ocean by land. It would cross the continent by way of the Great Lakes, the headwaters of the Mississippi, and the unmapped "Ouragon," pushing back the western margin northward until it came upon a great seaway falling into Hudson Bay. He was drafting a petition to the king to request an appropriation and would need their letters of support. Townshend and Campbell threw their considerable weight behind the idea.

On October 16 Rogers gained an audience with the 27-year-old George III at St. James's Palace, an honor most Americans, including Franklin, never attained. "Yesterday," reported *The New-Hampshire Gazette* some months later, "Major Rogers, who commanded his Majesty's Rangers in North-America during the last War, had the Honour to kiss his Majesty's Hand, on his being appointed to a Command in the Interior Country in America."[2] A tired but lucid king met Rogers. Earlier that year the king had suffered a mysteriously debilitating siege of coughing, chest pains, and fever, which may have presaged the health problems that would eventually rob him of his sanity. Despite the fatigue the young king, who would later win the nickname "Farmer George" for his plain tastes and simple interests, including a passion for agriculture, found Rogers an entertaining break from the tedious routines of court. Rogers could speak both about the fine details of life on the frontier (how to fashion snowshoes and ice-creepers, how to find a black bear in its winter den) and about the commanding big picture (the world-changing potential of the Northwest Passage and the procedures by which the Indians could be brought into accord with British imperial interests).

Millan had proved true to his word: Rogers bore with him two brown-leather volumes, gilt-lettered along their spine *Journals of Major Robert Rogers* and *A Concise Account of North America*, which he presented with deference and gratitude. Only days earlier he had learned that the king had ordered General Thomas Gage, now commanding British forces in North America, to appoint him commandant of Fort Michilimackinac, the Crown's westernmost outpost in the New World. The post would make Rogers the de facto viceroy of the west and offer him an ideal location from which to seek the Northwest Passage. He would serve as a major on full pay and receive £500 for "his disbursements during the Late War" and to repay his military debts. Rogers would return to America with his sovereign's blessing and a letter from a secretary of state, General Henry Seymour Conway, specifying details of his new assignment: "It is thought, from his Knowledge of that Part of the Country, and his Acquaintance with the Indians, he may be of Service by having some kind of Superintendence among those of the Neighborhood, particularly to the Westward of that Post."[3]

But the means of financing his supreme enterprise, the search for the Northwest Passage, remained in limbo. The Earl of Dartmouth, president of the Board of Trade, received Rogers's petition positively but directed it on September 6 to the War Office because such an expedition would involve the assigning of troops. The king evidently read Rogers's petition with interest and in early October put the matter before the Privy Council, a body of dignitaries who advised the sovereign on military, civil, and foreign policy.

No officer of the king's colonial subjects stood a better chance of bringing off a small-force transcontinental venture. But Rogers's petition hit the Privy Council at a difficult time. The prime minister had recently fallen, and his successor and the new cabinet were still finding their feet in a bitter political climate. Years of war in America and Europe, and Britain's new world-girdling empire, had drained the treasury; the national debt stood at £146,000,000 sterling—more than a year's gross national product. And that March Parliament, set on recovering a larger share of the mother country's war expenditures, overwhelmingly passed the Stamp Act, requiring that all legally binding documents, newspapers, and even playing cards bear a revenue stamp. It would become one of the impositions that drove the colonists to open rebellion.

Given this tension, the Privy Council postponed deciding on Rogers's proposal. But the door remained open.

After his audience Rogers had every reason to be happy, but he could not wait for the Privy Council's verdict, so set sail for America. In his three months in London he had met with the king, secured a commission, and published two truly substantial books. In December *The Gentleman's Magazine* commented on *Concise Account:* "The work is concise and yet full: and the knowledge it contains is acquired with pleasure, and retained with ease, by the regularity of the method, and the perspicuity of the stile."[4] *The Monthly Review or Literary Journal* wrote: "To this brave, active, judicious officer, it is, that the public are obliged for the most satisfactory account we have yet been favored with, of the interior parts of that immense continent."[5]

The next year Millan published the play *Ponteach; or, The Savages of America,* which Rogers had had a hand in writing before he left London. The early scenes appear authentic, but the middle and end devolve into clichéd melodrama. Understandably, critics panned the play. In its initial third, where Rogers's hand is evident, the action centers on traders and garrison troops who cheat Indians out of their hard-earned furs. Pontiac grows alarmed and challenges the fort commanders. *Ponteach* shows a serious moral purpose—Rogers was warning the British against taking advantage of the Indians, who he believed were essential to westward expansion and fur trading. It is not a romantic play; nor is Pontiac a noble savage but rather a man continuous with the civilized values of the advancing white man, exercised by real humanity, legitimate grievances, and concerns for dignity, liberty, and life.

Ponteach's deeper message fit with the *Concise Account* and Rogers's journals: the North American wilderness is not evil, corrupting all who touch it, but rather grand and extraordinary, capable of raising majestic qualities in its dwellers. If the woods of North America could breed such figures as Pontiac, then they too must be great and worthy of efforts to explore and develop them. At one point in the play the son of the embodiment of trespassed-upon native resistance cries, "My Blood runs high at the sweet Sound of Empire...And I'm impatient of the least Delay."

In the heady environment of imperial London, and not in the still rather provincial colonies of coastal North America, Rogers had found the place to nurture his dream of pressing the British Empire to the west coast of a continent that he was set on making his country's—and his own.

Rogers, product of the thin, glaciated soils of New Hampshire, knew that gold and all the world's precious elements counted little as compared to the rich earth of the North American heartland—and with it came the chance to make a new world. While back in New England the elite argued about the number of pennies in customs levies, Rogers boiled with impatience. Richness was right at their very fingertips, there for the taking. These were in deepest essence the words of an imperial thinker, a man striving to live in and grasp the many natures of a world that was beyond the ability of most to even imagine.

Decades later Rogers's visualization of the yet-newer world west would resonate with Thomas Jefferson, who made it his own; then, calling upon powers and resources that Rogers always lacked, he would send Lewis and Clark to turn that vision into continental power.

But for Rogers, the same scope of vision would bring upon him bitter rivalries in the New World with those who could understand neither the man nor the dynamic purpose of what lay toward the sunset. On hearing of Rogers's installation as commandant, General Gage wrote Indian Superintendent William Johnson, leaving no doubt about his judgment of a man so "wild, vain, of little understanding; and of as little Principle, but withal has a share of Cunning, No Modesty or veracity [who] sticks at Nothing."[6] More than anyone else, these two men would control Rogers's fate in the New World.

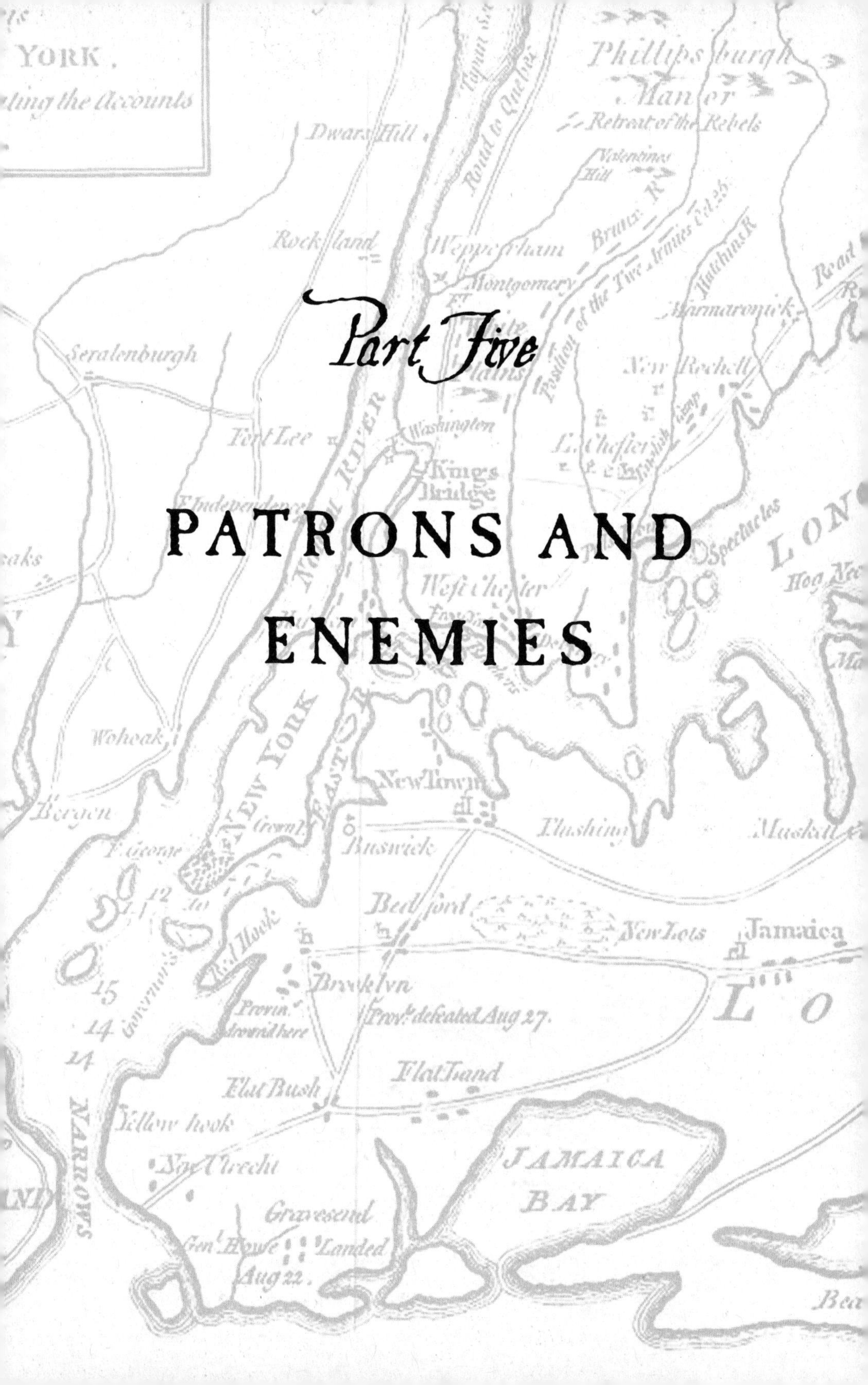

Part Five

PATRONS AND ENEMIES

Chapter 34

Trouble Brewing

My Dear Rogers,
This is the third time I've wrote you since our last meeting in New York...As I promised, you were remembered in my Conversations with the Minister of the King I now Serve [France]...
Maryland

"HOPKINS" LETTER TO ROGERS, ON THE BASIS
OF WHICH ROGERS WAS BROUGHT UP ON
CHARGES OF BEING A SPY

When the ship eased into New York's crowded harbor in 1766, its hold full of raw cane sugar from the Caribbean, few were likely to take notice. A third of the nearly 500 seagoing vessels coming into port that year bore the lucrative commodity that wharf-bound refineries would turn into "white gold."[1] But the craft that cast anchor on Thursday, May 1, raised eyebrows with its French flag.[2] Although no longer at war, Britain and France were competing vigorously in the triangular trade, the exploitative and extremely lucrative wheel of commerce involving slaves, sugar, and rum that bound the economies of the Caribbean to the New and Old Worlds. Sailing from Haiti with papers for Bordeaux, the vessel, two years into its round-trip, seemed a good thousand miles off course. Its captain pleaded distress of weather; a storm had battered her rigging, and she needed repairs.

At least one British colonial officer stationed in the city smelled a rat, confiding to his journals that "in my opinion the arrival of this French vessel is a mere Finesse."[3] And indeed he was right. A gentleman came ashore and walked up to General Gage's Broad Street headquarters, only a block or two from the batteries of Fort George at the tip of Manhattan.

Whoever he was saw to it that Gage received a passel of letters, which, he explained, came from "Mr. Hopkins"—whom the general knew as ex-captain Joseph Hopkins, late a Queen's Ranger from Maryland, now serving the French king.

One of the letters in particular, addressed to "Major Robert Rogers Governor of Detroit and its Dependences in North America," caught Gage's eye. The general could make out writing through its thin envelope. He instructed his secretary to open it in such a way that it could be resealed without the intended recipient any the wiser.

"*My Dear Rogers,*" began the ominous missive, "This is the third time I've wrote you since our last meeting in New York, and altho' our Absence has been long my Sentiments of Friendship are and always will be the same.—"[4] The letter then cut to its seductively treasonous point: "As I promised, you were remembered in my Conversations with the Minister of the King I now Serve, I have reason to think you would have a reasonable gracious Reception." More than any other single factor in Rogers's life, this letter would set off a chain of events that would forever stain Rogers's reputation. (See the transcribed letter in Appendix 3.)

Whoever had written this mysteriously skilled and explosive letter addressed the major several times, perhaps rather too often, as "dear friend" and recalled "the injustices we have suffered particularly yourself, nor is it in the power of England to recompense you for the disgraces you underwent for having Served them too faithfully." The writer warmly asserted his loyalties to the (presumably English-speaking) North Americans, insisting that he would risk his life and fortune "in being an Advocate for them for any Assistance or suplys that the present Circumstances of their Affairs may exige, there can be no Obstacle to their being a free and independant People." Spread the word through New England, he exhorted; "you have the means in your own hands, your numbers are far Superior to any Forces that can be sent against you." And furthermore "seize every opportunity of ingratiating yourself in the favor of the Indians where you are placed Governor."

Gage squinted over the idiosyncratic signature "Maryland," which was followed by a curious postscript: "and write me fully without signing your name—Mr. Hopkins is well, and you will address your Letters to me under Cover to him. there are Continual opportunitys from New York & Phil. for Monte O Christ or by the Missisippi to write me."[5] Gage had a hot piece in his hand and knew it.

Joseph Hopkins, originally of Kent County, Maryland, had commanded a company of Queen's Rangers during the French and Indian War, later serving with Rogers against Pontiac at Detroit. His command had seen a hard war, being almost totally annihilated by the Indians on Erie's lakeshore. As the threat to Detroit had all but dissolved, he had come near to swordpoints with many of the men he had fought alongside. Most unusually Rogers and 13 other officers endorsed one Lieutenant Cuyler's charge that Hopkins had acted extremely "ungentleman like" by overcharging his troops for rum and "necessary's furnished by him." For men living in close confinement, their numbers thinned by Pontiac's braves, few charges carried opprobrium darker than that of an officer's acting dishonorably toward the men he was responsible for. If his own company could not rely on him over blankets and rum, how could he be trusted to act the officer's part in matters of life and death? The charge's most damning point lay in its signatory's refusal "to do duty with him till such times as he clears his Character." Most such garrison disputes worked themselves out, particularly because the hardbitten provincials in the ranks preferred to solve their differences without resorting to authority. First to sign—with a confident flourish, its letters large and unmistakably clear—was Rogers.

Hopkins escaped criminal investigation—Amherst later chided his subordinate Major Gladwin for this leniency—and left for New York, then for London, where his appeals for compensation fell on deaf ears. In 1765 he entered the French service, apparently attaining the rank of colonel and serving in San Domingo, the thriving French colony on the eastern side of Hispaniola.

Hopkins found a receptive climate in France, which was still stinging from the loss of its continental empire in Canada and virtually all its holdings in India. Étienne François, duc de Choiseul, minister for foreign affairs during the war and still a powerful statesman, invested considerable effort in trying to inflame the smoldering relations between England and her colonists, who were no longer forced to defer by the French menace. Some in North America saw in the recent Stamp Act unrest evidence of a French plot. Choiseul seems to have recognized Hopkins's capacity to serve as a conduit through which to inject mistrust and distraction into the English colonies, whether or not his defector could recruit a single subversive. He became Hopkins's patron.

The letter's tone does not appear to be what a fellow ranger who had served in the same theater of war might write the most formidable member of his calling; nor does it allude to the unpleasantries that had passed between them. Instead it dwells on general abstract principles—rather strange talk between two men who had shared the extremities of war. It neither betrays much personal knowledge nor evinces any curiosity about old comrades. Had the real Hopkins sent it with the intent of incriminating Rogers, it surely would have more explicitly recalled Rogers's alleged treasonous outbursts. It appears strange also that Hopkins, should he be the sole author, did not just sign his name—he had nothing to lose as a well-known turncoat—but signed it "Maryland," keeping his identity altogether out of it. The elaborate reference to himself in the third person seems so ill disguised as to suggest that the writer was going out of his way to call attention to his letter's mysterious and secretive nature. Readers could no more ignore its implications than if the word *treason* had been bolded and italicized on the letterhead. The appeal to Rogers seems vague and impersonal, urging him to do no specific action but entangling him in strangely ill-concealed implications.

Nor is it likely that Hopkins had the power or resources to direct or pay for a ship to sail way off course. Could the letter have been written by some satellite figure? Taken all together, the evidence argues that the intended reader was not Rogers but those who would intercept it and place it directly into Gage's hands at the tip of Manhattan. Indeed, the French may have felt it far more important to compromise the powerful hero than to bring him on board—and to give their conquering rivals reason to fire at one another's shadows.

Two or more other missives in the packet were addressed to "Gentlemen of good Characters," Gage later wrote: these he promptly destroyed, because they clearly intended to "debauch them from their loyalty."[6] Sensible enough, but why did Gage destroy these letters yet retain the one addressed to Rogers?

Not only did Gage retain the letter to Rogers, but he asked his secretary to transcribe it; and two weeks later, on May 13, he called upon three men to witness that the transcription was correct.

He then resealed the letter and forwarded it to William Johnson in upcolony New York, putting him on his guard that "I am likewise to beg of you, for very particular Reason, which I can't now mention that you will give the strongest Orders to your Interpreters and Commissarys to watch Major Rogers's Transactions with the Indians and that they send you Information if he holds any bad Conversations with them." He continued that "Your People should keep their Instructions secret and not divulge what you write them on this Subject."[7] The superintendent opened the letter and promptly replied that he had made "a very extraordinary & alarming Discovery not to be mentioned at this time."[8] It was a strange communication to make to one's superior.

Unaware of this web of creative suspicion weaving so energetically behind him, Rogers nonetheless entertained little doubt that Gage and Johnson bore him ill will. Fresh from London, he had taken dispatches from Secretaries Barrington and Conway to Gage, which explicitly instructed the general not only to pass Rogers to his new post but to commission him a captain in the 60th Foot. Importantly from Rogers's perspective, the dispatch also encouraged Gage to settle Rogers's long-standing accounts. Gage then appointed a military commission, composed of men who would be quite clear about his intentions, to examine Rogers's claims for some £12,000 sterling.

Weeks later Rogers was aghast when Gage told him that only a fraction of his claims would be honored, compounding the insult with the declaration that Rogers himself could not see the report but only a lawyer of proven "Credit and Reputation." Rogers dashed off a letter of complaint to Lord Barrington but then had to leave for Michilimackinac.

As superintendent of Indian affairs, Johnson's nervousness about Rogers's ambitions as commandant of the empire's most western post is fairly clear. He confided to Gage his concern that Rogers "will have it in his power To confine the Trade in a great degree to himself & Friends," an odd concern from a man whose own proposals for a 100,000-acre parcel in the Illinois country and another principality near his home smacked of the kind of favoritism that was rampant then. (The age's greatest historian, Edward Gibbon, quipped that

corruption was the infallible sign of constitutional liberty.) "I am astonished," he wrote Gage, "that the Government could have thought
of Such an Employment for him."[9] The idea of the popular Scots-
Irish war hero deploying his vast energies on the edges of the aging
Johnson's not-yet-quite-sovereign domain was cause for serious alarm.

The source of Gage's animosity toward Rogers is less easy to
pinpoint. Rogers's propensity to incur debt certainly worried the
general, who was himself not getting enough money from Britain.
Gage's service in the field had taught him about Rogers's combat
record firsthand; Gage's shadowy but undying antagonism may have
had its roots in the forests outside Carillion in July 1758, during
Abercromby's ill-fated offensive, where Augustus Howe had died, if
not a truly sensible officer at least a brave one. Gage, thrust into field
command by Howe's death, had simply disappeared from the record
for many critical hours. Had Rogers, who covered the retreat, turned
with bitterness upon this command failure, the same indecision and
panic that had palsied Gage in the heat of battle at Monongahela under Braddock? Had the inarguable and effective courage of one man
deeply humiliated by its example another who was incapable of bearing up? The record, aside from Gage's demonstrably long silence on
the battlefield (or wherever he was), remains hidden, but Gage's subsequent and sustained efforts to ruin Rogers are bold and clear.

Yet to blame the unfolding events solely on personal friction
between these players overlooks a deeper truth: both Gage and
Johnson at one level or another understood that Robert Rogers was
capable of instituting fundamental change in everything he touched.
As events would prove, they were wise to pay attention.

On August 10, 1766, the schooner *Gladwin* pulled into the surf on
the southern edge of the Straits of Mackinac, four miles of wind-
tossed water that separate Michigan's Lower and Upper Peninsulas,
her hull slapped by chop. Eight miles to the northeast rose the
wooded outlines of Bois Blanc, Round, and Mackinac Islands; to the
west, St. Helena's Island. Figures on shore fired muskets into the air
in welcome.

Rogers and Betsy gained their first glimpse of the old French fort of Michilimackinac, which would be their home for the next two years. The 18-foot-high, deeply grayed cedar palisade enclosed a hexagonal fort of some two and a half acres, perched on the tip of an exposed tongue of sand and gravel. A pair of small cannons peered out from two waterside bastions. Near the shore to the east lay a smattering of birch-and-cedar-bark lodges and beached canoes; behind them stood dozens of bark-covered buildings, the summer dwellings and booths of traders and visiting Indians.

No more than 40 yards beyond the west and south bastions, the topography grew rugged—not by New Hampshire standards, Rogers noticed, but the steeply broken nature of the terrain made the post below unmistakably vulnerable. For the French, who first established a garrison here, proximity to a maize-cultivating Ottawa village and the lake counted most: a strong west wind would drive the waves right up to the palisade walls. In the summer the garrison shoveled sand from the palisades, as it did with snow in the winter.

Scrambling into a bateau, the small party rowed shoreward but soon ran aground in the stony shallows 50 yards out. Rogers jumped overboard and carried Betsy to land. Soldiers of the 17th splashed in as well, to lug armfuls of supplies and baggage onto the sand-swept beach.

Expecting the worst, Betsy was pleasantly surprised when they passed beneath a sentry box and through the water gate, then walked down the Rue Dauphiné, which ran only 350 feet, dividing the compound in half. Dogs barked and raced alongside the newcomers. Hard winters, rain, dampness, and frost had battered the exteriors into a worn, dull gray, but the officers' houses and some of the traders', most of French construction, were solidly built, even boasting pleasant-looking windows made of triangular glass pieces or seven-by-nine-inch rectangles, their shutters latched together with shutter dogs to protect against inclement weather. Many doors hung on pintles and bore massive locks. Twenty-penny spikes held the boards together, and cedar shingles topped most dwellings. New structures had arisen since Pontiac's warriors had swarmed inside the gates, two years earlier, under the pretense of retrieving a ball used during a game of *baggatiway*, or lacrosse, between the Sacs from Wisconsin and the Chippewas, and took the garrison.

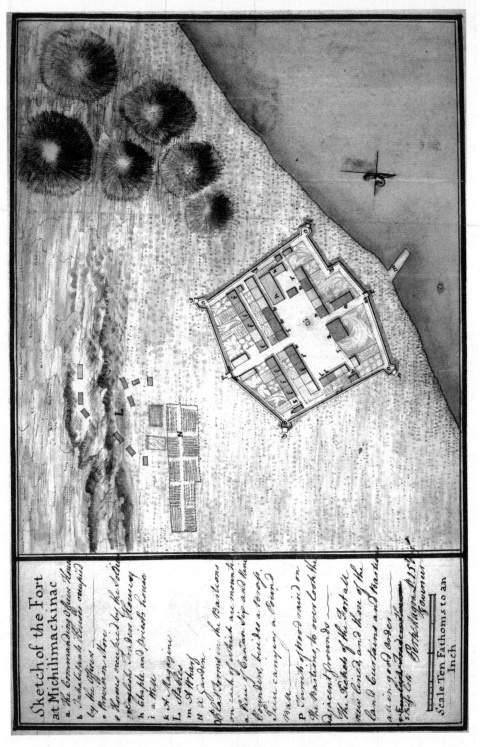

Fort Michilimackinac, 1766, by Lt. Perkins Magra

The short avenue opened onto a 120-by-168-foot parade ground of hard-stamped earth and sand, with a well at its center. To the right stood the Jesuit Church of Sainte-Anne, the patroness of voyageurs, topped with a belfry and cross; nearby sat the bark-shingled priest's house. A grassy mound in the southeast corner held the magazine. Kitchen gardens crowded between the houses, marked off by small pickets; woodpiles anticipating winter cold crowded against exterior walls. The rank smell of peltry hung thickly in the air, most intensely near the large barrackslike warehouses, where the skins of wildcat, bear, beaver, and deer were sorted, graded, beaten clean, and packed for shipment. Rough-hewn traders, such as Alexander Henry, with his twisted and busted nose, welcomed Rogers. Only the second English trader given a license for the Great Lakes region, the New Jerseyan had traveled west in 1761 disguised as an Indian, because the war still raged, and then nearly lost his life in Pontiac's War.[10] Others, such as John Askin and Ezekiel Solomon, came later. Short, dark-haired, French-speaking Canadians, dressed in colorful shirts, leggings, sashes, and garters, stared at the war hero with curiosity.

For Rogers, who rightly viewed this commission as his reward for wartime services rendered, the very act of entering the small fort as commandant was the fulfillment of many dreams. The small, remote, and dusty outpost might not look like much, but it was the hub of a complex fur-trading industry on the very edge of the British Empire, critically placed at the intersection of Lakes Michigan and Huron. Michilimackinac was the small beating heart at the center of a good many thousand square miles of territory stretching west across the Mississippi, far north of Lake Superior and far south into the Illinois country. The lifeblood of this immense trading center flowed through the rivers and lakes that made travel possible. The commandant, now a man of peace, could smell the possibility in this moment for British continental imperialism to burst beyond the Atlantic basin.

Bringing a new order to the old would not be easy, he later noted, because he "was not only to hold the Ballance of Justice between His Majestys Subjects and the Savages, but likewise to preserve Harmony and Peace between the different Nations of Savages, whose perpetual broils are highly obstructive of Trade: Moreover I had to Govern a Garrison of His Majesty's Officers and Soldiers with a great number of the English as well as the lately Conquered French Traders, and Inhabitants, whose different Interests Diametrically clashed with each other."[11]

While certainly remote, Michilimackinac did not lack material goods: during the fine weather, frequent packages from London and Liverpool arrived via Montreal or Albany, unbroken baling seals indicating that the shipment had arrived intact aboard canoes as long as 40 feet by 6 feet. Traders bought a license in Montreal that specified their destination and the amount of goods and listed the crewmen.[12] They were required to deliver a portion of their goods for the officers and the necessities of the garrison.[13] One inhabitant wrote that each incoming canoe "carries about 200 gallons of Rum & Wine."[14] In addition, the convoy might bear 300 pounds of shot and ball, 150 pounds of gunpowder, and a dozen and half trade guns.[15] Montreal traders came either via the St. Lawrence to Lake Ontario, then through Niagara and Detroit, enduring some three dozen portages,[16] or via the shorter northern route of the Ottawa River, Lake Nipissing, the French River, and Georgian Bay. Albany traders came west on the Mohawk River, up to Lake Ontario, and up the shore.[17]

When the winter froze the lake and brought *la poudrerie*, blowing snowstorms composed of hail that bit at exposed skin, the small garrison remained inside, entertaining themselves with eating, dances, drinking, and games. The British officers and their wives might sup on Queensware, Elers-type red stoneware, and continental Delft, drinking copious draughts of rum and wine out of cut-glass tumblers. During weekly balls at the post, the officers' wives dressed in gowns of damask and Russian sheeting, warmed in coats of imported Scottish Osnaburg, a rough textile made from flax or jute.

Betsy and Rogers settled into the two-story commanding officer's house on the north corner of the fort, only a few steps from the water gate. The second floor contained a billiards table.

All was not well at Michilimackinac. Two powerful nations, the Sioux and the Chippewa—the latter variously allied with the Cree, Pawnee, Assiniboine, and Mississauga—had levied a war for "40 winters." The Fox and Sauk habitually raided the Illinois, while the Potawatomi fought among themselves. The British and French traders were also discontented with new policies that limited trading to the immediate environs of the fort and that prohibited them from overwintering at far-flung Indian villages.

Johnson's appointment as northern Indian commissioner in 1754 came largely because the British feared that France's overtures to the Iroquois had come close to turning their allies. Johnson's vigorous diplomacy had held the Iroquois largely on the British side and kept the French at bay. War's end brought a major power shift but did not substantially interrupt the fur trade, for which Montréal and New York competed. Clearly interested in drawing peltry through his Iroquois middlemen along the Mohawk Valley and on to the merchants of Gotham, Johnson worked to confine all dealings to the posts of Niagara and Oswego. That enraged the powerful Montréal merchants, whose traders worked through Detroit and Michilimackinac. Johnson eventually relented and let Detroit and, later, Michilimackinac into the system. But he instituted rules restricting trade to the posts, a significant break with the decade-old trading practices by which traders traveled to Indian wintering grounds. That was no problem at Oswego and Niagara, where Indians lived nearby, but it proved difficult at the remote western outposts, where most of the trading Indians lived hundreds, sometimes many hundreds, of miles away. Restricting trade, wrote Johnson, "will make the Indians feel Wants" and prevent them from again going to war; he further argued that increased control over the traders would minimize their often-rapacious dealings with the Indians.

At Michilimackinac for the past two years Johnson's appointed commandant, Captain William Howard, operated according to Johnson's rules. He bent them only in 1765, when Indian hostility began to rise and the Great Lakes tribes began to head north to trade with the Hudson's Bay Company. Howard issued a limited number of licenses for overwintering without Johnson's authorization. Johnson reluctantly agreed, after the event. At Michilimackinac, merchants not chosen leveled allegations that Howard had benefited financially from his favoritism.

Amherst left under a cloud after Pontiac's War, and Gage threw his weight behind Johnson and his system, which prompted powerful Montreal merchants to petition the governor of Quebec to ease the restrictions. The merchants hired a lobbyist in London to pursue their cause. Theirs was not a tough sale: furs represented more than half the value of Canadian exports to England and had enriched many important English trading houses. In London, government and mercantile figures spoke to Rogers not long after he received his Michilimackinac command, outlining their designs on keeping London's control over the fur business.

The merchants at Michilimackinac received Rogers well; the presence of a military hero would go a long way to bring the Indians to some kind of order. Two days after his arrival 20 of Michilimackinac's principal merchants and traders gathered and read a letter to him expressing "particular Satisfaction" at his appointment, "more especially at a Time that many of the Indian Nations, almost worn out with repeated Solicitations for Traders, are on the Eve of Discontent." They expressed optimism that Rogers's experience in the past war had delivered him a "reputation you have by that Means gained amongst the Indians, will add Weight to your Councils, and re-establish the national Credit, through the most extensive and remotest Part of his Majesty's Dominions."[18]

Rogers immediately saw the difficulties of restricting trading to the fort: "Few if any Indians from the West of Lake Michigan or from the South and west of Lake Superior would ever visit that Post at all, some because they are at such a distance."[19] What could motivate Indians, he asked, to bring their pelts to the fort and "leave their Wives and Children not only in a distressed and Starving Condition but liable every day and Hour to become Slaves and their whole Country and Substance be left a prey to neighbouring Savages."[20] Without a trader nearby, the Indians who "are mostly poor must often Suffer great inconveniences" in any emergency or accident. A broken hatchet or loss of a knife "may lay a Whole Family under great inconveniences for six or eight Months together, the Spoiling of a Small quantity of Gunpowder, the breaking of a Spring of a gunLock &c may be the means of destroying a whole Seasons hunt and of distressing and Starving a numerous Family."[21] With these words Rogers gently reproached his audience for lack of enterprise, much as he had in his play about Pontiac, urging administrators to think beyond tomorrow's profits and overall more largely, even continentally, about the extraordinary profits to be made by establishing a dynamic web of trade with the Indians. He began to preach cooperation, in an attempt to reorganize the relationship between the cultures, based on an expansive, generous, and largely constructive vision of the Indians. Supply the Indians heavily, he implied, and they would return the favor with a heavy flow of furs. Rogers here exercised a trait later evident in the great industrialists who would not settle for small returns. He would apply ranger tactics to trade, expanding it by dynamic penetration, just as Bridger, Astor, and others would do forty to fifty years thence.

The traders were not disappointed. Daniel Claus, William Johnson's son-in-law and deputy commissioner for Indian affairs at Montreal, gleefully wrote Johnson that Rogers "immediately without hesitation, gave a general permit to all Trades to go wintering, for which he is vastly liked and applauded here. The Traders that came from there told me also that his behaviour towards the Indians was liked an approved of by them, as well as the people of the place."[22] But Johnson's reaction upon reading this news could not have been happy.

Yet as Rogers insisted in a letter responding to the traders' welcome, he had acted under the direction of Johnson: "This affectionate Address deserves my Gratitude. I cannot but be sensibly affected at the general Discontent among the Indians; but be assured, that I shall enforce every salutary Measure conducive to the Re-establishment of general Tranquility, consistent with the Instructions I have, and may, from Time to Time, receive from Sir William Johnson, under whom I act, from whose Judgment and extensive Knowledge in Indians Affairs, the Grievances you complain of, may speedily be removed."[23]

Chapter 35

The Northwest Passage

*The Rout Major Rogers proposes to take, is from the Great Lakes
towards the Head of the Mississippi, and from thence to the River called
by the Indians Ouragon, which flows into a Bay that projects North-
Eastwardly into the Country from the Pacific Ocean, and there to
Explore the said Bay and its Outletts, and also the Western Margin of
the Continent to such a Northern Latitude as shall be thought
necessary.*

ROGERS'S PETITION FOR FINANCING AN
EXPEDITION TO FIND THE NORTHWEST PASSAGE,
AUGUST 1765[1]

Rogers leaped into action. In his near-manic, constant motion can
be read astonishment at the failure of the French, who had been coming west for close to two centuries, to see the vast region as anything
more than a source of furs. He had certainly not forgotten his dreams
of finding the Northwest Passage by land. Soon after he arrived
Jonathan Carver and James Tute arrived at Michilimackinac, both
hired earlier by Rogers expressly to seek the passage. The latter had
fought under Rogers at the Battle on Snowshoes and led one of the
groups to safety on the harrowing return from Saint-François. Few
could match the 27-year-old's pathfinding skills. Jonathan Carver,
two decades older than Rogers, an amateur mapmaker and surveyor,
had served as a provincial soldier during the war, commanding a
Massachusetts company, in which capacity he had impressed Rogers
with his "firmness of mind and boldness of resolution." Both seemed
eminently qualified for the great overland venture, a critical capacity

because Rogers's responsibilities as commandant kept him at his post for extended periods.

Rogers found letters awaiting him at Michilimackinac from his patrons in London—Dr. John Campbell and Mr. Townshend—along "with various Letters from Sundry Gentlemen in England to the same effect" supporting his pursuit of the passage, although offering no money.[2] Rogers would have to be content with the prospect of the Admiralty's £20,000 prize awaiting the passage's discoverer. Undeterred by the shortage of funds, and again revealing an indomitable belief in his power to overcome any obstacles, Rogers planned to finance the small party by borrowing from traders, and he promised the men eight shillings a day, to be paid eventually by the king. Tute was instructed to return pelts to help defray costs.

Making Tute the commander, Rogers sent Carver out first on September 3 with a party of traders assigned to winter with the Sioux on the Mississippi. He instructed Carver to take "down an Exact Plan of the Country, by the way of marking down all Indian Towns with their numbers, as also to take Surveys of the Different Posts, Lakes and Rivers, as also the Mountains." Two weeks later he followed Carver, canoeing southwest along the northern shore of Michigan to Green Bay, then striking overland to the Mississippi at the site of present-day Minneapolis. Tute carried instructions "for the Discovery of the North West Passage from the Atlantic into the Pacific Ocean, if any such Passage there be, or for the Discovery of the Great River Ourigan that falls into the Pacific Ocean about the Latitude Fifty."[3] Accompanying him was the English trader James Stanley Goddard, instructed to take careful notes of their interactions with the Indians, for whom their canoes were filled with trade goods as presents. After wintering on the Mississippi, the small party was to travel northwest across the vast wilderness to a tiny French trading outpost at the forks of the Saskatchewan, to winter there awaiting supplies, then push west and northwest to the "great River Ourigan, and thence to the Western Sea."

News that Rogers had taken over command of Michilimackinac trickled out among the Indian nations of the western Great Lakes basin and beyond, and requests for audiences with him, sweetened by gifts of wampum, spilled in from werowances keen to assess the embodiment of the new power.

Rogers set out on his first tour six weeks after he arrived, when he canoed nearly 20 miles southwest to the Ottawa village of L'Arbre Croche ("Crooked Tree," near present-day Cross Village). Some 180 Ottawa families had moved there from Michilimackinac in 1741 after exhausting the soil. The Ottawas had cultivated large fields of maize in the vicinity of the recently abandoned Jesuit missionary Church of Saint-Ignace de Michilimackinac—corn on which the garrison had depended for years. The windswept village, spreading for a mile or two along the shore, had been nearly exterminated in 1757, when its triumphant warriors returned after sacking Fort William Henry, carrying not only plunder but the smallpox virus. The vectors of disease, probably garments, came from recently buried British soldiers, including Rogers's brother, whom the Indians had dug up in a blood frenzy.

Rogers met with Nissowaquet, the 51-year-old Ottawa chief known to the French and English as La Fourche, near Michilimackinac. His deft negotiating skills had helped his people survive and thrive during the transition from French to British ascendancy. During Pontiac's War and the attack on Michilimackinac, Nissowaquet had earned goodwill for harboring the military and civilian survivors, including Alexander Henry. His nephew was Charles Langlade, Rogers's formidable enemy at the Battle on Snowshoes.

Rogers recorded these negotiations and the many others following them in detail for Johnson, in one of the most remarkable documents of the interaction—lying, bluffing, enduring puzzlement, real respect, and mistrust—between the British and the western Indians. Twelve years earlier a 32-year veteran of the fur trade, Chevalier de Raymond, described negotiating with the Indians: "The diplomacy and care that are necessary to keep them faithful are incredible, because they are distrustful, vindictive, traitorous, perfidious, changeable, suspicious."[4] As a sign of the mutual respect that was growing between them, Rogers carefully noted the individual chiefs with whom he negotiated.

At L'Arbre Croche, Rogers sat with Nissowaquet in a longhouse, its floors swept clean, a small fire in the middle of the floor and a bundle of porcupine skins filled with bear grease stacked up against its walls. Nissowaquet and Rogers addressed each other formally. Years of experience had given Rogers an ability to communicate essentially with a patois and strong body language. But careful diplomacy between nations still required a translator.

Nissowaquet first assured Rogers of Ottawa friendship toward the British but said that "there is bad birds flying from the West side of the Missisipi to this part of the World." One Indian purported to have seen nine pieces of wampum sent to the Potawatomies of St. Joseph by Monsieur de Ange, "the officer that commands the uppermost Post on the West side of the Missisipi." Furthermore, this wampum "imports that two thousand French have arrived at that mouth of that River, & in the Spring are to come this way as soon as they take the English Fort at the Illinois, & reduce Michillimackinac & then to proceed to Detroit."[5]

Rogers gave Nissowaquet and another chief each a shirt and a ratteen, or thick twilled woolen coat, and presented the village with 20 gallons of rum. Then he said, "Brothers You greatly astonish me by your Speech, is it possible that such romantick foolish stories as those can enter into the Brain of an Ottawa, & give credit to it!" He continued, delivering a belt of wampum, "I tell you now, that the French have not one inch of Ground on the West side the Misisipi." He went on to remind them of the danger of engaging with Spanish traders, given their bloody record with the Indians. He encouraged the chiefs to send their young warriors to see with their own eyes if the rumor of a French army was true, and he reminded them of British superiority on the seas. He gave out more belts and strings of wampum and asked the Ottawa to bring him the nine strings of wampum come spring. "Be strong & wise behave like men & dont fall like a foolish child into the fire, I now bid Adieu to you, till I shall see you in the Spring at Michillimackinac, by that time you will be convinced from your Young Men, that you are to send to the Misisipi, that there's no such thing as your French Fathers, ever coming up the Misisipi with Troops while Water runs in that River."[6] They smoked from a pipe; if tobacco was short, they puffed on kinnikinnick, a mixture of bark and leaves, likely made from the bark of red osier and the leaves of sumac and bearberry.[7]

Back at Michilimackinac, a steady stream of Indians came to speak with Rogers, including a war party of young Mississaugas intent on attacking tribes to the west. Rogers dampened their ardor with a threat—"when you Strike the Sioux you strike the English also"—which broke off their plans. On December 12 a Mississauga chief arrived, again bearing the now-tired intelligence that the French were mounting another campaign in the far west. Instead of kicking the party out of the fort after humiliating its leader, a British commander's usual response to such behavior, Rogers calmly remarked that rumors of this kind were "a bad way to get drink," but he still presented the chief with rum and trade gifts, calling a bluff and raising the ante long before poker was invented. Such behavior, he signaled, would not be tolerated again; yet at the same time he preserved the chief's honor and gave implicit promise of a diplomatic response to good-faith initiatives in the future. And the chief knew that Rogers would expect a quid pro quo in time.

Upon others, Rogers bore down with a stronger hand. He forcibly prevented one party from stealing from the merchants, or "the first sight you shall have of me will be surrounding your Cabbins with a Bloody Hatchet, & all the Indians in this part of Country at my side." Interaction by interaction, Rogers was conveying a clear, consistent, trustworthy, and authoritative message to the Great Lakes Indians.

Unlike past commandants, whose policy had been pretty much to react to existing situations, Rogers shaped a long-term strategy to bring the Indian representatives to Michilimackinac annually to force a lasting peace. Rogers had no intention of maintaining the status quo, but he knew that he could bring the Indian nations together, stop war, bring them into line with British interests, shut out the French and Spanish, and revitalize the fur industry. Here in this remote outpost, far from the conventions and orthodoxies of the coastal colonies, his towering dreams could swell unconstrained.

Working with the Montreal traders, Rogers hatched a plan that was breathtaking in scope. Michilimackinac, he would later write, "ought to be a Beacon from which a most Extensive and as yet unknown Territory is Watched and observed—It is or ought to be a Store House frought with all manner of necessaries for the Constant Supply of almost innumerable Bands Tribes and nations of Savages— Savages removed from it five, Six & eight Hundred and some a thousand Leagues who cannot Annually nor ever in their Lives visit it as a Market."[8]

To the eager ears of the English traders and their French colleagues, Rogers outlined a plan to erect a civil government at Michilimackinac with its own governor, lieutenant governor, and twelve-member council that would manage the Indians, keep the French and Spanish interests from encroaching on trade and lands, and bring "a proper Subordination of Legislative and Executive Officers for the forming of proper Regulations from time to time and the due Administration of Justice."[9] Several companies of light infantry or rangers would help keep peace. "I here only subjoin that some national advantages may arise and those not inconsiderable from having a number of Subjects Annually Employed & for the most part resident four Six and eight Hundred Leagues and some further, west, Northwest and Southwest of Michilimakanac—who can say what valuable Discoveries may one Time or other be made by this Means?—and at any Rate would prevent any other European Nation from Secretly gaining any considerable footing in those remote regions that might be detrimental to us—it would bring a great number of British Subjects acquainted with the Rivers Mountains, Plains and Capes of the Country in a good Degree who would Serve for Guides and Conductors in case of any immergency."[10]

Rogers's plan, in part designed to consolidate his power and to detract from that of Gage and Johnson, was also an attempt to establish an organizational and legal presence over the far west that would expand British imperial interests beyond trade to settlement and true sovereignty. Rogers's idea had not come out of the blue: he had vetted the idea of a western colony with many influential British politicians. Lord Charles Townshend had accompanied Rogers to visit Lord Rockingham, the first lord of the Treasury, and outlined the full plan.[11] Implicit in the plan was Rogers's assuming the governorship and moving beyond Gage's authority.

After the war ended, the British Proclamation of 1763 forbade settlement west of the Alleghenies. The region reaching to the Mississippi, bounded by Hudson Bay to the north and French claims to the south thereafter knew no civil rule of law, aside from a clause inserted into the Mutiny Act of 1765 that enabled any officer to arrest civilians; military officers also had the authority to send the accused to the nearest colony for trial. But these conditions hardly constituted a workable and coherent system for administering justice.

Rogers's attempt to bring order to the westernmost edge of Britain's North American colonial power may have needed more fleshing out, but it certainly responded to an important need on the ground. To London officials in late 1765 it appeared a practical means of protecting British fur interests in the American west.

By the time that the proposal made its way to London, however, Rogers's fortunes had changed badly for the worse.

In mid-June 1767 the nearest Indians—Chippewa, Ottawa, Potawatomi, and Mississauga—were encamped outside the fort's cedar pickets, angry at Sioux and other western tribes. Rogers exhorted a series of councils to temper their anger, painting images of "Clearing the Path & Brightening the Chain of Peace that might extend through all the nations & Tribes of Indians from the Rising to the Seting Sun."[12] Gifts enhanced and cemented what had been determined at each powwow. Remarkably, Rogers convinced some of the Ottawas to travel out to guide the western tribes on their way there, giving them protection against potential Chippewa hostility. On June 25 a chief Rogers identified as Ragagumach declared for the assembled Sioux, Foxes, and Winnebagos that "our young Warriors have long been ready & eager to return the blows we have received, but because of your Words...we have restrained them."[13] Rogers underscored his desire for peace.

Over the next few days canoes continued to pull onto the sandy shores around Michilimackinac, disembarking one of the largest and most diverse gatherings of northwestern Indians in history. Typically, Rogers's journals rarely dwell on the details of what must have been an extraordinary scene. A nineteenth-century estimate that some 7,000 Indians attended probably overstated the numbers, but participation was still remarkable. Rogers's journal indicates the following attendees: Foxes from the Upper Fox River in central Wisconsin; Chippewas from Sault St. Marie, Lake Superior's northwestern shore, Pa Point, Rainy Lake, and Lake of the Woods; Menominees from Green Bay; Sauks from the Wisconsin River; Winnebagos from southeastern Wisconsin; Nipissings from Lake Nipigon; Crees from Lake Winnipeg; a combination of Foxes, Mascoutens, and Potawatomies from the present-day Milwaukee shoreline; and Sioux from the

Mississippi. The post's translator Jean-Baptiste Bernard de Jolicoeur noted that there were more nations—and more Indians—than he had seen in his thirty-eight years at Michilimackinac.[14]

Over the course of the next several days Rogers held several conferences with the various chiefs and warriors, observing that "I could not but observe a pretty general Hostile Temper to prevail & most of them upon the Point of an open war & rupture to the Westward, there had been Injuries Provocations and Bloodshed on both sides which joined to ye natural inclination of those Savages to frequent Wars, and the perfidious Conduct of the French and Spanish Traders from the other side of the Misissipi by instilling false notions into their Minds and Stiring them up to war among themselves and into a bad opinion of us and our Traders in that part of the Country at present."[15] He urged the western tribes "not to listen or hold any Commerce or converse with the French beyond the Misissipi as a thing Displeasing to the King to Sir William Johnson to me." In a whirlwind of activity Rogers convened small conferences with numerous Indian bands, especially the Chippewas, from whom he elicited promises of peace. On July 2, during the grand council, in which concerns were discussed, "after many Short Speeches Replys and Rejoinders," Rogers noted with satisfaction that "there was a general disposition to peace and Amity prevailing among them which I had before recommended to them separately." They all smoked the peace pipe, during which the chiefs "gave one another the Strongest assurances of Friendship and Love, Promised to forgive and forget all past Injuries and Affronts, to keep down and restrain the Fire of their young Warriors and use their utmost endeavours to prevent mischief on all sides for the future and to live in Harmony Concord & good Agreement like Brethren." And Rogers reiterated to them that traders would bring necessary goods to the villages.

In the midst of the grand council, like an albatross flying above an ocean-lashed ship, there arrived Benjamin Roberts, the newly appointed commissary of Michilimackinac, lately a lieutenant in the 46th Regiment, sent by William Johnson to keep an eye on Rogers. He brought a letter from Johnson ordering Rogers to cease all payments to Indians, out of concern for escalating costs. In the midst of the council Rogers could not stop handing out gifts to cement the peace process or the whole endeavor would crumble apart.

He carried on, making gifts of rum, stroud blankets, gimp, double bed gowns, coats, shirts, wampum, and vermilion. For the Sioux he finally had little to give, but the English and French traders banded together and donated £500 worth of trade goods out of the apprehension "that the presents Allotted by His Majesty for the Indians was insufficient at so Critical a Juncture."[16] They asked Rogers to dole out these gifts in the king's name.

Once the grand council wrapped up, Rogers gave Roberts his journals of the proceedings for him to send to Johnson. That Roberts bore Rogers no goodwill is evident in the accompanying letter he wrote Johnson. "Perhaps you can decypher [this; some] of us were puzzled about what Language it is Hebrew or Arabac I have laid a Wager you or [Guy Johnson] can do it pray make me Win my Wager."[17] While poking fun at Rogers, Roberts's note also suggested some confusion about Rogers's doings, a lack of understanding that the commandant was forging a new relationship with the Indians. Rogers had carefully noted in the journal that he looked upon the Indians neither as besotted idiots nor as vicious terrorists but as men and women not unlike the English, if less organized and less civilized.

Traders signed a note acknowledging the delivery of £481 of gifts to thirteen Indian nations, attaching a note that read, "We the Subscribers . . . are Confident that the within and other presents by him given to the Indians which we have this day Certify'd were absolutely Necessary and well Timed Otherwise an Indian War must have taken place in this Country Instead of a peace which he has with Great pains, care, and fatigue to himself settled amongst all the different Nations that Resort this post greatly to the advantage of His Majesty's Interest and to those of his Subjects Trading to this Country who must have been Totally Ruined by War."[18] Two months later Gage wrote to the Earl of Shelburne, one of the king's principal secretaries of state, that "All Accounts from Missilimakinac agree, that the Savages were never more Peaceable than at present or to appearance more disposed to remain so."[19] Within a year Rogers had stabilized British relations with the western Indians, which had been dangerously off balance since Pontiac's War; as a result of this stability, British commandants could work peacefully with the western nations for the next two decades or more.[20]

Rogers confessed to two Montreal merchants "my astonishment

as he [Roberts] is not Appointed by the Crown only a Warrant from Sir William Johnson." Gage and Johnson, he wrote, orchestrated the appointment out of "some Jealousy of me."[21] That spring Rogers sent to Gage by sleigh the Hopkins letter and his response to it. In an accident with far-reaching repercussions, the sleigh never made it, and the letter—and Rogers's response—was lost.

For all his concerns, he wrote Johnson that "it will afford me great pleasure to give [the new commissary] all the Assistance in my power towards Executing of his Office, and assure you sir that nothing shall be wanting by me on that head."[22] He had no conception of the extent of animosity that Roberts—and by extension, Johnson—bore toward him, let alone how quickly all his plans could unravel.

Chapter 36

Treason!

[Rogers] is a weak, Vain man, and however romantick his scheme may appear, I believe him capable of undertaking it or in short any thing else, and in the present State of affairs sho^d he escape he might I am certain give us some Trouble.

WILLIAM JOHNSON TO GAGE, OCTOBER 22, 1767[1]

A little after sunset on August 19, 1767, Rogers's English servant Andrew Stuart and two companions wrestled 40 small wooden kegs containing 189 gallons of rum outside the fort and into a waiting bateau. As darkness descended, the trio rowed to a nearby island, pulled the casks ashore, and rolled them into the nearby woods. They carried no passes or receipts for the rum. As Stuart would later claim in court, Rogers had given them the rum in lieu of payment, "being the only way he had to pay the Wages he owed." Rogers had yet to receive even a sixpence from Gage for his salary as commandant; and he had made good on debts with the most valuable currency of the frontier post, rum that could obtain valuable peltry in trade with the Indians.

Since Roberts arrived, the contents of the Hopkins letter had remained fresh in his mind. Meanwhile word of the rum's departure at dusk lit Roberts's imagination: could Rogers be stockpiling liquor for his traitorous conspiracy to raise the Indians against the British?

With evidence that he felt was tangible, Roberts ordered a sortie the following day, which easily found the rum and brought it back to the fort. When Roberts's party triumphantly pulled ashore near the water gate, the towering figure of Rogers awaited them on shore. A knot of traders gathered around to watch. Rogers directed the men to carry the casks to the king's provision storehouse, replying to Roberts's glance of anger:

"I have at present the honor of command here and will keep that authority until it is the pleasure of my superiors to order otherwise."

"I have as much command as you do," Roberts shot back. "If the rum goes to the king's warehouse, I want a receipt."

"You'll not have it," said Rogers.

If not a certainty, friction between post commandant and Indian agent was highly likely, due to overlap of responsibilities and a lack of clarity about authority. In 1764 Johnson had helped create the "Plan for the Future Management of Indian Affairs," a regulatory measure to restrict trade north of the Ohio to a number of posts. Overseeing the commerce would be a commissary, supported by a deputy commissioner and a blacksmith. The Crown never authorized the plan, in part out of concern over cost, although in 1766 it was agreed that appointments could be made. Still the commissaries' position lacked formal authority.[2] And the commissary, often of inferior grade to the commandant but elevated to authority over him in certain matters, could easily stress the relationship, should he choose to be aggressive. Commissary Benjamin Roberts had not shied away from confrontations, nearly coming to blows with his past two commandants: he argued violently with Captain Jonathan Rogers of the 17th at Fort Ontario and most recently with Captain John Brown of the 60th at Niagara. Angry letters had flown between Brown and Roberts for months. The commandant of Niagara had deluged Gage with letters protesting Roberts's high-handedness. He wrote Johnson contesting Roberts's authority. Johnson admitted that Parliament had not yet authorized the power of the commissary but urged him to try and work it out. Then in March 1767 Johnson recalled Roberts to Johnson Hall with a plan in mind worthy of Machiavelli. He would appoint Roberts to Michilimackinac, certain that he would raise trouble for the man he had come to hate: Robert Rogers.

As if the cantankerous and proud Roberts needed prompting, Johnson took him "into his closet and Shewed him the Copy of the Letter Captain Hopkins had wrote to Major Rogers ... Major Rogers had acknowledged to him the receipt of this letter, but had not communicated any part of the Contents to him or it to the General."

Johnson desired that Roberts "look out, whether any part of the Advice conveyed in said Letter was put into execution." Mention this to nobody, Johnson concluded, except if "matters carried to extremely, and to apply to the commanding Officer of the Troop, in case of Need."[3] Now he had only to sit back and wait for the fireworks.

Since Roberts arrived, he had complained about the size of his quarters and about innumerable of Rogers's decisions, including the number of wintering passes and Indian access to the fort. But more recently a person came to him and told him exactly what he wanted to hear: Rogers's secretary, Nathaniel Potter, entered Roberts's rooms and requested leave to go home. The once-strong friendship between Potter and the major had soured, he explained. Since he had returned from a trip in June, Potter had spent most of his time confined to trader Henry Bostwick's house, suffering from a debilitating sickness. (It would kill him some months later.) Rogers owed him money; his own fur-trading schemes had not worked out as well as planned. Deathly ill and in debt, Potter rather understandably no longer bought into Rogers's optimism about a future he would not see. A few days earlier Rogers had pressed him to travel to England and deliver his petition for a new civil government in Michilimackinac. Something in Potter snapped and he refused. They quarreled.

Roberts said that Potter told him Rogers "wanted to engage him in some bad Affairs, and had Villainous design in his head, that Major Rogers was in Correspondence with Captain Hopkins in the French Service, and Potter related the Substance of the Letter already mentioned, which he alledged Major Rogers had shewn him, and that he likewise had received, and also shewn to said Potter a second Letter from the same Person, acknowledging the receipt of one from Major Rogers, and acquiescing in the Proposals therein made; that Major Rogers had told him, Potter, he intended in the Spring sending a Party into Lake Superior, and another by La Baye, that he certainly intended making a Sweep of everything he could, and to join these Parties in order to go down by the Mississippi to New Orleans."[4] Roberts asked Potter why he should believe a man of such "bad Character," to which Potter replied that "his long Sickness had made him see his Errors...that what he now declared was the Truth."[5]

Potter's landlord, Henry Bostwick, told a different story.

Bostwick later testified that, aside from some disputes about money, "there could not be any great Disputes between them, as the Major sent Refreshments to, and Visited him every Day, while he lay sick."[6] He further testified that Potter had told him he knew a way of getting the money Rogers owed him. When Bostwick asked how, Potter had replied that "Lt. Roberts had promised him a Letter to Captain Claus, or Sir William Johnson, he does not Remember which, would pay or get him paid that money, but did not explain for what."

On the same day that Roberts recovered the rum, he had dashed off a letter to Guy Johnson about Potter's secrets and his belief that Rogers's Northwest Passage project was nothing more than a front to "go off in the Spring, and not empty handed." Roberts claimed to have great concern for his own "Life, Effects, and Reputation."[7]

It was Potter who had tipped off Roberts about the rum on the island, explained Roberts, which was "to be employ'd to the aforesaid purposes," in which he meant Rogers's alleged plans to go down the Mississippi and rendezvous with Hopkins. Rogers's insistence that the confiscated rum return to the king's provisions appeared to Roberts's inflamed vision to be an attempt to conceal his treasonous activities. His indignant righteousness broke into full flower.

"I have as much command as you," he declared. As the seizing officer, he insisted, he must have a receipt from the deputy commissary of provisions, William Maxwell, should the rum enter the king's storehouse.

"You will not have it," said Rogers, "untill such time it was Prved Seizable." He would order a court of inquiry about the matter tomorrow.

"You have already interfered to much with things relating to my office," fumed Roberts.

"You're very impertinent to tell me this," answered Rogers.

"You dare as well be damned to tell me I am impertinent out of the limits of the fort," Roberts yelled.

"Sir, do you challenge me?" Rogers asked. Turning to a couple of dozen traders, he ordered them to bear witness to Roberts's charge. Roberts then refused Rogers's order to go to his room, at which point the commandant called for the Royal American guard. Roberts bellowed to the now openly amazed traders that "Capt. Rogers was Guilty of High Treason and that he would Prove it...they are going to Murder me!" When Captain Spiesmaker appeared at his shoulder, he yelled out a warning that Rogers "was a Dangerous Person & if he went out of the Fort he might Depend on it he never would see him again."

The Royal Americans bore the squirming Roberts to his room, where he dashed off a statement to Captain Spiesmaker: "I impeach Robert Rogers Esqr. Commandant of Michilimackinac for holding Secret Correspondence with the Enimies of Great Britain, & forming Conspiracies, I desire you in your Allgiance to Seize his person & papers amongst which you will find Sufficient proof."[8] Once Roberts had cooled off overnight, he realized that his charges would have to wait for more conclusive proof, but the accusation lingered in the air. The next day he wrote a note to Spiesmaker saying that his outburst had stemmed from his anger over being sent to his room.

At that point Rogers, now justly certain that Johnson had shared the contents of the Hopkins letter with the commissary, dispatched sworn affidavits about Roberts's behavior to Johnson, whom he further informed that "the reason of my not sending him down the country was wholly on your account, I hope you will be pleased to Remove him from this Garrison."[9] Even Johnson had to write to Gage that "Mr. Roberts might have been more cool."[10]

Rogers and Roberts apologized to each other in the presence of Captain Spiesmaker, but Roberts's allegations and abuse could not be retracted. Rogers could brook no such open challenge to his authority.

A few days later the trio of Tute, Carver, and Goddard appeared exhausted at the water gate, after journeying about 750 miles. The sight of these worn explorers must have come as quite a shock for Rogers, who expected them by now to be wintering well to the northwest at Fort La Prairie. But Tute had mismanaged the expedition's resources. On July 20 Rogers had written to him, after receiving several letters from the party on its way up the Mississippi, that "it is very bad to me that you did not send me in the Peltrys that you promised me last Spring and am astonished at your heavy Drafts on me, but that Convinces me on the other hand that you must have now Goods enough with you to Compleat your Expedition and expect that Franco will make good Returns or am otherwise ruined by your Extravagance. I shall send more Boats up next Spring very Early and desire that you will push on your Journey with all Speed and be more prudent than you have hitherto been."[11]

Rogers's admonition proved vain: Tute had expended most of his trade goods in gifts to Indians but had no pelts to show for his efforts. Running extremely low on their own provisions, the small party had pushed eastward, arriving at the Grand Portage on Lake Superior on July 27 in order to meet their resuppliers as soon as possible. Six canoes with provisions soon arrived, but the larger ten-canoe provision train for the trip to Fort La Prairie, brought by François Le Blanc, carried only a small amount of the promised supplies, as well as Rogers's letter. Grumbling about being deceived, the venturers voted to paddle the 750 miles back to Michilimackinac for more trade goods and a fresh start.

Much to Roberts's delight, the homecoming proved fractious—Rogers was already deep in debt. That winter trade goods had failed to arrive by ship before the ice came, so Rogers himself had had to pay the traders' inflated prices for goods to feed the garrison. His bold gamble, launched with terribly few resources to spare and financed by borrowed money, had depended on the ingenuity and fortitude of his carefully selected group. Had Rogers himself accompanied the expedition, it might well have turned out differently, but he was mistaken in believing that others could bring to bear the same force of will that he could.

Two days later the unhappy Nathaniel Potter left the post accompanied by sawyer Jermiah MacCarty, who later testified that his companion "every day cursed and swore, if ever he could get to England, he would be revenged of the Major."[12] But Potter would never make it to London. After delivering an extraordinary deposition in which he claimed that Rogers had beaten him in front of witnesses—none of whom ever came forward—and that Rogers had corresponded with Hopkins, he died aboard an England-bound ship. Gage wrote to Lord Shelburne from New York on January 23, 1768, that Potter's affidavit stated that "Major Rogers had entertained very desperate Designs of plundering the Fort and other trading Posts, carrying away all he could, and retiring with his Booty to the French and Indians."[13] Curiously, he chose to ignore the judgment of the governor of Quebec, Guy Carleton, who observed that "Potter bears so bad a

Character and it appears so very surprising that Major Rogers, after a confidential Avowal of no less than the Acme of high Treason, should Quarrel with the Person whom he had entrusted with so dangerous a Secret, and let him quietly slip through his Fingers, that it must stagger the Faith of even those who are most inclined to entertain Suspicions of Rogers' conduct from his General Character, and the very great Distress his Extravagancies have involved him in."[14]

Reversing his quite recent tributes to Rogers having brought peace to the farther Great Lakes region, Gage claimed that Rogers had "lavished very considerable Sums on idle Pretences, upon his own Authority, and greatly hurt His Majesty's Affairs in the upper Lakes."[15] He soon sent Shelburne further innuendo, for instance suggesting that Rogers had acted in "a strange and extravagant Manner."[16]

In September Johnson wrote Gage that he kept hearing that Albany merchants were grousing that Rogers had amassed exorbitant drafts exceeding £5,000, "chiefly on pretence of making a peace between the Sioux & Chipeweighs, with wch I think we have very little to do, in good policy or otherwise." Rogers's greatest focus at Michilimackinac had been upon bringing peace between these habitually warring peoples, so that trade could be significantly opened up. More than anything else, this revealed the great differences between Rogers's and Johnson's visions of the west, a clash of new and old orders. In contrast to Johnson, who had much to lose if settlers pushed far west and upset the fur trade, Rogers saw only that once the French were gone, the British colonists, long nailed to the eastern edges of the great continent, could move virtually anywhere, as long as they maintained sensible relationships with the western Indians. Distance and geography were no obstacles; the resources of the west beckoned like a vast treasure chest, its imperializing pull making Rogers less British and less American and even more a citizen of further America, the America that would be. Only by a handful of people saw these gigantic possibilities, even as imperial possibility was in the air; soon Cook would be exploring the world's largest ocean basin, the British would spread into India, and the Russians would trek across Siberia. A generation or two later Rogers's ideas would be commonplace. But then, especially to Johnson, interested only in controlling the fur trade, the thought of Rogers brokering possibilities at the farthest edge of the empire was threatening.

Johnson concluded his letter to Gage: "I am induced to think there must be some particular motives for this Expense . . . I have reason to apprehend some thing more than common is in View (which may not be matter of surprise to you.)"—one more oblique reference to the Hopkins letter.[17]

The only recourse, urged Johnson, was Rogers's immediate removal. Gage replied that he would "put an immediate End to all the Mischiefs he may create, than to remove him immediately from his Command." Of course, none of Rogers's bills would be honored, because they were "undertaken soly by his own Authority . . . contrary to the orders and Instructions given him by you as well as by me, [and therefore] must be protested."[18] Gage would never be specific about exactly how Rogers had broken his and Johnson's orders, and the charge of extravagance bears little weight. In October 1767 Edward Cole, Johnson's Illinois commissary, submitted a bill on his "Accounts for the Last Six Months amounting Seven thousand and twenty pounds fifteen shillings & Eleven pence New England Cur'y for which I have drawn on you in Favour of Mess'rs Banyton, Wharton and Morgan, Merchants at Phil'a." So certain was Cole of Johnson's patronage—Johnson described him as having "a proper respectable Character"—he did not even bother to certify the expenditures; but Rogers, who lacked "principles," by contrast justified every expense to the shilling. Nor did Johnson display any compunction in sending payment to the Philadelphia merchants rather than to Rogers's creditors in Montreal. In the end Gage reimbursed Cole £10,742, far exceeding Rogers's expenses. And Cole continued in his position.[19]

On September 17 matters again came to a head between Rogers and Roberts, again by the latter's provocation. That Thursday Roberts approached the major asking to use the Royal Artillery forge for his Indian department blacksmith. Rogers allowed use of it for several days, until Roberts could arrange for his own shop. When Roberts demanded that he be given it permanently, Rogers answered that he could not do that. Roberts demanded that nearby witnesses note that he had asked Rogers for a smith's shop.

"If you don't be easy I will send you down the country," Rogers barked at Roberts.

"I want to be out of the garrison altogether," Roberts retorted.

"I wish you was out of the garrison," said Rogers, even offering to provide a pass.

"Sir, I will not take it, for I am not under your Command."

When Rogers again ordered the guard to take him to his room, Roberts bolted to plead his case with Captain Spiesmaker, but as in the episode the month before, the captain encouraged Roberts to follow Rogers's orders. As a guard led him away, Roberts said that "Major Roger was a Jail Breaking dog and that he wanted an Indian war should break out that he might get himself Clear of Debt."[20] Roberts again wrote Spiesmaker about Rogers's "Arbitrary illegal Malicious" actions and again suggested him culpable of "Crimes of the Blackest Nature" and "the total subversion" of Great Britain's constitution. Spiesmaker wrote to Johnson that Roberts was the subject of "so many complaints against him, which was Never Know to me before M[r]. Roberts Came here" and that, in his opinion, "Merchants Traders & Indians Seem'd well Sattisfy'd" with Rogers's command.[21] Rogers asserted to Spiesmaker that Roberts had "contracted to make Muteny under my Command" and dashed off a letter to an attorney asking his help in bringing suit against Roberts.

Before leaving for Detroit in early October, Roberts swore on the "Holy Evangelists" to Spiesmaker and several others that Potter had told him of Rogers's plan of engaging "some of the Soldiers to assist him in going off to Captain Hopkins by the Mississippi," which, Spiesmaker later testified, induced him "to be more on his Guard ever afterwards."[22]

In late October Johnson received Potter's affidavit and wrote to Gage that the material acted to "Confirm the Strong Suspicions we had before entertained concerning him." Johnson added: "He is a weak, Vain man, and however romantick his scheme may appear, I believe him capable of undertaking it or in short any thing else, and in the present State of affairs sho[d] he escape he might I am certain give us some Trouble... Potter with great difficulty escaped from his Clutches & got to Montreal."[23] No evidence has ever come to light that Rogers placed the faintest obstacle in the way of Potter's leaving Michilimackinac.

On October 19 Gage dispatched an order to Spiesmaker direct-
ing him to arrest Rogers for "holding Dangerous and Traiterous
Conferences with His Majesty's Enemies, and forming designs of the
most dangerous nature, with intent to raise Commotions and
Disturbances in the upper Countries, and to kindle a War betwixt the
Savages and His Majesty's Subjects."[24]

Chapter 37

Locked Up and Charged

I was put into very close Confinement and kept Night and day with a Guard over me of near Twenty men, with a Bolt of Iron of upwards of Six pounds Weight set across my Legs to prevent my Escaping at a Season of the Year (the Depth of Winter) when no Person ever so much at Liberty, could have left the Garrison with any human probability of any better Fortune than to Perish in the Woods, it being more than three hundred Miles to any English Settlement.

ROGERS, SPEAKING AT HIS COURT MARTIAL,
OCTOBER 1768[1]

On December 6, 1767, Captain Spiesmaker held Rogers in conversation on the parade ground while Lieutenant John Christie brought up an armed detail of Royal Americans. Spiesmaker read Gage's warrant, stating that Rogers would face trial in either Montreal or Detroit. The charges could not get more serious: a guilty verdict would mean execution. Rogers remained even-tempered, calmly asserting his innocence but declining to challenge his superior's orders. Rogers's equanimity under surprise and duress, so useful in an ambush, took a different cast on that parade ground, where suspicious minds found it to validate the coldest kind of calculation. To Christie, Rogers's cool response seemed "as subtil & deep as Hell itself." Ensign Johnston commented that Rogers "seemed to bear up with a good deal of Resolution ... even as this time he was forming the most horrid plot."[2]

Rogers was thrown into the guardhouse. After Spiesmaker searched his belongings, but found nothing incriminating, he ordered

Rogers's and Betsy's quarters boarded up. Realizing that the Hopkins letter had stirred the pot, Rogers wrote Gage acknowledging receipt of it but said that he had never written back.

That winter, while Rogers was confined awaiting spring and a ship to bear him to his trial, the rumors of his treason and nefarious intentions grew and fed on themselves like an infected blister; word soon spread around the garrison that Rogers, along with his Indian accomplices, had planned to cut the soldiers' and traders' throats and escape to New Orleans. The pitch of alarm grew so heated that even though his supposed Indian accomplices were hundreds of miles away and it was the middle of winter, he was "kept Night and day with a Guard over me of near Twenty men, with a Bolt of Iron of upwards of Six pounds Weight set across my Legs to prevent my Escaping at a Season of the Year (the Depth of Winter) when no person...could have left the Garrison with any human probability of any better Fortune than to Perish in the Woods, it being more than three hundred Miles to any English Settlement."[3] His wardens deprived him of food sometimes two days at a time and often failed to light the fire in his drafty prison.

Curious reports began appearing in papers back east, one—that the Indians had "cut MAJOR ROGERS to pieces...in resentment of his abuse of them in Trade"—probably originating with William Johnson.[4] Another said that only a heroic party from the garrison had been able to rescue the much-loathed commandant from a torturous death at the hands of his forest enemies. *The New-Hampshire Gazette* printed a letter from Spiesmaker that read, "I believe he has spirited up the savages against us...and the major is such a scoundrel as to under take any thing: we have therefore to take care that our throats are not cut in the night."[5] Ensign Robert Johnston wrote in *The New-York Gazette* that Rogers, "that experienced chief to all manner of wickedness and treachery," had intended to deliver the fort to Captain Hopkins and "formed a deep and horrid plot to kill me, send Captain Spiesmacher, and Lieut. Christie, prisoners to the Indian country, plunder the garrison, and put all the soldiers to death, who were not in the plot...He then with the Indians and what part of the troops that would follow him, was immediately to set off to surprize the garrison of Detroit and give it up to plunder... and then proceed to Old France...The Particulars of the dark Plot are many, the Proofs positive."[6] Christie added that Rogers was "a low Cunning Cheating back biting villain."[7] These frantic assertions tarnish Rogers's reputation to this day. Yet even as they damned him, the very power of their statements indirectly acknowledged his extraordinary capacities and command over others. His vilifiers as much as his adulators believed that he could pull off the miraculous. Spiesmaker cut Rogers off from any contact, including with Betsy.

Meanwhile Johnson remained deeply concerned about Rogers's capabilities in another sphere, the creation of a separate civil government at Michilimackinac. A friend had written that Rogers "was looked upon at London As A [not readable] very intelligent," which irritated Johnson sufficiently for him to growl back that "I raised him in 1755 from the lowest Station on accot of his Abilities as a Ranger for which duty he seemed well calculated, but how people at home or anywhere else could think him fit for any other purpost must appear surprising to those acquainted with him."[8]

Learning that Rogers's proposal was headed toward London, Johnson fired off a damning, well-crafted denunciation to Lord Shelburne, secretary of state, calling Rogers "a needy man, of bad circumstances, and worse principles, in the first authority . . . is too absurd to deserve any comment." But comment, of course, he did, warning against "dangerous projects . . . dangerous to the public in general. The public interest is always used as a cloak to private gain." Johnson, who himself stood to gain from a circulating proposal to establish a new colony in the Illinois country, understood better than almost anyone the way special interest, nepotism, and monopoly on trade could make a man rich.[9] Cleverly, Johnson evoked images of sedition and the idea of Rogers as an imperial juggler on the edge of civilization, fostering the anarchy in which he could best prosper.

The atmosphere at Michilimackinac grew even more hostile; even Betsy was not immune from salacious gossip and ill treatment. On May 27 the *Gladwin* pulled within sight of the fort, the ice finally clear.

Under armed guard, his leg irons removed after three months, Rogers limped down to a bateau waiting on the beach, past Ottawa and Chippewa braves who roared their displeasure at seeing Rogers so depart. Gage wrote Hillsborough how "Some Disturbance happened at Missilimakinac, on the Occasion of sending Major Rogers from that Fort...a disorderly Tribe of Chippewas, went there with their Arms; and threw their English Belts into the Lake, and invited other Nations to join them to release the Major from his Confinement. The officer Commanding, tryed to pacify them by various Methods, but at length put the Garrison under Arms, and by the help of two Armed Boats conveyed Major Rogers on Board a Vessel, and sent him to the Detroit."[10]

Betsy was led to a cabin. Even though another was available, Spiesmaker had her husband thrown into the hold upon a ballast of stones in his restored leg irons, to suffer through ten days of lurching and shuddering under the still-strong winds. Spiesmaker's fear of Rogers had grown so extreme that he no longer viewed Rogers with any humanity at all, seeing him as more wild beast than man. "From the pain I suffered," Rogers wrote, "together with the cold, the bone of my right leg was split, and the marrow forced its way out of the skin."[11]

On Thursday, October 20, 1768, more than ten months after his arrest, Rogers was brought before a court of twelve British officers, mostly captains, few of whom Rogers knew, presided over by Lieutenant Colonel Valentine Jones. They included George Ethrington, the commandant of Michilimackinac when the Chippewa lacrosse players surprised the garrison during Pontiac's War.

Rogers bowed to his peers and hobbled to a chair. Although he had long ago shed his shackles, their lingering effect still stiffened his gait. Rogers's relaxed demeanor certainly did not suggest that he was on trial for his life. As required in such proceedings, he had access to counsel but could not bring them into court. Requests for his papers, confiscated at Michilimackinac, had gone unheeded. He knew little more than from hearsay how Deputy Judge Advocate Hector Theophilus Cramahé would prosecute the case. But once more high adversity, which he knew so well, seemed to hone Rogers to a razor's edge.

He listened impassively as an officer of the court read the charges. First, he had "formed Designs of a Traiterous and Dangerous nature of Deserting to the French, after plundering the Traders and others of His Majesty's Subjects, and Stirring up the Indians against

His Majesty and His Government." Second, he had held "a Correspondence with His Majesty's Enemies." Third, he had "undertaken expensive Schemes and project, and lavished away money amongst the Savages, contrary to his Instructions, but Conformable to the Council given in a Letter to him (Major Rogers) by an Officer in the French Service." As Rogers later noted, Gage's original charge and explicit accusation—that he was a traitor to king and country—appeared nowhere in the indictment.

Over the course of the following week the Crown unfolded its case, beginning with Benjamin Roberts, who revealed how Johnson had taken him into his closet and showed him the Hopkins letter. The officers of the garrison testified, but when pressed they could provide no concrete examples to support the charges. William Johnson did not provide a scrap of evidence for the prosecution.

On Thursday, October 27, Rogers took the stand and addressed Gage's charge of being a traitor to king and country: "Under this heavy accusation my Name and Reputation have been blasted, and I have been branded with Infamy without the Ceremony of an Examination." Captain Spiesmaker, he said, had refused to deliver up his confiscated journals, letters, and other papers once he left Michilimackinac, which would have been "usefull to me on my Trial."

With devastating precision he walked through his accusers' arguments. That he had conducted private councils with the Indians was absurd; he could not speak the languages of the Great Lakes, and all the translators were present to testify that he had had no such meetings. He argued convincingly that Potter's testimony was inadmissible because he could not examine him.

As for the Hopkins letter, "great pains have been taken to blacken me in this Affair but without any Just Foundation; I don't deny the Receipt of a Letter, whereof that which the Judge Advocate has been pleased to Exhibit may be a True Copy, but I never was fully satisfied from whom that Letter Came...I never thought the Letter of any Material Consequence; I was to be a great Man whenever Mr. Maryland became Prime Minister of France, provided I should seduce the people of New England and the Indians of Michilimackinac to the French Interest, this it was which induced me to make no further inquiry about it; I abhorred the Scheme, and never entertained a thought about answering that Letter."[12] The idea that he and Mrs. Rogers planned to escape in the middle of the winter across a thousand miles of "uninhabited and Wild Country" to the Mississippi was not "within the Compass even of a Possibility." Furthermore, he added, where did it come up that Mr. Hopkins was at the Mississippi or in New Orleans? What had brought such wild ideas to Captain Spiesmaker he could not tell, but perhaps "the gloominess of the Place, or . . . some Imaginations he had Conceived concerning the Horrors of such a plot, or the Glory which he apprehended would redound to himself from the Discovery of it" induced him to "work himself into a Belief that a Plot had really been Concerted, and that himself and the Garrison were in the utmost Danger of being cutt off and Murdered."

Over the course of the next day Rogers called thirteen witnesses, all of whom he drew upon effectively to pick the prosecution's case apart. He submitted to the court an abstract of the distribution of goods made to the Indians during his time there, all signed by garrison officers and certified as "absolutely necessary and well Timed otherwise an Indian War must have taken place in this Country instead of a Peace which he has with great pains, care and fatigue to himself settled amongst all the Different Nations . . . greatly to the Advantage of His Majesty's Interest, and to those of His Subjects Trading to this Country, who must have been Tottally ruined by a War."[13]

Rogers's last witness, the merchant Gershon Levy, described the Hopkins letter's likely fate: a bateau had flipped, losing its contents in Lake Huron in the fall of 1766.

On Monday, October 31, 1768, the court found Rogers not guilty of all charges.

Despite the verdict, Gage was in no hurry to set Rogers free. Not until the middle of February did his order reach Montreal, permitting Rogers the freedom of the city's limits. In February Betsy, who had gone home while Rogers awaited trial, gave birth to a son, Arthur.

In the spring Deputy Judge Advocate Charles Gould wrote Gage "that His Majesty is pleased to approve the Opinion of the Court of Acquitting said Major Robert Rogers of each of the said Articles of Charge and to Order that he be released from the Confinement; at the same time it appears to His Majesty, that there was great reason to suspect the said Major Rogers entertaining an improper and dangerous correspondence, which Suspicion the Account afterwards given of his meditating an Escape tended to confirm."[14] Despite unequivocal evidence to the contrary, Rogers's copybook remained blotted. The Hopkins letter had somehow multiplied into a correspondence.

Gage needed no encouragement to blast Rogers's hopes to find work in North America forever, writing Lord Barrington in May that "unless His Majesty should be also of opinion, that he ought again to take upon him the Command of the Said Fort; I cannot Answer it, after Maturely considering all that has happened, to reinstate Major Rogers in the actual Command of Missilimakinac, or any other Post in the Indian Country."[15] Seven months after being cleared, Rogers was free to leave Montreal. He traveled to Portsmouth and visited his young son and family for nine days; then, keenly aware of the creditors close on his trail, he sailed for London, certain that there he could clear his name.

He and Gage would never meet again, but the commander-in-chief was still not finished with him. Well aware that Rogers would speak critically of him, Gage wrote Lord Barrington of Rogers's coming to London and said it was "needless to trouble you by giving you any Caution about his Assertions, as you have had some Experience of him."[16] Nor was Gage finished with his obsession. It remains unclear what would have moved him to inflict further injuries, but they hint at something deeper and darker than a vulnerability to French disinformation.

Chapter 38

Failing Fortunes

But kind Sir as you'r a Stranger
Down your Garnish you must lay
Or your coat will be in danger
You must either Strip or Pay.

W. PAGET, *HUMOURS OF THE FLEET*,
DESCRIBING A NEW PRISONER'S
WELCOME TO FLEET PRISON[1]

On October 16, 1772, Robert Rogers strode into Fleet Street Prison, and the jigger clanged the iron gate behind him. The inmates of London's most notorious debtors' prison welcomed him with their ominous chorus of "Garnish! Strip or pay!" demanding the newcomer pay an entrance fee or lose his coat.[2] Likely as not, Rogers glowered his way through the crowd into the broad courtyard and on to his new quarters.[3] Three years after arriving in London, having delivered a veritable library of petitions and memorials to the Privy Council, he had failed to obtain appropriations—or new career opportunities—from the Lords of Trade and the Treasury. He would spend the next two years in the Fleet, which, along with the time incarcerated at Michilimackinac and Montreal, meant that he spent more than half of those seven years in prison.

Situated on the east bank of the now-roofed-over Fleet River, the prison crammed some 250 prisoners, many accompanied by their families, into its small rooms. The satiric painter William Hogarth had spent five years as a child in the Fleet after his father's coffee-house had failed. By no means as rough as Newgate Prison, the Fleet still, wrote one contemporary, had "few hours in the night without riots and drunkenness," fueled by the easy availability of gin and beer.[4]

In 1759 one magazine writer had estimated that 20,000 people were imprisoned for debt in Great Britain and Ireland. "For debt only, are men condemned to languish in perpetual imprisonment, and to starve without mercy, redeemed only by the grave. Kings show mercy to traitors, to murtherers and thieves . . . but in debt we are lost to this world," wrote Daniel Defoe, the creator of *Robinson Crusoe*, who was well accustomed to debt and died on the run from his creditors.[5] The great poet John Donne and the erotic writer John Cleland both saw the inside of the Fleet.

Inmates had to pay the unsalaried warden for his room and board; most wretched inmates begged for alms from barred windows opening onto the street. Prisoners of some means could live more comfortably, and unmolested by creditors, just outside the prison's walls in an area known as the "Liberty of the Fleet." But no record indicates where Rogers lived, except a brief allusion in one of his land petitions that he was in "Close Confinement."

Not long after arriving in London, he had written Betsy that he would remain there "till my business is compleated . . . our Future happiness Depends on it."[6] Amid his cataract of petitions and memorials, of applications for testimonials, visits to possible patrons and begging deferments from his creditors, he had twice been cast into debtors' prison for short stints, but this time the £1400 owed eight creditors, including his publisher, John Millan, held him among the destitute shopkeepers, insolvent innkeepers, and occasional "broken gentleman" for the long term.

At the outset Rogers had returned to his Spring Garden apartments and beaten a path to his patrons. Before he left America, Gage had come through with his commandant's pay and the expenses associated with his imprisonment, but he had refused to meet the far greater outlays that Rogers had incurred with the Indians at Michilimackinac—monies that Rogers set out with indefatigable energy to recover, submitting a targeted and convincing brief to the Lords of the Treasury. They responded in early May 1770 "that a considerable sum of money is certainly due to Major Rogers from the public for the said services."[7] Despite Rogers's somewhat court-martial-tarnished record, a striking number of influential men still lined up to support him. "I cannot refuse the request of Major Rogers that I should say to you what I really think that the Case of his accounts now before the Treasury is attended with circumstances of great hardship inviting their Lordships compassion," wrote John Pownall, under secretary of state for the American colonies.[8] The Lords of the Treasury decided to remand the matter for Gage's recommendation, in what must have been a crushing blow to Rogers.

As he tirelessly continued petitioning, the press back home still avidly followed Rogers's activities. He was variously reported to be commanding a regiment in the East India Company's service, to be traveling to Quebec to establish an inland colony near Lake Superior, and to be commanding a company of British rangers that would harass the French in the event of war.[9]

As usual, Gage took months to respond to any issue concerning Rogers. When he got around to it this time, he came up with a deliberately ruinous reply. He did not deny that Rogers's accounts appeared "Authentic and Regular." Unlike Rogers's wartime paperwork, his Michilimackinac books had been kept carefully and were scrupulously corroborated. But Gage took another tack, explaining to the Lords that he wanted to "give their Lordships my Reasons for Refusing Payment thereof." Certainly he had granted Cole more than £10,000 in 1768, and Captain Beamsley Glazier, Rogers's replacement at Michilimackinac, had written him a letter confirming that "it is impossible, for a Commanding Officer to carry on the Service properly and keep the Indians upon good terms, with us without some Expense."[10] But Gage claimed that Rogers had "greatly exceeded his Powers in expending such considerable Sum." Not only that, he claimed that Rogers had spent fourteen times the usual annual disbursements to Indians at the post, a preposterously exaggerated figure. Clearly, Gage explained, such expenses, "if allowed at as Valid at one Post, would have served as an Example to the rest and soon Entail an annual Expence of between Thirty and Forty Thousand Pounds for Indian presents."[11]

No doubt appalled at these wild inflations, the Lords of the Treasury denied Rogers's claims on November 27, 1770, and thanked Gage for taking such good care of His Majesty's resources. "I am very happy that my Conduct respecting the Restrictions laid upon Major

Rogers on his taking Command at Missilimakinak have met the Approbation of the Lords Commissioners of His Majesty's Treasury," Gage wrote John Robinson in March 1771,[12] barely containing his delight at delivering a blow from which it would be difficult for Rogers to recover. At every step in the process, passing along the Hopkins letter while destroying others, fanning Johnson's fears—and despite Rogers's complete exoneration at the court martial and his long imprisonment—the supreme commander would feel some compelling need to lie and fabricate so as to throw Rogers into ruinous extremity with his creditors.

The ruling did not seem to slow the tireless Rogers, who continued to press petitions, one to the Board of Trade in late May for a grant of land near Lake Champlain, and another to the Privy Council for compensation for his sufferings incurred during the war. Both failed.[13]

In February 1772 he dusted off his ever-burning dream of finding the Northwest Passage. With fresh information gleaned by Carver while overwintering with the Sioux and from the explorations of some others since, he proposed a new expedition. It was vast in scope and ambition, yet far more modest in manpower and finances than his 1765 memorandum, cutting the original complement of 228 by three-quarters and the budget to £28,000 for the three-year expedition. He also reconceived the mission: his party would work their way to the western sea and then search every "Inlet, Nook, or Bay, from the Straits of Anian to Hudson's Bay" to find the saltwater passage that must link the western and eastern oceans.

This self-sustaining party of hunters and adventurers, supporting two draftsmen and a surgeon, would overwinter on the Mississippi at the Falls of St. Anthony near present-day Minneapolis, trapping beaver, gathering wild rice, and curing buffalo meat and venison. Come spring, they would push northwest up the Minnesota River to its source, then some 30 miles beyond that to the river "Ourigan" and thence down to the Pacific. Rogers's proposal anticipated the route that Meriwether Lewis and William Clark and their 42-man Corps of Discovery—close even in size to Rogers's projected party—would take more than three decades later.

For Rogers, getting west would be the easy part. He went on to outline how, after finding the passage, the expedition would voyage east to Hudson Bay, where a waiting ship would take them not back to England but to the Pacific and across to Asia. With his breathtaking ambition, Rogers believed that these hardy adventurers could travel via "Siberia, Russia, &ca: &ca: to Great Britain."[14]

The New-Hampshire Gazette reported that the proposal had drawn a warm response from the Lords of Trade, who passed it along with a favorable endorsement to the "Treasury Board, that a proper estimate may be made of the expence."[15] There, as so often in the past, for all the intervention of several patrons, including Customs Commissioner John Robinson, the proposal languished. How the history of North America might have changed had Rogers's proposal been approved remains mere speculation. Certainly he would not have discovered the passage, which lies north of the Bering Strait and would not be transited by water until the Norwegian explorer Roald Amundsen's 1906 expedition aboard the 47-ton *Gjøa*. But had he brought off his passage to the west coast—and no one else at that time stood a better chance of doing so—the implications might have had a bearing on the brewing discontent on the other side of the continent. Had Rogers established a separate western colony, would the British have held on to it, as they did Canada after the Revolution?

By early fall Rogers had exhausted every promise for extension, every clever refinancing scheme, every persuasive sales pitch, and entered the Fleet. Although the Fleet could easily pull a man into dissolution, there is little evidence that it had this effect on Rogers, who did not slow his petition-writing stride. In May the *Gazette* reported that he had secured an appointment as deputy governor of the Granada Islands.[16] A petition to the Privy Council in June for 60 square miles in North America was accompanied by testimonials of his contributions to victory in the lands thus won by an all-star cast, including Lord Loudoun, Abercromby, Amherst, Webb, and five colonels. Nonetheless the petition died.

Rogers took one last bold crack at his formidable rival, when the commander-in-chief returned to London on home leave. Rogers gave Gage one last opportunity to settle the outstanding debts by submitting another memorial, which the commander-in-chief again denied. Days later, on April 8, a London sheriff handed Gage a writ, suing him for damages, an action perhaps promoted by Rogers's creditors. Even if the chance of Gage's standing trial was minuscule, the publicity could again bring attention to Rogers's situation; but Gage sailed back to America with other things on his mind. While away he had missed the Boston Tea Party and the consequent closing of Boston's port by the garrison. In London the king informed his prime minister that Gage had brushed it off with rather jaunty assurances that "they will be Lyons, whilst we are Lambs but if we take the resolute part they will undoubtedly prove very meek."[17] Sixteen months later Gage would be recalled to London, largely because, as a secretary of state noted, he was "in a situation of too great importance for his talents."[18]

In late June changes in the bankruptcy laws enabled Rogers to petition for clemency. He won his release by signing over all his worldly goods to the king; on August 2, 1774, he walked out of the Fleet with 40 shillings in his pocket. Shortly thereafter he petitioned the Privy Council, more modestly and this time successfully, for a mere captain's half pay.

Throughout his imprisonment and his myriad futile petitions and memorials, Rogers had never lost interest in the Northwest Passage. On the contrary, the endeavor continued to engage his large imagination. He met up again with Jonathan Carver, and the pair managed to interest Richard Whitworth, a member of Parliament from Stafford, in an expedition. In May 1775 the three sat down to plot out a venture for the following spring. To support Whitworth's fund-raising efforts, Rogers wrote five carefully argued and effective memorandums that built upon and expanded his 1772 proposal. The first assessed the practicality of various routes in terms of portages, seasonality, and overall effort, settling on the Great Lakes, Missouri, and the Oregon. "It is plain that the health of the Men is a point that must be Guarded and preserved with care, as the whole Success of the Voyage intirely depends on them, but by taking the Route the propose has Determined upon, from Schinactady, one Month with be gained as the Spring opens much sooner on the Mohawk River, it being at Least 3 Degrees to the South of Montreal. The men wou'd take near one month to get over Lake Champlain to Montreal, which wou'd be a needless Expense and great loss of time and an unnecessary fategue to the Men."[19] The second, "Memorandum for forming Instructions for the intended Expedition," anchored command and authority at the most unassailable level by declaring that "all Orders respecting it's Execution should Originate from his Majesty and Ministers." The commander-in-chief in North America, all governors and post commandants, were "to give every aid and assistance as Occasion may require," giving the back of the hand to Gage.[20] The third, "Instructions for Major Robert Rogers late Commandant of our Rangers in North America," gave Rogers the authority to recruit "Fifty Common Hunters 4s. each per day."[21] The fourth document, "An Estimate of Necessaries for Major Rogers Expedition," lists some six dozen tools, pieces of equipment, Indian trade items, and navigational instruments: a pocket compass for each man, along with magnifying lanterns, two 24-inch reflecting telescopes, two astronomical quadrants, three theodolites, and six Gunter chains. He asked for "2 Compleat Setts" of carpenter, cooper, and blacksmith tools, and "1 Hundred Medals 50 of Silver and Fifty of Brass, with the Kings head on one side and the pipe of peace with the British flag on the other. The Silver to Weigh about three half Crowns, the Brass of the same Size."[22] Finally he wrote a treatise on the medical and commercial potential of North American "Herbs plants and Shrubs that possess uncommon Virtues," based on his "intimate Converse with the Indians." Running through dozens of plants from memory, he listed their potential economic and medical uses, ranging from an assortment of dyes to specific cures for venereal disease.[23]

On June 4, 1775, ten weeks after Concord and two weeks before Bunker Hill, Rogers sailed for North America aboard the *Baltimore*, content that he had given Whitworth documentation quite appetizing enough to raise the venture's expenses.

Part Six

HARD CHOICES

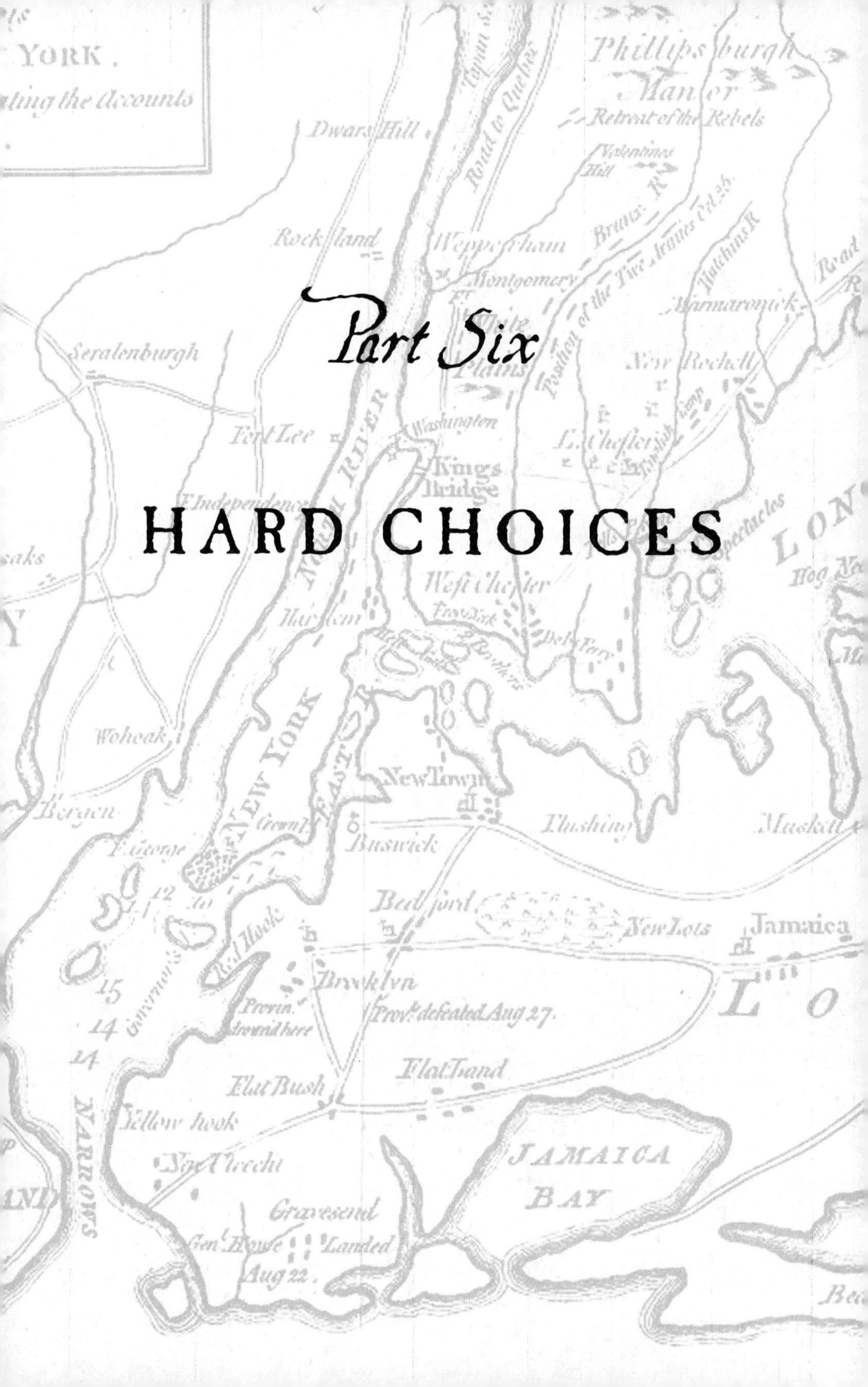

Chapter 39

A Bitter Homecoming

But yesterday two soldiers…on their return from Montreal, *informed me that our officers were assured by a* Frenchman, *a Captain of the artillery, whom they had taken captive, that Major* Rogers *was second in command under General* Carleton; *and that he had lately been in* Indian *habit through our encampments at* St. John's, *and had given a plan of them to the General; and suppose that he made his escape with the* Indians, *which were at* St. John's.

ELEAZAR WHEELOCK, PRESIDENT OF DARTMOUTH
COLLEGE, REPORTING WILD RUMORS ABOUT ROGERS
TO GENERAL WASHINGTON, DECEMBER 2, 1775[1]

Storms lashed the Atlantic during the early summer that year, and a crossing that could take as little as a few weeks dragged on for two months. The battered square-rigger *Baltimore* finally reached shore in August, as the weary passengers were extremely low on provisions. Rogers and several companions fought the wind-whipped seas and rowed ashore in search of supplies. Before they could return, conditions grew worse, the rolling Atlantic breakers becoming so powerful that even the seasoned bateau handler could not weather them. He watched as the *Baltimore* pulled away and disappeared, its captain fearful that the winds might cast it ashore.

With just the clothes on his back and only a few coins in his pocket, the 43-year-old Rogers headed north along the storm-ruined coast to Philadelphia where, as a half-pay officer in the king's service, he would need permission from the Continental Congress to travel.

He had few prospects, save the brightly burning promise of the Northwest Passage.

Anyone absent in Europe for the past six years could not have understood the seismic changes that had occurred in the British colonies, least of all Rogers, who had been incarcerated for so long and embroiled in an endless struggle for compensation. Revolutions, although often heralded by outbursts of violence, take years to come to a head, as antagonisms and resentments quietly bubble barely below the surface. When they do break out, they come with surprising energy and violence. But even after that April's bloodshed at Lexington and Concord, many colonists were still assessing their choices, convinced that the brewing conflict would end shortly. What could bind the southern plantation gentlemen of South Carolina (whom Rogers had come to know) to the steely Yankee ship merchants of Portsmouth, the large-minded Quakers of Philadelphia, and the rough fur dealers of Albany? It would be remarkably late in the turbulent events of the mid-1770s that many colonists would stop thinking of themselves first as Englishmen and only secondarily as Americans, a wrenching and momentous reidentification. During the next few months all colonists would have to declare themselves one way or the other.

Rogers lived in a strange netherworld, a place neither completely American nor altogether British, but as a citizen of a new and rapidly changing world, he was an American with British—in the wider, embracing sense—imperial vision. "I have leave to retire on my half-pay, and never expect to be called into service again," he would write General Washington. "I love North-America and I intend to spend the evening of my days in it."[2] He was deeply misjudging the changes under way in his home continent. The lands beyond the mountains and their extraordinary possibilities pulled at him, but most Americans would not seriously look west for another two generations. In the mid-1770s their gaze was directed solidly eastward, to their increasingly unsatisfactory relationship with Britain. These troubles distressed Rogers because they interfered with his continental plans. "I am exceedingly chagrin'd at my present Situation," Rogers wrote Whitworth a month and a half after landing, "and the more so on Account of our intended Expedition for the discovery of the North West passage, as the present times will not permit it to be carried on unless affairs were Settled between the Mother Country and her Colonies. For in the present Situation of affairs every man wou'd be made prisoners."[3] As his actions would reveal, Rogers intended to stay neutral in the conflict, wanting neither to alienate his British patrons and thereby shatter his Northwest Passage plans nor to fight against his countrymen in the deepest sense, his fellow Americans, to whose natural west-going destiny he was seeking to give practical form.

Indeed, events had proceeded apace: while Rogers endured the pitching seas aboard the *Baltimore*, the British had stormed the patriot strongpoint on Breed's Hill, at the Pyrrhic cost of 228 killed and more than 800 wounded, making the startling discovery that the rebels had the backbone to stand up in an open battle. Israel Putnam and John Stark had both played heroic parts. Rogers's old stomping grounds of Forts Ticonderoga and Crown Point had fallen in May. In June the Continental Congress bestowed the supreme command on George Washington. Rogers's fellow ranger Putnam became one of four major generals.

By late September Rogers had reached Philadelphia, paying a visit to John Adams on the twenty-first, who wrote, "He told me an old half Pay Officer, such as himself, would sell well next Spring. And when he went away, he said to S.A. [Sam Adams] and me, if you want me, next Spring for any Service, you know where I am, send for me."[4] The insolvent former ranger would consider service if the price was right.

The next day an officer with the Pennsylvania Committee of Safety brought Rogers in for questioning. Finding him suspicious only on the grounds that he remained a half-pay British officer, the committee let him go after he signed a statement saying that "on the honour of a soldier and a gentleman, . . . I will not bear arms against the *American* United Colonies, in any manner whatever, during the present contest between them and *Great Britain;* and that I will not, in that time, attempt to give intelligence to General *Gage,* the *British* Ministry, or any person or persons, of any matters relative to *America.*"[5] An irritated Rogers wrote Whitworth that "I had not been long in American before I was made a prisoner of War, and obliged to Sign my Parole not to Act Against them . . . otherwise go into Prison, the latter I have had too much of already."[6] He certainly felt the bite of irony with this rebuke: Gage would never have given him a position in the British forces in North America, even had Rogers desperately wanted one. His only consolation was earning official permission to travel the colonies at will.

In the following months Rogers could not breathe a word of his Northwest Passage plans to colonial authorities, although he would be subjected to more than one further interview about his intentions. The expedition's degree of British patronage would immediately arouse suspicions that he was heading west to incite the Indians against the colonists. His experience at Michilimackinac had taught him all too brutally the power of rumor and innuendo. Too often had loose talk ruined his plans, and on several occasions it had nearly cost him his life. American patriots, their senses sharpened for the least hint of betrayal, smelled that Rogers was not telling all, which deepened their suspicions of him. By mid-October the rumor mill was ginning new stories of Rogers's fabulous escapades: "A gentleman . . . saw Major Rogers not far from Virginia, in full march, with colours flying, at the head of a great body of Indians, in support of the Americans," reported *The Scots Magazine*.[7]

A week after that first note to Whitworth, Rogers reiterated his concerns: "I have great reason to wish for such reconciliation [between Britain and America] having not the least Dependence her Except the above Business shou'd be carried into Execution, & if it shou'd miscarry I must crave your friendly Interest in getting me into the East Indian Companys Service, a Pension from the Government, or some Employ that will enable me to support myself & Family."[8] He wanted no part in the current troubles—and should he win an appointment, he would like to serve elsewhere than North America. But he was leaving all his options open, not aware that the window of choice for so visibly enigmatic yet formidable a figure was rapidly slamming shut.

Traveling to New York, he met with William Smith, the colony's chief justice, who recommended that the penniless Rogers reinvigorate a petition for land grants in which he had joined in 1764 with other New Hampshire veterans, which now fell under the jurisdiction of York Colony, "especially as the Quarrels might soon Terminate in Negotiations for Peace."[9]

To that end, Rogers visited the royal governor of New York,

William Tryon, who evidently tried to wheedle some intelligence from him about his dealings in Philadelphia. Rogers did not break his parole, and the governor dubbed Rogers's information mere "sentiments." Nevertheless Tryon reissued some of the requested land grants.

On October 10 Rogers headed north, first to Albany and its environs to evaluate his claims, then eastward to visit his brother James in Kent, New York (now Londonderry, Vermont). Frontiers as well as loyalties were still indeterminate in those raw, shifting days. Stopping at Hanover, New Hampshire, he called upon the Reverend Eleazar Wheelock at Dartmouth College, which Wheelock had founded in 1769 for the education of Indians—indeed, in those early days, the bulk of the students had come from Saint-François. Rogers told Wheelock that he knew Lord Dartmouth in London, the school's namesake and prominent supporter. The ever-resourceful Rogers, who had not met Wheelock before, offered to help the school apply for large grants of land. Wheelock, while acknowledging that the "famous Major *Rogers*" treated him with great respect, looked askance at his visitor, describing him in "but ordinary habit for one of his character." In a letter to George Washington, he reported how Rogers had said that he "had been offered and urged to take a Commission in favour of the Colonies, but, as he was now on half pay from the Crown, he thought proper not to accept it."[10]

But Wheelock went on: "But yesterday two soldiers...on their return from *Montreal*, informed me that our officers were assured by a *Frenchman*, a Captain of the artillery, whom they had taken captive, that Major *Rogers* was second in command under General *Carleton;* and that he had lately been in *Indian* habit through our encampments at *St. John's*, and had given a plan of them to the General; and suppose that he made his escape with the *Indians*, which were at *St. John's*."[11] Fabulous tales and rumors seemed to bloom around Rogers wherever he went.

In early December he arrived in Portsmouth for a reunion with Betsy and to meet his son, Atty, for the first time. He had been absent a half dozen years, and none of the grand promises that had sent him back across the ocean had panned out. Forced as she was to live with her father and receiving little support from her husband, Betsy's fortunes had not bloomed bright, growing worse once her father died.

Betsy met his talk of land grants with a fair share of sadly earned skepticism. But then he was off again on urgent business to Boston.

The newly minted General Washington, alarmed by the rumors and by Rogers's rapid passages from colony to colony, instructed General John Sullivan of New Hampshire to interview him. Sullivan dined with Rogers at Winter Hill, the patriot position commanding the British on the Bunker Hill peninsula. Rogers explained that he was there to get Washington's authorization to travel, having indeed recently written to him asking for "permission for me to go unmolested where my private Business may take me as it will take some Months from this for me to settle with all my Creditors." At that time of brewing tensions, Rogers must still have viewed this as a straightforward request; but given his still-weighty standing and recent connections in a time verging on general war, it was a highly naïve one. Washington, not without justification, found his actions consistent with those of a spy. Rogers's reluctance to declare himself made Sullivan nervous, and while he lent little credence to the rumors of Rogers's doings in Canada, he wrote Washington that "as he was once Governour of *Michilimackinack*, it is possible he may have a commission to take that command, and stir up the *Indians* against us, and only waits for an opportunity to get there."[12] Everyone was frightened of Rogers's influence over the Indians. The net of suspicion was closing in tighter, yet Rogers still sought to maintain neutrality.

Sullivan's letter did not satisfy Washington's concerns. Rogers had traveled back to Albany to pursue further land grants; there he met General Philip Schuyler, whom Washington had instructed to interrogate the increasingly ambiguous wayfarer. Schuyler wrote Washington that the Canadian story was fiction but received a note back that even so, Rogers "being much suspected of unfriendly views to this country, his conduct should be attended to with some degree of vigilance and circumspection."[13]

In January 1776 Rogers returned to New York City, his portfolio filled with letters of recommendation, land deeds, and patents, ready to press his real estate claims with the royal government in New York, somehow believing that his declared neutrality would immunize him against tensions that were now heating to fever pitch. Fearing for his own personal safety, Tryon had moved aboard the

Duchess of Gordon—no act of panic, considering that in March rebels would burn him in effigy and destroy a tavern sign with his portrait.

Nearby the floating governor's mansion other warships lay anchored. They were joined in early February by General Sir Henry Clinton aboard HMS *Mercury*, who paused for a month on his way to shell Charles Town. Even while General Charles Lee, the outspoken British soldier turned Virginia planter who had served alongside Rogers at the Battle of Carillon in 1758, beefed up the patriot fortifications and called in more troops, small boats bore New Yorkers back and forth to the British ships. One of these took Rogers to Clinton, who promised to recommend him for employment should he rally to the king. Broke and desperate for employment though he was, Rogers yet countered—shrewdly, as he likely imagined it would preserve his options—that he would "if he could get rid of the oath."[14]

Meanwhile he stubbornly kept to his campaign for land grants and actually got his first gleam of hope in months with word that some of his petitions had made their way to the royal governor's council. His last recorded letter to Whitworth on February 22 reveals that he still clung to his vision of the Northwest Passage: "I sincerely wish you might be one of the comisioners should any be sent to this cuntry to settle those disagrable Broyls. I . . . hope one day to have the happiness to persue that much wishd for tour through North america, for the Discovery of the Interior cuntry, but by no means attempt it by the way of the mississippi. Partys are sent that way to intrupt any party, that go that way."[15]

All too soon Rogers would have to register how far the land had shifted underneath his feet.

Chapter 40

Confrontation with
George Washington

Upon information that Major Rogers was travelling through the
country under suspicious circumstances I thought it necessary to have
him secured.

GENERAL GEORGE WASHINGTON TO THE PRESIDENT
OF THE CONTINENTAL CONGRESS, JUNE 27, 1776[1]

Over the early months of 1776 New York City settled in for war; new recruits poured into town, trees were felled for barricades, and the waterfront was fortified. Tory and patriot fervors swelled. Parties unknown spiked cannons in the city defenses, and rumors flew about conspiracies in which certain prominent merchants were assisting the British war effort.

In the third week of March General William Alexander, who claimed the contested title Earl of Stirling, replaced Lee as the patriot commander in New York—and proved far less friendly to citizens consorting with the British in the harbor. With impeccably bad timing Rogers requested permission from Stirling for two associates of his to row out to visit Tryon with the land grants and petitions. Charles Lee, Rogers's old comrade-in-arms, may have cut him some slack for old times' sake, but Stirling simply took this request as trading with the enemy and point-blank forbade him any further transactions, banishing him from the city.

Rogers's options now contracted. He returned to Betsy in Portsmouth, but again without prospects or money, and with rumors of his divided loyalties now legion, it was not a happy reunion. Later, in her divorce filings, Betsy would write somewhat mysteriously that "he was in a situation, which as her peace and safety forced her *then* to shun & fly from him so Decency *now* forbids her to say more upon so indelicate a Subject."[2] Was this statement simply the flashpoint of years of neglect and hollow promises? There is certainly no suggestion that Rogers ever treated her violently. Or was there something more specific? Could Betsy have seen the telltale signs of venereal disease, for instance—the unquestionable proof of infidelity? Two years later the New Hampshire legislature would grant Betsy her divorce for a variety of reasons, "but especially by *Infidelity to her Bed.*"[3] Rogers would never see her or his son, Arthur, again.

Rogers had held his cards too long. The shadow of debtors' prison and suspicions of British loyalties lay heavily on his shoulders. With few options, he traveled toward Philadelphia in June, to throw his lot in with the patriots; that failing, he would head back to London. He crossed the Hudson at New Windsor, giving New York City a wide berth, and rode along the riverbank to South Amboy.

Tensions in the colonies, meanwhile, were coming to a boiling point. That June a provincial committee had uncovered evidence of loyalist plots, including an apparent conspiracy to assassinate Washington and other patriot leaders, for which one of Washington's own guards was arrested. Other Tory machinations were discerned, mounting in intensity as New Yorkers looked with dread to the impending arrival of General Sir William Howe, whose fleet of more than 100 square-rigged warships was working its way south from Halifax. Patriots rounded up suspected spies. Mobs tarred and feathered Tory sympathizers and ran them out of town. In these fraught times great things were clearly happening, but it was hard to know just what they were; many claimed that Governor Tryon was the dark mastermind behind these shadowy menaces.

Rogers's dealings with this elusive voice of empire, although they had taken place months earlier and with the permission of Congress, drew attention upon him and fueled even more speculation about his loyalties. Rogers was too big a figure, too capable of extraordinary feats, too unsettling a character, not to fall within the deepening shadows cast wide over the eastern seaboard as it sank into convulsively vast conflict.

In South Amboy, while he was waiting for some baggage from New York and perhaps yet another loan, patriot soldiers arrested him. "Upon information that Major Rogers was travelling through the country under suspicious circumstances," Washington wrote the president of Congress on June 27, "I thought it necessary to have him secured."[4] Jefferson wrote to a friend that "the famous Major Rogers is in custody on violent suspicion of being concerned in the conspiracy."[5]

Rogers arrived under armed escort at the rebel lines before New York, where Washington interviewed him. It would not be a happy meeting for Rogers.

These two charismatic, boldly ambitious alpha males, both more than six feet tall, both well proportioned and physically commanding, each a presence to the other for nearly two decades, now stood eyeing each other. Washington was now a thunderhead, risen in a matter of months to threaten Rogers's life vision. It is not known whether they had ever previously met, but they need not have laid eyes on each other to grasp each other's essence, their formidable reputations preceding them. North America had not known two greater English-speaking heroes. The summer before, a London correspondent had commented in *The New-Hampshire Gazette* that they were "two of the bravest and most experienced Officers in the King's Service."[6]

Only a year separated them in age. No better example exists in eighteenth-century America to illustrate the importance of family standing, good luck, and the ability to win friends in high places than the contrast between the unfolding fortunes of Washington and Rogers.[7] Their lives traveled dramatically different trajectories: Rogers had earned a much-sought-after commission in the British army, which Washington never attained. But the Virginian would return to a large estate and a rich fiancée, while Rogers would end up deeply in debt to Albany moneylenders and face charges of treason trumped up by his British superiors; such suspicions were most unlikely to attach themselves to a gentleman born. Both would know debt intimately: it had sent one to debtors' prison, the other digging his way out only with the help of influential friends and still having to borrow even to go to New York to assume the presidency. Nevertheless Washington went through life on a margin that Rogers never attained.

One was Scots-Irish, rough-hewn, and of little formal education, his life forged in the rugged New England wilderness; the other was a princely magnate in tidewater Virginia, whom Andrew Johnson later referred to as an "old English gentleman." Rogers grew up on the New Hampshire frontier, the violence of the hunter and the Indian wars' survivor such birthright as he possessed, never designated a leader of men by birth, nor tempted to treat war as an extreme sport. Never would Rogers have written as did Washington that "I have heard the Bullets whistle and believe me there was something charming in the sound."[8]

The seeds of mutual distrust lay deep: the coastal elites had never accepted the ever prickly Scots-Irishman, often changing the rules and laws right under Rogers's feet. Washington was involved in a revolution largely controlled by people of his own background, who justified their assertion of leadership by producing Washington, Jefferson, Madison, and Patrick Henry; their class would have come far short of filling an urban high school auditorium. To him the nascent democratic populism that would evolve fully flowered with Andrew Jackson and rail against the self-satisfied landed class was deeply unsettling. Washington, who had a great deal to lose to the rabble of the frontier, adopted, for reasons similar to those of the British officer class, a deep disdain for the unheeled immigrant who did not dream of playing by his rules and hacked out a hard livelihood on the colonies' brutal fringes. Rogers, by contrast, embodied frontier talent and insight and was less dismissible and much more frightening than mere muscled ax-wielding oafishness; so far from being one more face in the rabble crowd, he was a man capable of weaving unconstructive frontier individualism into formidable formations, a chilly portent to the saltwater quality who thought that it monopolized higher authority and powers of government.

Rogers and Washington epitomized two separate visions of America, neither one more or less American than the other. Each intended to shape all of America. Rogers did not stand in the path of 1776 but rather pointed along a different wilderness way that stretched to the setting sun, down which a power mighty on both sides of the Atlantic could master an entire continent; his horizon was neither Tory nor colonial but imperially cosmopolitan, a transforming vision of continental discovery and development. He did not hate the silks and pretensions of the settled world but rather proposed to leave them behind.

One look at Washington told Rogers that his fate was sealed. The tired and harried commander faced the imminent arrival of Howe's overwhelming seaborne force. The conspiracies to assassinate him must have deeply distressed even a man of Washington's iron nerve. An incoherent heap of circumstantial evidence, which would have evaporated under one hard look, just as had Gage and Johnson's fantasies of treason, had built up against yesterday's hero. The general did not have a shred of evidence that Rogers was a spy, only the certainty that he remained in half-pay service of the British army. Washington had overlooked that defect in Charles Lee and elevated him to a position of authority. Rogers's lack of enthusiasm for the war, his frantic search to recover opportunity, and his meetings with Tryon and Clinton all fed suspicions, even though Rogers had carefully sought permission for these all-too-necessary doings. No canny last-minute feints or clever tactical adjustments could burst through the gauzy web of innuendo and rumor.

But as with Gage and Johnson, something deeper and more fundamental unsettled Washington about the man standing before him, something far more menacing than his spy potential or even his unique leverage with the Indians. A tumbleweed of power, Rogers had no land—in essence, no roots. Most people of Rogers's background were a little dull and subservient, if not truculently alienated. Rogers, who somehow rose above that cramping background, manifested a dynamic, transforming force that made Washington and other authorities deeply nervous. He was a crystallization of the cultures on the edge, with hints of the biblical Adullamites, the plotting malcontents lurking in a cave on the edge of things. Washington quite rightly did not trust Rogers's loyalties, as defined not by the Tory-patriot divide but rather by his commitment to a different vision of America, the west, the continent, and the peoples within it. What was Rogers capable of? Where did his final commitments lie? Rogers remained, even after stints of disgrace and humiliating ruin in debtors' prison, an independent power still potentially capable of destabilizing Washington's still-being-shaped command authority.

Rogers explained that he was traveling to Philadelphia to make a secret offer of his services to the Continental Congress, no doubt still wishing to avoid alerting the British—for his half pay and any hopes of making a fortune in India rested upon London's goodwill should he be rebuffed. Were that rejected, he desired permission to travel back to Great Britain, because he had employment in the East Indies. (This employment did not materialize a year later, after America became a garden of ashes for Rogers. Had Rogers lied to Washington, or had his patrons deceived Rogers, or had an opportunity fallen through?) Thus this brief meeting ended.

Washington sealed Rogers's fate in a clever letter to Congress on June 27, 1776. The commander-in-chief never explicitly accused Rogers of spying but packed the document with so much pointed innuendo that the otherwise-uninformed reader could not but come to something like that conclusion. While clever, Washington's letter was also somewhat bewildering, so deeply out of the general's character, leaving so many questions hanging in the air, as to serve as an odd concession to Rogers's still-formidable power. By crossing "so far out of his proper and direct route to *Philadelphia*," Rogers could only have "pretended he was destined to *Philadelphia*, on business with Congress," even though the general later admitted that Rogers carried letters which "seem[ed] calculated to recommend him to Congress." Either Washington did not know or he chose to ignore that Rogers's circuitous route had been imposed largely by the need to bypass a New York City banned to him. "The Major's reputation, and his being a half-pay officer,—have increased my jealousies about him." Washington also noted that Rogers had come to ask for a commission, but if denied it he sought passage to Great Britain, as he had employ in the Indies. Unlike a would-be Tory, the continentalist Rogers clearly recognized the legitimacy of the Continental Congress. He did not need its permission to go to London; a quick trip up to New York, and he could easily catch a ship heading across the Atlantic.

"I submit it to their consideration," Washington ended, "whether it would not be dangerous to accept an offer of his services."[9] For a man who generally spoke his mind clearly and plainly, the whole letter bespeaks serious, rather painful ambivalence. (See transcription of Washington's letter in Appendix 4.) For political reasons, he could not tell Congress what it should do with this legendary talent, presenting itself to a cause desperate for all the talent it could muster. But the general had made up his own mind, so he charged the letter with hint and innuendo. Considering all he faced, Washington's decision would not be a wrong one, although Rogers was serious about serving the rebels and would have fought hard on their behalf.

Transported to the Philadelphia barracks, he lay in jail mulling his fate, as a few blocks away the Continental Congress drafted and signed its world-altering declaration. The half-pay ranger, falsely imprisoned by the British as a French agent, now by the Americans as a British spy, undertook a cold-eyed review of his options. The Congress decided to send him to New Hampshire for trial, hardly an encouraging prospect. The months inescapably to be spent in jail, even if he were exonerated of charges, would not deliver him from his troubles, as his previous court martial had revealed. His marriage was all but over, and his creditors were still on his track. His land grants were dust, as was his ultimate goal of locating and navigating the Northwest Passage, which had he attained the Pacific coast would have made him a shaper of continental history along with the great ones. And the reputation on which he rested his pride was already badly scarred under months of criticism, inquiry, and rumor.

On the evening of July 9 Rogers escaped and melted into the countryside. Despite a £50 bounty for his capture and soldiers sent after him, Rogers circled, backtracked, and finally made his way undetected in ten days to the British army, where he was warmly received. His imprisonment, Rogers believed, had voided his parole.

A few men of the time recorded a certain dismay at Rogers's treatment. John Stark's biographer recorded that the general, soon to fight valiantly for his new country at Bennington, "was of opinion that [Rogers] would have proved a true man to his native country, had not suspicions been entertained of his designs. He was denounced as a Tory before he had avowed his principles. Washington considered him a British agent, and as such, prohibited his entering the camp."[10] Stark rarely deviated from a flinty, indeed brutal, honesty. When Stark's older brother William, who had joined the loyalist New Hampshire Volunteers, was thrown from his horse and died,

John dryly observed that it "was the best thing William ever did in his life."[11] Josiah Bartlett, a delegate to the Continental Congress from New Hampshire and signer of the declaration, simply wrote that Rogers's imprisonment came about "though no absolute proof was made of his ill designs."[12]

For the vast majority of onlookers, especially when the Revolution played out for the patriots, Rogers's flight into the British lines was all the proof needed that he had held categorically to those allegiances ever since he returned to North America in 1775.

Rogers's subsequent actions under Howe suggest he served the British with some ambivalence. But not long after he joined the redcoats, he single-handedly engineered the most significant counterintelligence coup of the entire war by unmasking the patriots' most celebrated spy. And in the greatest irony, he did it by passing himself off as another spy, the closest he ever came actually to being one.

Chapter 91

Catching Nathan Hale

Colonel Rogers having for some days, observed Captain Hale, and suspected that he was an enemy in disguise; and to convince himself, Rogers thought of trying the same method, he quickly altered his own habit, with which he Made Capt Hale a visit at his quarters, where the Colonel fell into some discourse concerning the war, intimating the trouble of his mind, in his being detained on an island, where the inhabitants sided with the Britains against the American Colonies, intimating withal, that he himself was upon the business of spying out the inclination of the people and motion of the British troops. This intrigue, not being suspected by the Capt, made him believe that he had found a good friend, and one that could be trusted with the secrecy of the business he was engaged in; and after the Colonel's drinking a health to the Congress: informs Rogers of the business and intent.

CONNECTICUT SHOPKEEPER CONSIDER TIFFANY'S
ACCOUNT OF ROGERS'S CAPTURE OF NATHAN HALE[1]

On the evening of September 16, 1776, in the small Connecticut seaside town of Norwalk, two score miles from the New York City entrenchments, a young patriot captain shrugged off his uniform. His servant, Asher Wright, handed him the plain brown suit he had chosen to pass himself off as a New York Dutch schoolteacher.

Nathan Hale's escort, Sergeant Stephen Hempstead of New London, had known him as the master of the one-room schoolhouse in his hometown before war broke out. Everybody there knew the modest and sober young Yale graduate, who boasted an athletic if slightly plump frame, just a bit over average height. Blue eyes peered from a face that already bore the scars of a gunpowder explosion, which his always short-cropped sandy hair did little to hide.

Hale bent to unclip the silver buckles from his black leather shoes: such trappings would not fit his alleged standing as an itinerant schoolteacher. (As the proprietor himself of a small school of his own, Hale was part of the solid Norwalk bougeoisie.) Donning a round, broad-brimmed hat, he asked Hempstead in his sharp, rather piercing voice what he thought. Any concerns that Hempstead had he kept to himself. Hale handed the sergeant his commission and private papers, keeping only his college diploma as proof of his career. There would be no going back.

Hale bore a general order to all armed vessels to take him anyplace he desired, and that night a privateer carried him along Long Island Sound to a point near Huntington, Long Island. There Hale would spend several days working his way over the 50 miles to Brooklyn, gathering much-needed intelligence for General Washington en route.[2]

Howe's fleet had reached New York; on August 22 it landed 15,000 regulars at Brooklyn, where the American forward position had consolidated atop the wooded heights. Howe, grudgingly aware that the patriot army was capable of offering stern and punishing resistance to a frontal assault, as it had at Bunker Hill, devised an outflanking maneuver disguised by a frontal probe and caught the Americans flat-footed; Howe's regulars killed, wounded, or captured half the American force. The redcoats took Generals Sullivan and Stirling prisoner.

Desperate to know more of Howe's intentions, Washington called upon Colonel Thomas Knowlton of the rangers for volunteers to cross Long Island Sound and assess enemy strengths, plans, and movements, as well as the disposition of the Long Islanders. No one volunteered at the first call, but the eager young captain stepped forward on the second call, desperate for action. His unit's few sallies had not encountered the enemy. Had he waited a couple of days, he might well have gotten more action than he wanted, but he was already on his way north to Norwalk by the time Knowlton took a 120-strong reconnaissance party to probe Howe's position. During the previous war the colonel had cut his teeth as a teenager under Rogers, serving at the Battle of Fort Anne. He had confirmed his reputation at

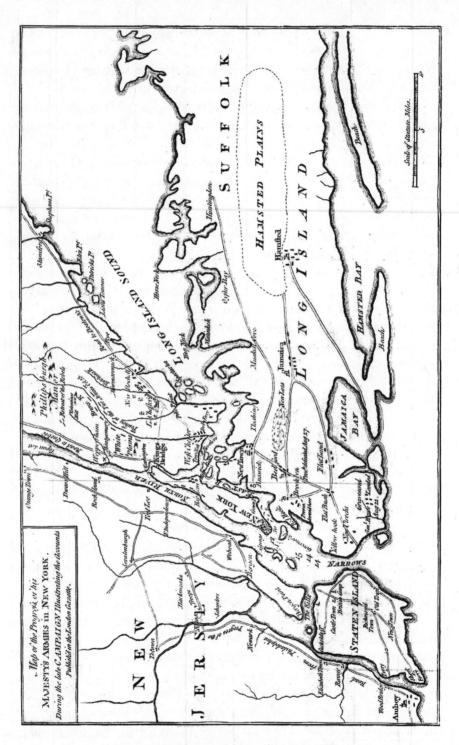

New York During the Revolutionary War

Bunker Hill a year before. Knowlton's rangers encountered a force of British light infantry three times their size south of Harlem Heights and, after a hot fight, drove them from the field. While Knowlton and some 30 other patriots lost their lives, the encounter checked Howe and lifted American spirits.

Late on the sixteenth two rebel privateers, *Schuyler* and her escort *Montgomery*, cruised over to Long Island, where Hale rowed to land.[3] Somehow Rogers got word of something suspicious, because of either the privateers' curious movements near shore or the appearance of an unfamiliar brown-suited schoolteacher. After Rogers's escape to the British, Howe had commissioned him a lieutenant colonel, tasked him with raising a battalion of provincial rangers, and given him the services of a ship to pick up recruits in New York and Connecticut. Thousands of loyalists flooded over to Long Island, fearing for their lives from patriot mobs. Among these refugees the young and strong Hale would have appeared ideal material. But something about Hale struck Rogers amiss. Somewhere in the vicinity of Huntington, he watched Hale for several days. Perhaps Hale had asked too many questions.[4]

Rogers decided to investigate Hale on the evening of September 20. He too shed his uniform for plain clothes and entered the roadside tavern where Hale was staying and now eating dinner. Taking a nearby table, he fell into conversation with his target, who was entirely unaware that he was speaking with a man he had heard about all his life, perhaps even from Knowlton himself.

Conversation grew warmer between the two, the talk centering on the war. Rogers intimated—perhaps not dishonestly—that he had a troubled mind. Hale gently pushed him for more. Rogers glanced around, then responded in a lowered voice that he was tired of being shut up on an island where the inhabitants favored the British over the Americans. Hale sucked in his breath. Rogers looked into Hale's eyes and further confided that he was spying on British troop movements and learning as much as he could about the inclination of the locals. He raised his glass, and the two men toasted the Continental Congress. Rogers had made his move: now it was the other's turn for confidences. Hale whispered to his newfound friend that he too was a spy.

Generations of historians have portrayed Hale as naïve, a judgment largely true of the manner in which he went about his business.

But even the simplest spy, desperate to serve his country, would not have revealed himself easily. Over the years at Amoskeag Falls, in Portsmouth taverns, and along deeply rutted roadsides so far from home, Rogers had interviewed, recruited, and lured hundreds, if not more, of similar young men, with the same gleam burning in their eyes, a similar intense desire to test themselves against the world. Rogers had felt that same power exercised by the larger-than-life counterfeiter Owen Sullivan, a man who could have been a serious player in the game of nations had life dealt him a more respectable hand. Rogers learned how to tap into these young men so well that they believed he had read and responded to their most intimately personal visions and ambitions. Hale was no different now in spilling the details of his mission to this worldly yet sympathetic elder.

As the evening wound down, Rogers suggested that they meet again the following night, this time at the nearby tavern where Rogers was staying, where he would introduce him to others of like mind. Hale readily agreed.

Hale's sharing of secrets gave Rogers more than enough grounds to arrest him on the spot, but something held him back. Did he want to stroke more information out of Hale? Or did his hard-bought familiarity with the court-martial system lead him to seek more witnesses? The unsettling possibility also exists that he enjoyed the game, much like a cat toying with a cornered mouse, or perhaps simply as a skilled player looking not merely to win but to win by the maximum number of points.

The next evening Hale and Rogers met again, this time joined by three or four others also posing as patriots. Again they raised their glasses to the Continental Congress; again they confided their allegiances. Emboldened by Rogers's attention, Hale again told all. At a signal from the colonel, one of the men left the room, and in moments the rapid tramp of boots sounded—and a squad of regular soldiers in bright red uniforms pushed into the tavern room and roughly seized the shaken Hale. Rogers calmly told him that he was under arrest as a spy. Equally as shocking to Hale as the deadly reversal of fortune, however, was the discovery that his supposed friend was none other than the famous partisan fighter Robert Rogers.

Armed with the evidence, Rogers may not have even bothered to go along with the regulars as they bore Hale to Howe's headquarters in Manhattan, instead sitting down with his comrades and ordering another round of drinks. According to the recently discovered account of the Connecticut Tory shopkeeper Consider Tiffany, "before [Hale] was carried far, several persons knew him and called him by name." Evidently this and Rogers's testimony left Sir William with no practical doubt as to Hale's guilt: that evening he signed an execution warrant—without the formalities of court martial—for the next morning, noting in his orderly book that Hale had made a full confession. At eleven A.M. on Sunday, September 22, on the seventh day of Hale's high-spirited venture onto Long Island, an executioner placed the noose around his neck at an artillery park near Dove Tavern, probably in the vicinity of today's 66th Street and Third Avenue.[5] Hale may or may not then have paraphrased a line from a popular play by the Whig dramatist Joseph Addison much adored by both sides, regretting that he had but one life to lose for his country. His corpse was left dangling for all to see. In the heat of war (and in an age that despised spies as less than soldiers), Hale's execution passed largely unnoticed. Captain William Bamford of the 40th Regiment notes in his journal that "Nathan Hale, a Cap't in ye Rebel Army, & a spy was taken by Maj'r Rogers & this mn'g hanged."[6]

Only decades later, as the stakes and complexities of war and espionage made themselves felt, would Hale gain national reverence as a young martyr for the patriot cause. The counterintelligence skills of the man who destroyed him would go unnoticed.

Chapter 42

End Games

A mind forever voyaging through strange seas of thought, alone.

WILLIAM WORDSWORTH, *THE PRELUDE*, 1850

On Tuesday morning, October 22, children at Mamaroneck in southern Westchester County had just settled into their desks at the schoolhouse on the Boston Post Road when the door burst open. In strode, as one child remembered years later, "a very rough looking man with red eyes," who dismissed the class and pushed the desks around to set up his headquarters. The frightened children, who could not take their eyes from this gargantuan being as they filed by him, may well have already known about Colonel Rogers.

Earlier that month, not far from where they sat, a rebel party had surprised the Tory William Lounsberry of Mamaroneck, only recently promoted by Rogers to a captain of the Queen's Rangers for his take-charge attitude and for his part in spiking 284 New York cannons with rat-tail files that spring.[1] Lounsberry had eagerly slipped back across the Sound to his old haunts with 14 men, certain that he could recruit from among the Westchester County loyalists. The promise of serving under the famous ranger fighter was a powerful incentive, even among those who proposed to wait and see how the war turned out.

Hemmed in by a large, well-armed rebel force, the intrepid Lounsberry refused to surrender and was cut down by the patriot commander. "In his Pocket Book," reported the New York Committee on Safety to Washington, "was found a Commission signed by Genl How to Major Rogers empowering him to raise a Battalion of Rangers with the Rank of Lt. Col° Command Rank."² Perhaps Washington had heard rumors of Rogers's activities, but this document confirmed the ranger's advancement and his aggressive recruiting. It deeply worried the general, especially when he discovered that the Crown offered a £10 bounty per recruit, far beyond what Congress could afford. In late September he wrote Governor Jonathan Trumbull of Connecticut about the enemy's success in recruiting and outlined his plans to deploy troops "to check and suppress, if possible, a practice so detrimental and injurious to our cause." Otherwise, he warned, "they will levy no inconsiderable Army of our own People." Washington based this on word that the enemy was now enlisting beyond the Sound, men agreeable "to serve under their banner and the particular Command of Major Rogers."³ The rebel general asked Trumbull to support his efforts to send a strong expedition against Huntington, Long Island.

Four days later Washington made an urgent request to Congress for better pay for his troops, who would otherwise not reenlist. He went so far as to imply that the enemy's dangerously competitive offers might make inroads among men who were already enlisted in the American cause. Congress should do no less but also should give the men and noncommissioned officers "a Suit of cloaths annually." Then Washington again cleverly used the specter of Rogers to drive his point home: the enemy, he wrote, "have got a Battalion under Major Rodgers nearly compleated on Long Island."⁴

The prospect of the great raider on the loose had raised more than Washington's concerns. On October 13 Trumbull wrote the general in a panic, passing along word that the "noted Maj. Rogers," who was acquainted with "every inlet and avenue into the Towns of Greenwich, Stamford & Norwalk," had plans to strike Connecticut suddenly by night "not only to take the Stores there but to Burn & destroy all before them there."⁵ To prevent a "Sudden invasion," the governor called upon some New Hampshire militiamen in the neighborhood to protect Norwalk in particular.

Eight days later Rogers and his corps of Queen's Rangers overcame scattered militia resistance and took Mamaroneck, a small town three miles north of New Rochelle, New York. Rogers's orders specified that he protect Howe's right flank as the main body moved up the East River and landed at Throg's Neck to assail Washington's position at White Plains. Rogers moved so swiftly that his force captured significant Continental Army stores of molasses, rum, and onions in the mills and houses along the Mamaroneck River, then camped on the flanks of Heathcote Hill, overlooking the town and the broad expanse of Long Island Sound beyond.

Upon hearing that Rogers lay exposed several miles from the main British army, Lord Stirling, who had been released by the British, assigned Colonel John Haslet and 600 men of his Delaware regiment, soldiers who had demonstrated their mettle during the patriots' devastating defeat at the Battle of Long Island in late August, to go after them. One hundred and fifty Maryland and Virginia soldiers, led by Major Green, would join them.

On the evening of October 22 Haslet's force, guided by local men, swept quietly in a wide loop around Mamaroneck, aware that Rogers had posted strong pickets to the north and east but had left the south only lightly guarded. Sometime that evening, with what can only be called a burst of practical intuition, Rogers ordered Captain John Eagles's company to set up a camp and outpost south of Heathcote Hill.

At about four A.M. Haslet's men stumbled on Eagles's mostly sleeping picket. Believing they had struck the main force, they awakened the rangers with cries of "Surrender, you Tory dogs!" The rangers escaped total annihilation only by themselves mimicking the Americans, some even pretending to fight one another. The darkness, plus the plain dress of the Queen's Rangers, who had not received uniforms, enabled many to escape.

Roused by the gunfire, Rogers raced out of the schoolhouse and up to the hill, where he mobilized his men. When Haslet's force, more than twice as strong, advanced on the hill, Rogers had the rangers hold their fire until the enemy had moved close, then let loose with several volleys; his voice rose above the ruckus with cries of "Fire!" and "Steady, boys, steady!" He had trained his men to reload efficiently, and the steady musket fire convinced Haslet to retire with the trophies won by his initial surprise, which included colors and many muskets.

Haslet took prisoner 28 rangers and 8 civilians, the latter evidently loyalists interested in enlisting. Twenty rangers died that evening, compared with only a handful of patriots. Haslet had given

Rogers and his outfit a bloody nose but certainly not a defeat. Rogers's much smaller force still controlled Mamaroneck. Eager to give the famous ranger a black eye and also to boost the failing patriot side, Haslet reported that "the late worthless Major; on the first Fire he skulked off in the dark,"[6] an account picked up with enthusiasm by Samuel Adams and patriot newspapers, one of which rather wishfully described the "terrible drubbing" that "utterly routed his whole corps."[7] General Howe's dispatch to London criticized the carelessness of Rogers's sentries but commended his "spirited Exertion," which "obliged them to retreat, leaving behind them some Prisoners, and several killed and wounded."[8]

Within a day or two Rogers and his rangers had raced off to Bedford, Connecticut, where they freed six or eight British naval officers and some other navy men kept prisoner there.[9] It was vintage Rogers.

In late October Howe's army pushed against Washington's position at White Plains, driving the Americans back but at great cost. On several occasions in the intervening weeks patriot Generals Sullivan, Glover, and Lee broke off their operations to take cracks at Rogers, but to no avail. As Howe moved his army to New Jersey in late November, Washington urgently needed reinforcement from General Lee's army, but his subordinate delayed the march so he could attack Rogers. Evidently Washington concurred: "Having formed an enterprize against Roger's &c I wish you may have succeeded."[10] A few days later Lee wrote to Washington with a little more brio than he felt: "I did not succeed with Rogers merely owing to the timidity or Caution of the Enemy who contracted themselves into a compact body very suddenly."[11]

Washington's bold Boxing Day attack on Trenton, which annihilated the Hessian garrison—a maneuver in the mold of Rogers himself—and his victory the following week at Princeton revived lagging patriot morale, prompting Washington to send a strong force under General William Heath toward New York in the early New Year of 1777. Its advance guard ran into Rogers's rangers, wintering as outliers of the British army at the northern end of Manhattan Island, near Fort Independence, a strongpoint taken from the rebels boasting two bastions, a moat, an abatis, a 12-pounder, and two four-pounders. The outnumbered rangers retreated into the fort, which

held a small Hessian contingent. Although Heath had no heavy artillery, the chance to corner Rogers caused him to lay siege. On
January 8 he offered terms of surrender to the 350 defenders.
Unsurprisingly Rogers refused, as did the Hessian major. *The Boston
Gazette* reported that "the infamous Major Rogers with about 1,500
tories is surrounded near King's Bridge and it is thought he must immediately fall into our hands."[12]

Snow and hard rains battered the patriot army in their huts as the
siege stretched on for a fortnight. After one particularly bad downpour Rogers, well aware that the enemy's powder was wet and
morale low, ordered a ranger sally into the enemy lines. There, according to Heath, they "surprised one of our out Guards; the
Regiment nearest the place was struck with a panic, and had quitted
their quarters, leaving their Baggage." In the two or three hours it
took the officers to gather their scattered men, the rangers had
moved on to other targets. Another ranger and Hessian unit marched
east, dislodging rebel soldiers from a small fort and a house. Heath
wrote Washington that "a diffidence & uneasiness were discovered in
even the bravest officers." That and a coming snowstorm convinced
him to withdraw northward.

News of the retreat of the vastly superior besieging force enraged
Washington: "Your Summons, as you did not attempt to fulfill your
threats, was not only Idle but farcical; and will not fail of turning the
laugh exceedingly upon us."[13]

Rogers had little time to relish the victory. Another storm cloud
blew in from London in the form of Lieutenant Colonel Alexander
Innes, recently appointed inspector general of the British provincial
forces and tasked with overhauling the army. The militia alone, he
wrote, "on their present plan will ever prove a useless, disorderly, destructive banditti."

Innes had no truck with enlisting "Negroes, Indians, Mulattoes,
Sailor and Rebel prisoners," which he considered would merely bring
about "the disgrace and ruin of the Provincial service," or with the
commissioning of commoners. The Queen's Rangers, one report observed, contained "men of mean extraction without any degree of
education sufficient to qualify them to bear His Majesty's Commission." Many "had been bred Mechanecks others had kept Public

Houses, and One or Two had even kept Bawdy Houses in the City of New York."[14] For Innes, the Queen's Rangers typified all the worst degradations of the provincial forces. Under Innes's pressure for reform, Howe removed Rogers from command and later the majority of Rogers's captains. While many of the latter complained, Rogers was strangely silent, for a man who usually responded to such adversity with a burst of energy and focus. After all, he had thrown together a battalion from slim pickings on short order and led it to inflict its share of damage.

Moments come about in life when the future suddenly crystallizes and a sense of new, unavoidable consequences comes to rest on a person's shoulders. Six months earlier the Declaration of Independence had signaled that revolution and nationhood trumped the hauntingly close imperial vision of an America stretching to the Pacific. Gone were Rogers's dreams of a Northwest Passage and continental expansion—they would have to wait for a new generation. And walking out of Howe's tent, for all the general's warm thanks and promise of future employ, Rogers could see himself as a man adrift, a refugee between two worlds.

In the next months—and years—he skittered among these unsupporting hard realities, a tragic figure unanchored and stripped of the substance of his hard-fought-for dreams. The future suddenly appeared a great deal cloudier and less certain. Howe retained Rogers's services—he still acted as an undismayed human face for increasingly difficult loyalist recruiting drives—but he appears to have started drinking heavily, and again debts mounted. A trip to London in 1779 secured endorsements that brought him a commission to raise two battalions of rangers, but the patriot army had survived the critical early years and now punished the British more often than not. Recruiting proved extremely difficult for someone whose heart did not seem in it.

Another blow came when Rogers discovered that Carver's just-published book, *Travels Through the Interior Parts of North America in Years 1766, 1767, and 1768*, gave him no credit for dreaming up and organizing Carver's trips. *Travels* became the first English account of the far west, embodying many of Rogers's own ideas. It used the word *Oregon*, which Rogers had been the first to commit to paper.

The book described Minnesota and Wisconsin for the first time and represented the first serious examination of the eastern Sioux. It would define much geographical thinking for the next generation.

The new commander of the Queen's Rangers barely lasted three months, resorting to advertising for men from his ranks who had drifted away. For many months after Rogers left, bandits from both sides or neither, ranging over the battle-scarred New York countryside, invoked the feared sobriquet of Rogers' Rangers to separate citizens from their worldly goods. But Washington never forgot Rogers's deadly capacities, writing Trumbull in April 1777 that the ranger belonged to a select few "villains, whose Crimes are of great enormity . . . Rogers is an Active instrument in the Enemy's hands, and his Conduct has peculiar claim to our notice."[15]

Rogers's Tory elder brother James wrote embarrassedly to a British general, "The conduct of my brother of late has almost unman'd me—when I was last at Quebec I wrote to him in regard to his conduct and as often he promised to reform—I am sorry his good talents should so unguarded fall a prey to Intemperance."[16]

In late 1780 Rogers was aboard a schooner sailing from Penobscot Bay to New York when it was taken by an American privateer brig. It was the first and only time he was made prisoner on active duty. He spent much of that year in the state prison at Philadelphia, his health deteriorating considerably, until he was exchanged.

He returned to London on a troop transport. Details of his last decade remain hazy, and the record remains incomplete, but many have discerned, perhaps with the eye of punitive hope, a long and sorry collapse. He endured yet another spell in prison, this time at the King's Bench, a term extended for assaulting a man, from early 1786 to 1789. He died in his apartment on Blackman Street on May 18, 1795, the day before his unlikely contemporary and quite different pioneer, James Boswell.

A handful of colorful anecdotes suggest that while Rogers's body was failing, his spirit was not. *The New-Hampshire Gazette* reprinted a report from an Irish paper in early 1785 but perhaps referring to two or three years before—often enough the lapse of time between an event and its recounting across the Atlantic. In 1782 and 1783 the

Irish Protestants seemed ready to revolt against high taxes and other grievances against the Crown. The British strengthened the Dublin garrison. Rogers may have traveled there in search of a commission or other work. He allegedly confronted five British officers at Daly's Chocolate House on Dame Street, affecting to behave that he had captured them in America, and "with his wonted complaisance, saluted them; one in a manner which would disgrace the gentleman, with an air of risible contempt, turned away his head, another smiled and some began to whistle." The major stood in silence and remained motionless for some moments.

"Do you not recollect me?" he asked, to which they said no. One accused him of stirring up trouble in Ireland.

"I see you are, one and all, the most ungrateful set of beings existing," said Rogers. Mine was "never the sword of rebellion, but the sword of liberty, and I sheathed it on the completion of it." His father had grown up in Ireland, he added, and he would see it rid of all enemies.

"Poh! Poh!" said one of the officers. "Sir, you mean to be insolent!"

"Ye young scoundrels, your insolence is as unbounded as your impudence is conspicuous—in the tented field it would be my pride to inflict on you the punishment you deserve; or, as a man, I should teach you the respect due to age, and how to treat a benefactor; and if you are gentlemen, DRAW." The "bucks slunk off," reported the paper.

Was this the hallucination of a man fantasizing that he fought for American liberty, a man unhinged? Perhaps. But as had been the case throughout his life, much about this crafty man did not meet the eye. Could he have chosen this very public display to subtly announce his interest in joining the Irish patriots? Could he even have been on a political espionage mission, setting up this act so he could ingratiate himself with the Irish leaders? He had certainly done it before with Hale. The record remains mute, but if anything is evident, it is never to count Rogers out of the game.

And finally an odd dispatch from *The Boston Gazette* reported a brief but intriguing visit that Rogers paid to America in 1785, the last he would make: "New London, Sept. 2. Tuesday last sailed, Ship *Peter Holden*, Wm. Dodds, Commander, for New-York, in whom went passenger, Col. Rogers, his Lady and suit consisting of a female bear, two dogs, a bitch, a brace of quails, and a young robin.—This redoubtable commander boasts of having, with seven others, taken three hundred rebels Cows, *Coupe de main*, and conducted them safely to New-York."

Just as in the old days on the shores of Lake Champlain, when he had bedeviled the French with one surprise after the other, this intensely private and deliberate man still managed to surprise those he encountered, much as he still does to those who look back at him from the twenty-first century.

Epilogue

Rangers Lead the Way

The qualifications indispensibly necessary to recommend a person to the chief command among [the Indians] are, that they must be fortunate, brave, and disinterested ... to which may be added that of secrecy in all his operations.

ROBERT ROGERS, *A CONCISE ACCOUNT*[1]

Every spring, some of the world's very toughest men gather in the humid and rainy scrub lowlands of southern Georgia for Fort Benning's Best Ranger Contest, an Olympian sixty-hour ordeal that requires near superhero strength, concentration, and endurance simply to finish. Two-man teams compete virtually without sleep, leaping into a lake from helicopters to drag 140-pound packages ashore, negotiating the four-story "skyscraper" on the infamous 1.5-mile Darby Queen obstacle course, and suffering through a twelve-hour night-orienteering exercise with 50-pound "ticks," the rucksacks so named because they suck the life out of those who must carry them.

A mere twenty-four hours into the competition, darkness rings the participants' sunken eyes; all healthy color has vanished from faces now set with gaunt determination, and most have adopted the stumbling shuffle of men pressed to the limit. As they drive themselves along the gauntlet, new life-sucking obstacles rise before them, to be only overcome by hard sustained reason as well as extreme exertion. The teams must perform medical and evacuation procedures on comrades under the scream of simulated shell fire, then dissemble and reassemble an M-1 rifle in minutes blindfolded.

On the second day, in the woods behind the broad green expanse of Todd Field, the pairs rotate through tests of skill. At one station grins break out even among the most exhausted as they set up behind a mark, grip a tomahawk, and eyeball the wooden target nailed to a tree trunk four or five yards away. The most natural keep their wrists stiff, positioning themselves more like dart throwers than fastball pitchers. A few with exceptional body awareness make small adjustments, moving back a half step or choking up on the handle, an acknowledgment that it takes between 12 and 14 feet for an ax to spin once fully through the air, varying according to a contestant's height and arm length, and the handle size. By the number of axes bouncing off the target, the exercise is far more difficult than it appears.

This event and much else pays tribute to Robert Rogers and his shaping influence upon what, a quarter of a millennium later, are called special operations. Ranger recruits today hear Rogers's name soon enough as it rings through their orientation booklets; they learn his rules of conduct, North America's first written and truly New World war manual; and his steely presence crowns the roster of most accomplished in the Ranger Hall of Fame on campus. Most of the veteran rangers speak fondly of the 1940 MGM film *Northwest Passage*, in which he was rather inaccurately depicted by Spencer Tracy. If the present generation of rangers know little more about his exploits than stories of single-day 50-mile snowshoe expeditions against French settler and Indian strongholds, they do innately understand a kinship when they grip the handles of their tomahawks.

It may at first be hard to understand how the tradecraft of the modern-day special operator, parachuting into the Hindu Kush after the Taliban, or a lightning strike force pushing into the dangerous Pakistani borderland, could echo the efforts of men from a preindustrial community struggling through New England winters on hickory and deergut snowshoes. But remarkably, the tone and spirit of Rogers's 250-year-old journals resonate—sometimes eerily—with the written accounts of SOG operations in Laos in the early 1970s and more recent SEAL actions in the central Asian mountains.

While much has certainly changed, the basic relationship of warriors to their technologies, environments, and enemies have not: the need to use them effectively and, in particular high-adrenaline moments, the ability to restate a problem and rework it in new, deadly effective—but above all in swift and confident—ways. The dynamics and tactics of small units aggressively penetrating hostile territory, often at night and in the teeth of extreme conditions, rely on the same critical factors for success then as now: a stress on mobility, security, surprise, and the pursuit of psychological ascendancy over an enemy. Terrain, foe, and date may change, but the basic challenges remain. The ability to cover great distances beyond the enemy's imaging and to infiltrate large tracts effectively has compelled rangers across the ages to use their command of topography as an indispensable tool. The risks are necessarily high, so rangers disproportionately incur higher mortality rates than forces on regular assignment.

The special operator must think harder and faster with less certain knowledge than the member of any other service, requiring a vast spectrum of evaluative skills from reading the environment and quickly adapting to the reactions and reinforcements of an almost always numerically superior enemy, to challenging weather conditions, and the inescapable freaks of illness, accident, and misfortune. Yet it is in the more intangible realm of raised consciousness and motivation of the extreme warrior that Rogers made his truly great and transforming changes. He stressed that the real index of a warrior was the ability to get up day after day—cold, wet, hungry, and often far worse—to march and fight again. Yet he knew as well that all that sheer endurance alone could do was to get a person killed farther away from home.

He synthesized several powerful forces—the Enlightenment's new concern with understanding as an instrument of mastery, the tenets of Native American woodcraft and skill, doctrines that united war endurance to daily life, the frontiersman's gradually unfolding focus on long hunting, and the Scots-Irish immigrants' raw democratic insistence that Jack is as good as his master—into forging an elite force, leveraging intense group identification and esprit de corps into an edged tool that would change the face of warfare. Motivation does not just soak down from the top but surges up from the bottom as well.

Watching the Best Ranger competitors, it becomes immediately clear that teams rarely quit—although nearly half often do not finish—out of a lack of will but rather from a torn hamstring, bruised heel, bad forearm fracture, or silver-dollar-sized blisters. One can concede that the superb physical training of these men is a function of youth, the legendary 61-day ranger boot camp, and ample discipline. But the self-command of these young warriors remains a mystery to the nonranger. Here lies the heart of the ranger mystique. Is it the result of a fitness regimen and training that enables a person to override the otherwise intolerable pain and cascade of nagging thoughts? Perhaps, partly. But such strategies alone would fail rangers in their pursuit of their ultimate goal: making outnumbered war in hostile environments where they must have all their wits merely to survive, let alone to destroy.

Rogers motivated not by instilling fear but by training his people to internalize a sense of never-satisfied transcendence about their skills and of pride in their brotherhood. Today the Ranger Creed holds its members to the knowledge that "as a Ranger my country expects me to move further, faster, and fight harder than any other soldier." Or the Navy SEALs mission statement holds that "I will never quit...if knocked down, I will get back up, every time." All other special forces units enforce such similar iron sentiments.

Rogers's 28 rules (which are listed in Appendix 1) exemplify the new traditions he was creating almost overnight, put forth in a brandnew American spirit, a cross between aphorism and hard-eyed Yankee practicality, which any soldier can remember and bring to mind to guide him under the nightmare stress and confusion of war. During Operation Husky, the Allied invasion of Sicily in July 1943, General George Patton urged 27 tactical adages upon his subordinate commands—borrowing liberally from Rogers in content and form. "Always fire low," reads number 7. "In case of doubt, attack," says number 22.[2] In Vietnam, Rogers's Rules printed on cards were laminated and handed to infantrymen.

But most importantly, Rogers's own physical toughness was not the defining force of his leadership, although it certainly played a part. It was the ability of this ultimate individualist to shape a group of Yankees into a unit defined by a collective mystique. Repeatedly the rangers defied all rational expectations: he taught his men to be undismayed before extraordinary odds, devilish conditions, and an enemy delighting in the most sadistic tortures. His rangers surprised and astonished, working in untested ways that even the most elite forces of the day could not come close to matching. Yet Rogers was not just trying things on to see if they worked; rather, he saw things that others did not. He trained his men rigorously, instilled in them his own self-devised corpus of rules, and taught them extraordinary practical skills. Above all, he treated them with a challengingly respectful and equal spirit, and taught them to overcome dread. Rogers's unique mark—the collective mystique—would not be fully seen again until World War II. In the woods of the New England frontier 250 years ago, a prescient man innovated and codified a particularly modern—and American—brand of warfare, one still taught today and used effectively in hostile situations the world over.

In the final analysis, the common perception of Rogers as the lone hero—a colonial Heracles—does disservice to his ultimate contributions. He is rightly seen as a man who got things done, but the means by which he did so have been little examined, yet are quite extraordinary. He believed in his men, the ultimate quality of a soldier of democracy. If they followed him, he promised that they would find within themselves the capacity to reach beyond what they ever thought themselves capable of. Certainly people of his day had learned to endure—surviving the Atlantic passage alone taught one that—but Rogers awoke in his comrades something new, a powerful sense of interior discipline and possibility. His teachings transcended the idea that greatness came only from the situation of one's birth but could be summoned up by anyone. On those remarkable scouts and sorties, Rogers was not just investing his men with courage but exploring their souls as they explored the continent.

American interest in developing skills and applying them to new problems has been such a strong theme of American warfare for so long that it is easy to take for granted and forget that it did not appear fully formed on the continent. Rogers's final rule, Number XXVIII, perhaps most clearly defined the enduring ranger modus operandi by stressing the necessity of maintaining "a firmness and presence of mind on every occasion." In the ranging service, he wrote, there are "a thousand occurrences and circumstances which may happen... every man's reason and judgment must be his guide."[3]

Twenty years later Rogers would come to believe that a continental vision of America in the end put him against his colonial brethren. But his ideas were one of the most intensely burning flames of the Revolutionary fire.

Acknowledgments

Isaac Newton's famous quote that "if I have seen a little further it is by standing on the shoulders of Giants" has certainly traversed the deeply rutted path that clichés take all too often. Yet in reflecting on the labors involved in writing a book, the great scientist's observations seems more apt than anything that I might freshly mint. What I've written would not have been possible without the scholarship and superb writing abilities of James Fenimore Cooper, Francis Parkman, and Kenneth Roberts, whose ability to bring the French and Indian War time period alive has inspired and enthralled me since I was little. Later, I would learn to balance carefully on the strong shoulders of this generation's fine batch of historians of the period, particularly David Hackett Fischer, Fred Anderson, Colin G. Calloway, Kevin M. Sweeney, and William Fowler, many of which have steered me in conversation and correspondence.

On the other side of academia lies a largely unacknowledged corps of devoted students of Robert Rogers and the French and Indian War. Though largely without formal training, these reenactors have sewed period clothing, tended to muzzle-loaders and poured their own bullet molds, refought long-finished skirmishes and battles, and marched endlessly through the woods. Their curiosity and love of the period and willingness to share their hard-earned insights into the nitty-gritty of eighteenth-century life proved invaluable. My thanks to all those reenactors who happily responded to my insistent questions, particularly George Bray, John-Eric Nelson, and Matt Wulff.

But I am perhaps most deeply indebted to a handful of amateur historians who have done the hard and important work of cutting trail that made my path possible, performing important scholarship and turning up revealing letters, journals, newspaper accounts, rosters, and a host of other documents. The work of John Cuneo, Burt Loescher, Tim Todish, Gary Zaboly, and Steve Brumwell became my constant companions over the last half-dozen years, until they seemed like old friends.

Ground zero for Rogers's activities over the war years was Fort Ticonderoga, and I have spent many days there attending French and Indian War congresses, plumbing the archives at the Thompson-Pell Research Center, walking the grounds, participating in the Grand Encampments, watching various reenactments, and generally bugging the dedicated workers there. My hat is off to the crew at Fort Ticonderoga National Historic Landmark, particularly the fort's long-time director, Nicholas Westbrook, who opened many new doors for me and was always unfailingly generous with his time and interest in arguing the finer points. My thanks also to the fort's curator, Chris Fox, a source of much valuable material and a font of period information. My thanks also to Rich Strum, Annie McCarty, and Karl Crannell, whose eagerness to help and share their knowledge have been a joy. Also, a bow to Virginia Westbrook, a terrific source of information and wisdom on all things local to the Lake Champlain area.

To the indefatigable and always cheerful Hubie Steward at the University of Maryland's Interlibrary Loan Department at McKeldin Library in College Park, Maryland, who over the years located obscure sources for me without seeming to break a sweat, I am deeply indebted. Thanks to all those who work on the third floor of the library, and to Michael Fry, maps librarian.

Of the many dozens of reference librarians, curators, and researchers who provided invaluable help, space will only permit me to mention a handful: Veronique Marier for wrestling through difficult translations and interpretations of colonial French documents; William Copeley, librarian at the New Hampshire Historical Society; Olga Tsapina, curator of American historical manuscripts at the Huntington Library; Rodrigo Brinkhaus at the Musée des Abénakis; Eileen Hannay, the manager of the Rogers Island Visitors Center; James Hutson, chief of manuscripts at the Library of Congress; Steve Brisson, chief curator at Mackinac State Historic Parks; Robert W. McRae, the property manager at St. Michael's Church in Charleston, South Carolina; David S. Stieghan, command historian at the U.S.

Army Infantry Branch and Fort Benning; and Brian Leigh Dunnigan, curator at the William L. Clements Library.

Thanks to the members of the Literary Society of Washington, D.C., and those of Mark Pachter's biography group—all of whom have been supportive of this project. Special thanks to two collectors of Rogers's materials and French and Indian War artifacts. First, Dr. Gary Milan for sharing with me some important unpublished journals and permitting me to publish parts of them. And, second, to Robert Maguire for his enthusiasm and interest in my project. His work on Rogers's Saint-François Map, featured in this book for the first time, is truly an important contribution to the history of this time period.

For numerous of my friends who have endured long hikes, week-long car journeys, and endless discussions about Rogers, my undying thanks for your patience, curiosity, and friendship: Stark Biddle, Robert Foster, Alexis Doster, Larry O'Reilly, Philip Kopper, Joe Meany, William Dean Howells, and Jim Ronda. To my friend Marc Choyt, who patiently taught me how to track and hunt elk and deer. And to other friends who have read parts or all of the manuscript, I am deeply grateful for their keen eyes and sharp insights, particularly Derek Leebaert, Sam Holt, and Tim Foote. To Tim Todish, who's the finest student of Rogers that I know, deep thanks for the many, many fine conversations, discussions, and arguments that we've had over the years. You are a true gentleman and scholar. I am particularly indebted to the polymath Timothy Dickinson, with whom I enjoyed dozens of lunches at the Zebra Room and Bangkok Bistro bouncing ideas around. His sharp eyes on the manuscript not only significantly enriched it but prevented me from making many missteps.

And, of course, my deep thanks to my crackerjack team at Bantam Dell, led by my editor, John Flicker, whose familiarity with the field and strong editorial instincts proved critical to the project. He let the project grow and evolve with great patience. His assistant, Jessica Waters, remained cheerful and attentive to detail throughout all the myriad details of publishing. Copyeditor Janet Biehl, production editor Dennis Ambrose, mapmaker Robert Bull, and designers Patrice Sheridan and Virginia Norey all worked hard on the project—with excellent results.

Thanks to my agent, Deborah Grosvenor of Kneerim & Williams, for her long-term enthusiasm and strong editorial judgment. Also, to my colleagues at *American Heritage* magazine, who patiently listened to all things Rogers and gave invaluable help from fonts to maps, particularly Edwin Grosvenor and Cindy Scudder.

And, finally, to my son, Forrister, and the Rangerettes (my wife, Diana, and daughter, Grace), the most invaluable small-unit force that anyone could ever want, who rarely complained when I asked them time and again to grab a paddle or their hiking shoes. If not for their love and patience as I worked with the words in the basement, this project would never have been completed. For one last time I resort to cliche: words cannot express the depth of gratitude and love that I have for my wife, Diana.

Appendix 1

Rogers's Rules of Ranging

I. All Rangers are to be subject to the rules and articles of war; to appear at roll-call every evening, on their own parade, equipped, each with a Firelock, sixty rounds of powder and ball, and a hatchet, at which time an officer from each company is to inspect the same, to see they are in order, so as to be ready on any emergency to march at a minute's warning; and before they are dismissed, the necessary guards are to be draughted, and scouts for the next day appointed.

II. Whenever you are ordered out to the enemies forts or frontiers for discoveries, if your number be small, march in a single file, keeping at such a distance from each other as to prevent one shot from killing two men, sending one man, or more, forward, and the like on each side, at the distance of twenty yards from the main body, if the ground you march over will admit of it, to give the signal to the officer of the approach of an enemy, and of their number, &c.

III. If you march over marshes or soft ground, change your position, and march abreast of each other to prevent the enemy from tracking you (as they would do if you marched in a single file) till you get over such ground, and then resume your former order, and march till it is quite dark before you encamp, which do, if possible, on a piece of ground that that may afford your centries the advantage of seeing or hearing the enemy some considerable distance, keeping one half of your whole party awake alternately through the night.

IV. Some time before you come to the place you would reconnoitre, make a stand, and send one or two men in whom you can confide, to look out the best ground for making your observations.

V. If you have the good fortune to take any prisoners, keep them separate, till they are examined, and in your return take a different route from that in which you went out, that you may the better discover any party in your rear, and have an opportunity, if their strength be superior to yours, to alter your course, or disperse, as circumstances may require.

VI. If you march in a large body of three or four hundred, with a design to attack the enemy, divide your party into three columns, each headed by a proper officer, and let those columns march in single files, the columns to the right and left keeping at twenty yards distance or more from that of the center, if the ground will admit, and let proper guards be kept in the front and rear, and suitable flanking parties at a due distance as before directed, with orders to halt on all eminences, to take a view of the surrounding ground, to prevent your being ambuscaded, and to notify the approach or retreat of the enemy, that proper dispositions may be made for attacking, defending, &c. And if the enemy approach in your front on level ground, form a front of your three columns or main body with the advanced guard, keeping out your flanking parties, as if you were marching under the command of trusty officers, to prevent the enemy from pressing hard on either of your wings, or surrounding you, which is the usual method of the savages, if their number will admit of it, and be careful likewise to support and strengthen your rear-guard.

VII. If you are obliged to receive the enemy's fire, fall, or squat down, till it is over; then rise and discharge at them. If their main body is equal to yours, extend yourselves occasionally; but if superior, be careful to support and strengthen your flanking parties, to make them equal to theirs, that if possible you may repulse them to their main body, in which case push upon them with the greatest resolution with equal force in each flank and in the center, observing to keep at a due distance from each other, and advance from tree to tree, with one half of the party before the other ten or twelve yards. If the enemy push upon you, let your front fire and fall down, and then let your rear advance thro' them and do the like, by which time those who before were in front will be ready to discharge again, and repeat the same alternately, as occasion shall require;

by this means you will keep up such a constant fire, that the enemy will not be able easily to break your order, or gain your ground.

VIII. If you oblige the enemy to retreat, be careful, in your pursuit of them, to keep out your flanking parties, and prevent them from gaining eminences, or rising grounds, in which case they would perhaps be able to rally and repulse you in their turn.

IX. If you are obliged to retreat, let the front of your whole party fire and fall back, till the rear hath done the same, making for the best ground you can; by this means you will oblige the enemy to pursue you, if they do it at all, in the face of a constant fire.

X. If the enemy is so superior that you are in danger of being surrounded by them, let the whole body disperse, and every one take a different road to the place of rendezvous appointed for that evening, which must every morning be altered and fixed for the evening ensuing, in order to bring the whole party, or as many of them as possible, together, after any separation that may happen in the day; but if you should happen to be actually surrounded, form yourselves into a square, or if in the woods, a circle is best, and, if possible, make a stand till the darkness of the night favours your escape.

XI. If your rear is attacked, the main body and flankers must face about to the right or left, as occasion shall require, and form themselves to oppose the enemy, as before directed; and the same method must be observed, if attacked in either of your flanks, by which means you will always make a rear of one of your flank-guards.

XII. If you determine to rally after a retreat, in order to make a fresh stand against the enemy, by all means endeavour to do it on the most rising ground you come at, which will give you greatly the advantage in point of situation, and enable you to repulse superior numbers.

XIII. In general, when pushed upon by the enemy, reserve your fire till they approach very near, which will then put them into the greatest surprize and consternation, and give you an opportunity of rushing upon them with your hatchets and cutlasses to the better advantage.

XIV. When you encamp at night, fix your centries in such a manner as not to be relieved from the main body till morning, profound secrecy and silence being often of the last importance in these cases. Each centry therefore should consist of six men, two of whom must be constantly alert, and when relieved by their fellows, it should be done without noise; and in case those on duty see or hear any thing, which alarms them, they are not to speak, but one of them is silently to retreat, and acquaint the commanding officer thereof, that proper dispositions may be made; and all occasional centries should be fixed in like manner.

XV. At the first dawn of day, awake your whole detachment; that being the time when the savages chuse to fall upon their enemies, you should by all means be in readiness to receive them.

XVI. If the enemy should be discovered by your detachments in the morning, and their numbers are superior to yours, and a victory doubtful, you should not attack them till the evening, as then they will not know your numbers, and if you are repulsed, your retreat will be favoured by the darkness of the night.

XVII. Before you leave your encampment, send out small parties to scout round it, to see if there be any appearance or track of an enemy that might have been near you during the night.

XVIII. When you stop for refreshment, chuse some spring or rivulet if you can, and dispose your party so as not to be surprised, posting proper guards and centries at a due distance, and let a small party waylay the path you came in, lest the enemy should be pursuing.

XIX. If, in your return, you have to cross rivers, avoid the usual fords as much as possible, lest the enemy should have discovered, and be there expecting you.

XX. If you have to pass by lakes, keep at some distance from the edge of the water, lest, in case of an ambuscade or an attack from the enemy, when in that situation, your retreat should be cut off.

XXI. If the enemy pursue your rear, take a circle till you come to your own tracks, and there form an ambush to receive them, and give them the first fire.

XXII. When you return from a scout, and come near our forts, avoid the usual roads, and avenues thereto, lest the enemy should have headed you, and lay in ambush to receive you, when almost exhausted with fatigues.

XXIII. When you pursue any party that has been near our forts or encampments, follow not directly in their tracks, lest they should be discovered by their rear guards, who, at such a time, would be most alert; but endeavour, by a different route, to head and meet them in some narrow pass, or lay in ambush to receive them when and where they least expect it.

XXIV. If you are to embark in canoes, battoes, or otherwise, by water, chuse the evening for the time of your embarkation, as you will then have the whole night before you, to pass undiscovered by any parties of the enemy, on hills, or other places, which command a prospect of the lake or river you are upon.

XXV. In padling or rowing, give orders that the boat or canoe next the sternmost, wait for her, and the third for the second, and the fourth for the third, and so on, to prevent separation, and that you may be ready to assist each other on any emergency.

XXVI. Appoint one man in each boat to look out for fires, on the adjacent shores, from the numbers and size of which you may form some judgment of the number that kindled them, and whether you are able to attack them or not.

XXVII. If you find the enemy encamped near the banks of a river or lake, which you imagine they will attempt to cross for their security upon being attacked, leave a detachment of your party on the opposite shore to receive them, while, with the remainder, you surprize them, having them between you and the lake or river.

XXVIII. If you cannot satisfy yourself as to the enemy's number and strength, from their fire, &c. conceal your boats at some distance, and ascertain their number by a reconnoitring party, when they embark, or march, in the morning, marking the course they steer, &c. when you may pursue, ambush, and attack them, or let them pass, as prudence shall direct you. In general, however, that you may not be discovered by the enemy upon the lakes and rivers at a great distance, it is safest to lay by, with your boats and party concealed all day, without noise or shew; and to pursue your intended route by night; and whether you go by land or water, give out parole and countersigns, in order to know one another in the dark, and likewise appoint a station every man to repair to, in case of any accident that may separate you.

Such in general are the rules to be observed in the Ranging service; there are, however, a thousand occurrences and circumstances which may happen, that will make it necessary in some measure, to depart from them, and to put other arts and stratagems in practice; and which cases every man's reason and judgment must be his guide, according to the particular situation and nature of things; and that he may do this to advantage, he should keep in mind a maxim never to be departed from by a commander, viz. to preserve a firmness and presence of mind on every occasion.

Appendix 2

Saint-François
Map of 1759

I am fortunate to publish for the first time in the United States a map of the Saint-François Raid (see insert) that was created with Robert Rogers's input. Not only does it help explain Rogers's route, but it reflects Rogers's strong geographic understanding. The topographical information is quite accurate. It is the most important piece of primary source material about Rogers in the last 50 years.

I am indebted to J. Robert Maguire for letting me publish the map from his private collection. I am including here a short piece he sent me in which he discusses the provenance of the map.

Robert Rogers's 1759 Map by J. Robert Maguire

Following his return from the attack on Saint-François, Robert Rogers informed General Amherst that, in response to the latter's request, he would soon be sending him "a Plan of all the Country I have travelled over." As promised, three months later, on March 20, 1760, he wrote from Crown Point enclosing what he described as "a Sketch of my Travels To and from Saint Francis."

Thus alerted, John Cuneo in his 1959 biography of Rogers noted that "Rogers sent a map of his route to Amherst but it cannot now be found." A few years after Cuneo's book appeared, however, the map turned up in England. It was eventually sold in October 1970 at auction by Parke-Bernet in New York. In response to an enquiry as to its whereabouts until then, the following information was provided by the original consignee, Parke-Bernet's London partner, Sotheby's:

I am afraid that I can only tell you that the map was bound in an eighteenth-century atlas with other manuscript maps relating to the wars in North America and one or two drawings of the campaigns. They came from the Worcestershire house of a direct descendant of a junior officer who served in these campaigns, and who regretfully but firmly wishes to remain anonymous.

Aside from its interest in tracing Rogers's route to and from Saint-François, the map—among the earliest topographic plans of the interior of the future state of Vermont—is notable for its accuracy. Measuring 22 by 18 inches, it bears a notation that its scale is based upon the distance "Allowd" between Montreal and Quebec (160 miles): "The other Part of it is Drew in proportion." The route followed by Rogers ("The way I came home") is clearly indicated: "The prict Line from Missisque Bay to Saint Francus [sic] is the way I March'd as also from Saint Francis to Connecticut River."

Evidence suggests the map to have been the work of Capt. James Abercrombie of the 42nd Regiment, an engineer and skilled cartographer, aide-de-camp to his uncle General James Abercromby and later to Amherst. It bears a marked similarity to another map by him of the same region and period, now in the Crown Collection in the British Library: a *Map of the Scene of Action*, dedicated to *His Excellency Major General Abercrombie*. (Apparently as a result of a misreading of the lettering on this map, it—as are other maps of his—is incorrectly attributed to an otherwise unknown "Captain *Thomas* Abercrombie.") In December 1759, Capt. James Abercrombie was summoned to England to attend the court martial of Major General Lord Charles Hay (charged with disrespectful speeches against Lord Loudoun) and therefore must have prepared the map at about this time for Rogers's use in furnishing the information requested by Amherst. Abercrombie was a friend and admirer of Rogers and accompanied the rangers on a number of occasions.

Appendix 3

The Hopkins Letter

Au Cap Francois ilsle de St. Domingue
The 9th of April 1766

My Dear Rogers,
This is the third time I've wrote you since our last meeting in
New York, and altho' our Absence has been long my Sentiments
of Friendship are and always will be the same.—

As I promised, you were remembered in my Conversations
with the Minister of the King I now Serve, I have reason to think
you would have a reasonable gracious Reception, but untill my
Affairs are entirely finished, and the promises which were made
me amply accomplished, I cannot think of persuading or enticeing
you on, untill there shall be a Certainty fixed for You, or such of
our Acquaintance as will follow my Example; you know the
injustices we have suffered particularly yourself, nor is it in the
power of England to recompense you for the disgraces you
underwent for having Served them too faithfully. Be assured my
Dear Friend of my doing and contributing every thing for your
Honour and Advantage, Seize every opportunity of ingratiating
yourself in the favor of the Indians where you are placed
Governor, by which means and your other merits, despair not in
case of a Change to be raised to the Rank that even the height of
your wishes could have expected. Mistrust all the World, have no
Confidence but in those of whom you have the greatest proofs of
their Friendship, so soon as the little difficulties I labor under are
raised, and my sort fixed, you shall know, and also the decision in
regard to yourself—A present Nous parterons des affaires
publiques—[Now let's turn to public affairs].

I am not unacquainted with the Disturbances of North
America, I foresaw the Storm when in London, that together
with the Injustice of the British Minister were my reasons for the
Steps I have taken, but my Dear Rogers although Detached from
the British interest intirely & Absolutely, believe me always
North American, and ready to render the Continent and my
Country men all the Services which may depend, or which can
be expected from me, in risqing for the Common Liberty not
only my Life and little Fortune, but also in being an Advocate for
them for any Assistance or suplys that the present Circumstances
of their Affairs may exige, there can be no Obstacle to their
being a free and independant People (preach this Doctrine in the
New England Provinces where you and your Family have so
much Interest) you have the means in your own hands, your
numbers are far Superior to any Forces that can be sent against
you—And I believe there are Powers who might think
themselves happy in being of the number of your Allies and
Friends, and of giving you the Proofs the most effectual of their
good Intentions for serving you—

Acquaint *Baube*, and all my Friends the Hurons, the
Potowatamys, the Chippowas, and Ottowas of the Change I have
made, and if you have an Interview with Pondiac take him by the
hand for me, and make known to him, I serve his Father the King
of France, the Reverende Pere Jesuite Portier pray him de me
Conserver toujours son amitie le famille de Monsr. Reaume & St.
Martin particulairment ma chere Catherine donnez moi aussi
souvent que possible de vos nouvelles & croyez moi sincerement
Votre [pray him to always keep his friendship for me and also the
family of Monsieur Reaume & St. Martin particularly my dear
Catherine also let me hear from you as frequently as possible and
believe me to be sincerely yours].

Maryland.

and write me fully without signing you name—Mr. Hopkins is
well, and you will address your Letters to me under Cover to
him. there are Continual opportunitys from New York & Phil. for
Monte O Christ or by the Missisippi to write me.

Appendix y

General Washington to
the President of Congress.

[Read July 1, 1776.]

New-York, June 27, 1776.

Sir: Upon information that Major *Rogers* was travelling through the country under suspicious circumstances, I thought it necessary to have him secured; I therefore sent after him. He was taken at *South-Amboy*, and brought up to *New-York*. Upon examination, he informed me that he came from *New-Hampshire*, the country of his usual abode, where he had left his family, and pretended he was destined to *Philadelphia*, on business with Congress.

As by his own confession, he had crossed *Hudson's River* at *New-Windsor*, and was taken so far out of his proper and direct route to *Philadelphia*, this consideration, added to the length of time he had taken to perform his journey; his being found in so suspicious a place as *Amboy*; his unnecessary stay there, on pretence of getting some baggage from *New-York* and an expectation of receiving money from a person here of bad character, and in no circumstances to furnish him out of his own stock; the Major's reputation, and his being a half-pay officer,— have increased my jealousies about him. The business which he informs me he has with Congress, is a secret offer of his services, to the end that, in case it should be rejected, he might have his way left open to an employment in the *East-Indies*, to which he is assigned; and in that case he flatters himself he will obtain leave of Congress to go to *Great Britain.*

As he had been put upon his parole by Congress, I thought it would be improper to stay his progress to *Philadelphia,* should he be in fact destined thither. I therefore send him forward, but (to prevent imposition) under the care of an officer, with letters found upon him, which, from their tenour, seem calculated to recommend him to Congress. I submit it to their consideration, whether it would not be dangerous to accept of the offer of his services.

I am, with the greatest respect and esteem, your most obedient servant,

George Washington

To the President of Congress.

Notes

Epigraph

1. *The Annual Register; or, A View of the History, Politics, and Literature for the Year 1763*, 7th ed. (London: 1796), pp. 28–29.

Introduction: The Bet

1. "London, October, 16," *Scots Magazine*, October 1775, p. 553.
2. Colin G. Calloway, *The Scratch of a Pen: 1763 and the Transformation of North America* (Oxford: Oxford University Press, 2006).
3. Michael Wigglesworth, "God's Controversy with New England" (1662), *Proceedings of the Massachusetts Historical Society* 12 (1871–73), pp. 83–84.
4. William Cronan, *Changes in the Land: Indians, Colonists, and the Ecology of New England* (New York: Hill and Wang, 1983), p. 50.

Chapter 1: Into the Wilderness

1. C. E. Potter, *The History of Manchester, Formerly Derryfield in New Hampshire; including that of Ancient Amoskeag, or the Middle Merrimack Valley* (Manchester: C. E. Potter, Publisher, 1856), p. 189; Charles E. Clark, *The Eastern Frontier: The Settlement of Northern New England, 1610–1763* (New York: Alfred A. Knopf, 1970), p. 275; and Jeremy Belknap, *The History of New-Hampshire* (New York: Arno Press, 1972), 2:118–21. For population figures for New Hampshire, see Thomas L. Purvis, *Colonial America to 1763*, Almanacs of American Life Series (New York: Facts on File, 1999), p. 128.
2. David Hackett Fischer, *Albion's Seed: Four British Folkways in America* (New York: Oxford University Press, 1989), p. 615.
3. John Greenleaf Whittier, *The Complete Writings of John Greenleaf Whittier* (New York: AMS Press, 1969), p. 251.
4. James G. Leyburn, *The Scotch-Irish: A Social History* (Chapel Hill: University of North Carolina Press, 1962), p. 241.

5. James Webb, *Born Fighting: How the Scots-Irish Shaped America* (New York: Broadway Books, 2004), pp. 89, 133.

6. Fischer, *Albion's Seed*, pp. 623–29.

7. Leyburn, *Scotch-Irish*, p. 168.

8. Fischer, *Albion's Seed*, p. 608.

9. Robert J. Rogers, *Rising Above Circumstances: The Rogers Family in Colonial America* (Bedford, Quebec: Sheltus and Picard, 1999), p. 2.

10. Fischer, *Albion's Seed*, p. 612.

11. Fred Anderson, *Crucible of War: The Seven Years' War and the Fate of Empire in British North America, 1754–1766* (New York: Knopf, 2000), p. 4.

12. Joseph S. Howe, *Historical Sketch on the Town of Methuen from Its Settlement to the Year 1876* (Methuen, Mass.: E. L. Houghton & Co., 1876), p. 17.

13. Gary Zaboly, *A True Ranger: The Life and Many Wars of Major Robert Rogers* (Garden City Park, N.Y.: Royal Block House, 2004), p. 17.

14. Henry David Thoreau, *A Week on the Concord and Merrimack Rivers* (Electronic Text Center, University of Virginia Library), p. 248.

15. Belknap, *History of New-Hampshire*, 3:74.

16. Purvis, *Colonial America*, p. 89.

17. Timothy Dwight, *Travels in New England and New York* (Cambridge, Mass.: Belknap Press, 1969), 1:21.

18. J. W. Meader, *The Merrimack River: Its Sources and its tributaries: embracing a history of manufactures, and of the towns along its course; their geography, topography, and products, with a descriptions of the magnificent natural scenery about its upper water* (Boston: B. B. Russell, 1869), p. 193.

19. Nathaniel Bouton, *The History of Concord, From Its First Grant in 1725 to the Organization of The City Government in 1853, With a History of the Ancient Penacooks* (Concord, N.H.: Benning W. Sanborn, 1856), p. 543.

20. Burt Feintuch and David H. Waters, eds., *The Encyclopedia of New England: The Culture and History of an American Region* (New Haven, Conn.: Yale University Press, 2005), p. 553.

21. Purvis, *Colonial America*, p. 7.

22. Edwin Tunis, *Frontier Living* (Cleveland and New York: World, 1961), p. 19.

23. David Freeman Hawke, *Everyday Life in Early America* (New York: Harper and Row, 1988), p. 49.

24. Thomas Williams, "Correspondence of Doctor Thomas Williams of Deerfield, Mass., a Surgeon in the Army. 1.—The Campaigns Against Crown Point in 1755 and 1756," *Historical Magazine*, 2nd ser., vol. 7, no. 4 (April 1870), p. 72.

25. Clark, *Eastern Frontier*, p. 196.

26. Tunis, *Frontier Living*, p. 17.

27. Clark, *Eastern Frontier*, p. 196.

28. Feintuch and Waters, *Encyclopedia*, p. 424.

29. Tunis, *Frontier Living*, p. 22.

30. Hawke, *Everyday Life*, p. 54.

31. Tunis, *Frontier Living*, p. 23.

32. Howe, *Historical Sketch*, p. 20.
33. Hawke, *Everyday Life*, p. 37.
34. John Josselyn, *New-England's Rarities Discovered* (Boston: Massachusetts Historical Society, 1972), pp. 311–12.
35. David M. Ludlum, *Early American Winters, 1604–1820* (Boston: American Meteorological Society, 1966), p. 49.
36. Ibid., pp. 49, 51, 78.
37. Ibid., p. 51.
38. Paul S. Boyer and Stephen Nissenbaum, eds., *The Salem Witchcraft Papers* (New York: Da Capo Press, 1977), p. 760.
39. Bouton, *History of Concord*, p. 526.
40. Robert Rogers, *A Concise Account of North America: containing a description of the several British colonies on that continent...* (London, 1765), p. 258.

Chapter 2: First Encounters on the Frontier

1. William C. Sturtevant, ed., *Handbook of North American Indians* (Washington, D.C.: Smithsonian Institution, 1978–2004), 15:159.
2. Nathaniel Bouton, *The History of Concord, From Its First Grant in 1725 to the Organization of The City Government in 1853, With a History of the Ancient Penacooks* (Concord, N.H.: Benning W. Sanborn, 1856), p. 579.
3. Henry Grace, *The History of the Life and Sufferings of Henry Grace of Basingstoke, in the County of Southampton* (Reading: Printed for the author, 1764), p. 12.
4. John Josselyn, *New-England's Rarities Discovered* (Boston: Massachusetts Historical Society, 1972), p. 14.
5. Bouton, *History of Concord*, p. 18.
6. Robert Rogers, *A Concise Account of North America: containing a description of the several British colonies on that continent...* (London, 1765), p. 212.
7. Ibid., p. 231.
8. Father Joseph-François Lafitau, *Customs of the American Indian Compared with the Customs of Primitive Times* (Toronto: Champlain Society, 1974), 2:138; and B. A. Botkin, *A Treasury of American Folklore: Stories, Ballads, and Traditions of the People* (New York: Crown, 1944), pp. 345–46.
9. Jeremy Belknap, *The History of New-Hampshire* (New York: Arno Press, 1972), 3:33, 35.
10. Andrew Gallup and Donald F. Shoffer, *La Marine: The French Colonial Soldier in Canada, 1745–1761* (Bowie, Md.: Heritage Books, 1992), p. 146.
11. Rogers, *Concise Account*, p. 246.
12. Ibid., p. 247.
13. Josselyn, *New-England's Rarities*, p. 39.
14. William Smith, *Expedition Against the Ohio Indians* (Ann Arbor, Mich.: University Microfilms, 1966), pp. 38–39.
15. Rogers, *Concise Account*, p. 209.

16. See the definition of *imagination* in the Oxford English Dictionary.
17. Lafitau, *Customs*, 2:135.
18. Theodore S. Van Dyke, *The Still-Hunter* (Norwood, Mass.: Norwood Press, 1912), pp. 24–25.
19. Lafitau, *Customs*, 2:138.
20. Smith, *Expedition*, p. 38.
21. Lafitau, *Customs*, 2:140.
22. J. W. Meader, *The Merrimack River: Its Sources and its tributaries: embracing a history of manufactures, and of the towns along its course; their geography, topography, and products, with a descriptions of the magnificent natural scenery about its upper water* (Boston: B. B. Russell, 1869), pp. 191–93.
23. On fishing at Amoskeag Falls, see William Little, *The History of Weare, New Hampshire, 1735–1888* (Lowell, Mass.: S.W. Huse & Co., 1888), p. 96.
24. *NHG*, May 23, 1760.
25. Meader, *Merrimack River*, p. 191.
26. Alfred E. Kayworth and Raymond G. Potvin, *The Scalp Hunters: Abenaki Ambush at Lovewell Pond, 1725* (Boston: Branden Books, 2002), p. 28.
27. Caleb Stark, *History of the Town of Dunbarton, Merrimack County, New-Hampshire, from the Grant By Mason's Assigns, in 1751, To the Year 1860* (Concord, N.H.: G. Parker Lyon, 1860), p. 142.
28. Charles E. Clark, *The Eastern Frontier: The Settlement of Northern New England, 1610–1763* (New York: Alfred A. Knopf, 1970), p. 260.
29. Botkin, *Treasury of American Folklore*, p. 3.
30. John Greenleaf Whittier, *The Complete Writings of John Greenleaf Whittier* (New York: AMS Press, 1969), 6:253.
31. Stark, *History of Dunbarton*, p. 142.

Chapter 3: Savage Justice

1. Reuben Gold Thwaites, ed., *The Jesuit Relations and Allied Documents: Travels and Explorations of the Jesuit Missionaries in New France, 1610–1791* (Cleveland, Ohio: Burrows Brothers, 1896–1901).
2. Maps of Concord (Rumford), 1892, 1928, NHHS; also NHHS manuscript no. 67993, Grace P. Amsden, "A Capital for New Hampshire," c. 1950.
3. Nathaniel Bouton, *The History of Concord, From Its First Grant in 1725 to the Organization of The City Government in 1853, With a History of the Ancient Penacooks* (Concord, N.H.: Benning W. Sanborn, 1856).
4. Gavin Cochrane Papers, Box 1, *FTA*.
5. Bouton, *History of Concord*, pp. 556–57.
6. Ibid., p. 562.
7. John Grenier, *The First Way of War: American War Making on the Frontier, 1607–1814* (New York: Cambridge University Press, 2005), p. 61.
8. *DRCHSNY*, 10:34.

9. Robert Rogers, *A Concise Account of North America: containing a description of the several British colonies on that continent*... (London, 1765), p. 228.

10. William Smith, *Expedition Against the Ohio Indians* (Ann Arbor, Mich.: University Microfilms, 1966), p. 39.

11. *BEP*, April 28, 1746, p. 3.

12. Francis Parkman, *A Half Century of Conflict* (New York: AMS Press, 1969), vol. 2, chap. 23.

13. Samuel Gardner Drake, *A particular history of the five years French and Indian war in New England and parts adjacent, from its declaration by the King of France, March 15, 1744, to the treaty with the eastern Indians, Oct. 16, 1749, sometimes called Governor Shirley's war. With a memoir of Major-General Shirley, accompanied by his portrait and other engravings* (Albany, N.Y.: J. Munsell, 1870), p. 98.

14. Timothy Walker, journal entry, June 12, 1746, in *Rev. Timothy Walker: The First and Only Minister of Concord, N.H., From his ordination November 18, 1730 to September 1, 1782.* ed. and ann. by Joseph B. Walker (Concord, N.H.: Ira C. Evans, printer, 1889), p. 133.

15. Bouton, *History of Concord*, pp. 54, 558.

16. "A Muster-Roll of the Company scouting under the command of Capt. Daniel Ladd, at Canterbury, &c.," in C. E. Potter, *The Military History of the State of New-Hampshire, from Its Settlement, in 1623, to the Rebellion, in 1861* (Concord, N.H.: McFarland and Jenks, 1866), pp. 94–95.

17. Britain and the colonies were still loyal to the Julian calendar, while in Canada it was already August 21 by Pope Gregory's reckoning, which the whole world now adopts.

18. Bouton, *History of Concord*, p. 157.

19. Ibid., p. 159.

20. Abner Clough, journal entries, July 14–September 28, 1746, in *Abner Clough's Journal, containing an account of the march of Capt. Daniel Ladd and his Men, who were sent by the Governor and Council of New Hampshire, to protect the inhabitants of Rumford, and the adjacent Town, against the incursion of the Indians. Copied from the original in the Secretary's office.* Collections of the New-Hampshire Historical Society (Concord: Marsh, Capen and Lyon, 1834), 4:201–14.

21. Bouton, *History of Concord*, p. 163; Benjamin L. Mirick, *The History of Haverhill, Massachusetts* (Haverhill: A. W. Thayer, 1832), pp. 78–84; and Samuel Penhallow, *The History of the Wars of New England with the Eastern Indians, or a Narrative of their Continued Perfidy and Cruelty, From the 10th of August 1703, To the Peace Reviewed 13th July, 1713* (New York: Kraus Reprint Co., 1969), p. 23.

22. For Ladd's muster roll, see Potter, *Military History*, pp. 94–95.

23. John Smith, *The General History of Virginia, New England, and the Summer Isles* (Chapel Hill: University of North Carolina, 2006), p. 152.

24. Ibid., p. 32.

25. *Proceedings and Acts of the General Assembly, January 1637/8–September 1665*, 1:228, Archives of Maryland Online.
26. Robert Rogers, *The Annotated and Illustrated Journals of Major Robert Rogers*, ed. Timothy Todish (Fleischmanns, N.Y.: Purple Mountain Press, 2002), p. 16.
27. Benjamin Church, *Diary of King Philips' War, 1675–76* (Chester, Conn.: Pequot Press, 1975), p. 247.
28. Penhallow, *History of the Wars*, p. 29.
29. John Ferling, *A Wilderness of Miseries: War and Warriors in Early America* (Westport, Conn.: Greenwood Press, 1980), p. 43.
30. *BEP*, August 10, 1747, p. 4.
31. John Grenier, *The First Way of War: American War Making on the Frontier, 1607–1814* (New York: Cambridge University Press, 2005), p. 65.
32. Father Joseph-François Lafitau, *Customs of the American Indian Compared with the Customs of Primitive Times* (Toronto: Champlain Society, 1974), 2:112.
33. *DRCHSNY*, 10:153.
34. Caleb Stark, *History of the Town of Dunbarton, Merrimack County, New-Hampshire, from the Grant By Mason's Assigns, in 1751, To the Year 1860* (Concord, N.H.: G. Parker Lyon, 1860), p. 214.

Chapter 4: Taken by Indians

1. Robert Rogers, *A Concise Account of North America: containing a description of the several British colonies on that continent…* (London, 1765), p. 233.
2. Amos Eastman and John Stark, deposition, in Nathaniel Bouton, ed. *Provincial Papers. Documents and Records Relating to the Province of New-Hampshire, from the Earliest Period of its Settlement: 1623–1686.* (Authority of the Legislature of New Hampshire, 1867–73), 6:305.
3. Thomas L. Purvis, *Colonial America to 1763*, Almanacs of American Life Series (New York: Facts on File, 1999), p. 95.
4. Ibid., p. 94.
5. Robert Rogers, *The Annotated and Illustrated Journals of Major Robert Rogers*, ed. Timothy Todish (Fleischmanns, N.Y.: Purple Mountain Press, 2002), p. 27.
6. For Stark's physical description, see his entry in *DAB*.
7. Edwin Tunis, *Frontier Living* (Cleveland and New York: World, 1961), p. 113.
8. Caleb Stark, *Memoir and official correspondence of Gen. John Stark: with notices of several other officers of the Revolution: also, a biography of Capt. Phinehas Stevens and of Col. Robert Rogers, with an account of his services in America during the "Seven Years' War"* (Concord, N.H.: G. P. Lyon, 1860), pp. 11–15.
9. Gordon M. Day, "Identity of the St. Francis Indians," in *In Search of New England's Native Past: Selected Essays* by Gordon M. Day. Michael K. Foster

and William Cowan, eds. (Amherst: University of Massachusetts Press, 1998), p. 268.

10. Henry Grace, *The History of the Life and Sufferings of Henry Grace of Basingstoke, in the County of Southampton* (Reading: Printed for the author, 1764), p. 12.

11. Thomas Brown, "A plain narrativ of the uncommon sufferings and remarkable deliverance of Thomas Brown, of Charleston, in New-England," *Magazine of History*, Extra, no. 4 (1908), p. 216.

12. Pierre de Charlevoix, *Journal of a Voyage to North America*, March of America Facsimile Series, no. 36 (Ann Arbor, Mich.: University Microfilms, 1966), 1:369–70.

13. C. E. Potter, *The Military History of the State of New-Hampshire, from Its Settlement, in 1623, to the Rebellion, in 1861* (Concord, N.H.: McFarland and Jenks, 1866), p. 278.

14. Charlevoix, *Journal*, 1:370.

15. Father Joseph-François Lafitau, *Customs of the American Indian Compared with the Customs of Primitive Times* (Toronto: Champlain Society, 1974), 2:157.

16. Rogers, *Concise Account*, p. 213.

17. Ibid., pp. 212–13.

18. Mark Warhus, *Another America: Native American Maps and the History of Our Land* (New York: St. Martin's Press, 1997), p. 146.

19. Rogers, *Concise Account*, pp. 235–36.

20. James Axtell, *The European and the Indian: Essays in the Ethnohistory of Colonial North America* (New York: Oxford University Press, 1982), p. 187.

21. James Smith, *Scoouwa: James Smith's Indian Captivity Narrative* (Columbus: Ohio Historical Society, 1978), pp. 21–25.

22. Rogers, *Concise Account*, p. 157.

23. Ibid., p. 26.

24. Captain Phineas Stevens, journal entry, June 27, 1752, in Newton D. Mereness, *Travels in the American Colonies* (New York: MacMillan, 1916), p. 311.

25. See www.vieux.montrea.qc.ca.

26. Phineas Stevens, "A Short Description of the City of Montreal in Canada," in Calloway, *North Country Captives*, pp. 43–44.

27. Peter Kalm, *Peter Kalm's Travels in North America; the America of 1750; the English version of 1770*, rev. and ed. Adolph B. Benson (New York: Dover, 1964), 2:403, 409.

28. Louis Franquet, *Voyages et Mémoires sur Le Canada par Franquet* (Quebec: Imprimérie Générale A. Coté et Cie, 1889), p. 5.

29. W. J. Eccles, "The Fur Trade and Eighteenth-Century Imperialism," *William and Mary Quarterly*, 3rd ser., vol. 40, no. 3 (July 1983), p. 346.

30. Ibid., pp. 355–56.

31. Louis Franquet, *Voyages et Mémoires sur Le Canada par Franquet* (Quebec: Imprimérie Générale A. Coté et Cie, 1889), pp. 69–74; in *FTA*, no. 2001.0036.

32. Captain Phineas Stevens, journal entry, July 4, 1752, in Newton D. Mereness, *Travels in the American Colonies* (New York: MacMillan, 1916), p. 311.
33. Atecouando entry, *DCB*.
34. Colin G. Calloway, *The Western Abenakis of Vermont, 1600–1800: War, Migration, and the Survival of an Indian People* (Norman and London: University of Oklahoma Press, 1990), p. 162.
35. *DRCHSNY*, 10:254.
36. Phineas Stevens, journal entry, in Calloway, *North Country Captives*, p. 38.

Chapter 5: The Counterfeiter

1. Caleb Stark, *History of the Town of Dunbarton, Merrimack County, New-Hampshire, from the Grant By Mason's Assigns, in 1751, To the Year 1860* (Concord, N.H.: G. Parker Lyon, 1860), pp. 12–13; and John B. Mills, "History of Dunbarton, N.H.," *Snowflake* (1883), p. 30.
2. *BG*, August 7, 1749.
3. James A. Cox, "Bilboes, Brands, and Branks: Colonial Crimes and Punishments," *Colonial Williamsburg Journal* (Spring 2003).
4. On Sullivan's previous experiences, see Kenneth Scott, *Counterfeiting in Colonial America* (New York: Oxford University Press, 1957), chap. 10; CG, March and April 1765; Owen Sullivan, *A Short account of the life of John ******, alias Owen Syllavan* (Leominister, Mass.: Adams & Wilder, 1802), pp. 1–12; and Kenneth Scott, "Counterfeiting in Colonial New Hampshire," *Historical New Hampshire* 13 (December 1957), pp. 3–38.
5. For the Sullivan and Rogers scene, see Elwin Page, "Notes Concerning Robert Rogers in New Hampshire Courts," typewritten ms., NHHS, no. 68036.
6. Thomas L. Purvis, *Colonial America to 1763*, Almanacs of American Life Series (New York: Facts on File, 1999), p. 117.
7. Charles E. Clark, *The Eastern Frontier: The Settlement of Northern New England, 1610–1763* (New York: Alfred A. Knopf, 1970), p. 239.
8. Scott, *Counterfeiting*, p. 10.
9. Sullivan, *Short account*, p. 12.

Chapter 6: The War Begins

1. Montreuil to Vaudreuil, June 12, 1756, cited in Francis Parkman, *Montcalm and Wolfe* (New York: AMS Press, 1969), p. 389.
2. For weather conditions, I have relied on Virginia Westbrook, correspondence with author. For a good description of bateaux, see Joseph F. Meany Jr., "Bateaux and 'Battoe Men': An American Colonial Response to the Problem of Logistics in Mountain Warfare," New York State Military Museum, online at www.dmna.state.ny.us/historic/articles/bateau.htm; and Robert Malcomson,

"Batteaux: Uniquely Canadian Crafts," *Beaver* 85, no. 4 (August–September 2005), pp. 40–44.

3. Robert Rogers, *The Annotated and Illustrated Journals of Major Robert Rogers*, ed. Timothy Todish (Fleischmanns, N.Y.: Purple Mountain Press, 2002), p. 82; and Godlsbrow Banyar to Johnson, September 21, 1755, in *The Sir William Johnson Papers* (Albany: State University of New York, 1921–65), 2:65.

4. Theodore Corbett, *A Clash of Cultures on the Warpath of Nations: The Colonial Wars in the Hudson-Champlain Valley* (Fleischmanns, N.Y.: Purple Mountain Press, 2002), p. 241.

5. Letter from a Gunner to his Cousin, *DRCHSNY*, 10:1005.

6. *NYM*, October 6, 1755, p. 2.

7. Ian K. Steele, *Betrayals: Fort William Henry and the "Massacre"* (Oxford: Oxford University Press, 1990), p. 8.

8. Corbett, *Clash of Cultures*, p. 230.

9. Theyanoguin entry, *DCB*, which also lists the images of the Indian chief that reveal his facial scarring.

10. Corbett, *Clash of Cultures*, pp. 232–33, 236.

11. The layout of the camp is well illustrated in Samuel Blodget, *A Prospect View of the Battle fought near Lake George on the 8th of Sept. 1755* (Boston, 1756).

12. Ibid., p. 2.

13. For a good account of the battle, see *BG*, September 29, 1755.

14. Letter from a Gunner to his Cousin, *DRCHSNY*, 10:1005.

15. Thomas Williams to his wife, September 11, 1755, *The Historical Magazine* 2nd ser., vol. 7, no. 4 (April 1870), p. 212.

16. Baron de Dieskau to Count d'Argenson, July 14, 1755, *DRCHSNY*, 10:317.

17. Corbett, *Clash of Cultures*, p. 240.

18. Williams to his wife, September 11, 1755, *The Historical Magazine*, p. 213.

19. *DRCHSNY*, 10:1012.

20. Edna V. Moffett, "The Diary of a Private on the First Expedition to Crown Point," *New England Quarterly* 5, no. 3 (July 1932), p. 609, n19.

21. Marshal Saxe and Baron de Dieskau, dialogue, *DRCHSNY*, 10:344.

22. Anne MacVicar Grant, *Memoirs of an American Lady; With Sketches of Manners and Scenes in America, as they Existed Previous to the Revolution* (New York: Appleton, 1846), p. 172.

23. Williams to his wife, June 6, 1755, *The Historical Magazine*, p. 210.

24. James Smith, *Scoouwa: James Smith's Indian Captivity Narrative* (Columbus: Ohio Historical Society, 1978), p. 170.

Chapter 7: First Sorties

1. Captain Louis-Antoine de Bougainville, journal entry for July 14–24, 1758, in *Adventures in the Wilderness: The American Journals of Louis Antoine de Bougainville, 1756–1760*, ed. and trans. Edward P. Hamilton (Norman: University of Oklahoma Press, 1964), p. 246.
2. Russell P. Bellico, *Chronicles of Lake George: Journeys in War and Peace* (Fleischmanns, N.Y.: Purple Mountain Press, 1995), p. 10.
3. Peter Kalm in ibid., p. 26.
4. For a good description of Crown Point, see Peter Kalm, *Peter Kalm's Travels in North America; the America of 1750; the English version of 1770*, rev. from the original Swedish and edited by Adolph B. Benson (New York: Dover, 1964), 2:391–92.
5. Robert Rogers, *The Annotated and Illustrated Journals of Major Robert Rogers*, ed. Timothy Todish (Fleischmanns, N.Y.: Purple Mountain Press, 2002), p. 34.
6. James Fenimore Cooper, *The Last of the Mohicans* (New York: Dover, 2003), p. 35.
7. Edna V. Moffett, "The Diary of a Private on the First Expedition to Crown Point," *New England Quarterly* 5, no. 3 (July 1932), p. 610.
8. Vaudreuil to Lotbinière, September 20, 1755, cited in Nicholas Westbrook, "Building Carillon," unpublished ms., pp. 3–4.
9. Seth Pomeroy, journal entry for October 1, 1755, in *The Journals and Papers of Seth Pomeroy*, ed. Louis Effingham DeForest (Society of Colonial Wars in the State of New York, 1926), p. 121.
10. William Johnson to William Shirley, October 10, 1755, in *The Sir William Johnson Papers* (Albany: State University of New York, 1921–65), 2:169.
11. *NYM*, October 20, 1755, p. 3.
12. Johnson to Hopkins, November 1, 1755, *Johnson Papers*, 2:262.
13. Wraxall to Johnson, October 3, 1755, ibid., 2:134.
14. Goldsbrow Banyar to William Johnson, October 27 (misdated, should be October 7), 1755, ibid., 2:242.
15. Johnson to Hardy, October 13, 1755, ibid., 2:190.
16. *BG*, November 3, 1755.
17. Examination of a French Deserter, October 16, 1755, *Johnson Papers*, 2:201.
18. *BG*, November 24, 1755, p. 2.
19. David Humphreys, *An Essay on the Life of the Honorable Major-General Israel Putnam* (Brattleboro: William Fessenden, 1812), pp. 27–28.
20. *BG*, November 24, 1755, p. 2.
21. *NYM*, November 17, 1755, p. 2.
22. Banyar to Johnson, November 11, 1755, *Johnson Papers*, 2:287.

Chapter 8: Honing Skills

1. Edward P. Hamilton, ed. and trans., *Adventures in the Wilderness: The American Journals of Louis Antoine de Bougainville, 1756–1760* (Norman: University of Oklahoma Press, 1964), p. 242.
2. Matt Wulff, reenactor and owner of period ice skates, correspondence with the author.
3. Gary Zaboly, *American Colonial Ranger: The Northern Colonies, 1724–64* (Oxford: Osprey, 2004), p. 32.
4. *BG*, February 9, 1756, p. 4.
5. M. Duchat, journal entry for July 15, 1756, cited in Francis Parkman, *Montcalm and Wolfe* (New York: AMS Press, 1969), 1:392.
6. *BG*, February 9, 1756, p. 4.
7. Captain Rogers's Report, Fort William Henry, January 29, 1756, in E. B. O'Callaghan, *The Documentary History of the State of New-York* (Albany: Charles Van Benthuysen, 1851), 4:184.
8. Thomas Williams to his wife, June 6, 1755, *Historical Magazine*, 2nd ser., vol. 7, no. 4 (April 1870), p. 210; Williams to his wife, August 23, 1755, ibid., p. 211.
9. William Buchan, *Domestic Medicine; or, A Treatise on the Prevention and Cure of Diseases* (1769), chapter "Of Surgery."
10. L. F. Newman, "Some Notes on Folk Medicine in Eastern Counties," *Folklore* 56, no. 4 (December 1945), p. 349.
11. Speculation about ranger singing is based on George Bray, reenactor, correspondence with the author, November 2, 2006.
12. *Harper's New Monthly Magazine* 12, no. 71 (April 1856), p. 579.
13. Seth Pomeroy, journal entry for October 8, 1755, in *The Journals and Papers of Seth Pomeroy*, ed. Louis Effingham DeForest (Society of Colonial Wars in the State of New York, 1926), p. 123.

Chapter 9: An Independent Company of Rangers

1. *BG*, February 14, 1757, p. 2.
2. *BEP*, March 29, 1756, p. 1.
3. Ibid.
4. Justin Winsor, ed., *Memorial History of Boston, including Suffolk County, Massachusetts, 1630–1880* (Boston: James R. Osgood & Co., 1882), 2:444.
5. Ibid., 2:xiv.
6. Ibid., 2:439.
7. Mary Caroline Crawford, *St. Botolph's Town: An Account of Old Boston in Colonial Days* (Boston: L. C. Page & Co., 1908), chap. 13.
8. The description of Province House is drawn from Samuel Adams Drake, *Old Landmarks and Historic Personages of Boston* (Boston: James R. Osgood & Co., 1875), pp. 235–36.

9. John Adams's diary is quoted in Winsor, *Memorial History*, 2:452, n1.
10. Robert Rogers, *The Annotated and Illustrated Journals of Major Robert Rogers*, ed. Timothy Todish and Gary Zaboly (Fleischmanns, N.Y.: Purple Mountain Press, 2002), p. 44.
11. Joseph F. Meany Jr., "Bateaux and 'Battoe Men': An American Colonial Response to the Problem of Logistics in Mountain Warfare," New York State Military Museum, online at www.dmna.state.ny.us/historic/articles/bateau.htm; and William Shirley to John Bradstreet, March 14, 1756, in *Correspondence of William Shirley, Governor of Massachusetts and Military Commander of America, 1731–1760*, ed. Charles Henry Lincoln (New York: Macmillan, 1912), 2:419.
12. Rogers, *Journals*, p. 44.
13. *BG*, April 26, 1756, p. 3.
14. Rogers, *Journals*, p. 46.
15. *BWNL*, July 29, 1756, p. 1.
16. For Rogers's route see *TGM* [London] 29 (May 1759), pp. 203–4, provided by Nicholas Westbrook; see also USGS New York quadrangle maps for Silver Bay, Whitehall, Putnam.
17. U.S. Naval Observatory, Astronomical Applications Department, Sun and Moon Data.
18. Thomas Williams to his wife, July 16, 1756, *The Historical Magazine*, 2nd ser., vol. 7, no. 4 (April 1870), p. 210; *BG*, July 26, 1756, p. 2.
19. Edward P. Hamilton, ed. and trans., *Adventures in the Wilderness: The American Journals of Louis Antoine de Bougainville, 1756–1760* (Norman: University of Oklahoma Press, 1964), pp. 46–47.
20. Montcalm to d'Argenson, July 20, 1756, *DRCHSNY*, 10:433.

Chapter 10: Ambush in the Snow

1. Thomas Brown, "A plain narrativ of the uncommon sufferings and remarkable deliverance of Thomas Brown, of Charleston, in New-England," *Magazine of History*, Extra, no. 4 (1908), p. 210.
2. *BFTM* 6, no. 4 (July 1742), p. 132.
3. On Lusignan, see his entry in *DCB*; also Peter Kalm, *Peter Kalm's Travels in North America; the America of 1750; the English version of 1770*, rev. from the original Swedish and edited by Adolph B. Benson (New York: Dover, 1964), 2:469.
4. David Curtis Skaggs, *The Sixty Years' War for the Great Lakes, 1754–1814* (East Lansing: Michigan State University Press, 2001), pp. 4–5, 81.
5. James Smith, *Scoouwa: James Smith's Indian Captivity Narrative* (Columbus: Ohio Historical Society, 1978), p. 91.
6. John Keegan, *Fields of Battle: The War for North America* (New York: Alfred A. Knopf, 1996), pp. 97–98.
7. Bougainville, journal entry for January 18, 1757, in *Adventures in the*

Wilderness: The American Journals of Louis Antoine de Bougainville, 1756–1760, ed. and trans. Edward P. Hamilton (Norman: University of Oklahoma Press, 1964), p. 79.

8. Smith, *Scoouwa*, p. 81.
9. *NYM*, February 7, 1757, p. 2.
10. Montcalm to Count d'Argenson, April 24, 1757, *DRCHSNY*, 10:548; "Account of Two Expeditions to Canada, in the course of the winter of 1757," *DRCHSNY*, 10:569–70.
11. *BNL*, February 10, 1757, p. 3.
12. Bernd Horn, "Hollow Death," *Canadian Military History* 14, no. 4 (Autumn 2005), p. 14.
13. Thomas Brown, "A plain narrativ of the uncommon sufferings and remarkable deliverance of Thomas Brown, of Charleston, in New-England," *Magazine of History*, Extra, no. 4 (1908), pp. 209–21.
14. *NYM*, February 7, 1757, p. 2.

Chapter 11: Tragedy at Fort William Henry

1. Loudoun to Cumberland, November 22, 1756, quoted in *Military Affairs in North America, 1740–1765: Selected Documents from the Cumberland Papers in Windsor Castle*, ed. Stanley Pargellis (New York: D. Appleton–Century, 1936), p. 269.
2. "Letter from a Correspondent at New-York," August 26, 1757, in *TGM*, October 1757, p. 442.
3. Mary Y. Mazzotta, "Nutrition and Wound Healing," *Journal of the American Podiatric Medical Association* (September 1994), p. 456.
4. Quoted in Isabel M. Calder, *Colonial Captivities, Marches and Journeys* (Port Washington, N.Y.: Kennikat Press, 1967), pp. 197–98.
5. Loudoun to Henry Fox, October 3, 1756, cited in John Grenier, "The Other American Way of War: Unlimited and Irregular Warfare in the Colonial Military Tradition," Ph.D. diss., University of Colorado at Boulder, 1999, p. 206.
6. "Journal of the Expedition Against Fort William Henry," *DRCHSNY*, 10:599; *Scots Magazine*, August 1757, p. 425; *Scots Magazine*, October 1757, p. 542.
7. Father Pierre Roubaud, letter, October 21, 1757, quoted in *The Jesuit Relations and Allied Documents: Travels and Explorations of the Jesuit Missionaries in New France, 1610–1791*, ed. Reuben Gold Thwaites (Cleveland, Ohio: Burrows Brothers, 1896–1901), 70:125–27.
8. Ibid., 70:179.

Chapter 12: Mutiny on Rogers' Island

1. James Wolfe to his father, May 20, 1758, in Beckles Willson, *The Life and Letters of James Wolfe* (London: Heinemann, 1909), p. 365.
2. David R. Starbuck, *The Great Warpath: British Military Sites from Albany to Crown Point* (Hanover, N.H.: University Press of New England, 1999), p. 66.
3. Rogers to Lord Loudoun, October 27, 1757, no. 4071, LO.
4. Luke Gridley, *Luke Gridley's Diary of 1757* (Hartford, Conn.: Acorn Club, 1907), p. 25.
5. For a good description of the construction of a hut, see Starbuck, *Great Warpath*, p. 60.
6. On cherry rum, see Jabez Fitch, journal entry for October 18, 1757, in Jabez Fitch, *The Diary of Jabez Fitch, Jr., in the French and Indian War 1757* (New York: Rogers Island Historical Association, 1966); on the raw fish bet, see Gridley, *Diary*, pp. 38, 25.
7. On salt pork as a staple, see Lois M. Feister, "Material Culture of the British Soldier at 'His Majesty's Fort of Crown Point' on Lake Champlain, New York, 1759–1783," *Journal of Field Archaeology* 11 (1984), p. 128.
8. *BG*, February 14, 1757.
9. Gridley, *Diary*, pp. 30–31.
10. Sylvia R. Frey, "Courts and Cats: British Military Justice in the Eighteenth Century," *Military Affairs* (February 1979), p. 7.
11. Gridley, *Diary*, p. 55.
12. Ibid., pp. 43, 52.
13. "A Court of Inquiry held on the island this 8th Decem. 1757 by order of Lieutenant Colonal Haviland," no. 4969, LO.
14. Lewis Butler, *The Annals of the King's Royal Rifle Corps* (London: Smith, Elder & Co., 1913), p. 1 (frontispiece).
15. Haviland to Abercromby, December 16, 1757, no. 6859, LO.
16. Ibid.

Chapter 13: Taunting His Foe

1. See Appendix 1.
2. Ibid.
3. Cumberland to Loudoun, cited in John R. Cuneo, *Robert Rogers of the Rangers* (Ticonderoga, N.Y.: Fort Ticonderoga Museum, 1988), pp. 54–55.
4. *The Annual Register; or, A View of the History, Politics, and Literature for the Year 1763*, 7th ed. (London, 1796), pp. 28–29.
5. Robert Rogers, *The Annotated and Illustrated Journals of Major Robert Rogers*, ed. Timothy Todish (Fleischmanns, N.Y.: Purple Mountain Press, 2002), p. 85.
6. "Journal of Occurrences in Canada, 1757, 1758," *DRCHSNY*, 10:837.

7. Burt Garfield Loescher, *The History of Rogers Rangers* (Bowie, Md.: Heritage Books, Inc., 2001), 1:357.

8. Abercromby to Loudoun, January 2, 1758, no. 5311, LO.

9. Loudoun, diary entry for January 13, 1758, cited in Gary Zaboly, *A True Ranger: The Life and Many Wars of Major Robert Rogers* (Garden City Park, N.Y.: Royal Block House, 2004), p. 201.

10. Jabez Fitch, journal entry for February 19, 1758, *The Diary of Jabez Fitch, Jr., May 20, 1757 to April 24, 1758* (New York: Rogers Island Historical Association, 1966), p. 49.

11. *BEP,* April 19, 1758.

12. Jabez Fitch, journal entry for March 6, 1758, *The Diary of Jabez Fitch, Jr.,* p. 51.

13. Rogers, *Journals*, p. 89.

14. Ibid.

Chapter 14: Battle on Snowshoes

1. Loudoun, notation next to Pottinger's name in a "list of Commissions Granted by His Excellency the Rᵗ Honᵇˡᵉ The Earl of Loudoun," cited in Joseph F. Meany, Jr., "Merchant and Redcoat: The Papers of John Gordon Macomb," Ph.D. diss., Fordham University, 1989, 1:413, n36–1.

2. James Pottinger to Loudoun, July 21, 1757, no. 3975, LO.

3. Robert Rogers, *The Annotated and Illustrated Journals of Major Robert Rogers,* ed. Timothy Todish (Fleischmanns, N.Y.: Purple Mountain Press, 2002), p. 90.

4. A. Theodore Steegmann Jr., ed., *Boreal Forest Adaptations: The Northern Algonkians* (New York: Plenum Press, 1983), p. 336.

5. Meany, "Merchant and Redcoat," 1:411, n35–1.

6. Rogers, *Journals*, p. 90.

7. Pouchot, Pierre, *Memoirs On The Late War In North America Between France and England,* Michael Cardy, trans., Brian Leigh Dunnigan, ed. (Youngstown, N.Y.: Old Fort Niagara Association, 2004), p. 138.

8. Robert Rogers, *A Concise Account of North America: containing a description of the several British colonies on that continent . . .* (London, 1765), p. 217.

9. Montcalm to de Paulmy, April 10, 1758, *DRCHSNY,* 10:693.

10. "Individual Weapons and Marksmanship," September 1966, extracts from ROTCM 145–30, online at www.pattonhq.com/garand.html.

11. Rogers, *Journals*, p. 91.

12. John Keegan, *The Face of Battle: A Study of Agincourt, Waterloo and the Somme* (New York: Penguin, 1978), p. 202.

Chapter 15: Blood on the Snow

1. See Appendix 1.
2. Robert Rogers, *The Annotated and Illustrated Journals of Major Robert Rogers*, ed. Timothy Todish (Fleischmanns, N.Y.: Purple Mountain Press, 2002), p. 91n.
3. Captain d'Hébecourt to the Chevalier de Bourlamaque, cited in Burt Garfield Loescher, *The History of Rogers' Rangers* (Bowie, Md.: Heritage Books, 2001), 1:387.
4. U.S. Naval Observatory, Astronomical Applications Department, http://aa.usno.navy.mil; Virginia Westbrook, communication to author.
5. Rogers, *Journals*, p. 91.
6. U.S. Naval Observatory, Astronomical Applications Department, http://aa.usno.navy.mil.
7. Jabez Fitch, journal entry, March 14, 1758, in *The Diary of Jabez Fitch, Jr.*, p. 53.
8. Ibid., p. 54.
9. Rogers, *Journals*, pp. 104–7.
10. Ibid., p. 104.
11. Joseph F. Meany, Jr., "Merchant and Redcoat: The Papers of John Gordon Macomb," Ph.D. diss., Fordham University, 1989, 2:571.
12. D'Hebecourt to Bourlamaque, cited in Loescher, *History*, 1:387.
13. Macomb to Greg and Cunningham, March 24, 1758, in Meany, "Merchant and Redcoat," 2:619.
14. Vaudreuil to Massiac, October 28, 1759, *DRCHSNY*, 10:924.

Chapter 16: Disaster at Carillon

1. Gary Paine, "Ord's Arks: Angles, Artillery, and Ambush on Lakes George and Champlain," *American Neptune* 58, no. 2 (Spring 1998), p. 105.
2. *Pennsylvania Journal*, July 27, 1758.
3. Paine, "Ord's Arks," p. 117.
4. Caleb Rea, "The Journal of Dr. Caleb Rea, Written During the Expedition Against Ticonderoga In 1758," *Historical Collections of the Essex Institute* 18 (1881), pp. 182, 187.
5. James Abercromby to William Pitt, June 29, 1758, in *Correspondence of William Pitt when Secretary of State with Colonial Governors and Military and Naval Commissioners in America*, ed. Gertrude Selwyn Kimball (New York: Macmillan, 1906), p. 286.
6. Richard Huck to Lord Loudoun, June 29, 1758, no. 5866, LO.
7. Huck notes them wearing breeches, in Huck to Loudoun, May 29, 1758, no. 5837, LO.
8. Narrative enclosed in Charles Lee to Miss Sidney Lee, September 16, 1758, in Charles Lee, *The Lee Papers*, Collections of the New-York Historical

Society for the Years 1871–1874 (New York: Printed for the Society, 1872), 1:11.

9. Abel Spicer, diary, quoted in Russell P. Bellico, *Chronicles of Lake George: Journeys in War and Peace* (Fleischmanns, N.Y.: Purple Mountain Press, 1995), p. 99.

10. Alfred A. Cave, *The French and Indian War* (Westport, Conn.: Greenwood Press, 2004), p. 79.

11. Bougainville, journal entry for July 6, 1758, in *Adventures in the Wilderness: The American Journals of Louis Antoine de Bougainville, 1756–1760*, ed. and trans. Edward P. Hamilton (Norman: University of Oklahoma Press, 1964), p. 227.

12. Cited in Russell P. Bellico, *Sails and Steam in the Mountains: A Maritime and Military History of Lake George and Lake Champlain* (Fleischmanns, N.Y.: Purple Mountain Press, 1992), p. 62.

13. Pitt to George Grenville, August 22, 1758, in Kimball, *Correspondence of Pitt*, 1:338–41, cited in Joseph Meany, *Howe Biography*, unpublished manuscript, pp. 37–38.

14. Cited in John R. Cuneo, *Robert Rogers of the Rangers* (Ticonderoga, N.Y.: Fort Ticonderoga Museum, 1988), p. 71.

15. Robert Rogers, *The Annotated and Illustrated Journals of Major Robert Rogers*, ed. Timothy Todish (Fleischmanns, N.Y.: Purple Mountain Press, 2002), p. 114.

16. George Ingalls, "Lord Howe," *Proceedings of the New York State Historical Association* (Albany: New York State Historical Association, 1902), 2:24–31, cited in Meany, *Howe*, pp. 37–38.

17. *BEP*, July 3, 1758, p. 2.

18. Anne MacVicar Grant, *Memoirs of an American Lady; With Sketches of Manners and Scenes in America, as they Existed Previous to the Revolution* (New York: Appleton, 1846), 1:223.

19. Ibid., 2:21.

20. Alexander Moneypenny, "Orderly Book," March 23, 1758–June 29, 1758, in *BFTM* 12, no. 5 (December 1969), pp. 328–57.

21. Grant, *Memoirs*, 1:226.

22. Huck to Loudoun, May 29, 1758, no. 5837, LO.

23. Narrative enclosed in Lee to Lee, in *Lee Papers*, 1:11; unnamed officer, *DRCHSNY*, 10:735.

24. Archelaus Fuller, "The Journal of Archelaus Fuller, May–Nov. 1758," in *BFTM* 13, no. 1 (December 1970), p. 9.

25. Abercromby, cited in Cuneo, *Robert Rogers*, p. 85.

26. Rogers, *Journals*, p. 119.

27. Moneypenny quoted in Ian M. McCulloch, " 'Like roaring lions breaking from their chains': The Battle of Ticonderoga, 8 July 1758," in *Fighting for Canada: Seven Battles, 1758–1945*, ed. Donald Graves (Toronto: Robin Brass Studio, 2000), p. 41.

28. Thomas Mante, quoted in Francis Parkman, *Montcalm and Wolfe* (New York: Little Brown and Company, 1897), 2:102.

29. Hamilton, *Adventures in Wilderness*, p. 228.
30. William Eyre, quoted in McCulloch, " 'Like roaring lions,' " p. 43.
31. Garrett Albertson, "A Short Account of the Life, Travels, and Adventures of Garrett Albertson, Sr., 1845," *BFTM* 4, no. 2 (1936), p. 44.
32. Hamilton, *Adventures in Wilderness*, p. 229.
33. Ibid., p. 231.
34. Garrett Albertson, "A Short Account," pp. 44–45.

Chapter 17: "Come Up, You French Dogs . . . Like Men!"

1. Archelaus Fuller, "The Journal of Archelaus Fuller, May–Nov. 1758," in *BFTM* 13, no. 1 (December 1970), p.11.
2. Montcalm, cited in René Chartrand, *Ticonderoga 1758: Montcalm's Victory Against All Odds* (Oxford: Osprey, 2000), p. 55.
3. Ian M. McCulloch, " 'Like roaring lions breaking from their chains': The Battle of Ticonderoga, 8 July 1758," in *Fighting for Canada: Seven Battles, 1758–1945*, ed. Donald Graves (Toronto: Robin Brass Studio, 2000), p. 60.
4. Abel Spicer, journal entry for July 8, 1758, in Russell P. Bellico, *Chronicles of Lake George: Journeys in War and Peace* (Fleischmanns, N.Y.: Purple Mountain Press, 1995), p. 101.
5. "Life of David Perry," *BFTM* 14, no. 1 (Summer 1981), p. 6.
6. Garrett Albertson, "A Short Account of the Life, Travels, and Adventures of Garrett Albertson, Sr., 1845," *BFTM* 4, no. 2 (1936), p. 45.
7. Archelaus Fuller, "The Journal of Archelaus Fuller, May–Nov. 1758," in *BFTM* 13, no. 1 (December 1970), p. 11.
8. Charles Lee, *The Lee Papers*, Collections of the New-York Historical Society for the Years 1871–1874 (New York: Printed for the Society, 1872), 1:7.
9. Narrative enclosed in Charles Lee to Miss Sidney Lee, September 16, 1758, ibid., 1:11.
10. McCulloch, " 'Like roaring lions,' " p. 71.
11. "Extract of a letter from a lieutenant in Howe's regiment, dated at Lake George, July 10," in *Scots Magazine*, August 1758, p. 439.
12. Joseph F. Meany, Jr., "Merchant and Redcoat: The Papers of John Gordon Macomb," Ph.D. diss., Fordham University, 1989, p. 390.
13. "Life of David Perry," *BFTM* 14, no. 1 (Summer 1981), p. 6.
14. Bougainville, journal entry for July 8, 1758, in *Adventures in the Wilderness: The American Journals of Louis Antoine de Bougainville, 1756–1760*, ed. and trans. Edward P. Hamilton (Norman: University of Oklahoma Press, 1964), p. 234.
15. Bougainville, journal entry for July 19, 1758, ibid., p. 235.
16. Pierre Pouchot, *Memoirs on the Late War in North America Between France and England*, Michael Cardy, trans., Brian Leigh Dunnigan, ed. (Youngstown, N.Y.: Old Fort Niagara Association, 2004), pp. 159–60.
17. Lee, *Lee Papers*, 1:14.

18. Caleb Rea, journal entry for July 10, 1758, in "The Journal of Dr. Caleb Rea, Written During the Expedition Against Ticonderoga In 1758," *Historical Collections of the Essex Institute* 18 (1881), pp. 106–7.
19. Spicer, journal entry for July 10, 1758, in Bellico, *Chronicles of Lake George*, p. 103.
20. Spicer, journal entry for July 14, 1758, ibid., p. 103.
21. Ibid., p. 95.
22. Captain Henry Champion, journal entry for July 27, 1758, cited in Robert Rogers, *The Annotated and Illustrated Journals of Major Robert Rogers*, ed. Timothy Todish (Fleischmanns, N.Y.: Purple Mountain Press, 2002), p. 130.
23. John Cleaveland, journal entry for July 31, 1758, in "Journal of the Rev. John Cleaveland, 14 June 1758—25 October 1758," *BFTM* 10, no. 3 (1959), p. 206.
24. Hamilton, *Adventures in Wilderness*, p. 258.
25. Spicer, journal entry, in Bellico, *Chronicles of Lake George*, p. 109.
26. Ibid.
27. Lieutenant Thomas Barnsley to Colonel Henry Bouquet, September 7, 1758, cited in Rogers, *Journals*, p. 146.

Chapter 18: Allegro Guerriero

1. See Appendix 1.
2. Robert Rogers, *The Annotated and Illustrated Journals of Major Robert Rogers*, ed. Timothy Todish and Gary Zaboly (Fleischmanns, N.Y.: Purple Mountain Press, 2002), p. 156.
3. Ibid., p. 155.
4. Geological display, Adirondack Museum, Blue Mountain Lake, N.Y.
5. Lieutenant Diederick Brehm, journal, *BFTM* 11, no. 1 (December 1962), p. 41.
6. Rogers, *Journals*, p. 155.
7. Ibid., p. 150.
8. Cited in John R. Cuneo, *Robert Rogers of the Rangers* (Ticonderoga, N.Y.: Fort Ticonderoga Museum, 1988), p. 94.
9. Ibid., p. 92.
10. Richard Huck to Loudoun, June 19, 1759, no. 6113, LO.
11. Rogers, *Journals*, p. 159.
12. William Shirley to Sir Thomas Robinson, November 5, 1755, in *Correspondence of William Shirley, Governor of Massachusetts and Military Commander of America, 1731–1760*, ed. Charles Henry Lincoln (New York: Macmillan, 1912), 2:319.
13. Thomas Dunbar and Thomas Gage to William Shirley, October 21, 1755, ibid., 2:313.
14. "Particulars of Major Robert Rogers's last Scout against the Enemy," *BG*, April 9, 1759, p. 4.

15. Thomas Gage to William Haldimand, February 20, 1759, quoted in Cuneo, *Robert Rogers*, p. 92.
16. Rogers, *Journals*, p. 156.
17. Thomas Gage to Jeffery Amherst, March 11, 1759, quoted in Gary Zaboly, *A True Ranger: The Life and Many Wars of Major Robert Rogers* (Garden City Park, N.Y.: Royal Block House, 2004), p. 253.
18. Henry Skinner journal, *BFTM* 15, no. 5 (1993), p. 367.
19. Gage to Amherst, February 18, 1759, cited in Zaboly, *True Ranger*, p. 251.
20. Amherst to Gage, cited ibid.
21. Rogers, *Journals*, p. 156.
22. Gage to Amherst, March 19, 1759, cited in Zaboly, *True Ranger*, p. 254.
23. Gage to Amherst, April 9, 1759, cited ibid., p. 255.
24. Gage to Haldimand, April 4, 1759, cited in Burt Garfield Loescher, *The History of Rogers' Rangers*, (Bowie, Md.: Heritage Books, 2001), p. 255, n52.
25. Cuneo, *Robert Rogers*, p. 94.
26. Amherst to Rogers, April 1, 1759, cited in Zaboly, *True Ranger*, p. 257.
27. Beckles Willson, *The Life and Letters of James Wolfe* (London: Heinemann, 1909), p. 369.
28. Rogers, *Journals*, p. 159.
29. *BG*, June 4, 1759, p. 1.
30. Rogers, *Journals*, p. 159.

Chapter 19: To Carillon Once Again

1. Jesse Parsons, "A Journal of an Expedition Design'd Against the French Possessions in Canada Kept by Jesse Parsons Philom." Reprinted courtesy of Dr. Gary Milan.
2. Dr. Thomas Haynes, Sr., "Memorandum of Collonial French War A.D. 1758," *BFTM* 12, no. 1 (1966), p. 202.
3. General Orders, *BFTM* 6, no. 3 (January 1942), p. 97.
4. Bourlamaque to Marshal de Belle Isle, November 1, 1759, *DRCHSNY*, 16:1055.
5. Ibid., 16:1054–55.
6. General Orders, *BFTM* 6, no. 3 (January 1942), p. 96.
7. Parsons, *A Journal*.
8. Reverend Eli Forbush, August 4, 1759, *BFTM* 1, no. 6 (July 1929), p. 22.
9. Parsons, *A Journal*.

Chapter 20: Mission Impossible

1. Dennis Lewis, "The Naval Campaign of 1759 on Lake Champlain," *BFTM* 14, no. 4 (Fall 1983), pp. 209–10.
2. Ibid., p. 205.

3. NASA, "Moon Phases: 1701–1800," online at http://sunearth.gsfc.nasa.gov.

4. *BEP,* September 24, 1759, p. 3.

5. Robert Webster, "Diary," *BFTM* 9, no. 5 (Summer 1954), p. 330.

6. Another explanation suggests that Williams touched off a booby-trapped skiff placed near Otter Creek by the French. Rogers notes the presence of such devices but remarks that his party fortunately avoided their ill effects. It seems unlikely that he would have omitted recording such a misfortune, had it befallen Williams.

7. *BEP,* October 1, 1759, p. 3.

8. Gary Zaboly, *A True Ranger: The Life and Many Wars of Major Robert Rogers* (Garden City Park, N.Y.: Royal Block House, 2004), p. 268.

9. Cited in Stephen Brumwell, *White Devil: A True Story of War, Savagery, and Vengeance in Colonial America* (Cambridge, Mass.: Da Capo Press, 2005), p. 176.

10. J. Clarence Webster, ed., *The Journal of Jeffrey Amherst: Recording the Military Career of General Amherst in America from 1758 to 1763* (Toronto: Ryerson Press, 1931), p. 171.

11. Pitt to Amherst, December 11, 1759, in Gertrude Selwyn Kimball, *Correspondence of William Pitt when Secretary of State with Colonial Governors and Military and Naval Commissioners in America* (New York: Macmillan, 1906), p. 216.

12. Webster, *Journal of Amherst,* p. 152. The entry is mislabeled August 15 but is clearly August 5.

13. Ibid., p. 167.

14. Robert Rogers, *The Annotated and Illustrated Journals of Major Robert Rogers,* ed. Timothy Todish (Fleischmanns, N.Y.: Purple Mountain Press, 2002), p. 170.

15. Cited in Francis Russell, "Oh Amherst, Brave Amherst...," *American Heritage* 12 (December 1960), www.americanheritage.com.

16. Brumwell, *White Devil,* p. 180.

17. *CM,* November 28, 1759.

18. Colin G. Calloway, *The Western Abenakis of Vermont, 1600–1800: War, Migration, and the Survival of an Indian People* (Norman and London: University of Oklahoma Press, 1990), p. 168.

19. Rogers, *Journals,* p. 179.

20. Grand atlas de la provincede Québec (St. Laurent: Cartotek Geo, 2006).

21. *NYG,* November 26, 1759.

22. Burt Garfield Loescher, *Genesis: The History of Rogers' Rangers,* 3:44.

23. Brumwell, *White Devil,* pp. 181–82.

24. Rogers, *Journals,* p. 179.

Chapter 21: Ordeal Through Spruce Bogs

1. "Wolf Research in Algonquin Provincial Park," www.sbaa.ca/projects.asp?cn=314.
2. For full rule, see Appendix 1.
3. *BNL*, February 7, 1760.
4. Robert Rogers, *The Annotated and Illustrated Journals of Major Robert Rogers*, ed. Timothy Todish (Fleischmanns, N.Y.: Purple Mountain Press, 2002), p. 179.
5. *BNL*, February 7, 1760.
6. John Cleaveland, journal entry for August 14, 1758, in "Journal of Rev. John Cleaveland, 14 June 1758–25 October 1758," *BFTM* 10, no. 3 (1959), p. 211.
7. Gordon M. Day, "Rogers' Raid in Indian Tradition," *HNH* (June 1962), pp. 3–17.
8. Peter Nabokov, *A Forest of Time: American Indian Ways of History* (Cambridge, U.K.: Cambridge University Press, 2002), p. 240.
9. Ibid., p. 239.
10. *NYG*, November 26, 1759.
11. Rogers, *Journals*, p. 172.
12. *BG*, November 26, 1759, p. 4.
13. *NCG*, October 18, 1759, cited in Gary Zaboly, *A True Ranger: The Life and Many Wars of Major Robert Rogers* (Garden City Park, N.Y.: Royal Block House, 2004), p. 280.
14. For number of houses, see Day, "Rogers' Raid," p. 15.
15. Marge Bruchac, *Reading Abenaki Tradition and European Records of Rogers' Raid*, unpublished manuscript, 2006.
16. For latitude and longitude of nearby Drummondville, Quebec, see U.S. Naval Observatory, Astronomical Applications Department, http://aa.usno.navy.mil.
17. *BG*, November 26, 1759.
18. *NYG*, November 26, 1759.
19. Luther Roby, *Reminiscences of the French War with Robert Rogers' Journal and a Memoir of General Stark* (Concord, N.H.: Luther Roby, 1831), pp. 179–80.
20. Rogers, *Journals*, p. 172.
21. Day, "Rogers' Raid," p. 13.
22. *NYG*, November, 26, 1759.
23. Rogers, *Journals*, p. 172.
24. Cited in Brumwell, *White Devil*, p. 302.
25. Bishop de Pontbriand, "An Imperfect Description of the Misery of Canada," *DRCHSNY*, 10:1058. See also Nicholas Sarrebource de Pontleroy to Bourlamaque, October 6, 1759, cited in Brumwell, *White Devil*, p. 302; Pierre Ponchot, *Memoirs*, p. 262.
26. Colin Calloway to author, May 31, 2007.

Chapter 22: Starvation

1. "A Ballad of Rogers' Retreat, 1759," *Vermont History* 46, no. 1 (Winter 1978), p. 22.
2. Gordon M. Day, "Western Abenaki," in *Handbook of North American Indians: Northeast*, ed. William C. Sturtevant (Washington, D.C.: Smithsonian Institution, 1978–2004), 15:156.
3. Father Pierre-Joseph Roubaud to Count Vergennes, March 2, 1776, National Archives of Canada, FM, 5, vol. 515, pp. 12–13. Later over the winter in Montréal, where he sought sanctuary, he delivered a sermon at the parish church that was a scathing indictment of the moral laxity of French troops, blaming them for losing Québec and by inference Saint-François.
4. Abbé Maurault, cited in Kenneth Roberts, *Northwest Passage*, vol. 2, appendix. Additional details are in Stephen Brumwell, *White Devil: A True Story of War, Savagery, and Vengeance in Colonial America* (Cambridge, Mass.: Da Capo Press, 2005), p. 199.
5. Thomas L. Purvis, *Colonial America to 1763*, Almanacs of American Life Series (New York: Facts on File, 1999), p. 169.
6. Rogers, *Journals*, p. 175.
7. *NYG*, September 3, 1759, p. 2.
8. *NYG*, September 24, 1759, p. 2.
9. *BEP*, September 17, 1759, p. 2.
10. *NYG*, September 24, 1759, p. 2; *BEP*, September 17, 1759, p. 2.
11. Cited in Gary Zaboly, *A True Ranger: The Life and Many Wars of Major Robert Rogers* (Garden City Park, N.Y.: Royal Block House, 2004), p. 285.
12. Rogers to Amherst, December 12, 1759, in Kenneth Roberts, *Northwest Passage*, vol. 2, appendix, p. 12.
13. Frederick Curtiss memorial, quoted in Brumwell, *White Devil*, p. 215.
14. *DRCHSNY*, 10:1042.
15. Curtiss memorial, quoted in Brumwell, *White Devil*, p. 216.
16. J. Clarence Webster, ed., *The Journal of Jeffrey Amherst: Recording the Military Career of General Amherst in America from 1758 to 1763* (Toronto: Ryerson Press, 1931), p. 175.
17. On symptoms of starvation, see Frederick Hocking, *Starvation: Social and Psychological Aspects of a Basic Biological Stress*, Australian Medical Association's Merwyn Archdall Medical Monograph Number 6 (Sydney: Australasian Medical Publishing Co., 1969), p. 17.
18. Ibid., pp. 17, 20.
19. Claude A. Piantadosi, *The Biology of Human Survival: Life and Death in Extreme Environments* (New York: Oxford University Press, 2003), p. 32.
20. Ibid.
21. Thomas Mante, *The history of the late war in North-America, and the islands of the West Indies, including the Campaign of MDCCLXIII and MDCCLXIV against his Majesty's Indian enemies* (London: W. Strahan and T. Cadell, 1772), pp. 223–24.

22. Robert Kirkwood claimed that Rogers killed the squaw, but his journal contains so many basic factual errors that it is difficult to believe that he accompanied the group. In addition, he acknowledged that the squaw was a good source of foraging material, another reason why Rogers would have been loath to kill her.
23. Cited in Zaboly, *True Ranger*, p. 287.
24. Luther Roby, *Reminiscences of the French War with Robert Rogers' Journal and a Memoir of General Stark* (Concord, N.H.: Luther Roby, 1831), pp. 180–81.

Chapter 23: Betrayal

1. Robert Rogers, *The Annotated and Illustrated Journals of Major Robert Rogers*, ed. Timothy Todish (Fleischmanns, N.Y.: Purple Mountain Press, 2002), p. 193.
2. Ibid., p. 180.
3. Kenneth Roberts, in the appendix of a special edition of *Northwest Passage*, lays some blame on Lieutenant McMullen, who may have misjudged how fast Rogers could reach the rendezvous on the Connecticut. This information, suggests Roberts, may have given Stevens the impression that Rogers was so long overdue that he was probably dead. Yet McMullen had left long before the rangers even reached Saint-François, so it's difficult to believe that Stevens could take his word so literally. By all accounts Stevens certainly did not give Rogers any benefit of doubt.
4. Jeffery Amherst, journal entry for October 30, 1759, in *The Journal of Jeffrey Amherst: Recording the Military Career of General Amherst in America from 1758 to 1763*, ed. J. Clarence Webster (Toronto: Ryerson Press, 1931), p. 185.
5. Rogers, *Journals*, p. 180.
6. Charles Francis Saunders, *Useful Wild Plants of the United States and Canada* (New York: Robert M. McBride & Co., 1920), pp. 2–3.
7. Henry David Thoreau, *The Maine Woods*, ed. Joseph J. Moldenhauer (Princeton, N.J.: Princeton University Press, 1972), Appendix VII: A List of Indian Words.
8. Rogers, *Journals*, p. 180.
9. Ibid., p. 181.
10. Ibid., pp. 180–81.
11. *NYG*, November 26, 1759.
12. Ibid.
13. Gary Zaboly, *A True Ranger: The Life and Many Wars of Major Robert Rogers* (Garden City Park, N.Y.: Royal Block House, 2004), p. 295.
14. *NHG*, February 1, 1760, p. 2.
15. *BWNL*, February 7, 1760, p. 1.
16. Ibid.

Chapter 24: Horror on the Ice

1. Rogers dates this as February 13, but Amherst's and Haviland's correspondence suggests it was a day earlier.
2. Amherst to Pitt, March 8, 1760, in *Correspondence of William Pitt when Secretary of State with Colonial Governors and Military and Naval Commissioners in America*, ed. Gertrude Selwyn Kimball (New York: Macmillan, 1906), 2:263–64.
3. Haviland to Gage, February 13, 1760, cited in Gary Zaboly, *A True Ranger: The Life and Many Wars of Major Robert Rogers* (Garden City Park, N.Y.: Royal Block House, 2004), p. 294.
4. *BNL*, February 28, 1760, supp., p. 2.
5. Haviland to Gage, February 13, 1760, cited in Zaboly, *True Ranger*, p. 294.
6. "The Memorial of Major Robert Rogers," May 23, 1760, cited ibid., p. 296.
7. Rogers to Amherst, May 11, 1761, cited ibid., pp. 293–94.
8. On Rogers's financial woes, see John R. Cuneo, *Robert Rogers of the Rangers* (Ticonderoga, N.Y.: Fort Ticonderoga Museum, 1988).
9. Robert Rogers, *The Annotated and Illustrated Journals of Major Robert Rogers*, ed. Timothy Todish (Fleischmanns, N.Y.: Purple Mountain Press, 2002), p. 198.
10. Ibid., p. 200.

Chapter 25: Pressing the French

1. For hardwood swamp details, see Richard M. DeGraaf et al., *Technical Guide to Forest Wildlife Habitat Management in New England* (Hanover, N.H.: University Press of New England, 2006), pp. 104–5.
2. Robert Rogers, *The Annotated and Illustrated Journals of Major Robert Rogers*, ed. Timothy Todish (Fleischmanns, N.Y.: Purple Mountain Press, 2002), p. 200.
3. *BG*, September 8, 1760, p. 2.
4. *BNL*, July 10, 1760, p. 3.
5. John Cuneo, unpublished notes to *Robert Rogers of the Rangers*, Chapter 10, fn. 18, *FTA*.
6. Rogers, *Journals*, p. 202.
7. Peter Kalm, *Peter Kalm's Travels in North America; the America of 1750; the English version of 1770*, rev. from the original Swedish and edited by Adolph B. Benson (New York: Dover, 1964), p. 397.
8. Ensign Donald Stuart of the 27th Regiment heard this while under a flag of truce and behind enemy lines. John R. Cuneo, *Robert Rogers of the Rangers* (Ticonderoga, N.Y.: Fort Ticonderoga Museum, 1988), p. 82.
9. Rogers, *Journals*, p. 202.
10. Ibid., p. 201.
11. Amherst to Rogers, June 26, 1760, ibid., p. 204.
12. Cuneo, *Robert Rogers*, p. 124.

13. *BWNL*, July 10, 1760, p. 3.
14. Cuneo, *Robert Rogers*, pp. 124–25.
15. Rogers, *Journals*, p. 207.
16. Ibid., p. 207.

Chapter 26: A Race West to Claim the Continent for Britain

1. B. Cole, engraver, "A Perspective View of the Town and Fortifications of Montreal in Canada," *Royal Magazine* [London] (1760).
2. Bernard De Voto, *The Course of Empire* (Boston: Houghton Mifflin, 1952), p. 240.
3. Rogers, *Journals*, p. 207.
4. *NHG*, February 13, 1761.
5. Robert Rogers, *The Annotated and Illustrated Journals of Major Robert Rogers*, ed. Timothy Todish (Fleischmanns, N.Y.: Purple Mountain Press, 2002), p. 208.
6. Charles Sanger, "The St. Lawrence and the Saguenay" (1856), lines 403–15.
7. Tim McNeese, *The St. Lawrence River* (Philadelphia: Chelsea House, 2005), p. 2.
8. Amherst, September 4, 1760, cited in Gary Zaboly, *A True Ranger: The Life and Many Wars of Major Robert Rogers* (Garden City Park, N.Y.: Royal Block House, 2004), p. 306.
9. René Chartrand, *French Fortresses in North America, 1535–1763: Quebec, Montreal, Louisbourg, and New Orleans* (Oxford: Osprey, 2005), pp. 37, 40.
10. Alexander Henry, *Travels and Adventures: In Canada and the Indian Territories Between the Years 1760 and 1776* (New York: Burt Franklin, 1969), p. 16.
11. H. Murray, "Historical Description of America," quoted in George Warburton, *The Conquest of Canada* (New York: Harper and Brothers, 1855), p. 112n.
12. Rogers, *Journals*, p. 210.
13. Ibid., p. 211.
14. Ibid.
15. Zaboly, *True Ranger*, p. 307.
16. Robert Rogers, *A Concise Account of North America: containing a description of the several British colonies on that continent...* (London, 1765), p. 173.
17. Robert Monckton, quoted in Rogers, *Journals*, p. 213.
18. John R. Cuneo, *Robert Rogers of the Rangers* (Ticonderoga, N.Y.: Fort Ticonderoga Museum, 1988), p. 133.
19. Rogers, *Journals*, p. 213.
20. George Croghan to William Johnson, November 1, 1760, in *The Sir William Johnson Papers* (Albany: State University of New York, 1921–65), 3:276.
21. Croghan, journal, quoted in *The Jesuit Relations and Allied Documents:*

Travels and Explorations of the Jesuit Missionaries in New France, 1610–1791, ed. Reuben Gold Thwaites (Cleveland, Ohio: Burrows Brothers, 1896–1901), p. 107.

22. Description of November 11–12, 2003, storm, at Great Lakes Storms Photo Gallery, Great Lakes Sea Grant Extension Office website, www.glerl.noaa.gov.

23. Rogers, *Concise Account*, p. 239.

24. There is some contention in academic circles about whether Rogers met Pontiac in November 1760, because he does not mention him by name in his journals. He does mention meeting an Ottawa sachem. Some believe that Rogers in his *Concise Account*, which was written in 1765, made up the meeting to add to the allure of his account. By then Pontiac had become well known, his name having been given to Pontiac's War. Not mentioning Pontiac's name remains consistent with Rogers's journal-keeping habits, in which he rarely if ever mentions Indians by name. It is certainly quite possible, even likely, that Pontiac would have come out to see the first British envoy westward. And while the *Concise Account* does retrospectively inflate Pontiac's importance—Rogers could have had no idea of Pontiac's power and upcoming role then—that does not mean that he made up the encounter. There still remains no proof that he did not meet the Ottawa chief.

25. Rogers, *Concise Account*, p. 240.

26. Ibid.

27. Croghan to Johnson, n.d., cited in Timothy J. Todish and Todd E. Harburn, *A "Most Troublesome Situation": The British Military and the Pontiac Indian Uprising of 1763–1764* (Fleischmanns, N.Y.: Purple Mountain Press, 2006), p. 19.

28. Rogers, *Concise Account*, pp. 223–24.

29. Ibid., pp. 241–43.

30. Rogers, *Journals*, p. 215.

31. Captain François-Marie Picoté de Belestre, *DCB* entry.

32. Rogers, *Journals*, p. 219.

33. Quoted in Todish and Harburn, *"Most Troublesome Situation,"* p. 22.

Chapter 27: Détroit

1. Robert Rogers, *The Annotated and Illustrated Journals of Major Robert Rogers*, ed. Timothy Todish (Fleischmanns, N.Y.: Purple Mountain Press, 2002), p. 220; George Croghan, journal entry for August 17, 1765, in *Early Western Travels, 1748–1846: A Series of Annotated Reprints of Some of the Best and Rarest Contemporary Volumes of Travel, Descriptive of the Aborigines and Social and Economic Conditions in the Middle and Far West, During the Period of Early American Settlement*, ed. Reuben Gold Thwaites (Cleveland: A. H. Clark, 1907), 1:152.

2. Colin G. Calloway, *The Scratch of a Pen: 1763 and the Transformation of North America* (Oxford: Oxford University Press, 2006), pp. 38–39; Brian Leigh Dunnigan, "Fortress Detroit, 1701–1826," in *The Sixty Years' War for*

the Great Lakes, 1754–1814, ed. David Curtis Skaggs (East Lansing: Michigan State University Press, 2001), pp. 167–85.

3. Gregory Evans Dowd, *War Under Heaven: Pontiac, the Indian Nations, & the British Empire* (Baltimore: Johns Hopkins University Press, 2002), p. 60.

4. Rogers, *Journals*, p. 221.

5. Henry Bouquet, *Bouquet Papers*, ed. S. K. Stevens, Donald H. Kent, and Autumn L. Leonard (Harrisburg: Pennsylvania Historical and Museum Commission, 1951–94), 5:204.

6. Cited in John R. Cuneo, *Robert Rogers of the Rangers* (Ticonderoga, N.Y.: Fort Ticonderoga Museum, 1988), p. 139.

7. Rogers, *Journals*, p. 224.

8. Ibid., pp. 207–8.

9. *NHG*, February 27, 1761.

10. Theda Perdue and Michael D. Green, *The Cherokee Nation and the Trail of Tears* (New York: Viking, 2007), p. 13.

11. Calloway, *Scratch*, pp. 36–37.

12. Duane H. King, ed., *The Memoirs of Lt. Henry Timberlake: The Story of a Soldier, Adventurer, and Emissary to the Cherokees, 1756–1765* (Cherokee, N.C.: Museum of the Cherokee Indian Press, 2007), pp. xvii–xix; John L. Nichols, "John Stuart, Beloved Father of the Cherokees," *Highlander Magazine* 31, no. 5 (September–October 1993), pp. 37–40.

13. Amherst to Grant, February 27, 1761, cited in Gary Zaboly, *A True Ranger: The Life and Many Wars of Major Robert Rogers* (Garden City Park, N.Y.: Royal Block House, 2004), p. 318.

14. Ibid., pp. 318–19.

15. For the financial hurdles faced by Rogers, see Cuneo, *Robert Rogers*.

16. Thomas L. Purvis, *Colonial America to 1763*, Almanacs of American Life Series (New York: Facts on File, 1999), pp. 86, 89.

17. On Portsmouth, see Thomas Bailey Aldrich, *An Old Town by the Sea* (Boston: Houghton Mifflin, 1893), pp. 1–125; the Strawbery Banke Museum website, www.strawberybanke.org; Purvis, *Colonial America*, pp. 142, 252.

18. Franklin Ware Davis, "Old St. John's Parish, Portsmouth," *New England Magazine* 11, no. 1 (September 1894), p. 324.

19. On the trial of Penelope Kenny and Sarah Simpson, see Christopher Benedetto, " 'A Warning to All Others': The Story of the First Executions in New Hampshire History," *New England Ancestors* 6, no. 5 (Holiday 2005).

20. Rogers to Betsy, May 1762, quoted in Zaboly, *True Ranger*, p. 331.

Chapter 28: To South Carolina

1. Robert Rogers, *A Concise Account of North America: containing a description of the several British colonies on that continent* . . . (London, 1765), p. 140.

2. Ibid.

3. Pelatiah Webster, "Journal of a Visit to Charleston, 1765," in *The Colonial*

South Carolina Scene: Contemporary Views, 1697–1774, ed. H. Roy Merrens (Columbia: University of South Carolina Press, 1977), pp. 220–21; John Bartram and Francis Harper, "Diary of a Journey Through the Carolinas, Georgia, and Florida," *Proceedings of the American Philosophical Society*, new ser., vol. 33, no. 1 (December 1942), p. 23. On uniforms of South Carolina Independents, see Fitzhugh McMaster, *Soldiers and Uniforms: South Carolina Military Affairs, 1660–1775* (Columbia: University of South Carolina Press, 1971).

4. McMaster, *Soldiers and Uniforms*, pp. 72–73.

5. Rogers, *Concise Account*, p. 141.

6. Bishop Roberts and William Henry Toms, *Prospect of Charles Town, 1737–1739*, reproduced in Gloria Gilda Deak, *Picturing America* (Princeton, N.J.: Princeton University Press, 1988), vol. 2, illus. 90.

7. Rogers, *Concise Account*, p. 141.

8. Thomas L. Purvis, *Colonial America to 1763*, Almanacs of American Life Series (New York: Facts on File, 1999), p. 11, 224.

9. B. R. Carroll, *Historical Collections of South Carolina* (New York: Harper and Brothers, 1836), 2:476.

10. Carl Bridenbaugh, *Myths and Realities: Societies of the Colonial South* (New York: Atheneum, 1971), pp. 57, 70–71.

11. Colin G. Calloway, *The Scratch of a Pen: 1763 and the Transformation of North America* (Oxford: Oxford University Press, 2006), pp. 31–32.

12. Bridenbaugh, *Myths and Realities*, p. 64.

13. Ibid., p. 57.

14. *BEP*, September 19, 1761, p. 4.

15. Anna Wells Rutledge, "After the Cloth Was Removed," *Winterthur Portfolio* 4 (1968), p. 47.

16. George Roupell, *Mr. Peter Manigault and His Friends* (1760), reprinted ibid., p. 49.

17. Webster, "Journal of a Visit," p. 221.

18. Bridenbaugh, *Myths and Realities*, p. 79.

19. Cited in Alan D. Watson, ed., *Society in Early North Carolina: A Documentary History* (Raleigh: North Carolina Department of Cultural Resources, 2000), p. 307.

20. *BEP*, November 20, 1769, p. 4.

21. Amherst to Grant, July 13, 1761, cited in Gary Zaboly, *A True Ranger: The Life and Many Wars of Major Robert Rogers* (Garden City Park, N.Y.: Royal Block House, 2004), p. 325.

22. See "Frontier Outposts," South Carolina Department of Archives and History, www.state.sc.us/scdah/exhibits/cherokee/5a-Frontieroutposts.htm.

23. *NYM*, August 3, 1761, p. 1.

24. *BPB*, October 19, 1761, p. 1.

25. Rogers to Amherst, October 19, 1761, cited in Zaboly, *True Ranger*, p. 326.

26. On "seasoning," see William Tryon to Sewallis Shirley, July 26, 1765, excerpted in Watson, *Society in Early North Carolina*, p. 161.

27. Rogers, *Concise Account*, p. 140.
28. H. Roy Merrens and George D. Terry, "Dying in Paradise: Malaria, Mortality, and the Perceptual Environment in Colonial South Carolina," *Journal of Southern History* 50, no. 4 (November 1984), p. 540.
29. Bartram and Harper, "Diary of a Journey," p. 21.
30. Merrens and Terry, "Dying in Paradise," p. 549.
31. Webster, "Journal of a Visit," p. 224.

Chapter 29: A Dream Is Born

1. On Dobbs's mansion, see Stanley A. South, " 'Russellborough': Two Royal Governors' Mansions at Brunswick Town," *North Carolina Historical Review* 44 (1967), pp. 361–72.
2. "Correspondence of Doctor Thomas Williams, of Deerfield Mass., A Surgeon in the Army," *Historical Magazine*, 2nd ser., vol. 7, no. 4 (April 1870), p. 214.
3. Arthur Dobbs entry, *DAB*.
4. Desmond Clarke, *Arthur Dobbs Esquire 1689–1765: Surveyor-General of Ireland, Prospector and Governor of North Carolina* (London: Bodley Head, 1958), frontispiece.
5. J. Russell Snapp, "Arthur Dobbs," *American National Biography* (New York: Oxford University Press, 1999), 6:658; Clarke, *Arthur Dobbs*, p. 31.
6. Cited in Gary Zaboly, *A True Ranger: The Life and Many Wars of Major Robert Rogers* (Garden City Park, N.Y.: Royal Block House, 2004), p. 328.
7. Arthur Dobbs, "A Letter from Arthur Dobbs Esq; to Charles Stanhope Esq; F. R. S. concerning Bees, and Their Method of Gathering Wax and Honey," *Philosophical Transactions* 46 (1749), pp. 536–49.
8. Frank N. Egerton, "A History of the Ecological Sciences, Part 25. American Naturalists Explore Eastern North America: John and William Bartram," *Bulletin of the Ecological Society of America* 88, no. 3 (July 2007), p. 257.
9. Peter Whitfield, *New Found Lands: Maps in the History of Exploration* (New York: Routledge, 1998), p. 140.
10. Brendan Lehane, *The Northwest Passage* (Alexandria, Va.: Time-Life Books, 1981), p. 72.
11. Eric Hinderaker, "The 'Four Indian Kings' and the Imaginative Construction of the First British Empire," *WMQ*, 3rd ser., vol. 53, no. 3 (July 1996), p. 487.
12. Arthur Dobbs, *An Account . . .* (London: Printed for J. Robinson, 1749).
13. Byram Scott and David G. Lewis, "Ourigan: Wealth of the Northwest Coast," *Oregon Historical Quarterly* 102, no. 2 (Summer 2001), p. 136.
14. Dobbs, *Account*, p. 13.
15. Hennig Cohen, *The South Carolina Gazette, 1732–1775* (Columbia: University of South Carolina Press, 1953), p. 242.
16. Ibid., p. 159.

17. Or $240, calculated using the retail price index.

18. Rogers to Amherst, March 20, 1762, cited in Zaboly, *True Ranger*, p. 330.

19. Rogers to Amherst, July 10, 1762, cited in John R. Cuneo, *Robert Rogers of the Rangers* (Ticonderoga, N.Y.: Fort Ticonderoga Museum, 1988), p. 155.

20. Rogers to Betsy, May 4, 1762, Rogers/Roche Papers, Clements Library, cited in Zaboly, *True Ranger*, p. 330.

21. Amherst to Rogers, August 23, 1762, cited ibid., p. 331.

22. Fred Anderson, *Crucible of War: The Seven Years' War and the Fate of Empire in British North America, 1754–1766* (New York: Alfred A. Knopf, 2000), p. 501.

23. Arthur Browne to Rogers, May 12, 1763, cited in Zaboly, *True Ranger*, p. 337.

24. William R. Nester, *"Haughty Conquerors": Amherst and the Great Indian Uprising of 1763* (Westport, Conn.: Praeger, 2000), p. 23.

25. Amherst to Rogers, December 26, 1762, cited in Zaboly, *True Ranger*, p. 334.

Chapter 30: Great Lakes Tribes Declare War

1. *BG*, August 15, 1763, p. 1.

2. On the height of the bluffs, Raymond Buyce (Mercyhurst College geology department), communication to author.

3. For descriptions of the attack on Fort Presque Isle, see Francis Parkman, Jr., *The History of the Conspiracy of Pontiac, and the War of the North American Tribes Against the English Colonies After the Conquest of Canada* (Boston: Little, Brown and Company, 1855); "Extract of a Court of Enquiry Held by Order of Major Gladwin to Enquire into the Manner of the Taking of Presque Isle, Detroit. July 10, 1763," in Extracts of Letters, Declaration Etc. in *Historical Collections, Michigan Pioneer and Historical Society* 27 (1897), pp. 638–39; Samuel P. Bates, *History of Erie County, Pennsylvania* (Chicago: Warner, Beers & Co., 1884), chap. 7.

4. *NYM*, September 5, 1763, p. 2.

5. Rogers to Betsy, July 15, 1763, quoted in Gary Zaboly, *A True Ranger: The Life and Many Wars of Major Robert Rogers* (Garden City Park, N.Y.: Royal Block House, 2004), p. 340.

6. William R. Nester, *"Haughty Conquerors": Amherst and the Great Indian Uprising of 1763* (Westport, Conn.: Praeger, 2000), p. 22.

7. Amherst to Johnson, February 22, 1761, cited in Timothy J. Todish and Todd E. Harburn, *A "Most Troublesome Situation": The British Military and the Pontiac Indian Uprising of 1763–1764* (Fleischmanns, N.Y.: Purple Mountain Press, 2006), pp. 37–38.

8. For an excellent discussion of the intricacies of gift giving, see Gregory Evans Dowd, *War Under Heaven: Pontiac, the Indian Nations, & the British Empire* (Baltimore: Johns Hopkins University Press, 2002), pp. 70–75.

9. Walters to Johnson, April 5, 1762, in *The Sir William Johnson Papers* (Albany: State University of New York, 1921–65), 10:427.

10. Thomas Hutchins to Croghan, cited in Todish and Harburn, *"Most Troublesome Situation,"* p. 40.

11. Campbell to Amherst, November 28, 1761, cited ibid.

12. Dowd, *War Under Heaven,* p. 65; Richard Middleton, *Pontiac's War: Its Causes, Course and Consequences* (New York: Routledge, 2007), p. 67.

13. Dowd, *War Under Heaven,* p. 66.

14. Robert Navarre, "The Journal of Pontiac's Conspiracy," in Milo Milton Quaife, *The Siege of Detroit in 1763: The Journal of Pontiac's Conspiracy and John Rutherfurd's Narrative of a Captivity* (Chicago: Lakeside Press, 1958), p. 22.

15. Fred Anderson, *Crucible of War: The Seven Years' War and the Fate of Empire in British North America, 1754–1766* (New York: Alfred A. Knopf, 2000), p. 538.

16. Amherst to Gladwin, May 29, 1763, in *Johnson Papers,* 4:98.

17. Anderson, *Crucible,* p. 538.

18. Alexander Henry, *Travels and Adventures: In Canada and the Indian Territories Between the Years 1760 and 1776* (New York: Burt Franklin, 1969), pp. 78–82.

19. Amherst to Gladwin and Bouquet, quoted in Howard H. Peckham, *Pontiac and the Indian Uprising* (Princeton, N.J.: Princeton University Press, 1947), pp. 226–27.

20. Navarre, "Journal of Pontiac's Conspiracy," pp. 114–15.

21. *NYM,* August 8, 1763, p. 3.

22. Rogers to Lord Hillsborough, November 17, 1771, cited in Zaboly, *True Ranger,* p. 339.

23. *BG,* August 8, 1763, p. 2.

Chapter 31: Encounter with Pontiac

1. Robert Rogers, *Ponteach; or, The Savages of America,* in *Representative Plays by American Dramatists,* ed. Montrose J. Moses (New York: Benjamin Blom, 1964), p. 128.

2. *NYM,* September 5, 1763, p. 2; *NYM,* August 8, 1763, p. 2.

3. Robert Rogers, *A Concise Account of North America: containing a description of the several British colonies on that continent . . .* (London, 1765), p. 244.

4. Ibid.

5. There's much confusion in the historical record about how many men formed the attack party. The best source is the "List of the Detachment commanded by Capt. Dalyell, At Detroit, the 31st of July, 1763," in *NYM,* September 5, 1763, p. 3, which breaks down the number of officers and rank and file. Added to the list were eight traders and two habitant guides mentioned in *NYM,* same date, p. 2.

6. U.S. Naval Observatory, Astronomical Applications Department, Sun and Moon Data for July 31, 1763.

7. Jehu Hay, journal, in Milo Milton Quaife, *The Siege of Detroit in 1763: The*

Journal of Pontiac's Conspiracy and John Rutherfurd's Narrative of a Captivity (Chicago: Lakeside Press, 1958), p. 218.

8. Details of Detroit are from John Montressor's "Plan of Detroit and Its Environs, 1763," in Seymour I. Schwartz, *The French and Indian War, 1754–1763: The Imperial Struggle for North America* (Edison, N.J.: Castle Books, 1994), p. 156.
9. *NYM*, September 9, 1763, p. 2.
10. Mante's account of the Battle of Bloody Run is in Robert Rogers, *The Annotated and Illustrated Journals of Major Robert Rogers*, ed. Timothy Todish (Fleischmanns, N.Y.: Purple Mountain Press, 2002), p. 279.
11. Hay journal, entry for July 31, 1763, in Quaife, *Siege of Detroit*, p. 219.
12. *TGM*, October 1763; Quaife, *Siege of Detroit*, p. 219; *NYM*, September 5, 1763, p. 2.
13. *NYM*, September 5, 1763, p. 2.

Chapter 32: Imperial Capital

1. Heinrich Heine, quoted in *Knopf Guides: London* (New York: Alfred A. Knopf, 1992), pp. 118–19.
2. Rogers to Betsy, "on Board the Ship ye 27th 1765," *FTA*. For types of London buildings, see Richard B. Schwartz, *Daily Life in Johnson's London* (Madison: University of Wisconsin Press, 1983), p. 3; and Frederick A. Pottle, *Boswell's London Journal, 1762–1763* (New Haven, Conn.: Yale University Press, 2004), p. 44.
3. Rosamond Bayne-Powell, *Eighteenth-Century London Life* (New York: E. P. Dutton, 1938), p. 8.
4. For a good description of mid-eighteenth-century London, see Alan Charles Kors, ed., *The Encyclopedia of the Enlightenment* (New York: Oxford University Press, 2003), entry for "London."
5. *Monthly Review* 24 (January 1766), p. 79.
6. "In Defense of Americans," *London Chronicle*, May 12, 1759.
7. John Adams, diary entry for December 27, 1765, in *Adams Family Papers: An Electronic Archive*, Massachusetts Historical Society, online at www.masshist.org.
8. *Public Advertiser*, August 3, 1765, p. 2.
9. *BEP*, November 18, 1765, p. 3.
10. *BNL*, December 19, 1765.
11. Tobias Smollett, *The Expedition of Humphry Clinker* (London: Oxford University Press, 1966), p. 88.
12. Penelope J. Corfield, "Walking the City Streets: The Urban Odyssey in Eighteenth-Century England," *Journal of Urban History* 16, no. 2 (February 1990), pp. 132–62.
13. Aileen Ribeiro, *The Art of Dress: Fashion in England and France, 1750–1820* (New Haven, Conn.: Yale University Press, 1995), p. 46.
14. Rogers mentions the New England Coffee House in a letter to Betsy, quoted

in Gary Zaboly, *A True Ranger: The Life and Many Wars of Major Robert Rogers* (Garden City Park, N.Y.: Royal Block House, 2004), p. 357. Ned Ward is quoted in J. Pelzer and L. Pelzer, "Coffee Houses of Augustan London," *History Today* (October 1982), p. 40.

15. George Winchester Stone, Jr., and George M. Kahrl, *David Garrick: A Critical Biography* (Carbondale: Southern Illinois University Press, 1979), p. 667; Bayne-Powell, *Eighteenth-Century London Life*, pp. 164–65.

16. Robert Rogers, *The Annotated and Illustrated Journals of Major Robert Rogers,* ed. Timothy Todish (Fleischmanns, N.Y.: Purple Mountain Press, 2002), introduction.

17. Robert Rogers, *A Concise Account of North America: containing a description of the several British colonies on that continent . . .* (London, 1765), p. vi.

18. Ibid., p. 233.

19. Ibid., pp. 151–52.

Chapter 33: *A Concise Account of North America*

1. Charles Townshend to Dr. Richard Brocklesby, August 24, 1765, quoted in Gary Zaboly, *A True Ranger: The Life and Many Wars of Major Robert Rogers* (Garden City Park, N.Y.: Royal Block House, 2004), p. 360.

2. *NHG*, December 20, 1765, p. 1.

3. Henry S. Conway to Gage, St. James's, October 12, 1765, in *The Correspondence of General Thomas Gage with the Secretaries of State, 1763– 1775,* ed. Clarence Edwin Carter (New Haven, Conn.: Yale University Press, 1931), 2:26–27.

4. *TGM*, December 1765.

5. *Monthly Review; or, Literary Journal*, January 1766.

6. Gage to Johnson, January 13, 1766, cited in Zaboly, *True Ranger*, p. 367.

Chapter 34: Trouble Brewing

1. Based on 1768 figures; see Thomas L. Purvis, *Colonial America to 1763,* Almanacs of American Life Series (New York: Facts on File, 1999), p. 122.

2. *NYG*, May 5, 1766, p. 3.

3. John Montresor, journal entry for May 3, 1766, in G. D. Scull, *Journals of Captain John Montresor* (Philadelphia: Pennsylvania Historical Society, 1882), p. 364.

4. David A. Armour, *Treason? At Michilimackinac: The Proceedings of a General Court Martial Held at Montreal in October 1768 for the Trial of Major Robert Rogers* (Mackinac Island, Mich.: Mackinac Island State Park Commission, 1972), pp. 44–45.

5. Ibid.

6. Gage to Barrington, March 12, 1768, in *The Correspondence of General*

Thomas Gage with the Secretaries of State, 1763–1775, ed. Clarence Edwin Carter (New Haven, Conn.: Yale University Press, 1931), 2:454.

7. Johnson to Gage, June 2, 1766, cited in Gary Zaboly, *A True Ranger: The Life and Many Wars of Major Robert Rogers* (Garden City Park, N.Y.: Royal Block House, 2004), p. 372.

8. Johnson to Gage, June 12, 1766, ibid.

9. Johnson to Gage, January 25, 1766, in William Johnson, *The Sir William Johnson Papers* (Albany: State University of New York, 1921–65), 12:9.

10. Alexander Henry entry, *DCB*.

11. Armour, *Treason?*, p. 93.

12. David A. Armour and Keith R. Widder, *At the Crossroads: Michilimackinac During the American Revolution* (Mackinac Island, Mich.: Mackinac Island State Park Commission, 1978), p. 25.

13. Eugene T. Petersen, *Gentlemen on the Frontier: A Pictorial Record of the Culture of Michilimackinac* (Mackinac Island, Mich.: Mackinac Island State Park Commission, 1964), p. 42.

14. Ibid., p. 27.

15. Armour and Widder, *At the Crossroads*, p. 40.

16. Ibid., p. 26.

17. Ibid., p. 12.

18. *BG*, November 3, 1766, p. 2.

19. W. L. Clements, ed., "Rogers's Michillimackinac Journal," in *American Antiquarian Society Proceedings*, new ser., vol. 28 (1918), pp. 262–63.

20. Ibid., p. 264.

21. Ibid., pp. 263–64.

22. Claus to Johnson, October 16, 1766, in *Johnson Papers*, 12:212.

23. *BG*, November 3, 1766.

Chapter 35: The Northwest Passage

1. "A Proposal by Robert Rogers, Esq.," cited in Gary Zaboly, *A True Ranger: The Life and Many Wars of Major Robert Rogers* (Garden City Park, N.Y.: Royal Block House, 2004), p. 359.

2. David A. Armour, *Treason? At Michilimackinac: The Proceedings of a General Court Martial Held at Montreal in October 1768 for the Trial of Major Robert Rogers* (Mackinac Island, Mich.: Mackinac Island State Park Commission, 1972), p. 63.

3. Ibid., p. 49.

4. Cited in Keith R. Widder, "The 1767 Maps of Robert Rogers and Jonathan Carver: A Proposal for the Establishment of the Colony of Michilimackinac," *Michigan Historical Review* 30, no. 2 (Fall 2004).

5. W. L. Clements, ed., "Rogers's Michillimackinac Journal," in *American Antiquarian Society Proceedings*, new ser., vol. 28 (1918), p. 232.

6. Ibid., p. 233.

7. U. P. Hedrick, *The Land of the Crooked Tree* (New York: Oxford University Press, 1948), p. 58.
8. Clements, "Rogers's Michillimackinac Journal," pp. 268–69.
9. Ibid., p. 270.
10. Ibid., p. 266.
11. Widder, "1767 Maps of Rogers."
12. Clements, "Rogers's Michillimackinac Journal," p. 254.
13. Ibid., pp. 255–56.
14. Armour, *Treason?*, p. 79.
15. Clements, "Rogers's Michillimackinac Journal," p. 256.
16. John R. Cuneo, *Robert Rogers of the Rangers* (Ticonderoga, N.Y.: Fort Ticonderoga Museum, 1988), p. 204.
17. Cited in Zaboly, *True Ranger*, p. 389.
18. Clements, "Rogers's Michillimackinac Journal," p. 258.
19. Gage to Shelburne, August 24, 1767, in *The Correspondence of General Thomas Gage with the Secretaries of State, 1763–1775*, ed. Clarence Edwin Carter (New Haven, Conn.: Yale University Press, 1931), p. 148.
20. Widder, "1767 Maps of Rogers."
21. Cited in Louise Phelps Kellogg, *The British Regime in Wisconsin and the Northwest* (Madison: State Historical Society of Wisconsin, 1935), p. 77.
22. Cited in Zaboly, *True Ranger*, p. 389.

Chapter 36: Treason!

1. Johnson to Gage, October 22, 1767, *DHSNY*, 2:513.
2. Peter Marshall, "The Michilimackinac Misfortunes of Commissary Roberts," in *The Fur Trade Revisited: Selected Papers of the Sixth North American Fur Trade Conference, Mackinac Island, Michigan, 1991*, ed. Jennifer S. H. Brown, W. J. Eccles, and Donald P. Heldman (East Lansing/Mackinac Island: Michigan State University Press, 1994), pp. 286–87.
3. John R. Cuneo, *Robert Rogers of the Rangers* (Ticonderoga, N.Y.: Fort Ticonderoga Museum, 1988), p. 210.
4. David A. Armour, *Treason? At Michilimackinac: The Proceedings of a General Court Martial Held at Montreal in October 1768 for the Trial of Major Robert Rogers* (Mackinac Island, Mich.: Mackinac Island State Park Commission, 1972), pp. 17–18.
5. Ibid., p. 20.
6. Ibid., p. 67.
7. Roberts to Guy Johnson, August 20, 1767, cited in Gary Zaboly, *A True Ranger: The Life and Many Wars of Major Robert Rogers* (Garden City Park, N.Y.: Royal Block House, 2004), p. 391.
8. Benjamin Roberts to Fre. Christopher Spiesmacher, August 20, 1767, in William Johnson, *The Sir William Johnson Papers* (Albany: State University of New York, 1921–65), 10:629–30.

9. Cited in Zaboly, *True Ranger*, p. 392.
10. Johnson to Gage, December 6, 1767, *DHSNY*, 2:896.
11. Armour, *Treason?*, p. 55.
12. Ibid., p. 74.
13. Gage to Shelburne, January 23, 1768, in *The Correspondence of General Thomas Gage with the Secretaries of State, 1763–1775*, ed. Clarence Edwin Carter (New Haven, Conn.: Yale University Press, 1931), 1:161.
14. Cuneo, *Robert Rogers*, p. 222.
15. Gage to Shelburne, January 23, 1768, in Carter, *Correspondence of Gage*, 1:161.
16. Gage to Shelburne, March 12, 1768, ibid., 1:164.
17. Johnson to Gage, September 11, 1767, *DHSNY*, 2:502.
18. Johnson to Gage, September 21, 1767, *DHSNY*, 2:502–3.
19. Cuneo effectively lays out the Cole materials in his unpublished footnotes, *FTA*, Chapter 22, fn. 59.
20. The transactions between Rogers and Roberts are taken from a series of memorandums in August and September 1767 of witnesses to the altercation at Fort Michilimackinac, in the Burton Historical Collection, Detroit Public Library.
21. Spiesmaker to Johnson, September 22, 1767, Johnson Papers, 5:696–97.
22. Armour, *Treason?*, p. 25.
23. Johnson to Gage, October 22, 1767, *DHSNY*, 2:513.
24. Armour, *Treason?*, p. 25.

Chapter 37: Locked Up and Charged

1. David A. Armour, *Treason? At Michilimackinac: The Proceedings of a General Court Martial Held at Montreal in October 1768 for the Trial of Major Robert Rogers* (Mackinac Island, Mich.: Mackinac Island State Park Commission, 1972), p. 94.
2. John R. Cuneo, *Robert Rogers of the Rangers* (Ticonderoga, N.Y.: Fort Ticonderoga Museum, 1988), p. 225.
3. Armour, *Treason?*, p. 94.
4. *BG*, February 29, 1768, cited in Gary Zaboly, *A True Ranger: The Life and Many Wars of Major Robert Rogers* (Garden City Park, N.Y.: Royal Block House, 2004), p. 399.
5. *NHG*, July 1, 1768.
6. *NYG*, June 12, 1768, cited in Cuneo, *Robert Rogers*, p. 228.
7. Cuneo, *Robert Rogers*, p. 288.
8. Gavin Cochrane to Johnson, October 30, 1767, in *The Sir William Johnson Papers* (Albany: State University of New York, 1921–65), 4:769; Johnson to Cochrane, November 14, 1767, ibid., 4:788.
9. Cited and discussed in Zaboly, *True Ranger*, p. 399.
10. Gage to Hillsborough, August 17, 1768, in *The Correspondence of General*

Thomas Gage with the Secretaries of State, 1763–1775, ed. Clarence Edwin Carter (New Haven, Conn.: Yale University Press, 1931), 1:184.

11. Memorial of Robert Rogers to Hillsborough, December 21, 1769, cited in Cuneo, *Robert Rogers*, p. 231.

12. Armour, *Treason?*, p. 62.

13. Ibid., p. 87.

14. Gould to Gage, March 1, 1769, cited in Zaboly, *True Ranger*, p. 413.

15. Gage to Barrington, May 11, 1769, in Carter, *Correspondence of Gage*, 2:506.

16. Gage to Barrington, July 22, 1769, ibid., 2:518.

Chapter 38: Failing Fortunes

1. Peter Okun, *Crime and the Nation: Prison Reforms and Popular Fiction in Philadelphia, 1786–1800* (London: Taylor and Francis, 2002), p. 120.

2. John Ashton, *The Fleet: Its River, Prison and Marriages* (London: T. Fisher Unwin, 1889), p. 297.

3. Benjamin Roberts noted that in an early brief stay at King's Bench Prison, Rogers "fought his Way thro the jailers & turnkeys, would pay no fees," as cited in John R. Cuneo, *Robert Rogers of the Rangers* (Ticonderoga, N.Y.: Fort Ticonderoga Museum, 1988), p. 246.

4. George M. Dorothy, *London Life in the Eighteenth Century* (New York: Capricorn Books, 1965), p. 300.

5. Rosamond Bayne-Powell, *Eighteenth-Century London Life* (New York: E. P. Dutton, 1938), p. 216.

6. Rogers to Betsy, 1770, cited in Gary Zaboly, *A True Ranger: The Life and Many Wars of Major Robert Rogers* (Garden City Park, N.Y.: Royal Block House, 2004), p. 418.

7. Ibid.

8. Cuneo, *Robert Rogers*, p. 247.

9. *NHG*, September 21, 1770; *BEP*, September 24, 1770, and November 19, 1770, as cited in Zaboly, *True Ranger*, p. 419.

10. Cuneo unpublished footnotes, *FTA*, Chapter 22, fn. 59.

11. Gage to Grey Cooper, September 8, 1770, in *The Correspondence of General Thomas Gage with the Secretaries of State, 1763–1775*, ed. Clarence Edwin Carter (New Haven, Conn.: Yale University Press, 1931), 2:558–59.

12. Gage to John Robinson, March 6, 1771, ibid., 2:568.

13. Zaboly, *True Ranger*, p. 420.

14. Ibid., p. 422.

15. *NHG*, May 22, 1772.

16. *NHG*, August 6, 1773.

17. Gage entry, *DCB*.

18. Lord George Germain, quoted ibid.

19. John C. Dann, "North West Passage Revisited" in *The American Magazine* 2, no. 1 (Spring–Summer 1986), p. 31.

20. Ibid., p. 32.
21. Ibid., p. 33.
22. Ibid., pp. 33–35.
23. Ibid., pp. 36–44.

Chapter 39: A Bitter Homecoming

1. Wheelock to Washington, December 2, 1775, in Peter Force, ed., "Correspondence, Proceedings, &c., December, 1775," in *American archives: consisting of a collection of authentick records, state papers, debates, and letters and other notices of publick affairs, the whole forming a documentary history of the origin and progress of the North American colonies; of the causes and accomplishment of the American revolution; and of the Constitution of government for the United States, to the final ratification thereof.* (Washington, D.C.: M. St. Clair Clarke and Peter Force, 1848–53), ser. 4, vol. 4, p. 159.
2. John R. Cuneo, *Robert Rogers of the Rangers* (Ticonderoga, N.Y.: Fort Ticonderoga Museum, 1988), p. 260.
3. John C. Dann, "North West Passage Revisited" in *The American Magazine* 2, no. 1 (Spring–Summer 1986), p. 24.
4. John Adams, diary entry for September 21, 1775, cited in Gary Zaboly, *A True Ranger: The Life and Many Wars of Major Robert Rogers* (Garden City Park, N.Y.: Royal Block House, 2004), p. 431.
5. "Minutes of the Pennsylvania Committee of Safety, September 1775," *American Archives*, ser. 4, vol. 3, p. 866.
6. Dann, "North West Passage Revisited," p. 24.
7. *Scots Magazine*, October 1775, p. 553.
8. Dann, "North West Passage Revisited," p. 24.
9. Zaboly, *True Ranger*, p. 433.
10. Wheelock to Washington, December 2, 1775, in Peter Force, ed., "Correspondence, Proceedings, &c., December, 1775," in *American Archives*, ser. 4, vol. 4, p. 158.
11. Ibid., p. 159.
12. Sullivan to Washington, December 17, 1775, Peter Force, ed., "North Carolina Provincial Council, December, 1775," in *American Archives*, ser. 4, vol. 4, p. 300.
13. Washington to Schuyler, January 16, 1776, Peter Force, ed., "Correspondence, Proceedings, &c., January, 1776," in *American Archives*, ser. 4, vol. 4, p. 696.
14. Sir Henry Clinton, cited in Cuneo, *Robert Rogers*, p. 261.
15. Dann, "North West Passage Revisited," p. 25.

Chapter 40: Confrontation with George Washington

1. Washington to President of Congress, June 27, 1776, Peter Force, ed., "Correspondence, Procedures, &c., June, 1776," in *American Archives*, ser. 4, vol. 6, pp. 1108–9.
2. John R. Cuneo, *Robert Rogers of the Rangers* (Ticonderoga, N.Y.: Fort Ticonderoga Museum, 1988), p. 262.
3. Gary Zaboly suggests that venereal disease was the reason for their split. See *A True Ranger: The Life and Many Wars of Major Robert Rogers* (Garden City Park, N.Y.: Royal Block House, 2004), p. 439.
4. Washington to President of Congress, June 27, 1776, Peter Force, ed., "Correspondence, Procedures, &c., June, 1776," in *American Archives*, ser. 4, vol. 6, p. 1108.
5. Jefferson to William Fleming, Philadelphia, July 1, 1776, in *The Papers of Thomas Jefferson*, ed. Julian P. Boyd (Princeton, N.J.: Princeton University Press, 1950), 1:412.
6. *NHG*, August 15, 1775.
7. John E. Ferling, review of Cuneo, *Robert Rogers*, in *Journal of American History* 75, no. 2 (September 1988), p. 597.
8. Washington to his brother Jack, 1754, *The Papers of George Washington: Colonial Series* (Charlottesville: University of Virginia Press, 1983), 1:118.
9. Washington to President of Congress, June 27, 1776, Peter Force, ed., "Correspondence, Procedures, &c., June, 1776," in *American Archives*, ser. 4, vol. 6, pp. 1108–9.
10. Luther Roby, *Reminiscences of the French War with Robert Rogers' Journal and a Memoir of General Stark* (Concord, N.H.: Luther Roby, 1831), p. 161.
11. Ibid., p. 162.
12. John Bartlett to John Langdon, Philadelphia, July 15, 1776, Peter Force, ed., "Correspondence, Proceedings, &c., July 1776," in *American Archives*, ser. 5, vol. 1, p. 348.

Chapter 41: Catching Nathan Hale

1. James Hutson, "Nathan Hale Revisited: A Tory's Account of the Arrest of the First American Spy," *Library of Congress Information Bulletin* (July–August 2003).
2. Hale's physical description, and details of his actions, come from George Dudley Seymour, *Documentary Life of Nathan Hale*, excerpted in "The Last Days and Valiant Death of Nathan Hale," *American Heritage* 15, no. 3 (April 1964).
3. Alexander Rose, *Washington's Spies: The Story of America's First Spy Ring* (New York: Bantam Dell, 2006), p. 19.
4. Hutson, "Nathan Hale Revisited," includes a transcription of the recently

discovered Tiffany journal entry that reveals Rogers's part in the Hale capture.

5. "Nathan Hale Blundered into a Trap, Papers Show," *New York Times*, September 21, 2003.
6. William Bamford, diary entry for September 22, 1776, in *Maryland Historical Magazine* 28 (1938), p. 10.

Chapter 42: End Games

1. Otto Hufeland, *Westchester County During the American Revolution, 1775–1783* (White Plains, N.Y.: Westchester County Historical Society, 1926), p. 99.
2. New York Committee of Safety to Washington, August 30, 1776, in *George Washington Papers at the Library of Congress, 1741–1700*, ser. 4, *General Correspondence, 1697–1799*.
3. Washington to Trumbull, September 30, 1776, *George Washington Papers at the Library of Congress, 1741–1799*, ser. 3c, *Varick Transcripts*, Letterbook 1.
4. Washington to Continental Congress, October 4, 1776, *George Washington Papers at the Library of Congress, 1741–1799*, ser. 3c, *Varick Transcripts*, Letterbook 2.
5. Trumbull to Washington, October 13, 1776, in *George Washington Papers at the Library of Congress, 1741–1700*, ser. 4, General Correspondence, *1697–1799*.
6. Extract of a letter from Colonel Haslet to General Rodney, October 28, 1776, Peter Force, ed., in *American Archives*, ser. 5, vol. 2, p. 1270.
7. *NHG*, November 26, 1776, cited in Gary Zaboly, *A True Ranger: The Life and Many Wars of Major Robert Rogers* (Garden City Park, N.Y.: Royal Block House, 2004), p. 451.
8. *NYG*, March 17, 1776.
9. Frederick Mackenzie, *Diary of Frederick Mackenzie, giving a daily narrative of his military service as an officer of the regiment of Royal Welch fusiliers during the years 1775–1781 in Massachusetts, Rhode Island and New York* (Cambridge, Mass.: Harvard University Press, 1930), 1:87.
10. Washington to Lee, November 27, 1776, in *George Washington Papers at the Library of Congress, 1741–1700*, ser. 4, General Correspondence, *1697–1799*.
11. Lee to Washington, November 30, 1776, ibid.
12. *BG*, February 10, 1777, p. 456.
13. Washington to Heath, February 4, 1777, in *George Washington Papers at the Library of Congress, 1741–1700*, ser. 4, General Correspondence, *1697–1799*.
14. Quoted in John R. Cuneo, *Robert Rogers of the Rangers* (Ticonderoga, N.Y.: Fort Ticonderoga Museum, 1988), p. 268.

15. Washington to Trumbull, April 12, 1777, in *George Washington Papers at the Library of Congress, 1741–1700*, ser. 4, General Correspondence, *1697–1799*.
16. James Rogers to Haldimand, April 29, 1780, cited in Zaboly, *True Ranger*, p. 466.

Epilogue

1. Rogers, *Concise Account*, p. 231.
2. Rick Atkinson, *The Day of Battle: The War in Sicily and Italy, 1943–1944* (New York: Henry Holt, 2007), pp. 43–44.
3. Robert Rogers, *The Annotated and Illustrated Journals of Major Robert Rogers*, ed. Timothy Todish (Fleischmanns, N.Y.: Purple Mountain Press, 2002), p. 78.

Map Credits

1. Penacook, New Hampshire, later Rumford and Concord. Nathaniel Bouton, *The History of Concord*, 1856.

2. Rogers's Sketch of the French Garrison at Crown Point, 1755. Library of Congress.

3. Fort Edward to Crown Point, 1759. Rogers's secret trail over the mountains labeled as "C." *Gentlemen's Magazine*, May 1759.

4. Plan of Fort Edward and Rogers' Island, 1759. Thomas Mante, *History of the Late War in North America*, 1772.

5. Battle on Snowshoes Schematic, 1758. Gary Zaboly.

6. British Approach to Carillon, 1758. John Almon, *Remembrancer*, 1778.

7. Thomas Jeffery's Map of Carillon and Attack by Abercromby's Forces, 1758. Fort Ticonderoga.

8. Fort Detroit and Environs, 1763. Author's Collection.

9. Fort Michilimackinac, 1766, by Lt. Perkins Magra. The Clements Library, University of Michigan, Ann Arbor.

10. New York During the Revolutionary War. *The London Gazette*.

A Note on Sources and Usage

Following the movements of the peripatetic Rogers has proved a challenge, but in every possible case I have attempted to cover the ground that he did, although I had the benefit of the car, vibram soles, kevlar canoes, and topographical maps where he obviously did not. This took me on rivers, all along the early New Hampshire, New York, and Vermont frontier, to Canada, South Carolina, and London, up many mountains, and scouring places where it's believed battles were fought and into the remains of old forts and outposts.

In addition to "ground truthing," I've relied on a wide array of sources and experts on topography, seasons, botany, and climate to reconstruct life and events in the eighteenth century. Where relevant, I've pulled on my past experiences as an extreme adventurer to suggest what Rogers and his men might have gone through on some of their scouts.

A great joy and frustration of doing research involving eighteenth-century documents is deciphering the cramped hand and sometime atrocious spelling of journal keepers and letter writers. I've not attempted to correct misspelling, nor clutter the quotations with "sic" notations. Rogers himself spelled his own name differently on occasion, sometimes as "Roger" or "Rodgers." As most style guides recommend, I've used the "apostrophe-plus-s" spelling for Rogers in the singular and plural possessive, except in the case of Rogers' Rangers and Rogers' Island, which have been spelled that way for generations in scholarly and popular literature.

Selected Bibliography

Bibliographic Abbreviations
Journals/Compendiums

BFTM   *Bulletin of the Fort Ticonderoga Museum*
CWJ   *Colonial Williamsburg Journal*
DAB   *Dictionary of American Biography*
DCB   *Dictionary of Canadian Biography Online*
DHSNY   *Documentary History of the State of New York*
DRCHSNY   *Documentary Records of the Colonial History of the State of New York*
HNH   *Historical New Hampshire*
TGM   *The Gentleman's Magazine*
WMQ   *The William & Mary Quarterly*

Colonial Newspapers

BEP   *The Boston Evening-Post*
BG   *The Boston Gazette*
BNL   *The Boston News-Letter*
BPB   *The Boston Post-Boy*
BWNL   *The Boston Weekly News-Letter*
CM   *The Caledonian Mercury*
CG   *The Connecticut Gazette*
NCG   *The North Carolina Gazette*
NHG   *The New-Hampshire Gazette*
NYM   *The New-York Mercury*
PG   *The Pennsylvania Gazette*
SCG   *The South Carolina Gazette*

Archives

LO papers   Loudoun Papers, Huntington Library, San Marino, Calif.
AB papers   Abercromby Papers, Huntington Library, San Marino, Calif.
Rogers/Roche Papers   William L. Clements Library, University of Michigan, Ann Arbor
FTA   Fort Ticonderoga Archives
NHHS   New Hampshire Historical Society, Concord, N.H.

Selected Bibliography

Albertson, Garrett. "A Short Account of the Life, Travels, and Adventures of Garrett Albertson, Sr., 1845." *BFTM* 4, no. 2 (1936).

Anderson, Fred. *A People's Army: Massachusetts Soldiers and Society in the Seven Years' War.* Chapel Hill and London: University of North Carolina Press, 1984.

———. "Why Did Colonial New Englanders Make Bad Soldiers? Contractual Principles and Military Conduct During the Seven Years' War." *WMQ*, 3rd ser., vol. 38, no. 3 (1981), pp. 395–417.

———. *Crucible of War: The Seven Years' War and the Fate of Empire in British North America, 1754–1766.* New York: Alfred A. Knopf, 2000.

Armour, David A. *Treason? At Michilimackinac: The Proceedings of a General Court Martial Held at Montreal in October 1768 for the Trial of Major Robert Rogers.* Mackinac: Mackinac Island State Park Commission, 1972.

Armour, David A., and Keith R. Widder. *At the Crossroads: Michilimackinac During the American Revolution.* Mackinac Island, Mich.: Mackinac Island State Park Commission, 1978.

Axtell, James. *The European and the Indian: Essay in Ethnohistory of Colonial North America.* New York: Oxford University Press, 1982.

———. "Babel of Tongues: Communicating with the Indians in Eastern North America." In *The Language Encounter in the Americas, 1492–1800: A Collection of Essays.* Edited by Edward G. Gray and Norman Fiering. New York: Berghahn Books, 2000.

Axtell, J., and W. C. Sturtevant. "The Unkindest Cut, or Who Invented Scalping?" *WMQ*, 3rd ser., vol. 37, no. 3. (July 1980), pp. 451–72.

Aykroyd, W. R. "Definition of Different Degrees of Starvation." In *Famine: A Symposium Dealing with Nutrition and Relief Operations in Times of*

Disaster. Edited by G. Blix, Y. Hofvander, and B. Vahlquist. Uppsala: Almquist and Wiksells, 1971.

Bailey, Kenneth P., ed. and trans. *Journal of Joseph Marin: French Colonial Explorer and Military Commander in the Wisconsin County, August 7, 1753–June 20, 1754.* Self-published, 1975.

Baldwin, Thomas Williams, ed. *The Revolutionary Journal of Col. Jeduthan Baldwin, 1775–1778.* Bangor: Printed for the De Burians, 1906.

Bayne-Powell, Rosamond. *Eighteenth-Century London Life.* New York: E. P. Dutton, 1938.

Bearor, Bob. *Leading by Example: Partisan Fighters and Leaders of New France, 1660–1760.* Bowie, Md.: Heritage Books, 2002.

Beattie, Daniel J. "The Adaptation of the British Army to Wilderness Warfare, 1755–1763." In *Adapting to Conditions: War and Society in the Eighteenth Century.* Edited by Ultee Maarten. University, Ala.: University of Alabama Press, 1986.

Beauchamp, W. M. "Rhymes from Old Powder-Horns." *Journal of American Folklore* 2, no. 5 (April–June 1889), pp. 117–22.

Belknap, Jeremy. *The History of New-Hampshire.* 3 vols. New York: Arno Press, 1972.

Bellico, Russell P. *Sails and Steam in the Mountains: A Maritime and Military History of Lake George and Lake Champlain.* Fleischmanns, N.Y.: Purple Mountain Press, 1992.

———. *Chronicles of Lake George: Journeys in War and Peace.* Fleischmanns, N.Y.: Purple Mountain Press, 1995.

Benes, Peter, ed. "New England/New France, 1600–1850." *Dublin Seminar for New England Folklife Annual Proceedings 1989.* Boston: Boston University, 1992.

Beston, Henry. *The Saint Lawrence.* New York: Farrar and Rinehart, 1942.

Blodget, Samuel. *A Prospective-Plan of the Battle near Lake George on the Eighth Day of September, 1755.* Boston: Richard Draper, 1755.

Botkin, B. A. *A Treasury of American Folklore: Stories, Ballads, and Traditions of the People.* New York: Crown, 1944.

Bouquet, Henry. *Bouquet Papers.* Edited by S. K. Stevens, Donald H. Kent, and Autumn L. Leonard. 6 vols. Harrisburg: Pennsylvania Historical and Museum Commission, 1951–94.

Bouton, Nathaniel. *The History of Concord, From Its First Grant in 1725 to the Organization of The City Government in 1853, With a History of the Ancient Penacooks.* Concord, N.H.: Benning W. Sanborn, 1856.

————., ed. *Provincial Papers. Documents and Records Relating to the Province of New-Hampshire, from the Earliest Period of its Settlement: 1623–1686.* Authority of the Legislature of New Hampshire, 1867–73.

Boyer, Paul S., and Stephen Nissenbaum, eds. *The Salem Witchcraft Papers.* New York: Da Capo Press, 1977.

Bridenbaugh, Carl. *Myths and Realities: Societies of the Colonial South.* New York: Atheneum, 1971.

Brown, Jennifer S. H., W. J. Eccles, and Donald P. Heldman, eds. *The Fur Trade Revisited: Selected Papers of the Sixth North American Fur Trade Conference, Mackinac Island, Michigan, 1991.* East Lansing/Mackinac Island: Michigan State University Press, 1994.

Brown, Thomas. "A plain narrativ of the uncommon sufferings and remarkable deliverance of Thomas Brown of Charlestown in New England." *Magazine of History.* Extra, No. 4, 1908.

Brumwell, Steve. " 'A Service Truly Critical': The British Army and Warfare with the North American Indians, 1755–1764." *War in History* 5, no. 2 (April 1998).

————. *Redcoats: The British Soldier and War in the Americas, 1755–1763.* Cambridge: Cambridge University Press, 2002.

————. *White Devil: A True Story of War, Savagery, and Vengeance in Colonial America.* Cambridge, Mass.: Da Capo Press, 2005.

Calder, Isabel M. *Colonial Captivities, Marches, and Journeys.* Port Washington, N.Y.: Kennikat Press, 1967.

Calloway, Colin G. "An Uncertain Destiny: Indian Captivities on the Upper Connecticut River." *Journal of American Studies* 17 (1983).

————. "Gray Lock's War." *Vermont History* 55 (1987).

————. *The Western Abenakis of Vermont, 1600–1800: War, Migration, and the Survival of an Indian People.* Norman and London: University of Oklahoma Press, 1990.

————., ed. *Dawnland Encounters: Indians and Europeans in Northern New England.* Hanover and London: University Press of New England, 1991.

————., ed. *North Country Captives: Selected Narratives of Indian Captivity from Vermont and New Hampshire.* Hanover, N.H.: University Press of New England, 1992.

————. *New Worlds for All: Indian, Europeans, and the Remaking of Early America.* Baltimore: Johns Hopkins University Press, 1997.

————. *The Scratch of a Pen: 1763 and the Transformation of North America.* Oxford: Oxford University Press, 2006.

Canup, John. *Out of the Wilderness: The Emergence of an American Identity in Colonial New England*. Middletown, Conn.: Wesleyan University Press, 1990.

Carroll, Joy. *Wolfe and Montcalm: Their Lives, Their Times, and the Fate of a Continent*. Buffalo, N.Y.: Firefly Books, 2004.

Carter, Clarence Edwin, ed. *The Correspondence of General Thomas Gage with the Secretaries of State, 1763–1775*. New Haven, Conn.: Yale University Press, 1931.

Cave, Alfred A. *The French and Indian War*. Westport, Conn.: Greenwood Press, 2004.

Charlevoix, Pierre de. *Journal of a Voyage to North America, Vol. 1*. March of America Facsimile Series, No. 36. Ann Arbor, Mich.: University Microfilms, 1966.

Chartrand, René. *French Fortresses in North America, 1535–1763: Quebec, Montreal, Louisbourg, and New Orleans*. Oxford: Osprey, 2005.

Chet, Guy. *Conquering the American Wilderness: The Triumph of European Warfare in the Colonial Northeast*. Amherst: University of Massachusetts Press, 2003.

Christie, Ian R., and Benjamin W. Labaree. *Empire or Independence, 1760–1776: A British-American Dialogue on the Coming of the American Revolution*. New York: W. W. Norton, 1976.

Clark, Charles E. *The Eastern Frontier: The Settlement of Northern New England, 1610–1763*. New York: Alfred A. Knopf, 1970.

Clarke, Desmond. *Arthur Dobbs Esquire, 1689–1765: Surveyor-General of Ireland, Prospector and Governor of North Carolina*. London: Bodley Head, 1958.

Cleaveland, John. "Journal of the Rev. John Cleaveland, 14 June 1758–25 October 1758." *BFTM* 10, no. 3 (1959).

Cleland, John. *Tombo-Chiqui; or, The American Savage. A Dramatic Entertainment in Three Acts*. London: S. Hooper, 1758.

Clements, W. L., ed. "Rogers's Michillimackinac Journal." *American Antiquarian Society Proceedings*, new series, 28 (1918).

Corbett, Theodore. *A Clash of Cultures on the Warpath of Nations: The Colonial Wars in the Hudson-Champlain Valley*. Fleischmanns, N.Y.: Purple Mountain Press, 2002.

Corfield, Penelope J. "Walking the City Streets: The Urban Odyssey in Eighteenth-Century England." *Journal of Urban History* 16, no. 2 (February 1990).

Cox, James A. "Bilboes, Brands, and Branks: Colonial Crimes and Punishments." *CWJ* (Spring 2003).

Cronan, William. *Changes in the Land: Indians, Colonists, and the Ecology of New England.* New York: Hill and Wang, 1983.

Cuneo, John R. *Robert Rogers of the Rangers.* Ticonderoga, N.Y.: Fort Ticonderoga Museum, 1988.

Darling, Anthony D. *Red Coat and Brown Bess.* Bloomfield, Ont.: Museum Restoration Service, 1971.

Darlington, Mary C., ed. *History of Col. Henry Bouquet and the Western Frontiers of Pennsylvania, 1747–1764.* New York: Arno Press, 1971.

Day, Gordon M. "Rogers' Raid in Indian Tradition." *Historical New Hampshire* (June 1962), pp. 3–17.

———. "Western Abenaki." In *Handbook of North American Indians.* Edited by William C. Sturtevant (Washington, D.C.: Smithsonian Institution, 1978–2004), vol. 15.

———. "Identity of the St. Francis Indians," in *In Search of New England's Past: Selected Essays by Gordon M. Day.* Edited by Michael K. Foster and William Cowan. (Amherst: University of Massachusetts Press, 1998.)

DeGraaf, Richard M., et. al. *Technical Guide to Forest Wildlife Habitat Management in New England.* Hanover, N.H.: University Press of New England, 2006.

Demos, John Putnam. *Entertaining Satan: Witchcraft and the Culture of Early New England.* New York: Oxford University Press, 1982.

De Voto, Bernard. *The Course of Empire.* Boston: Houghton Mifflin, 1952.

Dixon, David. *Never Come to Peace Again: Pontiac's Uprising and the Fate of the British Empire in North America.* Norman: University of Oklahoma Press, 2005.

Dodge, L. W. "Along the John Stark River, From Agiocochook to the Connecticut." *Granite Monthly* 5, no. 11 (August 1882).

Dowd, Gregory Evans. *A Spirited Resistance: The North American Struggle for Indian Unity, 1745–1815.* Baltimore: Johns Hopkins University Press, 1992.

———. *War Under Heaven: Pontiac, the Indian Nations, and the British Empire.* Baltimore: Johns Hopkins University Press, 2002

Drake, Samuel Adams. *Old Landmarks and Historic Personages of Boston.* Detroit, Mich.: Singing Tree Press, 1970.

Drake, Samuel Gardner. *A particular history of the five years French and Indian war in New England and parts adjacent, from its declaration by the King of France, March 15, 1744, to the treaty with the eastern Indians, Oct. 16, 1749, sometimes called Governor Shirley's war. With a memoir of Major-General Shirley, accompanied by his portrait and other engravings. By Samuel G. Drake.* Albany, N.Y.: J. Munsell, 1870.

Dupuy, R. Ernest, and Trevor N. Dupuy. *The Harper Encyclopedia of Military History: From 3500 BC to the Present.* New York: HarperCollins, 1993.

Dwight, Timothy. *Travels in New England and New York.* Cambridge, Mass.: Belknap Press, 1969.

Eames, Steven C. "Rustic Warriors: Warfare and the Provincial Soldier on the Northern Frontier, 1689–1748." Ph.D. diss., University of New Hampshire, 1989.

Eastburn, Robert. *A faithful narrative, of the many dangers and sufferings, as well as wonderful deliverances of Robert Eastburn during his late captivity among the Indians: together with some remarks upon the country of Canada, and the religion, and policy of its inhabitants,* 1758.

Eccles, W. J. *The Canadian, 1534–1760.* Albuquerque: University of New Mexico Press, 1983.

———. "The Fur Trade and Eighteenth-Century Imperialism." *WMQ,* 3rd ser., vol. 40, no. 3 (July 1983).

Eid, Leroy V. "The Cardinal Principle of Northeast Woodland Indian War." *Papers of the Thirteenth Algonquian Conference.* Ottawa: Carleton University, 1982.

———. " 'A Kind of Running Fight': Indian Battlefield Tactics in the Late Eighteenth-Century." *Western Pennsylvania Historical Magazine* 71, no. 2 (April 1988).

Feintuch, Burt, and David H. Waters, eds. *The Encyclopedia of New England: The Culture and History of an American Region.* New Haven, Conn.: Yale University Press, 2005.

Ferling, John. *A Wilderness of Miseries: War and Warriors in Early America.* Westport, Conn.: Greenwood Press, 1980.

Fischer, David Hackett. *Albion's Seed: Four British Folkways in America.* New York: Oxford University Press, 1989.

Fitch, Jabez. *The Diary of Jabez Fitch, Jr. May 20, 1757 to April 24, 1758.* New York: Rogers Island Historical Association, 1966.

Force, Peter, ed. *American archives: consisting of a collection of authentick records, state papers, debates, and letters and other notices of publick affairs, the whole forming a documentary history of the origin and progress of the North American colonies; of the causes and accomplishment of the American revolution; and of the Constitution of government for the United States, to the final ratification thereof.* Washington, D.C.: M. St. Clair Clarke and Peter Force, 1848–53.

Foster, Michael K., and William Cowan, eds. *In Search of New England's Native Past: Selected Essays by Gordon M. Day.* Amherst: University of Massachusetts Press, 1998.

Franquet, Louis. *Voyages et Mémoires sur Le Canada par Franquet.* Montreal: Institut Canadien de Québec, 1974.

Fuller, Archelaus. "The Journal of Archelaus Fuller—May–November 1758." *BFTM* 13, no. 1 (December 1970).

Fuller, J.F.C. *British Light Infantry in the Eighteenth Century.* London: Hutchison & Co. Paternoster Row, 1925.

Gallay, Alan. *Colonial Wars of North America, 1512–1763: An Encyclopedia.* New York: Garland, 1996.

Gallup, Andrew, and Donald F. Shoffer. *La Marine: The French Colonial Soldier in Canada, 1745–1761.* Bowie, Md.: Heritage Books, 1992.

Gipson, Lawrence Henry. "The American Revolution as an Aftermath of the Great War for the Empire, 1754–1763." *Political Science Quarterly* 65, no. 1 (March 1950).

Grace, Henry. *The History of the Life and Sufferings of Henry Grace of Basingstoke, in the County of Southampton.* Reading, England: Printed for the Author, 1764.

Grant, Anne MacVicar. *Memoirs of an American Lady; With Sketches of Manners and Scenes in American, as they Existed Previous to the Revolution.* New York: Appleton, 1846.

Graves, Donald E., ed. *Fighting for Canada: Seven Battles, 1758–1945.* Toronto: Robin Brass Studio, 2000.

Grenier, John E. " 'Of Great Utility': The Public Identity of Early American Rangers and Its Impact on American Society." *War and Society* 21, no. 1 (May 2003).

———. *The First Way of War: American War Making on the Frontier, 1607–1814.* New York: Cambridge University Press, 2005.

Gridley, Luke. *Luke Gridley's Diary of 1757.* Hartford, Conn.: Acorn Club, 1907.

Griffin, Patrick. *The People with No Name: Ireland's Ulster Scots, America's Scots Irish, and the Creation of a British Atlantic World, 1689–1764.* Princeton, N.J.: Princeton University Press, 2001.

Haefeli, Evan, and Kevin Sweeney. "Revisiting the Redeemed Captive: New Perspectives on the 1704 Attack on Deerfield." *WMQ* 52 (January 1995).

———. *Captors and Captives: The 1704 French and Indian Raid on Deerfield*. Amherst and Boston: University of Massachusetts Press, 2003.

Hall, Dennis Jay. *The Journal of Sir William Johnson's Scouts 1755 and 1756: The Early Scouts of Robert Rogers & Co. Along the Shores of Lake George & Lake Champlain*. Panton, Vt.: Essence of Vermont, 1999.

Hamilton, Edward P., ed. and trans. *Adventures in the Wilderness: The American Journals of Louis Antoine de Bougainville, 1756–1760*. Norman: University of Oklahoma Press, 1964.

Harris, R. Cole. *Historical Atlas of Canada*, vol. 1, *From the Beginning to 1800*. Toronto: University of Toronto Press, 1987.

Hawke, David Freeman. *Everyday Life in Early America*. New York: Harper and Row, 1988.

Hedrick, U. P. *The Land of the Crooked Tree*. New York: Oxford University Press, 1948.

Henry, Alexander. *Travels and Adventures: In Canada and the Indian Territories Between the Years 1760 and 1776*. New York: Burt Franklin, 1969.

Higginbotham, Don. "The Early American Way of War: Reconnaissance and Appraisal." *WMQ*, 3d ser., vol. 44, no. 2 (April 1987), pp. 230–73.

Hinderaker, Eric, and Peter C. Mancall. *At the Edge of Empire: The Backcountry in British North America*. Baltimore: Johns Hopkins University Press, 2003.

Hirsch, Adam J. "The Collision of Military Cultures in Seventeenth-Century New England." *Journal of American History* 74, no. 4 (March 1988).

Hocking, Frederick. *Starvation: Social and Psychological Aspects of a Basic Biological Stress*. Australian Medical Association's Merwyn Archdall Medical Monograph Number 6. Sydney: Australasian Medical Publishing Company, 1969.

Holmes, Richard. *Redcoat: The British Soldier in the Age of Horse and Musket*. New York: W. W. Norton, 2001.

Howe, Joseph S. *Historical Sketch on the Town of Methuen from Its Settlement to the Year 1876*. Methuen, Mass.: E. L. Houghton & Co., 1876.

Hubbard, Jake T. "Americans as Guerrilla Fighters: Robert Rogers and His Rangers." *American Heritage* 5, no. 22 (August 1971).

Huber, Thomas M. *Compound Warfare: That Fatal Knot.* Fort Leavenworth, Kans.: U. S. Army Command and General Staff College Press, 2002.

Huden, J. C. "The White Chief of the St. Francis Abenakis—Some Aspects of Border Warfare, 1690–1790." *Vermont History* 24 (1956).

Jackson, Donald. *Thomas Jefferson and the Stony Mountains: Exploring the West from Monticello.* Norman: University of Oklahoma Press, 1993.

Jefferson, Thomas. *Notes on the State of Virginia.* New York: Harper and Row, Publishers, 1964.

Johnson, William. *The Sir William Johnson Papers.* Albany: University of the State of New York, 1921–65.

Josselyn, John. *New-England's Rarities Discovered.* Boston: Massachusetts Historical Society, 1972.

Kalm, Peter. *Peter Kalm's Travels in North America; the America of 1750; the English version of 1770, rev. from the original Swedish and edited by Adolph B. Benson.* New York: Dover, 1964.

Kayworth, Alfred E., and Raymond G. Potvin. *The Scalp Hunters: Abenaki Ambush at Lovewell Pond—1725.* Boston: Branden Books, 2002.

Keegan, John. *Fields of Battle: The War for North America.* New York: Alfred A. Knopf, 1996.

Kellogg, Louise Phelps. *The British Regime in Wisconsin and the Northwest.* Madison: State Historical Society of Wisconsin, 1935.

Kidder, Frederick. "The Adventures of Capt. Lovewell." *New England Historical and Genealogical Register* 7 (January 1853).

Kimball, Gertrude Selwyn. *Correspondence of William Pitt when Secretary of State with Colonial Governors and Military and Naval Commissioners in America,* 2 vols. New York: Macmillan, 1906.

King, Duane H., ed. *The Memoirs of Lt. Henry Timberlake: The Story of a Soldier, Adventurer, and Emissary to the Cherokees, 1756–1765.* Cherokee, N.C.: Museum of the Cherokee Indian Press, 2007.

Knowles, Nathaniel. "The Torture of Captives By the Indians of Eastern North America." *Proceedings of the American Philosophical Society* 82 (1940).

Knox, Captain John. *An Historical Journal of the Campaign in North America For the Years 1757, 1758, 1759, 1760.* Toronto: Champlain Society, 1914.

Kopperman, Paul E. *Braddock at the Monongahela.* Pittsburgh: University of Pittsburgh Press, 1977.

Lafitau, Father Joseph-François. *Customs of the American Indian Compared with the Customs of Primitive Times,* 2 vols. Toronto: Champlain Society, 1974.

Langlade, Charles de. *Memoir of Charles de Langlade*, vol. 7, *Report and Collections of the State Historical Society of Wisconsin*. Madison, Wis.: E. B. Boleno, 1876.

Leach, Douglas Edward. *Roots of Conflict: British Armed Forces and Colonial America, 1677–1763*. Chapel Hill and London: University of North Carolina Press, 1986.

Lee, Charles. *The Lee Papers, 1754–1776*, vol. 1, *Collections of the New-York Historical Society for the Year 1871*. New York: Printed for the Society, 1872.

Lehane, Brendan. *The Northwest Passage*. Alexandria, Va.: Time-Life Books, 1981.

Leyburn, James G. *The Scotch-Irish: A Social History*. Chapel Hill: University of North Carolina Press, 1962.

Lincoln, Charles Henry, ed. *Correspondence of William Shirley, Governor of Massachusetts and Military Commander of America, 1731–1760*. New York: Macmillan, 1912.

Little, William. *The History of Weare, New Hampshire, 1735–1888*. Lowell, Mass.: S. W. Huse & Co., 1888.

Lock, J. D. *"To Fight with Intrepidity..."*: *The Complete History of the U. S. Army Rangers 1622 to Present*. Tucson, Ariz.: Fenestra Books, 2001.

Loescher, Burt Garfield. *The History of Rogers Rangers*. 4 vols. Bowie, Md.: Heritage Books, 2001.

Ludlum, David M. *Early American Winters, 1604–1820*. Boston: American Meteorological Society, 1966.

Lynch, Jack. "Of Sharpers, Mumpers, and Fourberies: Some Early American Imposters and Rogues." *CWJ* (Spring 2005).

Mahon, J. K. "Anglo-American Methods of Indian Warfare, 1676–1794." *Mississippi Valley Historical Review* 45 (September 1958).

Malone, Patrick M. *The Skulking Way of War: Technology and Tactics Among the New England Indians*. Lanham, Md.: Madison Books, 1991.

Mante, Thomas. *The history of the late war in North-America, and the islands of the West Indies, including the Campaign of MDCCLXIII and MDCCLXIV against his Majesty's Indian enemies*. London: W. Strahan and T. Cadell, 1772.

McCardell, Lee. *Ill-Starred General: Braddock of the Coldstream Guards*. New York: University of Pittsburgh Press, 1958.

McConnell, Michael N. *Army and Empire: British Soldier on the American Frontier, 1758–1775*. Lincoln and London: University of Nebraska Press, 2004.

McCulloch, Ian M. " 'Like roaring lions breaking from their chains': The Battle of Ticonderoga, 8 July 1758." In Donald Graves, ed., *Fighting for Canada: Seven Battles, 1758–1945*. Toronto: Robin Brass Studio, 2000.

McCulloch, Ian M., and Timothy J. Todish. *Through So Many Dangers: The Memoirs and Adventures of Robert Kirk, Late of the Royal Highland Regiment*. Fleischmanns, N.Y.: Purple Mountain Press, 2004.

McMaster, Fitzhugh. *Soldiers and Uniforms: South Carolina Military Affairs, Tricentennial Booklet Number 10, 1670–1775*. Columbia: University of South Carolina Press, 1971.

McNeese, Tim. *The St. Lawrence River*. Philadelphia: Chelsea House, 2005.

Meader, J. W. *The Merrimack River: Its Sources and its tributaries: embracing a history of manufactures, and of the towns along its course; their geography, topography, and products, with descriptions of the magnificent natural scenery about its upper water*. Boston: B. B. Russell, 1869.

Meany, Joseph. *Howe Biography*. Unpublished manuscript.

Meany, Jr., Joseph F. *Merchant and Redcoat: The Papers of John Gordon Macomb*. Ph.D. diss., Fordham University, 1989.

Mereness, Newton D. *Travels in the American Colonies*. New York: MacMillan, 1916.

Middleton, Richard. *Pontiac's War: Its Causes, Course and Consequences*. New York: Routledge, 2007.

Miller, John C. *The First Frontier: Life in Colonial America*. New York: Dell, 1974.

Mills, John B. "History of Dunbarton, N.H." *Snowflake* (1883).

Mirick, Benjamin L. *The History of Haverhill, Massachusetts*. Haverhill: A. W. Thayer, 1832.

Moneypenny, Alexander. "Orderly Book." *BFTM*. March 23–June 29, 1758, in vol. 12, no. 5 (December 1969), pp. 328–57; June 30–August 7, 1758, in vol. 12, no. 6 (December 1970), pp. 434–61; August 8, 1758–October 26, 1758, in vol. 13, no. 1 (December 1970), pp. 89–116; October 27, 1758–May 6, 1759, in vol. 13, no. 2 (June 1971), pp. 151–84; July 15–August 3, 1759, in vol. 2, no. 6 (July 1932), pp. 219–25.

Morgan, Edmund S. *The Mirror of the Indian: An Exhibition of Books and Other Source Materials by Spanish, French, and English Historians and Colonists of North America from the 16th Throughout the 18th Century*. Providence: Association of the John Carter Brown Library, 1958.

Morgan, Ted. *Wilderness at Dawn: The Settling of the North American Continent*. New York: Simon and Schuster, 1993.

Moses, Montrose J. *Representative Plays by American Dramatists*. New York: Benjamin Blom, 1964.

Mott, Frank Luther. *Golden Multitudes: The Story of Best Sellers in the United States*. New York: Macmillan, 1947.

Nabokov, Peter. *A Forest of Time: American Indian Ways of History*. Cambridge, U.K.: Cambridge University Press, 2002.

Nester, William R. *The First Global War: Britain, France, and the Fate of North America, 1756–1775*. Westport, Conn.: Praeger, 2000.

————. *"Haughty Conquerors": Amherst and the Great Indian Uprising of 1763*. Westport, Conn.: Praeger, 2000.

Neuburg, Victor E. "Chapbooks in America: Reconstructing the Popular Reading of Early America." In *Reading in America: Literature and Social History*. Edited by Cathy N. Davidson. Baltimore: Johns Hopkins University Press, 1989.

Nicolai, Martin L. "A Different Kind of Courage: The French Military and the Canadian Irregular Soldier During the Seven Years' War." *Canadian Historical Review* 70, no. 1 (1989).

Nobles, Gregory H. "Breaking into the Backcountry: New Approaches to the Early American Frontier, 1750–1800." *WMQ*, 3rd ser., vol. 46 (1989), pp. 641–70.

O'Callaghan, E. B. *The Documentary History of the State of New-York*. Albany, N.Y.: Charles Van Benthuysen, 1851.

O'Toole, Finton. *White Savage: William Johnson and the Invention of America*. New York: Farrar, Straus, and Giroux, 2005.

Padeni, Scott A. "Forgotten Soldiers: The Role of Blacks in New York's Northern Campaign of the Seven Year's War." *BFTM* 16, no. 2 (1999), pp. 152–69.

Paine, Gary. "Ord's Arks: Angles, Artillery, and Ambush on Lakes George and Champlain." *American Neptune* 58, no. 2 (Spring 1998), pp. 105–22.

Paret, Peter. "Colonial Experience and European Military Reform at the End of the Eighteenth Century." *Bulletin of the Institute of Historical Research* 37 (1964), pp. 47–59.

Pargellis, Stanley. *Lord Loudoun in North America*. New Haven, Conn.: Yale University Press, 1933.

————., ed. *Military Affairs in North America, 1748–1765: Selected Documents from the Cumberland Papers in Windsor Castle*. New York: D. Appleton–Century, 1936.

Parker, King Lawrence. "Anglo-American Wilderness Campaigning, 1754–

1764: Logistical and Tactical Developments." Ph.D. diss., Columbia University, 1970.

Parkman, Francis. *Montcalm and Wolfe*. New York: Little, Brown and Company, 1897.

———. *The Conspiracy of Pontiac*. New York: Collier Books, 1962.

———. *A Half Century of Conflict*. New York: AMS Press, 1969.

Patten, Matthew. *The Diary of Matthew Patten of Bedford, N.H., 1754–1788*. Camden, Me.: Picton Press, 1993.

Peckham, Howard H. *Pontiac and the Indian Uprising*. Princeton, N.J.: Princeton University Press, 1947.

———., ed. "Thomas Gist's Indian Captivity, 1758–1759." *Pennsylvania Magazine of History and Biography* 80 (1956), pp. 285–311.

Pelzer, J., and L. Pelger. "Coffee Houses of Augustan London." *History Today* (October 1982), pp. 40–47.

Penhallow, Samuel. *The History of the Wars of New England with the Eastern Indians; or, A Narrative of their continued Perfidy and Cruelty, From the 10th of August 1703, To the Peace reviewed 13th July, 1713*. New York: Kraus Reprint Co., 1969.

Perdue, Theda, and Michael D. Green. *The Cherokee Nation and the Trail of Tears*. New York: Viking, 2007.

Petersen, Eugene T. *Gentlemen on the Frontier: A Pictorial Record of the Culture of Michilimackinac*. Mackinac Island, Mich.: Mackinac Island State Park Commission, 1964.

Piantadosi, Claude A. *The Biology of Human Survival: Life and Death in Extreme Environments*. New York: Oxford University Press, 2003.

Potter, C. E. *The History of Manchester, Formerly Derryfield in New Hampshire; including that of Ancient Amoskeag, or the Middle Merrimack Valley*. Manchester: C. E. Potter, Publisher, 1856.

———. *The Military History of the State of New-Hampshire, from Its Settlement, in 1623, to the Rebellion, in 1861*. Concord: McFarland and Jenks, 1866.

Pottle, Frederick A. *Boswell's London Journal, 1762–1763*. New York: McGraw-Hill, 1950.

Pouchot, Pierre. *Memoirs on the Late War in North America Between France and England*. Translated by Michael Cardy and edited by Brian Leigh Dunnigan. Youngstown, N.Y.: Old Fort Niagara Association, 2004.

Pound, Arthur. *Nature Stock: The Rise of the American Spirit Seen in Six Lives*. New York: Macmillan, 1931.

Purvis, Thomas L. *Colonial America to 1763.* Almanacs of American Life Series. New York: Facts on File, 1999.

Quaife, Milo Milton. *The Siege of Detroit in 1763: The Journal of Pontiac's Conspiracy and John Rutherfurd's Narrative of a Captivity.* Chicago: Lakeside Press, 1958.

Rath, Richard Cullen. *How Early America Sounded.* Ithaca and London: Cornell University Press, 2003.

Rea, Caleb. "The Journal of Dr. Caleb Rea, Written During the Expedition Against Ticonderoga in 1758." *Historical Collections of the Essex Institute* 18, nos. 4, 5, 6, 7, 8, 9 (April, May, June, July, August, September 1881), pp. 81–120, 177–200.

Ribeiro, Aileen. *The Art of Dress: Fashion in England and France, 1750–1820.* New Haven, Conn.: Yale University Press, 1995.

Richter, Daniel K. *The Ordeal of the Longhouse: The People of the Iroquois League in the Era of European Colonization.* Chapel Hill: University of North Carolina Press, 1992.

Roberts, Kenneth. *Northwest Passage.* Garden City, N.Y.: Doubleday Doran, 1937.

Roby, Luther. *Reminiscences of the French War with Robert Rogers' Journal and a Memoir of General Stark.* Concord, N.H.: Luther Roby, 1831.

Rogers, Mary Cochrane. *Glimpses of an Old Social Capital (Portsmouth, New Hampshire) as Illustrated by the Life of the Reverend Arthur Browne.* Boston: privately printed, 1923.

Rogers, Robert. *The Annotated and Illustrated Journals of Major Robert Rogers.* Edited by Timothy Todish and illustrated by Gary Zaboly. Fleischmanns, N.Y.: Purple Mountain Press, 2002.

———. *A Concise Account of North America: containing a description of the several British colonies on that continent* . . . London, 1765.

Rogers, Robert J. *Rising Above Circumstances: The Rogers Family in Colonial America.* Bedford, Quebec: Sheltus and Picard, 1999.

Russell, Peter E. "Redcoats in the Wilderness: British Officers and Irregular Warfare in Europe and America, 1740 to 1760." *WMQ* 35 (October 1978), pp. 650–51.

Sagard, Father Gabriel. *The Long Journey to the Country of the Hurons.* Toronto: Champlain Society, 1939.

Saunders, Charles Francis. *Useful Wild Plants of the United States and Canada.* New York: Robert M. McBride & Co., 1920.

Sayre, Gordon M. *The Indian Chief as Tragic Hero: Native Resistance and the Literatures of America, from Moctezuma to Tecumseh.* Chapel Hill: University of North Carolina Press, 2005.

Schutz, John A. *William Shirley: King's Governor of Massachusetts.* Chapel Hill: University of North Carolina Press, 1961.

Schwartz, Richard B. *Daily Life in Johnson's London.* Madison: University of Wisconsin Press, 1983.

Schwartz, Seymour I. *The French and Indian War, 1754–1763: The Imperial Struggle for North America.* Edison, N.J.: Castle Books, 1994.

Scott, Kenneth. *Counterfeiting in Colonial America.* New York: Oxford University Press, 1957.

Scull, G. D., ed. *The Montresor Journals.* In *Collections of the New-Historical Society For the Year 1881.* New York: Printed for the Society, 1882.

Silcox, Jr., Major James H. "Rogers and Bouquet: The Origin of American Light Infantry." *Military Review* (December 1985), pp. 62–74.

Skaggs, David Curtis, and Larry L. Nelson, eds. *The Sixty Years' War for the Great Lakes, 1754–1814.* East Lansing: Michigan State University Press, 2001.

Slotkin, Richard. *Regeneration Through Violence: The Mythology of the American Frontier, 1600–1860.* Middletown, Conn.: Wesleyan University Press, 1973.

Smith, James. *Scoouwa: James Smith's Indian Captivity Narrative.* Columbus: Ohio Historical Society, 1978.

Smith, John. *The General History of Virginia, New England, and the Summer Isles.* Chapel Hill: University of North Carolina Press, 2006.

Smith, William. *Expedition Against the Ohio Indians.* Ann Arbor, Mich.: University Microfilms, 1966.

Smoyer, Stanley C. "Indians as Allies in the Intercolonial Wars." *New York History* (October 1936).

Somers, Rev. A. N. *History of Lancaster, New Hampshire.* 1898.

Starbuck, David R. *The Great Warpath: British Military Sites from Albany to Crown Point.* Hanover, N.H.: University Press of New England, 1999.

Stark, Caleb. *History of the Town of Dunbarton, Merrimack County, New-Hampshire, from the Grant By Mason's Assigns, in 1751, To the Year 1860.* Concord, Mass: G. Parker Lyon, 1860.

———. *Memoir and official correspondence of Gen. John Stark: with notices of several other officers of the Revolution: also, a biography of Capt. Phineas Stevens and of Col. Robert Rogers, with an account of his services in America during the "Seven Years' War."* Concord: G. P. Lyon, 1860.

Starkey, Armstrong. *European and Native American Warfare*. Norman: University of Oklahoma Press, 1998.

———. "War and Culture, a Case Study: The Enlightenment and the Conduct of the British Army in America, 1755–1781." *War and Society* 8 (May 1990).

Steegmann, Jr., A. Theodore, ed. *Boreal Forest Adaptations: The Northern Algonkians*. New York: Plenum Press, 1983.

Steele, Ian K. *Betrayals: Fort William Henry and the "Massacre."* Oxford: Oxford University Press, 1990.

Sturtevant, William C., ed. *Handbook of North American Indians*. Washington, D.C.: Smithsonian Institution, 1978–2004.

Sullivan, Owen. *A Short Account of the Life of John ******, alias Owen Syllavan*. Leominster, Mass.: Adams & Wilder, 1802.

Sylvester, Herbert Milton. *Indian Wars of New England*. Vol. 3. Boston: W. B. Clarke, 1910.

Symmes, Thomas. *Brief History of the Battle which was fought on the 8ᵗʰ of May, 1725, Between Capt. John Lovewell with his Associates, and a body of Indians Under the Command of Paugus, sachem of the Pigwacket Tribe*. Portland, Me.: A. and V. Shyrley, 1818.

Thwaites, Reuben Gold, ed. "The Jesuit Relations and Allied Documents." *Travels and Explorations of the Jesuit Missionaries in New France, 1610–1791*. Cleveland, Ohio: Burrows Brothers, 1896–1901.

Todish, Timothy J., and Todd E. Harburn. *A "Most Troublesome Situation": The British Military and the Pontiac Indian Uprising of 1763–1764*. Fleischmanns, N.Y.: Purple Mountain Press, 2006.

Turney-High, Harry Holbert. *Primitive War: Its Practice and Concepts*. Columbia: University of South Carolina Press, 1971.

Tunis, Edwin. *Frontier Living*. Cleveland and New York: World, 1961.

Van Deventer, David E. *The Emergence of Provincial New Hampshire, 1623–1741*. Baltimore: Johns Hopkins University Press, 1976.

Van Dyke, Theodore S. *The Still-Hunter*. Norwood, Mass.: Norwood Press, 1912.

Waghelstein, John David. "Preparing for the Wrong War: The United States Army and Low-Intensity Conflict, 1755–1890." Ph.D. diss., Temple University, 1990.

Warhus, Mark. *Another America: Native American Maps and the History of Our Land*. New York: St. Martin's Press, 1997.

Watson, Alan D., ed. *Society in Early North Carolina: A Documentary*

History. Raleigh: North Carolina Department of Cultural Resources, 2000.

Weatherford, Jack. *How the Indian Enriched America*. New York: Ballantine Books, 1992.

Webb, James. *Born Fighting: How the Scots-Irish Shaped America*. New York: Broadway Books, 2004.

Webster, J. Clarence, ed. *The Journal of Jeffrey Amherst: Recording the Military Career of General Amherst in America from 1758 to 1763*. Toronto, Ont.: Ryerson Press, 1931.

White, Richard. *The Middle Ground: Indians, Empires, and Republics in the Great Lakes Region, 1650–1815*. Cambridge: Cambridge University Press, 1991.

White, William Chapman. *Adirondack County*. New York: Alfred A. Knopf, 1983.

Whittier, John Greenleaf. *The Complete Writings of John Greenleaf Whittier*. New York: AMS Press, 1969.

Williams, Glyndwr. *The British Search for the Northwest Passage in the Eighteenth Century*. London: Longman, Green and Co., 1962.

Williams, Thomas. "Correspondence of Doctor Thomas Williams, of Deerfield, Mass., a Surgeon in the Army. 1.—The Campaigns Against Crown Point, in 1755 and 1756." *The Historical Magazine*, 2nd. ser., vol. 7, no. 4 (April 1870).

Williamson, Peter. *French and Indian Cruelty*. New York, 1757.

Winsor, Justin, ed. *Memorial History of Boston, including Suffolk County, Massachusetts, 1630–1880*. 4 vols. Boston: James R. Osgood & Co., 1882.

Wiseman, Frederick Matthew. *The Voice of the Dawn: An Autohistory of the Abenaki Nation*. Hanover and London: University Press of New England, 2001.

Wulff, Matt. *Robert Rogers' Rules for the Ranging Service: An Analysis*. Westminster, Md.: Heritage Books, 2006.

Zaboly, Gary. *American Colonial Ranger: The Northern Colonies, 1724–64*. Oxford, England: Osprey, 2004.

———. *A True Ranger: The Life and Many Wars of Major Robert Rogers*. Garden City Park, N.Y.: Royal Block House, 2004.

Zielinski, Gregory A., and Barry D. Keim. *New England Weather, New England Climate*. Hanover, N.H.: University Press of New England, 2003.

Index

Italic page numbers indicate a map or illustration reference.

Champlain campaign, 115; Loudoun as replacement for, 115; and opening months of French and Indian War, 67–68; rangers' views of, 149; Rogers's meeting with, 107–8, 109, 111–13; Rogers's recruitment of volunteers for, 67–68; Rogers's relations with, 192; Rogers's views of, 112; and sacking of Louisbourg, 112; and small-unit woods fighting, 216; and snowshoe men, 36; views about Rogers of, 112–13

Sioux Indians, 380, 385, 390–91, 392, 414, 448

sleigh convoy (Montressor's), French attack on, 207–8, 312

smallpox, 138, 141, 206, 323, 341; Rogers dies of, 139

Smith, James, 53–54

Smith, John, 9, 43

Smith, William, 30, 424

snowshoe men. *See* rangers

snowshoes, 124, 127, 183

Snowshoes, Battle on (1758), 3, 166, 167, 170–75, *173*, 176–84, 188, 193, 196, 214, 225, 240, 272, 384, 386

South Carolina: and life in Charles Town, 317–21; Rogers's description of, 317, 323; Rogers in, 316, 317–24, 330–33

The South Carolina Gazette, 320, 321, 330

South Carolina independent company, 309, 318, 320

Speakman, Thomas, 124, 125, 126, 127–28, 129, 131–32, 133–34, 137

Spicer, Abel, 190, 206, 210

Spiesmaker, Captain, 398, 402, 403, 404, 405, 406, 407, 408, 409

Stamp Act, 365, 374

Standing Bear, Luther, 247

Stark, Caleb, 4, 10, 54

Stark, John, xxi; portrait of, *insert*; and Abercrombie (Captain), 152–54, 161, 199; in American Revolution, 49, 227, 423; and attack on Carillon, 163, 189, 198, 199, 201; and attack on Fort William Henry, 138; on brother's death, 435; commissions in French and Indian War of, 49, 68; discharge of rangers under, 154; as hunter and trapper, 48, 49, 50; illness/injuries of, 103, 139, 240; as Indian prisoner, 50–59, 240; and Indian raids near Rumford, 48; and Langlade-Ottawa attack, 129, 130, 133; as leader of Speakman rangers, 137; and Louisbourg expedition, 139;

and New Hampshire motto, 49; as ranger captain, 162; ransom of, 59; and recruitment of rangers, 114; and Rogers in American Revolution, 434; and Rogers's prosecution for counterfeiting, 67; and Rogers prosecution for Saint-François Raid, 240; Rogers's relationship with, 4, 17, 33, 49; and Rogers's return from Battle on Snowshoes, 182; and Sullivan-Rogers deal, 66; as surveyor, 62; and wintering near Lake Champlain, 124, 125, 127

Stark, William, 48, 49, 50, 58, 59, 434–35

Starkstown, New Hampshire, land titles in, 61

starvation, 261–62

Stevens, Phineas, xxi, 55–59, 62

Stevens, Samuel, xxi, 260, 263, 264, 268–69, 285

Stinson, David, 48, 50

Stirling, William Alexander, possibly Earl of, 428, 437, 444

Stockbridge Indians: and attack on Carillon, 189; disease among, 233–34; and King George's War, 37; as rangers, 220, 221, 236, 241, 249, 250, 282; and Rogers's financial affairs, 311; and Rogers's scouting/raids into Canada, 277, 282; and Saint-François Raid, 249, 250; in South Carolina, 318, 322–23

Sullivan, Owen, xxi, 63, 64–65, 66, 67, 440

Sullivan, Richard, 63, 437, 445

Theyanoguin, xxi, 75, 77

Thousand Islands, 295

Three Fires Confederacy, 122

Tiffany, Consider, 436, 441

Timothy, Peter, 320, 330–31

Titigaw, Francis, 50, 51, 58

torture, of Indian prisoners, 52–53

Townshend, Charles, 363, 385, 389

Townshend, Roger, 221, 227

trade/traders: and accusations against Rogers, 394; Amherst's views of, 338; in beaver pelts, 47, 48, 49–50; in Boston, 110; and British relations with Great Lakes Indians, 337; British-French competition for, 371; and Carver expedition, 385; and gift-giving, 338; and Indian-French relations, 37; Montréal as center of, 55, 381–82, 388; and Ottawa-Huron relations, 124; in Portsmouth, New Hampshire, 313–14;

About the Author

John F. Ross is the executive editor of *American Heritage* and *Invention & Technology* magazines and a former senior editor of *Smithsonian* magazine. On assignment, he has chased scorpions in Baja, dived 3,000 feet underwater in the Galapagos, and dogsledded with the Polar Inuit in Greenland. He has published more than two hundred articles and spoken at the Explorers Club of New York, the Smithsonian Institution, NASA's Ames Research Center, and BMW's Herbert Quandt Foundation.

While doing research for *War on the Run*, Ross walked and kayaked many parts of Rogers's tracks, giving him valuable on-the-ground experience with which to bring Rogers's experiences vividly to life. He is the author of *The Polar Bear Strategy: Reflections on Risk in Modern Life* and lives in Bethesda, Maryland.

See www.WarontheRun.com for more information.